THE ROUTLEDGE
DICTIONARY OF
LATIN
QUOTATIONS

Also by Jon R. Stone

Latin for the Illiterati (1996)

More Latin for the Illiterati (1999)

and

The Craft of Religious Studies (1998)

The Essential Max Müller: On Language, Mythology, and Religion (2002)

Expecting Armageddon: Essential Readings in Failed Prophecy (2000)

A Guide to the End of the World (1993)

On the Boundaries of American Evangelicalism (1997)

Prime-Time Religion: An Encyclopedia of Religious Broadcasting (1997)

THE ROUTLEDGE DICTIONARY OF

LATIN QUOTATIONS

The Illiterati's Guide to Latin Maxims,
Mottoes, Proverbs, and Sayings

Jon R. Stone

ROUTLEDGE
NEW YORK AND LONDON

Published in 2005 by

Routledge
270 Madison Avenue
New York, NY 10016
www.routledge-ny.com

Published in Great Britain by

Routledge
2 Park Square
Milton Park, Abingdon,
Oxon OX14 4RN U.K.
www.routledge.co.uk

Routledge is an imprint of the Taylor & Francis Group.

Library of Congress Cataloging-in-Publication Data

The Routledge dictionary of Latin quotations : the illiterati's guide to Latin maxims, mottoes, proverbs and sayings / Jon R. Stone.
p. cm.
Latin with English translations.
Includes bibliographical references and index.
ISBN 0-415-96908-5 (alk. paper)—ISBN 0-415-96909-3 (pbk. : alk. paper)—ISBN 0-415-97431-3 (jacketed hardback)
1. Quotations, Latin. 2. Quotations, Latin—Translations into English. I. Stone, Jon R., 1959-
PN6080.R68 2004
398.9'71--dc22   2004002081

For Benton Johnson

A Gifted Teacher, An Inspiring Mentor —
With Great Admiration

CONTENTS

PREFACE

In a recent airing of a PBS travel program, a group of San Francisco-area college students were filmed visiting China, their ancestral home. After arriving in a wayside village, one of the women students quoted the ancient proverb, "When you drink water, remember the source," and then asserted, "That's very Chinese!" There is a similar Chinese aphorism that rebukes those who would drink from a fountain without first giving thought to the ancestor who had dug the well. In both instances, the notion is the same: we owe our lives, but also our daily conveniences, to those who came before us. Whether Chinese or American, Asian or Western, the proverb aptly applies to all. Our ancestors planted the trees whose fruits we now eat; they built the roads and bridges over which we now drive. Indeed, it is they who handed down to us the storehouse of folk wisdom that we draw upon daily to guide, enrich, and inform our lives.

For those of us who study cultural history, much of what we find in ancient proverbial wisdom centers around themes of memory and connection. Ancient wisdom encourages us to be ever mindful of our ties, as well as our obligations, to the past. The way we go in this life follows after those who came before us. "Via trita, via tuta," the old Roman adage asserts, "The beaten path is the safe path." There is a certain comfort and assurance in knowing that the road we travel upon is a familiar one and that it will not lead us astray. The image that emerges, then, is of one generation after another following a trail blazed by revered ancestors—of following and then of passing on a tradition set down in custom as well as in word.

At the same time, the connection is not only from past to present, but also from present to future. A people's life continues onward ever mindful of their connection to their forebears, but also of what guideposts or markers they will leave for their descendants. Someday, we too will be ancestors, and the wisdom we have gleaned from our experiences will guide those who follow after us—or so we hope.

Four centuries ago, Sir Francis Bacon published *De Sapientia Veterum* (*On the Wisdom of the Ancients*), a delightful book of Classical myths and fables in which he sought to recover examples of "humane wisedome" from antiquity that had been "buried in obliuion [oblivion] and silence." In his Preface, Bacon observed that "There is found among men ... a two-fold use of Parables, and those ... referred to contrary ends; conducing as well to foulding [folding] up and keeping of things under a vaile [veil], as to the inlightening [enlightening] and laying open of obscurities." These Parables, he noted, must be "accounted … as Sacred reliques [relics] or abstracted ayres [airs] of better times, which by tradition from more ancient Nations fell into the Trumpets and Flutes of the Græcians," and had since found their way to his own time.

For his part, Bacon was much more interested in the second of these two uses, that is, of laying open obscurities and enlightening those who might encounter them. But from another perspective, Bacon's observation that fables, allegories, parables, similes, and "ænigmaes" hide as well as reveal knowledge, remains the more intriguing of the two aims of ancient wisdom, despite his waving it aside. To shroud something is not merely to conceal it, but, at the same time, to protect and preserve it. A culture's "sacred reliques" are not for "rude and impatient" hands to mishandle, lest they become profaned. It is for this reason that we frequently find ancient wisdom couched in the abstractions, subtleties, and nuances of metonymy and metaphor, of analogy and pun.

Much like Bacon's small book, this present collection of nearly 8,000 proverbs, mottoes, and quotations also seeks to gather and preserve *De Sapientia Veterum* of the Latin tradition, ancient wisdom written down and passed on from the birth of the Republic to the Fall of the Empire, and into the age of Renaissance and Reformation. To be sure, Roman customs and mores were deeply rooted in tradition and upheld the conservative cultural values that characterized the Republic. But beyond that, their aim was to safeguard the sacred *genius* of a people who had forged a social and political system that brought predictability and order within an otherwise chaotic world. Much of this wisdom fell into the "Flutes and Trumpets" of the Romans through Rome's contact with and admiration of Greek civilization. "Aurea Mediocritas" (the golden mean), moderation in all things, was among these ideals that the Romans borrowed from the Greeks, but then added their own emphasis on social obligation and the caution not to tempt Fate. *Virtus* (virtue), *aretê*, the highest Greek ideal, translated easily into Roman thought as maintaining balance between one's social and familial duties and the striving after personal honor through heroic acts of valor. In fact, *Honos* or *Honor* meant everything to the Romans and strongly shaped the Roman ethos, as did *Fides* (faith) and *Magnanimitas* (greatness of spirit). "Facte nova virtute, puer; sic itur ad astra," encouraged Virgil: "go on and increase in valor, young man; thus is the path to the stars."

The use of proverbs, mottoes, and maxims appears common to all cultures. Such pith expresses the essence of a culture's customs and traditions in the form of mnemonic or memory devices meant to inform as well as to entertain. For instance, the Hebrew Book of Proverbs makes very effective use of parallel phrasings that are preserved when rendered in English, such as "pride goeth before destruction, and a haughty spirit before a fall" (16:18), and "a soft answer turns away wrath, but a harsh word stirs up anger" (15:1). For their part, Latin authors and orators made effective use of meter and rhyme as mnemonic devices. As with "via trita, via tuta," the phrase "mox nox" (soon night, or night is approaching) likewise employs meter and rhyme. The same is the case with "mone sale" (advise with salt), and "nec habeo, nec careo, nec curo" (I have not, I want not, I care not), which are both fairly easy to remember.

Another interesting mnemonic device is the tongue twister, examples of which we also encounter in Latin literature. One clever tongue twister is "mala mali malo mala contulit omnia mundo" (man's jaw and an apple brought all evils in the world). Another is the phrase "sunt pueri pueri, pueri puerilia tractant" (children are children, and children occupy themselves with childish things), which features a repetition of the same word bracketed by two words that closely rhyme. Elsewhere in the literature, we chance upon examples of the *chiasmus* or cross pattern, such as the menacing phrase from Plautus that goes "altera manu fert lapidem, panem ostentat altera" (he shows us bread in one hand, but holds a stone in the other). Notice that the phrase begins and ends with "altera," and, at least in terms of its syllabic sounds, closely resembles a palindrome.

Apart from being witty, the mnemonic cast of ancient proverbial wisdom served to teach children and remind adults of the way they should go in life. The phrase *way of life* is itself a metaphor for how life is to be lived in *mimesis* or imitation of great cultural heroes. Across traditions, this same motif predominates. At times, the *way* is presented in terms of a choice between two roads, as in the "bivium virtutis et vitii" (the two paths of virtue and of vice). At other times, virtue, in Horace's words, "est medium vitiorum et utrinque reductum" (is the middle between two vices, and is equally removed from either extreme). In Juvenal, we find the admonition, "semita certe tranquillæ per virtutem patet unica vitæ" (only one path in this life leads to tranquility: the path of virtue). And, as a last example, there is the anonymous saying, "errantem in viam reductio" (lead the wanderer back into the right way).

In addition, these types of literary devices served to reinforce traditional methods of teaching by example, methods likewise embraced by the Romans, who preferred practical to theoretical knowledge. Accordingly, we find instances, such as in Seneca, who expressed this idea using the *path* or *road* metaphor in a rhyming doublet: "longum iter est per præcepta, breve et efficax per exempla" (teaching by precept is a long road, but brief and beneficial is the way by example). Moreover, wisdom is at times personified both in terms of its mimetic and its mnemonic aspects. One such example is in Lucius Afranius, who wrote: "Usus me genuit, mater peperit Memoria. Sophiam vocant me Graii, vos Sapientiam" (Practice was my father, Memory my mother. The Greeks call me Sophia, you call me Wisdom).

In this way, ancient wisdom served both mimetic and mnemonic aims. It is in memory and a culture's connection to its past that tradition and custom and a people's way of life are preserved and protected against change. For, as Cicero wrote, "memoria est thesaurus omnium rerum e custos" (memory is the treasury and guardian of all things).

As with my two previous books, *Latin for the Illiterati* (1996) and *More Latin for the Illiterati* (1999), both published by Routledge, the creation of this third Latin lexicon presented a number of problems that need to be mentioned here as a sort of "caveat lector," a caution to the reader. First, as much as I would have liked to have gathered together all the wisdom of the ancients into one volume, because of page constraints I have had to content myself with a text of fewer than 400 pages. Even so, the selections contained in this treasury of proverbs and quotations represent the widest possible survey of that literature, including such authors and orators as Cato, Juvenal, Seneca, Pliny, Ovid, Cicero, Virgil, Publilius Syrus, Terence, Horace, Plautus, Lucretius, and many others. These are persons whose wisdom and humor spoke to their own time, but speak to ours as well.

Second, because this collection draws from a wide range of sources in the Classical, Medieval, Renaissance, and later periods, there exist noticeable variations and inconsistencies in spelling and syntax that cannot be reconciled. For example, the letters "j" and "y" came to indicate the letter "i" when consonated. The aspirated letter "h" is sometimes inserted after "c" and between double vowels, usually to distinguish hard from soft sounds and to mark double vowels that were not diphthongs. Consequently, the reader will encounter such spelling changes as *jus* and *judex* for *ius* and *iudex*, *inclytus* for *inclitus*, *lacrymis* or *lachrymis* for *lacrimis*, *ahereus* for *aereus*, and so on. Apart from these types of irregularities, it should be pointed out that not all irregular spellings or syntactical "errors" can be corrected to satisfy everyone's tastes. I still receive letters from conscientious readers who chastise me for having retained the use of "j" and "corrupted" Medieval syntax in my earlier lexicons.

But these "corruptions" should not surprise us. All languages become corrupted with use. What should amaze us is that many people fail to see change as a natural development of human cultural life. All things change from being stretched, even language. To think of language as "corrupted" assumes that there was an original point of perfection from which the language began to degrade, such as the Fall in the Garden or the confusion of tongues at the Tower of Babel. Much to the contrary, language is a tool for communicating among people as well as a means of communicating across space and time. As the conversation moves forward, some words change their spellings and meanings, some become obsolete and later discarded, and new words are introduced either to replace worn-out expressions or to express new or emerging ideas. Witness the archaic forms in the quotes from Sir Francis Bacon cited above. Shall we consider Jacobean English as the true and pure form and Modern Standard English as its defilement? Of course not. There is no pure language, for language, as a human creation, is neither fixed nor constant, but changes with the needs and conventions of the times.

In addition to irregularities in spelling and syntax, I have also had to wrestle with variant and contradictory versions of quotations, as well as discrepancies over the original authorship of proverbs and maxims. In the case of variant renderings of quotations and sayings, it seemed best to consult multiple sources (including Web-based, such as *The Latin Library on-line*) and then select the version that appeared most frequently in published form (even then, I encountered a number of typographical errors in books and mis-scanned or miskeyed texts on the Web). With respect to author attribution, in most cases I simply listed all the authors to whom the quote had been ascribed.

While, for the sake of convenience, the main text has been divided into three sections—Proverbs and Maxims, Mottoes and Phrases, and Familiar Quotations—not all entries fit neatly into these categories. Some proverbs and maxims appear as mottoes on ancient and modern crests. What is more, some of the authored proverbs and maxims are lengthy and would thus seem better suited to the section of quotations. And, of course, not all readers will know in which sections to look for the entries that fall between these categories—or will even agree with where they have been placed. For these inconveniences, these slight mea culpas, I beg the reader's kind indulgence. Doubtless these, and all other faults and omissions in the text, will pursue me through this life like the Furies, and then follow me to the shades below.

Finally, as I had observed in the Prefaces of my earlier Latin texts, there is much in Latin literature to offend modern sensibilities. Racial and sexist epithets are not unique to our time nor even to Western culture. All traditional societies felt threatened by differences both within and without, and many viciously attacked dissenters—and still do. Doubtless, such phrases as "Æthiopiem lavare" (to wash an Ethiopian) and "Græculus esuriens" (ever the hungry young Greek) are racially offensive. In terms of sexist remarks, one tends to find jabs at both men and women. For instance, Publilius Syrus wrote that "women surpass men at scheming evil" (In Latin, "malo in consilio feminæ vincunt viros"); while, at about the same time, Ovid, his contemporary, penned the phrase: "forma viros neglecta decet," or "neglect of appearance becomes men." While both comments can be read as sheer sarcasm, they can also be seen as offensive. Though a few selections such as these have been included in this text, their appearance is merely for historical purposes. I did not (and do not) believe that it was my role as a lexicographer to sanitize Roman cultural attitudes toward race, class, or gender.

Notwithstanding these minor imperfections, it is hoped that *The Routledge Dictionary of Latin Quotations* will offer to the reader, both now and in future generations, a treasury of ancient wisdom that, to quote Horace, "delectando pariterque monendo," delights while at the same time instructs.

Vita enim mortuorum in memoria vivorum est posita — Cicero

Jon R. Stone
August 2003

REFERENCES AND SOURCES

Adkins, Lesley and Roy A. Adkins. *Handbook to Life in Ancient Rome*. New York: Oxford University Press, 1994.

Bacon, Sir Francis. *The Wisedome of the Ancients* (*de Sapientia Veterum*, 1609), translated by Arthur Gorges. Amsterdam: Da Capo Press, 1968 [facsimile of 1619 edition].

Boardman, John, et al. (Eds.). *The Oxford History of the Classical World*. New York: Oxford University Press, 1986.

Cassell's Concise Latin-English/English-Latin Dictionary (compiled by D.P. Simpson). New York: Macmillan Publishing Co., 1977.

Champion, Selwyn G. *Racial Proverbs* (2nd ed.). London: Routledge and Kegan Paul, 1950.

Collins, John F. *A Primer of Ecclesiastical Latin*. Washington, D.C.: The Catholic University of America Press, 1985.

Grant, Michael. *History of Rome*. New York: Charles Scribner's Sons, 1978.

Greenough, J.B. et al. (Eds.). *Allen & Greenough's New Latin Grammar*. New Rochelle, NY: Aristide D. Caratzas, 1983 [reprint of 1903 edition].

Guterman, Norbert. *A Book of Latin Quotations*. New York: Anchor Books, 1966.

Harbottle, Thomas Benfield. *Dictionary of Quotations (Classical)*. New York: Macmillan, 1897.

King, W. Francis H. *Classical and Foreign Quotations: A Polyglot Dictionary of Historical and Literary Quotations, Proverbs and Popular Sayings* (2nd ed.). New York: Frederick Ungar Publishing Co., 1965.

Lewis, James John. *The Collegiate Law Dictionary*. Brooklyn, New York: The American Law Book Co., 1925.

MacDonnel, D.E. *A Dictionary of Quotations, in Most Frequent Use, Taken Chiefly from Latin and French, but Comprising Many from the Greek, Spanish, and Italian Languages, Translated into English, with Illustrations Historical and Idiomatic* (8th edition, revised and corrected). London: G. & W.B. Whittaker, 1822.

Mawson, C.O. Sylvester and Charles Berlitz (Eds.). *Dictionary of Foreign Terms* (2nd ed.). New York: Barnes & Noble Books, 1979.

Meissner, C. *Latin Phrase-Book* (H.W. Auden, trans.). London: Macmillan & Co., 1938.

Novum Testamentum Latine: Textum Vaticanum (11th ed., Eberhard Nestle, Ed.). Stuttgart: Württembergische Bibelanstalt, 1971.

Nunn, H.P.V. *An Introduction to Ecclesiastical Latin.* Cambridge University Press, 1922.

The Oxford Dictionary of Quotations (2nd ed.). New York: Oxford University Press, 1955.

Shelton, Jo-Ann. *As the Romans Did* (2nd ed.). New York: Oxford University Press, 1998.

Sidwell, Keith. *Reading Medieval Latin.* Cambridge: Cambridge University Press, 1995.

Simpson, D.P. *Cassell's Latin Dictionary.* New York: Macmillan, 1977.

Smith, Sir William. *Smaller Classical Dictionary.* New York: E.P. Dutton & Co., 1958.

Stevenson, Burton. *Stevenson's Book of Proverbs, Maxims and Familiar Phrases.* London: Routledge and Kegan Paul, 1949.

Stone, Jon R. *Latin for the Illiterati.* New York and London: Routledge, 1996.

——. *More Latin for the Illiterati.* New York and London: Routledge, 1999.

Trayner, John. *Latin Phrases and Maxims.* Edinburgh: William Patterson, 1861.

Webster's II: New Riverside University Dictionary. Boston: Houghton Mifflin Co., 1984.

Webster's New World Dictionary of the English Language. New York: World Publishing Company, 1964.

Wheelock, Frederick M. *Latin* (College Outline Series). New York: Barnes & Noble Books, 1962.

Wood, James. *Dictionary of Quotations from Ancient and Modern, English and Foreign Sources,* etc. London and New York: Frederick Warne and Co., 1893.

PRONUNCIATION GUIDE

Most Latin word sounds have corresponding English word sounds, following the same rules for short and long pronunciation of vowels. For example, the long *a* in *father* is the same sound as the long *a* in the Latin word *pater*. The short *a* in the English words *par* and *far* are very similar in sound to that of the Latin words *pax* and *fax*. The short *e* in *pet* is similar in sound to the Latin *et*, as the short *i* in *twig* is the same as the *i* in the Latin word *signum*. The long *o* in *Ohio* sounds very much like the *o* in the Latin word *dolor*. In the same way, the short *o* in *pot* is pronounced similarly to the short *o* in *populas*. Likewise, the Latin *u* in *runa* and *pudicus*, one long and the other short, sound the same as the long and short *u* vowels in *rude* and *put*.

The reader should also keep in mind that in Latin, unlike English, all syllables in words are pronounced, including the final e and es of words, such as *arte* and *artes*, *duce* and *duces*, *fide* and *fides*, *opinione*, and *legiones*, and the like.

With respect to Latin consonants, one should nearly always pronounce them as those in English (e.g., b = b, d = d, f = f, l = l, m = m, n = n, p = p, r = r, s = s, t = t, etc.), with the exception of c , g, h, and v, which are always pronounced like k (as in *kirk*), g (as in *give, gave,* and *go*), h (as in *hard*), and w (as in *we* and *was*) respectively. The letters i–j, when placed before another vowel, such as *iam/jam* and *ius/jus*, are pronounced like the consonant y (as in *you, yam,* and *use*), not the consonant j. The convention of substituting the letter j for i when used as a consonant appeared after the Classical period. Although its use is vexing to most Latin purists today, for the sake of simplicity, its use is retained here.

Finally, with respect to vowel diphthongs, most Classical Latin linguists prefer to pronounce them as follows: æ as if it were a long *i* (as in *pine*); œ as *oi* (as in *boy*); au as *ou* or *ow* (as in *bough* or *now*); ei as a long *a* (as in *weight*); eu as *eu* (as in *feud*); and ui as *wee* (as in the French *oui*).

LATIN PROVERBS AND MAXIMS

A

a cane non magno sæpe tenetur aper: a boar is often held by a not-so-large dog (Ovid)

a facto ad jus non datur consequentia: the inference from the fact to the law is not allowed

a fonte puro pura defluit aqua: from a pure spring pure water flows

a fronte præcipitium a tergo lupi: a precipice before (me), wolves behind (me) (i.e., caught between death and dismemberment)

a minimis quoque timendum: one ought to fear even the tiniest of creatures

a prima descendit origine mundi causarum series: even from the first beginnings of the world descends a series of causes (Lucan)

a proximis quisque minime anteiri vult: no one likes to be surpassed by those of his own level (Livy)

a verbis legis non est recedendum: from the words of the law there is no departure

ab abusu ad usum non valet consequentia: (fig.) the abuse of a thing is no argument against its use

ab actu ad posse valet illatio: it is possible to infer the future from the past

ab alio expectes, alteri quod feceris: what you do to others, you may expect another to do to you (Laberius and Publilius Syrus)

ab alto speres alteri quod feceris: expect from Heaven what you have done to another

ab hoc et ab hac et ab illa: from this and from this and from that (i.e., from here, there, and everywhere; confusedly)

ab honesto virum bonum nihil deterret: nothing deters a good man from what honor requires of him (Seneca)

ab inopia ad virtutem obsepta est via: the way from poverty to virtue is an obstructed one

ab uno disce omnes: from one learn all (i.e., from one sample we judge the rest) (Virgil)

abeunt studia in mores: pursuits become habits (Ovid)

abi in malam crucem: (fig.) to the devil with you!

abores serit diligens agricola, quarum adspiciet baccam ipse numquam: the diligent farmer plants trees of which he himself will never see the fruit (Cicero)

absens hæres non erit: the absent one will not be the heir (i.e., out of sight, out of mind)

absentem lædit cum ebrio qui litigat: to quarrel with a drunk is to dispute with a man who is not there (Publilius Syrus)

absque argento omnia vana: without money all is vain

abstineto a fabis: abstain from beans (i.e., have nothing to do with elections—the ballot having been cast with beans)

absurdum est ut alios regat, qui seipsum regere nescit: it is absurd that he should rule others who knows not how to rule himself

abundans cautela non nocet: abundant caution does no harm

abusus non tollit usum: abuse does not take away use

accensa domo proximi, tua quoque periclitatur: when your neighbor's house is on fire, yours is likewise in danger

acceptissima semper munera sunt, auctor quæ pretiosa facit: those gifts are always the most acceptable that owe their value to the giver (Ovid)

accidit in puncto, et toto contingit in anno: it happens in a moment, and happens all year long

accidit in puncto quod non contingit in anno: what does not occur in the whole course of the year may happen in a moment

accipere quam facere præstat injuriam: it is better to receive than to do an injury (Cicero)

acclinus falsis animus meliora recusat: the mind attracted by what is false refuses better things (Horace)

accusare nemo se debet nisi coram Deo: no one is bound to accuse himself unless it be before God

acer et ad palmæ per se cursurus honores, si tamen horteris fortius ibit equus: the spirited horse, which will of itself strive to win the race, will run still more swiftly if encouraged (Ovid)

acer et vehemens bonus orator: a good orator is pointed and impassioned (Cicero)

acerrima proximorum odia: the hatred of those closest to us is the most bitter (Tacitus)

acerrimus ex omnibus nostris sensibus est sensus videndi: the keenest of all our senses is the sense of sight (Cicero)

acribus initiis, incurioso fine: alert (or energetic) at the beginning, careless (or negligent) at the end (Tacitus)

acta deos nunquam mortalia fallunt: the deeds of men never escape the gods (Ovid)

acta exteriora indicant interiora secreta: external actions indicate internal secrets

acti labores jucundi: the remembrance of past labors is pleasant

actio personalis moritur cum persona: a personal action (or right) dies with the person

actis ævum implet, non segnibus annis: his lifetime is full of deeds, not of indolent years (Ovid)

actum ne agas: do not do what is done (i.e., leave well enough alone) (Terence and Cicero)

actus Dei nemini facit injuriam: the act of God does injury to no one

actus Dei nemini nocet: the act of God brings harm to no one

actus legis nulli facit injuriam: the act of the law does injury to no one

actus me invito factus, non est meus actus: an act done against my will is not my act

actus non facit reum, nisi mens sit rea: the act does not make the person guilty, unless the mind be guilty

ad auctores redit sceleris coacti culpa: the guilt of enforced crimes lies on those who impose them (Seneca)

ad calamitatem quilibet rumor valet: any rumor is sufficient against calamity (i.e., when a disaster happens, every report confirming it obtains ready credence)

ad damnum adderetur injuria: that would be adding insult to injury (Cicero)

ad Græcas kalendas soluturos: they will pay at the Greek calends (i.e., never; there is no Greek calends) (Cæsar Augustus)

ad mala quisque animum referat sua: let each recall his own woes (Ovid)

ad nocendum potentes sumus: we all have power to do harm (Seneca)

ad perditam securim manubrium adjicere: to throw the handle after the hatchet (i.e., to give up in despair)

ad perniciem solet agi sinceritas: honesty is often goaded to ruin (Phædrus)

ad pœnitendum properat, cito qui judicat: the one who judges in haste repents in haste (Publilius Syrus)

ad præsens ova cras pullis sunt meliora: eggs today are better than chickens tomorrow (i.e., a bird in the hand is worth two in the bush)

ad quæstionem legis respondent judices, ad quæstionem facti respondent juratores: it is the judge's business to answer to the question of law, the jury's to answer to the question of fact

ad tristem partem strenua est suspicio: one is quick to suspect where one has suffered harm before (or, the losing side is full of suspicion) (Publilius Syrus)

ad vivendum velut ad natandum is melior qui onere liberior: he is better equipped for life, as for swimming, who has the lesser to carry (Apuleius)

addecet honeste vivere: it much becomes us to live honorably

addere legi justitiam decus: it is to one's honor to combine justice with law

adeo facilius est multa facere quam diu: it is much easier to try one's hand at many things than to concentrate one's powers on one thing (Quintilian)

adeo in teneris consuescere multum est: so much depends upon habit in the tender years (i.e., such are the advantages of an early education) (Virgil)

adhibenda est in jocando moderatio: moderation should be used in joking (Cicero)

adhuc tua messis in herba est: your crop is still in grass (Ovid)

adjuvat in bello pacatæ ramus olivæ: in war the olive branch of peace is of use (Ovid)

adolescentem verecundum esse decet: it becomes a young man to be modest (Plautus)

adsit regula, peccatis quæ pœnas irroget æquas: have a rule apportioning to each offense its appropriate penalty (Horace)

adversæ res admonent religionum: adversity reminds men of religion (Livy)

adversus miseros … inhumanus est jocus: jokes directed against the unfortunate are inhumane (Quintilian)

adversus solem ne loquitor: neither speak against the sun (i.e., do not dispute with what is obvious)

ædificatum solo, solo cedit: the thing built on the land goes with the land

ægrescit medendo: he grows worse with the treatment (i.e., the remedy is worse than the disease) (adapted from Virgil)

ægroto, dum anima est, spes est: to the sick, while there is life there is hope (Cicero)

æmulatio æmulationem parit: emulation begets emulation

æqua lege necessitas, sortitur insignes et imos: necessity apportions impartiality to the high and the low (Horace)

æqua tellus pauperi recluditur regumque pueris: the impartial earth opens alike for the child of the pauper and that of the king (Horace)

æquabit nigras candida una dies: one single bright day will equal the black ones

æquari pavet alta minori: a lofty thing fears being made equal with a lower

æquo animo pœnam, qui meruere, ferant: let those who have deserved their punishment bear it patiently (Ovid)

æquum est peccatis veniam poscentem reddere rursus: the one who asks pardon for faults should grant the same to others (Horace)

ære quandoque salutem redimendam: safety must sometimes be bought with money

ærugo animi, rubigo ingenii: rusty mind, blighted genius (i.e., idleness is the blight of genius)

æs debitorem leve, gravius inimicum facit: a slight debt produces a debtor, a large one an enemy (Laberius)

æstimatio delicti præteriti ex post facto non crescit: the nature of a crime is not altered by subsequent acts

ætatem non tegunt tempora: our temples do not conceal our age

ævo rarissima nostro simplicitas: simplicity is nowadays very rare (Ovid)

age officium tuum: act your office

agentes, et consentientes, pari pœna puniendi: those acting and those consenting ought to bear equal punishment

agite pro viribus: act according to your strength

alia res sceptrum, alia plectrum: ruling men is one thing, entertaining them is another

aliæ nationes servitutem pati possunt, populi Romani est propria libertas: other nations may be able to put up with slavery, but liberty is peculiar to the Roman people (Cicero)

aliena nobis, nostra plus aliis placent: other people's things are more pleasing to us, and ours to other people (Publilius Syrus)

aliena opprobria sæpe absterrent vitiis: we are often deterred from crime by the disgrace of others (Horace)

aliena optimum frui insania: it is best to profit by the madness of others

aliena pericula, cautiones nostræ: others' dangers are our warnings

aliena vitia in oculis habemus, a tergo nostra sunt: the vices of others we have before our eyes, our own are behind our backs (Seneca)

alieno in loco haud stabile regnum est: the throne of another is not stable (i.e., sovereignty over a foreign land is insecure) (Seneca)

alienos agros irrigas tuis sitientibus: you water the fields of others while your own are parched

alienum est omne quicquid optando evenit: what we obtain merely by asking is not really our own (Publilius Syrus)

alii sementem faciunt, alii metentem: some do the planting, others the reaping

aliis lætus, sapiens sibi: cheerful for others, wise for himself

aliorum medicus, ipse ulceribus scates: a physician to others, while you yourself are full of ulcers

aliquando bonus dormitat Homerus: sometimes even the good Homer nods off (Horace)

aliquando et insanire jucundum est: it is pleasant at times to play the madman (Seneca)

aliquid mali propter vicinum malum: something bad from a bad neighbor (i.e., to be harmed because of an evil neighbor)

aliquis malo sit usus ab illo: let us derive some use or benefit from that evil

aliquis non debet esse judex in propria causa: no one should be a judge in his own cause

aliter catuli longe olent, aliter sues: puppies and pigs have a very different smell (Plautus)

alitur vitium vivitque tegendo: the taint is nourished and lives by being concealed (i.e., vice lives and thrives by secrecy) (Virgil)

aliud est celare, aliud tacere: it is one thing to conceal, another to be silent

aliud legunt pueri, aliud viri, aliud senes: boys read books one way, men another, old men another (Terence)

alium silere quod valeas (or **voles**), **primus sile:** to make another person hold his tongue, be first silent (Seneca)

alius est amor, alius cupido: love is one thing, lust another (Lucius Afranius)

alius peccat, alius plectitur: one man sins, the other is punished

allegans contraria non est audiendus: no one is to be heard whose evidence is contradictory

alta sedent civilis vulnera dextræ: deep-seated are the wounds dealt out in civil conflict (or civil wars) (Lucan)

alteri sic tibi: do to another as to yourself

alterum alterius auxilio eget: one thing needs the help of another

altissima quæque flumina minimo sono labuntur: the deepest rivers flow with the least noise (i.e., still waters run deep) (Curtius)

ama et fac quod vis: love and do what you will (adapted from St. Augustine)

amabit sapiens, cupient cæteri: the wise man loves, the others are lecherous (Lucius Afranius)

amans iratus multa mentitur: an angry lover tells himself many lies (Publilius Syrus)

amantes amentes: in love, in delirium (Terence)

amantes sunt amentes: lovers are lunatics (Terence)

amantium iræ amoris redintegratio est: the quarrels of lovers are the renewal of love (Terence)

amare et sapere vix deo conceditur: even a god finds it hard to love and be wise at the same time (Publilius Syrus and Laberius)

amarus vitiorum fructus: the fruit of sin is bitter

amat victoria curam: victory and care are close friends

ambiguum pactum contra venditorem interpretandum est: an ambiguous contract is to be interpreted against the seller

amici probantur rebus adversis: friends are proved by adversity (Cicero)

amici vitium ni feras, prodis tuum: unless you bear with the faults of a friend, you betray your own (Publilius Syrus)

amicitia fucata vitanda: feigned friendship [is] to be avoided

amicitia semper prodest, amor et nocet: friendship always benefits, love sometimes injures (Seneca and Publilius Syrus)

amicitiæ immortales, mortales inimicitias debere esse: friendships should be immortal, enmities should be mortal (Livy)

amico ficto nulla fit injuria: no injury is done to a feigned friend

amicorum esse communia omnia: friends' goods are common property

amicos esse fures temporis: friends are thieves of time (Francis Bacon)

amicum ita habeas, posse ut fieri hunc inimicum scias: be on such terms with your friend as if you knew that he might one day become your enemy (Laberius)

amicum perdere est damnorum maximum: to lose a friend is the greatest of all losses (Publilius Syrus)

amicus certus in re incerta cernitur: a true friend is certain when certainty is uncertain (i.e., a friend in need is a friend indeed) (Ennius)

amicus est unus animus in duobus corporibus: a friend is one soul in two bodies (Aristotle)

amicus in necessitate probatur: a friend is proven in time of necessity (or, a friend in need is a friend indeed)

amicus Plato, amicus Socrates, sed magis amica veritas: Plato is my friend, Socrates is my friend, but truth is more my friend

amicus Plato, sed magis amica veritas: Plato is my friend, but truth is more my friend

amicus verus rara avis: a true friend is a rare bird

amicus vitæ solatium: a friend is the solace of life

amittimus iisdem modis quibus acquirimus: we gain and lose by the same means

amittit famam qui se indignis comparat: he loses repute who compares himself with unworthy people (Phædrus)

amittit merito proprium, qui alienum appetit: the one who covets what is another's deservedly loses what is his own (Phædrus)

amor animi arbitrio sumitur, non ponitur: we choose to love, we do not chose to cease loving (Publilius Syrus)

amor Dei et proximi summa beatitudo: the love of God and our neighbor is the highest happiness

amor et melle et felle est fecundissimus: love has both honey and gall in abundance (Plautus)

amor gignit amorem: love begets love

amor omnibus idem: love is the same in all (Virgil)

amor tussisque non celantur: love, and a cough, are not concealed (Ovid)

amoris vulnus idem sanat qui facit: love's wounds are cured by love itself (Publilius Syrus)

an nescis longas regibus esse manus?: do you not know that kings have long hands? (Ovid)

an quisquam est alius liber, nisi ducere vitam cui licet, ut voluit?: is any man free except the one who can pass his life as he pleases? (Persius)

anguillam cauda tenes: you hold an eel by the tail (i.e., you have caught a lion by the tail)

anguis in herba latet: a snake concealed in the grass

animi cultus quasi quidam humanitatis cibus: cultivation is as necessary to the soul as food is to the body (Cicero)

animi scrinium servitus: servitude [is] the cage of the soul

animo ægrotanti medicus est oratio: kind words are as a physician to an afflicted spirit

animum rege, qui nisi paret imperat: rule your spirit well, for if it is not subject to you, it will rule over you (Horace)

animus æquus optimum est ærumnæ condimentum: a patient mind is the best remedy for trouble (Plautus)

animus est nobilitas: the soul is the nobility

animus hominis est anima scripti: the intention of the person is the intention of the written instrument

animus tamen omnia vincit; ille etiam vires corpus habere facit: courage conquers all things; it even gives strength to the body (Ovid)

annus inceptus habetur pro completo: a year begun we reckon as completed

ante victoriam ne canas triumphum: do not celebrate your triumph before you have conquered

antiquissima quæque commenticia: all that is most ancient is a lie (or, a fiction)

antiquitas sæculi juventus mundi: ancient times were the youth of the world (Francis Bacon)

aperit præcordia liber: wine opens the seals of the heart (Horace)

aperte mala cum est mulier, tum demum est bona: when a woman is openly bad, she then is at the best (i.e., open dishonesty is preferable to concealed hypocrisy)

apex est autem senectutis auctoritas: the crown of old age is authority (Cicero)

appetitus rationi pareat: let your desires be governed by reason (Cicero)

aqua profunda est quieta: still water runs deep

aquam a pumice nunc postulas: you are trying to get water from a stone (Plautus)

arbore dejecta quivis (or **qui vult**) **ligna colligit:** when the tree is thrown down, anyone who wishes may gather the wood (i.e., even the lowliest will gather the fruits of the fallen tyrant)

arbores serit diligens agricola, quarum aspiciet baccam ipse nunquam: the industrious husbandman plants trees, not one berry of which he will ever see (Cicero)

arcanum demens detegit ebrietas: mad drunkenness discloses every secret (Virgil)

arcum intensio frangit, animum remissio: straining breaks the bow, and relaxation the mind (Publilius Syrus)

ardua deturbans vis animosa quatit: the strength of courage shatters higher things

ardua enim res famam præcipitantem retrovertere: it is a hard thing to prop up a falling reputation (Francis Bacon)

ardua res hæc est opibus non tradere mores: it is a hard thing not to surrender morals for riches (Martial)

arma pacis fulcra: arms are the props (or buttresses) of peace

arma tenenti omnia dat, qui justa negat: the one who refuses what is just, gives up everything to an enemy in arms (Lucan)

ars fit ubi a teneris crimen condiscitur annis: where crime is taught from early years, it becomes a part of nature (Ovid)

ars prima regni posse te invidiam pati: the first art to be learned by a ruler is to endure envy (Seneca)

ars varia vulpis, ast una echino maxima: the fox has many tricks, the hedgehog has one, and it is the greatest of them

artes serviunt vitæ; sapientia imperat: the arts are the servants of life; wisdom its master (Seneca)

asinus asino, et sus sui pulcher: as an ass is beautiful to an ass, so a pig is to a pig

asperæ facetiæ, ubi nimis ex vero traxere, acrem sui memoriam relinquunt: a bitter jest, when it comes too near the truth, leaves a sharp sting behind it (Tacitus)

asperius nihil est humili cum surgit in altum: nothing is more harsh (or galling) than a low man raised to a high position (Claudian)

aspirat primo Fortuna labori: Fortune smiles upon our first effort (Virgil)

assiduus usus uni rei deditus et ingenium et artem sæpe vincit: constant practice devoted to one subject often outdoes both intelligence and skill (Cicero)

at caret insidiis hominum, quia mitis, hirundo: the swallow is not ensnared by men because of its gentle nature (Ovid)

at pulchrum est digito monstrari et dicier: his est: it is pleasing to be pointed at with the finger and to have it said: there he goes (Persius)

atria regum hominibus plena sunt, amicis vacua: the courts of kings are full of men, empty of friends (Seneca)

atrocitatis mansuetudo est remedium: gentleness is the remedy for cruelty (Phædrus)

attendite vobis: attend to yourselves

auctor pretiosa facit: the giver makes the gift precious (adapted from Ovid)

audacter calumniare, semper aliquid hæret: hurl calumny boldly, some of it always sticks (Francis Bacon)

audax ad omnia fœmina, quæ vel amat vel odit: a woman, when she either loves or hates, will dare anything

audendo magnus tegitur timor: great fear is concealed under daring (Lucan)

audi alteram partem: hear the other party (i.e., listen to both sides) (St. Augustine)

audi, vide, tace, si vis vivere in pace: use your ears and eyes, but hold your tongue, if you would live in peace

audiatur et altera pars: let the other side also have a hearing (Seneca)

audire est operæ pretium: it is worth your while to hear (Horace)

auri sacra fames quid non?: what does the accursed greed for gold not drive men to do?

auro loquente nihil pollet quævis ratio: when gold speaks, not even the least reason avails

auro quæque janua panditur: a golden key opens any door

aurum omnes victa jam pietate colunt: all men now worship gold, all other types of reverence being done away

auscultare disce, si nescis loqui: if you do not know how to talk, learn to listen (Pomponius Bononiensis)

aut disce, aut discede; manet sors tertia, cædi: either learn, or depart; a third course is open to you, and that is, submit to be flogged

aut non tentaris, aut perfice: either do not try it or go through with it (Ovid)

aut nunquam tentes aut perfice: either never attempt or accomplish (i.e., try not, do!; after Ovid)

aut prodesse volunt aut delectare poëtæ: poets wish either to profit or to please (Horace)

aut regem aut fatuum nasci oportere: a man ought to be born either a king or a fool (Seneca)

auxilia humilia firma consensus facit: union gives strength to the humblest of aids (Laberius and Publilius Syrus)

auxilium non leve vultus habet: a pleasing countenance is no small advantage (Ovid)

avarus, nisi cum moritur, nil recte facit: a miser does nothing right except when he dies

B

barbæ tenus sapientes: men are wise as far as their beards (referring to those who pretend to have knowledge they do not in fact possess)

barbaris ex fortuna pendet fides: the fidelity of barbarians depends on fortune (Livy)

bastardus nullius est filius, aut filius populi: a bastard is the son of no one, or the son of the people

beati monoculi in regione cærcorum: blessed is the one-eyed person in the country of the blind

beatus autem esse sine virtute nemo potest: no one can be happy without virtue (Cicero)

beatus enim nemo dici potest extra veritatem projectus: no one can be called happy who is living a life of falsehood (Seneca)

bella gerant alii: leave war to others (Ovid)

bellum nec timendum nec provocandum: war ought neither to be dreaded nor provoked (Pliny the Younger)

bene agendo nunquam defessus: never weary of doing good (after Galatians 6:9)

bene dormit, qui non sentit quod male dormiat: he sleeps well who is not conscious that he sleeps ill

bene est cui Deus obtulit parca quod satis est manu: well for him to whom God has given enough with a sparing hand

bene orasse est bene studuisse: to have prayed well is to have striven well (Ovid)

bene qui latuit bene vixit: well has he lived who has lived a retired life (i.e., he who has lived in obscurity has lived in security) (Ovid)

bene qui pacifice: he lives well who lives peacefully

bene qui sedulo: he lives well who lives industriously

beneficia dare qui nescit, injuste petit: the one who knows not how to confer a kindness has not the right to ask any for himself

beneficia plura recipit qui scit reddere: he receives the most favors who knows how to return them (Publilius Syrus)

beneficium accipere libertatem vendere est: to accept a favor is to sell one's liberty (Publilius Syrus and Laberius)

beneficium dignis ubi des, omnes obliges: where you confer a benefit on those worthy of it, you confer a favor on all (Publilius Syrus)

beneficium invito non datur: no benefit can be conferred upon one who will not accept it

beneficium non est, cujus sine rubore meminisse non possum: a favor that a person cannot recall without a blush is not a favor (Seneca)

beneficium non in eo quot fit aut datur consistit sed in ipso dantis aut facientis animo: a benefit consists not in what is done or given, but in the intention of the giver or doer (Seneca)

benignus etiam dandi causam cogitat: even the benevolent man reflects upon the cause of giving

bibamus, moriendum est: let us drink, death is certain (Seneca the Elder)

bilingues cavendi: one should beware of the double-tongued

bis dat qui cito dat: he gives twice who gives quickly (Cervantes)

bis dat qui temptestive donat: he gives twice who gives on time

bis est gratum quod opus est, si ultro offeras: the kindness is doubled if what must be given is given willingly

bis interimitur qui suis armis perit: he dies twice who perishes by his own weapons (i.e., by his own devices) (Publilius Syrus)

bis peccare in bello non licet: it is not permitted to err twice in war

bis pueri senes: old men are twice children

bis repetita placent: that which pleases is twice repeated (Horace)

bis vincit qui se vincit: he conquers twice who conquers himself

bis vivit qui bene vivit: he lives twice who lives well

bona nemini hora est, ut non alicui sit mala: there is no hour good for one man that is not bad for another (Publilius Syrus)

bonæ leges malis ex moribus proceantur: good laws grow out of evil acts (Macrobius)

bonarum rerum consuetudo pessima est: nothing is worse than being accustomed to good things (or good fortune) (Publilius Syrus)

boni judicis est lites dirimere: a good judge is one who prevents litigation

boni pastoris est tondere pecus, non deglubere: it is the duty of a good shepherd to shear his sheep, not to flay them (Emperor Tiberius, in reference to taxation)

bonis a divitibus nihil timendum: good men ought to fear nothing from the rich

bonis nocet quisquis pepercerit malis: he hurts the good who spares the bad (Publilius Syrus)

bonis quod bene fit (or **benefit**) **haud perit:** whatever good is done for good men is never done in vain (Plautus)

bonitas non est pessimis esse meliorem: it is not goodness to be better than the worst (Seneca)

bonum ego quam beatum me esse nimio dici mavolo: I would rather be called good than well off (Plautus)

bonum est fugienda aspicere in alieno malo: it is good to see in the misfortune of another what we should shun ourselves (Publilius Syrus)

bonum est, pauxillum amare sane, insane non bonum est: it is good to be moderately sane in love, but it is not good to be insanely in love (Plautus)

bonum magis carendo quam fruendo cernitur: that which is good is perceived more strongly in its absence than in its enjoyment

bonum vinum lætificat cor hominis: good wine makes men's hearts rejoice

bonum virum facile crederes, magnum libenter: you might believe a good man easily, a great man with pleasure (Tacitus)

bonus animus in mala re dimidium est mali: good courage in a bad circumstance is half of the evil overcome (Plautus)

bonus atque fidus judex honestum prætulit utili: a good and faithful judge ever prefers the honorable to the expedient (Horace)

bonus dux bonum reddit militem: the good leader makes good soldiers

bonus judex damnat improbanda, non odit: the good judge condemns the crime, but does not hate the criminal (Seneca)

bonus vir semper tiro: a good man is always learning

bos lassus fortius figit pedem: the tired ox plants its foot more firmly

brevis ipsa vita est sed malis fit longior (also, **brevis ipsa vita est sed longior malis**): life itself is short but evils make it longer (Publilius Syrus)

brevis voluptas mox doloris est parens: short-lived pleasure is the parent of pain

brevissima ad divitias per contemptum divitiarum via est: the shortest way to wealth lies in the contempt of wealth (Seneca)

C

cadit ira metu: fear causes anger to subside (Ovid)

cæca invidia est: envy is blind (Livy)

cæcus non judicat de colore: the blind do not judge of colors

cælum (or **cœlum**) **non animum mutant qui trans mare currunt:** they change the sky, not their soul, who run across the sea (Horace)

Cæsar non supra grammaticos: Cæsar has no authority over the grammarians

cæteris major qui melior: the one who is better than all others is greater

calamitosus est animus futuri anxius: dreadful is the state of that mind that is anxious about the future (Seneca)

calumniam contra calumniatorem virtus repellit: virtue turns calumny back against the calumniator

camelus desiderans cornua etiam aures perdidit: the camel, begging for horns, was deprived of its ears as well

candida pax homines, trux decet ira feras: white-robed peace becomes men, savage anger becomes wild beasts (Ovid)

candide secure: honesty is the best policy

canis timidus vehementius latrat quam mordet (pl. **canes timidi vehementius latrant quam mordent**): a timid dog barks more violently than it bites (Curtius)

cantabit vacuus coram latrone viator: the empty-handed traveler sings before the robber (i.e., the penniless man has nothing to lose) (Juvenal)

capiat qui capere possit: let him take who can (i.e., catch as catch can)

captantes capti sumus: we catchers have been caught (i.e., the biter is bitten)

cara Deo nihilo carent: God's beloved are in want of nothing

caret periculo, qui etiam (cum est) tutus cavet: he is most free from danger, who, even when safe, is on his guard (Publilius Syrus)

carior est illis homo quam sibi: man is dearer to them (the gods) than to himself (Juvenal)

carpe diem, quam minimum (or **minime**) **credula postero:** seize the day, trusting little in tomorrow (Horace)

carpent tua poma nepotes: your descendants will pick your fruit

caseus est sanus quem dat avara manus: cheese is healthy when given with a sparing hand

casta ad virum matrona parendo imperat: a chaste wife acquires an influence over her husband by obeying him (Laberius and Publilius Syrus)

casus quem sæpe transit, aliquando invenit: chance (or misfortune) will at some time or another find the one whom it has often passed by (Publilius Syrus)

catus amat pisces, sed non vult tingere plantas: a cat likes fish, but it does not like to wet its paws

causarum ignoratio in re nova mirationem facit: in extraordinary events ignorance of their causes produces astonishment (Cicero)

cautionis is in re plus quam in persona: goods are better sureties than the debtor's person

cautis pericula prodesse aliorum solent: prudent people are ever ready to profit from the experiences of others (Phædrus)

cautus metuit foveam lupus: the cautious wolf fears the snare

cave ab homine unius libri: beware of the man of one book (adapted from St. Thomas Aquinas)

cave ignoscas: take care not to overlook or forgive

cave ne cadas: take heed you do not fall (i.e., beware of falling from your high position)

cave ne quidquam incipias, quod post pœniteat: take care not to begin anything of which you may repent (Publilius Syrus)

cave quid dicis, quando et cui: beware what you say, when, and to whom

cavendi nulla est dimittenda occasio: no occasion to be alert is to be overlooked

cavendum a meretricibus: one ought to beware of prostitutes

cedant arma togæ, concedant laurea laudi: let arms yield to the toga, laurels to pæans (Cicero)

celsæ graviore casu decidunt turres: lofty towers fall with a heavier crash (Horace)

certa amittimus dum incerta petimus: we lose things certain in pursuing things uncertain (Plautus)

certanti et resistenti victoria cedit: victory yields to the one who struggles and resists

certe ignoratio futurorum malorum utilius est quam scientia: it is more advantageous not to know than to know the evils that are coming upon us (Cicero)

certis rebus certa signa præcurrunt: certain signs precede certain events (Cicero)

certum pete finem: aim at a certain end (i.e., aim at a sure thing)

certum voto pete finem: set a definite limit to your desire (Horace)

charitas non quærit quæ sua sunt: love does not seek things for itself

charta non erubescit: a document does not blush

cineri gloria sera est (or **cineri gloria sera venit**): glory paid to ashes (the dead) comes too late (Martial)

citius venit periculum cum contemnitur: the danger we despise comes quickest upon us (Publius Syrus and Laberius)

cito enim arescit lacrima, præsertim in alienis malis: for a tear is quickly dried, especially when shed for the misfortunes of others (Cicero)

cito maturum, cito putridum: soon ripe, soon rotten

cito rumpes arcum, semper si tensum habueris, at si laxaris, quum voles, erit utilis: a bow kept taut will quickly break, but kept loosely strung, it will serve you when you need it (Phædrus)

cito scribendo non fit, ut bene scribatur; bene scribendo fit, ut cito: write quickly and you will never write well; write well, and you will soon write quickly (Quintilian)

claude os, aperi oculos: close your mouth, open your eyes

cœlum (or **cælum**) **non animum mutant qui trans mare currunt:** those who cross the sea change their climate, but not their character (Horace)

cogas amantem irasci, amare si velis: you must make a lover angry if you wish him to love (Publilius Syrus)

cogenda mens est ut incipiat: the mind must be stimulated for it to make a beginning (Seneca)

cogi qui potest nescit mori: the one who can be compelled knows not how to die (Seneca)

cogitationis pœnam nemo meretur: no one deserves punishment for a thought

colossus magnitudinem suam servabit etiam si steterit in puteo: a giant will keep his size even though he will have stood in a well (Seneca)

comes jucundus in via pro vehiculo est: a pleasant companion on the road is as good as a vehicle (Publilius Syrus)

commune naufragium omnibus est consolatio: a shipwreck that is common to all is a consolation

commune periculum concordiam parit: a common danger begets unity

communia esse amicorum inter se omnia: all things are common among friends (Terence)

communis error facit jus: sometimes common error makes law

compendia dispendia: short cuts are roundabouts

compendiaria res improbitas, virtusque tarda: wickedness takes the shorter road, and virtue the longer

compesce mentem: control your temper (Horace)

concordia res parvæ crescunt, discordia maximæ dilabuntur: with concord small things increase, with discord the greatest things go to ruin (Sallust)

conjunctio maris et fœminæ est de jure naturæ: the conjuction of man and woman is of the law of nature

conscia mens recti famæ mendacia risit (or **ridet**): the mind conscious of integrity scorns the lies of rumor (Ovid)

conscientia rectæ voluntatis maxima consolatio est rerum incommodarum: the consciousness of good intention is the greatest solace of misfortunes (Cicero)

consilia res magis dant hominibus quam homines rebus: men's plans should be regulated by the circumstances, not circumstances by the plans (Livy)

consiliis nox apta ducum, lux aptior armis: night is the time for counsel, day for arms (Caius Rabirius)

consilio melius vinces quam iracundia: you will conquer more surely by prudence than by passion (Publilius Syrus)

constans et lenis, ut res expostulet, esto: be firm or mild as the occasion may require (Cato)

consuetudo manerii et loci est observanda: the custom of the manor and the place is to be observed

contemni est gravius stultitiæ quam percuti: to be despised is more galling to a foolish man than to be whipped

contemptum periculorum assiduitas periclitandi dabit: constant exposure to dangers will breed contempt for them (Seneca)

contentum vero suis rebus esse, maximæ sunt certissimæque divitiæ: to be content with what one has is the greatest and truest of riches (Cicero)

continua messe senescit ager: a field becomes exhausted by constant tillage (Ovid)

contra malum mortis, non est medicamen in hortis: against the evil of death there is no remedy in the garden

contraria contrariis curantur: opposite cures opposite

contumeliam si dicis, audies: if you utter abuse, you must expect to receive it (or, if you speak insults you will hear them as well) (Plautus)

conventio privatorum non potest publico juri derogare: an agreement between individuals cannot set aside public law

corpora lente augescunt, cito extinguuntur: bodies are slow in growth, rapid in decay (Horace and Tacitus)

corpus non animæ domicilium sed diversum est: the body is not the abode of the soul but its enemy

corpus onustum hesternis vitiis animum quoque prægravat una: the body, loaded with yesterday's excess, also bears down the mind (Horace)

corrumpunt mores bonos colloquia mala: bad company corrupts good morals (1 Corinthians 15:33)

corruptio optimi pessima: the corruption of the best is the worst

corruptissima (in) republica plurimæ leges: in the most corrupt state exist the most laws (or, the more corrupt the state, the more the laws) (Terence and Tacitus)

crede mihi; miseros prudentia prima relinquit: believe me; it is prudence that first forsakes the wretched (Ovid)

crede quod est quod vis: believe that that is which you wish to be (Ovid)

crede quod habes, et habes: believe that you have it, and you have it

crescit amor nummi quantum ipsa pecunia crescit: the love of money increases as wealth itself increases (Juvenal)

cressa ne careat pulchra dies nota: let not a day so fair be without its white mark (Horace)

crimen quos inquinat, æquat: crime puts on an equal footing those whom it defiles

crimina qui cernunt aliorum, non sua cernunt; hi sapiunt aliis, desipiuntque sibi: those who see the faults of others, but not their own, are wise for others and fools for themselves

crimine ab uno disce omnes: from the guilt (or crime) of one learn the nature of them all (Virgil)

crudelem medicum intemperans æger facit: a disorderly patient makes the physician cruel (Publilius Syrus)

crux est si metuas quod vincere nequeas: it is torture to fear what you cannot overcome (Ausonius)

cucullus non facit monachum: the cowl does not make the monk

cui licitus est finis, etiam licent media: for whom the end is lawful, the means are also lawful (i.e., the end justifies the means)

cui placet alterius, sua nimirum est odio sors: when a person envies another's lot, it is natural for him to be discontented with his own

cui placet obliviscitur, cui dolet meminit: we forget our pleasures, we remember our pains (Cicero)

cui prodest scelus, is fecit: he has committed the crime who has derived the profit (Seneca)

cuilibet in arte sua perito credendum est: every skilled man is to be trusted in his own art

cuisvis (or **cujusvis**) **hominis est errare, nullius nisi insipientis in errore perseverare:** any man is liable to err, [but] no one except a fool will persevere in error (Cicero)

cujus est solum, ejus (est) usque ad cœlum: the one who owns the soil owns everything above it to the sky

cujus sit vita indecoris mortem fugere turpem haut convenit: one whose life has been disgraceful is not entitled to escape a disgraceful death (Accius)

cujus vita fulgor, ejus verba tonitrua: his words are thunderbolts whose life is as lightning

culpa sua damnum sentiens non intelligitur damnum pati: he who suffers by his own fault is not deemed a sufferer

culpam pœna premit comes: punishment presses hard upon the heels of crime (Horace)

cum altera lux venit jam cras hesternum consumpsimus: when another day has arrived, we will find that we have consumed our yesterday's tomorrow (Persius)

cum corpore mentem crescere sentimus pariterque senescere: we find that, as the mind strengthens with the body, it decays with it in like manner (Lucretius)

cum fortuna manet, vultum servatis amici: while fortune lasts you will see your friend's face (Petronius)

cum frueris felix quæ sunt adversa caveto: when fortune is lavish of her favors beware of adversity (Cato)

cum larvis non luctandum: one ought not to wrestle with ghosts

cum licet fugere, ne quære litem: do not seek the quarrel, or the suit, of which there is an opportunity of escaping

cum odio sui cœpit veritas: the first reaction to truth is hatred (Tertullian)

cum plus sunt potæ, plus potiuntur aquæ: the more they have been drinking, the more water they drink (often said of the thirst for knowledge)

cum quod datur spectabis, et dantem adspice: while you look at what is given, look also at the giver (Seneca)

cum vitia prosint, peccat qui recte facit: if vices were profitable, the virtuous man would be the sinner

cuncta complecti velle, stultum: it is foolish to wish to encompass all things

cupias non placuisse nimis: do not aim at too much popularity (Martial)

cupiditas ex homine, cupido ex stulto numquam tollitur: a man can be cured of his lust, but never a fool of his greed (Lucilius)

cupido dominandi cunctis affectibus flagrantior est: the desire to rule is the most ardent of all the affections of the mind (Tacitus)

cur ante tubam tremor occupat artus?: why should a tremor seize the limbs before the trumpet sounds? (Virgil)

cur omnium fit culpa, paucorum scelus?: why should the wickedness of a few be laid to the account of all?

cura facit canos: care brings grey hairs

cura ut valeas: take care that you keep well (Cicero)

curæ leves loquuntur, ingentes stupent: light griefs find utterance, great ones hold silence (Seneca)

curis tabescimus omnes: we are all consumed by cares

cutis vulpina consuenda est cum cute leonis: the fox's skin must be sewn to that of the lion

D

da fidei quæ fidei sunt: give to faith that which belongs to faith (Francis Bacon)

da locum melioribus: give place to your betters (Terence)

da requiem; requietus ager bene credita reddit: take rest; a field that has rested gives a bountiful crop (Ovid)

da spatium tenuemque moram; male cuncta ministrat impetus: allow time and slight delay; haste and violence ruin everything (Statius)

damna minus consueta movent: losses to which we are accustomed affect us little (Juvenal)

damnosa quid non imminuit dies?: what is there that corroding time does not damage? (Horace)

damnum appellandum est cum mala fama lucrum: gain made at the expense of reputation must be reckoned as loss

damnum sentit dominus: the master suffers the loss

damnum sine injuria esse potest: loss without injury is deemed possible

dat Deus immiti cornua curta bovi: God gives short horns to the cruel ox

de calceo sollicitus, at pedem nihil curans: anxious about the shoe, but careless about the foot

de duobus malis, minus est semper eligendum: of two evils, always choose the lesser (Thomas à Kempis)

de gustibus non est disputandum (or **de gustibus non disputandum**): there is no disputing about tastes

de inimico non loquaris male sed cogites: do not speak ill of your enemy, but plan it (Publilius Syrus)

de male quæsitis vix gaudet tertius hæres: a third heir seldom enjoys what is dishonestly acquired (Juvenal)

de morte hominis nulla est cunctatio longa: no delay is long when it concerns the death of a man

de mortuis nihil nisi bonum: of the dead say nothing but good (Chilon, one of the Seven Sages of Greece)

de mortuis nil nisi bene: of the dead say nothing but what is favorable

de mortuis nil nisi verum: of the dead say nothing but what is true

de multis grandis acervus erit: out of many things a great heap will be formed (Ovid)

de parvis grandis acervus erit: small things will make a large pile

de paupertate tacentes plus poscente ferent: those who are silent about their poverty fare better than those who beg (Horace)

de principiis non est disputandum: there is no disputing about principles

de similibus idem est judicium: in similar cases, the judgment is the same (i.e., follow precedent)

de te fabula narratur: the story relates to you (Horace)

de vita hominis nulla cunctatio longa est: when the life of a man is at stake, no delay that is afforded can be too long

de vitiis nostris scalam nobis facimus, si vitia ipsa calcamus: we make a ladder for ourselves of our vices, if we trample those same vices underfoot (St. Augustine)

debile fundamentum fallit opus: a weak foundation destroys the work upon which it is built

decet patriam nobis cariorem esse quam nosmetipsos: our country ought to be dearer to us than ourselves (Cicero)

decet verecundum esse adolescentem: it becomes a young man to be modest (Plautus)

decipimur specie recti: we are deceived by the appearance of rectitude (Horace)

decipit frons prima multos: the first appearance deceives many

decorum ab honesto non potest separari: propriety cannot be separated from what is honorable (Cicero)

dedecet philosophum abjicere animum: it dishonors a philosopher to be disheartened (Cicero)

dediscit animus sero quod didicit diu: the mind is slow in unlearning what it has been long learning (Seneca)

defectio virium adolescentiæ vitiis efficitur sæpius quam senectutis: loss of strength is more frequently due to faults of youth than old age (Cicero)

deficit omne quod nascitur: everything that is born passes away (Quintilian)

degeneranti genus opprobrium: to the degenerate man his good family is a disgrace

degeneres animos timor arguit: fear betrays ignoble souls (Virgil)

dei pherein ta ton theon: we must bear what the gods lay upon us (a Greek saying)

delegatus non potest delegare: a delegate cannot delegate

deliberando sæpe perit occasio: an opportunity (or occasion) is often lost through deliberation (Publilius Syrus)

deliberandum est diu, quod statuendum semel: that should be considered at length, which can be decided but once (Publilius Syrus)

deliberare utilia, mora est tutissima: to deliberate about useful things is the safest delay

delicta majorum immeritus lues: undeservedly you will atone for the sins of your fathers (Horace)

deligas tantum quem diligas: choose only the one whom you love

delphinum natare doces: you are teaching a dolphin to swim (i.e., you are wasting your time)

deme supercilio nubem: remove the clouds from your brow (i.e., come down from your cloud)

demonstratio longe optima est experientia: the best proof by far is experience (Francis Bacon)

denique non omnes eadem mirantur amantque: not all men admire or love the same things (Horace)

dente lupus, cornu taurus petit: the wolf attacks with its fang, the bull with its horn (Horace)

Deo dante nil nocet invidia, et non dante, nil proficit labor: when God gives, envy injures us not, and when He does not give, labor avails not

deos fortioribus adesse: the gods are said to aid the stronger (Tacitus)

deos placatos pietas efficiet et sanctitas: piety and holiness of life will propitiate the gods (Cicero)

deprendi miserum est: it is wretched to be found out (Horace)

derelicta fertilius revivescunt: fields left fallow recover their fertility (Pliny the Elder)

derelicto communis utilitatis contra naturam: the abandonment of what is for the common good is a crime against nature

derivativa potestas non potest esse major primitiva: the power derived cannot be greater than that from which it is derived

desidiam abjiciendam: idleness ought to be rejected

desine fata Deum flecti sperare precando: cease to hope that the decrees of Heaven can bend to prayer (Virgil)

desubito famam tollunt si quam solam videre in via: the moment they see a woman alone in the street, they cry scandal (Nævius)

desunt inopiæ multa, avaritiæ omnia: poverty is in want of many things, avarice of everything (Publilius Syrus)

det ille veniam facile, cui venia est opus: the one who needs pardon should readily grant it (Seneca)

Deus scitur melius nesciendo: God is best known in not knowing him (St. Augustine)

di irati laneos pedes habent: the gods, when angry, have their feet covered with wool

di nos quasi pilas homines habent: the gods treat us mortals like so many balls to play with (Plautus)

dicere enim bene nemo potest, nisi qui prudenter intelligit: no one can speak well, unless he thoroughly understands his subject (Cicero)

dicique beatus ante obitum nemo supremaque funera debet: no one should be called happy before he is dead and buried (Ovid)

dies adimit ægritudinem: time cures our griefs

difficile est crimen non prodere vultu: it is difficult not to betray guilt by the countenance (Ovid)

difficile est longum subito deponere amorem: it is difficult to give up suddenly a long love (Catullus)

difficile est plurimum virtutem revereri, qui semper secunda fortuna sit usus: it is difficult for one who has enjoyed uninterrupted good fortune to have a due reverence for virtue (Cicero)

difficile est proprie communia dicere: it is difficult to say what is common in a distinct way (Horace)

difficile est tenere quæ acceperis nisi exerceas: it is difficult to retain what you may have learned unless you should practice it (Pliny the Younger)

difficile est tristi fingere mente jocum: it is difficult to feign jocularity when one is in a sad mood (Tibullus)

difficilem oportet aurem habere ad crimina: one should not lend an easy ear to criminal charges (i.e., accusations should be taken with skepticism) (Publilius Syrus)

difficilia quæ pulchra: beauty is difficult to attain

difficilis in otio quies: tranquility is difficult if one has leisure

difficilius est sarcire concordiam quam rumpere: it is more difficult to restore harmony than to sow dissension

dignus est decipi qui de recipiendo cogitavit cum daret: the man who gives, thinking to receive, deserves to be deceived (Seneca)

dii laboribus omnia vendunt: the gods sell all things to hard labor

dilationes in lege sunt odiosæ: delays in the law are odious

diligentia maximum etiam mediocris ingeni subsidium: diligence is a very great help even to a mediocre intelligence (Seneca)

diligentia, qua una virtute omnes virtutes reliquæ continentur: diligence, the one virtue that embraces in it all the rest (Cicero)

diligitur nemo, nisi cui fortuna secunda est: only he who is the favorite of fortune is loved (Ovid)

dimidium facti qui (bene) cœpit habet: sapere aude: what is well begun is already half done: dare to be wise (Horace)

discipulus est prioris posterior dies: each day succeeding is the student of the one preceding (Publilius Syrus)

discite justitiam moniti: having been warned, learn justice

disputandi pruritas ecclesiarum scabies: an itch for disputation is the mange of the Church (Henry Wotton, reputedly said of King Charles)

dissidia inter æqualies, pessima: dissensions among equals are the worst

distrahit animum librorum multitudo: a multitude of books distracts the mind (i.e., his learning is wide but shallow) (Seneca)

dives aut iniquus est aut iniqui hæres: a rich man is either an unjust man or the heir of one

dives est, cui tanta possessio est, ut nihil optet amplius: rich is the one who wishes no more than he has (Cicero)

dives qui fieri vult, et cito vult fieri: the one who desires to become rich desires to become rich quickly (Juvenal)

divitis servi maxime servi: servants to the rich are the most abject

dociles imitandis turpibus ac pravis omnes sumus: we are all easily taught to imitate what is base and depraved (Juvenal)

docti rationem artis intelligunt, indocti voluptatem: the learned understand the principles of art, the unlearned feel its pleasure (Quintilian)

doctos doctis obloqui nefas esse: it is a sacrilege for scholars to malign scholars

doctrina est ingenii naturale quoddam pabulum: learning is a kind of natural food for the mind (Cicero)

doctrina sed vim promovet insitam rectique cultus pectora roborant: but instruction improves the innate powers (of the mind), and good discipline strengthens the heart (Horace)

dolendi modus, non est timendi: to suffering there is a limit, to being in fear there is none (Pliny the Younger)

dolendi modus, timendi non autem: there is a limit to grief, but not to fear (Francis Bacon, after Pliny the Younger)

doli non doli sunt, nisi astu colas: fraud is not fraud, unless craftily planned (Plautus)

dolium volvitur: an empty cask is easily rolled

dolosus versatur in generalibus: a deceiver deals in generalities

dolus versatur in generalibus: deceit deals in generalities

domi manere convenit felicibus: those who are happy at home should stay there

dominium a possessione cœpisse dicitur: a right is said to have its beginning from possession

dominus videt plurimum in rebus suis: the master sees best in his own affairs (Phædrus)

domus amica domus optima: the house of a friend is the best house

domus sua cuique tutissimum refugium: the safest place of refuge for everyone is his own home (Coke)

dona præsentis cape lætus horæ, et linque severa: gladly enjoy the gifts of the present hour, and banish serious thoughts (Horace)

donec eris felix, multos numerabis amicos; tempora si fuerint nubila, solus eris: as long as you are lucky, you will have many friends; if cloudy times come, you will be alone (Ovid)

dormit aliquando jus, moritur nunquam: a right sometimes sleeps, but never dies (i.e., sometimes in abeyance, but never abolished) (Coke)

dormiunt aliquando leges, nunquam moriuntur: the laws sometimes sleep, but never die

dos est magna parentum virtus: the virtue of parents is a great dowry (Horace)

dos est uxoria lites: strife is the dowry of a wife (Ovid)

dubiam salutem qui dat afflictis, negat: the one who offers the afflicted a doubtful deliverance denies all hope (Seneca)

dubitando ad veritatem pervenimus: by way of doubting we arrive at the truth (Cicero)

ducis ingenium, res adversæ nudare solent, celare secundæ: disasters are wont to reveal the abilities of a leader, good fortune to conceal them (Horace)

ducunt volentem fata, nolentem trahunt: fate leads the willing and drags the unwilling (Seneca, after Cleanthes)

dulce bellum inexpertis: war is delightful to the inexperienced (Erasmus)

dulce est desipere in loco: it is sweet to be silly in places (i.e., to unwind upon occasion) (Horace)

dulce est miseris socios habuisse doloris: it is a comfort to the wretched to have companions in misfortune

dulce et decorum est pro patria mori: sweet and seemly it is to die for one's country (Horace)

dulcia quandoque amara fieri: sometimes sweet things become bitter

dulcibus est verbis alliciendus amor: love is to be won by affectionate words

dulcibus est verbis mollis alendus amor: with soft words must love be fostered (Ovid)

dulcis inexpertis cultura potentis amici; expertus metuit: the cultivation of friendship with the powerful is pleasant to the inexperienced, but he who has experienced it dreads it (Horace)

dum fata fugimus, fata stulti incurrimus: while we flee from our fate, we like fools run into it (Buchanan)

dum in dubio est animus, paulo momento huc illuc impellitur: while the mind is in doubt, a very little sways it one way or the other (Terence)

dum inter homines sumus, colamus humanitatem: so long as we live among men, let us cherish humanity (Seneca)

dum lego, assentior: whilst I read, I give assent (Cicero)

dum loquor, hora fugit: while I am speaking, time flies (Ovid)

dum potes vive: live while you can

dum singuli pugnant, universi vincuntur: so long as they fight separately, the whole are conquered (Tacitus)

dum vitant stulti vitia, in contraria currunt: while fools try to avoid one error, they fall into its opposite (Horace)

dummodo morata recte veniat, dotata est satis: provided she comes with virtuous principles, a woman brings dowry enough (Plautus)

dumque punitur scelus, crescit: while crime is punished it yet increases (Seneca)

duo quum faciunt idem non est idem: when two do the same thing, it is not the same thing (Terence)

duos qui sequitur lepores neutrum capit: the one who follows two hares is sure to catch neither

dura lex, sed lex: the law is hard, but it is the law

dura usu molliora: difficult things become easier with practice

durate et vosmet rebus servate secundis: carry on and preserve yourselves for better times (Virgil)

durum et durum non faciunt murum: hard and hard do not make a wall (i.e., brick against brick, without mortar)

E

e flamma cibum petere: to fetch food from the flames (i.e., to live by desperate means) (Terence)

e labore dulcedo: pleasure arises out of labor

e multis paleis paulum fructus collegi: from much chaff I have gathered little grain

e tardegradis asinis equus non prodiit: the horse is not the progeny of the slow-paced ass

e tenui casa sæpe vir magnus exit: a great man often steps forth from a humble cottage

ea libertas est qui pectus purum et firmum gestitat; aliæ res obnoxiosæ nocte in obscura latent: liberty is having a pure and dauntless heart; all else is slavery and hidden darkness (Ennius)

ea molestissime ferre homines debent quæ ipsorum culpa ferenda sunt: men ought to be most annoyed by the sufferings that come from their own faults (Cicero)

eamus quo ducit gula: let us go where our appetite prompts us (Virgil)

effodiuntur opes, irritamenta malorum: riches, the incentives to evil, are dug out of the earth (Ovid)

effugere non potes necessitates, potes vincere: you cannot escape necessity, but you can overcome it (Seneca)

effugit mortem, quisquis contempserit; timidissimum quemque consequitur: whoever despises death escapes it, while it overtakes the one who is afraid of it (Curtius)

ego apros occido, alter fruitur pulpamento: I kill the boars, another enjoys their flesh

ego mihimet sum semper proximus: I am ever my nearest neighbor (or, I am always my own best friend)

eheu!, fugaces labuntur anni: alas!, the years glide swiftly away (Horace)

eheu!, quam brevibus pereunt ingentia causis (or **fatis**)**:** alas!, by what slight means are great affairs brought to destruction (Claudian)

ei, qui semel sua prodegerit, aliena credi non oportere: he who has once squandered his own ought not to be trusted with another's

elati animi comprimendi sunt: minds that are too much elated ought to be kept in check

elige eum cujus tibi placuit et vita et oratio: choose the one who recommends. himself to you by his life as well as by his speech (Seneca)

elucet maxime animi excellentia magnitudoque in despiciendis opibus: excellence and greatness of soul are most conspicuously displayed in contempt of riches

emas non quod opus est, sed quod necesse est; quod non opus est, asse carum est: buy not what you want, but what you need; what you do not want is costly at a penny (Cato the Elder)

emendatio pars studiorum longe utilissima: correction and revision of what we write is by far the most useful part of our studies (Quintilian)

emere malo quam rogare: I had rather buy than beg

emitur sola virtute potestas: virtue alone can purchase power (Claudian)

empta dolore docet experientia: experience bought with pain teaches

enim vero di nos quasi pilas homines habent: truly the gods use us men as footballs (Plautus)

eodem animo beneficium debetur, quo datur: a benefit is estimated according to the mind of the giver (Seneca)

epistola ... non erubescit: a letter ... does not blush (Cicero)

equi et poëtæ alendi, non saginandi: horses and poets should be fed, not pampered (Charles IX of France)

equo frænato est auris in ore: the ear of the bridled horse is in the mouth (Horace)

ergo hoc proprium est animi bene constituti, et lætari bonis rebus, et dolere contrariis: this is a proof of a well-constituted mind, to rejoice in what is good and to grieve at the opposite (Cicero)

eripe te moræ: tear yourself from all that detains you (Horace)

eripere vitam nemo non homini potest; at nemo mortem; mille ad hanc aditus patent: anyone may take life from man, but no one death; a thousand gates stand open to it (Seneca)

eripit interdum, modo dat medicina salutem: medicine sometimes destroys health, sometimes restores it (Ovid)

errantem in viam reductio: lead back the wanderer into the right way

error qui non resistitur approbatur: an error that is not resisted is approved

esse bonum facile est, ubi quod vetet esse remotum est: it is easy to be good when all that prevents it is far removed (Ovid)

esse oportet ut vivas, non vivere ut edas: you should eat to live, not live to eat (Cicero)

esse quam videri malim: I should wish to be rather than to seem

est aliquid fatale malum per verba levare: it is some alleviation of an incurable disease to speak of it to others (Ovid)

est aliquid valida sceptra tenere manu: it is something to hold the scepter with a firm hand (Ovid)

est ars etiam male dicendi: there is even an art of maligning

est aviditas dives, et pauper pudor: avarice is rich, while modesty is poor (Phædrus)

est (enim) demum vera felicitas, felicitate dignum videri: true happiness consists in being considered deserving of it (Pliny the Younger)

est deus in nobis, agitante calescimus illo: there is a god in us, who, when he stirs, sets us all aglow (Ovid)

est deus in nobis, et sunt commercia cœli: there is a god within us, and we hold commerce with heaven (Ovid)

est etiam miseris pietas, et in hoste probatur: regard for the wretched is a duty, and deserving of praise even in an enemy (Ovid)

est etiam quiete et pure et eleganter actæ ætatis placida ac lenis senectus: a life of peace, purity, and refinement leads to a calm and untroubled old age (Cicero)

est etiam, ubi profecto damnum præstet facere, quam lucrum: there are occasions when it is certainly better to lose than to gain (Plautus)

est genus hominum qui esse primos se omnium rerum volunt, nec sunt: there is a class of men who wish to be first in everything, and are not (Terence)

est in aqua dulci non invidiosa voluptas: there is no small pleasure in sweet water (Ovid)

est ipsa cupiditati tarda celeritas: to passion, even haste is slow (Publilius Syrus)

est miserorum, ut malevolentes sint atque invideant bonis: it is the tendency of the wretched to be ill-disposed toward and to envy the fortunate (Plautus)

est modus in rebus: there is a mean (or method) in all things (Horace)

est natura hominim novitatis avida: it is human nature to hunt for novelty (Pliny the Elder)

est nobis voluisse satis: to have willed suffices us (Tibullus)

est pater ille quem nuptiæ demonstrant: he is the father whom marriage points to as such

est pii Deum et patriam diligere: it is part of a good man to love God and country

est procax natura multorum in alienis miseriis: there are many who are only too ready to take advantage of the misfortunes of others (Pliny the Elder)

est profecto animi medicina, philosophia: philosophy is the true medicine of the mind (Cicero)

est proprium stultitiæ aliorum cernere vitia, oblivisci suorum: it is characteristic of folly to judge the faults of others and to forget its own (Cicero)

est quædam flere voluptas; expletur lacrymis egeriturque dolor: there is a certain pleasure in weeping; pain is soothed and alleviated by tears (Ovid)

est quoque cunctarum novitas carissima rerum: in all things, novelty is what we prize most (Ovid)

est unusquisque faber ipsæ suæ fortunæ: every man is the maker of his own fortune (or fate) (Appius Claudius)

esto prudens ut serpens et simplex scut columba: be as wise as the serpent and gentle as the dove (after St. Matthew 10:16)

esto, ut nunc multi, dives tibi, pauper amicis: be, as many now are, rich to yourself, poor to your friends (Juvenal)

estque pati pœnas quam meruisse minus: it is less to suffer punishment than to deserve it (Ovid)

esurienti ne occurras: do not throw yourself in the way of a hungry man

et credis cineres curare sepultos?: and do you think that the ashes of the dead concern themselves with our affairs? (Virgil)

et genus et formam regina pecunia donat: money, like a queen, bestows both rank and beauty (Horace)

et genus et proavos, et quæ non fecimus ipsi, vix ea nostra voco: we can scarcely call birth and ancestry, and what we have not ourselves done, our own

et genus et virtus, nisi cum re, vilior alga est: without money, both birth and virtue are as worthless as seaweed (Horace)

et mala sunt vicina bonis: there are bad qualities near akin to good (Ovid)

et male tornatos incudi reddere versus: and take ill-formed verses back to the anvil (Horace)

et minimæ vires frangere quassa valent: a little force will break that which has been cracked already (Ovid)

et monere, et moneri, proprium est veræ amicitiæ: to give counsel, as well as to take it, is a feature of true friendship (Cicero)

et qui nolunt occidere quenquam posse volunt: even those who have no wish to kill anyone, would like to have the power (Juvenal)

et quiescenti agendum est, et agenti quiescendum est: the active should occasionally rest, and the inactive should occasionally labor (Seneca)

et sanguis et spiritus pecunia mortalibus: money is both blood and life to mortal men

et sceleratis sol oritur: the sun shines even on the wicked (Seneca)

et semel emissum volat irrevocabile verbum: and a word once uttered flies abroad never to be recalled (Horace)

eternitatem cogita: think on eternity

etiam capillus unus habet umbram: even one hair has a shadow (Publilius Syrus)

etiam celeritas in desiderio mora est: in desire, swiftness itself is delay (Publilius Syrus)

etiam fera animalia, si clausa teneas, virtutis obliviscuntur: even wild animals, if you keep them in confinement, forget their fierceness

etiam ferocissimos domari: even the fiercest are overcome

etiam fortes viros subitis terreri: even brave men are alarmed by sudden terrors (Tacitus)

etiam illud quod scies nesciveris; ne videris quod videris: know not what you know, and see not what you see (Plautus)

etiam innocentes cogit mentiri dolor: pain makes even the innocent man a liar (Publilius Syrus)

etiam oblivisci qui (or **quid**) **sis interdum expedit:** it is sometimes expedient to forget who (or what) you are (Publilius Syrus)

etiam oblivisci quod scis interdum expedit: it is sometimes expedient to forget what you know (Publilius Syrus)

etiam quod esse videris: be what you seem to be

etiam sapientibus cupido gloriæ novissima exuitur: even for the wise, the desire for glory is the last of all passions to be laid aside (Tacitus)

eum ausculta, cui quatuor sunt aures: listen to the one who has four ears (i.e., one who is readier to hear than to speak)

eventus stultorum magister (**est**)**:** experience is the teacher of fools (Livy)

ex abusu non arguitur ad usum: no argument can be drawn from the abuse of a thing against its use

ex abusu non argumentum ad desuetudinem: the abuse of a thing is no argument for its disuse

ex Africa semper aliquid novi: out of Africa there is always something new (Pliny the Elder)

ex damno alterius, alterius utilitas: one man's loss is another man's gain

ex desuetudine amittuntur privilegia: it is from disuse that rights are lost

ex factis non ex dictis amici pensandi: friends are to be estimated from deeds, not words (Livy)

ex facto jus oritur: the law goes into effect after the fact

ex falsis, ut ab ipsis didicimus, verum effici non potest: from the false, as they have themselves taught us, we can obtain nothing true (Cicero)

ex granis fit acervus: many grains make a heap

ex inimico cogita posse fieri amicum: think that you may make a friend of an enemy (Seneca)

ex ipso ore procedit benedictio et maledictio: out of the same mouth comes blessing and cursing (St. James 3:10)

ex magno certamine magnas excitari ferme iras: it is when great issues are at stake that men's passions are more easily roused (Livy)

ex malis eligere minima: of evils to choose the least (Cicero)

ex malis moribus bonæ leges natæ sunt: from bad manners (or morals) good laws have sprung (Coke)

ex ore parvulorum veritas: out of the mouth of little children comes truth

ex otio plus negotii quam ex negotio habemus: our leisure gives us more to do than our business

ex parvis sæpe magnarum momenta rerum pendent: events of great consequence often spring from trifling circumstances (Livy)

ex vitio alterius sapiens emendat suum: from the faults of another a wise man will correct his own (Laberius)

exceptio probat regulam: the exception proves the rule (i.e., gives greater definition)

excessus in jure reprobatur: all excess is condemned by the law

excusatio non petita fit accusatio manifesta: an excuse not called for betrays the guilt of him who makes it

exemplo plus quam ratione vivimus: we live more by example than by reason

exemplumque dei quisque est in imagine parva: each person is the image of God in miniature (or, everyone is in a small way the image of God) (Manilius)

exercitatio optimus est magister: practice is the best teacher

exercitato artem parat (or, **exercitatio artem parat**): exercise gives skill (i.e., practice makes perfect)

exhæreditare filium non potest pater, nisi: the father may not disinherit the son, never (Justinian)

exigua pars est vitæ quam nos vivimus: the part of life that we really live is short (Seneca)

exiguum est ad legem bonum esse: it is but a small matter to be good in the eye of the law (Seneca)

exitus acta probat: the ending proves the deeds (i.e., all's well that ends well)

expedit esse deos, et, ut expedit esse putemus: it is expedient that gods exist, and, given it is expedient, let us believe it (Ovid)

experientia docet stultos: experience teaches fools

experto crede (or **experto credite**): believe one who has had experience (i.e., trust the expert) (Virgil)

expertus dico, nemo est in amore fidelis: I say as an expert, no one is faithful in love (Propertius)

expetendæ opes ut dignis largiamur: we should seek riches so that we may give to the deserving

expetuntur divitiæ ad perficiendas voluptates: riches are desired to bring about our pleasures

explorant adversa viros: adversity tries men

expressa nocent, non expressa non nocent: what is expressed may be hurtful, what is not expressed cannot do any injury (a principle of legal contracts)

expressio unius est exclusio alterius: the naming of one is the exclusion of the other

expressum facit cessare tacitum: a matter expressed causes that to cease which otherwise would have been implied

exstinctus (or **extinctus**) **amabitur idem:** [though hated in life,] the same man will be loved after he is dead (Horace)

extant recte factis præmia: the rewards of good deeds endure

extra lutum pedes habes: you have got your feet out of the mud

extrema gaudii luctus occupat: grief treads on the confines of gladness

extrema manus nondum operibus ejus imposita est: the finishing hand has not yet been put to his works

extrema primo nemo tentavit loco: no one tries extreme remedies at first (Seneca)

F

fabas indulcet fames: hunger sweetens beans (i.e., hunger makes everything taste good)

faber (est) quisque fortunæ suæ: each person is the architect of his own fortune (Sallust, Appius Claudius, and Francis Bacon)

fabricando fabri fimus: we become workmen by working

fac tibi consuescat. Nil adsuetudine majus: accustom her to your companionship. There is nothing more powerful than custom (Ovid)

facies qualis mens talis: as is the face so is the mind

facies tua computat annos: your years are counted on your face (Juvenal)

facile est imperium in bonis: it is easy to rule over the good (Plautus)

facile est inventis addere: it is easy to add to what has already been invented

facile largiri de alieno: it is easy to be generous with what is another's

facilis descensus Averno (est) (or, facilis [est] descensus Averni): the descent to hell is easy (Virgil)

facilius crescit dignitas quam incipit: dignity increases more easily than it begins (Seneca)

facilius crescit quam inchoatur dignitas: it is easier to increase dignity than to acquire it in the first place (Laberius)

facilius est se a certamine abstinere quam abducere: it is easier to keep out of a quarrel than to get out of one (Seneca)

facilius in amore finem impetres quam modum: love is more easily quenched than moderated (Seneca the Elder)

facinus audax incipit, qui cum opulento pauper homine cœpit rem habere aut negotium: the poor man who enters into partnership with a rich man makes a risky venture (Plautus)

facinus quos inquinat æquat: crime levels all whom it defiles (i.e., puts all on equal terms) (Lucan)

facit indignatio versum: indignation gives inspiration to verse (Juvenal)

facit occasio furem (or, occasio furem facit): opportunity makes the thief

facito aliquid operis, ut semper te diabolus inveniat occupatum: be sure to keep busy, so that the devil may always find you occupied (St. Jerome)

factum abiit; monumenta manent: the event is past; the memorial remains (Ovid)

factum est illud; fieri infectum non potest: it is done; it cannot be undone (Plautus)

facundia difficilis: eloquence is difficult

fallaces sunt rerum species: the appearances of things are deceptive (Seneca)

falsus in uno, falsus in omnibus: false in one thing, false in everything

fama crescit eundo: rumor grows as it goes (Virgil)

fama fert: rumor runs away

fama malum quo non aliud velocius ullum: there is no evil swifter than a rumor (Virgil)

fama nihil est celerius: nothing is swifter than rumor (Livy)

famæ damna majora (sunt), quam quæ æstimari possint: the damage done to reputation is greater than can be possibly estimated (Livy)

famæ laboranti non facile succurritur: it is not easy to repair a damaged reputation

famæ quidem ac fidei damna majora esse quam quæ æstimari possent: it is impossible to estimate the injury that may be done to us by an attack on our credit and our reputation (Livy)

fames et more bilem in nasum conciunt: hunger and delay stir up one's bile in the nostrils

fames optimum condimentum: hunger is the best of seasonings

fames, pestis, et bellum, populi sunt pernicies: famine, pestilence, and war are the destruction of a people

familiare est hominibus omnia sibi ignoscere: it is common to man to pardon all his own faults

fas est (et) ab hoste doceri: it is permitted to learn even from an enemy (Ovid)

fas est præteritos semper amare viros: our reverence is ever due to those who have passed on (Propertius)

fastidientis est stomachi multa degustare: it proves a dainty stomach to taste of many things (Seneca)

Fata volentem ducunt, nolentem trahunt: the Fates lead the willing and drag the unwilling

fatetur facinus (is) qui judicium fugit: the one who flees the law confesses his guilt (Publilius Syrus)

fatigatis humus cubile est: to the weary, the bare ground is a bed (Curtius)

fatuis levia committito: entrust trifles to fools

fecundi calices quem non fecere disertum?: whom have flowing cups not made eloquent? (Horace)

felicitas multos habet amicos: happiness (or prosperity) has many friends

felicitas nutrix est iracundiæ: prosperity is the nurse of an angry disposition

felicitate corrumpimur: we are corrupted by good fortune (Tacitus)

feliciter is sapit, qui periculo alieno sapit: he is happily wise who is wise at the expense of another (Plautus)

felis demulcta mitis: the stroked cat is meek

felix ille tamen corvo quoque rarior albo: a lucky man is rarer than a white crow (Juvenal)

felix quem faciunt aliena pericula cautum!: happy are they who can learn caution from the danger of others!

felix qui nihil debet: happy is the one who owes nothing

felix qui potuit rerum cognoscere causas: happy is the one who understands the causes of all things (Virgil)

felix qui quod amat, defendere fortiter andet: happy is the one who dares courageously to defend what he loves (Ovid)

fere fit malum malo aptissimum: one misfortune is generally followed closely by another (Livy)

feriis caret necessitas: necessity knows no holiday

ferme fugiendo in media fata ruitur: how often it happens that men fall into the very evils they are striving to avoid (Livy)

ferreus assiduo consumitur annulus usu: by constant use an iron ring is worn away (Ovid)

ferto, fereris: forgive and you will be forgiven

fervet olla, vivit amicitia: as long as the pot boils, friendship lasts

festinatio tarda est: haste is late (or, haste is slow)

ficta voluptatis causa sit proxima veris: fictions meant to please should have as much resemblance as possible to truth (Horace)

fide abrogata, omnis humana societas tollitur: if good faith be abolished, all human society is dissolved (Livy)

fide sed cui vide: trust but see in whom you are trusting

fideli certa merces: the faithful are certain of their reward

fidelius rident tiguria: the laughter of the cottage is more hearty and sincere than that of the court

fidem qui perdit perdere ultra nil potest: the one who loses his honor has nothing else he can lose (Publilius Syrus)

fides probata coronat: faith approved confers a crown

fides ut anima, unde abiit, eo nunquam redit: honor, like life, when once it is lost, is never recovered (Publilius Syrus)

filii non plus possessionum quam morborum hæredes sumus: we sons are heirs no less to diseases than to estates

finis finem litibus imponit: the end put an end to litigation

finis unius diei est principium alterius: the end of one day is the beginning of another

finiunt pariter renovantque labores: they finish at the same time and renew their labor

firmissima convelli non posse: what stands firmest cannot be overthrown

firmum in vita nihil: nothing in life is permanent

fit cito per multas præda petita manus: the spoil that is sought by many hands quickly accumulates (Ovid)

fit erranti medicina confessio: confession is as healing medicine to the one who has erred

fit fabricando faber: a smith becomes a smith by working at the forge

fit fastidium copia: from abundance comes disgust (or boredom) (Livy)

fit in dominatu servitus, in servitute dominatus: in masterhood is servanthood, in servanthood masterhood (also, in the master there is the servant, in the servant there is the master) (Cicero)

fit scelus indulgens per nubila sæcula virtus: in times of trouble leniency becomes crime

flagiti principium est nudare inter cives corpora: the beginning of shame is baring the body in public (Ennius)

flamma fumo est proxima: flame is close to smoke (i.e., where there is smoke, there is fire) (Plautus)

flamma per incensas citius sedatur aristas: the flames are sooner to be extinguished when once spread amongst the standing corn (a reference to the rapid spread of destructive views) (Propertius)

flectere si nequeo superos, Acheronta movebo: if I cannot bend heaven then I shall move (or stir up) Acheron (i.e., hell) (Virgil)

flectimur non frangimur undis: we are bent but not broken by waves

flectimur obsequio non viribus: we bend out of compliance and not because of force

fœcundi calices quem non fecere disertum?: whom has not the inspiring chalice [of wine] made elegant? (Horace)

fœdum inceptu, fœdum exitu: foul in the beginning, foul in the end

fœnum habet in cornu: he carries hay upon his horn (i.e., he shows signs of madness)

fontes ipsi sitiunt: even the fountains complain of thirst

forma bonum fragile est: beauty is a fragile good (i.e., a transitory blessing) (Ovid)

forma viros neglecta decet: neglect of appearance becomes men (Ovid)

formidabilior cervorum exercitus, duce leone, quam leonum cervo: an army of deer would be more formidable commanded by a lion than one of lions commanded by a deer

formosa facies muta commendatio est: a handsome face is a silent recommendation (Liberius; also attributed to Publilius Syrus)

forte scutum, salus ducum: a strong shield is the safety of leaders

fortem facit vicina libertas senem: the approach of liberty makes even an old man brave (Seneca)

fortem posce animum: pray for a strong will (Juvenal)

fortes creantur fortibus et bonis: brave sons spring from the steadfast and good (Horace)

fortes semper monstrant misericordiam: the brave always show mercy

forti et fideli nihil (or nil) difficile: to the brave and faithful, nothing is difficult

fortia facere et pati Romanum est: to do brave deeds and to suffer is Roman

fortior et potentior est dispositio legis quam hominis: the disposition of the law is stronger and more potent than that of man

fortis cadere, cedere non potest: the brave may fall, but they cannot yield

fortis et constantis animi est, non perturbari in rebus asperis: it shows a brave and resolute spirit not to be agitated in exciting circumstances (Cicero)

fortis sub forte fatiscet: the brave man will yield to a braver man

fortissima minimis interdum cedunt: the strongest sometimes yield to the smallest

fortiter ferendo vincitur malum quod evitari non potest: by bravely enduring it, an evil that cannot be avoided is overcome

fortiter in re, (et) suaviter in modo: firmly in the matter (and) gently in the manner (or, resolute in the deed, but gentle in the approach)

fortuna cæca est: fortune is blind

fortuna magna magna domino est servitus: a great fortune is a great slavery to its owner (Publilius Syrus)

fortuna miserrima tuta est: the most wretched fortune is safe (Ovid)

fortuna multis dat nimium, nulli satis: to many fortune gives too much, to none does it give enough (Martial and Publilius Syrus)

Fortuna, nimium quem fovet, stultum facit: Fortune, when she caresses a man too much, makes him a fool (Publilius Syrus)

fortuna non mutat genus: fortune does not change nature (Horace)

fortuna obesse nulli contenta est semel: fortune is not content to do someone an ill turn only once (Publilius Syrus)

fortuna opes auferre, non animum potest: fortune may steal our wealth, but it cannot take away our courage (Seneca)

fortuna parvis momentis magnas rerum commutationes efficit: fortune in brief moments works great changes in our affairs

fortuna vitrea est, tum cum splendet frangitur: fortune is like glass; when it sparkles, it is broken (Publilius Syrus)

fortunam citius reperias quam retineas: it is easier to find fortune than to keep hold of it (Publilius Syrus)

fortunam debet quisque manere suam: everyone ought to live within his means (Ovid)

fortunato omne solum patria est: to the fortunate, every land is his country

fortunatus et ille deos qui novit agrestes: happy the person who knows the rural gods (Virgil)

fragrat post funera virtus: virtue smells sweet after death

fraudare eos qui sciunt et consentiunt nemo videtur: a fraud upon those who are aware of and consent to it is not deemed a fraud

fraus est celare fraudem: it is fraud to conceal fraud

fraus meretur fraudem: deceit deserves deceit

frigidam aquam effundere: to throw cold water on a business

fructu non foliis arborem æstima: judge a tree by its fruit, not by its leaves (Phædrus)

frustra fit per plura, quod fieri potest per pauciora: that is idly done by many, which may be done by a few

frustra Herculi: it is vain to speak against Hercules

frustra laborat qui omnibus placere studet: he labors in vain who tries to please everybody

fugere est triumphus: to flee [evil] is a triumph

fugiendo in media sæpe ruitur fata: by fleeing, men often meet the very fate they seek to avoid (Livy)

fugientes afflictio sequitur: suffering follows those who flee

fuimus Troës; fuit Ilium: we have been Trojans; Troy was (Virgil)

fulgente trahit constrictos gloria curru, non minus ignotos generosis: glory draws all bound to her shining carriage, low-born and high-born alike (Horace)

fundamentum justitiæ est fides: the fountain of justice is good faith (Cicero)

furiosi solo furore punitur: a madman is to be punished by his madness alone

furiosus absentis loco est: a madman is like a man who is absent (Coke, adapted from Justinian)

furiosus furore suo punitur: a madman is punished by his madness

furor fit læsa sæpius patientia: patience, when too often offended, is turned into rage

furor iraque mentem præcipitant: rage and anger hurry on the mind (Virgil)

futurum invisibile: the future is inscrutable

G

galeatum sero duelli pœnitet: after donning the helmet, it is too late to repent of war (Juvenal)

gallus in sterquilinio suo plurimum potest: the cock is proudest on his own dungheap (Seneca)

gaudeamus igitur (juvenes dum sumus): let us be joyful, therefore (while we are young)

gaudent magni viri rebus adversis non aliter, quam fortes milites bellis: great men rejoice in adversity just as brave soldiers triumph in war (Seneca)

gaudium est miseris socios habere pœnarum: it is joy to the unhappy to have companions in misfortune (i.e., misery loves company) (Dominicus de Gravina)

genus est mortis male vivere: to live an evil life is a type of death (Ovid)

gladiator in arena consilium capit: the gladiator takes counsel in the arena (i.e., he asks for advice after it is too late to heed it)

gloria virtutem tanquam umbra sequitur: glory follows virtue as if it were its shadow (Cicero)

gloriæ et famæ jactura facienda est, publicæ utilitatis causa: a surrender of glory and fame must be made for the public advantage (Cicero)

gloriam qui spreverit, veram habet: the one who despises glory will have true glory (Livy)

grata superveniet quæ non sperabitur hora: the hour of happiness will come, the more welcome when it is not expected (Horace)

gratia atque honos opportuniora interdum non cupientibus: fame and honor sometimes fall more fitly on those who do not desire them (Livy)

gratia pro rebus merito debetur inemtis: thanks are justly due for things we do not pay for (Ovid)

gratior et pulchro veniens in corpore virtus: virtue is all the fairer when it comes in a beautiful body (Virgil)

gratus animus est una virtus non solum maxima, sed etiam mater virtutum omnium reliquarum: a thankful heart is not only the greatest virtue, but the parent of all the other virtues (Cicero)

grave nihil est homini quod fert necessitas: no burden is really heavy to a man that necessity lays on him

grave paupertas malum est, et intolerabile, quæ magnum domat populum: the poverty that oppresses a great people is a grievous and intolerable evil

grave senectus est hominibus pondus: old age is a heavy burden to man

gravior multo pœna videtur, quæ a miti viro constituitur: a punishment always appears far more severe when it is inflicted by a merciful man (Seneca)

graviora quæ patiantur videntur jam hominibus quam quæ metuant: present sufferings seem far greater to men than those they merely dread (Livy)

graviora quædam sunt remedia periculis: some remedies are worse than the disease (Publilius Syrus)

gravis ira regum (est) semper: the wrath of kings is always severe (Seneca)

gravissimum est imperium consuetudinis: the power of custom is most weighty (Publilius Syrus)

grex totus in agris unius scabie cadit: the entire flock in the fields dies of the disease introduced by one (Juvenal)

gutta cavat lapidem, non vi, sed sæpe cadendo: the drop hollows the stone, not by force but by constant dripping (Ovid)

gutta fortunæ præ dolio sapientiæ: a drop of good fortune rather than a cask of wisdom

H

habent insidias hominis blanditiæ mali: under the fair words of a bad man there lurks some treachery (Phædrus)

habeo senectuti magnam gratiam, quæ mihi sermonis aviditatem auxit: I owe it to old age, that my desire for conversation is so increased (Cicero)

habere non potest Deum patrem qui ecclesiam non habet matrem: one cannot have God for a father who does not have the Church for a mother (St. Cyprian)

habet et bellum suas leges: even war has its laws

habet et musca splenem: even a fly gets angry

hac urget lupus, hac canis: on one side a wolf besets you, on the other a dog (Horace)

hæ nugæ in seria ducent mala: these trifles will lead to serious evils (Horace)

hæc a te non multum abludit imago: this picture bears no resemblance to yourself (Horace)

hæc brevis est nostrorum summa malorum: such is the short sum of our evils (Ovid)

hæc olim meminisse juvabit: it will be a pleasure to remember these things hereafter (Virgil)

hæredis fletus sub persona risus est: the weeping of an heir is laughter under a mask (i.e., in disguise) (Publilius Syrus)

hæreditas nunquam ascendit: the right of inheritance never ascends

hæres legitimus est quem nuptiæ demonstrant: he is the lawful heir whom marriage points out as such

haud æquum facit, qui quod didicit, id dediscit: he does not do right who unlearns what he has learned (Plautus)

haud ignara mali miseris succurrere disco: not unfamiliar with misfortune myself, I have learned to aid the wretched (Virgil)

haud semper errat fama; aliquando et elegit: fame does not always err; sometimes it chooses well (Tacitus)

haud sidit inane: it does not sink when empty

hei mihi!, quod nullis amor est medicabilis herbis: ah me!, love cannot be cured by herbs (Ovid)

heu!, nihil invitis fas quenquam fidere divis!: alas!, it is not well for anyone to feel confident when the gods are adverse! (Virgil)

heu!, quam difficile est crimen non prodere vultu!: alas!, how difficult it is not to betray guilt by our looks! (Ovid)

heu!, quam difficilis gloriæ custodia est!: alas!, how difficult is the custody of glory! (Publilius Syrus)

heu!, quam miserum est ab eo lædi, de quo non ausis queri!: alas!, how galling it is to be injured by one against whom you dare not make a complaint! (Publilius Syrus)

hi sunt inimici pessumi fronte hilaro corde tristi: your worst enemies are those whose faces are cheerful while their hearts are bitter (Cæcilius)

hic est aut nusquam quod quærimus: what we seek is either here or nowhere (Horace)

hic funis nihil attraxit: this line has taken no fish (i.e., this scheme has failed)

hilarisque tamen cum pondere virtus: virtue may be happy, but with dignity (Statius)

his nunc præmium est, qui recta prava faciunt: nowadays those are rewarded who make right appear wrong (Terence)

historia quo quomodo scripta delectat: history, however written, is always a pleasure to us (Pliny the Younger)

hoc erat in more majorum: this was in the custom (or manner) of our ancestors

hoc est vivere bis, vita posse priore frui: it is to live twice, when you can enjoy recalling your former life (Martial)

hoc habeo quodcunque dedi: whatever I have given, I still possess (Caius Rabirius)

hoc maxime officii est, ut quisquis maxime opus indigeat, ita ei potissimum opitulari: it is our prime duty to aid him first who most stands in need of our assistance (Cicero)

hoc pretium ob stultitiam fero: this reward I gain for my folly (Terence)

hoc sustinete, majus ne veniat malum: endure this evil lest a greater come upon you (Phædrus)

hoc tempore obsequium amicos, veritas odium parit: these days flattery wins friends, truth begets hatred (Terence)

hodie vivendum, amissa (or **omissa**) **præteritorum cura:** let us live today, forgetting the cares that are past (an Epicurean maxim)

hominem improbum non accusari tutius est quam absolvi: it is safer that a bad man should not be accused, than that he should be acquitted (Livy)

hominem non odi sed ejus vitia: I do not hate the man, but his vices (Martial)

homines amplius oculis quam auribus credunt: men are readier to believe their eyes than their ears (Seneca)

homines dum docent discunt: even while they teach, men learn (Seneca)

homines (enim) ad deos nulla re propius accedunt quam salutem hominibus dando: in nothing are men more like gods than when they save (or heal) their fellow men (Cicero)

homines nihil agendo discunt male agere: men, by doing nothing, learn to do ill (Cato)

homines plus in alieno negotio videre, quam in suo: men see better into other people's business than into their own (Seneca)

homines proniores sunt ad voluptatem, quam ad virtutem: men are more prone to pleasure than to virtue (Cicero)

homines, quo plura habent, eo cupiunt ampliora: the more men have, the more they want (Justinian)

homines voluptatibus transformantur: men are transformed by pleasures

homini ne fidas nisi cum quo modium salis absumpseres: trust no man till you have eaten a peck of salt with him (i.e., have known him for a long time)

homini plurima ex homine sunt mala: most of man's misfortunes are due to man (Pliny the Elder)

homini potentiam quærenti egentissumus quisque opportunissumus: to someone seeking power, the poorest man is the most useful (Sallust)

hominibus plenum, amicis vacuum: full of men, vacant of friends (Seneca)

hominis est errare, insipientis (vero) perseverare: to be human is to err, but it is (truly) the fool who perseveres in error

hominum immortalis est infamia; etiam tum vivit, cum esse credas mortuam: disgrace is immortal, and it lives even when one thinks it dead (Plautus)

hominum sententia fallax: the opinions of men are fallible (Ovid)

homo doctus in se semper divitias habet: a learned person always has wealth (or riches) within (Phædrus)

homo extra est corpus suum cum irascitur: a man, when angry, is beside himself (Syrus Publilius)

homo fervidus et diligens ad omnia paratur: the man who is earnest and diligent is prepared for all things (Thomas à Kempis)

homo homini aut Deus aut lupus: man is to man either a God or a wolf (Erasmus)

homo homini deus est si suum officium sciat: man is to man a god when he recognizes his duty (Cæcilius)

homo multi consilii et optimi: a man always ready to give advice, and that the most judicious

homo proponit, sed Deus disponit: man proposes, but God disposes (Thomas à Kempis)

homo solus aut Deus aut Dæmon: man alone is either a God or a Demon (Erasmus)

homo sum; humani nihil a me alienum puto: I am a man; nothing that relates to man do I consider foreign to me (Terence)

homo totiens moritur quotiens amittit suos: a man dies as often as his friends (or loved ones) die (Publilius Syrus)

homo vitæ commodatus non donatus: a man is lent, not given, to life (Publilius Syrus)

homunculi quanti sunt!, cum recogito: how insignificant men are!, when I think of it (Plautus)

honesta mors turpi vita potior: an honorable death is better than a dishonorable life (Tacitus)

honesta quædam scelera successus facit: success makes some crimes honorable (Seneca)

honestum non est semper quod licet: what is lawful is not always respectable

honora medicum propter necessitatem: honor physicians for the sake of necessity

honos alit artes, omnesque incenduntur ad studia gloria: honors encourage the arts, for all are incited toward studies by glory (or fame) (Cicero)

honos habet onus: honor has its burdens (i.e., honor carries responsibility)

horæ momento, cita mors venit aut victoria læta: in a moment comes either sudden death or joyful victory (Horace)

horrea formicæ tendunt ad inania nunquam; nullus ad amissas ibit amicus opes: just as ants never bend their way to visit empty storehouses, so no friend will visit departed wealth (Ovid)

horrent commota moveri: what has been disturbed shrinks from being stirred up again

hos ego versiculos feci, tulit alter honores: I wrote these lines, another has taken the credit (Virgil)

hosti etiam servanda fides: faith must be kept even to the enemy

hostis est uxor invita quæ ad virum nuptum datur: the wife who is given in marriage to a man against her will becomes his enemy (Plautus)

hostis honori invidia: envy is the foe of honor

humanitati qui se non accommodat, plerumque pœnas oppetit superbiæ: the one who does not conform to courtesy generally pays the penalty for his haughtiness (Phædrus)

humanius est deridere vitam quam deplorare: it is better for a man to laugh at life than to lament over it (Seneca)

humanum amare est, humanum autem ignoscere est: it is human to love, and it is also human to forgive (Plautus)

humanum genus est avidum nimis auricularum: man suffers from the plague of itching ears (Lucretius)

humiles laborant ubi potentes dissident: the humble are in danger when the powerful disagree (Phædrus)

hunc laborem sumas laudem qui tibi ac fructum ferat: accept tasks that bring you praise as well as profit (Lucilius)

hypocritæ progenies viperarum: hypocrites are the offspring of vipers

I

ibit eo quo vis, qui zonam perdidit: the one who has lost his girdle (i.e., wallet or purse), will go wherever you wish (Horace)

id agas tuo te merito ne quis oderit: take care that no one hates you justly (Publilius Syrus)

id arbitror adprime in vita esse utile, ne quid nimis: this I consider to be a valuable principle in life, not to do anything in excess (Terence)

id cinerem, aut manes credis curare sepultos?: do you think that spirits or ashes of the dead care for such things? (Virgil)

id commune malum; semel insanivimus omnes: it is a common calamity; we have all been mad once (Mantuanus)

id demum est homini turpe, quod meruit pati: that only brings disgrace on a man which he has deserved to suffer (Phædrus)

id facere laus est quod decet, non quod licet: he is deserving of praise who considers not what he may do, but what it becomes him to do (Seneca)

id maxime quemque decet, quod est cujusque suum maxime: the best becomes every person, which is more peculiarly his own (Cicero)

id nobis maxime nocet, quod non ad rationis lumen sed ad similitudinem aliorum vivimus: this is especially ruinous to us, that we shape our lives not by the light of reason, but after the fashion of others (Seneca)

id quoque, quod vivam, munus habere Dei: this also, that I live, I consider a gift of God (Ovid)

idem est ergo beate vivere et secundum naturam: to live happily is the same thing as to live in accordance with nature's laws (Seneca)

idem velle atque idem nolle, ea demum firma amicitia est: to have the same likes and dislikes, this, after all, is what defines a solid friendship (Sallust)

idque petit corpus, mens unde est saucia amore: the body seeks that which has wounded the mind with love (Lucretius)

ignavis precibus Fortuna repugnat: Fortune spurns the prayers of cowards (Ovid)

ignavis semper feriæ sunt: to the indolent every day is a holiday

ignem ne gladio fodito: do not stir the fire with a sword

ignis aurum probat, miseria fortes viros: fire tests gold, adversity brave men (Seneca)

ignis gladio non fodiendus: the fire should not be stirred by the sword

ignis, quo clarior fulsit, citius exstinguitur: the more brightly the fire has burnt, the sooner it is extinguished (Seneca)

ignorantia juris non excusat: ignorance of the law does not excuse

ignorantia legis neminem excusat: ignorance of the law excuses no one

ignorantia non excusat legem: ignorance does not excuse the law

ignoratione rerum bonarum et malarum, maxime hominum vita vexatur: through ignorance of the distinction between good and bad, the life of men is greatly vexed (Cicero)

ignoscas aliis multa, nil tibi: you should forgive many things in others, but nothing in yourself (Ausonius)

ignoscito sæpe alteri nunquam tibi: forgive others often, yourself never

ignoti nulla cupido: there is no desire for what is unknown (i.e., ignorance is bliss)

illa dolet vere quæ sine teste dolet: one grieves sincerely who grieves unseen (Martial)

ille crucem sceleris pretium tulit, hic diadema: that one man found a cross the reward of his guilt, this one, a diadem (Juvenal)

ille sinistrorsum, hic dextrorsum, abit: unus utrique error, sed variis illudit partibus: one wanders to the left, another to the right: both are equally wrong, but in different directions (Horace)

ille terrarum mihi præter omnis angulus ridet: that corner of the world smiles for me more than anywhere else (Horace)

illi mors gravis incubat, qui, notus nimis omnibus, ignotus moritur sibi: death presses heavily on that man who, being but too well known to others, dies in ignorance of himself (Seneca)

illic apposito narrabis multa Lyæo: there, with the wine of Bacchus in front of you, you will tell many a tale (Ovid)

illicitum non sperandum: what is unlawful should not be hoped for

ima permutat brevis hora summis: but one short hour will change the lot of the highest and of the lowest (Seneca)

imago animi sermo est: speech is the mirror of the mind (Seneca)

immensum gloria calcar habet: the love of glory gives an immense stimulus (Ovid)

immersabilis est vera virtus: true virtue cannot be overwhelmed

immortalia ne speres, monet annus et almum quæ rapit hora diem: not to hope for things to last forever is what the year teaches, and even the hour that speeds the pleasant day (Horace)

impedit ira animum, ne possit cernere verum: anger so clouds the mind that it cannot perceive the truth (Dionysius Cato)

impendendus homo est, deus esse ut possit in ipso: man must be so weighed as though there were a god within him (Manilius)

impensa monumenti supervacua est; memoria nostra durabit si vita meruimus: a monument is an unnecessary expense; our memory will endure if we have earned it by our life (Pliny the Younger)

imperat aut servit collecta pecunia cuique: money is either our master or our slave (Horace)

imperator ... intra ecclesiam, non supra ecclesiam est: the emperor is in the Church, not above the Church (St. Ambrose)

imperia dura tolle, quid virtus erit?: remove severe restraints and what will become of virtue? (Seneca)

imperium cupientibus nihil medium inter summa et præcipitia: in the struggle between those seeking power there is no middle course (Tacitus)

imperium facile iis artibus retinetur, quibus initio partum est: power is easily retained by those arts by which it was at first acquired (Sallust)

imperium, flagitio acquisitum, nemo unquam bonis artibus exercuit: the power that was acquired by disgraceful means has never been directed to any good purpose (Tacitus)

impetrare oportet, quia æquum postulas: you ought to obtain what you ask, as you only ask for what is fair (Plautus)

impia sub dulci melle venena latent: deadly poisons are concealed under sweet honey (Ovid)

implacabiles plerumque læsæ mulieres: women, when offended, are generally implacable

importunitas evitanda: importunity (or insolence) should be avoided

impossibilium nulla obligatio est: there is no legal obligation to perform impossibilities (Celsus)

impotentia excusat legem: impotency excuses law (i.e., laws that do not apply to the disabled or infirm)

imprimis venerare deos: before all things reverence the gods (Virgil)

imprimisque hominis est propria veri inquisitio atque investigatio: the first duty of man is seeking after and investigating the truth (Cicero)

improbe Neptunum accusat, qui naufragium iterum facit: the one who suffers shipwreck twice is unjust to blame Neptune (Publilius Syrus)

improbi hominis est mendacio fallere: it is the act of a bad man to deceive by falsehood (Cicero)

improbis aliena virtus semper formidolosa est: to wicked men the virtue of others is always a matter of dread (Sallust)

improbus a nullo flectitur obsequio: the wicked are not swayed by obsequiousness

impunitas ferociæ parens: impunity is the parent of ferocity

impunitas semper ad deteriora invitat: impunity is always an invitation to a greater crime (Coke)

in alio pediculum, in te ricinum non vides: you see a louse on someone else, but not a tick on yourself (Petronius)

in angustis amici boni apparent: good friends appear in difficulties

in animo perturbato, sicut in corpore, sanitas esse non potest: in a disturbed mind, as in a body in the same state, health cannot exist (Cicero)

in annulo Dei figuram ne gestato: do not wear the image of God in a ring (i.e., do not be frivolous in your use of God's name)

in audaces non est audacia tuta: against the daring, daring is unsafe (Ovid)

in beato omnia beata: with the blessed, all things are blessed (Horace)

in calamitoso risus etiam injuria est: even to smile at the unfortunate is to do them injury (Publilius Syrus)

in candore decus: there is honor in sincerity

in casu extremæ necessitatis omnia sunt communia: in a case of extreme emergency all things are common

in causa facili, cuivis licet esse diserto: in an easy cause, any person may be eloquent (Ovid)

in civitate libera linguam mentemque liberas esse debere (jactabat): in a free state there should be freedom of speech and thought (Tiberias, as quoted by Suetonius)

in cœlo nunquam spectatum impune cometam: a comet is never seen in the sky without indicating disaster (Claudian)

in contingentibus et liberis tota ratio facti stat in voluntate facientis: in contingent and free things, all the reason of the fact lies in the will of the doer

in cute curanda plus æquo operata juventus: youth unduly busy with pampering the outer man (Horace)

in dubiis benigniora semper sunt præferenda: in doubtful cases we must always prefer the mildest sentence

in eadem re, utilitas et turpitudo esse non potest: usefulness and baseness cannot exist in the same thing (Cicero)

in fuga fœda mors est; in victoria gloriosa: in flight death is disgraceful; in victory, glorious (Cicero)

in generalibus latet dolus: in generalities lurks deception

in generalibus latet error: in generalities lurks error

in judicando criminosa est celeritas: in pronouncing judgment, haste is criminal

in magnis et voluisse sat est: in great things, it is enough even to have willed (Propertius)

in malis sperare bonum, nisi innocens, nemo potest: in adversity, only the virtuous can entertain hope

in maxima fortuna minima licentia est: in the greatest fortune lies the least liberty (Sallust)

in maxima potentia minima licentia (est): in the greatest power lies the least liberty

in medio tutissimus ibis: safety is in going the middle course (Ovid)

in morte alterius spem tu tibi ponere noli: beware of placing your hopes in the death of others (Cato)

in nocte consilium: in the night is counsel (i.e., sleep on it)

in nomine Domini incipit omne malum: in the name of the Lord every evil begins

in nullum avarus bonus est, in se pessimus: the avaricious man is kind to no person, but most unkind to himself

in omni adversitate fortunæ infelicissimum est genus infortunii fuisse felicem: in every kind of adversity, the bitterest part of a person's affliction is to remember that he was once happy (Boëthius)

in omni re vincit imitationem veritas: in everything, truth surpasses its imitation (Cicero)

in omnibus fere minori ætati succurritur: in all cases, relief is afforded to persons under age

in omnibus quidem, maxime tamen in jure, æquitas est: in all things, but particularly in law, regard is to be given to equity

in pace leones, in prælio cervi: in peace they are lions, in battle they are deer

in pace ut sapiens aptarit idonea bello: in peace, like the wise man, make preparations for war (Horace)

in pertusum ingerimus dicta dolium, operam ludimus: we are pouring our words into a perforated cask, and lose our labor (Plautus)

in pœnam sectatur et umbra: for punishment even a shadow is pursued

in proverbium cessit, sapientiam vino adumbrari: it has passed into a proverb, that wisdom is overshadowed by wine (Pliny the Elder)

in re dubia melius est verbis edicti serviri: in uncertain cases it is best to follow orders

in rebus prosperis, superbiam, fastidium arrogantiamque magno opere fugiamus: in prosperity let us most carefully avoid pride, disdain, and arrogance (Cicero)

in se magna ruunt: great things are apt to rush against each other (i.e., to clash) (Lucan)

in tanta inconstantia turbaque rerum nihil nisi quod preteriit certum est: in the great inconstancy and crowd of events, nothing is certain except the past (Seneca)

in toto et pars continetur: in the whole, the part is also contained

in turbas et discordias pessimo cuique plurima vis: in seasons of tumult and discord, the worst men have the greatest power (Tacitus)

in unoquoque virorum bonorum habitat Deus: God has his dwelling within every good man (Seneca)

in vindicando, criminosa est celeritas: in revenge, haste is criminal

in virtute posita est vera felicitas: true happiness is centered in virtue (Seneca)

in virtute sunt multi ascensus: in the ascent to virtue there are many steps (i.e., there are many degrees of excellence) (Cicero)

in vitium ducit culpæ fuga: in fleeing one vice we are sometimes caught by another (Horace)

in vota miseros ultimus cogit timor: fear of death drives the wretched to prayer (Seneca)

incendit omnem feminæ zelus domum: the jealousy of a woman sets a whole house aflame

incerta pro nullis habetur: what is uncertain is to be treated as non-existent

incerti sunt exitus belli: the results of war are uncertain (Cicero)

incertum est quo te loco mors expectet; itaque in omni loco illam expecta: it is uncertain in what place death awaits you; therefore, be ready for it in every place (Seneca)

incipe quidquid agas: pro toto est prima operis pars: begin whatever you have to do: the beginning of a work stands for the whole (Ausonius)

incitantur enim homines ad agnoscenda quæ differuntur: our inquisitive disposition is excited by having its gratification deferred (Pliny the Younger)

inclusio unius est exclusio alterius: the mention by name of the one is the exclusion of the other

inde datæ leges ne fortior omnia posset: laws have been ordained so that the stronger may not have everything their own way

index animi sermo est: speech is an indicator of thought

indigna digna habenda sunt hæres quæ facit: things unbecoming are to be held becoming if the master does them (Plautus)

indigne vivit per quem non vivit alter: he by whom another does not live does not deserve to live

indulgentia parentum, filiorum pernicies: the indulgence of parents is the bane of children

ingenii largitor venter: the belly is the giver of genius (i.e., poverty inspires genius) (Persius)

ingenio experior funera digna meo: I suffer ruin worthy of mine own invention

ingenio facies conciliante placet: when the disposition wins us, the features please (Ovid)

ingenio non ætate adipiscitur sapientia: wisdom is a gift of nature, not of years

ingenio stat sine morte decus: the honor accorded to genius is immortal (Propertius)

ingenio stimulos subdere fama solet: the love of fame usually spurs on the mind (Ovid)

ingeniorum cos æmulatio: rivalry is the whetstone of talent

ingenita levitas et erudita vanitas: levity is inborn, but vanity is instilled (Cicero)

ingenium mala sæpe movent: misfortunes often stir up genius (Ovid)

ingenium res adversæ nudare solent, celare secundæ: as a rule, adversity reveals genius and prosperity conceals it (Horace)

ingens telum necessitas: necessity is a powerful weapon (Seneca)

ingentia marmora findet caprificus: the fig tree splits huge blocks of marble

ingenuas didicisse fideliter artes emollit mores, nec sinit esse feros: a faithful study of the liberal arts refines the manners and corrects their harshness (Ovid)

ingratis servire nefas: to serve the ungrateful is an offense to the gods

ingrato homine terra pejus nil creat: the earth does not produce anything worse than an ungrateful man (Ausonius)

ingratum si dixeris, omnia dicis: if you pronounce a man ungrateful, you say all that can be said against him

ingratus est qui remotis testibus agit gratiam: he is an ungrateful man who is unwilling to acknowledge his obligation before others (Seneca)

ingratus unus miseris omnibus nocet: one ungrateful man does an injury to all who are wretched (Publilius Syrus)

inhumanitas omni ætate molesta est: inhumanity is harmful in every age (Cicero)

inhumanum verbum est ultio: revenge is an inhuman word (Seneca)

inimicorum dona, infausta: gifts of enemies are unlucky

inimicus et invidus vicinorum oculus: an enemy and an envious man is an eye over his neighbor (i.e., carefully watches his neighbor)

iniqua nunquam regna perpetua manent: authority, founded on injustice, does not remain perpetual (Seneca)

iniquissimam pacem justissimo bello antefero: I prefer the most unjust peace to the most just war (Cicero)

iniquum est aliquem rei sui esse judicem: it is unjust that anyone should be the judge in his own cause (Coke)

iniquum est collapsis manum non porrigere: commune hoc jus generis humani est: it is no sin to stretch out your hand to the fallen: that is a common law of the human race (Seneca the Elder)

initia magistratuum nostrorum meliora ferme, et finis inclinat: our magistrates discharge their duties best at the beginning and fall off toward the end (Tacitus)

initium est salutis, notitia peccati: the first step toward salvation is the recognition of sin (Seneca)

initium sapientiæ est timor Domini: the beginning of wisdom is the fear of the Lord (also, the beginning of wisdom is the fear of **domini,** the master)

injuria non excusat injuriam: one wrong does not justify another

injuriæ spretæ exolescunt, si irascaris agnitæ videntur: injuries that are slighted and unnoticed are soon forgotten; if you are angry, they are seen to be acknowledged

injuriam qui facturus est jam facit: the one who is bent on doing an injury has already done it (Seneca)

injuriarum remedium est oblivio: the best remedy for injuries is to forget them (Publilius Syrus)

injuriis infirmitas subjecta: weakness is subject to injuries (or wrongs)

injusta ab justis impetrare non decet; justa autem ab injustis petere, insipientia est: to ask what is unreasonable from the reasonable is not right; to ask what is reasonable from the unreasonable is folly (Plautus)

inopi beneficium bis dat, qui dat celeriter: the one who gives quickly gives a double benefit to the needy (Publilius Syrus and Seneca)

inopiæ desunt multa, avaritiæ omnia: poverty is the lack of many things, but avarice is the lack of all things (Publilius Syrus)

inops, potentem dum vult imitari, perit: it is destruction to the weak man to attempt to imitate the powerful (Phædrus)

inquinat egregios adjuncta superbia mores: the best manners are stained by the addition of pride (Claudian)

insania scire se non potest, non magis quam cæcitas se videre: insanity cannot recognize itself any more than blindness can see itself (Apuleius)

insanus omnis furere credit cæteros: every madman thinks all others insane (Publilius Syrus)

insipientis est dicere, non putarem: it is the part of a fool to say, I should not have thought so

insita hominibus libidine alendi de industria rumores: innate to all persons is a natural desire to spread rumors

insita hominibus natura violentiæ resistere: it is natural to man to resist violence (Tacitus)

insita mortalibus natura, propere sequi quæ piget inchoare: people are naturally ready enough to follow in matters in which they are disinclined to take the lead (Tacitus)

insperata accidunt magis sæpe quam quæ speres: what you do not expect happens more frequently than what you do (Plautus)

inspicere tanquam in speculum in vitas omnium jubeo, atque ex aliis sumere exemplum sibi: the lives of other men should be regarded as a mirror from which we may take an example and a rule of conduct for ourselves (Terence)

integra mens augustissima possessio: a sound and vigorous mind is the highest possession

intelligenti pauca: to the understanding, few words suffice

intemperans adolescentia effœtum corpus tradit senectuti: an intemperate youth transfers to old age a worn-out body (Cicero)

intentio cæca mala: a hidden intention is an evil one

inter amicos omnium rerum communitas: among friends all things are common (Cicero)

inter arma leges silent: in time of war, the laws are silent (Circero)

inter delicias semper aliquid sævi nos strangulat: in the midst of our enjoyments there is always some wrong to torture us

inter nos sanctissima divitiarum majestas: among us the most sacred majesty is that of riches (Juvenal)

inter sylvas Academi quærere verum: amid the woods of the Academy to seek for truth (Horace)

inter utrumque tene: keep between both extremes (Ovid)

intera fortunam quisque debet manere suam: every man should stay within his own fortune (Ovid)

interdum lacrimæ pondera vocis habent: even tears at times have the weight of speech (Ovid)

interdum requiescendum: sometimes we must rest

interdum stultus bene loquitur: sometimes a fool speaks well

interdum vulgus rectum videt, est ubi peccat: sometimes the common people see what is right, at other times they err (Horace)

intererit multum Davusne loquatur an heros: there is a great difference when the servant Davus is speaking and when a hero speaks (Horace)

intolerabilius nihil est quam fœmina dives: there is nothing more insufferable than a rich woman (Juvenal)

intra fortunam quisque debet manere suam: everyone should confine himself within the bounds of his own fortune (Ovid)

intret amicitiæ nomine tectus amor: love will enter cloaked in friendship's name (Ovid)

intus si recte, ne labora: if inwardly right, don't worry

intuta quæ indecora: what is unseemly is unsafe (Tacitus)

invidiam ferre aut fortis aut felix potest: only the brave or the fortunate are able to endure envy (Publilius Syrus)

invidiam placare paras, virtute relicta?: are you trying to appease envy by the abandonment of virtue?

invidiam, tanquam ignem, summa petere: envy, like fire, always makes for the highest points (Livy)

invidus alterius macrescit rebus opimis: the envious man grows lean at the prosperity of another (Horace)

invisa numquam imperia retinentur diu: hated governments never last long (Seneca)

invitat culpam qui peccatum præterit: the one who overlooks one sin (or crime) invites the commission of another (Publilius Syrus)

invitum fortuna fovet: fortune helps a man even against his will

invitum qui servat idem facit occidenti: the one who saves a man against his will does the same as if he killed him (Horace)

involuta veritas in alto latet: truth lies wrapped up and hidden in the depths (Seneca)

ipsa quidem virtus pretium sibi: virtue is indeed its own reward (Claudian)

ipsa scientia potestas est: knowledge itself is power (Francis Bacon)

ipsa se fraus, etiamsi initio cautior fuerit, detegit: treachery, though at first very cautious, betrays itself in the end (Livy)

ipse decor, recti facti si præmia desint, non movet: men do not value a good deed unless it brings a reward (Ovid)

ipse fecit nos, et non ipsi nos: He (God) made us, and not we ourselves (after Psalm 100:3)

ipse Jupiter, neque pluens omnibus placet, neque abstinens: even Jupiter himself cannot please all, whether he sends rain or fair weather

ira furor brevis est: anger is a brief madness (Horace)

ira quæ tegitur nocet; professa perdunt odia vindictæ locum: resentment that is concealed is dangerous; hatred avowed loses its opportunity of vengeance (Seneca)

iram qui vincit, hostem superat maximum: the one who subdues his anger conquers his greatest enemy

iratus cum ad se redit, sibi tum irascitur: when an angry man returns to himself, he is angry with himself (Publilius Syrus)

is demum miser est, cujus nobilitas miserias nobilitat: wretched, indeed, is the man whose fame makes his misfortunes famous (Accius)

is maxime divitiis fruetur (or **utitur**), **qui minime divitiis indiget:** he most enjoys wealth who least desires wealth (Seneca)

is plurimum habebit qui minimum desiderabit: he will have most who desires least (Ausonius)

is sapiens qui se ad casus accommodet omnes; stultus pugnat in adversis ire natator aquis: he is a wise man who adapts himself to all contingencies; the fool struggles like a swimmer against the stream

ista parentum est vita vilis liberis, ubi malunt metui quam vereri se ab suis: children hold cheap the life of parents who would rather be feared than respected (Lucius Afranius)

isthuc est sapere non quod ante pedes modo est videre, sed etiam illa quæ futura sunt prospicere: true wisdom consists not in seeing that which is immediately before our eyes, but in the foresight of that which may happen (Terence)

istuc est sapere, qui, ubicunque opus sit, animum possis flectere: you are a wise man if you can easily direct your attention to whatever may require it (Terence)

ita comparatam esse naturam omnium, aliena ut melius videant et dijudicent, quam sua: the nature of all men is so formed that they see and discriminate in the affairs of others much better than in their own (Terence)

ita cuique comparatum est in ætate hominum; ita divis est placitum, voluptatem ut mæror comes consequatur: it is our human lot, it is heaven's will, for sorrow to come after joy (Plautus)

ita finitima sunt falsa veris, ut in præcipitem locum non debeat se sapiens committere: falsehood often borders so nearly on the truth that a wise man should not trust himself to the precipice (Cicero)

itidemque ut sæpe jam in multis locis, plus insciens quis fecit quam prodens boni: and so it happens oft in many instances; more good is done without our knowledge than is intended by us (Plautus)

Iuppiter ex alto perjuria ridet amantum: Jupiter from on high laughs at the lies of lovers (Ovid)

J

jejunus raro stomachus vulgaria temnit: a hungry stomach rarely despises common fare (also translated: the stomach that is rarely hungry despises common fare) (Horace)

jocos et dii amant: even the gods love jokes (Plato)

jucunda est memoria præteritorum malorum: the recollection of past miseries is pleasant (Cicero)

jucunda oblivia vitæ: it is pleasant to forget [the calamities of] life

jucundi acti labores: past labors are pleasant (Cicero)

jucundiorem autem faciet libertatem servitutis recordatio: liberty is made even more precious by the recollection of servitude (Cicero)

jucundum et carum sterilis facit uxor amicum: a wife who has no children makes a dear and delightful friend (to her husband's heirs) (Juvenal)

jucundum nihil est, nisi quod reficit varietas: nothing is pleasant to which variety does not give relish

judex damnatur cum nocens absolvitur: the judge is condemned when the guilty is acquitted (Publilius Syrus)

judex non potest esse testis in propria causa: a judge cannot be a witness in his own cause (Coke)

judicandum est legibus, non exempli: the judgment must be pronounced from law, not from precedent

judicata res pro veritate accipitur: a matter that has been adjudged is accepted as a truth

judicia Dei sunt ita recondita ut quis illa scrutari nullatenus possit: the purposes of God are so abstruse that no one can possibly scrutinize them (Cicero)

judicis est innocentiæ subvenire: it is the duty of the judge to support innocence (Cicero)

judicis est judicare secundum allegata et probata: it is the judge's duty to decide in accordance with what is alleged and proved

judicis est jus dicere non dare: it is the judge's duty to enunciate the law, not to make it

judicis officium est, ut res, ita tempora rerum quærere: it is the judge's duty to inquire into not only the facts, but the circumstances (Ovid)

judicium a non suo judice datum nullus est momenti: judgment given by a judge in a matter outside his jurisdiction is of no legal force

Jupiter est quodcumque vides, quocumque moveris: Jupiter is whatever you see, whichever way you move (Lucan)

jura inventa metu injusti fateare necesse est, tempora si fastosque velis evolvere mundi: if you examine the history of the world you will have to admit that fear of injustice brought justice into being (Horace)

jurare est Deum in testem vocare: to swear is to call God to witness

jurgia præcipue vino stimulata caveto: above all, avoid quarrels excited by wine (Ovid)

jus civile neque inflecti gratia, neque perfringi potentia, neque adulterari pecunia debet: the law ought neither to be warped by favor, nor shattered by power, nor corrupted by money (Cicero)

jus est ars boni et æqui: law is the art of the good and the just

jus summum sæpe summa malitia est: extreme law (or justice) is often extreme wrong (Terence)

justæ causæ facilis est defensio: the defense of a just cause is easy

justitia erga Deum religio dicitur, erga parentes pietas: the discharge of our duty toward God is called religion, toward our parents, piety (Cicero)

justitia est constans et perpetua voluntas jus suum cuique tribuens (or **tribuendi**): justice is the constant and perpetual wish to render to everyone his due (Justinian)

justitia est obtemperatio scriptis legibus: justice is conformity to the written laws (Cicero)

justitia nihil expetit præmii: justice seeks no reward (Cicero)

justitia suum cuique distribuit: justice renders to every one his due (Cicero)

justitia virtutum regina: justice is the queen of virtues

justitiæ partes sunt, non violare homines verecundiæ non offendere: it is the office of justice to injure no one, of property, to offend none (Cicero)

justo geminantur anni: the years are doubled for the just

juvant aspera probum: misfortunes benefit the good man

juvenile vitium regere non posse impetum: it is the fault of youth that it cannot govern its own impulses (Seneca)

L

labitur occulte, fallitque volubilis ætas: time rolls on steadily and eludes us as it steals past (Ovid)

labor est etiam ipsa voluptas: even pleasure itself is a toil (Manilius)

labor improbus omnia vincit (or, **labor omnia vincit improbus**): great labor overcomes everything

labor ipse voluptas: work is itself a pleasure (i.e., labor is its own reward)

labor optimos citat: work summons forth the best men (Seneca)

lacrimæ nobis deerunt antequam causæ dolendi: our tears will fail before we cease to have cause for grief (Seneca)

lactuca innatat acri post vinum stomacho: lettuce after wine floats on the acrid stomach (Horace)

lætus sorte tua vives sapienter: you will live wisely if you live contented with your lot

lætus sum laudari a laudato viro: I am pleased to be praised by a man of such praise (Cicero)

lapis qui volvitur algam non generat: a rolling stone gathers no moss

largitio fundum non habet: giving has no bottom

latere semper patere, quod latuit diu: leave in concealment what has long been concealed (Seneca)

laterem laves: you wash a brick (i.e., you may as well wash a clay brick white) (Terence)

latet anguis in herba: a snake lies hid in the grass (Virgil)

lathe biosas: remain hidden in life (Epicurus, from the Greek)

latrante uno, latrat statim et alter canis: when one dog barks, another immediately begins to bark as well

laudari a viro laudato maxima est laus: to be praised by a man himself deserving of praise is the greatest possible praise

laudat venales qui vult extrudere merces: he praises his wares who wishes to palm them off upon another (Horace)

laudato ingentia rura, exiguum colito: praise a large estate, but cultivate a small one (Virgil)

laus est facere quod decet, non quod licet: it is doing what we ought to do, and not merely doing what we may do, that is the ground of praise

laus in ore proprio vilescit: the praise one bestows upon oneself is of little value

laus in proprio ore sordescit: self-praise is offensive

laus magna natis obsequi parentibus: great praise is the reward of children who respect the wishes of their parents (Phædrus)

laus propria sordet: self-praise is base

laus vera et humili sæpe contingit viro; non nisi potenti falsa: true praise is often the lot of him who is humble; false praise reaches none but the powerful (Seneca)

lege totum si vis scire totum: read the whole if you wish to know the whole

legem brevem esse oportet quo facilius ab imperitis teneatur: a law ought to be short, that it may be the more easily understood by the unlearned (Seneca)

leges ad civium salutem, civitatumque incolumitatem conditæ sunt: laws were framed for the welfare of the citizens and the security of states (Cicero)

leges arma tenent sanctas: arms cause laws to be respected

leges bonæ ex malis moribus procreantur: from bad morals good laws are produced (Macrobius)

leges mori serviunt: laws are subservient to custom (Plautus)

leges neminem in paupertate vivere neque in anxietate mori permittunt: it is never the intention of the law that anyone shall live in poverty or die in anguish (Justinian)

leges posteriores priores contrarias abrogant: later laws repeal prior contrary laws

leges sunt inventæ quæ cum omnibus semper una atque eadem voce loquerentur: laws are so devised that they may always speak with one and the same voice to all (Cicero)

legis constructio non facit injuriam: the construction of the law does injury to no one

lenior et melior fis, accedente senecta: you become milder and better as old age advances (Horace)

leonem larva terres: you frighten a lion with a mask

leonum ora a magistris impune tractantur: the mouths of lions are handled by their keepers with impunity (Seneca)

leve æs alienum debitorem facit, grave inimicum: a small debt makes a man your debtor, a large one your enemy (Seneca)

leve fit quod bene fertur onus: light is the load that is cheerfully borne (Ovid)

leve incommodum tolerandum est: a slight inconvenience must be endured

leves homines futuri sunt improvidi: light-minded men are improvident of the future (Tacitus)

levia perpessi sumus, si flenda patimur: we have suffered lightly, if we have suffered what we should weep for (Seneca)

leviores sunt injuriæ, quæ repentino aliquo motu accidunt, quam eæ quæ meditate præparata inferuntur: the injuries that befall us unexpectedly are less severe than those that we are deliberately anticipating (Cicero)

levis est consolatio ex miseria aliorum: the comfort derived from the misery of others is slight (Cicero)

levis est dolor qui capere consilium potest: light is the grief that can take counsel (Seneca)

levius fit patientia quicquid corrigere est nefas: patience makes more tolerable that which it is impossible to correct (Horace)

levius solet timere qui propius timet: he fears less who fears what is nearer to him (Seneca)

lex aliquando sequitur æquitatem: law is sometimes according to equity

lex citius tolerare vult privatum damnum quam publicum malum: the law will sooner tolerate a private loss than a public evil (Coke)

lex neminem cogit ad impossibilia: the law compels no one to do what is impossible

lex prospicit non respicit: the law is prospective, not retrospective

lex universa est quæ jubet nasci et mori: there is a universal law that commands that we shall be born and we shall die (Publilius Syrus)

libenter homines id quod volunt credunt: men willingly believe that which they wish for (Julius Cæsar)

libera te metu mortis: deliver yourself from the fear of death (Seneca)

liberæ sunt enim nostræ cogitationes: our thoughts are free (Cicero)

liberatem natura etiam mutis animalibus datam: liberty is given by nature even to mute animals (Tacitus)

libertas est potestas faciendi id quod jure licet: liberty consists in the power of doing what the law permits (Cicero)

libertas inæstimabile res est: liberty is a thing of inestimable value (Justinian)

libidinosa et intemperans adolescentia effœtum corpus tradit senectuti: a sensual and intemperate youth transfers to old age a worn-out body (Cicero)

libido effrenata effrenatam appententiam efficit: unbridled gratification produces unbridled desire

libra justa justitiam servat: a just balance preserves justice

licentiam retrœna: abstain from license

licet superbus ambules pecunia, Fortuna non mutat genus: though you walk proud of your money, yet Fortune has not changed your birth (Horace)

licuit semperque licebit parcere personis, dicere de vitiis: it has been, and ever will be, lawful to spare the individual and to attack the vice

limæ labor et mora: the labor and delay of the file (i.e., the tedious revising of a literary work before publication) (Horace)

lingua mali loquax malæ mentis est indicium: an evil tongue is the proof of an evil mind (Publilius Syrus)

lingua mali pars pessima servi: the tongue is the worst part of a bad servant (Juvenal)

linguam compescere, virtus non minima est: to restrain the tongue is not the least of the virtues

litem parit lis, noxa item noxam parit: strife engenders strife, and injury likewise engenders injury

litem quod lite resolvit: resolving one controversy by creating another (Horace)

litera scripta manet, verbum ut inane perit: the written word remains, what is spoken perishes

littera enim occidit, spiritus autem vivificat (or, **littera occidit, spiritus vivicat**): for the letter kills, but the spirit breathes life (2 Corinthians 3:6)

littore quot conchæ, tot sunt in amore dolores: there are as many pangs in love as shells on the seashore (Ovid)

litus ama; altum alii teneant: keep close to the shore; let others venture into the deep (Virgil)

locus est et pluribus umbris: there is room for even more guests at the feast (Horace)

longa mora est nobis omnis, quæ gaudia differt: every delay that postpones our joys is long (Ovid)

longissimus dies cito conditur: the longest day soon comes to an end (Pliny the Younger)

longum iter est per præcepta, breve et efficax per exempla: teaching by precept is a long road, but brief and beneficial is the way by example (Seneca)

loquendum ut vulgus, sentiendum ut docti: we should speak as the populace, think as the learned (Coke)

lubrici sunt fortunæ gressus: the footsteps of fortune are slippery

lubricum linguæ non facile in pœnam est trahendum: a slip of the tongue ought not to be rashly punished

lucri bonus (est) odor ex re qualibet: money smells good no matter its source (Emperor Vespasian, in reference to his tax on public latrines)

lucrum malum æquale dispendio: an evil gain equals a loss (Publilius Syrus)

lucrum sine damno alterius fieri non potest: there is no profit without another's loss (Publilius Syrus)

lupo ovem commisisti: you have entrusted the wolf with the sheep (Terence)

lupum auribus tenere: to hold a wolf by its ears

lupus est homo homini: man is a wolf to his fellow man

lupus non curat numerum ovum: the wolf is not scared by the number of the sheep

lupus pilum mutat, non mentem: the wolf changes its coat, not its disposition

lusus animo debent aliquando dari, ad cogitandum melior ut redeat sibi: the mind ought sometimes to be amused, that it may the better return to thought and to itself (Phædrus)

luxuriæ desunt multa, avaritiæ omnia: luxury is in want of many things, avarice of everything (Publilius Syrus)

M

macte virtute diligentiaque esto: persevere in virtue and diligence (Livy)

magis gauderes quod habueras, quam mœreres quod amiseras: better to have loved and lost, than not to have loved at all (Seneca)

magis gaudet quam qui senectam exuit: he rejoices more than an old man who has put off old age (i.e., has become young again)

magis magni clerici non sunt magis sapientes: the greatest scholars are not the wisest men

magister alius casus: misfortune is a second master (Pliny the Elder)

magistratum legem esse loquentem, legem autem mutum magistratum: a judge is a speaking law, law a silent judge (Cicero)

magistratus indicat virum: the office shows the man

magna civitas, magna solitudo: great city, great solitude

magna di curant, parva neglegunt: the gods care about great matters, but they neglect small ones (Cicero)

magna est vis consuetudinis; hæc ferre laborem, contemnere vulnus et dolorem docet: great is the force of habit, teaching us as it does to bear fatigue and to despise wounds and pain (Cicero)

magna inter molles concordia: there is great unanimity among the dissolute (Juvenal)

magna pars hominum est, quæ non peccatis irascitur sed peccantibus: the greater part of mankind is angry with the sinner and not with the sin (Seneca)

magna pars vulgi levis odit scelus spectatque: most of the giddy rabble hate the evil deed they come to see (Seneca)

magna servitus est magna fortuna: a great fortune is a great slavery (Seneca)

magnæ felicitates multum caliginis mentibus humanis objiciunt: great and sudden prosperity has a deadening effect on the human mind (Seneca)

magnæ fortunæ comes adest adulatio: adulation is ever the attendant on great wealth

magnam fortunam magnus animus decet: a great mind becomes a great fortune (Seneca)

magni animi est injurias despicere: it is the mark of a great mind to despise injuries (Seneca)

magni animi est magna contemnere, ac mediocria malle quam nimia: it is a sign of a great mind to despise greatness, and to prefer things in measure to things in excess (Seneca)

magni est ingenii revocare mentem a sensibus, et cogitationem a consuetudine abducere: it is a proof of great talents to call back the mind from the senses, and separate thought from habit (Cicero)

magni pectoris est inter secunda moderatio: moderation is the mark of a great heart (Seneca the Elder)

magni refert quibuscum vixeris: it matters a great deal with whom you live (i.e., the company you keep betrays your character)

magno cum periculo custoditur, quod multis placet: that is guarded at great risk which is coveted by many (Publilius Syrus)

magnos homines virtute metimur, non fortuna: we measure great men by their virtue, not their fortune (Cornelius Nepos)

magnum est argumentum in utroque fuisse moderatum: it speaks volumes for a man that, when placed in quite different situations, he displays in each the same spirit of moderation

magnum hoc vitium vino est, pedes captat primum; luctator dolosu 'st: this is the great fault of wine, it first trips up the feet; it is a cunning wrestler (Plautus)

magnum pauperies opprobrium jubet quidvis aut facere aut pati: poverty, that deep disgrace, bids us do or suffer anything (Horace)

magnum vectigal est parsimonia: economy (or thrift) is a great revenue (Cicero)

magnus animus remissius loquitur et securius: the talk of a great soul is at once more quiet and confident than that of other men (Seneca)

magnus sibi ipse non facit finem dolor: great grief does not of itself put an end to itself (Seneca)

magnus sine viribus ignis incassum furit: a great fire, unless you feed it, spends its rage in vain (Virgil)

majestatem res data dantis habet: the gift derives its value from the rank of the giver (Ovid)

major e longinquo reverentia: respect is greater at a distance (Tacitus)

major erat natu; non omnia possumus omnes: he was older; there are some things we cannot all do (Lucilius)

major famæ sitis est quam virtutis; quis enim virtutem amplectitur ipsam, præmia si tollas?: the thirst of fame is greater than that of virtue; for who would embrace virtue itself, if you take away its rewards? (Juvenal)

major hæreditas venit unicuique nostrum a jure et legibus, quam a parentibus: a greater inheritance comes to each of us from our rights and laws than from our parents (Cicero)

major ignotarum rerum est terror: greater is the terror of something unknown (Livy)

majore tumultu planguntur nummi quam funera: money is bewailed with a greater tumult than death (Juvenal)

majores fertilissium is agro oculum domini esse dixerunt: our fathers used to say that the master's eye was the best fertilizer (Pliny the Elder)

majus et minus non variant speciem: greater and less do not change the nature of a thing

mala causa silenda est: it is best to be silent in a bad cause (Ovid)

mala gallina, malum ovum: bad hen, bad egg

mala grammatica non vitiat chartam: bad grammar does not vitiate a contract (or deed)

mala mens, malus animus: bad mind, bad designs; bad mind, bad heart (Terence)

mala ultro adsunt: misfortunes come unsought

male cuncta ministrat impetus: anger manages everything badly (Statius)

male facere qui vult numquam non causam invenit: those who would do evil never fail to find a reason (Publilius Syrus)

male imperando summum imperium amittitur: the greatest empire may be lost by the misrule of its governors (Syrus Publilius)

male irato ferrum committitur: do not trust an angry man with a sword (Seneca)

male parta male dilabuntur: ill-gotten, ill-spent (i.e., easy come, easy go) (Cicero)

male partum male disperit: property ill got is property ill spent (i.e., easy come, easy go) (Plautus)

male secum agit æger, medicum qui hæredem facit: a sick man acts foolishly for himself who makes his doctor his heir

male verum examinat omnis corruptus judex: a corrupt judge does not carefully search for the truth (Horace)

male vivunt qui se semper victuros putant: they live ill who think they will live forever (Publilius Syrus)

maledicus a malefico non distat nisi occasione: an evil-speaker differs from an evil-doer in nothing but want of opportunity (Quintilian)

malevolus animus abditos dentes habet: the malevolent have hidden teeth (Publilius Syrus)

malim inquietam libertatem quam quietum servitium: I would rather have a restless liberty than a quiet slavery

maliuolum solacii genus est turba miserorum: A crowd of fellow sufferers is a miserable kind of comfort (Seneca)

malo benefacere tantumdem est periculum quantum bono malefacere: to do good to the bad is a danger just as great as to do bad to the good (Plautus)

malo in consilio feminæ vincunt viros: women surpass men at scheming evil (Publilius Syrus)

malo indisertam prudentiam, quam loquacem stultitiam: I prefer silent prudence to loquacious folly (Cicero)

malo mihi male quam molliter esse: I would rather be ill than idle (Seneca)

malo mori quam fœdari: I would rather die than be dishonored (i.e., better death than dishonor)

malo nodo malus quærendus cuneus: for a hard knot a hard tool must be sought

malo undique clades: disaster awaits the wicked on every side

malorum facinorum ministri quasi exprobrantes aspiciuntur: accomplices in evil actions are always regarded as reproaching the deed (Tacitus)

malum consilium consultori pessimum: bad advice is often fatal to the adviser (Verrius Flaccus)

malum (est) consilium quod mutari non potest: bad is the plan that is incapable of change (Publilius Syrus)

malum nascens facile opprimitur; inveteratum fit pleurumque robustius: an evil habit is easily subdued in the beginning, but when it becomes inveterate it gains strength (Cicero)

malum vas non frangitur: a worthless vessel is seldom broken (i.e., cheap things are secure from harm)

malus bonum ubi se simulat, tunc est pessimus: a bad man, when he pretends to be a good man, is the worst man of all (Publilius Syrus)

malus usus abolendus est: a bad custom is to be abolished

manet insontem gravis exitus: a grim end awaits the innocent

manus justa nardus: the just hand is as precious ointment

marcet sine adversario virtus: valor becomes feeble without an opponent (Seneca)

Mars gravior sub pace latet: a more severe war lurks under the guise of peace (Claudian)

mater artium necessitas: necessity is the mother of the arts (i.e., of invention)

materiam (or materiem) superabat opus: the workmanship surpassed the material (Ovid)

matre pulchra filia pulchrior: a daughter more beautiful than her beautiful mother (Horace)

matrem timidi flere non solere: the mother of a timid man seldom has reason to weep (Cornelius Nepos)

maturas cœlo non cadit ante diem: he who is ripe for heaven falls not before his day

mature fieri senem, si diu velis esse senex: you must become an old man soon if you would be an old man long (Cicero)

maxima debetur puero reverentia (or, **maxima reverentia pueris debetur**): the greatest respect is due to a child (Juvenal)

maxima illecebra est peccandi impunitatis spes: the greatest incitement to guilt is the hope of sinning with impunity (Cicero)

maxima quæque domus servis est plena superbis: every great house is full of haughty servants (Juvenal)

maximæ cuique Fortunæ minime credendum est: it is when Fortune is most propitious that she is least to be trusted (Livy)

maximas virtutes jacere omnes necesse est, voluptate dominante: where pleasure prevails, all the greatest virtues must lie dormant (or, lose their power) (Cicero)

maximeque admirantur eum, qui pecunia non movetur: above all is he admired who is not moved by money (Cicero)

maximum ornamentum amicitiæ tollit, qui ex ea tollit verecudiam: he takes the greatest ornament from friendship, who takes modesty from it (Cicero)

maximum remedium iræ mora est (or **dilatio est**): the best remedy for anger is delay (Seneca)

maximus novator tempus: time is the greatest innovator

medici, causa morbi inventa, curationem inventam putant: physicians, when they have found out the cause of a disease, believe they have found out the cure (Cicero)

medici graviores morbos asperis remediis curant: doctors cure the more serious diseases with harsh remedies (Curtius)

medio maxima turba mari est: the roughest seas are far from land (Propertius)

medio tutissimus ibis: the middle way is the safest for you to go (Ovid)

mediocribus utere partis: make moderate use of possessions

medium tenuere beati: blessed are they who have kept a middle course

mega biblion mega kakon: a great book is a great evil (Callimachus, from the Greek)

melior est conditio possidentis: better is the condition of the one in possession (i.e., possession is nine-tenths of the law)

melior tutiorque est certa pax quam sperata victoria: better and safer is the certainty of peace than the hope of victory (Livy)

meliora sunt ea quæ natura, quam quæ arte perfecta sunt: the things that are perfect by nature are better than those that are perfect by art (Cicero)

melius est cavere semper quam pati semel: it is better to be always on our guard than to suffer once

melius est pati semel, quam cavere semper: it is better to suffer once than always to be cautious (Julius Cæsar)

melius est peccata cavere quam mortem fugere: it is better to avoid sin than to flee from death (Thomas à Kempis)

melius in malis sapimus, secunda rectum auferunt: we become wiser by adversity; prosperity destroys our appreciation of the right (Seneca)

mellitum venenum, blanda oratio: flattering speech is honey-sweetened poison

meminerunt omnia amantes: lovers remember everything (Ovid)

memorem immemorem facit, qui monet quod memor meminit: the one who reminds someone of what he already remembers makes him forget (Plautus)

memoria est thesaurus omnium rerum e custos: memory is the treasury and guardian of all things (Cicero)

memoria minuitur, nisi eam exerceas: your power of memory will diminish unless you exercise it (Cicero)

mendacem memorem esse oportet (or **oportere**)**:** a liar should have a good memory (Quintilian)

mendaci homini, ne verum quidem dicenti credere solemus: we give no credit to a liar, even when he speaks the truth (Cicero)

mendico ne parentes quidem amici sunt: to a beggar not even his own parents show affection

mens bona regnum possidet: a good mind possesses a kingdom (Seneca)

mens cujusque is est quisque: the mind is the true self (Cicero)

mens sine pondere ludit: the mind is playful when unburdened

mens sola loco non exsulat: the mind alone cannot be exiled (Ovid)

mensque pati durum sustinet ægra nihil: a mind diseased cannot bear anything harsh (Ovid)

mercenarius fugit a grege: the hired hand flees from the flock

merces virtutis laus est: applause is the reward of virtue

meret qui laborat: he is deserving who is industrious

meritus augentur honores: honors are enhanced by merit

merx ultronea putret: proffered service stinks (i.e., it is despised)

messe tenus propria vive: live within the harvest (i.e., live within your means)

metiri se quemque suo modulo ac pede verum est: it is right that every man should measure himself by his own model and standard (Horace)

metus autem non est, ubi nullus irascitur: there is no fear where none is angry (Lactantius)

militat omnis amans: every lover is engaged in a war (Ovid)

militiæ species amor est: love is a kind of warfare (Ovid)

mille animos excipe mille modis: treat a thousand dispositions in a thousand ways (Ovid)

mille mali species, mille salutis erunt: there are a thousand forms of evil; there will be a thousand remedies (Ovid)

minatur innocentibus qui parcit nocentibus: he threatens the innocent who spares the guilty (Coke)

minimæ vires frangere quassa valent: very little avails to break a bruised thing (Ovid)

minime sibi quisque notus est, et difficilime de se quisque sentit: every one is least known to himself, and it is very difficult for a man to know himself (Cicero)

minimum decet libere cui multum licet: he who has great power should use it lightly (Seneca)

minor est quam servus, dominus qui servos timet: a master who fears his servants is lower than a servant

minuentur atræ carmine curæ: black care will be soothed by song (Horace)

minuit præsentia famam: presence diminishes fame (Claudian)

minus afficit sensus fatigatio quam cogitatio: bodily fatigue affects the mind less than intense thought (Quintilian)

minus (or minor) in parvis Fortuna furit, leviusque ferit leviora Deus: the rage of Fortune is less directed against the humble, and God strikes more lightly upon the low (Seneca)

minuti semper et infirmi est animi exiguique voluptas ultio: revenge is ever the delight of a stinted and weak and petty mind (Juvenal)

mira quædam in cognoscendo suavitas et delectatio: there is a certain wonderful sweetness and delight in gaining knowledge

miramur ex intervallo fallentia: we admire at a distance the things that deceive us

misce stultitiam consiliis brevem; dulce est desipere in loco: mix a little foolishness with your serious plans; it is sweet to be silly in places (Horace)

misera est magni custodia census: the custody of a large fortune is a wretched business (Juvenal)

misera est servitus ubi jus est aut vagum aut incognitum: obedience to the law is a hardship where law is either unsettled or unknown

miseram pacem vel bello bene mutari: an unhappy peace may be profitably exchanged for war (Tacitus)

miseranda vita, qui se metui, quam amari malunt: pitiable is the life of those who prefer being feared to being loved (Cornelius Nepos)

miserias properant suas audire miseri: the wretched hasten to hear of their own miseries (Seneca)

misero datur quodcunque, fortunæ datæ: whatever we give to the wretched, we lend to fortune (Seneca)

miseros prudentia prima relinquit: prudence is the first thing to forsake the wretched (Ovid)

miserrima est fortuna quæ inimico caret: most wretched is the fortune of him who has no enemy (i.e., who is not envied) (Publilius Syrus)

miserum est aliorum incumbere famæ: it is a wretched thing to lean upon the fame of others (Juvenal)

miserum est opus, igitur demum fodere puteum, ubi sitis fauces tedet: it is a wretched business to be digging a well just as thirst is mastering you (Plautus)

miserum est tacere cogi, quod cupias loqui: you are in a pitiable condition when you have to conceal what you wish to tell (Publilius Syrus)

mitte hanc de pectore curam: dismiss these anxieties from your heart (Virgil)

mitte sectari, rosa quo locorum sera moretur: stop looking for the place where a late rose may yet linger (Horace)

mobile mutatur semper cum principe vulgus: the fickle populace always changes with the prince (Claudian)

mobilis et varia est ferme natura malorum: misfortunes generally are of a variable and changeable nature (Juvenal)

moderari animo et orationi, cum sis iratus, non mediocris ingenii est: to be able to temper your indignation and language when you are angry is evidence of a chastened disposition (Cicero)

modestia famæ neque summis mortalibus spernenda est: fame, modestly courted, is not to be despised by persons of the highest character (Tacitus)

modica voluptas laxat animos et temperat: moderate pleasure relaxes the spirit and moderates it (Seneca)

modo, et modo, non habebent modum: by-and-by has no end (St. Augustine)

modus omnibus in rebus, soror, optimum est habitu; nimia omnia nimium exhibent negotium hominibus ex se: in everything the middle course is best; all things in excess bring trouble to men (Plautus)

mollis educatio nervos omnes et mentis et corporis frangit: an easy education weakens all powers both of mind and body (Quintilian)

mora omnis odio est, sed facit sapientiam: all delay is hateful, but it produces wisdom (Publilius Syrus)

morbi perniciores pluresque animi quam corporis: the diseases of the mind are more and more destructive than those of the body (Cicero)

morborum in vitio facilis medicina recenti: the cure is easy if the malady be recent (Gratius Faliscus)

mores amici noveris, non oderis: know well, but take no offense at the manners of a friend

mori est felicis antequam mortem invocet: happy is the one who dies before he must call on death (Publilius Syrus)

moribus et forma conciliandus amor: pleasing manners and a handsome form conciliate love (Ovid)

mors et fugacem persequitur virum: death pursues the man even as he flees from it (Horace)

mors ipsa refugit sæpe virum: death itself often takes flight at the presence of a man (Lucan)

mors laborum ac miseriarum quies est: death is repose from all our toils and miseries (Cicero)

mors sola fatetur quantula sint hominum corpuscula: death alone reveals how small are men's bodies (Juvenal)

mors ultima linea rerum est: death is the last boundary of things (Horace)

mortalia acta nunquam deos fallunt: the deeds of mortals can never be hid from the gods

mortem effugere nemo potest: no one can escape death

mortem misericors sæpe pro vita dabit: mercy often inflicts death (Seneca)

mortui non mordant: the dead do not bite (i.e., dead men tell no tales)

mortuo leoni et lepores insultant: even hares strike (or insult) a dead lion

motus in fine velocior: motion drawing to its end is swifter

mulier quæ sola cogitat male cogitat: the thoughts of a woman when alone tend toward mischief

mulier recte olet ubi nihil olet: a woman smells sweetest when she smells not at all (Plautus)

multa cadunt inter calicem supremaque labra: many things fall between the cup and the lip (Laberius)

multa ceciderunt ut altius surgerent: many things have fallen only to rise higher (Seneca)

multa docet fames: hunger teaches many things

multa fidem promissa levant: many promises weaken faith (Ovid)

multa magis quam multorum lectione formanda mens: the mind is formed by reading deep rather than reading wide (Quintilian)

multa novit vulpis, sed felis unum magnum: the fox knows many devices, the cat only one great one (i.e., to run up a tree)

multa petentibus desunt multa: those who long for much are in want of much (Horace)

multa senem circumveniunt incommoda: many are the discomforts that gather around old age (Horace)

multa trepidus solet detegere vultus: the fearful face usually betrays great guilt (Seneca)

multæ hominibus at malitam viæ sunt: many are the ways of malice in men (Justinian)

multæ manus onus levius faciunt: many hands make work light

multæ regum aures et oculi: kings have many ears and eyes

multæ terricolis linguæ cœlestibus una: the inhabitants of earth have many tongues, those of heaven have one

multas amicitias silentium diremit: silence (or neglect) dissolves many friendships

multi adorantur in ara qui cremantur in igne: many are worshipped at the altar who are burning in flames (St. Augustine)

multi multa, nemo omnia novit: many know many things, no one everything (Coke)

multi nil rectum nisi quod placuit sibi ducunt: many deem nothing right but what suits their own conceit (Horace)

multi quidem facilius se abstinent ut non utantur, quam temperent ut bene utantur: to many, total abstinence is easier than perfect moderation (St. Augustine)

multi sunt vocati, pauci vero electi: many are called but few are chosen (St. Matthew 22:14)

multi te oderint, si teipsum ames: many will hate you if you love yourself

multis minatur, qui uni facit injuriam: the person who injures one threatens many (Publilius Syrus)

multis terribilis caveto multos: if you are a terror to many, then beware of many (Ausonius)

multitudinem decem faciunt: ten constitute a crowd (Coke)

multo enim multoque seipsum quam hostem superare operosius est: it is harder, much harder, to conquer yourself than it is to conquer your enemy (Valerius Maximus)

multo plures satietas quam fames perdidit viros: many more die of excess than of hunger

multos in summa pericula misit venturi timor ipse mali: the mere apprehension of coming evil has driven many into positions of great peril

multos ingratos invenimus, plures facimus: we come upon many ungrateful men and, by being kind, we make more (said of benefactors)

multum sapit qui non diu desipit: he is very wise who does not long persist in folly

munditiis capimur: we are captivated by neatness (Ovid)

mundus est Dei viva statua: the world is the living image of God (Campanella)

mundus est ingens deorum omnium templum: the world is the mighty temple of the gods (Seneca)

mundus universus exercet histrioniam (or, **totus mundus agit histrionem**): all humanity practices the art of acting (Petronius)

mundus vult decipi; ergo decipiatur: the world wishes to be deceived; therefore let it be deceived

murus æneus conscientia sana: a sound conscience is a wall of bronze

mus non uni fidit antro: a mouse does not rely on just one hole (Plautus)

mutata forma interimitur prope substantia rei: the form being changed, the substance of the thing is destroyed

mutato nomine, de te fabula narratur: change but the name, and the tale is told of you (Horace)

mutum est pictura poëma: a picture is a silent poem

N

næ amicum castigare ob meritam noxiam immune est facinus: truly, it is a thankless office to censure a friend for a fault when he deserved it (Plautus)

nam dives qui fieri vult, et cito vult fieri: for the one who wishes to become rich wishes to become rich quickly (Juvenal)

nam et ipsa scientia potesta(s) est: for knowledge is itself power (Francis Bacon)

nam genus et proavos et quæ non fecimus ipsi vix ea nostra voco: for birth and ancestry, and that which we have not ourselves achieved, we can scarcely call our own (Ovid)

nam homo proponit, sed Deus disponit: for man proposes, but God disposes (Thomas à Kempis)

nam inimici famam non ita ut nata est ferunt: enemies carry a report in a form different from the original (Plautus)

nam non solum scire aliquid, artis est, sed quædam ars etiam docendi: not only is there an art in knowing a thing, but also a certain art in teaching it (Cicero)

nam nunc mores nihil faciunt quod licet, nisi quod lubet: nowadays it is the fashion to make nothing of what is proper, but only what is pleasant (Plautus)

nam quum magna malæ superest audacia causæ, creditur a multis fiducia: when great impudence comes to the help of a bad cause, it is taken by many for honest confidence (Juvenal)

nam risu inepto res ineptior nulla est: for there is nothing sillier than a silly laugh (Catullus)

nam scelus intra se tacitum qui cogitat ullum facti crimen habet: the one who secretly meditates a crime has all the guilt of the deed (Juvenal)

nam sera nunquam est ad bonos mores via: quem pænitet peccasse, pæne est innocens: it is never too late to turn from the errors of our ways: the one who repents of his sins is almost innocent (Seneca)

nam si violandum est jus, regnandi gratia violandum est: aliis rebus pietatem colas: if you must break the law, do it only to seize power: in all other cases, observe it (Julius Cæsar)

nam tanto brevius omne, quanto felicius tempus: the happier the moments, the shorter the time (Pliny the Younger)

nam tua res agitur, paries cum proximus ardet: you too are in danger when your neighbor's house is on fire (Horace)

nam ut quisque est vir optimus, ita difficillime esse alios improbos suspicatur: the more virtuous any man is, the less easily does he suspect others of being wicked (Cicero)

nam vitiis nemo sine nascitur; optimus ille est qui minimis urgetur: for no one is born without faults, and the best is the one who has the fewest (Horace)

nam(que) inscitia est adversum stimulum calces: it is ignorance to struggle against the spur (or goad) (Terence)

nascentes morimur, finisque ab origine pendet: we are born but to die, the end hangs from the beginning (Manilius)

nascimur poëtæ, fimus oratores: we are born poets, we become orators (Cicero)

natura hominum novitatis avida: human nature is greedy of novelty (Pliny the Elder)

natura inest in mentibus nostris insatiabilis quædam cupiditas veri videndi: nature has planted in our minds an insatiable desire to seek the truth (Cicero)

natura semina scientiæ nobis dedit, scientiam non dedit: nature has given us the seeds of knowledge, not knowledge itself (Seneca)

natura vero nihil hominibus brevitate vitæ præstitit melius: nature has granted man no better gift than the brevity of life (Pliny the Elder)

naturæ enim non imperatur, nisi parendo: we cannot command nature except by obeying her (Francis Bacon)

naturæ vis maxima: the greatest force is that of nature

naturalia non sunt turpia: natural things are without shame

naturam expellas furca, tamen usque recurret: you may drive out nature with a pitchfork, but she will keep coming back (Horace)

ne cede malis, sed contra audentior ito: yield not to misfortunes, but rather go more boldly to meet them (Virgil)

ne depugnes in alieno negotio: do not fight in another man's affairs

ne discedas a statione: do not desert your post

ne e quovis ligno Mercurius fiat: not every wood is fit for a statue of Mercury (Erasmus)

ne puero gladium: do not entrust a sword to a boy

ne quid detrimenti respublica capiat: take care to protect the republic from harm

ne quid nimis: nothing too much (i.e., avoid excess) (Terence)

ne scutica dignum horribili sectere flagello: do not pursue, with a weighty scourge, the person who deserves only a slight whip (Horace)

ne sutor supra crepidam (judicaret) (also, ne sutor ultra crepidam): let not the shoemaker judge beyond his last (i.e., speak of things he does not know) (Pliny the Elder)

ne te quæsiveris extra: seek not yourself from outside yourself

ne tempora perde precando: do not lose time by praying (Ovid)

ne tentes, aut perfice: attempt not, or accomplish (i.e., do not attempt what you do not intend to accomplish)

nec amor nec tussis celatur: neither love nor a cough can be hidden

nec cui de te plusquam tibi credas: do not believe any man more than yourself about yourself

nec deus intersit, nisi dignus vindice nodus: nor let a god intervene, unless the knot be worthy of such an intervention (Horace)

nec domo dominus, sed domino domus honestanda est: the master should not be graced by the mansion, but the mansion by the master (Cicero)

nec est ad astra mollis e terris via: the way from the earth to the stars is no easy one (Seneca)

nec grata est facies cui gelasinus abest: unpleasing is the face that does not smile (Martial)

nec lex est æquior ulla, quam necis artifices arte perire sua: nor is there any law more just than that the one seeking to harm should perish by his own devices (Ovid)

nec lusisse pudet, sed non incidere ludum: there is no shame in having sported, but in not having broken off play (Horace)

nec quicquam acrius quam pecuniæ damnum stimulat: nothing stings more deeply than the loss of money (Livy)

nec rationem patitur, nec æquitate mitigatur nec ulla prece flectitur, populus esuriens: a hungry populace listens not to reason, nor cares for justice, nor is bent by any prayers (Seneca)

nec scire fas est omnia: neither is it permitted to know all things (Horace)

nec semper feriet quodcunque minabitur arcus: the arrow will not always hit the object that it threatens

nec si non obstatur propterea etiam permittitur: that an act is not prohibited, it does not follow that it is permitted (Cicero)

nec sibi, sed toti genitum se credere mundo: to think that he was born not for himself alone, but for the whole world (Lucan)

nec sidera pacem semper habent: nor is heaven always at peace (Claudian)

nec te quæsiveris extra: do not seek out the opinion of another beside yourself (Persius)

nec tecum possum vivere, nec sine te: neither can I live with you nor without you (Martial)

nec ulla major pœna nequitiæ est, quam quod sibi et suis displicet: there is no greater punishment of wickedness than that it is dissatisfied with itself and its deeds (Seneca)

nec verbo, nec facto, quenquam lædendum: neither in word nor in deed should anyone be injured (or, harm no one, neither by word nor by deed)

nec vero superstitione tollenda religio tollitur: we do not destroy religion by destroying superstition (Cicero)

nec vitia nostra nec remedia pati possumus: neither can we endure our vices nor the remedies for them (Livy)

nec vixit male qui natus moriensque fefellit: neither has he lived ill whose birth and death has passed unnoticed by the world (Horace)

nec vultu destrue dicta tuo: do not discredit your words by the expression on your face (Ovid)

necesse est cum insanientibus furere, nisi solus relinqueris: it is necessary to be mad with the insane, unless you wish to be left quite alone (Petronius)

necesse est facere sumptum, qui quærit lucrum: it is necessary that the one who seeks gain should incur expense (Plautus)

necesse est in immensum exeat cupiditas quæ naturalem modum transiliit: when once ambition has passed its natural bounds, its progress is sure to be immense (Seneca)

necesse est multos timeat quem multi timent: he must fear many, whom many fear (Laberius, alluding to Julius Cæsar)

necessitas dat legem non ipsa accipit: necessity gives law without itself accepting one (Publilius Syrus)

necessitas fortiter ferre docet, consuetudo facile: necessity teaches us to bear misfortunes bravely, habit to bear them easily (Seneca)

necessitas ultimum et maximum telum est: necessity is the last and strongest weapon (Livy)

necessitudinis et libertatis infinita est æstimatio: necessity and liberty require the greatest consideration

nefas nocere vel malo fratri puta: you should esteem it a crime to hurt even an evil brother (Seneca)

nega, si fecisti (also, **si fecisti, nega**): if you did it, deny it

neglecta solent incendia sumere vires: a fire, if neglected, always gathers in strength (Horace)

neglecta virescunt: neglected things flourish

negligentia semper habet infortuniam comitem: negligence always has misfortune for a companion

negligere quid de se quisque sentiat, non solum arrogantis est, sed etiam omnino dissoluti: to be careless of what others think of us not only indicates an arrogant, but an altogether dissolute, character (Cicero)

neminem id agere, ut ex alterius prædetur nescitia: no one should so act as to take advantage of another's folly (Cicero)

nemini fidas, nisi cum quo prius multos modios salis absumpseris: trust no one unless you have eaten much salt with him (Cicero)

nemo agit in se ipsum: no one sues himself

nemo allegans suam turpitudinem audiendus est: no one testifying to his own baseness ought to be heard (i.e., do not trust the words of the debased)

nemo autem regere potest, nisi qui et regi: no one can rule who cannot also submit to authority (Seneca)

nemo bis punitur pro eodem delicto: no one is punished twice for the same crime

nemo dat quod non habet: no one can give what he does not have

nemo debet bis puniri pro uno delicto: no one shall be punished twice for the same offense (i.e., the principle of double jeopardy)

nemo debet bis vexari pro una et eadem causa: no one shall be harassed twice for the same cause

nemo debet esse judex in propria causa: no one ought to be judge in his own cause

nemo debet ex aliena jactura lucrari: no one ought to gain by another person's loss

nemo doctus mutationem consilii inconstantiam dixit esse: no sensible person ever charged someone with inconstancy who had merely changed his opinion (Cicero)

nemo (enim) est tam senex qui se annum non putet posse vivere: no one is so old that he does not think it possible to live another year (Cicero)

nemo (enim) potest personam diu ferre fictam: no one can wear a mask for very long (Seneca)

nemo est hæres viventis: no one is heir of the living

nemo est tam fortis quin rei novitate perturbetur: no one is so courageous as not to be upset by an unexpected turn of events (Julius Cæsar)

nemo ex proprio dolo consequitur actionem: no one can bring suit for his own fraud

nemo facile cum fortunæ suæ conditione concordat: no one is perfectly satisfied with what fortune allots him

nemo fit fato nocens: no one becomes guilty by fate (Seneca)

nemo impetrare potest a papa bullam nunquam moriendi: no one can ever obtain from the pope a dispensation from death (Thomas à Kempis)

nemo in amore videt: no one in love sees (Propertius)

nemo in sese tentat descendere: nemo!: no one is able to descend into his own bosom [to examine his faults]: no one! (Persius)

nemo ita pauper vivit, quam pauper natus est: no one is so poor in life as he was poor at birth (after Seneca)

nemo læditur nisi a seipso: no one is harmed but by himself

nemo liber est qui corpori servit: no one is free who is a slave to the body (Seneca)

nemo malus felix: no evil person is happy (Juvenal)

nemo mortalium omnibus horis sapit: no one is wise at all times (Pliny the Elder)

nemo patriam in qua natus est exuere nec ligeantiæ debitum ejurare possit: no one can cast off his native country or abjure his allegiance to his sovereign

nemo plus juris in alium transferre potest quam ipse habet: no one can transfer to others rights more extensive than those that he possesses

nemo potest duobus dominis servire: no one can serve two masters (St. Matthew 6:24)

nemo potest mutare consilium suum in alterius injuriam: no one can change what he proposes to enact to the injury of another

nemo potest nudo vestimenta detrahere: you cannot strip the garment off a naked man

nemo præsumitur alienam posteritatem suæ prætulisse: no one is presumed to have preferred another's offspring to his own

nemo punitur pro alieno delicto: let no one be punished for the fault of another

nemo repente fuit (or **fit**) **turpissimus:** no one ever became suddenly base (i.e., became evil all at once) (Juvenal)

nemo risum præbuit qui ex se cœpit: no one becomes a laughingstock who eagerly laughs at himself (Seneca)

nemo sibi nascitur: no one is born for himself

nemo solus satis sapit: no one alone is sufficiently wise (or, no one is wise enough by himself) (Plautus)

nemo sua sorte contentus: no one is satisfied with his lot

nemo tam pauper vivit quam natus est: no one is so poor in life as he was at birth (Seneca)

nemo tenetur se ipsum accusare: no one is bound to accuse himself

nemo timendo ad summum pervenit locum: no one reaches a high position without daring (Publilius Syrus)

nemo umquam neque poëta neque orator fuit, qui quemquam meliorem quam se arbitraretur: no poet or orator has ever existed who thought there was another better than himself (Cicero)

nemo unquam sapiens proditori credendum putavit: no wise man ever thought that a traitor should be trusted (Cicero)

nemo unquam sine magna spe immortalitatis se pro patria offerret ad mortem: no one could ever meet death for his country without the hope of immortality (Cicero)

nemo vir magnus sine aliquo afflatu divino unquam fuit: no man was ever great without some divine inspiration (Cicero)

neque cæcum ducem neque amentem consultorem: do not take either a blind guide or a weak advisor (from Aristophanes)

neque cuiquam mortalium injuriæ suæ parvæ videntur; multi eas gravius æquo habuere: no one underestimates the wrongs he suffers; many take them more seriously than they ought (Julius Cæsar, as quoted by Sallust)

neque culpa neque lauda teipsum: neither blame nor applaud yourself

neque enim est quisquam tam malus, ut videri velit: no one is wicked enough to wish to appear wicked (Quintilian)

neque enim lex est æquior ulla, quam necis artifices arte perire sua: nor is there any law more just than that he who has plotted death shall perish by his own plot (Ovid)

neque fœmina, amissa pudicitia, alia abnuerit: when a woman has lost her chastity, she will not shrink from any other crime (Tacitus)

neque laus in copia neque culpa in penuria consistit: it is no credit to be rich and no disgrace to be poor (Apuleius)

neque mala vel bona quæ vulgus putet: the views of the multitude are neither bad nor good (also, things are not to be viewed either good or bad merely because the public thinks so) (Tacitus)

neque opinione sed natura constitutum est jus: not in opinion, but in nature, is law founded (Cicero)

neque (enim) quies gentium sine armis: the quiet of nations cannot be maintained without arms, nor can arms be maintained without pay, nor pay without taxation (Tacitus)

nequicquam sapit qui sibi non sapit: he is wise to no purpose who is not wise regarding himself

nervos belli, pecuniam infinitam (also, **nervi belli, pecunia infinita**): the sinews of war: unlimited money (Cicero)

nescia mens hominum fati sortisque futuræ, et servare modum, rebus sublata secundis: the mind of man is ignorant of fate and future destiny, and cannot keep within due bounds when elated by prosperity (Virgil)

nescio quid curtæ semper abest rei: something is always wanting to our imperfect fortune (Horace)

nescire quædam magna pars sapientiæ est: ignorance of certain subjects is a great part of wisdom (Hugo de Groot, 1670)

nescis tu quam meticulosa res sit ire ad judicem: you do not know what a frightful thing it is to go to court (Plautus)

nescit vox missa reverti: a word once spoken can never be recalled (Horace)

neutiquam officium liberi esse hominis puto, cum is nihil promereat, postulare id gratiæ apponi sibi: a man of liberal sentiments will not stoop to ask that as a favor, which he cannot claim as a reward (Terence)

nihil a Deo vacat; opus suum ipse implet: nothing is void of God; his work everywhere is filled with himself (Seneca)

nihil aliud est ebrietas quam voluntaria insania: drunkenness is nothing but voluntary madness (Seneca)

nihil aliud necessarium ut sis miser, quam ut te miserum credas: nothing else is necessary to make you wretched than to believe you are so

nihil amanti durum: nothing is hard for one who loves

nihil amori injuriam est: there is no wrong that love will not forgive

nihil cum fidibus graculo: jackdaws have nothing to do with a lute (Aulus Gellius)

nihil dat qui non habet: a person gives nothing who has nothing

nihil dictum quod non dictum prius: nothing can be said that has not been said before

nihil difficile amanti: nothing is difficult for the lover (Cicero)

nihil enim æque gratum est adeptis, quam concupiscentibus: an object in possession seldom retains the same charms that it had when it was longed for (Pliny the Younger)

nihil enim lacryma citius arescit: nothing dries sooner than a tear (Cicero)

nihil eripit Fortuna nisi quod et dedit: Fortune takes nothing away but what she also gave (Publilius Syrus)

nihil esse præcipue cuiquam dolendum in eo, quod accidat universis: no one has the right to be sorry for himself for a misfortune that strikes everyone (Cicero)

nihil est ab omni parte beatum: there is nothing that is blessed in every respect (i.e., there are no unmixed blessings) (Horace)

nihil est aliud falsitas nisi veritatis imitatio: falsehood is nothing but an imitation of truth (Justinian)

nihil est aliud magnum quam multa minuta: every great thing is composed of many things that are small

nihil est annis velocius!: nothing is swifter than the years! (Ovid)

nihil est autem tam voluere: nothing is so swift as calumny (Cicero)

nihil est enim tam miserabile quam ex beato miser: nothing is more deserving of pity than a poor man who has seen better days (Cicero)

nihil est miserum, nisi cum putes: nothing is lamentable unless you think it so (Boëthius)

nihil est quod credere de se non possit: there is nothing of which it (power) cannot believe itself capable (Juvenal)

nihil est quod Deus efficere non possit: there is nothing that God cannot do (Cicero)

nihil est tam utile, quod in transitu prosit: nothing is so useful as to be of profit after only a hasty study of it (Seneca)

nihil hic nisi carmina desunt: nothing is wanting here except a song (Virgil)

nihil honestum esse potest, quod justitia vacat: nothing can be honorable where justice is absent (Cicero)

nihil inimicius quam sibi ipse: man is his own worst enemy (Cicero)

nihil ita sublime est, supraque pericula tendit non sit ut inferius suppositumque Deo: nothing is so high and above all danger that is not below and in the power of God (Ovid)

nihil magis consentaneum est quam ut iisdem modis res dissolvatur, quibus constituitur: nothing is more equitable than that everything should be dissolved by the same means by which it was first constituted

nihil morosius hominum judiciis: there is nothing so peevish as men's judgments of one another (Erasmus)

nihil non aggressuros homines, si magna conatis magna præmia proponantur: there is nothing men will not attempt when great enterprises hold out the promise of great rewards (Livy)

nihil potest rex nisi quod de jure potest: the king can do nothing but what the law allows

nihil quod est inconveniens est licitum: nothing that is inconvenient is lawful

nihil scire est vita jucundissima: to know nothing at all is the happiest life (i.e., ignorance is bliss)

nihil simul inventum est et perfectum: nothing is invented and brought to perfection all at once (Coke)

nihil sub sole novum (or, **nihil sub sole novi,** or, **nil novi sub sole**): there is nothing new under the sun (after Ecclesiastes 1:9)

nihil tam absurdum dici potest ut non dicatur a philosopho: there is nothing so absurd but it may be said by a philosopher (Cicero)

nihil tam firmum est, cui periculum non sit etiam ab invalido: nothing is so steadfast as to be free of danger from even the weakest person (Curtius)

nihil tam incertum nec tam inæstimabile est quam animi multitudinis: nothing is so uncertain or so inestimable as the disposition of a crowd (Livy)

nihil tam munitum est, quod non expugnari pecunia possit: nothing is so strongly fortified that it cannot be taken by money (Cicero)

nihil volitum quin præcognitum: nothing can be said to be desired that is not first known

nil actum reputa si quid superest agendum: do not consider that anything has been done if anything is left to be done (Lucan)

nil agit exemplum litem quod lite resolvit: that example does nothing, which, in removing one difficulty, introduces another (Horace)

nil dictum quod non dictum prius: there can be nothing said now that has not been said before

nil enim prodest, quod lædere non possit idem: nothing can be of advantage that is not also convertible to purposes of injury (Ovid)

nil est amore veritatis celsus: nothing is loftier than the love of truth (Prudentius)

nil feret ad manes divitis umbra suos: the spirit of the rich man will carry nothing to the shades below (Ovid)

nil habet infelix paupertas durius in se, quam quod ridiculos homines facit: the misfortunes of poverty carry with them nothing harder to bear than that it exposes men to ridicule (Juvenal)

nil homine terra pejus ingrato creat: earth produces nothing worse than an ungrateful man (Ausonius)

nil homini certum est: there is nothing assured to men (Ovid)

nil magnum nisi bonum: nothing is great unless it is good

nil mortalibus arduum est; cœlum ipsum petimus stultitia: nothing is too difficult for mortals; in our folly we strive to reach heaven itself (Horace)

nil peccant oculi, si oculis animus imperet: the eyes do not err if the mind governs them (Publilius Syrus)

nil posse creari de nilo: nothing can be created of nothing (Lucretius)

nil proprium ducas quod mutari potest: never deem anything your own that can be transferred (Publilius Syrus)

nil similius insano quam ebrius: nothing is more like a madman than a man who is drunk

nil sine magno vita labore debit mortalibus: life has given nothing great to mortals without labor (Horace)

nil spernat auris, nec tamen credat statim: let the ear despise nothing, nor yet be too ready to believe (Phædrus)

nil tam difficile est quod non solertia vincat: there is nothing so difficult that skill will not overcome it

nil tam inæstimabile est quam animi multitudinis: nothing is so valueless as the sentiments of the mob (Seneca)

nil temere novandum: make no rash innovations

nil unquam longum est, quod sine fine placet: nothing is ever long that never ceases to please

nimia cura deterit magis quam emendat: too much concern may injure rather than improve your work

nimia est miseria nimis pulchrum esse hominem: it is a great affliction to be too handsome a man (Plautus)

nimia est voluptas, si diu abfueris a domo domum si redieris, si tibi nulla est ægritudo animo obviam: it is a very great pleasure if, on your return home after a long absence, you are not confronted with anything to vex you (Plautus)

nimia familiaritas parit contemptum: familiarity breeds contempt (Publilius Syrus)

nimis uncis naribus indulges: you indulge too much in turning up the nose

nimium altercando veritas amittitur: in too much disputing, truth is apt to be lost (Publilius Syrus)

nimium (enim) risus pretium est, si probitatis impendio constat: we pay too much for a laugh if it is at the expense of our honesty (Quintilian)

nimium ne crede colori: trust not too much in a beautiful complexion (i.e., trust not too much to appearances) (Virgil)

nimium ne lætare secundis: do not rejoice too much in prosperity

nimium rebus ne fide secundis: do not trust prosperity too much

nisi caste, saltem caute: if not chastely, then at least cautiously

nisi pariter, non pugnant: there is no battle unless there be two (Seneca)

nisi utile est quod facias, stulta est gloria: unless what we do is useful, our pride is foolish (Phædrus)

nitamur semper ad optima: let us always strive for the best

nitimur in vetitum semper, cupimusque negata: we are ever striving after what is forbidden, and coveting what is denied us (Ovid)

nobilitatis virtus non stemma character: virtue, not pedigree, is the mark of nobility

nocet empta dolore voluptas: pleasure bought by pain is injurious (Horace)

nodum in scirpo quærere: to look for a knot in the rushes (i.e., to look for difficulty where none exists) (Terence)

noli altum sapere: do not aim at lofty things

noli barbam vellere mortuo leoni: do not pluck the beard of a dead lion (Juvenal)

noli tuba canere Eleemosynam: do not trumpet your almsgiving

nolite dare sanctum canibus: do not give that which is sacred to dogs (St. Matthew 7:6)

nolite deficere bene facientes: do not cease to do good (2 Thessalonians 3:13)

nolite judicare ut non judicemini: judge not that you be not judged (St. Matthew 7:1)

nomen amicitia est; nomen inane fides: friendship is but a name; fidelity but an empty name (Ovid)

nomina stultorum parietibus hærent: fools' names stick to the walls (i.e., fools' names and fools' faces are always found in public places)

non ætate verum ingenio adipiscitur sapientia: wisdom is not attained with years, but by ability (Plautus)

non aliunder pendere: do not rely on others

non bene conveniunt, nec in una sede morantur majestas et amor: majesty and love do not consort well together, nor do they dwell in the same place (Ovid)

non bene imperat, nisi qui paruerit imperio: no one makes a good commander except the one who has been trained to obey commands

non bene olet, qui bene semper olet: (fig.) the one who uses perfume has good reasons for using it (Martial)

non cuicunque datum est habere nasum: not everyone is gifted with a nose (i.e., has the powers of discernment) (Martial)

non cuivis homini contingit adire Corinthum: it is not every man that can go to Corinth (i.e., not everyone possesses the same opportunities) (Horace)

non damnatio sed causa hominem turpem facit: it is not the condemnation but the crime that disgraces a man (Seneca)

non decipitur qui scit se decipi: no one is deceived who is knowingly deceived

non deest generoso in pectore virtus: there is no lack of courage in a noble heart

non defendi homines sine vituperatione fortasse posse, neglegenter defendi sine scelere non posse: it might be pardonable to refuse to defend some men, but to defend them negligently is nothing short of criminal (Cicero)

non enim potest quæstus consistere, si eum sumptus superat: there can be no profit if the expense exceeds it (Plautus)

non enim tam auctoritatis in disputando, quam rationis momenta quærenda sunt: in every disputation, we should look more to the weight of reason than to the weight of authorities (Cicero)

non est ab homine nunquam sobrio postulanda prudentia: prudence must not be expected from a man who is never sober (Cicero)

non est alius ingenio alius animo color: genius does not have one form (or appearance) and courage another (Seneca)

non est ars quæ ad effectum casu venit: that which achieves its effect by accident is not art (Seneca)

non est bonum ludere cum diis: it is not good to trifle with the gods

non est discipulus super magistrum nec servus super dominum suum: the student is not above the teacher, nor is the servant above his master (St. Matthew 10:24)

non est ejusdem et multa et opportuna dicere: the same person will not both talk much and to the purpose

non est jocus esse malignum: there is no joke in being malignant (Horace)

non est princeps super leges, sed leges supra principem: The prince is not above the laws, but the laws above the prince (Pliny the Younger)

non est sine pulvere palma: the palm (honor) is not obtained without toil

non est vivere, sed valere, vita (est): life is not mere living but the enjoyment of health (Martial)

non ex verbo verbum sed ad sensu curabis reddere fidus interpres: as a faithful translator, be careful not to render (or translate) word for word but the meaning

non exercitus, neque thesauri, præsidia regni sunt, verum amici: the safety of a kingdom does not depend so much upon its armies, or its treasures, as on its alliances (Sallust)

non exiguum temporis habemus; sed multa perdidimus: it is not that we have so little time, but that we have lost so much (Seneca)

non facile solus serves quod multis placet: it is not easy to keep to yourself what many desire (Publilius Syrus)

non facit nobilem atrium plenum fumosis imaginibus: it is not a hallway filled with dusty portraits that makes a man a nobleman (Seneca)

non faciunt meliorem equum aurei freni: a gilded bit does not make for a better horse (Seneca)

non generant aquilæ columbas: eagles do not beget doves

non id quod magnum est pulchrum est, sed id quod pulchrum magnum: not that which is great is beautiful, but that which is beautiful is great

non in caro nidore voluptas summa, sed in teipso est, tu pulmentaria quære sundando: the pleasure [of eating] does not lie in the costly flavor, but in yourself; seek the relish, therefore, from hard exercise (Horace)

non intelligitur quando obrepit senectus: we do not perceive old age, seeing it creeps on apace (Cicero)

non intelligunt homines quam magnum vectigal sit parsimonia: men do not understand what a great revenue is thrift (Cicero)

non licet in bello bis peccare: in war, it is not permitted to err twice

non licet omnibus adire Corinthum: not everyone is permitted to go to Corinth (i.e., we cannot all be wealthy or have the same opportunities) (after Horace)

non metuit mortem, qui scit contemnere vitam: he fears not death who has learned to despise life (Dionysius Cato)

non mihi sapit qui sermone, sed qui factis sapit: not the one who is wise in speech, but the one who is wise in deeds, is wise for me (Gregory of Agrigentum)

non missura cutem, nisi plena cruoris hirudo: a leech that will not leave the skin until it is gorged with blood (Horace)

non omne quod licet honestum est (also, **non omne licitum honestum**): what is permissible is not always honorable (Justinian)

non omnem molitor quæ fluit unda videt: the miller does not see everything that floats by his mill (i.e., no one can be expected to see everything that might pass his way)

non omnes eadem mirantur amantque: all men do not admire and love the same things (Horace)

non omnes qui habent citharam sunt citharœdi: not all who own a lyre are lyre-players (Varro)

non omnia possumus omnes: we cannot all do all things (Virgil)

non omnibus ægris eadem auxilia conveniunt: the same remedies do not suit every patient (Celsus)

non omnis error stultitia est dicendus: not every error is to be called folly

non opus est verbis, credite rebus: there is no need of words; believe facts (Ovid)

non parcit populis regnum breve: a short reign brings no respite to the masses (Statius)

non parvum est seipsum noscere: it is not a little thing to know oneself

non posse bene geri rempublican multorum imperiis: a republic cannot be well conducted under the command of many (Cornelius Nepos)

non potest severus esse in judicando, qui alios in se severos esse judices non vult: he cannot be strict in judging who does not wish others to be strict judges of himself (Cicero)

non progredi est regredi: not to go forward is to go backward

non propter vitam faciunt patrimonia quidam, sed vitio cæci propter patrimonia vivunt: some men do not get estates for the purpose of enjoying life, but, blinded by error, live only for their estates (Juvenal)

non purgat peccata qui negat: the one who denies his sins does not atone for them

non quam diu, sed quam bene vixeris refert: not how long, but how well you have lived, is the main thing (Seneca)

non quam multis placeas, sed qualibus stude: do not care how many you please, but whom (Publilius Syrus)

non qui parum habet, sed qui plus cupit, pauper est: it is not the one who has little, but the one who craves more, who is the poor man (Seneca)

non satis est puris versum perscribere verbis: it is not enough to write your verse in plain words (Horace)

non scholæ, sed vitæ discimus: we learn not at school, but in life; or, we learn not for school, but for life (modified version of Seneca's **non vitæ, sed scholæ discimus**)

non scribit, cujus carmina nemo legit: no man writes whose verses no one reads (Martial)

non semper erit æstas: it will not always be summer (Hesiod)

non semper erunt Saturnalia: it will not always be Saturnalia (i.e., the carnival will not last forever)

non semper temeritas est felix: rashness is not always fortunate (Livy)

non sentire mala sua non est hominis et non ferre non est viri: not to feel one's misfortunes is not human, not to bear them is not manly (Seneca)

non sentiunt viri fortes in acie vulnera: in the stress of battle brave men do not feel their wounds (Cicero)

non si male nunc et olim sic erit: if matters go on badly at present, they may take a better turn in the hereafter (Horace)

non tua te moveant, sed publica vota: let not your own, but the public wishes, motivate you

non uti libet, sed uti licet, sic vivamus: we must live not as we like, but as we can

non vi sed virtute, non armis sed arte paritur victoria: not by force but by virtue, not with arms but with art is victory won

non vitæ, sed scholæ discimus: in school, we learn not the lessons of life, but of school (Seneca)

non vixit male, qui natus moriensque fefellit: he has not lived ill whose birth and death have passed unnoticed by the world (Horace)

nondum omnium dierum sol occidit: the sun of all days has not yet set

nondum victoria, jam discordia erat: not yet victory, and there was already dissension (Tacitus)

nonum(que) prematur in annum: let it (your first draft) be kept back from publication until the ninth year (Horace)

nos numerus sumus et fruges consumere nati: we are a mere cipher, and born to consume the fruits of the earth (Horace)

noscitur a sociis ejusdem generis: one is known by his companions of the same type (i.e., it takes one to know one)

nosse omnia hæc salus est adolescentulis: it is salutary for young men to know all these things (Terence)

nosse volunt omnes, mercedem solvere nemo: all wish to know, but no one wishes to pay the fee (Terence)

nostra nos sine comparatione delectant; nunquam erit felix quem torquebit felicior: what we have pleases us if we do not compare it with what others have; no person will be happy to whom a happier person is a torture (Seneca)

notatio naturæ, et animadversio peperit artem: art is born of the observation and investigation of nature (Cicero)

notissimum quodque malum, maxime tolerabile: the best known evils are the easiest to bear (Livy)

novos amicos dum paras, veteres cole: while you seek new friendships, take care to cultivate the old ones (Hermes)

noxiæ pœna par esto: let the punishment equal the crime (Cicero)

nudus amor formæ non amat artificem: naked love loves not the beauty that is due to art (Propertius)

nulla aconita bibuntur fictilibus: no poison is drunk out of earthenware (i.e., the poor and powerless need not fear being poisoned) (Juvenal)

nulla ætas ad perdiscendum est: there is no time of life past learning something (St. Ambrose)

nulla dies mærore caret: there is no day without sorrow (Seneca)

nulla (enim) res tantum ad dicendum proficit, quantum scriptio: nothing so much assists learning as writing down what we wish to remember (Cicero)

nulla est igitur excusatio peccati, si amici causa peccaveris: it is certainly no excuse for sin if we have sinned for the sake of a friend (Cicero)

nulla est sicera voluptas; sollicitumque aliquid lætis intervenit: no joy comes unmixed; and something of anxiety intervenes with every pleasure (Ovid)

nulla falsa doctrina est, quæ non permisceat aliquid veritatis: there is no doctrine so false that it does not contain some mixture of truth

nulla fere causa est, in qua non fœmina litem moverit: there is hardly a [bad] cause in which a woman has not been a prime mover (Juvenal)

nulla fides regni sociis, omnisque potestas impatiens consortis erit: there is no trust among colleagues in power, and all power will be impatient of a colleague (Lucan)

nulla fides umquam miseros elegit amicos: loyalty never chose the unfortunate as friends (Lucan)

nulla lex satis commoda omnibus est: no law is sufficiently convenient to all (Livy)

nulla placere diu nec vivere carmina possunt quæ scribuntur aquæ potoribus: no song can give pleasure for long, nor can it last, that is written by drinkers of water (Horace)

nulla res carius constat quam quæ precibus empta est: nothing costs so much as what is bought by prayers (Seneca)

nulla res tantum ad discendum profuit quantum scripto: nothing so much assists learning as writing down what we wish to remember

nulla unquam de vita hominis cunctatio longa est: no delay is too long when the life of a man is at stake (Juvenal)

nulli est homini perpetuum bonum: no man has perpetual good fortune (Plautus)

nulli jactantius mœrent, quam qui maxime lætantur: none mourn with more affection of sorrow than those who inwardly rejoice (Tacitus)

nulli sapere casu obtigit: no one was ever wise by chance (Seneca)

nulli te facias nimis sodalem, gaudebis minus et minus dolebis: be on too intimate terms with no one; if your joy be less, so will your grief (Martial)

nullis amor est medicabilis herbis: love is not to be cured by medicinal herbs (Ovid)

nullius boni sine socio jucunda possessio (est): without friends to share it, no good we possess is truly enjoyable (Seneca)

nullum ad nocendum tempus angustum est malis: no time is too short for the wicked to injure their neighbors

nullum caruit exemplo nefas: no crime has been without a precedent (Seneca)

nullum cum victis certamen et æthere cassis: brave men never warred with the dead and conquered (Virgil)

nullum enim officium referenda gratia magis necessarium est: there is no duty more obligatory than the repayment of a kindness (Cicero)

nullum est jam (or nunc) dictum quod non sit dictum prius: nothing is said now that has not been said before (Terence)

nullum est malum majus, quam non posse ferre malum: there is no greater misfortune than not to be able to endure misfortune

nullum est sine nomine saxum: no stone without a name (or, without a tale to tell) (Lucan, said of the fate of Troy)

nullum imperium tutum, nisi benevolentia munitum: no government is safe unless it be fortified by good will (Cornelius Nepos)

nullum iniquum in jure præsumendum est: nothing unjust is to be presumed in the law

nullum magnum ingenium sine mixtura dementiæ fuit: there has not been any great genius without an element of madness (Seneca)

nullum magnum malum quod extremum est: no evil is great which is the last (i.e., people have endured all manner of ills believing that there was no more to come) (Cornelius Nepos)

nullum majus boni imperii instrumentum quam bonos amicos esse: there can be no more effectual instrument of good government than good friends (Tacitus)

nullum numen abest, si sit prudentia: where there is prudence, a protecting deity is not far away

nullum sæculum magnis ingeniis clausum est: no era is closed to great intellects (Seneca)

nullum scelus rationem habet: no crime has a reason (i.e., no crime can be defended on rational grounds) (Livy)

nullum simile quatuor pedibus currit: no simile runs on all fours (i.e., applicable in every case)

nullum tempus occurrit regi: no lapse of time bars the rights of the king

nullus argento color est avaris abdito terris: silver has no shine while it is hidden in the miserly earth (Horace)

nullus argento color est, nisi temperato splendeat usu: silver has no splendor of its own unless it shines by temperate use (Horace)

nullus commodum capere potest de injuria sua propria: no one can take advantage of a wrong committed by himself

nullus dolor est quem non longinquitas temporis minuat ac molliat: there is no pain that length of time will not diminish and soothe (Cicero)

nullus est liber tam malus ut non aliqua parte prosit: there is no book so bad that it is not profitable in some part (attributed to Pliny the Elder)

nullus est locus domestica sede jucundior: there is no place more delightful than one's own domestic space (Cicero)

nullus tantus quæstus, quam quod habes parcere: there is no gain so certain as that which arises from sparing what you have (i.e., economy is a more certain road to wealth)

numero omnia impare gaudet: odd numbers bring luck (Virgil)

nunc vino pellite curas!: now drive away your cares with wine! (Horace)

nunquam acquiescere: never acquiesce

nunquam ad liquidum fama perducitur: fame (or rumor) never reports things in their true light

nunquam ædepol temere tinniit tintinnabulum; nisi quis illud tractat aut movet, mutum est, tacet: the bell never rings of itself; unless someone handles or moves it, it is silent (Plautus)

nunquam aliud natura, aliud sapientia dicit: nature never says one thing and wisdom another (Juvenal)

nunquam erit alienis gravis, qui suis se concinnat levem: he will never be disagreeable to others who makes himself agreeable to his own relations (Plautus)

nunquam est fidelis cum potente societas: never trust an alliance with the powerful (Phrædrus)

nunquam imperator ita paci credit, ut non se præparet bello: no ruler can be so confident of peace as not to prepare for war (Seneca)

nunquam libertas gratior extat quam sub rege pio: liberty is never more enjoyable than under a pious king (Claudian)

nunquam minus solus quam cum solus: never less alone than when alone (Cicero)

nunquam nimis dicitur, quod nunquam satis discitur: that is never too often repeated that is never sufficiently learned (Seneca)

nunquam potest non esse virtuti locus: there must ever be a place for virtue (Seneca)

nunquam procrastinandum: one ought never to procrastinate

nunquam scelus scelere vincendum est: it is unlawful to overcome crime by crime (Seneca)

nunquam vera species ab utilitate dividitur: the truly beautiful is never separated from the useful (Quintilian)

nunquam vir æquus dives evasit cito: no just man ever became rich quickly (Menander)

nusquam est qui ubique est: the man who is everywhere is never anywhere (Seneca)

nusquam tuta fides: nowhere is trust safe; or, nowhere is there true fidelity (or honor) (Virgil)

O

oblatam occasionem tene: seize the opportunity that is offered

obsequium amicos, veritas odium parit: obsequiousness brings us friends, the truth brings forth enemies (Terence)

occasio ægre offertur, facile amittitur: a good opportunity is seldom presented, and is easily lost (Publilius Syrus)

occasio furem facit (or, **facit occasio furem**): opportunity makes the thief

oculi sunt in amore duces: in love the eyes are our leaders (Propertius)

oculi tanquam speculatores altissimum locum obtinent: the eyes, like sentinels, occupy the highest place in the body (Cicero)

oculis magis habenda fides quam auribus: it is better to trust our eyes than our ears

oculus domini saginat equum: the master's eye makes the horse fat

oderunt di homines injuros: the gods hate unjust men (Nævius)

oderunt hilarem tristes, tristemque jocosi: the sad detest the cheerful, and the cheerful the sad (Horace)

oderunt peccare boni virtutis amore: good men hate to sin out of their love of virtue (Horace)

odia qui nimium timet, regnare nescit: the one who dreads hostility too much is unfit to rule (Seneca)

odit verus amor, nec patitur, moras: true love hates, and does not suffer, delay (Seneca)

officii fructus sit ipsum officium: let the reward of duty be duty itself (Cicero)

officium natura docet: nature teaches one duty

oi pleiones kakoi: the greater part of humankind is bad (Bias, one of the Seven Greek Sages, from the Greek)

olim meminisse juvabit: it will delight us to recall these things (i.e., some day we will look back at this and laugh) (Virgil)

omina sunt aliquid: there is something in omens (Ovid)

omne actum ab agentis intentione (est) judicandum: every act is to be judged by the intention of the agent

omne ævum curæ: cunctis sua displicet ætas: every age has its own care: each one thinks his own time of life is disagreeable (Ausonius)

omne animal seipsum diligit: every animal loves itself (Cicero)

omne animi vitium tanto conspectius in se crimen habet, quanto major qui peccat habetur: every vice of the mind makes its guilt the more conspicuous in proportion to the rank of the offender (Juvenal)

omne bellum sumi facile, ceterum ægerrume desinere: war is always easy to start, but very hard to end (Sallust)

omne homini natale solum: the whole world is a man's birthplace (Statius)

omne ignotum pro magnifico (est): everything unknown is thought to be magnificent (Tacitus)

omne in præcipiti vitium stetit: every vice ever stands on a precipice (Juvenal)

omne malum nascens facile opprimitur; inveteratum fit plerumque robustius: every evil is easily crushed at its birth; when grown old, it generally becomes more obstinate (Cicero)

omne nimium vertitur in vitium: every excess develops into a vice

omne quod dulce est cito satiat: all sweet things quickly bring satiety (or satisfaction) (Macrobius)

omne supervacuum pleno de pectore manat: everything that is superfluous overflows from the full bosom (Horace)

omnem crede diem tibi diluxisse supremum: believe that each day that shines on you is your last (Horace)

omnes pari sorte nascimur: sola virtute distinguimur: men are equal by birth: merit alone makes the difference

omnes sapientes decet conferre et fabulari: all wise people ought to confer and hold converse with each other (Plautus)

omnes sibi malle melius esse, quam alteri: it is human nature that every individual should wish for his own advantage in preference to that of others (Terence)

omnes sub regno graviore regnum est: every monarch is subject to a mightier one (Seneca)

omnes una manet nox, et calcanda semel via lethi: one night awaits us all, and the path of death must be trodden once (Horace)

omni ætati mors est communis: death is common to every age (Cicero)

omnia conando docilis solertia vincit: by application a docile shrewdness conquers every difficulty (Manilius)

omnia cum amico delibera, sed de (te) ipso prius: consult your friend on everything, but particularly on what concerns yourself (Seneca)

omnia enim plerumque quæ absunt vehementius hominum mentes perturbant: as a rule, men's minds are more deeply disturbed by what they do not see (Julius Cæsar)

omnia fert ætas, animum quoque: age carries everything away, even the mind (Virgil)

omnia inconsulti impetus cœpta, initiis valida, spatio languescunt: all enterprises that are entered into with hasty zeal may be pursued with great vigor at first, but are sure to languish in the end (Tacitus)

omnia mala exempla ex rebus bonis orta sunt (also, **omnia mala exempla orta sunt ex bonis initiis**): every bad precedent originated as a justifiable measure (Sallust)

omnia mors æquat: death levels all things (Claudian and Cicero)

omnia mors poscit. Lex est, non pœna, perire: death claims all things. It is law, not punishment, to die (Seneca)

omnia munda mundis: to the pure all things are pure

omnia mutantur, nihil interit: all things merely change, nothing perishes (Ovid)

omnia mutantur, nos et mutamur in illis: all things change, and we ourselves change with them (Borbonius)

omnia non pariter rerum sunt omnibus apta: all things are not equally fit for all men (Propertius)

omnia non properanti clara certaque erunt; festinatio improvida est, et cæca: all things will be clear and distinct to the man who does not hurry; haste is blind and improvident (Livy)

omnia orta occidunt, et aucta senescunt: everything that rises sets, and everything that grows grows old (Sallust)

omnia perversas possunt corrumpere mentes: all things tend to corrupt perverted minds (Ovid)

omnia præclara rara: all excellent things are rare (Cicero)

omnia præsumuntur rite et solenniter esse acta: all things are presumed to have been done duly and in the usual manner

omnia prius experiri, quam armis, sapientem decet: it becomes a wise man to try all methods before having recourse to arms (Terence)

omnia rerum principia parva sunt: all beginnings are small (Cicero)

omnia Romæ cum pretio: all things at Rome may be bought for a price (Juvenal)

omnia sunt hominum tenui pendentia filo; et subito casu, quæ valuere, ruunt: all things human hang by a slender thread; and that which seemed to stand strong of a sudden falls and sinks in ruins (Ovid)

omnia vincit amor, nos et cedamus amori: love conquers all things, let us also yield to love (Virgil)

omnibus bonis expedit rempublicam esse salvam: it is for the interest of every good man that the republic shall be safe (Cicero)

omnibus in rebus voluptatibus maximis fastidium finitimum est: the greatest pleasures are only narrowly separated from disgust (Cicero)

omnis amans amens: every lover is demented

omnis ars imitatio est naturæ: all art is an imitation of nature (Seneca)

omnis commoditas sua fert incommoda secum: every convenience brings its own inconveniences along with it

omnis homines ... qui de rebus dubiis consultant, ab odio, amicitia, ira atque misericordia vacuos esse decet: those who deliberate on controversial matters should be free from hatred, friendship, anger, and pity (Julius Cæsar, as quoted by Sallust)

omnis mutatio loci jucunda fiet: every change of place becomes a delight (Seneca)

omnis nimium longa properanti mora est: every delay is too long to one who is in a hurry (Seneca)

omnis pœna corporalis, quamvis minima, major est omni pœna pecuniaria, quamvis maxima: the slightest corporal punishment falls more heavily than the largest pecuniary penalty

omnis sors ferendo superanda est: every fate is to be overcome by enduring

omnis stultitia laborat fastidio sui: all folly is afflicted with a disdain of itself (Seneca)

omnium consensu capax imperii, nisi imperasset: he would have been universally deemed fit for empire, if he had never reigned (Tacitus, said of Emperor Galba)

omnium rerum, heus, vicissitudo est: there are changes, mark you, in all things (Terence)

omnium rerum principia parva sunt: the beginnings of all things are small (Cicero)

onus segni impone asello: lay the burden on the lazy ass

operæ pretium est: there is a reward for work (i.e., it is worth doing) (Terence)

operæ pretium non est: it is work not worthy of doing (i.e., it is not worthwhile)

opere in longo fas est obrepere somnum: in a long work it is allowable for sleep to steal upon us (or, upon the writer) (Horace)

opes regum, corda subditorum: the wealth of kings is in the affections of their subjects

opinionem quidem et famam eo loco habeamus, tamquam non ducere sed sequi debeat: as for rumor and reputation, let us consider them as matters that must follow, not guide, our actions (Seneca)

opinionum commenta delet dies, naturæ judicia confirmat: time erases the comments of opinion, but it confirms the judgments of nature (Cicero)

optanda mors est, sine metu mortis mori: to die without fear of death is something to be desired (Seneca)

optat ephippia bos piger optat arare caballus: the lazy ox covets the horse's saddle, the slow horse would rather plough (Horace)

optima mors Parca quæ venit apta die: the best death is that which comes on the day that Fate determines (Propertius)

optimi consiliarii mortui: the best counselors are the dead

optimum custodem ovium quem dicunt esse lupum!: what a fine shepherd a wolf must be!

optimum obsonium labor: work is the best of relishes (or, work is the best means to eating)

optimus est portus pœnitenti mutatio consilii: the safest haven for the penitent is a change in conduct (Cicero)

optimus est qui optime facit: the best is he who does the best

opulentia tyranni, paupertas subjectorum: the wealth of a tyrant is the poverty of his subjects

opus artificem probat: the work proves the craftsman (i.e., the worker is known by his work)

orandum est ut sit mens sana in corpore sano: we should pray for a sound mind in a sound body (Juvenal)

orare est laborare, laborare est orare: to pray is to work, to work is to pray

orationis summa virtus est perspicuitas: the greatest virtue of speech is perspicuity (Quintilian)

orator improbus leges subvertit: a morally corrupt orator subverts the law

ostendite modo bellum, pacem habebitis: you need only a show of war to have peace (Livy)

otia dant vitia: leisure begets vices

otia si tollas, periere Cupidinis arcus: remove leisure, and the bow of Cupid will lose its effect (Ovid)

otiosi semper egentes: the idle are always needy

otiosis nullus adsistit deus: no god assists the idle

otium sine litteris mors est et hominis vivi sepultura: leisure without literature is death, or rather the burial of a living man (Seneca)

otium sortem exspectat: idleness awaits its destiny (i.e., hopes for good fortune)

P

pacem hominibus habe, bellum cum vitiis: maintain peace with men, war with their vices

pactum non pactum est; non pactum pactum est, quod vobis lubet: an agreement is not an agreement; no agreement is an agreement, as it pleases you (Plautus)

palam mutire plebeio piaculum est: for a common man to mutter what he thinks is a risky venture

par in parem imperium non habet: an equal has no authority over an equal

paratæ lacrimæ insidias non fletum indicant: ready tears are a sign of treachery, not of grief (Publilius Syrus)

parcite paucarum diffundere crimen in omnes: refrain from laying the guilt of the few upon the many (Ovid)

parem delinquentis et suasoris culpam esse: the fault belongs alike to the wrong-doer and to the persuader

pares cum paribus ut est in veteri proverbio facillime congregantur: as in the old proverb, like associates more easily with like (Cicero)

paritur pax bello: peace is produced by war (Cornelius Nepos)

pars beneficii est quod petitur si belle neges: to refuse graciously is to confer a favor (Publilius Syrus)

pars beneficii est quod petitur si cito neges: to refuse a favor quickly is to grant one (Publilius Syrus)

pars minima est ipsa puella sui: the girl herself is the least part of herself (Ovid)

pars sanitatis velle sanari fuit: it is a step to the cure to be willing to be cured (Seneca)

parsimonia est magnum vectigal: thrift is a great revenue (Cicero)

parta tueri: defend what you have won

parva leves capiunt animas (or **animos**)**:** little minds are caught (or captured) by little things (Ovid)

parvam culinam duobus ganeonibus non sufficere: a small kitchen does not suffice for two gluttons

parvi enim sunt foris arma, nisi est consilium domi: an army abroad is of little use unless there are prudent counsels at home (Cicero)

parvula scintilla sæpe magnum suscitavit incendium: a very small spark has often kindled a great conflagration

parvum parva decent: small things become the small (Horace)

pati necesse est multa mortales mala: mortals must bear many ills (Nævius)

patientia casus exsuperat omnes: patience masters all chances

patientia læsa fit furor: patience abused becomes fury

patria cuique chara: each person's homeland is dear to him

patriæ fumus igne alieno luculentior: the smoke of one's own country is brighter than any fire in a foreign land

patriæ quis exsul se quoque fugit?: what fugitive from his homeland can flee from himself? (Horace)

patriæ solum omnibus carum est: the soil of their native land is dear to the hearts of all (Cicero)

pauci dignoscere possunt vera bona, atque illis multum diversa: few men can distinguish the truly good from the reverse (Juvenal)

pauci libertatem, pars magna justos dominos volunt: few men desire liberty; the majority are satisfied with a just master (Sallust)

paucis carior fides quam pecunia fuit: there were few who preferred honor to money (Sallust)

paullum (or **paulum**) **sepultæ distat inertiæ celata virtus:** virtue (or excellence) when concealed, differs but little from buried idleness (Horace)

pauper enim non est, cui rerum suppetit usus: that man is not poor who has a sufficiency for all his wants (Horace)

pauper ubique jacet: everywhere the poor man is despised (Ovid)

paupertas est, non quæ pauca possidet, sed quæ multa non possidet: poverty is not possessing few things, but lacking many things (Seneca)

paupertas fugitur, totoque arcessitur orbe: poverty is shunned and treated as a crime throughout the world (Lucan)

paupertatem summis ingeniis obesse, ne provehantur: poverty hinders the greatest talents from advancing

paupertatis onus patienter ferre memento: patiently bear the burden of poverty (Dionysius Cato)

pavore carent qui nihil commiserunt; at pœnam semper ob oculos versari putant qui peccarunt: the innocent are free from fear; but the guilty have always the dread of punishment before their eyes

pax paritur bello: peace is produced by war (Cornelius Nepos)

pax potior bello: peace is preferable to war

peccare licet nemini: no one has license to sin (Cicero)

peccare pauci nolunt, nulli nesciunt: few are unwilling to sin, all know how (Publilius Syrus)

pectus est quod disertos facit: it is the heart that makes one eloquent (Quintillan)

pecunia obediunt omnia: all things are obedient to money

pecunia regimen est rerum omnium: money controls all things (Publilius Syrus)

pecuniam in loco negligere interdum maximum est lucrum: to despise money on occasion sometimes leads to very great gain (Terence)

pecuniam perdidisti; fortasse illa te perderet manens: you have lost your money; perhaps, if you had kept it, it would have lost you

pejor est bello timor ipse belli: the dread of war is worse than war itself (Seneca)

per difficile est, cum prestare cæteris concupieris, servare æquitatem: it is very difficult to preserve equity aiming to surpass others (Cicero)

per multum risum, poteris cognoscere stultum: by his redundant laughter, you can always distinguish a fool

per scelera semper sceleribus certum est iter: the way to wickedness is always through wickedness (Seneca)

percunctatorem fugito; nam garrulus idem est: avoid the inquisitive person, for he is sure to be a talker (i.e., secrets entrusted to idle gossips are no longer secrets) (Horace)

perdidit arma, locum virtutis deseruit, qui semper in augenda festinat et obruitur re: he has lost his weapons and deserted the cause of virtue who is ever eager and engrossed in increasing his wealth (Horace)

pereant amici, dum una inimici intercidant: let our friends perish, provided our enemies fall along with them (a Greek proverb in Latin, condemned by Cicero)

pereant qui ante nos nostra dixerunt: may they perish who said our good things before us (said humorously of ideas borrowed from predecessors)

perfer et obdura; dolor hic tibi proderit olim: bear and endure to the end; one day this pain will be useful to you (Ovid)

perfer et obdura; multo graviora tulisti: bear and endure to the end; you have borne much heavier misfortunes than these (Ovid)

periculosior casus ab alto: even more dangerous is a fall from high

periculosum est credere et non credere: it is equally dangerous to believe and to disbelieve (Phædrus)

periculum in mora: there is danger in delay

perimus licitis: we come to ruin by permitted things (i.e., we died for a good cause)

perit omnis in illo nobilitas, cujus laus est in origine sola: he loses all nobility whose only merit is noble birth (Saleius Bassus)

perituræ parcite chartæ: spare the paper that is fated to perish (adapted from Juvenal)

perjuria ridet amantum Juppiter: Jupiter laughs at lovers' deceits

perjurii pœna divina exitium, humana dedecus: the punishment of perjury at the hands of the gods is perdition; at the hands of man, it is disgrace (from *The Twelve Tables*)

pessimum genus inimicorum, laudantes: the worst kind of enemies: flatterers (Tacitus and Publilius Syrus)

philosophia simulari potest, eloquentia non potest: philosophy can be feigned, eloquence cannot (Quintilian)

phobou to geras, ou gar erchetai monon: fear old age, for it does not come alone (a Greek proverb)

pigmæi gigantum humeris impositi plusquam ipsi gigantes vident: pygmies on a giant's back see more than the giant himself (Didacus Stella)

pinguis venter non gignit sensum tenuem: a fat belly does not produce fine sense (St. Jerome)

placeat homini quicquid (or **quidquid**) **Deo placuit:** whatever is God's pleasure should be man's pleasure (Seneca)

plebeia ingenia magis exemplis quam ratione capiuntur: vulgar minds are more impressed by examples than by reasons (Macrobius)

plerumque gratæ divitibus vices: changes are generally agreeable to the wealthy (Horace)

plerumque modestus occupat obscuri speciem, taciturnus acerbi: usually, the modest man passes for a reserved man, the silent for a sullen one (Horace)

ploratur lacrimis amissa pecunia veris: the loss of money is bewailed with true tears (Juvenal)

plura consilio quam vi perficimus: we accomplish more by prudence than by force (Tacitus)

plura faciunt homines e consuetudine quam e ratione: men do more things from habit than from reason

plures adorant solem orientem quam occidentem: more do homage to the rising sun than to the setting one

plures crapula quam gladius: drunkenness kills more than the sword

plures tegit Fortuna quam tutos facit: Fortune shields more than it makes safe (Publilius Syrus)

pluribus intentus minor est ad singula sensus: a person engaged in various pursuits minds none of them well

plurima sunt quæ non audent homines pertusa dicere læna: there are very many things that men, when their cloaks have holes in them, dare not say (Juvenal)

pluris est oculatus testis unus quam auriti decem: one eyewitness is better than ten who have heard (Plautus)

plus aloës quam mellis habet: she has more of aloes than of honey (i.e., the bitter outweighs the sweet) (Juvenal)

plus animi est inferenti periculum, quam propulsanti: there is always more spirit in attack than in defense (Livy)

plus apud me (or nos) tamen vera ratio valebit quam vulgi opinio: sound argument will have more weight with me (or us) than popular opinion (Cicero)

plus dolet quam necesse est, qui ante dolet quam necesse est: the one who grieves before it is necessary grieves more than necessary (Seneca)

plus exemplo quam peccato nocent: they do more mischief by the example than by the sin

plus impetus, majorem constantiam, penes miseros: we find more violence and greater perseverance among the wretched (Tacitus)

plus in amicitia valet similitudo morum quam affinitas: similarity of manners is more conducive to friendship than affinity by marriage (Cornelius Nepos)

plus in posse quam in actu: more in possibility than in actuality

plus potest qui plus valet: the stronger always succeeds (Plautus)

plus ratio quam vis cæca valere solet: reason can generally effect more than blind force (Cornelius Gallus)

plus salis quam sumptus: more of good taste than expense (also, more relish than meat) (Cornelius Nepos)

plus scire satius est, quam loqui: it is well for one to know more than he says (Plautus)

plus vetustis nam favet invidia mordax, quam bonis præsentibus: biting envy is more merciful to good things that are old than such that are new (Phædrus)

poësis est vinum dæmonum: poetry is the wine of demons

poëta nascitur, non fit: a poet is born, not made

pompa mortis magis terret quam mors ipsa: the solemnity associated with death awes us more than death itself (Seneca, as quoted by Bacon)

ponderanda sunt testimonia, non numeranda: testimonies are to be weighed, not counted

populus me sibilat, at mihi plaudo: the people boo me, but I applaud myself (Horace)

populus vult decipi; (ergo) decipiatur: the people wish to be deceived; (therefore) let them be deceived

poscunt fidem secunda, at adversa exigunt: prosperity asks for fidelity; adversity exacts it (Seneca)

post amara dulcia: sweet things come after bitter things

post amicitiam credendum est, ante amicitiam judicandum: after friendship, you should render implicit belief; before friendship, you should exercise judgment (Seneca)

post cineres gloria sera venit: glory comes too late after one has died (Martial)

post coitum omne animal triste: after sexual intercourse, every animal is sad

post epulas stabis vel passus mille meabis: after eating, you should either stand or walk a mile (variation of Schola Salern)

post factum nullum consilium: counsel is of no effect after the fact

post malam segetem serendum est: after a bad crop, immediately begin to sow (Seneca)

post mortem nulla voluptas: after death no pleasure remains

post prandium stabis, post cœnem ambulabis: after lunch rest a while, after supper walk a mile (Schola Salern)

posteriores cogitationes sapientiores solent esse: second thoughts are generally wiser thoughts (Cicero)

posthac occasio calva: later, opportunity is bald (i.e., has passed)

postremo nemo ægrotus quidquam somniat tam infandum, quod non aliquis dicat philosophus: in short, no sick man ever dreamed of anything so absurd that one or another philosopher has not said it (Varro)

potentiam cautis quam acribus consiliis tutius haberi: power is more safely retained by cautious than by severe counsels (Tacitus)

potentissimus est, qui se habet in potestate: he is the most powerful who has himself in his power (Seneca)

potest ex casa magnus vir exire: a great man can come from a hut (Seneca)

potest melior vincere, non potest non pejor esse qui vicerit: the better man may win, but he cannot fail to be the worse for his victory (Seneca)

potius ignoratio juris litigiosa est quam scientia: the litigious spirit is more often found with ignorance than with knowledge of law (Cicero)

potuit fortasse minoria piscator quam piscis emi: the fisherman could perhaps be bought for less than the fish (Juvenal)

præcedentibus insta: follow close on those who go before (or precede)

præcepta ducunt, at exempla trahunt: precepts guide, but examples drag along

præceptores suos adulescens veneratur et suspicit: a young man respects and looks up to his teachers (Seneca)

præcipue autem lignum, sive virga, versus superiorem partem curva est: every staff of empire is truly crooked at the top (Francis Bacon)

præcocia non diuturna: precocious things do not last long

præferre patriam liberis regem decet: a king should prefer his country to his children (Seneca)

præmium virtutis honor (pl. præmia virtutis honores): honor is the reward of virtue

præsis ut prosis: be first, that you may be of service

præstatur laus virtuti, sed multo ocius verno gelu tabescit: praise is bestowed on virtue but vanishes more quickly than frost in the Spring (Livius Andronicus)

prævalent illicita: things forbidden have a secret charm (Tacitus)

presto maturo, presto marcio: soon ripe, soon rotten

pretio parata vincitur pretio fides: fidelity bought with money is overcome by money (Seneca)

pretiosum quod utile: what is useful is valuable

prima caritas incipit a seipso: charity begins at home

prima enim sequentem, honestum est in secundis, tertiisque consistere: when you are aspiring to the highest place, it is honorable to stand in the second or even the third rank (Cicero)

prima est hæc ultio, quod se judice nemo nocens absolvitur: this is the first of punishments, that no guilty man is acquitted if judged by himself (Juvenal)

prima et maxima peccantium est pœna peccasse: the first and greatest punishment of sinners is the conscience of sin (Seneca)

prima quæ vitam dedit hora, carpit: the hour that gives us life begins to take it away (Seneca)

prima societas in ipso conjugio est; proxima in liberis; deinde una domus, communia omnia: the first bond of society is marriage; the next, our children; then the whole family and all things in common (Cicero)

primus in orbe deos fecit timor: it was fear that first produced gods in the world (Petronius and Statius)

primus sapientiæ gradus est falsa intelligere: the first step toward wisdom is to distinguish what is false

princeps qui delatores non castigat, irritat: the prince who does not punish informers encourages them (Domitian, as quoted by Suetonius)

principes mortales, rempublicam æternam: princes are mortal, the republic is eternal (Tacitus)

principibus placuisse viris non ultima laus est: to have won the approval of important people is not the last degree of praise (Horace)

principis est virtus maxima nosse suos: it is the greatest merit of a prince to know his subjects (Martial)

prius quam (or **priusquam**) **incipias consulto, et ubi consulueris mature facto opus est:** before you begin, consider; but having considered, use dispatch (Sallust)

privatorum convento juri publico non derogat: no bargain between individuals derogates from a law

privilegium est quasi privata lex: privilege is, as it were, private law

probæ etsi in segetem sunt deteriorem datæ fruges, tamen ipsæ suaptæ natura enitent: a good seed, planted even in poor soil, will bear rich fruit by its own nature (Accius)

probis probatum potius quam multis fore: the praise of the honorable is worth more than that of the multitude (Accius)

probitas laudatur et alget: honesty is praised and is left out to freeze (Juvenal)

probitas verus honor (or **honos**)**:** honesty (or integrity) is true honor

probum non pœnitet: the honest man does not repent

procellæ quanto plus habent virium tanto minus temporis: the more violent the storms are, the sooner they are over (Seneca)

proditor pro hoste habendus: we must take the traitor for an enemy (attributed to Cicero)

prohibetur ne quis faciat in suo, quod nocere possit (or **potest**) **in alieno:** no one is allowed to do on his own property what may injure that of a neighbor

promissio boni viri fit obligatio: the promise of an honest man is a bond

propra vivere et singulos dies singulas vitas puta: make haste to live, and consider each day a life (Seneca)

proprium humani ingenii est odisse quem læseris: it is a weakness of human nature to hate those whom one has wronged (Tacitus)

prosperum et felix scelus virtus vocatur: crime, when it succeeds, is called virtue (Seneca)

proximorum incuriosi longinqua sectamur: uninterested in things near, we pursue those that are at a distance (Pliny)

proximus a tectis ignis defenditur ægre: a fire is difficult to ward off when the neighboring house is in flames (Ovid)

prudens interrogatio quasi dimidium sapientiæ: prudent questioning is, as it were, the half of knowledge

prudens quæstio dimidium scientiæ: half of science is putting forth the right questions (Francis Bacon)

prudens qui patiens: he is prudent who has patience

prudentes vino abstinent: prudent men abstain from wine

prudentis est mutare consilium; stultus sicut luna mutatur: a prudent man may, on occasion, change his opinion; but a fool changes as often as the moon

publicum bonum privato est præferendum: the public good is to be preferred to private advantage

pudor doceri non potest, nasci potest: modesty is inborn, it cannot be learned (Publilius Syrus)

pulchra mulier nuda erit quam purpurata pulchrior: a beautiful woman is more beautiful undressed than dressed in fine purple (Plautus)

pulchrum est accusari ab accusandis: it is an honorable circumstance to be accused by those who are themselves deserving of accusation

pulchrum est digito monstrari et dicier, hic est: it is pleasant to be pointed at with the finger and to have it said, there he is (Persius)

pulvis et umbra sumus, fruges consumere nati: we are but dust and shadows, born to consume the fruits of the earth (Horace)

punitis ingeniis gliscit auctoritas: when men of talents are punished, authority is strengthened (Tacitus)

puras Deus non plenas adspicit manus: God looks to pure hands, not to full ones (Publilius Syrus)

purgamenta hujus mundi sunt tria: pestis, bellum, et frateria: this world is purified by three means: by plague, by war, and by monastic seclusion

Q

qua dii vocant, eundum: where the gods call, there one must go

qua flumen placidum est, forsan latet altius unda: where the river flows calmly, there perchance is it the deepest (Dionysius Cato)

quæ amissa salva: things lost are safe

quæ e longinquo magis placent: things are more pleasant from a distance

quæ fuerant vitia mores sunt: what were once vices are now customs (Seneca)

quæ fuit durum pati meminisse dulce est: what was hard to suffer is sweet to remember (Seneca)

quæ in terris gignuntur omnia ad usum hominum creantur: the produce of the earth was all created for humanity's use (Cicero)

quæ nimis apparent retia, vitat avis: if the net be spread too openly, the bird avoids the snare (Ovid)

quæ nocent docent: that which hurts, teaches

quæ peccamus juvenes ea luimus senes: we pay when old for the excesses of our youth

quæ serata secura: things locked up are safe

quæ virtus et quanta, boni, sit vivere parvo!: how great, my friends, is the virtue of living upon a little! (Horace)

quæ volumus et credimus libenter, et quæ sentimus ipsi, reliquos sentire speramus: what we desire we readily believe, and what we ourselves think, we expect the rest to think (Julius Cæsar)

quædam non jura scripta sed omnibus scriptis certiora sunt: some laws are unwritten, but they are better established than all written ones (Seneca the Elder)

quære adolescens, utere senex: youth seek, the old use

quærit, et inventis miser abstinet, ac timet uti: the miser is ever on the search, yet fears to use what he has acquired (Horace)

quæsitam meritis sume superbiam: assume the honors that are justly due to your merits (Horace)

quæstio fit de legibus, non de personis: the question must refer to the laws, not to persons

quævis terra alit artificem: every land supports the artisan

qualem commendes etiam atque etiam aspice, ne mox incutiant aliena tibi peccata pudorem: study carefully the character of the one you recommend, lest his misdeeds bring you shame (Horace)

quales sunt summi civitatis viri talis est civitas: a community is as those who rule it (Cicero)

qualis ab incepto processerit et sibi constet: let him proceed as he began, and be consistent with himself (Horace)

qualis avis, talis cantus; qualis vir, talis oratio: as is the bird, so is its song; as is the man, so is his manner of speech

quam angusta innocentia est, ad legem bonum esse: what narrow innocence it is for one to be good only according to the law (Seneca)

quam continuis et quantis longa senectus plena malis!: how incessant and great are the ills with which a prolonged old age is replete! (Juvenal)

quam magnum vectigal sit parsimonia!: what a wonderful revenue lies in thrift! (Cicero)

quam multa injusta ac prava fiunt moribus!: how many unjust and improper things are authorized by custom! (Terence)

quam multum interest quid a quo fiat!: what a difference it makes by whom the deed is done! (Pliny the Younger)

quam parva sapientia regitur mundus!: with how little wisdom the world is governed!

quam prope ad crimen sine crimine!: how near to guilt a man may approach without being guilty!

quam quisque novit artem, in hac se exerceat: let a man practice the profession he best knows (Cicero)

quam sæpe forte temere eveniunt, quæ non audeas optare: how often things occur by mere chance, for which we dared not even to hope (Terence)

quam temere in nosmet legem sancimus iniquam!: how rashly do we sanction an unjust law against ourselves! (Horace)

quam veterrimus homini optimus est amicus: a man's oldest friend is his best (Plautus)

quamlibet infirmas adjuvat ira manus: anger assists hands however weak (Ovid)

quamvis tegatur proditur vultu furor: anger, though concealed, is betrayed by the countenance (Seneca)

quando aliquid prohibetur, prohibetur et omne per quod devenitur ad illud: when anything is forbidden, whatever leads to it is at the same time forbidden

quanti est sapere!: what a great thing it is to be wise! (Terence)

quanto quisque sibi plura negaverit, a dis plura feret: the more a person denies himself, the more will he receive from the gods (Horace)

quantum caliginis mentibus nostris objicit magna felicitas!: how much does great prosperity overspread the mind with darkness! (Seneca)

quantum est in rebus inane!: what emptiness there is in things! (i.e., in human affairs) (Persius)

quantum instar in ipso est: none but himself can be his parallel (Virgil)

quantum quisque sua nummorum servat in arca tantum habet et fidei: the faith (or credit) of every person is in proportion to the number of coins he keeps in his chest (Juvenal)

quantum religio potuit suadere malorum!: to how many evils does not religion persuade! (Lucretius)

quas dederis, solus semper habebis opes: the wealth which you give away will ever be your own (Martial)

quem di diligunt, adolescens moritur, dum valet, sentit, sapit: the one whom the gods love dies young, while he has strength and senses and wits (Plautus)

quem dies vidit veniens superbum, hunc dies vidit fugiens jacentem: the man whom the new day sees in his pride is by its close seen prostrate

quem Juppiter vult perdere, prius dementat: whom Jupiter wishes to destroy, he first dements

quem metuit quisque, perisse cupit: every one wishes that the man whom he fears would perish (Ovid)

quem metuunt oderunt; quem quisque odit periise expetit: whom men fear, they hate; whom a man hates he wishes dead (Ennius)

quem pœnitet peccasse pene est innocens: the one who repents of having sinned is almost innocent (Seneca)

quem res plus nimio delectavere secundæ, mutatæ quatient: whom prosperity has charmed too much, adversity will shatter (Horace)

quemcunque miserum videris, hominem scias: whenever you see a fellow creature in distress, remember that he is a man (Seneca)

qui a nuce nucleum esse vult, frangat nucem: the one who wishes to eat the kernel must crack the nut (Plautus)

qui alta contemplantur, cadere: those who contemplate the heights, fall

qui alterum incusat probri eum ipsum se intueri oportet: the one who accuses another of improper conduct ought to look to himself (Plautus)

qui amat, tamen hercle si esurit, nullum esurit: a man in love, though he is hungry, is not hungry (Plautus)

qui bene amat bene castigat: the one who loves well chastises well

qui bene conjiciet, hunc vatem perhibeto optimum: hold him the best prophet who forms the best conjectures

qui bene imperat, paruerit aliquando necesse est: the one who is good at commanding must have at some time been good at obeying (Cicero)

qui capit, ille facit: the one who takes it, the same makes it (i.e., if the shoe fits, let the cobbler wear it)

qui de contemnenda gloria libros scribunt, nomen suum inscribunt: those who write books condemning fame inscribe their own names on the cover (i.e., they wish for the very fame they condemn)

qui dedit beneficium taceat; narrat qui accepit: let him who has given a favor be silent; let he who has received it tell it (Seneca)

qui dedit hoc hodie, cras, si volet, auferet: the one who has given today may, if he so please, take away tomorrow (Horace)

qui desiderat pacem, præparet bellum: the one who wishes for peace must prepare for war (Vegetius)

qui docet discit: the one who teaches, learns

qui e nuce nucleum esse vult, frangat nucem: the one who wishes to eat the kernel must crack the nut (Plautus)

qui ex errore imperitæ multitudinis pendet, hic in magnis viris non est habendus: the one who hangs on the errors of the ignorant multitude must not be counted among great men (Cicero)

qui facit per alium est perinde ac si faciat per seipsum: the one who acts through an agent is responsible as though he acted himself (Pope Boniface VIII)

qui facit per alium facit per se: the one who does a thing by another does it himself (Coke)

qui fert malis auxilium, post tempus dolet: the one who aids the wicked suffers in the end (Phædrus)

qui finem quæris amoris, cedet amor rebus; res age tutus eris: you who seek an end of love, love will yield to business; be busy, and you will be safe (Ovid)

qui fugiebat, rursus prœliabitur: the one who flees will fight again (Tertullian, citing a Greek proverb)

qui genus jactat suum aliena laudat: the one who boasts of his descent boasts of what he owes to others (Seneca)

qui gratus futurus est statim dum accipit de reddendo cogitet: let the man who would be grateful think of repaying a kindness even while receiving it (Seneca)

qui homo mature quæsivit pecuniam, nisi eam mature parcit, mature esurit: the one who has acquired wealth in time, unless he saves it in time, will in time come to starvation (Plautus)

qui honeste fortiter: he who acts honestly acts bravely

qui in amore præcipitavit pejus perit, quam si saxo saliat: he who falls in love meets a worse fate than he who leaps from a rock (Plautus)

qui invidet minor est: the one who envies is inferior

qui ipse si sapiens prodesse non quit, nequiquam sapit: a wise man whose wisdom does not serve him is wise in vain (Ennius)

qui jacet in terra non habet unde cadat: the one who lies upon the ground cannot fall (Allain de Lille)

qui jure suo utitur, neminem lædit: the one who enjoys his own right injures no one

qui lingua jurat, mentem non injuratam gerit: the one who swears with his tongue carries a mind unsworn

qui male agit, odit lucem: the one who commits evil shuns the light

qui medice vivit, misere vivit: the one who lives by medical prescription lives a miserable life

qui mentiri aut fallere insuevit patrem, tanto magis is audebit cæteros: the one who has made it a practice to lie or to deceive his father, the more daring will he be in deceiving others (Terence)

qui modeste paret, videtur qui aliquando imperet dignus esse: the one who obeys with modesty appears worthy of being some day a commander (Cicero)

qui nescit dissimulare, nescit regnare: the one who knows not how to dissemble knows not how to rule (Louis XI)

qui nescit dissimulare, nescit vivere: the one who knows not how to dissemble, knows not how to live

qui nil potest sperare, desperet nihil: the one who can hope for nothing should despair of nothing (Seneca)

qui nimium probat, nihil probat: he who proves too much proves nothing

qui nolet fieri desidiosus, amet: he who would not be idle, let him fall in love (Ovid)

qui non est hodie, cras minus aptus erit: the one who is not prepared today will be less prepared tomorrow (Ovid)

qui non improbat, approbat: the one who does not disapprove, approves

qui non laborat, non manducet: the one who does no work shall not eat (2 Thessalonians 3:10)

qui non libere veritatem pronunciat, proditor est veritatis: the one who does not speak the truth freely is a betrayer of the truth

qui non moderabitur iræ infectum volet esse, dolor quod suaserit et mens: the one who does not restrain his anger will wish that undone that his irritation and temper prompted him to do (Horace)

qui non proficit, deficit: the one who does not make progress loses ground

qui non prohibet quod prohibere potest assentire videtur: the one who does not prevent what he can prevent is seen to consent

qui non vetat peccare cum possit, jubet: the one who does not prevent a crime when he can encourages it (Seneca)

qui peccat ebrius luat sobrius: let the one who sins when drunk be punished when sober

qui per alium facit seipsum facere videtur: the one who has a thing done by another does it himself

qui per virtutem peritat, non interit: the one who dies for virtue does not perish (Plautus)

qui prægravat artes, infra se positas, extinctus amabitur idem: the one whose excellence causes envy in his lifetime shall be revered when he is dead (Horace)

qui proficit in literis et deficit in moribus, plus deficit quam proficit: the one who is proficient in learning and deficient in morals is more deficient than proficient

qui pulchra affectat ardua perferat: he who strives after beauty, let him endure the arduous

qui quæ vult dicit, quod non vult audiet: the one who says what he likes will hear what he does not like (Terence)

qui scribit bis legit: the one who writes reads twice

qui se exaltat, humiliabitur: the one who exalts himself will be humbled

qui sentit commodum, sentire debet et onus: the one who derives the advantage should endure the burden

qui sibi amicus est, scito hunc amicum omnibus esse: you may be sure that the one who is a friend to himself is a friend to all (Seneca)

qui socius est in malo, consors erit in supplicio: a partner in evil will also be a partner in punishment

qui spe aluntur, pendent, non vivunt: those who feed on hope, they hang on, but they do not live

qui stat, caveat ne cadat: let the one who stands be careful lest he fall (1 Corinthians 10:12)

qui stultus videri eruditi volunt stulti eruditis videntur: those who wish to appear learned to fools will appear fools to the learned (Quintilian)

qui sustinet hamos, novit, quæ multo pisce natentur aquæ: the one who holds the hook is aware in what waters many fish are swimming (Ovid)

qui tacet consentire videtur: the one who is silent is seen to consent (Pope Boniface VIII)

qui tacet, non utique fatetur, sed tamen verum est eum non negare: though silence is not necessarily an admission, neither it is a denial (Justinian)

qui terret plus ipse timet: the one who terrifies others is himself more afraid (Claudian)

qui timide rogat, docet negare: the one who asks timidly courts denial (Seneca)

qui uti scit, ei bona: he should possess wealth who knows how to use it (Terence)

qui vicit non est victor nisi victus fatetur: the victor is not truly victor unless the vanquished admits it (Ennius)

qui vivens lædit morte medetur: he who hurts in life heals in death

qui vult decipi, decipiatur: the one who wants to be deceived, let him be deceived

quicquid agas, prudenter agas, et respice finem: whatever you do, do it with intelligence, and keep the end in view (Thomas à Kempis)

quicquid cœpit, et desinit: whatever begins also ends (Seneca)

quicquid crescit in cinere perit: whatever grows perishes in ashes

quicquid erit, superanda omnis fortuna ferendo est: whatever the event many be, we must subdue our fortune by bearing it (Virgil)

quicquid excessit modum pendet instabili loco: whatever has overstepped its due bounds is always in a state of instability (Seneca)

quicquid præcipies, esto brevis: whatever precepts you give, be brief (Horace)

quicquid servatur, cupimus magis: we covet what is guarded (Ovid)

quicunque turpi fraude semel innotuit, etiamsi verum dicit, amittit fidem: whoever has once become known for a shameful fraud is not believed, even if he speaks the truth (Phædrus)

quid æternis minorem consiliis animum fatigas?: why weary with eternal purposes a mind too weak to grasp them? (Horace)

quid cæco cum speculo?: what has a blind man to do with a mirror?

quid clarius astris?: what is brighter than the stars?

quid crastina volveret ætas scire nefas homini: it is not permitted to man to know what tomorrow may bring forth (Statius)

quid datur a divis felici optatius hora?: what thing more to be wished do the gods bestow than a happy hour? (i.e., a golden opportunity) (Catullus)

quid de quoque viro, et cui dicas, sæpe caveto: take special care what you say of any person, and to whom it is said (Horace)

quid domini facient, audent quum (or cum) talia fures?: what would the masters do when their own servants dare such things? (Virgil)

quid enim ratione timemus aut cupimus?: what do we fear or desire with reason? (i.e., how void of reason are our hopes and fears) (Juvenal)

quid enim salvis infamia nummis?: what does disgrace matter when the money is safe? (Juvenal)

quid est enim novi, hominem mori, cujus tota vita nihil aliud quam ad mortem iter est?: what new thing is it then for a man to die, whose whole life is nothing else but a journey to death? (Seneca)

quid est somnus gelidæ nisi mortis imago?: what is sleep but the image of cold death? (Ovid)

quid est turpius quam senex vivere incipiens?: what is more disgraceful than an old man just beginning to live? (Seneca)

quid faciant leges, ubi sola pecunia regnat?: what power has law where only money rules? (Petronius)

quid faciunt pauci contra tot millia fortes?: what can a few brave men do against so many thousand? (Ovid)

quid furor est census corpore ferre suo!: what madness it is to carry one's fortune on one's back! (Ovid)

quid leges sine moribus vanæ proficiunt?: what good are laws when there are no morals? (Horace)

quid leone fortius?: what is braver than a lion?

quid non dedit Fortuna non eripit: Fortune cannot take away what she did not give (Seneca)

quid non mortalia pectora cogis, auri sacra fames?: to what lust do you not drive mortal hearts, you accursed hunger for gold? (Virgil)

quid obseratis auribus fundis preces?: why do you pour prayers into ears that are stopped? (Horace)

quid opus est verbis?: what need is there for words?

quid quisque vitet, nunquam homini satis cautem est in horas: man never takes sufficient and hourly care against that which he ought to avoid (Horace)

quid sit futurum cras fuge quærere, et quem Fors dierum cunque dabit, lucro appone: avoid asking what the future will bring, and every day that Fortune shall grant you, set down as gain (Horace)

quid tam ridiculum quam appetere mortem, cum vitam tibi inquietam feceris metu mortis?: what can be so ridiculous as to seek for death, when it is merely the fear of death that makes your life so restless? (Seneca)

quid te exempta juvat spinis de pluribus una?: what pleasure does it give to be rid of one thorn out of many? (Horace)

quid terras alio calente, sole mutamus?: why do we change for soils warmed only by another sun? (Horace)

quid tibi cum pelago? Terra contenta fuisses: what have you to do with the sea? You should have been content with the land (Ovid)

quid tristes querimoniæ si non supplicio culpa reciditur?: what do sad complaints avail if the offense is not cut down by punishment? (Horace)

quid turpius quam sapientis vitam ex insipientis sermone pendere?: what is more contemptible than to estimate the life of a wise man from the talk of a fool?

quid vesper ferat, incertum est?: who knows what the evening may bring us? (Livy)

quid violentius aure tyranni?: what is more violent than the ear of a tyrant? (Juvenal)

quidquid agas, prudenter agas, et respice finem: whatever you do, do prudently, and look to the result

quidquid erit, superanda omnis fortuna ferendo est: our fate, whatever it be, is to be overcome by our patience under it (Virgil)

quidquid id est, timeo Danaos et dona ferentes: whatever it is, I fear the Greeks even when they bring gifts with them (Virgil)

quidquid in altum fortuna tulit, ruitura levat: whatever fortune has raised to a height, it has raised only that it might fall (Seneca)

quidquid multis peccatur inultum est: the guilt that is committed by many must pass unpunished (Lucan)

quidquid præcipies, esto brevis: whatever you teach, be brief (Horace)

quieta non movere: do not disturb things at rest (i.e., let sleeping dogs lie)

quiete et pure atque eleganter actæ ætatis placida et lenis recordatio: placid and soothing is the remembrance of a life passed with quietness, innocence, and elegance (Cicero)

quietem nemo impune lacesset: though I am peaceful, no one will attack me with impunity

quin etiam leges latronum esse dicuntur, quibus pareant, quas observent: even thieves are said to have laws that they obey, that they observe (Cicero)

quis ... bene celat amorem?: who can successfully conceal love? (Ovid)

quis custodiet ipsos custodes?: who shall guard the guards themselves? (Juvenal)

quis desiderio sit pudor aut modus tam cari (or **chari**) **capitis?:** what shame or measure can there be in our grief for one so dear? (Horace)

quis enim virtutem amplectitur ipsam, præmia si tollas?: for who would embrace virtue itself if you took away the reward? (Juvenal)

quis fallere possit amantem?: who can deceive a lover? (Virgil)

quis memorabitur tui post mortem?: who will remember you after you are dead? (Thomas à Kempis)

quis scit an adjiciant hodiernæ crastina summæ tempora di superi?: who knows whether the gods above will add tomorrow's hours to the sum of today? (Horace)

quis vitia odit, homines odit: the one who hates vice, hates humanity (Pliny the Younger)

quisnam igitur liber? Sapiens qui sibi imperiosus: who then is free? The one who is wisely in command of himself (Horace)

quisnam igitur sanus? Qui non stultus: who then is sane? The one who is not a fool (Horace)

quisque sibi proximus: everyone is nearest to himself

quisque suos patimur manes: [in the nether world,] each one suffers his own spirit's doom (also rendered, each one suffers from the spirits of his own past) (Virgil)

quo Fata trahunt retrahuntque, sequamur: let us follow the Fates wherever they may lead us, or divert our steps (Virgil)

quo minime credas gurgite, piscis erit: in the eddies where you least expect it, there will be a fish (Ovid)

quo semel est imbuta recens servabit odorem testa diu: the jar will long retain the odor of that with which it was once filled (Horace)

quo spinosior fragrantior: the more thorns, the greater the fragrance

quocirca vivite fortes fortiaque adversis opponite pectora rebus: wherefore live as brave men, and face adversity with stout hearts

quocunque trahunt Fata, sequamur: wherever the Fates direct us, let us follow (Virgil)

quod ab initio non valet, tractu temporis convalescere non potest: that which has no force in the beginning, can gain no strength from the lapse of time

quod alias bonum et justum est, si per vim aut fraudem petatur, malum et injustum est: what otherwise is good and just, if it be aimed at by violence or fraud, becomes evil and unjust

quod antecedit tempus, maxima venturi supplicii pars est: the time that precedes punishment is the severest part of it (Seneca)

quod certaminibus ortum ultra metam durat: that which arises from struggle often goes beyond the mark (Velleius Paterculus)

quod cito fit, cito perit: what is done quickly, perishes quickly

quod commune cum alio est, desinit esse proprium: what we share with another ceases to be our own (Quintilian)

quod decet honestum est et quod honestum est decet: what is becoming is honorable, and what is honorable is becoming (Cicero)

quod dubitas, ne feceris: which you doubt, then neither do (Pliny the Younger)

quod enim mavult homo verum esse, id potius credit: for what a man would like to be true, that he more readily believes (Francis Bacon)

quod enim munus reipublicæ afferre majus, meliusve possumus, quam si docemus atque erudimus juventutem?: what greater or better gift can we offer the republic than to teach and instruct our youth? (Cicero)

quod est ante pedes nemo spectat; cœli scrutantur plagas: no one sees what is before his feet; they scan the tracks of heaven (Ennius and Cicero)

quod est inconveniens et contra rationem non est permissum in lege: whatever is inconvenient and contrary to reason is not permitted in law

quod est violentum, non est durabile: what is violent is not durable

quod exemplo fit, id etiam jure fieri putant: men think they may justly do that for which they have a precedent (Cicero)

quod fors dedit, hoc capit usus: what fortune gives, habit soon makes its own (Calpurnius)

quod gratis asseritur, gratis negatur: what is asserted without reason (or proof), may be denied without reason (or proof)

quod in te est, prome: bring forth what is in you

quod latet ignotum est; ignoti nulla cupido: what is hid is unknown; for what is unknown there is no desire (Ovid)

quod licet ingratum est, quod non licet acrius urit: what is lawful is less desirable, what is unlawful is more keenly desired (Ovid)

quod male fers, assuesce; feres bene: accustom yourself to that which you bear ill, and you will bear it well (Seneca)

quod nimis miseri volunt, hoc facile credunt: whatever the wretched anxiously wish for, this they readily believe (Seneca)

quod non legitur non creditur: what is not read is not believed

quod non opus est, asse carum est: what you do not need is costly at a penny (Cato the Elder, as quoted by Seneca)

quod non potest, vult posse, qui nimium potest: the one who is all powerful still aims at possessing greater power (Seneca)

quod non vetat lex, hoc vetat fieri pudor: modesty (or shame) forbids what the law does not (Seneca)

quod nunc ratio est, impertus ante fuit: what is now reason was formerly impulse (Ovid)

quod optanti divum promittere nemo auderet, volvenda dies, en!, attulit ultro: what none of the gods could have promised to your prayers, lo!, the turning of time has supplied (Virgil)

quod petis id sane invisum est acidumque duobus: what you seek is disagreeable and distasteful to two others (i.e., there is no compromise among three) (Horace)

quod quisque vitet, nunquam homini satis cautum est in horas: man is never sufficiently aware of the dangers that await him hourly (Horace)

quod ratio nequiit (or **non quit**)**, sæpe sanavit mora:** what reason could not avoid has often been cured by delay (Seneca)

quod sapit, nutrit: what pleases, nourishes

quod satis est cui contingit, nihil amplius optet: the one who has enough for his share should wish for nothing more (Horace)

quod sis esse velis, nihilque malis: summum nec metuas diem, nec optes: be content to be what you are, and prefer nothing to it; neither fear nor wish for your last day (Martial)

quod sors (or **fors**) **feret, feremus æquo animo:** whatever fate (or fortune) shall bring, let us bear with a firm and equal mind (Terence)

quod volumus bonum; quod placet sanctum: what we wish is good; what we please is sacred (Austin)

quod vos jus cogit, id voluntate impetret: what the law insists upon, let your adversary obtain from your own free will (Terence)

quod vult habet qui velle quod satis est potest: he has what he desires who can limit his desires to what is enough (Publilius Syrus)

quondam etiam victis redit in præcordia virtus: valor sometimes returns even into the bosom of the conquered (Virgil)

quoniam diu vixesse denegatur, aliquid faciamus quo possimus ostendere nos vixisse: as length of life is denied to us, we should at least do something to show that we have lived (Cicero)

quoniam dociles imitandis turpibus ac pravis omnes sumus: we are all too prone to imitate whatever is base and depraved (Juvenal)

quoniam id fieri quod vis non potest, velis id quod possit: as that which you wish cannot be effected, you should wish for that which may be obtained (Terence)

quos amor verus tenuit tenebit: those whom true love has held it will go on holding (Seneca)

quos Deus vult perdere prius dementat: whom God would ruin he first deprives of reason (after Euripides)

quos læserunt et oderunt: whom they have injured they also hate (Seneca)

quot capitum vivunt, totidem studiorum millia: there are as many thousands of pursuits as there are individuals

quot homines, tot sententiæ: suus cuique mos: so many men, so many sentiments: each has his own way (Terence)

quum Romæ fueris, Romano vivite more: when you are at Rome, live after the Roman fashion

R

rabiem livoris acerbi nulla potest placare quies: nothing can allay the rage of biting envy (Claudian)

radix (enim) omnium malorum est cupiditas: the love of money is a root to all kinds of evil (1 Timothy 6:10)

rapiamus, amici, occasionem de die: let us, my friends, snatch our opportunity from the passing day (Horace)

rara est adeo concordia formæ atque pudicitiæ: so rare is the union of beauty with modesty (Juvenal)

rara fides pietasque viris qui castra sequuntur: faith and piety are rare among the men who follow the camp (whether political or military) (Lucan)

raram facit misturam cum sapientia forma: rarely are beauty and wisdom found together

raro antecedentem scelestum deseruit pede pœna claudo: rarely does punishment, even at a slow pace, fail to overtake the criminal in his flight (Horace)

raro simul hominibus bonam fortunam bonamque mentem dari: men are seldom given good fortune and good sense at the same time (Livy)

rarus concubitus corpus excitat, frequens solvit: the body is excited by infrequent coitus, by frequent it relaxes (Celsus)

rarus enim ferme sensus communis in illa fortuna: common sense is generally rare in that condition (i.e., in those of high position) (Juvenal)

ratio est legis anima: reason is the spirit and soul of the law

ratio et auctoritas, duo clarissima mundi lumina: reason and authority, the two brightest luminaries of the world (Coke)

ratio et consilium propriæ ducis artes: judgment and deliberation are the proper qualities of a leader (Tacitus)

ratio quasi quædam lux lumenque vitæ: reason is, as it were, the guide and light of life (Cicero)

re opitulandum non verbis: we should assist by deeds, not by words

rebus cunctis inest quidam velut orbis: in all things there is a kind of law of cycles (Tacitus)

rebus in angustis facile est contemnere vitam; fortiter ille facit qui miser esse potest: it is easy in misfortune to despise life; but he does bravely who can endure misery (Martial)

rebus secundis etiam egregios duces insolescere: in the hour of prosperity even the best leaders become haughty and insolent (Tacitus)

recedant vetera: let old things recede

recepto dulce mihi furere est amico: it is delightful to indulge in extravagance on the return of a friend (Horace)

recte quod honeste: that is rightly done which is honestly done

regia, crede mihi, res est, succurrere lapsis: it is a regal act, believe me, to succor the fallen (Ovid)

regula ex jure, non jus ex regula, sumitur: we draw this rule from the law, and not the law from the practice

religentem esse oportet, religiosum nefas: a man should be religious, not superstitious (quoted by Aulus Gellius)

rem, facias rem recte, si possis; si non, quocunque modo rem: fortune, make a fortune by honest means, if you can; if not, by any means make a fortune (Horace)

rem tibi quam nosces aptam dimittere noli; fronte capillata, post est occasio calva: let nothing pass that will give you advantage; though hairy in front, opportunity is bald behind (Dionysius Cato)

rem tu strenuus auge: labor vigorously to increase your property (Horace)

remedia in arduo, mala in prono esse: there are benefits in what is difficult, evils in what is easy

remissio animum frangit; arcum intensio: much bending breaks the bow; much unbending, the mind (Publilius Syrus)

rempublicam duabus rebus contineri dixit, præmio et pœna: a state is regulated by two things, reward and punishment (Cicero, attributed to Solon)

repente dives nemo factus est bonus: no good person ever became suddenly rich (Publilius Syrus)

repente nemo fit turpissimus: no one becomes extremely wicked all at once

reperit Deus nocentem: God finds out the guilty

repetitio est mater studiorum: repetition is the mother of study

rerum cognitio vera, e rebus ipsis est: the true knowledge of things is from the things themselves (Scaliger)

res age, tute eris: be busy and you will be safe (Ovid)

res amicos invenit: fortune finds us friends (Plautus)

res est ingeniosa dare: giving requires good sense (Ovid)

res est sacra miser: the afflicted person is sacred (or, a person in misery is a sacred matter) (Ovid)

res est solliciti plena timoris amor: love is a thing full of anxious fears (Ovid)

res humanæ in summo declinant: at their summit, human affairs decline

res nolunt diu male administrari: things refuse to be mismanaged long

res non posse creari de nilo: it is not possible to create matter from nothing

res perit suo domino: the loss falls upon its owner

res sunt humanæ flebile ludibrium: human affairs are a jest to be wept over

respondeat superior: let the superior answer (i.e., let the principal answer for the actions of his agent)

rex est major singulis, minor universis: the king is greater than each singly, but less than all universally (Bracton)

rex est qui metuit nihil; rex est qui cupit nihil: a king is one who fears nothing; a king is one who desires nothing (Seneca)

rex non potest fallere nec falli: the king cannot deceive or be deceived

rex non potest peccare: the king can do no wrong

rex regnat sed non gubernat: the king reigns but does not govern

rhinoceros nunquam victus ab hoste cedit: the rhinoceros never turns away defeated from the enemy

rident stolidi verba Latina: fools laugh at the Latin language (Ovid)

ridentem dicere verum quid vetat?: what forbids a person, when laughing, from speaking the truth? (Horace)

ridetur chorda qui semper oberrat eadem: that person makes himself ridiculous who is ever harping on one string (Horace)

ridiculum acri fortius ac melius magnas plerumque secat res: ridicule often settles matters of importance better and with more effect than severity (Horace)

ridiculus æque nullus est, quam quando esurit: no one is so ridiculous as when he is hungry (Plautus)

risu inepto res ineptior nulla est: there is nothing more foolish than a foolish laugh (Catullus)

risus abundat in ore stultorum: laughter abounds in the mouth of fools

rivalem patienter habe: bear patiently with a rival (Ovid)

S

sæpe creat molles aspera spina rosas: often the prickly thorn produces tender roses (Ovid)

sæpe decipimur specie recti: we are often misled by the appearance of truth (Horace)

sæpe est etiam sub palliolo sordido sapientia: wisdom is often found even under a tattered coat

sæpe ignavavit fortem ex spe expectatio: expectation based on hope has often disappointed the courageous (Accius)

sæpe in conjugiis fit noxia, cum nimia est dos: quarrels often arise in marriages when the dowry is excessive (Ausonius)

sæpe in magistrum scelera redierunt sua: crime often falls back upon its author's head (Seneca)

sæpe ingenia calamitate intercidunt: genius often goes to waste through misfortune (Phædrus)

sæpe intereunt aliis meditantes necem: those who plot the destruction of others very often fall themselves the victims

sæpe ne utile quidem est scire quid futurum sit: often it is not even advantageous to know what will be (Cicero)

sæpe nihil inimicus homini quam sibi ipse: often a man is his own worst enemy (Cicero)

sæpe premente deo, fert deus alter opem: often when we are oppressed by one god, another comes to our help

sæpe satius fuit dissimulare quam ulcisci: it is often better not to see an insult than to avenge it (Seneca)

sæpe stylum vertas: turn the stylus often (i.e., correct freely, if you want to write anything of merit)

sæpe summa ingenia in occulto latent: the greatest talents often lie buried out of sight (Plautus)

sæpe tacens vocem verbaque vultus habet: often a silent face has a voice and speaks (i.e., has expression) (Ovid)

sæpe venit magno fœnore tardus amor: love that comes late in life bears great interest (Propertius)

sæpe via obliqua præstat quam tendere recta: it is often better to go the circuitous way than the direct one

sæpius in auro bibitur venenum: poison is more often drunk from a gold cup

sævis inter se convenit ursis: even savage bears agree among themselves (Juvenal)

sal sapit omnia: salt seasons everything

salus ubi multi consiliarii: there is safety in many advisors

sanctio justa, jubens honesta, et prohibens contraria: a just decree, commanding what is honorable and forbidding the contrary (Bracton)

sanctum est vetus omne poëma: every old poem is sacred (Horace)

sapere aude, incipe: dare to be wise, begin at once

sapere isthac ætate oportet, qui sunt capite candido: those who have white hair are old enough to be wise (Plautus)

sapiens nihil facit invitus, nihil dolens, nihil coactus: a wise man does nothing against his will, nothing from sorrow, nothing under coercion (Cicero)

sapiens qui prospicit: the one who is wise looks ahead

sapiens qui vigilat: he is wise who watches

sapiens virtuti honorem præmium, haud prædam petit: the wise man seeks honor, not profit, as the reward of virtue (Cicero)

sapientem locupletat ipsa Natura: Nature herself makes the wise man wealthy (Cicero)

sapientes pacis causa bellum gerunt, laborem spe otii sustentant: the wise wage war for the sake of peace, and endure toil in the hope of leisure (Sallust)

sapientes principes sapientum congressu: princes become wise by associating with the wise (i.e., from the council of wise advisors) (after Plato)

sapientia prima est, stultitia caruisse: the first step toward wisdom is by being exempt from folly (Horace)

sapimus animo, fruimur anima; sine animo anima est debilis: we discern with the mind, enjoy with the heart; without the mind, the heart is feeble (Accius)

satis eloquentiæ, sapientiæ parum: enough eloquence, not enough wisdom (i.e., those who speak well do not always think well) (Sallust)

satis est superare inimicum, nimium est perdere: it is enough to defeat an enemy, too much to destroy him (Publilius Syrus)

satis quod sufficit: what suffices is enough

satius est recurrere, quam currere male: it is better to run back than to run on the wrong way

scandala removenda sunt: things causing offense must be removed

scelere velandum est scelus: one crime is to be concealed by another (i.e., a crime committed to mask a greater crime) (Seneca)

scelus intra se tacitum qui cogitat ullum, facti crimen habet: the one who meditates upon a crime possesses all the guilt of the crime (Juvenal)

scientia nihil aliud est quam veritatis imago: science is but an image of the truth (Francis Bacon)

scientia quæ est remota a justitia, calliditas potius quam sapientia est appellanda: knowledge that is divorced from justice may be called cunning rather than wisdom (Cicero)

scientia ultima stat pretio ultime: ultimate knowledge costs the ultimate price

scilicet expectes, ut tradet mater honestos atque alios mores, quam quos habet?: can you expect that the mother will teach good morals or ones other than her own? (Juvenal)

scilicet insano nemo in amore videt: certainly everyone is blind when maddened by love (Propertius)

scilicet, ut fulvum spectatur in ignibus aurum, tempore sic duro est inspicienda fides: as the yellow gold is tested in the fire, so the faith of friendship can only be known in the time of adversity (Ovid)

scinditur incertum studia in contraria vulgus: the uncertain multitude is divided by contrary opinions (Virgil)

scire tuum nihil est, nisi te scire hoc sciat alter: it is nothing for you to know a thing unless another knows that you know it (Persius)

scire ubi aliquid invenire possis, ea demum maxima pars eruditionis est: to know where you can find a thing is the chief part of learning

scire volunt omnes, mercedem solvere nemo: everyone wishes to know, but no one is willing to pay the price (Juvenal)

scribendi recte sapere est et principium et fons: knowledge is the foundation and source of good writing (Horace)

scribere est agere: to write is to act

scribimus indocti, doctique: learned and unlearned, we all write (Horace)

scribit in marmore læsus: the injured man writes in marble

scripta non temere edenda: writings should not be published readily

secrete amicos admone, lauda palam: admonish your friends secretly, but praise them openly (Publilius Syrus)

secunda felices, adversa magnos probent: prosperity proves the fortunate, adversity the great (Pliny the Younger)

secundas fortunas decent superbiæ: pride is the fitting companion of fortune (Plautus)

securior quo paratior: the better prepared, the more secure

sed fugit interea, fugit inreparabile (or **irreparabile**) **tempus:** but meanwhile it is flying, irretrievable time is flying (Virgil)

sed jam serpentum major concordia: but nowadays there is more agreement among snakes (than among men) (Juvenal)

sed mulier cupido quod dicit amanti in vento et rapida scribere oportet aqua: but what a woman says to her lover it is best to write in the wind and in the swiftly flowing water (Catullus)

sed quis custodiet ipsos custodes?: but who will guard the guardians themselves? (Juvenal)

sed tacitus pasci si posset corvus, haberet plus dapis, et rixæ multo minus invidiæque: if the crow had been satisfied to eat his prey in silence, he would have had more meat and less quarreling and envy (Horace)

sedit qui timuit ne non succederet: the one who feared he would not succeed sat still (Horace)

seditio civium hostium est occasio: the dissatisfaction of the citizenry gives occasion to the enemy

seditiosissimus quisque ignavus: the most seditious is the most cowardly (Tacitus)

segnius homines bona quam mala sentire (or **sentiunt**): men are slower to recognize blessings than misfortunes (Livy)

segnius irritant animos demissa per aurem, quam quæ sunt oculis subjecta fidelibus: what we learn merely through the ear makes less impression upon our minds than what is presented to the trustworthy eye (Horace)

semel in anno licet insanire: it is allowed once in the year to be mad

semel insanivimus omnes: we have all at one time been insane

semel malus, semper præsumitur esse malus: once bad is to be presumed always bad

semita certe tranquillæ per virtutem patet unica vitæ: only one path in this life leads to tranquility, the path of virtue (Juvenal)

semper ad eventum festinat: he always hastens to the issue (or the crisis) (Horace)

semper aliquid novi Africam affere: there is always something new out of Africa (Pliny the Elder)

semper autem in fide quid senseris, non quid dixeris, cogitandum: a promise must be kept not merely in the letter, but in the spirit (Cicero)

semper avarus eget; certum voto pete finem: the miser is ever in want; let your desire aim at a fixed limit (Horace)

semper bonus homo tiro: a good man is always a learner (Martial)

semper et infirmi est animi exiguique voluptas ultio: revenge is always the weak pleasure of a little and narrow mind (Juvenal)

semper in dubiis benigniora præferenda sunt: in doubtful cases, the more liberal interpretation must always be preferred (Justinian)

semper in fide quid senseris, non quid dixeris, cogitandum: in an honorable dealing you should consider what you intended, not what you said or thought (Cicero)

semper inops, quicunque cupit: always poor is the one who desires more (Claudian)

semper nocuit differre paratis: delay has always been injurious to those who are prepared (Lucan)

semper pluris feci ego potioremque habui libertatem quam pecuniam: I have always valued freedom more highly than money, and preferred it (Nævius)

semper præsto esse infortunia: misfortunes are always at hand

semper tibi pendeat hamus; quo minime credas gurgite, piscis erit: have your hook always baited; in the pool where you least think it, there will be a fish (Ovid)

semper timidum scelus: crime is always fearful

senectus insanabilis morbus est: old age is an incurable disease (Seneca)

senectus ipsa morbus est: old age is itself a sickness (or disease) (Terence)

senex bis puer: an old man is twice a boy

septem convivium, novem convitium: seven is a banquet, nine a brawl

septem horas dormisse sat est juvenique, senique: seven hours of sleep is enough, both for young and old

sepulchri mitte supervacuos honores: discard the superfluous honors at the grave (Horace)

sequitur superbos ultor a tergo deus: the avenging god follows in the steps of the proud (Seneca)

sequiturque patrem non passibus æquis: he follows his father, but not with equal steps (Virgil)

sera in fundo parsimonia: thrift is too late when you are at the bottom of your purse (Seneca)

serit arbores quæ alteri sæclo prosint: he plants trees to benefit another generation (Statius)

serius aut citius sedem properamus ad unam: sooner or later we hasten to one home (Ovid)

sermo animi est imago; qualis vir, talis et oratio est: conversation is the image of the mind; as the man, so is his speech (Publilius Syrus)

sermo datur cunctis, animi sapientia paucis: speech is given to all, wisdom to few (Dionysius Cato)

sermo hominum mores et celat et indicat idem: the same words conceal and declare the thoughts of men (Dionysius Cato)

sero clypeum post vulnera sumo: I am too late in taking my shield after being wounded

sero venientibus ossa: bones for those who come late (i.e., first come, first served)

serpens ni edat serpentem, draco non fiet: unless a serpent devour a serpent, it will not become a dragon (i.e., unless one power absorb another, it will not become a great power) (Erasmus)

serum auxilium post prælium: help comes too late when the fight is over

serum est cavendi tempus in mediis malis: the time for caution is too late when we are in the midst of evils (Seneca)

servare cives, major est virtus patriæ patri: to preserve the lives of citizens is the greatest virtue in the father of his country (Seneca)

servetur ad imum qualis ab incepto processerit, et sibi constet: let the character be kept up to the very end, just as it began, and so be consistent (Horace)

serviet æternum, quia parvo nescit uti: he will always be a slave because he knows not how to live upon little (Horace)

servus curru portatur eodem: the slave rides in the same chariot

si ad naturam vivas, nunquam eris pauper; si ad opinionem, nunquam dives: if you live according to nature, you will never be poor; if according to the notions of men, you will never be rich (Seneca)

si animus est æquus tibi satis habes, qui bene vitam colas: if you are content, you have enough to live comfortably (Plautus)

si cadere necesse est, occurrendum discrimini: if one must fall, let him meet the hazard head on (Tacitus)

si cæcus cæco ducatum prebet, ambo in foveam cadent: if the blind leads the blind, they will both fall into the ditch

si caput dolet omnia membra languent: if the head aches, all the members languish

si claudio cohabites, subclaudicare disces: if you live with a lame man, you will learn to limp

si Deus pro nobis, quis contra nos?: if God is for us, who is against us? (Romans 8:31)

si dixeris, æstuo, sudat: if you say that you are warm, he sweats (said of a sycophant)

si duo dicunt idem, non est idem: if two [languages] say the same thing, it is not the same thing

si fecisti, nega (or, **nega, si fecisti**): if you did it, deny it

si finis bonus est, totum bonum erit: if the end is good, all will be good

si fortuna juvat, caveto tolli; si fortuna tonat, caveto mergi: if fortune favors you, do not be elated; if fortune frowns, do not sink in despair (Ausonius)

si gravis, brevis; si longus, levis: if severe, short; if long, light

si judicas, cognosce; si regnas, jube: if you judge, inquire; if you reign, command (Seneca)

si libenter crucem portas portabit te: if you willingly bear the cross, it will bear you (Thomas à Kempis)

si mens non læva fuisset: if the mind had not been on the left side (i.e., had not been unlucky) (Virgil)

si mortuorum aliquis miseretur, et non natorum misereatur: if anyone pities the dead, he must also pity those who have not been born (Seneca)

si natura negat, facit indignatio versum: even if nature denies power, indignation makes verse (Juvenal)

si possis recte, si non, quocumque modo rem: uprightly if possible, if not, then make money somehow (Horace)

si possis suaviter, si non, quocunque modo: gently if you can, if not, then by some means or another

si post fata venit gloria, non propero: if glory comes after death, then I am in no hurry (Martial)

si qua voles apte nubere, nube pari: if you wish to marry suitably, marry your equal (in years) (Ovid)

si quid novisti rectius istis, candidus imperti; si non, his utere mecum: if you know anything better than these maxims, frankly impart them to me; if not, then use them like me (Horace)

si quidem potest vi et metu extortum honorarium nominari?: if it is extorted by force or by fear, how can we call it an honorarium? (Cicero)

si Romæ fueris, Romano vivito more; si fueris alibi, vivito sicut ibi: if you are at Rome, live as they do at Rome; if elsewhere, live as they do there (St. Ambrose)

si sine amore jocisque nil est jucundum, vivas in amore jocisque: if nothing appears to you delightful without love and sports, then live in love and sports (Horace)

si tibi deficiant medici, medici tibi fiant hæc tria; mens hilaris, requies, moderata diæta: if you stand in need of medical advice, let these three things be your physician: a cheerful mind, rest, and a moderate diet (Schola Salern)

si tibi vis omnia subjicere, te subjice rationi: if you wish to subject everything to yourself, subject yourself to reason (Seneca)

si vir es, suspice, etiam si decidunt, magna conantes: if you are a man, admire those who attempt great things, even though they fail (Seneca)

si vis ad summum progredi ab infimo ordire: if you wish to reach the highest, begin at the lowest (Publilius Syrus)

si vis amari, ama: if you want to be loved, then love (Seneca)

si vis incolumem, si vis te reddere sanum, curas tolle graves, irasci crede profanum: if you wish to preserve yourself in health and safety, avoid all serious cares, and believe wrathful passions as something profane

si vis pacem, para bellum: if you wish for peace, prepare for war

si vultis nihil timere, cogitate omnia esse timenda: if you wish to fear nothing, think that everything is to be feared (Seneca)

sibi servire gravissima est servitus: the most severe slavery is to be a slave to oneself (Seneca)

sibimet merces industria: industry is a recompense to itself (i.e., work is its own reward)

sic fac omnia ... tanquam spectat aliquis: do everything as in the eye of another (Seneca)

sic multa quæ honesta natura videntur esse, temporibus fiunt non honesta: thus many things that seem honorable by their nature are rendered dishonorable by circumstances (Cicero)

sic omnia fatis in pejus ruere et retro sublapsa referri: thus all things are fated to change for the worse and to retrograde (Virgil)

sic præsentibus utaris voluptatibus, ut futuris non noceas: enjoy your present pleasures so as not to injure those which are to come (Seneca)

sic utere tuo ut alienum non lædas: make use of your own property in such a manner as not to injure that of another

sic vive cum hominibus, tamquam Deus videat; sic loquere cum Deo, tamquam homines audiant: live among men as if God were watching; speak with God as if men were listening (Seneca)

sic volo, sic jubeo, stat pro ratione voluntas: thus I wish, thus I order, my will stands in place of reason (Juvenal)

sic vos non vobis: thus do you, but not for you (i.e., you do the work, another takes the credit) (Virgil)

signum pacis amor: love is the token of peace

sile et philosophus esto: be silent and you will pass for a philosopher

silent leges inter arma (or, **silent enim leges inter arma**): the laws are silent in time of war (Cicero)

simia quam similis turpissima bestia nobis!: the monkey, so base a creature, how like ourselves! (Ennius and Cicero)

sincerum est nisi vas, quodcumque infundis acescit: unless the vessel is clean, everything you pour into it turns sour (Horace)

sine amicitia vitam esse nullam: there is no life without friendship (Cicero)

sine doctrina vita est quasi mortis imago: without learning, life is but the image of death (Dionysius Cato)

sine virtute esse amicitia nullo pacto potest: there cannot be friendship without virtue (Sallust)

singula de nobis anni prædantur euntes: as the years pass, they rob us of one thing after another (Horace)

sis pacem, para bellum: if you want peace, then prepare for war

sit jus liceatque perire poëtis: leave poets free to perish as they will (Horace)

sit piger ad pœnas princeps, ad præmia velox: a prince should be slow to punish and swift to reward (Ovid)

societatis vinculum est ratio et oratio: reason and speech are the bond of society (Cicero)

socius fidelis anchora tuta est: a faithful companion is a sure anchor

sol crescentes decedens duplicat umbras: the setting sun doubles the increasing shadows (Virgil)

sol non occidat super iracundiam vestram: let not the sun set on your anger (Ephesians 4:26)

sola bona que honesta: only those things are good that are honest

solamen miseris socios habuisse doloris: it is a comfort to the wretched to have others to share their sorrow (i.e., misery loves company) (Virgil)

solem enim e mundo tollere videntur qui amicitiam e vita tollunt: robbing life of friendship is like robbing the world of the sun (Cicero)

solem quis dicere falsum audeat?: who would dare to call the sun a liar? (Virgil)

solent mendaces luere pœnas malefici: the liar will pay the penalty for his crime (Phædrus)

sollicitæ mentes speque metuque pavent: minds that are ill at ease are agitated both with hope and fear (Ovid)

solo cedit, quicquid solo plantatur: whatever is planted in the soil goes with it

solum ut inter ista certum sit nihil esse certi: in these matters the only certainty is that there is nothing certain (Pliny the Elder)

solvitur ambulando: it is solved by walking (i.e., a theory is tested by practice)

somnus est imago mortis: sleep is the image of death (Cicero)

sorex suo perit indicio: the mouse perishes by betraying itself

sperate miseri, cavete felices: let the wretched live in hope and the happy be on their guard

sperate, et vosmet rebus servate secundis: live in hope and reserve yourselves for more prosperous circumstances (Virgil)

sperne voluptates: nocet empta dolore voluptas: despise pleasure: pleasure bought by pain is injurious (Horace)

spes sibi quisque: let each be a hope unto himself (i.e., each must rely on himself alone)

spiritus durissima coquit: a noble mind digests even the most painful injuries

spiritus promtus (est), caro autem infirma: the spirit is ready, but the flesh is weak (St. Matthew 26:41)

stat fortuna domus virtute: the fortune of the household stands by its virtue

stat nulla diu mortalibus usquam fortuna titubante, fides: not long will man's faith endure when fortune is tottering (Silius Italicus)

stateræ ordo non transiliendus: the balance should not be overladen with weight (Paradin)

stemmata quid faciunt?: of what use are pedigrees? (Juvenal)

stillicidi casus lapidem cavat: a constant drip hollows a stone

stipendia enim peccati mors (also, **stipendium peccati mors est**): for the wages of sin is death (Romans 6:23)

strenuorum immortale nomen: the fame of men of action is immortal

struit insidias lacrimis cum femina plorat: when a woman weeps, she is setting traps with her tears (Dionysius Cato)

studiis invigilandum: one must pay attention to studies

studio sapientia crescit: wisdom grows by study

stulti sunt innumerabiles: fools are without number (Erasmus)

stultitia est timore mortis mori: it is folly to die of the fear of death (Seneca)

stultitiam dissimulare non potes nisi taciturnitate: there is no concealing folly except by silence

stultitiam patiuntur opes: riches allow one to be foolish (Horace)

stultitiam simulare loco prudentia summa est: it is sometimes prudent to feign stupidity (Dionysius Cato)

stultitiam simulare loco sapientia summa est: to feign stupidity is, in certain situations, the highest wisdom (Horace)

stulto intellegens quid interest!: what a difference between a wise man and a fool! (Terence)

stultorum eventus magister est: experience is the teacher of fools (Livy)

stultorum incurata malus pudor ulcera celat: the false shame of fools makes them hide their uncured sores (Horace)

stultorum plenea sunt omnia: all places are filled with fools (Cicero)

stultorum quanto status sublimior, tanto manifestior turpitudo: the higher the status of fools, the more manifest is their baseness

stultum est dicere, putabam: it is foolish to say, I did not think

stultum est in luctu capillum sibi evellere, quasi calvito mæror levaretur: it is foolish to pluck out one's hair for sorrow, as if grief could be assuaged by baldness (Cicero)

stultum est timere quod vitare non potes (or **non potest**): it is foolish to fear what you cannot avoid (or what cannot be avoided) (Publilius Syrus)

stultum facit Fortuna quam vult perdere: Fortune makes a fool of him whom she would ruin (Publilius Syrus)

stultus es, rem actam agis: you are a fool, doing what has already been done (Plautus)

stultus labor est ineptiarum: foolish is the labor that is bestowed on foolish things (Martial)

stultus nisi quod ipse facit, nil rectum putat: the fool thinks nothing well done except what he does

stultus semper incipit vivere: the fool is always beginning to live

stultus, qui, patre occiso, liberos relinquat: the one who kills the father and leaves the children is a fool

sua cuique deus fit dira cupido: each one makes his own dire passion a god (Virgil)

sua cuique quum sit animi cogitatio, colorque proprius: each person has his own way of thinking, and a peculiar disposition (Phædrus)

sua cuique sunt vitia: everyone has his or her own vices

sua cuique vita obscura est: everyone's life is dark to himself

sua munera mittit cum hamo: he sends his gift with a hook attached

sua quisque exempla debet æquo animo pati: everyone ought to bear patiently with what is done after his own example (Phædrus)

suave est ex magno tollere acervo: it is pleasant to take from a great heap (Horace, said of the miser)

suavis laborum est præteritorum memoria: sweet is the memory of past labor (or trouble) (Cicero, citing a Greek proverb)

subditus fidelis regis et salus regni: a subject faithful to his king is the safety of the kingdom

sublata causa, tollitur effectus: when the cause is removed, the effect ceases

sublato fundamento cadit opus: remove the foundation and the structure falls

sufficit ad id, natura quod poscit: we have a sufficiency, when we have what nature requires (Seneca)

sufficit unum lumen in tenebris: a single light suffices in the darkness

suffundere malis hominis sanguinem, quam offundere: seek rather to make a man blush for his guilt than to shed his blood (Terence)

sui cuique fingunt fortunam: one's character fashions his fate (Cornelius Nepos)

sui cuique mores fingunt fortunam: each one's fortune is shaped for him by his own mores (Cornelius Nepos)

sume superbiam quæsitam meritis: assume the proud place your merits have won (Horace)

sumite materiam vestris qui scribitis æquam viribus: let those who write fix on a subject to which their force is equal (Horace)

summa bona putas, aliena vivere quadra: you think it the chief good to live on another's crumbs (Juvenal)

summa petit livor: envy aims very high (i.e., it attacks the highest things) (Ovid)

summa sedes non capit duos: the highest seat does not hold two

summæ opes inopia cupiditatum: he is richest who is poorest in his desires (Seneca)

summum crede nefas animam præferre pudori, et propter vitam vivendi perdere causas: count it the greatest sin to prefer your existence to your honor, and for the sake of life to lose every reason for living (Juvenal)

summum jus sæpe summa injuria est: the highest justice is often the greatest injustice (Cicero)

summum (or **summam**) **nec metuas diem, nec optes:** neither fear nor wish for your last day (Martial)

sumptus censum ne superet: let not your spending exceed your income

sunt bona mixta malis, sunt mala mixta bonis: good is mixed with evil, and evil is mixed with good (a definition of human existence)

sunt et belli sicut pacis jura: the same laws hold for peace as for war (Livy)

sunt lacrimæ rerum et mentem mortalia tangunt: tears are the nature of things and the mind touched by human mortality (Virgil)

sunt pueri pueri, pueri puerilia tractant: children are children, and children occupy themselves with childish things (also, boys are boys, …)

sunt superis sua jura: even the gods above are subject to law (Ovid)

superanda omnis fortuna ferendo est: every misfortune is to be subdued by patience (Virgil)

superstitio mentes occupavit: superstition has taken hold of their minds

superstitione tollenda religio non tollitur: religion is not abolished by abolishing superstition (Cicero)

suppressio veri suggestio falsi: suppression of the truth is the suggestion of falsehood

surdo fabulam narras: you are telling your story to a deaf man

suspectum semper invisumque dominantibus, qui proximus destinaretur: those in supreme power always suspect and hate their next heir (Tacitus)

sutor, ne supra crepidam: cobbler, stick to your last (i.e., mind your own business)

suum cuique decus posteritas rependit: posterity gives to everyone what is his due (Tacitus)

suum cuique pulchrum: to each his own beauty

suum cuique tribuere, ea demum summa justitia est: to give everyone his due, that is supreme justice (Cicero)

suus cuique mos (est): to each his own custom (i.e., different strokes for different folks) (Terence and Horace)

T

tacere multis discitur vitæ malis: silence is learned by the many misfortunes of life (Seneca)

tacita bona est mulier semper quam loquens: it more becomes a woman to be silent than to talk (Plautus)

tacitæ magis et occultæ inimicitiæ sunt, quam indictæ et opertæ: enmities unavowed and concealed are more to be feared than when open and declared (Cicero)

talis hominibus fuit oratio qualis vita: as was his speech so was his life (Seneca)

tam deest avaro quod habet, quam quod non habet: the miser is as much in want of that which he has, as of that which he has not (Publilius Syrus)

tam diu discendum est, quum diu nescias, et, si proverbio credimus, quam diu vivas: you must continue learning as long as you do not know, and, if we believe the proverb, as long as you live (Seneca)

tamquam scopulum, sic fugias inauditum atque insolens verbum: avoid a strange and unfamiliar word as you would a dangerous reef (Julius Cæsar)

tantæne animis cælestibus (or cœlestibus) iræ?: can wrath so great dwell in heavenly minds? (Virgil)

tanti eris aliis, quanti tibi fueris: you will be of as much value to others as you have been to yourself (Cicero)

tanto brevius omne, quanto felicius tempus: the happier the moments, the shorter the time (Pliny the Younger)

tanto est accusare quam defendere, quanto facere quam sanare vulnere, facilius: it is just so much easier to accuse than to defend, as it is easier to inflict than to heal a wound (Quintilian)

tanto major famæ sitis est quam virtutis; quis enim virtutem amplectitur ipsam præmia si tollas?: the thirst for fame is much greater than that for virtue; for who would embrace virtue itself if you take away its rewards? (Juvenal)

tantum de medio sumptis accedit honoris: so much of honor is due to subjects taken from what is common place (Horace)

tantum series juncturaque pollet: of so much force are system and connection (Horace)

tantus amor laudum, tantæ est victoria curæ: as great the love of praise, so great the anxiety for victory (Virgil)

tarda solet magnis rebus inesse fides: men are slow to rest their confidence in undertakings of magnitude (Ovid)

tarde venientibus ossa: to those who come late the bones

tarde, quæ credita lædunt, credimus: we are slow to believe that which, if believed, would work us harm (Ovid)

tardiora sunt remedia quam mala: remedies are slower in their operation than diseases (Tacitus)

tarditas et procrastinatio odiosa est: delay and procrastination is hateful (Cicero)

taurum tollet qui vitulum sustulerit: the one who has carried the calf will be able, eventually, to carry the ox

te digna sequere: follow what is worthy of you

te hominem esse memento: remember that you are a man

tecum habita; noris quam sit tibi curta supellex: live with yourself; get to know how poorly furnished you are (Persius)

temeritas est damnare quod nescias: it is rash to condemn what you do not know (Seneca)

temeritas est (videlicet) florentis ætatis, prudentia senescentis: rashness is (clearly) a characteristic of youth, prudence of old age (Cicero)

tempora mutantur, et nos mutamur in illis: times change, and we change with them (attributed to Emperor Lothar I)

tempora si fuerit nubila, solus eris: if the stormy season should arrive, you will be alone (i.e., adversity finds few companions) (Ovid)

tempore cuncta mitiora: everything becomes mellower with time

tempore difficiles veniunt ad aratra juvenci; tempore lenta pati frena docentur equi: in time the unmanageable young oxen come to the plow; in time the horses are taught to endure the restraining bit (Ovid)

tempore ducetur longo fortasse cicatrix; horrent admotas vulnera cruda manus: a wound may, perhaps, through time be closed; but, when fresh, it shrinks from the touch (Ovid)

tempore felici multi numerantur amici; si fortuna perit, nullus amicus erit: in happy times we reckon many friends; but if fortune fails, we will have no friends (Ovid)

tempore ruricolæ patiens fit taurus aratri: in time the bull is brought to wear the yoke (Ovid)

tempori parendum: one must move with the times

temporibus mores sapiens sine crimine mutat: the wise man does no wrong in changing his habits with the times (Dionysius Cato)

temporis ars medicina fere est: time is the best of the healing arts (Ovid)

tempus erit quo vos speculum vidisse pigebit: the time will come when it will disgust you to look in a mirror (Ovid)

tempus fugit: time flies

tenere lupum auribus: to hold a wolf by the ears (i.e., to hold danger in your hands; also, to take the bull by the horns)

teneros animos aliena opprobria sæpe absterrent vitiis: the disgrace of others often deters tender minds from vice (Horace)

tenet insanabile multos scribendi cacoëthes, et ægro in corde senescit: many have an incurable itch for writing that takes full possession of their disordered faculties (Juvenal)

terra es, terram ibis: you are earth, and to the earth you will return (Genesis 3:19)

terra malos homines nunc educat, atque pusillos: the earth now supports many bad and weak men (Juvenal)

tibi seris, tibi metis: you sow for yourself, you reap for yourself (i.e., as you sow, so shall you reap) (Cicero)

timendi causa est nescire: ignorance is the cause of fear (Seneca)

timidi est optare necem: to wish for death is a coward's part (Ovid)

timidi mater non flet: the mother of the coward has no occasion to weep

timidus se vocat cautum, parcum sordidus: the coward calls himself cautious, the miser thrifty (Publilius Syrus)

timor mortis morte pejor: the fear of death is worse than death

timor non est diuturnus magister officii: fear is not a lasting teacher of duty (Cicero)

tolle jocos; non est jocus esse malignum: away with such jests; there is no joking where there is ill will

tolle moras—semper nocuit differre paratis: away with all delays—it is ever injurious to postpone, when you are in readiness (Lucan)

tolle periclum, jam vaga prosiliet frænis natura remotis: take away the danger, remove the restraint, and vagrant nature bounds forth free (Horace)

tolluntur in altum, ut lapsu graviore ruant: they are raised to a great height, that they may tumble with a heavier fall (Claudian)

torrens dicendi copia multis et sua mortifera est facundia: to many, a torrent flow of speech and their own eloquence is fatal (Juvenal)

tota hujus mundi concordia ex discordibus constat: the complete harmony of this world consists in discords (Seneca)

tota in minimis existit natura: the whole of nature exists in the very smallest things (quoted by Emerson)

tota vita nihil aliud quam ad mortem iter est: the whole of life is nothing but a journey to death (Seneca)

totus mundus agit histrionem (or, **mundus universus exercet histrioniam**): all the world plays the comedian (or actor) (Petronius)

trahimur omnes laudis studio, et optimus quisque maxime gloria ducitur: we are all drawn by our eagerness for praise, and the noblest are most influenced by glory (Cicero)

trahit sua quemque voluptas: each one is drawn by his own delight (Virgil)

tranquillas etiam naufragus horret aquas: the man who has suffered shipwreck shudders even at a calm sea (Ovid)

translata proficit arbos: a tree makes progress when transplanted

tristia mæstum vultum verba decent; severum, seria dictu: sorrowful words become the sorrowful; serious words suit the grave (Horace)

tristis eris si solus eris: you will be sad if you are alone (i.e., if you keep company with only yourself) (Ovid)

tritissima quæque via et celeberrima maxime decipit: we most often go astray on a well-beaten path and a much traveled road (Seneca)

tu ne cede malis, sed contra audentior ito quam tua te fortuna sinet: do not surrender to evil but go boldly against it, as your fortune shall permit you (Virgil)

tu ne quæsieris, scire nefas: do not inquire, for it is not permitted to know such things (Horace)

tu pol si sapis, quod scis nescis: you, if you are wise, will not know what you do know (Terence)

tu recte vivis, si curas esse quod audis: you live a true life if you make it your care to be what you seem (Horace)

tu si animum vicisti, potius quam animus te, est quod gaudeas: if you have conquered your inclination, rather than your inclination you, you have something to rejoice at (Plautus)

tu si hic sis, aliter sentias: if you were in my place, you would think differently (Terence)

tua res agitur, paries cum proximus ardet: your property is in danger when the neighboring wall (house) is on fire (Horace)

tui animi compote es, ne quid fraudis stuprique ferocia pariat: be master of your soul, lest your untamed nature bring forth deceit and disgrace (Appius Claudius)

tum denique homines nostra intelligimus bona, quom quæ in potestate habuimus, ea amisimus: we men only realize the value of our blessings when we have lost them (Plautus)

tunc tua res agitur, paries cum proximus ardet: then your property is in danger when the neighboring wall (house) is on fire

turpe est aliud loqui, aliud sentire; quanto turpius aliud scribere, aliud sentire!: it is base to say one thing and to think another; how much more base to write one thing and think another! (Seneca)

turpe est in patria peregrinari, et in eis (or iis) rebus quæ ad patriam pertinent hospitem esse: it is disgraceful to live as a stranger in one's country, and to be uninformed of its interests and affairs (Manutius)

turpe est laudari ab illaudatis: it is degrading to be commended by those who are not themselves worthy of praise

turpe est odisse quam laudes: it is disgraceful to hate the one whom you praise

turpe est viro, id in quo quotidie versatur ignorare: it is shameful that a person should be ignorant of that in which he is everyday employed

turpe quid ausurus, te sine teste time: when about to commit a base deed, respect yourself, even though there is no witness (Ausonius)

turpis autem fuga mortis omni est morte pejor: a dishonorable flight from death is worse than any death (Cicero)

turpiter obticuit, sublato jure nocendi: he was shamefully silent when he had lost the power to injure

turpius ejicitur quam non admittitur hospes: it is more disgraceful to turn a guest out than not to admit one (Ovid)

tuta scelera esse possunt, non secura: wickedness may be safe, but not secure (Seneca)

U

ubi amici ibidem opus: (fig.) friends are sometimes troublesome (Plautus)

ubi amici, ibi opes: where there are friends, there is wealth (Plautus)

ubi amor condimentum inerit cuivis placiturum credo: where love enters to season a dish, I believe it will please anyone (Plautus)

ubi desinit philosophus, ibi incipit medicus: where the philosopher ends, there the physician begins (after Aristotle)

ubi est autem dignitas, nisi ubi honestas?: where is dignity unless there is honesty? (Cicero)

ubi idem et maximus et honestissimus amor est, aliquando præstat morte jungi quam vita distrahi: where there exists the greatest and most honorable love, it is sometimes better to be joined in death than separated in life (Valerius Maximus)

ubi innocens damnatur, pars patriæ exsulat: when an innocent man is condemned, part of his country is exiled (Publilius Syrus)

ubi jus, ibi remedium: where there is law, there is remedy

ubi jus incertum, ibi jus nullum: where the law is uncertain, there is no law

ubi major pars est, ibi est totum: where the greater part is, there [by law] is the whole

ubi nihil erit quod scribas, id ipsum scribito: where you have nothing to write, write and say so (Cicero)

ubi solitudinem faciunt pacem appellant: where they create a desolation they call it peace (Tacitus)

ubi timor adest, sapientia adesse nequit: where fear is present, wisdom cannot be (Lactantius)

ubi velis nolunt, ubi nolis cupiunt ultro: where you are willing, they are disinclined, where you are averse, they are willing (Terence)

ubi vinci necesse est, expedit cedere: where defeat is inevitable, it is expedient to yield (Quintilian)

ubicunque ars ostentatur, veritas abesse videtur: wherever art is displayed, truth seems to be wanting

ubique Mors est; optime hoc cavit Deus: Death is everywhere; God has provided well for that

ulterius ne tende odiis: do not go forward in your hatred (Virgil)

ultimum malorum e vivorum numero exire, antequam moriaris: there is no more dire misfortune than to quit the ranks of the living before you are dead (Seneca)

ultra posse nemo obligatur: no one is obligated to do more than he or she is able

una dies aperit, conficit una dies: in one day it opens its blossoms, in one day it decays (Ausonius, said of the rose)

una salus victis nullam sperare salutem: the only salvation (or safety) for the vanquished is not to hope for salvation (Virgil)

unde fames homini vetitorum tanta ciborum est?: why does man hunger so much after forbidden fruit? (Ovid)

unde habeas quærit nemo; sed oportet habere: no man inquires how you obtained your wealth; but it is necessary to possess it (Juvenal)

unde tibi frontem libertatemque parentis, cum facias pejora senex?: how do you derive your privilege as a parent when you, as an adult, do worse things? (Juvenal)

undique enim ad inferos tantundem viæ est: from all sides there is equally a way to the lower world (i.e., to hell) (Cicero, after Anaxagoras)

undique mors est: death is everywhere

unicumque homo est, ibi beneficio locus est: wherever there is a human being, there is an opportunity for a kindness (Seneca)

unius compendium, alterius dispendium: the gain of the one is the loss of the other

unius dementia dementes efficit multos: the madness of one makes many mad

universus hic mundus sit una civitas communis deorum atque hominum existimanda: we must conceive of this whole universe as one community of which both gods and men are citizens (Cicero)

universus mundus exercet histrioniam: all the world practices the art of acting

unum bonum est, quod beatæ vitæ causa et firmamentum est, sibi fidere: there is only one good, which is the cause and support of a blessed life: to trust (or believe) in yourself (Seneca)

unum nihil, duos plurimum posse: one man can do nothing, two can do much

unus utrique error; sed variis illudit partibus: the same error belongs to each, but it mocks them in different ways (Horace)

urbes constituit ætas: hora dissolvit: it takes an age to build a city, an hour to ruin it (Seneca)

urticæ proxima sæpe rosa est: the stinging nettle is often next to the rose (Ovid)

usque adeo nulli sincera voluptas, solicitique aliquid lætis intervenit: no one possesses unalloyed pleasure; there is some anxiety mingled with the joy (Ovid)

usque adeone mori miserum est?: is it then so very wretched a thing to die? (Virgil)

usque adeone scire tuum nihil est, nisi te scire hoc sciat alter?: is then your knowledge to pass for nothing unless others know of that knowledge? (Persius)

usus est optimum magister: use is the best teacher

usus libri, non lectio prudentes facit: the use, not the reading, of a book makes men wise

usus promptos facit (also, **usus promptum facit**): use (or practice) makes one ready (i.e., practice makes perfect)

ut acerbum est, pro benefactis quum mali messem metas: it is a bitter thing to have sown good deeds and to reap a harvest of evils (Plautus)

ut adversas res, secundas immoderate ferre, levitatis est: it shows a weak mind not to bear prosperity as well as adversity with moderation (Cicero)

ut ager, quamvis fertilis, sine cultura fructuosus esse non potest, sic sine doctrina animus: as a field, however fertile, can yield no fruit without cultivation, so neither can the mind without education (Seneca)

ut ameris, amabilis esto: to be loved, be lovable (Ovid)

ut amnis vita labitur: like a brook, life flows away

ut desint vires, tamen est laudanda voluntas: though strength may be lacking, yet the will is to be praised (Ovid)

ut enim non omne vinum, sic non omnis ætas vetustate coacescit: neither every wine, nor every life, turns to vinegar with age (Cicero)

ut fragilis glacies interit ira mora: like fragile ice, anger passes away in time (Ovid)

ut homines sunt, ita morem geras; vita quam sit brevis, simul cogita: as men are, so must you humor them; think, at the same time, how short life is (Plautus)

ut homo est, ita morem geras: as a man is, so must you humor him (i.e., conduct yourself) (Terence)

ut metus ad omnes, pœna ad paucos perveniret: that fear may reach all, punish but a few

ut placeas, debes immemor esse tui: that you may please others you must be forgetful of yourself (Ovid)

ut plerique solent, naso suspendis adunco ignotos: as is the way with most people, you turn up your nose at men of obscure origin (Horace)

ut quimus, quando ut volumus non licet: when we cannot act as we wish, we must act as we can (Terence)

ut quisque contemtissimus et ludibrio est, ita solutæ linguæ est: the more despicable and ridiculous a man is, the readier he is with his tongue (Seneca)

ut quisque est vir optimus, ita difficillime esse alios improbos suspicatur: the better the man is, the harder it is for him to suspect dishonesty in others (Cicero)

ut quisque suum vult esse, ita est: as everyone wishes his offspring to be, so it is (Terence)

ut ridentibus arrident, ita flentibus adflent, humani vultus: human countenances, as they smile on those who smile, so they weep with those that weep (Horace)

ut sæpe summa ingenia in occulto latent!: how often does it happen that great genius is hidden in obscurity! (Plautus)

ut sementem feceris ita (et) metes: as you have sown, so (also) shall you reap (Cicero)

ut sit mens sana in corpore sano: may we have a sound mind in a sound body (Juvenal)

ut sunt humana, nihil est perpetuum: as human affairs go, nothing is everlasting (Plautus)

ut sunt molles in calamitate mortalium animi!: how weak are the hearts of mortals under calamity! (Tacitus)

ut tibi sic alteri: as to yourself so to another (i.e., do unto others as you would have others do unto you)

ut vera laus ornat, ita falsa castigat: true praise is an honor, false praise a rebuke (Sidonius Apollinaris)

utatur motu animi, qui uti ratione non potest: let the one be guided by his passions, who can make no sense of his reason

utendum est ætate; cito pede labitur ætas: use the occasion, for it passes swiftly by (Ovid)

utilem pete finem: seek a useful end

utilis interdum est ipsis injuria passis: sometimes those who suffer injury find it beneficial (Ovid)

utitur in re non dubia testibus non necessariis: he uses unnecessary proofs on an indisputable point (Cicero)

utque in corporibus, sic in imperio, gravissimus est morbus qui a capite diffunditur: and as in men's bodies, so in government, that disease is most serious which proceeds from the head (Pliny the Younger)

utrum horum mavis accipe: take whichever you prefer

utrumque vitium est, et omnibus credere et nulli: it is equally an error to trust (or confide) in all and in none (Seneca)

V

vacuus cantat coram latrone viator: the traveler who has nothing sings before the robber (Juvenal)

validius est naturæ testimonium quam doctrinæ argumentum: the testimony of nature is weightier than the arguments of the learned (St. Ambrose)

vanitas est longam vitam optare, et de bona vita parum curare: it is vanity to desire a long life, and to care little whether that life be well spent (Thomas à Kempis)

varia vita est: life is changeable (Plautus)

varietas delectat: variety is delighting (Phædrus)

varii hominum sensus: various are the opinions of men

varium et mutabile semper fœmina: woman is ever fickle and changeable (Virgil)

vectigalia nervos esse rei publicæ: taxes are the sinews of the republic (i.e., essential to its strength) (Cicero)

vel capillus habet umbram suam: even a hair has its shadow (Publilius Syrus)

velis quod possis: aim at what you can accomplish

velle suum cuique, nec voto vivitur uno: each person has his own wish, the inclinations of all cannot be the same (Persius)

velocitas juxta formidinem, cunctatio propior constantiæ est: (fig.) haste is next door to panic, delay is nearer to firm courage (Tacitus)

velox consilium sequitur pœnitentia: hasty counsels are followed by repentance (Laberius and Publilius Syrus)

venalis populus venalis curia patrum: the people are venal, and the senate is equally venal (i.e., everyone has his or her price)

venenum in auro bibitur: poison is drunk from a gold cup (Seneca)

venia necessitati datur: pardon is conceded to necessity (i.e., necessity knows no law) (Cicero)

venienti occurrite morbo: confront disease at its onset (i.e., prevention is better than cure) (Persius)

venter, pluma, Venus, laudem fugiunt: the belly, featherbed, and Venus run away from praise (i.e., gluttony, sloth, and lust shun fame)

ventum seminabant et turbinem metent: they were sowing the wind, and they shall reap the whirlwind (Hosea 8:7)

verba dat omnis amans: every lover makes fair speeches (Ovid)

verba facit mortuo: he is talking to a dead man (i.e., he is wasting his words) (Plautus)

verba ligant homines, taurorum cornua funes: words bind men, cords the horns of a bull

verba volant, scripta manent: spoken words fly, written words remain

verbaque provisam rem non invita sequentur: words will not fail when the matter is well considered (Horace)

verbum Dei manet in æternum: the word of God endures through eternity

verbum emissum non est revocabile: a word once spoken cannot be recalled

verbum sat sapienti: a word to the wise is sufficient

verbum verbo reddere, fidus interpres: as a faithful interpreter, render (or translate) word for word (after Horace; a variation of the negative form, **nec verbum verbo curabis reddere fidus interpres**)

vere magnum habere in se fragilitatem hominis ac securitatem Dei: it is true greatness to have in one's self the frailty of a man and the security of a God

veritas, a quocunque dicitur, a Deo est: truth, by whomever it is spoken, comes from God

veritas jam attributa vino est: truth is indeed an attribute of wine (Pliny the Elder)

veritas nihil veretur nisi abscondi: truth fears nothing but concealment

veritas nimium altercando amittitur: truth is lost through too much altercation

veritas non recipit magis ac minus: truth admits not of greater or lesser (Wilkins)

veritas odit moras: truth hates delays (Seneca)

veritas odium parit: truth begets hatred

veritas premitur non opprimitur: truth may be kept down, but not crushed

veritas vel mendacio corrumpitur vel silentio: truth is violated by falsehood or by silence (Cicero)

veritas visu et mora, falsa festinatione et incertis valescunt: truth is established by inspection and delay; falsehood thrives by haste and uncertainty (Tacitus)

veritatem dies aperit: time reveals the truth (Seneca)

veritatem laborare nimis sæpe, aiunt, exstingui nunquam: it is said that truth is often eclipsed but never extinguished (Livy)

veritatis simplex oratio est: the language of truth is simple (Seneca)

versate diu, quid ferre recusent, quid valeant humeri: often try what weight you can bear, and what your shoulders cannot support (Horace)

versibus exponi tragicis res comica non vult: a comic matter cannot be expressed in tragic verse (Horace)

verum est aviditas dives, et pauper pudor: but greed is rich and modesty poor (Phædrus)

verum illud est, vulgo quod dici solet, omnes sibi malle melius esse quam alteri: the common assertion is certainly true, that we all wish matters to be better with ourselves than others (Terence)

verum opere in longo fas est obrepere somnum: but in a long work it is allowable that sleep may creep on (Horace)

verum putas haud ægre, quod valde expetas: you believe that easily, which you hope for earnestly

verus amicus est is qui est tanquam alter idem: a true friend is the one who is, as it were, a second self (Cicero)

verus amor nullum novit habere modum: true love knows no limits (i.e., knows not moderation) (Propertius)

vestibulum domus ornamentum est: the hall is the ornament of a house (i.e., the first impression makes a lasting impression)

vestigia nulla retrorsum: footprints do not go backwards

vetera extollimus, recentium incuriosi: we extol what is old, and are not interested in the new (i.e., we extol the past and are indifferent to our own times) (Tacitus)

vetera semper in laude, presentia in fastidio: old things are always in good repute, present things in disfavor (Tacitus)

vetus consuetudo naturæ vim obtinet: an ancient custom obtains force of nature (Cicero)

vetustas pro lege semper habetur: ancient custom is always held as law

via trita est tutissima: the beaten path is the safest one (Coke)

viam qui nescit qua deveniat ad mare, eum oportet amnem quærere comitem sibi: the one who knows not his way to the sea should seek the river for his companion (Plautus)

victor volentes per populos dat jura: the victor dictates his laws to a willing people

victores victosque numquam solida fide coalescere: victor and vanquished never unite in substantial agreement (Tacitus)

victrix patientia duris: in difficulty, win by patience

vigilando, agundo, bene consulundo prospera omnia cedunt: prosperity comes through vigilance, energy, and wise counsel (Cato, as quoted by Sallust)

vigilandum est semper; multæ insidiæ sunt bonis: always be on your guard; there are many snares for the good (Accius)

vigilantibus, non dormientibus, subveniunt jura (or, **vigilantibus non dormientibus servit lex**): the laws assist those who watch, not those who sleep

vigor ætatis fluit ut flos veris: the vigor of youth passes away like a spring flower

vile latens virtus: virtue when concealed is a worthless thing (Claudian)

vilius argentum est auro, virtutibus aurum: as gold is worth more than silver, so is virtue worth more than gold (Horace)

vim vi repellere omnia jura clamant: every right calls upon man to repel by force

vincit qui se vincit: he conquers who conquers himself

vincula de linguæ vel tibi linguæ dabit: bind your tongue or your tongue will have you bound

vindicta nemo magis gaudet quam fœmina: no one rejoices more in revenge than woman (Juvenal)

vino diffugiunt mordaces curæ: wine diffuses the bite of cares (adapted from Horace)

violenta nemo imperia continuit diu; moderata durant: no one ever held power long by violence; it lasts only when wielded with moderation (Seneca)

vir sapiens forti melior: a wise man is better than a strong one

vir sapit qui pauca loquitur: wise is the person who talks little

virgo formosa etsi sit oppido pauper, tamen abunde dotata est: a beautiful girl, though she indeed be poor, is yet abundantly dowered (Apuleius)

viri infelicis procul amici: friends stay far away from an unfortunate person (Seneca)

viris fortibus non opus est mœnibus: brave men have no need of walls

virtus auro præferenda: virtue is to be preferred to gold

virtus dabit, cura servabit: valor will give, care will keep

virtus est medium vitiorum et utrinque reductum: virtue is the middle between two vices, and is equally removed from either extreme (Horace)

virtus est vitium fugere: to flee vice is the beginning of virtue (Horace)

virtus in astra tendit, in mortem timor: courage leads to heaven, fear, to death (Seneca)

virtus ipsa suis firmissima nititur armis: true virtue relies on its own arms

virtus laudatur et alget: virtue is praised and left out to freeze (Juvenal)

virtus, repulsæ nescia sordidæ, intaminatis fulget honoribus: that virtue which is unconscious of a base repulse, shines with unstained honors (Horace)

virtute acquiritur honos: honor is the reward of virtue

virtute enim ipsa non tam multi præditi esse, quam videri volunt: fewer possess virtue than those who wish us to believe that they possess it (Cicero)

virtute nulla possessio major: no possession is greater than virtue

virtute orta occidunt rarius: things sprung from virtue rarely perish

virtutem doctrina paret, naturane donet?: does training produce virtue, or does nature bestow it? (Horace)

virtutem incolumem odimus; sublatam ex oculis quærimus invidi: we hate virtue when it is safe and flourishing; but when it is removed from our sight, even envy itself regrets it (Horace)

virtutem videant intabescantque relicta: let them recognize virtue and rot for having left it behind (Persius)

virtuti sis par, dispar fortunis patris: be like your father in virtue, unlike him in fortune (Accius)

virtutibus obstat res angusta domi: straitened circumstances at home obstruct the path of virtue (Juvenal)

virtutis enim laus omnis in actione consistit: the whole praise of virtue consists in the practice of virtue (Cicero)

vis consilii expers mole ruit sua: strength (or force), lacking judgment, collapses by its own weight (Horace)

vita brevis nulli superest, qui tempus in illa quærendæ sibi mortis habet: life is so short, there is no time to seek for death (Lucan)

vita cedat, uti conviva satur: let him take leave of life, as a guest satisfied with his entertainment (Horace)

vita enim mortuorum in memoria vivorum est posita: the life of the dead is placed in the memory of the living (Cicero)

vita hominis sine litteris (or **literis**) **mors est:** the life of a man without literature is death

vita, si scias uti, longa est: life, if you know how to use it, is long enough (Seneca)

vita sine proposito vaga est: a life without purpose is an aimless one (Seneca)

vitæ est avidus, quisquis non vult mundo secum pereunte mori: he is greedy of life who is unwilling to die when the world around him is perishing (Seneca)

vitæ summa brevis spem nos vetat inchoare longam: the short span of life forbids us from entering into long hopes (Horace)

vitam regit fortuna, non sapientia: fortune, not wisdom, rules this life (Cicero)

vitanda est improba siren Desidia: you must avoid that wicked siren Sloth (Horace)

vitaque mancipio, nulli datur, omnibus usu: and life is given to none to possess fully, but for all to use (Lucretius)

vitavi denique culpam, non laudem merui: I have avoided what is censurable, not merited what is commendable (Horace)

vitia nobis sub virtutum nomine obrepunt: vices steal upon us under the name of virtues (Seneca)

vitia otii negotio discutienda sunt: the vices of sloth are only to be shaken off by doing something (Seneca)

vitiant artus ægræ contagia mentis: when the mind is ill at ease, the body is in a certain degree affected (Ovid)

vitiis nemo sine nascitur; optimus ille qui minimis urgetur: no one is born without faults; he is the best who is plagued by the fewest (Horace)

vitiosum est ubique, quod nimium est: too much of anything is in every case a defect (Seneca)

vitium commune omnium est, quod nimium ad rem in senecta attenti sumus: it is a fault that is common to all, that in old age we are too much attached to our property and interests (Terence)

vitium fuit, nunc mos est, assentatio: flattery, which was formerly a vice, is now grown into a custom (Publilius Syrus)

vitium impotens virtus vocatur: vice that is powerless is called virtue (Seneca)

vivas ut possis quando nec quis ut velis: live as you can since you cannot live as your would (Cæcilius)

vive memor Lethi; fugit hora: live ever mindful of death; the hour flies (Persius)

vivit post funera virtus: virtue lives on after the grave (Emperor Tiberias)

vivite felices quibus est fortuna peracta jam sua!: may those be happy whose fortunes are already completed! (Virgil)

vivite fortes, fortiaque adversis opponite pectora rebus: live as brave men, and stand against adversity with stout hearts (Horace)

vix decimus quisque est, qui ipse sese noverit: hardly one man in ten knows himself (Plautus)

vix ulla tam iniqua pax, quin bello vel æquissimo sit potior: scarcely is there any peace so unjust that it is better than even the fairest war (Erasmus)

volenti non fit injuria: no injury is done to the willing

voluntas habetur pro facto: the will is taken for the deed

voluntas non potest cogi: the will cannot be forced

voluptas vivere cœpit, vita ipsa desiit: pleasure begins to live when life itself is departing (Pliny the Elder)

voluptates commendat rarior usus: pleasures rarely used are greatly enjoyed (Juvenal)

vos exemplaria Græca nocturna versate manu, versate diurna: by night and day thumb through the pages of your Greek exemplars (Horace)

vos vestros servate, meos mihi linquite mores: you keep to your own ways and leave mine to me (Petrarch)

votis subscribunt fata secundis: destiny makes wishes come true

vox audita perit, litera scripta manet: the voice that is heard perishes, the letter that is written remains

vox nihil aliud quam ictus aër: the voice is nothing but beaten air (Seneca)

vulgare amici nomen, sed rara est fides: the name of friend is common, but a faithful friend is rare (Phædrus)

vulgare Græciæ dictum, semper Africam aliquid novi afferre: a common Greek saying: there is always something new being brought from Africa (Pliny the Elder)

vulgo dicitur multos modios salis simul edendos esse, ut amicitia munus expletum sit: it is a common saying that many pecks of salt must be eaten before the duties of friendship can be discharged (Cicero)

vulgo enim dicitur: jucundi acti labores: for it is commonly said: completed labors are pleasant (Cicero)

vulgus amicitias utilitate probat: the common crowd seeks friendships for their usefulness

vulgus ex veritate pauca, ex opinione multa, æstimat: the masses judge of few things by the truth, of most things by opinion (Cicero)

vulnera dum sanas, dolor est medicina doloris: when you are dressing a wound, pain is pain's medicine (Dionysius Cato)

vult plane virtus honorem, nec est virtutis ulla alia merces: virtue clearly desires honor and has no other reward (Cicero)

vultus est index animi: the face is the index of the soul

LATIN MOTTOES AND PHRASES

A

a capite ad calcem: from head to heel; from top to bottom

a cœlo usque ad centrum: from the heavens to the center of the earth

a cruce salus: salvation is by (or from) the Cross

a crux nostra corona: the Cross is our crown

a cuspide corona: from a spear a crown (i.e., honor for military exploits)

a Deo et rege: from God and the king

a Deo lux nostra: our light comes from God

a fortiori: with stronger force

a Jove principium: beginning with Jove

a mari usque ad mare: from sea to sea (motto on Canada's coat of arms)

a posse ad esse: from possibility to actuality

a re decedunt: they wander from the point

a solis ortu usque ad occasum: from the rising to the setting of the sun

a te pro te: from thee for thee

a verbis ad verbera: from words to blows

ab igne ignem: fire from fire

ab initio: from the beginning

ab insomni non custodita Dracone: not guarded by the sleepless dragon

ab Jove principium: from Jove is the beginning of all things (Virgil)

ab ovo usque ad mala: from the egg to the apples (i.e., from appetizer to dessert; from beginning to end)

ab uno ad omnes: from one to all

ab urbe condita (A.U.C.): from the founding of the city (i.e., Rome)

aberrare a scopo: to miss the mark

abiit ad plures: he is gone to the majority (i.e., he has died) (Petronius)

abnormis sapiens: abnormally wise; wise without learning (Horace)

abscissa virescit: by pruning it grows green

absit omen: may the omen augur no evil

absque labore nihil: nothing without labor

abundat dulcibus vitiis: he abounds with delightful faults (Quintilian)

abyssus abyssum invocat: deep calls unto deep

Acherontis pabulum (or, Acheruntis pabulum): food for Acheron (i.e., marked for death; bound for hell) (Plautus)

acta est fabula: the play is over (the dying words of Cæsar Augustus)

actum est de me: it is all over with me! (i.e., all is lost!)

actum est de nobis: it is all over with us!

actum est de republica: it is all over with the Republic!

aculei irriti: ineffectual stings

ad alta virtute: to the heights of my virtue

ad amussim: made exactly by rule

ad aperturam: wherever a book may be opened

ad astra: to the stars (motto of University College, Dublin)

ad astra per ardua: to the stars by steep paths

ad astra per aspera: to the stars through adversities (motto of Kansas)

ad augusta per angusta: to honors through difficulties

ad captandum vulgus: to catch or capture the rabble (i.e., something offered for the entertainment of the masses)

ad cœlos volans: flying to the heavens

ad cœlum tendit: he directs his course toward heaven

ad eundem gradum (or, **ad eundem**): to the same rank (which one previously held)

ad finem: to the end

ad finem fidelis: faithful to the end

ad Græcas kalendas (or **calendas**): at the Greek calends (i.e., never; there is no Greek calends)

ad instar omnium: in the likeness of all

ad kalendas (or **calendas**) **Græcas:** at the Greek calends (i.e., never; there is no Greek calends)

ad majorem Dei gloriam (A.M.D.G.): to the greater glory of God (motto of the Society of Jesus, the Jesuits)

ad meliora vertamur: let us turn to better things

ad metam: to the mark

ad mortem fidelis: faithful till death

ad omnem libidinem projectus homo: a man addicted to every lust

ad perpetuam rei memoriam: for the perpetual remembrance of a thing (or, of the matter)

ad summum: to the highest point

ad unguem: to a nail; to a T

ad unguem factus homo: a man accomplished to his fingertips (Horace)

ad unum omnes: all to a one; unanimously

ad utrumque paratus: prepared for either case

ad virtus astra: virtue to the stars

ad vitam aut culpam: for life or fault (i.e., till some misconduct be proved)

addere legi justitiam Deo: to add the justice of God to the law

adjutorium nostrum in nomine Domini: our help is in the name of the Lord

adjuvante Deo labor proficit: with God's help, work prospers

adscriptus glebæ: attached to the soil

adstrictus necessitate: bound by necessity (Cicero)

adulescentia deferbuit: the fires of youth have cooled

adversa virtute repello: I repel adversity by valor

ægis fortissima virtus: virtue is the strongest shield

ægrescitque medendo: the medicine increases the disease (Virgil)

ægri somnia vana: the idle or delusive dreams of a sick man (Horace)

æmulus atque imitator studiorum ac laborum: a rival and imitator of his studies and labors (Cicero)

Æneadum genetrix, hominum divomque voluptas: mother of Aeneas, pleasure of men and gods (Lucretius)

æquabiliter et diligenter: by equity and diligence

æquam servare mentem: to preserve an equal mind (or even temper)

æquanimiter: with equanimity

æquitas sequitur legem: equity follows the law

æque tandem: equally at length (e.g., when perched, the small bird is as tall as the tallest tree)

æquo animo: with an even or equitable mind

ære perennius: more lasting than bronze (Horace)

æternum inter se discordant: they are eternally in discord with each other (Terence)

æternum servans sub pectore vulnus: tending an eternal wound within the heart

Æthiopiem lavare: to wash an Ethiopian

afflavit Deus et dissipantur: God sent forth his breath and they are scattered (an inscription commemorating the English defeat of the Spanish Armada in 1588)

age quod agis: do what you are doing (i.e., attend to the work you have at hand; mind your own business)

agedum virtus antecedat, tutum erit omne vestigium: if virtue precede us, every step will be safe (Seneca)

agere pro aliis: to act for others

albæ gallinæ filius: the son of a white hen (i.e., a lucky person)

album calculum addere: to give a white stone (i.e., to cast a favorable vote)

alea belli: the uncertainty of war

alea jacta est: the die is cast (Julius Cæsar, after crossing the Rubicon in 49 BCE)

alea judiciorum: the uncertainty of law

alere flammam: to feed the flame (Ovid)

ales volat propriis: a bird flies to its own (i.e., birds of a feather flock together)

alia tentanda via est: another way must be tried (Virgil)

aliam excute quercum: go, shake some other oak [for your acorns]

alieni temporis flores: flowers of other days

alieno more vivendum est mihi: I must live according to another's whim (Terence)

alio sub sole: under another sun

alis aspicit astra: flying, he keeps his eye on the stars

alis volat propriis: she flies by her own wings (motto of Oregon)

aliud et idem: another and the same

aliusque et idem: another, yet the same (Horace)

alliciunt somnos tempus motusque merumque: time, motion, and wine cause sleep (Ovid)

allos ego: alter ego (Zeno's definition of a friend)

alma mater: a dear mother (applied to one's school; also applied to Mother Earth)

alnus semper floreat: may the Alder always flourish (motto of the Alder family)

alte fert aquila: the eagle bears me on high

alter alterius auxilio eget: the one stands in need of assistance of the other (Sallust)

alter ego: another or second self

alter ego est amicus: a friend is another self (Zeno)

alter ipse amicus: a friend is a second self

altera manu scabunt, altera feriunt: they tickle with one hand and smite with the other

alterius non sit qui suus esse potest: let no man be slave of another who can be his own master (motto of Paracelsus)

altiora peto: I seek higher things

amabilis insania: a fine frenzy

ambigendi locus: room for doubt

amentium, haud amantium: of lunatics, not lovers

amici, diem perdidi: friends, I have lost a day (Emperor Titus, as quoted by Suetonius)

amicis semper fidelis: always faithful to friends

amicitia, etiam post mortem durans: friendship enduring even after death

amicitia reddit honores: friendship gives honors

amicitia sine fraude: friendship without deceit

amicum lædere ne joco quidem licet: a friend must not be injured, even in jest (Publilius Syrus)

amicus amico: a friend to a friend

amicus animæ dimidium: a friend is half of one's soul

amicus curiæ: a friend to the court (i.e., an impartial adviser in a case)

amicus est tanquam alter idem: a friend is, as it were, a second self (Cicero)

amicus humani generis: a friend of the human race

amicus usque ad aras: a friend as far as the altar (i.e., a friend in everything save religion; or, a friend to the point of sacrifice or death)

amo: I love

amo probos: love proved

amo ut invenio: I love as I find

amor et honor: love and honor

amor et obœdientia: love and obedience

amor et pax: love and peace

amor patriæ: love of country

amor proximi: love of neighbor

amor vincit omnia: love conquers all things

amore patriæ vincit: the love of country conquers

amore sitis uniti: be united in love

anchora salutis: the anchor of salvation

anguis in herba: a snake in the grass

anima in amicis una: one mind among friends

anima mundi: the soul of the world

animæ dimidium meæ: the half of my own life (Horace)

animis illabere nostris: you will steal into our hearts

animis opibusque parati: prepared in minds and resources (a motto of South Carolina)

animo et fide: by courage and faith

animo, non astutia: by courage, not by craft

animus et prudentia: courage and discretion

animus homini, quicquid sibi imperat, obtinet: the mind of man can accomplish whatever it resolves to do

animus non deficit æquus: a well-balanced mind is not wanting (i.e., equanimity does not fail us)

animus, non res: mind, not property (or possessions)

animus tamen idem: my mind is still the same

animus valet: courage avails

anno Domini (A.D.): in the year of our Lord

anno urbis conditæ (A.U.C.): in the year of the founding of the city (i.e., Rome)

annona cara est: corn is dear

annoso robore quercus: an oak in aged strength

annuit cœptis: He (God) has favored our undertaking (a motto of the United States of America)

annus mirabilis: the wonderful year (i.e., a year filled with wonders)

ante ferit, quam flamma micet: it strikes before the flame flickers

ante omnia: before everything else

ante tubam trepidat: he trembles before the trumpet sounds (i.e., he cries before he is hurt) (Virgil)

anthropos physei zoön politikon: man is by nature a political being (Aristotle, from the Greek)

antidoti salubris amaror: the bitterness of the healing antidote

antiqua homo virtute ac fide: a man of ancient virtue and fidelity (Terence)

antiquam obtinens: possessing antiquity

antiquum assero decus: I claim ancient honor

apage Satanus! (also, **apage Satana!**): away with you, Satan!

aperto vivere voto: to live with unconcealed desire (i.e., to live life as an open book or as an honest person) (Persius)

apio opus est: there is need of parsley (i.e., someone is dying, parsley being strewn over a person's grave)

aquila non capit muscas: an eagle does not catch flies

aquilæ senectus: the old age of the eagle (Terence)

aranearum telas texere: to weave spiders' webs (i.e., spinning a tall tale or weaving an intricate argument)

arbiter bibendi: the judge of the drinking (i.e., the master of the feast)

arbiter elegantiarum: the judge of elegant affairs (i.e., the master of ceremonies)

arbiter formæ: the judge of beauty

arbitrii mihi jura mei: my laws are my will

Arcades ambo: Arcadians both (Virgil)

arcana imperii: state secrets

arcus, artes, astra: the bow, arts, and stars

ardenter amo: I love fervently

ardentia verba: glowing words

ardua petit ardea: the heron seeks high places

arena sine calce: sand without cement (i.e., an unconnected or disjointed speech) (Suetonius)

arenæ mandas semina: you are sowing grain in the sand

arma parata fero: I carry arms in readiness

arma tuentur pacem: arms maintain peace

armat spinat rosas: the thorn arms the rose

arrectis auribus adsto: I wait with listening ears (Virigil)

ars adeo latet arte sua: so art lies hid by its own artifice (Ovid)

ars æmula naturæ: art is nature's rival (Apuleius)

ars artium omnium conservatrix: the art of preserving all other arts (i.e., printing)

ars deluditur arte: craft deceived by craft

ars est celare artem: true art is to conceal art (Ovid)

ars gratia artis: art for art's sake (motto of Metro-Goldwyn-Mayer)

ars longa, vita brevis: art is long, life is short (adapted from Hippocrates)

ars naturam adjuvans: art aiding nature

arte conservatus: preserved by skill

arte et marte: by skill and valor

arte magistra: by the aid of art (Virgil)

arte perire sua: to perish by one's own trickery (i.e., to be caught in one's own trap)

artes honorabit: he will honor (or adorn) the arts

artes, scientia, veritas: arts, science, truth (motto of the University of Michigan)

ascendo: I rise

asinum sub fræno currere docere: to teach an ass to obey the rein (i.e., to labor in vain)

asinus ad lyram: an ass at the lyre (i.e., to be unmusical or all thumbs)

asinus asinum fricat: the ass rubs the ass (i.e., one fool rubs another fool's back; mutual praise)

asinus in tegulis: an ass on the roof tiles

asinus in unguento: an ass among perfumes (i.e., one who cannot appreciate the finer things)

asinus inter simias: an ass among apes (i.e., a fool among people who make a fool of him)

aspice et imitare: look and imitate

aspicit unam: it sees one only

aspiro: I aspire

astra castra, numen lumen: the stars my camp, the gods my light

astra regunt homines, sed regit astra Deus: the stars govern men, but God governs the stars

astræa redux: return of the goddess of justice

astutior coccyge: craftier than a cuckoo (i.e., a bird that lays its eggs in another bird's nest)

at spes infracta (or, **at spes non fracta**): but hope is not broken

Athanasius contra mundum: Athanasius against the world (a reference to the stand made by St. Athanasius against heresy in the early fourth century CE)

aucto splendore resurgo: I rise again with increase of splendor

auctor ego audendi: I am the author of my daring

audaces fortuna juvat: fortune helps the brave

audaces fortuna juvat timidosque repellit: fortune assists the bold and repels the coward

audaces juvo: I assist the bold

audacia et industria: boldness and diligence

audacia pro muro habetur: courage protects like a wall (Sallust)

audacter et sincere (or, **audaciter et sincere**): boldly and sincerely

audax et celer: bold and swift

aude aliquid dignum: dare something worthy

aude contemnere opes: dare to despise riches (Virgil)

aude sapere: dare to be wise

aude, tace, fuge: listen, be silent, flee

audemus jura nostra defendere: we dare to defend our rights (motto of Alabama)

audentes Deus ipse juvat: God himself favors the brave (Ovid)

audentes (or **audaces**) **fortuna juvat:** fortune aids (or favors) the bold (Virgil)

audentum Forsque Venusque juvant: Fortune and Love favor the brave (Ovid)

audio sed taceo: I hear, but say nothing

auditque vocatus Apollo: and Apollo hears when called upon (a reference to poetic inspiration) (Virgil)

Augiæ cloacas purgare: to cleanse the Augean stables (i.e., to accomplish a difficult and disagreeable work) (Seneca)

Augusto felicior, Trajano melior: a more fortunate man than Augustus, a more excellent man than Trajan (Eutropius)

aura popularis: the popular breeze (i.e., popular favor) (Cicero)

aurea mediocritas (or, **auream mediocritatem**): the golden mean (Horace)

aureæ compedes: golden shackles

auream quisquis mediocritatem diligit: someone who loves the golden mean (Horace)

aureo hamo piscari (or, **aureo piscari hamo**): to fish with a golden hook (i.e., gold is the surest of lures)

auri sacra fames: accursed hunger for gold (Virgil)

auribus teneo lupum: I hold a wolf by the ears (i.e., I am in desperate trouble) (Terence)

aurora musis amica (est): dawn is the friend of the Muses

aurum e stercore: gold from dung

aurum huic olet: he smells the money (Plautus)

auspice Christo: under the guidance of Christ

auspicium melioris ævi: a pledge of better times (motto of the Order of St. Michael and St. George)

Austriæ est imperare orbi universo (A.E.I.O.U.): all the world is to be ruled by Austria (motto of Frederick III)

ausus est vana contemnere: he dared to scorn vain fears

aut amat aut odit mulier: nil (or **nihil**) **est tertium:** woman either loves or hates: there is no(thing) in between (Publilius Syrus)

aut bibat aut abeat: either drink or go away

aut Cæsar aut nihil: either Cæsar or nothing (motto of Cæsar Borgia)

aut Cæsar aut nullus: he will be either Cæsar or nobody

aut cum hoc aut in hoc: either with this or on this

aut disce aut discede: either learn or depart

aut inveniam viam aut faciam: either I will find a way or make one

aut mors aut victoria: either death or victory

aut suavitate aut vi: either by gentleness or by force

aut vincam aut periam: either win or perish

aut vincere aut mori: either victory or death

autumnus—libitinæ quæstus acerbæ: autumn—the harvest of bitter death (Horace)

auxilium ab alto: help from on high

auxilium meum a Domino: my help comes from the Lord

auxilium meum ab alto: my help is from above

avaritia huius sæculi: the avarice of this generation

ave atque vale: hale (or hail) and farewell

ave Maria, gratia plena (also, **ave Maria, plena gratia**): hail Mary, full of grace

140

avi memorantur avorum: my ancestors recall their ancestors (i.e., my ancestral line is long)

avi numerantur avorum: I follow a long line of ancestors

avitæ gloriæ memor: mindful of ancestral glory

avito viret honore: he flourishes upon ancestral honors (i.e., his honor is not of his own doing)

B

basis virtutum constantia: constancy is the foundation of virtue

beatæ memoriæ: of blessed memory

beati pacifici: blessed are the peace makers (St. Matthew 5:9)

beati pauperes spiritu: blessed are the poor in spirit

beati qui durant: blessed are they that endure

bella, detesta matribus: wars, the horror of mothers (Horace)

bella, horrida bella: wars, horrible wars (Virgil)

bella matronis detestata: wars detested by mothers (Horace)

bellicæ virtutis præmium: the reward of valor in war

bello ac pace paratus: prepared in war and peace

bello palmam fero: I bear the palm in war

bellua multorum capitum: the many-headed monster (i.e., the mob)

bellum omnium in omnes: a war of all against all

bellum, pax rursus: a war, and again a peace (Terence)

bene dissere est finis logices: to dispute well the chief end of logic

bene est tentare: it is as well to try

bene merentibus: to the well-deserving

bene tenax: rightly tenacious

benedictus qui tollit crucem: blessed is the one who bears the Cross

benedictus qui venit in nomine Domini: blessed is the one who comes in the name of the Lord (St. Matthew 21:9)

benigno numine: by the favor of heaven; by divine favor

bibere venenum in auro: to drink poison from a golden cup

bivium virtutis et vitii: the two paths (or crossroads) of virtue and of vice

blandæ mendacia linguæ: the lies of a flattering tongue

bona fide: in good faith

bona fide polliceor: I promise in good faith

bonis avibus: under favorable auspices

bonis omnia bona: all things are good to the good

bonis vel malis avibus: under good or evil auspices

bos in lingua: an ox on the tongue (i.e., hush money: certain coins in Athens were imprinted with an ox)

brutum fulmen (or, **fulmen brutum**): a harmless thunderbolt (i.e., an empty threat)

C

cacoëthes carpendi: an itch for finding fault

cacoëthes loquendi: an itch for speaking

cacoëthes scribendi: an itch for writing

cadenti porrigo dextram: I extend my right hand to one who is falling

cæca regens vestigia filo: guiding blind steps by a thread

cælestis veritas origo: the source of heavenly truth

cæli enarrant gloriam Dei: the heavens tell of the glory of God

cælitus impendet: it hangs in the heavens

cælitus mihi vires: my strength is from heaven

cælo imperium Jovis extulit ales: the bird of Jupiter raised the empire to the heavens

cælum, non animum: the clime, not the mind

calco sub pedibus: I trample it under my feet

callida junctura: skillful arrangement (Horace)

candide et caute: with candor and caution

candide et constanter: with candor and constancy; frankly and firmly

candide sincere: candidly and sincerely

candor dat viribus alas: sincerity gives wings to strength

candor illesus: purity unharmed

cane pejus et angue: worse than a dog or a snake

canina facundia: dog eloquence (i.e., snarling) (Appius)

canis in præsepi: a dog in the manger (neither will it let the ox eat the hay nor will it eat the hay itself)

capistrum maritale: the matrimonial halter (Juvenal)

capitis nives: the snowy locks of the head (Horace)

captivus ob gulam: captured by gluttony

captus nidore culinæ: caught by the odor of the kitchen

caput inter nubila condit: it hides its head amid the clouds (i.e., fame) (Virgil)

caput mortuum: dead head (i.e., the worthless remains; a numbskull)

caput mundi: the head of the world (i.e., Rome)

caret: it is wanting

caret initio et fine: it lacks beginning and end

caritas fructum habet: charity bears fruit

carmen triumphale: a song of triumph

carpe diem: seize the day (i.e., make the most of the present) (Horace)

carpere et colligere: to pick and gather

Carthago delenda est: Carthage must be destroyed (Cato the Elder)

cassis tutissima virtus: virtue is the safest helmet

casta moribus et integra pudore: of chaste morals and unblemished modesty (Martial)

castigat ridendo mores: it corrects manners by laughing at them (i.e., comedy)

Cato contra mundum: Cato against the world

caute, non astute: cautiously, not craftily

cautus semper viret: the cautious man always flourishes

cave a signatis: beware of those who are marked

cave!, adsum: beware!, I am present

cave canem: beware of the dog

cave!, Deus videt: beware!, God sees

cave paratus: beware while prepared

caveat actor: let the doer beware (of the consequences)

caveat emptor: let the buyer beware

caveat venditor: let the seller beware

caveat viator: let the traveler beware

cavendo tutus: safe by taking heed

cavete a canibus: beware of the dogs

cedamus amori: let us yield to love

cedant arma: let arms yield

cedant arma togæ: let arms yield to the toga (i.e., let the military yield power to civil authority) (Cicero; motto of Wyoming)

cede Deo: yield to God (Virgil)

cede nullis: yield to no one

cedo nulli: I yield to no one

celer et audax: swift and daring

celer et fidelis: swift and faithful

celer et vigilans: quick and watchful

celeritas: swiftness

celeritas et veritas: swiftness and truth

celeriter: swiftly

cernit omnia Deus vindex: there is an avenging God who sees all

certa salutis anchora: the sure anchor of salvation

certavi et vici: I have fought and conquered

certior in cœlo domus: a surer home in heaven

certum scio: I know for certain

cervus lacessitus leo: the stag provoked becomes a lion

cessit victoria victis: victory has yielded to the vanquished

cetera quis nescit?: the rest who does not know?

ceterum censo: but my decided opinion is (Cato)

chalepa ta kala: what is good (or excellent) is difficult (a Greek phrase)

chaos, rudis indigestaque moles: chaos, a rough and unordered mass (Ovid)

Christi crux est mea lux: the Cross of Christ is my light

Christo duce feliciter: happily, under the guidance of Christ

Christo duce vincamus: let us conquer with Christ as leader

Christo et Ecclesiæ: for Christ and for the Church

cicatrix manet: the scar remains

cita mors ruit: death is a swift rider (Horace)

citius, altius, fortius: faster, higher, stronger (motto of the modern Olympic Games)

civilitas successit barbarum: civilization succeeds barbarism (territorial motto of Minnesota)

civis Romanus sum: I am a citizen of Rome (Cicero)

civium in moribus rei publicæ salus: the welfare of the state [depends upon] the morals of its citizens (motto of the University of Florida)

clamamus, Abba, Pater: whereby we cry, Abba, Father (after Galatians 4:6)

clarior e tenebris (also, **clarior ex tenebris**): [I shine] more brightly from the darkness (or from obscurity)

clarior ex obscuro: [I shine] more brightly from obscurity

clarior hinc honos: hence the brighter honor

clariora sequor: I follow brighter things

claris dextra factis: a right hand employed in glorious deeds

claritate dextra: with a bright light to the right

clarum et venerabile nomen: a bright and venerable name

classicum canit: the trumpet sounds attack

clementia in potentia: clemency in power

cœlestem spero coronam: I hope for a heavenly crown

cœlitus datum: given by heaven

cœlitus mihi vires: my strength is from heaven

cœlo solo salo potentes: rely on heaven alone

cœlum non animum: you may change your climate, not your mind

cœlum non solum: heaven not earth

cœlum versus: heavenward

cœtus dulces valete: fare you well (Catullus)

cogito ergo sum (also, **ego cogito, ergo sum**): I think, therefore I am (Descartes)

colligavit nemo: no one has bound me

colubrem in sinu fovere: to hold a snake in one's bosom (Phædrus)

comitas inter gentes: comity among nations

commodum non damnum: a convenience not an injury

communi consensu: by common consent

communia proprie dicere: to express commonplace things with propriety (said of accomplished actors) (Horace)

compos mentis: of sound mind

compositum jus fasque animi: law and equity (Persius)

conabimur: we will try

conanti dabitur: it will be given to him who strives

conantia frangere frangunt: they break those which are trying to break them

concordia: harmony

concordia discors (or, **discors concordia**): harmony in discord; a dissonant harmony (i.e., agreeing to differ) (Horace and Ovid)

concordia insuperabilis: unconquerable harmony

concussus surgo: though shaken, I rise (or, when struck I rise)

confide recte agens: doing rightly be confident

confido: I trust

confido et conquiesco: I trust and I am completely at rest

confido in probitate: I trust in my probity (i.e., honesty or uprightness)

conjuncta virtuti fortuna: fortune is joined to bravery

Consanguineus Lethi Sopor: Sleep, the Brother of Death

conscia mens recti: a mind conscious of integrity (Ovid)

conscientia mille testes: conscience is as a thousand witnesses

consensus audacium: an agreement of rash men (i.e., a conspiracy) (Cicero)

consensus facit legem: consent makes law

consensus tollit errorem: consent takes away error

consequitur quodcunque petit: he attains whatever he attempts

consilia et facta: by thought and deed

consilio et animis: by counsel (wisdom) and courage

consilio et prudentia: by counsel (wisdom) and prudence

consilio manque: by work and by counsel (wisdom)

consilio, non impetu: by counsel (wisdom), not impulse

constans et fidelis: constant and faithful

constans et fidelitate: constant and with faithfulness

constantia comes victoriæ: perseverance, a companion of victory

constantia et virtute: by constancy and virtue (or valor)

consuetudinis magna vis est: great is the force of habit (Cicero)

consuetudo est altera lex: custom is a second law

consuetudo est secunda natura: custom is a second nature (St. Augustine)

consuetudo pro lege servatur: custom is observed as law

consuetudo quasi altera natura: habit is as second nature (Cicero)

consule Planco: when Plancus was consul (i.e., in my younger days; in the good old days) (Horace)

consummatum est: it is finished (St. John 19:30; one of the Seven Last Words of Christ)

contemnit tuta procellas: secure, she despises storms

contra bonos mores: against good morals

contra stimulum calces: you kick against the goad (i.e., your opposition is in vain) (Terence)

copiose et opportune: plentiful and in time

cor ad cor loquitur: heart speaks to heart (Cardinal Newman)

cor et manus: heart and hand

cor mundum crea in me, Deus: create in me a clean heart, O God (Psalm 51:10)

cor nobile, cor immobile: a noble heart is an immovable heart

cor unum, via una: one heart, one way

coram Domino Rege: before the Lord our King (also, **coram domino rege**: before our lord the king)

coram nobis: before us

coram populo: in the presence of the people (Horace)

corda serata fero: I carry a heart locked up (pun on Lockhart family name)

coronat virtus cultores suos: virtue crowns her votaries

corpus sine pectore: a body without a soul (Horace)

cos ingeniorum: a whetstone to their wit

crambe repetita: warmed-over cabbage (i.e., the same old thing) (Juvenal)

cras credemus, hodie nihil: tomorrow we will believe, not today

crede Byron: trust Byron (motto of Lord Byron)

credite posteri: believe it, posterity (Horace)

credo, Domine: Lord, I believe

credo et videbo: I believe, and I shall see

credo quia absurdum (est): I believe it because it is absurd (Tertullian)

credo quia impossibile (est): I believe it because it is impossible (attributed to Tertullian)

credo ut intelligam: I believe so that I might understand (i.e., belief precedes knowledge) (St. Augustine)

credula res amor est: a credulous thing is love (Ovid)

crescat scientia, vita excolatur: where knowledge increases, life is enriched (motto of the University of Chicago)

crescere ex aliquo: raising oneself through the fall of another

crescit eundo: it grows as it goes (motto of New Mexico)

crescit occulto velut arbor ævo: it grows as a tree with a hidden life (Horace)

crescit sub pondere virtus: virtue grows under oppression

crescite et multiplicamini: increase and multiply (motto of Maryland)

crescitur cultu: it is increased by cultivation

creta an carbone notandum: whether to be marked with chalk or charcoal (i.e., as good or bad)

cribro aquam haurire: to draw water with a sieve

crocodili lacrimæ: crocodile tears (Erasmus)

cruce, dum spiro, fido: while I have breath, I trust in the Cross

cruci dum spiro fido: while I breathe, I trust in the Cross

crux mea stella: the Cross is my star

crux mihi ancora: the Cross is my anchor

crux mihi grata quies: the Cross is my pleasing rest

crux salutem confert: the Cross confers salvation

cui bono?: for whose benefit is it? (Cicero)

cui debeo fidus: faithful to whom I owe faith

cui malo?: to whose detriment?; whom does it harm? (Cicero)

cuique suum: to each his own

cujus regio, ejus religio: whose region, his religion (i.e., the faith of the people is determined by their king)

cum corde: with the heart

cum crepitat, sonora silent: when it rattles, loud words subside

cum dilectione hominum et odio vitiorum: with love for humanity and hatred of sins (St. Augustine)

cum grano salis: with a grain of salt (i.e., with some allowance or room for doubt) (Pliny the Elder)

cum plena est, sit emula solis: when full, she may rival the sun

cum pudore læta fœcunditas: happy fecundity accompanied by modesty

cum tacent, clamant: with their silence, they cry out (i.e., silence speaks louder than words) (Cicero)

cum tempore mutamur: we change with time

cunctando restituit rem: he restored the cause of Rome by delay (Ennius, said of Fabius)

cuneus cuneum trudit: wedge drives wedge

cur (or **quid**) **me persequeris?:** why do you persecute me? (after Acts 9:5)

cura cura repulsa nova: the new drives out the old (Ovid)

curiosa felicitas: nice felicity of expression (Petronius)

curiosis fabricavit inferos: he fashioned hell for the inquisitive (St. Augustine)

currente calamo: with a running pen (i.e., quickly or fluently)

currentem tu quidem: (fig.) you spur a willing horse

currus bovem trahit: the cart draws the ox (i.e., to put the cart before the horse)

cursum intendimus alis: we wing our way

curta supellex: scanty supply of furniture (i.e., meager stock of knowledge)

custodi civitatem, Domine: keep the city, O Lord

custos morum: a guardian of customs (or morals)

D

da gloriam Deo: give glory to God

d-a p-e-c-u-n-i-a-m: give money (C.J. Weber, who called this phrase the Vatican's Ten Commandments in Ten Letters)

da veniam lacrymis: forgive these tears

dabit qui dedit: he will give who gave

dant vires gloriam: strength gives glory

dapes inemptæ: dainties unbought (i.e., home produce) (Horace)

dare cervices: give the neck (i.e., submit to the executioner)

dare fatis vela: to give the sails to fate (Virgil)

dare pondus idonea fumo: to give weight to smoke (i.e., to give importance to trifles) (Persius)

dat Deus incrementum: God gives the increase

data fata secutus: following what is decreed by fate (Virgil)

de die in diem: from day to day

de filo pendet: it hangs by a thread

de fumo in flammam: out of the smoke into the flame (i.e., out of the frying pan and into the fire)

de industria: industriously

de lana caprina: concerning goat's wool (i.e., a worthless matter)

de minimis non curat lex: the law does not concern itself with trifles

de monte alto: from a high mountain

de nihilo nihil: from nothing, nothing can come (Persius)

de nimium: not too much

de pilo pendet: it hangs by a hair

de præscientia Dei: of the foreknowledge of God

de profundis: out of the depths

de propaganda fide: for propagating the faith

de publico est elatus: he was buried at the public expense (Livy)

De Sapientia Veterum: On the Wisdom of the Ancients (Francis Bacon, title of a work)

debellare superbos: to overthrow the proud (Virgil)

debit Deus his quoque finem: God will put an end to these as well (Virgil)

debito justitiæ: by debt of justice

decet imperatorem stantem mori: an emperor ought to die standing (i.e., at his post) (Vespasian)

decies repetita placebit: though ten times repeated, it still is pleasing (usually said of a play or a musical masterpiece) (Horace)

decori decus addit avito: he adds honor to his ancestral honor

decrevi: I have decreed

decus et tutamen: honor and defense

dedimus potestatem: we have given power

defendit numerus junctæque umbone phalanges: their numbers and their compact array protect them (Juvenal)

defensor fidei: defender of the faith (a motto of the English monarchy)

deficiunt vires: strength is wanting

Dei gratia: by the grace of God (a motto of Canada)

Dei gratias: thanks be to God

Dei irati: the wrath of God

Dei memor, gratus amicis: mindful of God, grateful to friends

Dei plena sunt omnia: all things are full of God (Cicero)

Dei providentia juvat: God's providence assists

delectando pariterque monendo: by giving pleasure and at the same time instructing (Horace; said of a well-written book)

delectare in Domino: to delight in the Lord

delenda est Carthago: Carthage must be destroyed (Cato the Elder)

deliciæ humani generis: the delight of mankind (a reference to the Emperor Titus)

deliramenta doctrinæ: the madness of scholars (i.e., delirious with too much learning)

denique cælum (or, **denique cœlum**): heaven at last (Crusaders' battle cry)

dens theonina: a slanderous tooth

dente superbo: with a disdainful tooth (Horace)

Deo adjuvante non timendum: with God's help, nothing need be feared

Deo date: give unto God

deo dignus vindice nodus: a knot worthy of a god to unloose (i.e., a great dilemma)

Deo duce, ferro comitante: God for guide, sword for companion

Deo duce, fortuna comitante: God for guide, fortune for companion

Deo ducente: with God's guidance

Deo et Patriæ: for God and Country (motto of the University of Saskatchewan)

Deo et regi fidelis: loyal to God and king

Deo favente: with God's favor

Deo fidelis et patria: faithful to God and country

Deo fidelis et regi: faithful to God and the king

Deo fidens persistas: always faithful to God

Deo gloria noster: our glory to God

Deo gratias: thanks be to God

Deo honor et gloria: to God the honor and glory

Deo ignoto: to the unknown God

Deo juvante: with God's help (motto of Monaco)

Deo monente: with God's warning (i.e., a warning from God)

Deo, non fortuna: from God, not fortune (or chance)

Deo, Optimo, Maximo (D.O.M.): to God, the Best, the Greatest (motto of the Benedictines)

Deo patria tibi: for God, homeland, and yourself

Deo, patriæ, amicis: for God, homeland, and friends

Deo patriæque fidelis: faithful to God and country

Deo, regi, patriæ: to God, king, and country

Deo, regi, vicino: for God, king, and neighbor

Deo, reipublicæ, amicis: to God, the republic, and friends

Deo servire regnare est: to serve God is to reign

Deo volente (D.V. or d.v.): God willing

deorum cibus est: it is food for the gods

depressus extollor: having been depressed, I am exalted

desideratum: a thing desired (but sadly lacking)

desiderium spe vacuum: a desire devoid of hope

despicio terrena: I despise earthly things

detur digniori: let it be given to those most worthy

detur pulchriori: let it be given to the most beautiful (the inscription on the golden apple of discord)

Deum cole, regem serva: worship God, serve the king

Deum colit, qui novit: the one who knows God worships Him (Seneca)

deum esse credimus: we believe in the existence of God

Deus alit eos: God feeds them

Deus avertat!: God forbid!

Deus clypeus meus: God is my shield

Deus dabit vela: God will fill the sails

Deus det!: God grant!

deus est in pectore nostro: there is a god within our heart (Ovid)

Deus est regit qui omnia: there is a God who rules all things

Deus est summum bonum: God is the greatest good

Deus est suum esse: God is his own being

deus ex machina: a god from a machine

Deus fortitudo mea: God is my strength

Deus gubernat navem: God pilots the ship

Deus id vult (or simply, Deus vult): God wills it (rallying cry of the First Crusade)

Deus major columna: God is the greatest of supports

Deus mihi providebit: God will provide for me

Deus misereatur: God be merciful

Deus nobis hæc otia fecit: God has given us this place of rest (Virgil)

Deus nobiscum, quis contra?: God with us, who can be against us?

Deus non reliquit memoriam humilium: God hath not forgotten the humble

Deus noster refugium: our God is our refuge

Deus omnibus quod sat est suppeditat: God supplies enough to all

Deus pascit corvos: God feeds the ravens

Deus pastor meus: God is my shepherd

Deus protector noster: God is our protector

Deus providebit: God will provide

Deus salutaris noster: God our Savior

Deus sive natura: God or nature (Spinoza)

Deus solamen: God is my comfort

Deus tuetur: God defends

Deus vobiscum: God be with you

Deus vult (also, **Deus id vult**): God wills [it] (rallying cry of the First Crusade)

dextra cruce vincit: my right hand conquers by the Cross

dextra fideque: by my right hand and my fidelity

dextra mihi Deus: my right hand is to me as a god (Virgil)

dextras dare: to give right hands (i.e., to greet one another or to promise mutual support)

dextro tempore: at the right time; at a lucky moment

di me tuentur: the gods my protectors (Horace)

di meliora: God forbid!

di (or **dii**) **pia facta vident:** the gods see virtuous deeds (Ovid)

dicamus bona verba: let us speak words of good omen (Terence)

dicta docta pro datis: smooth words in place of gifts (Plautus)

dicta fides sequitur: the promise is no sooner given than fulfilled (Ovid)

dicta tibi est lex: the law is laid before you (Horace)

dictis facta suppetant: let deeds suffice for words (Plautus)

dictum factum (also, **dictum ac factum**): said and done (i.e., no sooner said than done)

dictum sapienti sat est: a word to the wise is sufficient (Plautus and Terence)

diem perdidi: I have lost a day (i.e., I have done nothing of worth) (attributed to Titus)

dies faustus: a lucky day

dies infaustus: an unlucky day

dignum et justum est: it is right and fitting

dignus hoc indice nodus: a knot worthy to be untied by such hands (i.e., a difficulty calling for experienced hands) (Horace)

dii majores et minores: gods of a higher and lower degree

Dii rexque secundent: may God and the king favor us

diis aliter visum: it has seemed otherwise to the gods (Virgil)

diligenter et fideliter: diligently and faithfully

diligentia: diligence

diligentia ditat: industry enriches

diligentia fortior: stronger by diligence

dira necessitas: cruel necessity (Horace)

dirige nos, Domine: direct us, O Lord

dirigo: I direct (motto of Maine)

dis aliter visum: it seemed otherwise to the gods (Virgil)

dis bene juvantibus: with the help of the gods

dis ducibus: under the direction of the gods

disce aut discede: learn or leave

disce et doce: learn and teach (motto of the University of Sheffield)

disce pati: learn to endure

discere docendo: to learn by teaching

disciplina, fide, perseverantia: by discipline, fidelity, and perseverance

disciplina præsidium civitatis: the instruction and protection of the state (motto of the University of Texas)

discors concordia (or, **concordia discors**): harmony in discord; a dissonant harmony (i.e., agreeing to differ) (Horace and Ovid)

discretis sua virtus inest: when separated, each has its own virtue

disjecti membra poëtæ: limbs of a dismembered poet (sometimes said of a plagiarized work) (Horace)

disponendo me, non mutando me: by disposing of me, not by changing me

distantia jungit: it joins things that were apart

ditat Deus: God enriches (motto of Arizona)

ditat servata fides: faith preserved enriches

diversa ab illis virtute valemus: we are strong because our skill differs from theirs

divide et impera: divide and rule

divina natura dedit agros, ars humana ædificavit urbes: divine nature gave us the fields, human art built our cities (Latin version of the Spanish motto over the Santa Barbara County Court House) (Varro)

divinitus accidit: it happened miraculously

divitiæ virum faciunt: riches make the man

dixit Dominus: the Lord has spoken it

do ut des: I give that you may give (a maxim of Bismarck)

doce ut discas: teach that you may learn

docendo discimus: we learn by teaching

docta ignorantia: learned ignorance (Nicolas of Cusa)

domi militiæque: at war and at peace

domina omnium et regina ratio: reason is the mistress and queen of all things (Cicero)

Domine, dirige nos: O Lord, direct us (motto of the city of London)

Domine, illuminatio mea!: O Lord, my light!

Domine, non sum dignus: O Lord, I am not worthy

domini pudet, non servitutis: I am ashamed of my master, not of my servitude (Seneca)

Domini quid reddam?: what shall I render unto the Lord?

Domino, Optimo, Maximo (D.O.M.): to the Lord, the best, the greatest (alternate motto of the Benedictine Order)

Dominus a dextris: the Lord is on my right hand

Dominus fecit: the Lord hath done it

Dominus fortissima turris: the Lord is the strong tower

Dominus illuminatio mea: the Lord is my light (motto of Oxford University)

Dominus illuminatio mea, et salus mea, quem timebo?: the Lord is my light and my salvation, whom shall I fear? (Psalm 26:1)

Dominus petra mea: the Lord is my rock

Dominus providebit: the Lord will provide

Dominus vobiscum: the Lord be with you

domitæ naturæ: of a tame nature

domus et placens uxor: a home and a pleasing wife (Horace)

dona nobis pacem: grant us peace

donatio mortis causa: a gift made in prospect of death

donec impleat: until it fill

donec impleat orbem: until it fill the globe

donec totum impleat orbem: until it fills the whole world (motto of the Knights of the Crescent)

dono dedit: given as a gift

dormitat Homerus: even Homer nods off (i.e., sometimes even the best of us is caught napping) (Horace)

duabus sellis sedere (also, **duabus sedere sellis**): to sit in two saddles (or, on two stools)

ducat amor Dei: let the love of God lead us

duce et auspice: under his guidance and auspices

duces tecum: bring with you

ducit amor patriæ: love of country leads me

ducit Dominus: the Lord leads

ducitur, non trahitur: he is led, not drawn

ductor dubitantium: a guide to those in doubt

dulce domum: sweet home

dulce periculum: sweet danger

dulce quod utile: what is useful is sweet

dulce sodalicium (or, **dulce sodalitium**): sweet society (i.e., sweet association of friends)

dulcior melle: sweeter than honey

dulcis pro patria labor: labor for one's country is sweet

dulcius ex asperis: sweeter after difficulties

dum fortuna fuit: while fortune lasted

dum se bene gesserit: so long as his behavior is good

dum spiritus hos regit artus: so long as the spirit of life controls these limbs (Virgil)

dum spiro, spero: while I breathe, I hope (a motto of South Carolina)

dum tacent clamant: though they are silent, they cry aloud (i.e., their silence speaks loudly)

dum vita est, spes est: while there is life, there is hope

dum vivimus, vivamus: while we live, let us live (motto of the Epicureans)

dum vivo, prosum: while I live, I do good

duplici spe uti: to have a double hope

durante bene placito (or, **durante beneplacito**). during his good pleasure; at the pleasure of

durante vita: during life

durum telum necessitas: necessity is a hard weapon

dux fœmina facti (or, **dux femina facti**): the leader of the action was a woman (Virgil)

dux vitæ ratio: reason is the guide of life

E

e fungis nati homines: men born of mushrooms (i.e., upstarts)

e pluribus unum: out of many one (motto of the United States of America)

e se finxit velut araneus: he spun from himself like a spider (i.e., he relied on his own resources)

e tellure effodiuntur opes: our wealth is dug out of the earth

ea fama vagatur: that report is in circulation

ecce Agnus Dei: behold the Lamb of God

ecce homo: behold the man (Pontius Pilate, St. John 19:5)

ecce iterum Crispinus!: here's that Crispinus again! (i.e., said of someone who shows up at every event) (Juvenal)

ecce quam bonum: behold, how good (motto of the University of the South)

ecce signum: behold the sign (i.e., here is the proof)

Ecclesia non moritur: the Church does not die

edo, ergo ego sum (also, **edo, ergo sum**): I eat, therefore I am

effloresco: I flourish

ego cogito, ergo sum (also, **cogito, ergo sum**): I think, therefore I am (Descartes)

ego ero post principia: I will keep behind the first rank (i.e., I will stay out of harm's way) (Terence)

ego et rex meus: I and my king (an insolent remark attributed to Cardinal Wolsey)

ego hoc feci: I have done this; this was my doing

ego me bene habeo: with me all is well (last words of Burrus)

ego meorum solus sum meus: I myself am the only friend I have (Terence)

ego nolo Cæsar esse: I don't want to be Cæsar (Florus)

ego primum tollo, nominor quoniam leo: I will take first, for my name is lion (i.e., because I am the strongest) (Phædrus)

ego spem pretio non emo: I do not purchase hope for a price (i.e., I do not buy a pig in a poke) (Terence)

ego sum, ergo omnia sunt: I am, therefore all things are

ego sum lux mundi: I am the light of the world (St. John 8:12)

ego sum ostium ovium: I am the gate of the sheep (St. John 10:7)

ego sum pastor bonus: I am the good shepherd (St. John 10:11)

ego sum resurrectio et vita: I am the resurrection and the life (St. John 11:25)

ego sum vitis vera: I am the true vine (St. John 15:1)

ego te intus et in cute novi: I know you even under the skin (Persius)

egomet mi ignosco: I myself pardon myself (Horace)

egomet sum mihi imperator: I am my own ruler (Horace)

elatum a deo non deprimat: upheld by God, I am not depressed

elegantiæ arbiter: the master of taste (Tacitus)

elegit: he has chosen

elephantem ex musca facis: you are making an elephant out of a fly (i.e., making a mountain out of a molehill)

eloquentia fortitudine præstantior: eloquence, surpassing strength

eloquentia sagitta: eloquence [is] my arrow

emeritus (fem. **emerita;** pl. **emeriti**): a veteran (i.e., an honorary title for a person who has retired from official duties)

emunctæ naris: of nice scent (i.e., discernment) (Horace)

en altera quæ vehat Argo: behold, another Argo to carry them

ense et aratro: with sword and plow

ense petit placidam sub libertate quietem: by the sword she seeks peaceful quiet under liberty (motto of Massachusetts)

eo instanti: at that instant

eo magis præfulgebant quod non videbantur (pl.): they shone with a greater splendor the more they were not seen (Tacitus)

eo magis præfulgebat quod non videbatur (sing.): he shone with a greater splendor the more he was not seen (Tacitus)

eodem collyrio mederi omnibus: to cure all by the same ointment

eodem genere mali: in the same kind of evil

Epicuri de grege porcus (or **porcum**): a hog from the drove of Epicurus (i.e., a glutton) (Horace)

epulis accumbere divum: to recline at the feast of the gods (Virgil)

eques ipso melior Bellerophonte: a better horseman than Bellerophon himself (Horace)

equis virisque: with horse and foot (i.e., with all one's might)

equo ne credite, Teucri: do not trust the horse, Trojans

erectus, non elatus: exalted but not elated

eripuit cœlo fulmen sceptrumque tyrannis: he snatched the lightning from heaven and the scepter from tyrants (said of Benjamin Franklin)

eris mihi magnus Apollo: you shall be my great Apollo (Virgil)

erit altera merces: the one or the other will be my reward

ero quod spero: I will again hope

errare humanum est: to err is human

errores Ulixis: the wanderings of Ulysses

esse quam videri: to be rather than to seem (motto of North Carolina)

est concordia fratrum: harmony becomes brothers

est deus in nobis: there is a god within us (Ovid)

est egentissimus in sua re: he is in very straitened circumstances

est mihi honori: it reflects well on me

est mihi sorte datum: it is given to me by chance

est nulla fallacia: there is no deceit

est voluntas Dei: it is the will of God

esto fidelis: be faithful

esto perpetua: may she be everlasting (dying words of Paolo Sarpi, said of Venice; also, motto of Idaho)

esto perpetuum: let it be everlasting

esto quod esse videris: be what you seem to be

esto semper fidelis: be ever faithful

et decus et pretium recti: both the ornament and the reward of virtue

et in Arcadia ego: I too am in Arcadia (a tomb inscription)

et manu et corde: both with hand and heart

et mea messis erit: my harvest will also arrive

et omnes sancti: and all the saints

et sic de ceteris: and so of the rest

et sic de similibus: and so of the like (i.e., this also applies in similar cases)

et vitam impendere vero: keep the truth at the hazard of life (a motto of Rousseau)

etiam periere ruinæ: even the ruins have perished (i.e., there is nothing left) (Lucan)

euge, poëta!: well done, poet! (Persius)

eureka: I have found it (motto of California, from the Greek)

ex abrupto: without preparation

ex abundante cautela: from excessive precaution

ex æquo et bono: justly and equitably

ex arduis perpetuum nomen: from difficulties, lasting fame

ex auribus cognoscitur asinus: an ass is known by its ears

ex bello, pax: from war, peace

ex campo victoriæ: from the field of victory

ex concordia victoriæ spes: hope of victory through union

ex debito justitiæ: from what is due to justice; from a regard to justice

ex dono Dei: by the gift of God

ex duris gloria: from suffering arises glory

ex fide fortis: strong through faith

ex fumo dare lucem: to give light from smoke

ex maximo minimum: from the greatest, least

ex merito: from merit

ex mero motu: from a mere motion, (i.e., of one's own volition)

ex necessitate rei: from the necessity of the thing

ex nihilo nihil fit: from nothing, nothing is made

ex officio: by virtue of office (i.e., as a matter of duty)

ex pace ubertas: from peace, plenty

ex pede Herculem: from the foot we judge Hercules

ex pluribus unum facere: from many to make one (St. Augustine)

ex post facto: after the fact

ex scintilla incendium: from a spark a conflagration

ex tempore: on the spur of the moment; unrehearsed (Cicero)

ex umbra in solem: from the shade into the sun

ex umbris et imaginibus in veritatem: from shadows and types to the reality (Cardinal Newman)

ex undis aratra: plows from the waves

ex ungue leonem: from a claw, the lion (i.e., the lion is known by its claws)

ex uno disce omnes: from one learn all (i.e., from one we judge the rest)

ex uno omnia: all things are from one

ex urna resurgam: I shall rise again from the urn (i.e., from the tomb)

ex vitulo bos fit: from a calf an ox grows up

ex vulnere salus: healing (or salvation) from a wound

exaltabit honore: it will exalt with honor

excelsior: ever higher (motto of New York State)

exceptis excipiendis: the requisite exceptions being made

excessere metum mea jam bona: the blessings I now enjoy transcend fear (Ovid)

excessit ex ephebis: he exceeds twenty years (i.e., he has come to the age of manhood)

excitabat fluctus in simpulo: he was stirring up billows in a ladle (i.e., a tempest in a teapot) (Cicero)

excitari, non hebescere: to be spirited, not sluggish (Terence)

exclusa opes omnes: all hope is gone (Plautus)

exeat: let him depart

exegi monumentum ære perennius: I have raised a monument more lasting than bronze (Horace)

exempla sunt odiosa: examples are odious

exercitatio potest omnia: perseverance conquers all things (also, practice makes perfect)

exoriare aliquis nostris ex ossibus ultor: an avenger shall arise from my bones (Virgil)

expectada dies aderat: the longed for day is at hand (Virgil)

expende Hannibalem: weigh the dust of Hannibal (Juvenal)

experientia docet: experience teaches (Tacitus)

experimentum crucis: the experience of the cross (i.e., a guidepost for others; also, truth elicited by force, such as torture)

expertus dico: I speak from experience

expertus loquitur: he speaks from experience

expertus metuit: the expert is afraid (i.e., once burnt, twice shy) (Horace)

extinguo: I extinguish

extra ecclesiam nulla salus: there is no salvation outside the Church

extra muros: beyond the walls

extra telorum jactum: beyond throwing range; out of range

extremis malis extrema remedia: extreme remedies for extreme evils

F

faber suæ fortunæ: the maker of his own fortune (Sallust)

fac et excusa: do it and so justify yourself

fac et spera: do and hope

fac simile: do the like (i.e., a close imitation of an original)

facere non possum quin: I cannot but

facile princeps: easily the first (i.e., an undisputed leader)

facilius sit Nili caput invenire: it would be easier to discover the source of the Nile

facinus majoris abollæ: a crime of a very deep dye (i.e., one committed by a respected person) (Juvenal)

facio liberos ex liberi libris libraque: I make free men out of children with books and balance (motto of St. John's College, Annapolis)

facta non verba: deeds not words

factotum: a "do everything" (i.e., a jack-of-all-trades)

factum est: it is done

fæx populi: the dregs of the people

fama clamosa: a current scandal

fama perennis erit: your fame shall be enduring

fama semper vivat!: may his/her fame live forever!

fama volat: the report (or rumor) flies (Virgil)

famam extendere factis: to extend one's fame by valiant deeds (Virgil)

fare fac: speak and act

fari quæ sentiat: to say what one feels (Horace)

farrago libelli: the medley of that book of mine (Juvenal)

fasti et nefasti dies: lucky and unlucky days

Fata obstant: the Fates oppose (Virgil)

Fata viam invenient: the Fates will find a way (Virgil)

Fata vocant: the Fates call (Virgil)

faveat fortuna: let fortune favor

favente Deo: by God's favor

favete linguis: favor with your tongues (i.e., be respectful; be silent) (Horace and Ovid)

fax mentis honestæ gloria: glory is the torch of an honorable mind

fax mentis incendium gloriæ: the flame of (or passion for) glory is the torch of the mind

fecit: he did it

felices errore suo: happy in their error (Lucan)

felix culpa!: O fault most fortunate! (St. Augustine's allusion to the Fall of humanity that necessitated the coming of the Redeemer)

felix hora: a lucky occasion (i.e., a golden opportunity)

felix, heu nimium felix: happy, alas, too happy (Virgil)

feræ naturæ: of a wild nature

ferendo non feriendo: by bearing not by striking

feret ad astra virtus: virtue will bear us to the sky

feriunt summis fulmina (or **fulgura**) **montes:** lightning strikes the mountain tops

ferro, non gladio: by iron, not by sword

ferrum ferro acuitur: iron is sharpened by iron

fert palmam mereat: he bears the palm, let him deserve it

fervet opus: the work boils (Virgil)

festina lente: make haste slowly (Suetonius, attributed to Cæsar Augustus)

FIAT (Flatus Ignis Aqua Terra), or **fiat:** let it be done (air, fire, water, earth)

fiat Dei voluntas: God's will be done

fiat experimentum in corpore vili: let the experiment be done upon a worthless body (or object)

fiat ignem: let there be fire

fiat justitia: let justice be done

fiat justitia et pereat mundus: let justice be done though the world perish (motto of Emperor Ferdinand I)

fiat justitia, ruat cælum (or **cœlum**): let justice be done, though the heavens fall

fiat justitiam, pereat mundus: let justice be done, and the world perish

fiat lux: let there be light (Genesis 1:3; motto of the University of California)

fiat pax florent justitia: let peace be made, justice be done

fiat voluntas tua: Thy will be done (St. Matthew 6:10)

fictio cedit veritati: fiction yields to truth

fide et amore: by faith and love

fide et fiducia: by faith and confidence

fide et fortitudine: by faith and fortitude

fide et labore: by faith and labor

fide et literis: by faith and learning

fide et virtute: by faith and valor

fide fortuna forti: faith is stronger than fortune

fide, non armis: by faith, not by arms

fide, sed cui vide: trust, but be careful whom

fidei coticula crux: the Cross is the touchstone of faith

fidei defensor: defender of the faith (a motto of the English monarchs)

fidelis ad urnam: faithful to the urn (i.e., until death)

fidelis et audax: faithful and daring

fidelis usque ad mortem: faithful even to death

fidelitas vincit: fidelity prevails

fideliter: faithfully

fideliter et constanter: faithfully and firmly

fidem servabo genusque: I will serve faith and family

fidem servo: I keep faith

fidens et constans: faithful and constant

fides ante intellectum: faith before understanding

fides et justitia: fidelity and justice

fides facit fidem: faith creates faith; confidence begets confidence

fides hoc uno, virtusque probantur: virtue and faith are tested by this alone

fides non timet: faith does not fear

fides nos loricat: faith is our breastplate

fides probata coronat: faith approved confers a crown

fides Punica: Punic faith (i.e., treachery)

fides servanda est: faith must be kept (Plautus)

fides sit penes auctorem: credit this to the author (i.e., let the person supplying the facts be responsible for their accuracy)

fides, spes, charitas: faith, hope, love (1 Corinthians 13:13)

fidus Achates: faithful Achates (a trustworthy friend of Aeneas) (Virgil)

fidus et audax: faithful and daring (or courageous)

fieri facias: cause it to be done; see that it be done

filius istarum lacrymarum: a child of those tears (St. Augustine)

filius nullius: the son of no one (i.e., a bastard son)

filius terræ: the son of the earth (i.e., a person of low birth)

finem respice: look to the end (i.e., consider the outcome)

finem transcendit habendi: he goes beyond the proper limit of acquiring wealth (Paradin)

finis coronat opus: the end crowns the work

firmior quo paratior: the stronger the better prepared

firmor ad fidem: I am true to the faith

firmus maneo: I remain steadfast

fit via vi: a way is made by force

flagrante bello: while the war blazes (i.e., during hostilities)

flagrante delicto: while the crime blazes (i.e., caught in the act)

flebile ludibrium: a farce to weep at (i.e., a tragic farce)

flecti, non frangi: to be bent, not broken

flet victus, victor interiit: the conquered one weeps, the conqueror is ruined

floreat domus: may this house flourish

floreat Etona: may Eton flourish (motto of Eton College)

floreat majestas: let majesty flourish

floreat qui laborat: let the one who labors flourish

flores curat Deus: God takes care of the flowers

floriferis ut apes in saltibus omnia libant: as bees taste of everything in the flowery meadows (Lucretius)

flos ipse civitatis: the very flower of the state (Apuleius)

flos juventutis (or, **flos juvenum**): the flower of youth (or, the flower of young men) (Livy)

flosculi sententiarum: florets of thought

fluctuat nec mergitur: she is tossed by the waves but she does not sink (motto of Paris, which has a ship as its emblem)

fluctus in simpulo exitare: to raise a tempest in a teapot (Cicero)

fluvius cum mari certas: you but a river, and contending with the ocean

fons et origo: the source and origin

fons et origo mali: the source and origin of the evil

fons malorum: the origin of evil

fons omnium viventium: the fountain of all living things

forensis strepitus: the clamor of the forum

forma flos, fama flatus: beauty is a flower, fame is a breath

fors et virtus miscentur in unum: fortune and valor are mixed into one (Virgil)

fors juvat audentes: fortune favors the brave (Claudian)

forte et fidele: strong and loyal

fortem te præbe: be brave!

fortes fortuna (ad)juvat: fortune favors the strong (or brave) (Terence)

forti non ignavo: to the brave man, not to the coward

fortis atque fidelis: strong and faithful

fortis est ut mors dilectio: love is strong as death (Song of Solomon 8:6)

fortis est veritas: strong is the truth

fortis et celer: strong and swift

fortis et egregius: brave and distinguished

fortis et fidelis: brave and faithful

fortis et hospitalis: strong and hospitable

fortis et liber: strong and free (motto of Alberta)

fortis et velox: strong and swift

fortis fortuna adjuvat: fortune aids the brave (Terence)

fortis in arduis: brave in difficulties

fortiter: boldly

fortiter et fidelis: brave and faithful

fortiter et fideliter: boldly and faithfully

fortiter et honeste: boldly and honorably
fortiter et recte: bravely and uprightly
fortiter et suaviter: firmly and mildly
fortiter, fideliter, feliciter: fearlessly, faithfully, successfully
fortiter geret crucem: he will bravely bear the Cross
fortitudine: with fortitude
fortitudine et decore: by boldness and gracefulness
fortitudine et labore: by fortitude and labor
fortitudine et prudentia: by courage and prudence
fortitudo et prudentia: fortitude and prudence
fortuna favente: by the favor of fortune
fortuna favet fatuis: fortune favors fools
fortuna favet fortibus: fortune favors the strong (or brave)
fortuna juvat audaces: fortune favors the brave
fortuna mea in bello campo: fortune is mine in a fair fight
fortuna meliores sequitur: fortune follows the better man (Sallust)
fortuna sequatur: let fortune follow
fortunæ cætera mando: I commit the rest to fortune (Ovid)
fortunæ filius: a child of fortune; a favorite son (Horace)
fortunæ naufragium: a shipwreck of fortune (Apuleius)
fortunæ objectum esse: abandoned to fate
fortunæ vicissitudines: the vicissitudes of fortune
fossoribus orti: sprung from ditch diggers (i.e., from humble origins)
fragrat, delectat, et sanat: it smells sweet, is pleasing, and healthful
frangas, non flectes: you may break me, but you shall not bend me
frons est animi janua: the forehead is the door of the mind (Cicero)
frons hominem præfert: the forehead reveals the man
fronte capillata, post est occasio calva: hairy in front, occasion is bald behind (Dionysius Cato)
fronti nulla fides: there is no trusting to appearances (Juvenal)
fructo cognoscitur arbor: a tree is known by its fruit
fruges consumere nati: born to consume the fruits of the earth (Horace)
frustra operam: they work in vain; labor lost (Terence)
frustra vigilant: they keep watch in vain; they stand guard in vain
fugaces labuntur anni: the fleeting years glide by
fugam fecit: he has taken to flight
fugit hora: the hour flies (or, time flies) (Ovid)
fugit irreparabile (or irreparabile) tempus: irretrievable time flies (Virgil)
fuimus: we have been (i.e., we have made our mark)
fuimus et sub Deo ermus: we have been, and we shall be under God
fuimus Troës: we were once Trojans (i.e., our day is over) (Virgil)

fuit Ilium: Troy was (i.e., its day is over) (Virgil)

fulcrum dignitotis virus: virtue is the support of dignity

fulget virtus: virtue shines forth

fulmen brutum (or, **brutum fulmen**): a harmless thunderbolt (i.e., an empty threat)

fulminis instar: like lightning

fumos vendere: to sell smoke (Martial)

functus officio: discharged of duty

furens quid fœmina possit: that which an enraged woman can accomplish (Virgil)

furor arma ministrat: rage supplies arms (Virgil)

furor loquendi: a rage for speaking

furor poëticus: the poet's frenzy

furor scribendi: a rage for writing

G

galea spes salutis: hope is the helmet of salvation

Gaude, Maria Virgo: Rejoice, Virgin Mary

gaudeamus (igitur): let us be joyful (therefore)

gaudeo: I rejoice

gaudet tentamine virtus: virtue rejoices in trial (i.e., in being tested)

gaudium adfero: I bring good tidings

genius loci: the presiding genius of the place (Virgil)

gens togata: the nation with the toga (i.e., Rome)

genti æquus utrique: worthy of both families

genus irritabile vatum: the irritable race of poets (Horace)

Gloria in Excelsis Deo: Glory be to God Most High (the "greater doxology")

gloria invidiam vicisti: glory has vanquished envy (Sallust)

Gloria Patri: Glory be to the Father (the "lesser doxology")

Gloria Tibi, Domine: Glory be to Thee, O Lord

gloria virtutis umbra: glory is the shadow of virtue (i.e., its attendant and companion)

gradatim: by degrees; step by step

gradatim plena: full by degrees

gradatim vincimus: we conquer by degrees

gradu diverso, via una: the same way by different steps

Græculus esuriens: hungry young Greek (Juvenal, meant disparagingly)

grandescunt aucta labore: they grow with increase of toil

grata naturam vincit: grace overcomes nature

grata quies: rest is pleasing

grata testudo: the pleasing lyre

gratia Dei: by the grace of God

gratia gratiam parit: kindness produces kindness

gratia misericordia et pax: grace, mercy, and peace

gratia placendi: the grace (or satisfaction) of pleasing

gratia vobis et pax: grace to you and peace

gratiam referendam: a favor ought to be returned

gratias agimus Tibi: we give Thee thanks

gratis asseritur: brought forth for nothing (i.e., it is asserted without being proved)

gratis dictum: said for nothing

grato animo: with grateful heart (or mind)

graviora manent: more grievous perils remain (i.e., the worst is yet to come)

grex venalium: a venal flock (Suetonius)

H

habemus confitentem reum: we have an accused person who pleads guilty (Cicero)

habent sua fata libelli: books have their own destiny (Terentianus Maurus; also attributed to Horace)

habeo non habeor: I hold but am not held

habere derelictui rem suam: to neglect one's affairs (Aulus Gellius)

habere et dispertire: to have and to distribute

habere, non haberi: to hold, not to be held

habes confitentem reum: the robber confesses the crime (Petronius)

habet salem: he has wit; he is witty

habitarunt di quoque sylvas: the gods also dwelt in the woods (Virgil)

hac illac perfluo: I flow this way and that

hac mercede placet: I accept the terms

hac sunt (in) fossa Bedæ venerabilis ossa: in this grave lie the bones of the Venerable Bede (the inscription on Bede's tomb)

hac virtutis iter: this is the path to virtue

hæc generi incrementa fides: this faith will bring an increase to our race

hæc omnia transeunt: all these things pass away

hæc studia oblectant: these studies are our delight

hæc tibi dona fero: these gifts I bear to thee (motto of Newfoundland)

hærent infixi pectore vultus: his face is engraved on her heart (Virgil)

Hannibal ad portas: Hannibal is at the gate (i.e., the enemy is close at hand) (adapted from Cicero)

haud facile emergunt: they do easily rise up

haud ignara ac non incauta futuri: neither ignorant nor careless of the future (Horace)

haud ignota loquor: I speak of things by no means unknown (i.e., I speak of well-known events)

haud inscia ac non incauta futuri: neither ignorant nor careless of the future (Virgil)

haud nomine tantum: not in name alone

haud passibus æquis: with unequal steps (Virgil)

helluo librorum: a devourer of books (i.e., a book worm)

heroum filii: sons of heroes (motto of Wellington College)

heu pietas!, heu prisca fides!: alas for piety!, alas for the ancient faith! (Virgil)

hiatus maxime deflendus: an opening (or deficiency) very much to be deplored

hibernicis ipsis hibernior: more Irish than the Irish themselves

hic domus, hæc patria est: here our home, this our country (Virgil)

hic est mucro defensionis tuæ: this is the point of your defense (Cicero)

hic et nunc: here and now

hic et ubique: here and everywhere; also, here, there, and everywhere

hic et ubique terrarum: here and everywhere throughout the world (motto of the University of Paris)

hic finis fandi: here was an end to the discourse (i.e., here the speech ended) (Virgil)

hic hæret aqua!: here the water stops! (i.e., here is the difficulty!)

hic jacet: here lies

hic jacet lepus: here lies the hare (i.e., here lies the difficulty)

hic murus aheneus esto: let this be your brazen wall of defense

hic niger est: that one has a dark heart (Horace)

hic Rhodos, hic salta: here is Rhodes, here leap

hic terminus hæret (or **hærit**): here is the end of all things (Paradin)

hic vigilans somniat: he sleeps awake (Plautus)

hiems subest: winter is at hand

hiera picra: the sacred bitter (i.e., a medicine) (a Greek saying)

hinc illæ lacrymæ (or **lacrimæ**)!: hence these tears! (Cicero, Horace, and Virgil)

hinc lucem et pocula sacra: from hence we receive light and sacred drafts (motto of Cambridge University)

hinc orior: hence I rise

hinc sola salus: this is my only salvation

hinc spes effulget: hence hope shines forth

his ducibus: with these as guides

hoc age: this attend (i.e., concentrate)

hoc certum est: this much is certain

hoc erat in votis: this was in my prayers

hoc est corpus meum: this is my body (St. Matthew 26:26)

hoc fac et vives: do this and you shall live

hoc habet!: he has hit! (the cry of the spectators at gladiatorial contests)

hoc indictum volo: I wish this unsaid (i.e., I withdraw the statement)

hoc Latio restare canunt: they predict that this awaits Rome

hoc loco: in this place

hoc majorum virtus: this is the valor of my ancestors

hoc opus: this is (my) work

hoc opus, hic labor est: this is the task, this is the toil (i.e., there's the rub) (Virgil)

hoc opus, hoc studium: this work, this pursuit (Horace)

hoc signo vinces: by this sign you will conquer

hoc tibi est honori: this reflects well on you

hoc uno Iupiter ultor: with this alone Jupiter punishes

hoc vince: by this conquer (a variation of **in hoc signo vinces**)

hoc virtutis opus: this is virtue's work

hoc volo, hoc jubeo: this I wish, this I require (Juvenal)

hoc voluerunt: they wished this (Julius Cæsar, after the Battle of Munda in 45 BCE)

hodie animi nostri, postridie orbis: today our souls, tomorrow the world

hodie mihi, cras tibi: today for me, tomorrow for thee (i.e., mine today, yours tomorrow)

hodie nihil, cras credo: tomorrow I will trust, not today (Varro)

hodie, non cras: today, not tomorrow

hodie tibi, cras mihi: today you, tomorrow me (Marlowe, in reference to execution)

hoi polloi: the masses (a Greek phrase)

hominem pagina nostra sapit: our page relates to man (Martial)

hominem quæro: I am looking for a man (Phædrus, after Diogenes)

hominem te esse memento: remember that you are a man

homini necesse est mori: man must die (Cicero)

hominis est errare: to err is human

homo fuge!: fly, oh man!

homo homini lupus: man is a wolf to man (Plautus)

homo mensura: man is the measure (of all things) (Protagoras)

homo multarum literarum: a man of many letters (i.e., of great learning)

homo nullius coloris: a man of no party

homo sum: I am a man

homo trium literarum: a man of three letters (i.e., "fur," a thief) (Plautus)

homo unius libri: a man of one book (Thomas Aquinas's definition of a learned man)

homunculi quanti sunt!: how insignificant men are! (Plautus)

honesta paupertas prior quam opes malæ: poverty with honor is better than ill-gotten wealth

honesta quam splendida: honorable rather than showy

honeste audax: bold but honest

honestum præfero utili: I prefer honesty to utility

honestum prætulit utili: he has preferred honesty to advantage

honor Deo: honor be to God

Honor est a Nilo: Honor is from the Nile (anagram for Admiral **H**oratio **N**elson, who won the Battle of the Nile)

honor est præmium virtutis: honor is the reward of virtue (Cicero)

honor et virtus: honor and virtue

honor fidelitatis præmium: honor is the reward of fidelity

honor sequitur fugientem: honor follows the one who flees from her

honor virtutis præmium: honor is the reward of virtue

honorat mors: death confers honor

honores et præmia: honors and rewards

honores mutant mores: honors alter manners

honos alit artes: honor (or fame) nourishes the arts (Cicero)

honos (or honor) virtutes satilles: honor, the attendant of virtue

hora fugit: the hour flies (or, time flies)

horas non numero nisi serenas: I number none but shining hours (an inscription on a sun dial)

horresco referens: I shudder to relate it (sometimes said facetiously) (Virgil)

horribile dictu!: horrible to tell!

horribile visu!: horrible to see!

horror ubique: terror everywhere (motto of the Scots Guards)

horror vacui: abhorrence of a vacuum

hostis humani generis: an enemy of the human race

huic habeo non tibi: I hold it for him, not for you

humani nihil alienum: nothing that relates to man is alien to me (Terence; a motto of the Stone family)

humanum est errare: to err is human

humilitate: with humility

hypotheses non fingo: I frame no hypothesis (i.e., I deal entirely with the facts) (Sir Isaac Newton)

hysteron proteron: the last put first (i.e., to put the cart before the horse) (a Greek saying)

I

i secundo omine: go, and may all good go with you (Horace)

iacta alea esto (also, **jacta alea esto**): let the die be cast (Julius Cæsar, as quoted by Suetonius)

iam iam (or, **jam jam**): now now (i.e., forthwith)

iamque opus exegi: and now I have finished the work (Ovid)

id genus omne: all the persons of that ilk (Horace)

idem velle atque idem nolle: to like and dislike the same things (Sallust)

idoneus homo: a fit man (i.e., a person of proven ability)

Iesus Hominum Salvator (I.H.S.): Jesus, the Savior of Humanity

ignem gladio scrutare modo: only stir the fire with a sword (Horace)

ignis fatuus (pl. **ignes fatui**): a foolish fire (i.e., specious words; a will-o'-the-wisp)

ignobile vulgus: the ignoble multitude

ignoramus: we are ignorant

ignorantia facti excusat: ignorance of the fact excuses

ignoratio elenchi: ignoring the point at issue

ignosco tibi: I forgive you (Catullus)

ignotum argenti pondus et auri: an unknown (or untold) mass of silver and gold (Virgil)

ignotum per ignotius: the unknown explained by the unknown

Ilias malorum: an Iliad of woes

illa victoria viam ad pacem patefecit: by that victory he opened the way of peace

illæso lumine solum: an undazzled eye to the sun (said of an eagle)

ille mi par esse deo videtur: he seems to me to be equal to a god (Catullus)

imitari quam invidere: to imitate rather than envy

imitatores, servum pecus: ye imitators, servile herd (Horace)

immotus: immoveable; ummoved

imo pectore: from the bottom of the heart

impavide: fearlessly

impavidum ferient ruinæ (or, **impavidum ruinæ ferient**): the ruins strike him undaunted (Horace)

impendam expendar: I will spend and be spent

impera parendo: command by obeying

imperio regit unus æquo: one [God] rules with just government

imperium et libertas: empire and liberty (Cicero)

imperium in imperio: an empire within an empire (motto of Ohio)

imponere Pelion Olympo: to pile Pelion on Olympus (i.e., to attempt to scale heaven)

imprimis: first of all

in æternum: forever

in altum: toward heaven

in ambiguo: in doubt

in anima vili: on a subject of little worth

in aqua scribis: you are writing in water (i.e., it is without effect)

in arena ædificas: you are building on sand (i.e., it is in vain)

in articulo mortis: at the point of death

in caducum parietem inclinare: to lean against a falling wall

in cælo quies: in heaven is rest

in cælo salus: in heaven is salvation

in cauda venenum: in the tail is poison (i.e., beware of danger)

in Christi nomine: in Christ's name

in cœlo quies: in heaven there is rest

in cœlum jacularis: you are aiming at the heavens (i.e., your anger is in vain)

in concussa virtus: unshaken virtue

in copia cautus: cautious amid plenty

in cruce glorior: glory in the Cross

in cruce salus: salvation in the Cross

in cruce spero: I hope in the Cross

in crucifixo gloria mea: I glory in the Crucified One

in Deo confido: I trust in God

in Deo sola spec mea: my hope in God alone

in Deo speramus: in God we trust (motto of Brown University)

in Deo speravi: in God have I trusted

in Deo spero: in God I hope

in diem vivere: to live from hand to mouth

in dies meliora: better things to come

in Domino confido: in the Lord we trust

in Domino et non in arcu meo sperabo: I will rest my hope on the Lord, and not in my bow

in Domino speravi: in the Lord I have placed my hope

in dubis constans: firm amid dangers

in dulci jubilo: now sing and be joyful (Peter of Dresden)

in dutus virtute ab alto: endued with virtue from above

in eburna vagina plumbeus gladius: a leaden sword in an ivory sheath (Diogenes, said of a finely dressed person)

in ferrum pro libertate ruebant: for freedom they rushed upon the sword

in fide et in bello fortis: strong both in faith and in war

in fidelitate et veritate universas ab æternitate: in universal faithfulness and truth from eternity

in flammam flammas, in mare fundis aquas: you add fire to fire, and water to the sea

in forma pauperis: as a pauper; as a poor man

in foro conscientiæ: before the court of conscience

in hac spe vivo: in this hope I live (from Shakespeare's *Pericles*)

in hoc salus: there is safety in this

in hoc signo spes mea: in this sign is my hope (a reference to the Cross of Christ)

in hoc signo vinces: by this sign (the Cross) you will conquer (Emperor Constantine's vision at the Battle of the Milvian Bridge, 312 CE, which inspired the Chi-Rho, XP, monogram, the labarum)

in Jehovah fides mea: in Jehovah is my trust

in libris libertas: in books there is freedom (motto of the Los Angeles Public Library)

in lumine lucem: I may shine in the light

in lumine tuo videbimus lumen: in Thy light we shall see the light (motto of Columbia University)

in malos cornu: my horn against the bad

in medias res: into the midst of things (Horace)

in mediis malis: into the midst of evils (Seneca)

in medio virtus: virtue lies in the mean (i.e., the middle course)

in memoriam: in memory of; to the memory of

in necessariis unitas, in dubiis libertas, in omnibus caritas (or **charitas**): in things essential unity, in things doubtful liberty, in all things love (Melanthon, after St. Augustine; a motto of the Disciples of Christ)

in nomine Domini: in the name of the Lord

in nomine Patris et Filii et Spiritus Sancti: in the name of the Father, the Son, and the Holy Spirit (from the Catholic Mass)

in nova fert animus: my mind inclines to new things

in nubibus: in the clouds

in nuce Iliad: an Iliad in a nutshell

in omnia paratus: in all things prepared; prepared for everything

in omnibus caritas: in all things love

in partibus infidelium: in the unbelieving parts of the world

in periculis audax: bold in dangers

in perpetuam rei memoriam: in everlasting remembrance of an event or thing

in pertusum ingerimus dicta dolium: we are pouring our words into a perforated cask (Plautus)

in pios usus: for pious uses

in portu quies: rest in port

in propria persona: in his or her own person

in puris naturalibus: in a purely natural state

in recto fides: faith in rectitude

in rerum natura: in the nature of things

in sæcula sæculorum: for ages and ages; forever and ever

in sanguine fœdus: a covenant ratified in blood

in scientia veritas, in arte honestas: in science truth, in art honor

in se contexta recurrit: intertwined together, it returns to itself

in se(ipso) totus, teres, atque rotundus: perfect in himself, polished, and rounded (i.e., a well-rounded man) (Horace)

in serum rem trahere: to draw out the matter to a late hour; to drag on the discussion (Livy)

in silvam ligna ferre: to carry wood to the forest

in solo Deo salus: salvation in God alone

in statu quo ante bellum: the state in which before the war

in te omnia sunt: everything depends on you

in te, Domine, speravi: in thee, O Lord, have I set my hope

in tempestate floresco: I flourish in the tempest

in tenui labor, at tenuis non gloria: the object of the labor was small, but not the fame (Virgil)

in terrorem: in terror; as a warning

in theatro ludus: like a scene in a play

in totidem verbis: in so many words

in transitu: in transit; on the passage

in trinitate robur: my strength lies in the Trinity (also, my strength lies in triunity)

in tuo lumine videbimus lumen: In Thy Light we shall see light (motto of Ohio Wesleyan University)

in utramvis dormire aurem: to sleep on both ears (i.e., to sleep soundly)

in utraque fortuna paratus: prepared for any change of fortune

in utroque fidelis: faithful in both

in utrumque paratus: prepared for both; ready for both

in veritate religionis confido: I trust in the truth of religion

in veritate triumpho: I triumph in the truth

in veritate victoria: victory lies with the truth

in vino veritas: in wine is truth (i.e., under wine's influence, the truth is spoken)

inanis verborum torrens: an empty torrent of words (Quintilian)

incerta animi decreta resolvet: she will dispel the uncertainties of the mind

incessu patuit dea: by her gait the goddess was revealed (Virgil)

incipe: begin

inclinata resurgit: when pressed down, it raises itself again

inclytus virtute: illustrious by virtue

incoctum generoso pectus honesto: a heart imbued with generous honor (Persius)

incredulus odi: being skeptical, I detest it (Horace)

incudi reddere: to return to the anvil (i.e., to revise or retouch) (Horace)

inde iræ: hence this anger

inde iræ et lacrimæ: hence this anger and these tears (Juvenal)

indictum sit: be it unsaid

indignante invidia florebit justus: the just will flourish in spite of envy

indocilis pauperiem pati: one who cannot learn to endure poverty (Horace)

indocilis privata loqui: one incapable of telling secrets (Lucan)

industria et spe: by industry and hope

industria floremus: by industry we flourish

industria naturam corrigit: industry corrects nature

industria veritas et hospitalis: industry, truth, and hospitality

industriæ nil impossibile: to industry, nothing is impossible

indutus virtute ab alto: anointed with virtue from above

inest clementia forti: clemency belongs to the brave

inest et formicæ sua bilis: even the ant has its bile (i.e., even ants become angry)

inest sua gratia parvis: even little things have a grace (or charm) of their own

infandum renovare dolorem: to renew an unspeakable grief (adapted from Horace)

infecta pace: without effecting a peace (Terence)

infinita est velocitas temporis: the swiftness of time is infinite (Seneca)

infixum est mihi: I have firmly resolved; I am determined

infra dignitatem: beneath one's dignity

infringit solido: it breaks against a solid

ingenio et labore: by natural ability and work (motto of the University of Auckland)

ingenio maximus, arte rudis: greatest in genius, rough in skill (Ovid, said of Ennius)

ingenium superat vires: genius overcomes strength

inopem copia fecit: abundance has made him poor (after Ovid)

inopem me copia fecit: abundance made me poor (Ovid)

insanabile cacoëthes scribendi: an incurable passion to write (Juvenal)

inservi Deo et lætare: serve God and rejoice

instar omnium: like all the others

intaminatis fulget honoribus: he shines with unstained honors

intaminatis honoribus: with unstained (or untarnished) honors

integer vitæ scelerisque purus: blameless of life and free from crime (Horace)

integros haurire fontes: to drink from pure fountains

integrum est mihi: I am at liberty

intellectus merces est fidei: understanding is the reward of faith (St. Augustine)

intelligabilia, non intellectum, fero: I provide you with things intelligible, but not with intelligence

intemerata fides: faith undefiled

inter canem et lupum: between dog and wolf (i.e., at twilight)

inter cruces triumphans in cruce: amongst troubles, being triumphant in the Cross

inter malleum et incudem: between the hammer and the anvil

inter pocula: over their cups (Persius)

inter pueros senex: an old man among boys

inter sacrum saxumque sto: standing between the knife and the victim (i.e., between the hammer and the anvil) (Plautus)

inter spem et metum: between hope and fear

inter vivos: among the living

interim fit aliquid: meanwhile, something is going on (Terence)

interiora vide: look within

interminabilis humanæ vitæ labor: the unending labor of human life

intra verba peccare: to offend in words only

intrepidus maneo: I stand or remain intrepid

introibo ad altare Dei: I will go to the altar of God (from the Catholic Mass)

introite, nam et hic dii sunt: enter, for here too are gods (after Heraclitus)

intus et in cute novi hominem: I know the man inside and out (Persius)

invia virtuti nulla est via: no way is impassable to virtue (Ovid)

invicta labore: by labor unconquered

invicta veritate: by unconquered (or invincible) truth

invictus arduis: unconquered in difficulties

invictus maneo: I remain unconquered

invidia gloriæ comes: envy is the attendant of glory (Ovid)

invidia major: superior to envy

inviolabiles telo Cupidinis: those immune to Cupid's arrow

invita Minerva: Minerva being unwilling (i.e., lacking inspiration)

invitum sequitur honos (or **honor**): honors follow him unsolicited

Ioannes est nomen eius: John is his name (St. Luke 1:63; motto of Puerto Rico)

ipse amicus: I am my own friend

ipse dixit Dominus: the Lord himself has spoken it

ira leonis nobilis: the anger of the lion is noble

irremeabilis unda: the river from which there is no return (i.e., the river Styx) (Virgil)

irrevocabile: irrevocable

irritabis crabones: you will stir up the hornets (Plautus)

isthæc in me cudetur faba: that bean will hit me (i.e., I shall have to suffer for this) (Terence)

it prex cæli: prayer goes heavenward

ita: thus

ita et virtus: thus also virtue

ita lex scripta (est): thus the law is written; such is the law

ita voluerunt, ita factum est: so they willed, so it will be done

ite, missa est: go, the mass is over

iterum virescit: again it grows green

Iupiter merentibus offert: Jupiter rewards the deserving

J

jacta alea esto (or, **iacta alea esto**): let the die be cast (Julius Cæsar, as quoted by Suetonius)

jacta est alea (or, **jacta alea est**): the die is cast (words attributed to Julius Cæsar upon crossing the Rubicon)

jam jam (or, **iam iam**): now now (i.e., forthwith)

jam redit et Virgo: now returns the Virgin

jamque opus exegi: and now I have finished the work (Ovid)

januæ mentis: gates of the mind

Jesus Christus esto mihi: let Jesus Christ be mine

Jesus (or Iesus) Hominum Salvator (I.H.S.): Jesus, the Savior of Humanity

Joannes est nomen ejus: his name is John (St. Luke 1:63; motto of Puerto Rico)

Jovis omnia plena: all things are full of Jove

Jubilate Deo: rejoice in God

jucunda rerum vicissitudo: a delightful change of circumstances

judex est lex loquens: a judge is the law speaking

judicio acri perpendere: to weigh with keen judgment (Lucretius)

judicium Dei: the judgment of God (i.e., trial by ordeal)

judicium parium aut leges terræ: judgment of one's peers or else the laws of the land (Magna Carta)

judicium subtile videndis artibus: a judgment subtle in discriminating works of art (Horace)

jugulare mortuos: to stab to death

juncta juvant: things united aid each other (i.e., union is strength)

juniores ad labores: the younger men for labors (i.e., for the heavier work)

Jupiter tonans: Jupiter the thunderer

jurare in verba magistri: to swear by the words of the master

jure divino: by Divine right; by Divine law

jure humano: by human law; by the will of the people

jure, non dono: by right, not by gift

jure repræsentationis: by right of representation

jus et norma loquendi: the rule and law of language

jus gentium: the law of nations (Cicero)

jus gladii: the law of the sword

justi ut sidera fulgent: the just shine as the stars

justissimus unus et servantissimus æqui: just and observant of what is right, as no other is (Virgil)

justitia et fortitudo invincibilia sunt: justice and fortitude are invincible

justitia et pax: justice and peace

justitia omnibus: justice for all (motto of the District of Columbia)

justitiæ soror fides: faith, the sister of justice

justitiæ tenax: tenacious of justice

justum et tenacem propositi: just and firm of purpose

justum et tenacem propositi virum: a man upright and firm of purpose (Horace)

justus autem ex fide vivit: the just shall live by faith (Romans 1:17)

justus et fidelis: just and faithful

justus et propositi tenax: just and firm of purpose

justus propositi tenax: a just person steadfast to his purpose (Horace)

justus ut palma florebit: the just shall flourish as a palm tree

juvant arva parentum: the fields of our ancestors delight [me]

juvante Deo: God helping

K

kairon gnothi: know your opportunity (Pittachus, from the Greek)

Kalendæ Græcæ: the Greek calends (i.e., never; the Greek calendar did not mark the calends)

kat' eksochen: by way of excellence; with distinction (a Greek phrase)

Kyrie eleison: Lord, have mercy on us (from the Greek)

L

labor irritus: useless toil; vain labor

labor omnia vincit: labor conquers all things (motto of Oklahoma, the University of Illinois, and the American Federation of Labor)

labor omnia vincit improbus: persevering labor conquers all things (Virgil)

labora ut in æternum vivas: strive that you may live forever

laborare est orare: to work is to pray

labore: by labor

labore et honore: by labor and honor

labore vinces: by labor will you conquer

laborum dulce lenimen: the sweet solace of my labors (Horace, to his lyre)

labuntur et imputantur: the moments slip away and are entered into our account (a popular saying for a sundial)

lacrimæ rerum: the tears of things

lacrimæ simulatæ: simulated tears (i.e., crocodile tears)

læso et invicto militi: for our wounded but unconquered soldiery

lambendo paulatim figurant: (fig.) licking a cub into shape (Pliny the Elder)

lapsus linguæ: a slip of the tongue

lapsus ubi?, quid feci?: where did I err?, what did I accomplish? (Alciato)

lascivi soboles gregis: the offspring of a wanton herd (Horace)

lateat scintillula forsan: perchance a little spark of life may lie hidden (motto of the Humane Society)

latitat: he lurks; he is hidden

laudant quod non intelligunt: they praise what they do not understand

laudari a laudato viro (or, laudari a viro laudato): to be praised by a man of praise (Cicero)

laudator temporis acti: a praiser of times past (i.e., one who prefers the good old days) (Horace)

laudatur ab his, culpatur ab illis: praised by some, blamed by others (Horace)

laudes cano heroum: I sing the praise of heroes

laudis avidi, pecuniæ liberales: greedy of praise, lavish of money (Sallust)

laudumque immensa cupido: and an immense desire for praise (i.e., a passion for praise) (Virgil)

laus Deo: praise be to God

leberide cæcior: blinder than a serpent's sloughed skin

legale judicium parium: the legal judgment of my peers

lege, quæso: I beg you read (a note appended to the top of student papers inviting tutors to read their work)

leges juraque servat: he observes the laws and statutes

legimus, ne legantur: we read that others may not read (Lactantius, referring to censors and reviewers)

legite et discite: read and learn

legant prius et postea despeciant: let them read first, and despise afterward (Lope de Vega)

lene tormentum: gentle torment

lente sed opportune: slowly, but opportunely

Leo de Juda est robur nostrum: the Lion of Judah is our strength

leone fortior fides: faith is stronger than a lion

leonina societas: partnership with a lion (i.e., a "lion's corporation" in which the whole of the profits is controlled by the strongest and most powerful member)

leporis vitam vivit: he lives the life of a hare (i.e., always full of fear)

leve et reluis: arise and re-illumine

levis sit tibi terra: may the earth lie light upon you (a tombstone inscription)

levius fit patientia: patience makes it (one's burden) lighter

liber et erectus: free and upright

libera nos a malo: deliver us from evil

liberavi animam meam: I have freed my soul (St. Bernard)

libertas: liberty

libertas et natale solum: liberty and my native land

libertas in legibus: liberty in the laws

libertas sub rege pio: liberty under a pious king

libido dominatur: the passions have gained control

liceat concedere veris: we are free to yield to truth (Horace)

licentia poëtica: poetic license (Seneca)

ligonem ligonem vocat: he calls a hoe a hoe (i.e., to call a spade a spade)

limæ labor: the labor of the file (i.e., polishing and revising one's work)

linguæ verbera: lashings of the tongue

lis litem generat: strife begets strife

litem lite resolvere: to settle strife by strife

litera canina: the canine letter (i.e., the letter R, when pronounced very hard)

Literæ Bellerophontis: a Bellerophon's letter (i.e., a letter requesting that the bearer be dealt with summarily for an offense)

littera occidit, spiritus vivicat: the letter kills, the spirit gives life (after 2 Corinthians 3:6)

littera scripta manet: the written letter remains

litteræ non erubescunt: a letter does not blush (Cicero)

litteris dedicata omnibus artibus: dedicated to the letters and all the arts (motto of the University of Nebraska)

locus penitentiæ: place for repentance

longe aberrat scopo: he wanders far from the goal (i.e., he is wide of the mark)

longe absit: far be it from me; God forbid!

longo sed proximo intervallo: the next, but after a long interval (Virgil)

longo splendescit in usu: with long use it shines

lotis manibus: with washed hands

luce lucet aliena: it shines with a borrowed light (e.g., the moon)

luceat et crescat: let it shine and grow

lucent in tenebris: they shine in darkness

lucernam olet: it smells of the lamp (i.e., of late night toil)

lucis et pacis: light and peace

lucrum Christi mihi: to me, Christ is gain

ludere cum sacris: to play or trifle with sacred things

ludibrium Fortunæ: the plaything of Fortune

ludus, luctus, luxus: gambling, grief, debauchery (i.e., the fruits of drunkenness)

lugete, O Veneres Cupidinesque: weep, all you Venuses and Cupids (Catullus)

lumen cœleste sequamur: may we follow heavenly inspiration

lumen est in Deo: the Light is in God

lumenque juventæ purpureum: the light of purple youth (i.e., the radiant bloom of youth) (Virgil)

lupus in fabula: the wolf in the fable (i.e., speak of the devil)

lux: light (motto of the University of Northern Iowa)

lux esto: let there be light (motto of Kalamazoo College)

lux et lex: light and law (motto of the University of North Dakota)

lux et veritas: light and truth (motto of Yale University)

lux hominum vita: light, the life of men (motto of the University of New Mexico)

lux in homine factum: the light has been made in man

lux in tenebris: light in darkness

lux in tenebris lucet: the light shines in the darkness

lux/libertas: light/liberty (motto of the University of North Carolina)

lux mihi laurus: the laurel is my light

lux mundi: light of the world (motto of Jessup University)

lux perpetua luceat eis: let perpetual light shine on them

lux sit: let there be light (motto of the University of Washington)

lux sum mundi: I am the light of the world (St. John 9:5)

lux tua via mea: thy light is my way

lux tua vita mihi: your light is my life (from Shakespeare's *Pericles*)

lux venit ab alto: light comes from above

lux vitæ: the light of life

M

macte virtute: persevere in virtue (sometimes said sarcastically)

magalia quondam: formerly humble huts stood here (Virgil)

magis mutus quam piscis: quieter than a fish

magister dixit: the master has said so

Magna Carta (or **Magna Charta**): the Great Charter, signed by King John in 1215

magna comitante caterva: a great crowd accompanying (Virgil)

magna est veritas et prævalebit: truth is mighty and will prevail

magna est vis consuetudinis: great is the force of habit (Cicero)

magnæ spes altera Romæ: another hope of mighty Rome (i.e., a youth of promise)

magnanimiter crucem sustine: bear afflictions with magnanimity (also rendered, bear up bravely under the Cross)

magnas inter opes inops: poor amid great riches (Horace)

magni nominis umbra: the shadow of a great name (Lucan)

magnificat: it magnifies

magnificat anima mea Dominum: my soul magnifies the Lord (St. Luke 1:46)

magnis excidit ausis: he failed in bold attempts (Ovid)

magno conatu magnas nugas: a great effort for great trifles (i.e., so much work for so little gain) (Terence)

magnorum haud unquam indignus avorum: never unworthy of his illustrious ancestors (Virgil)

magnum in parvo: a great amount in a small space

magnus Alexander corpore parvus erat: the great Alexander was small in stature

Magnus Apollo: Great Apollo (i.e., a great oracle)

major sum quam cui possit Fortuna nocere: I am too great for Fortune to harm (Ovid)

majores pennas nido: wings greater than the nest (i.e., to rise above the position to which one is born) (Horace)

majoresque cadunt altis de montibus umbræ: and the greater shadows fall from the lofty mountains (Virgil)

majori cedo: I yield to the one who is greater

majorum consuetudini deditus: devoted to the tradition of his ancestors (Seneca)

mala fides: bad faith

maledicat Dominus: may the Lord curse him

malesuada fames: hunger that impels the crime (Virgil)

mali principii malus finis: the bad end of a bad beginning (i.e., bad beginnings have bad endings)

malignum spernere vulgus: to scorn the wicked rabble (Horace)

malis avibus: with bad birds (i.e., with a bad omen) (Cicero)

malum in se: a thing evil in itself

malum prohibitum: a prohibited evil (i.e., a crime because it is forbidden by law)

manebant vestigia morientis libertatis: there still remained traces of dying liberty (Tacitus)

manent optima cœle: the best things await us in heaven

manet alta mente repostum: it remains stored deep in the mind (Virgil)

manibus pedibusque: with hands and feet; with might and main

manibus victoria dextris: victory by my right hand

manliana: a Manlian (i.e., a harsh and severe sentence; a reference to Titus Manlius, who ordered his son to be scourged and beheaded for defying his orders)

manu e nubibus: with a hand from the clouds (i.e., help from above)

manu et corde: with hand and heart

manu et mente: with hand and mind (motto of the University of New South Wales)

manu forti: with a strong hand

manum de tabula!: hand of the picture! (i.e., hold!, enough!; do not touch up!) (Cicero)

manus e nubibus: a hand from the clouds

manus hæc inimica tyrannis: this hand is an enemy to tyrants

manus manum fricat: one hand rubs the other

manus manum lavat: one hand washes the other

mare cœlo miscere: to confound sea and sky

mare ditat, rosa decorat: the sea enriches, the rose adorns

margarita e stercore: a pearl from a dunghill

margaritas ante porcos: pearls before swine (after St. Matthew 7:6)

martem accendere cantu: to excite war by song (Virgil)

maturandum: one must make haste

maturato opus est: (fig.) there is need of haste (Livy)

mature fias senex: may you early prove an old man (i.e., may you learn wisdom beyond your years)

maximus in minimis: greatest in the least; very great in very little things

me, me adsum qui feci: I, the one before you, did the deed (Virgil)

me pompæ provexit apex: the summit of glory has led me on (or has inspired me) (from Shakespeare's *Pericles*)

me stante virebunt: while I stand they will flourish

mea gloria fides: faith is my glory

mea nihil interest: it is all the same to me

mea pila est: I have won

medicas adhibere manus: to touch with a healing hand (Serenus Samonicus)

medice, cura te ipsum: physician, heal thyself (St. Luke 4:23)

mediocria firma: the middle course is most secure (i.e., moderation is safer than extremes)

medius fidius!: so help me God!

melete to pan: industry is everything (a Greek saying, attributed to Periander)

meliora: better things; or, always better (motto of the University of Rochester)

meliora supersunt: better things remain

meliores priores: the better ones first

melioribus auspiciis: under more favorable auspices

memento mori: remember death

memor esto: be mindful of; think upon

memor et fidelis: mindful and faithful

memorabilia: things to be remembered

memoria in æterna: in eternal remembrance

memoria pii æterna: the memory of the pious is eternal

mendaces, ebriosi, verbosi: liars, drunkards, and wordy people

mendici, mimi, balatrones, et hoc genus omne: beggars, actors, buffoons, and all that sort of people (i.e., a group of contemptible folk) (Horace)

menin áeide, Thea: sing of wrath, O Goddess (the opening words, in Greek, of Homer's *Iliad*)

mens æqua (rebus) in arduis: a mind undisturbed in adversities

mens agitat molem: mind moves matter (Virgil; motto of the University of Oregon)

mens conscia recti: a mind conscious of uprightness (or integrity)

mens et manus: mind and hand (motto of the Massachusetts Institute of Technology)

mens immota manet: the mind remains unmoved

mens interrita lethi: a mind undaunted by death (Ovid)

mens invicta manet: the mind remains unconquered

mens sana in corpore sano: a sound mind in a healthy body (Juvenal)

mens sibi conscia recti: a mind conscious of its own integrity (i.e., a good conscience) (Horace)

mente manuque: with heart and hand

mentis gratissimus error: a most delightful reverie of the mind (i.e., an hallucination) (Horace)

merces sublimis honorum: the high reward of honor

merum sal: pure salt; genuine Attic wit

metuenda corolla draconis: fear the dragon's crest

meum et tuum: mine and thine

micat inter omnes: it shines among all (i.e., it outshines all) (Horace)

mihi consulit Deus: God cares for me

mihi cura futuri: my care is for the future (motto of Hunter College)

mihi est propositum in taberna mori: I purpose to end my days in a tavern

mihi et meæ: for me and for mine (motto of Anne Boleyn)

mihi persuasum est: I am persuaded; I firmly believe

mihi pondera, luxus: excess is a burden to me

mihi terra, lacusque: the land and the waters are mine

miles gloriosus: the bragging soldier (Plautus)

militamus sub spe: we fight under [the banner of] hope

minima de malis: the lesser of two evils

minor jurare non potest: a minor cannot swear (i.e., serve on a jury)

mirabile dictu!: wonderful to tell!

mirabile visu!: wonderful to behold!

mirandum naturæ opus: amazing is the work of nature

misera contribuens plebs!: the poor tax-paying people! (Verböczy)

miserrima vidi: I have seen most miserable things

mitis et fortis: gentle and brave

mobilium turba Quiritium: a crowd of fickle citizens (i.e., Romans) (Horace)

moderata durant: things used in moderation endure (Seneca)

modo et forma: in manner and form

modo vir, modo femina: now as a man, now as a woman (Ovid)

mole ruit sua: it is crushed under its own weight (Horace)

molesta et importuna salutantium frequentia: a troublesome and annoying crowd of visitors

mollia tempora fandi: favorable occasions for speaking (Horace and Virgil)

mollissima fandi tempora (or, **mollissima tempora fandi**)**:** the most favorable (or fitting) occasions for speaking (Virgil and Horace)

molliter manus imposuit: he gently laid hands

molliter ossa cubent: let his bones softly rest (Ovid)

mone sale: advise with salt (i.e., with discretion)

moneo et munio: I advise and defend

moniti meliora sequamur: being admonished, let us follow better counsel (Virgil)

monstrant regibus astra viam: the stars show the way to kings

montani semper liberi: mountaineers are always free (motto of West Virginia)

montes auri pollicens: promising mountains of gold (Terence)

monumentum ære perennius: a monument more lasting than bronze (Horace)

more majorum: after the custom (or manner) of our ancestors

morem fecerat usus: habit had made the custom (Ovid)

mores multorum vidit: he saw the customs of many men (Horace, of Ulysses)

moriamur et in media arma ruamus: let us die, even as we rush into the thick of the fight (Virgil)

moribus antiquis stat Roma: Rome stands by its ancient morals

moriendo vivo: in dying I live

morior invictus: I die unconquered (i.e., death before defeat)

morituri morituros salutant: those about to die salute those about to die (a gladiator salute)

morituri te salutamus: we who are about to die salute thee (a gladiator salute)

mors aut honorabilis vita: death or a life of honor

mors Christi mors mortis mihi: Christ's death is to me the death of death

mors janua vitæ: death is the gate of life

mors omnia solvit: death dissolves all things

mors omnibus communis: death is common to all things

mors potius macula: death rather than disgrace

mors sceptra ligonibus æquans: death makes scepters equal with hoes

mors tua, vita mea: your death, my life (i.e., you die that I might live)

mortales inimicitias, sempiternas amicitias: be our enmities for time, our friendships for eternity (Cicero)

mortalitate relicta vivit immortalitate indutus: having left mortality, he lives clad in immortality

mos pro lege: custom for law

moveo et proficior: I proceed and am more prosperous

moveo et propitior: I rise and am appeased

mox nox: soon night (i.e., night is approaching)

mox nox in rem: night is approaching, let's get on with the matter

mugitus labyrinthi: the bellowing of the labyrinth (i.e., a weak and predictable theme from an amateur writer) (Juvenal)

multa acervatim frequentans: crowding together a number of thoughts

multa gemens: groaning deeply; with many a groan (Virgil)

multa paucis: much in little

multa tacere loquive paratus: ready to speak little or to speak much

multa tulit fecitque: much has he suffered and done

multarum palmarum causidicus: an advocate who has won many causes

multis e gentibus vires: from many peoples, strength (motto of Saskatchewan)

multitudo sapientium sanitas orbis: a multitude of the wise is the health of the world (motto of the University of Victoria, British Columbia)

multum abludit imago: the picture is by no means like (i.e., there is no real resemblance here) (Horace)

multum demissus homo: a very modest or unassuming man (Horace)

multum in parvo: much in little

multum, non multa: much, not many (Pliny)

mundus vult decipi: the world wishes to be deceived

munit hæc et altera vincit: this one defends and the other conquers (motto of Nova Scotia)

munus Apolline dignum: a gift worthy of Apollo (Horace)

munus ornare verbis: to enhance the value of a present by words (Terence)

mus in pice: a mouse in tar (i.e., struggling in vain)

musicam diis curæ esse: music is in the care of the gods

mutare vel timere sperno: I spurn either to change or to fear

mutua fœcunditas: mutual fecundity

N

nascentes morimur: we are born but to die (Manilius)

nati natorum: the children of our children (i.e., posterity) (Virgil)

natio comœda est: it is a nation of comics (Juvenal, referring to the Greeks)

natura abhorret a vacuo: nature abhors a vacuum

natura appetit perfectum: nature desires perfection

natura majora facit: nature does greater things

natura nihil agit frustra: nature does nothing in vain

natura non facit saltum (or **saltus**)**:** nature makes no leaps (i.e., there are no gaps in nature) (Linnæus)

naturæ non artis opus: a work of nature, not of art

natus nemo: not a born soul (Plautus)

naufragium in portu facere: to become shipwrecked in port (Quintilian)

ne cede malis: neither yield to misfortunes (or evils)

ne fronti crede: trust not to appearances

ne Hercules quidem contra duos: not even Hercules could contend against two at once

ne Jupiter (or **Juppiter**) **quidem omnibus placet:** not even Jupiter can please everyone

ne me perdas: let me not be lost

ne nimium: not too much

ne obliviscaris: do not forget

ne parcas nec spernas: neither spare nor scorn

ne plus ultra: no more beyond (i.e., nothing beyond it; unsurpassed)

ne quid falsi: nothing false

ne teruncius quidem: (fig.) not a penny!

ne timeo nec sperno: I neither fear nor despise

ne vile fano: bring no vile thing to the temple

ne vile velis: incline to nothing vile (or base)

nec ab ordine cedunt: nor do they depart from their rank

nec ab oriente, nec ab occidente: neither from the east nor from the west

nec aspera terrent: not even hardships deter us

nec caput nec pedes: neither head nor tail (i.e., in confusion)

nec cito, nec tarde: neither swiftly nor slowly

nec cupias, nec metuas: neither desire nor fear

nec elatus nec dejectus: neither elated nor dejected

nec fas est, nec posse reor: I deem it neither lawful nor possible

nec habeo, nec careo, nec curo: I have not, I want not, I care not

nec male notus eques: a knight of no stigma (i.e., of good repute)

nec me meminisse pigebit: nor shall I regret to remember

nec metuas, nec optes: neither fear nor desire

nec mora, nec requies: neither delay, nor rest (Virgil)

nec morti esse locum: there is no room for death (Ovid)

nec obolum habet unde restim emat: neither has he a penny left to buy a rope (i.e., he doesn't even have money enough to hang himself)

nec omnia, nec semper, nec ab omnibus: neither all, nor always, nor by all

nec placida contentus quiete est: neither is he contented with quiet repose

nec pluribus impar: not equal to many (i.e., a match for the whole world) (motto of Louis XIV of France)

nec prece nec pretio: neither by entreaty nor by bribery

nec quærere nec spernere honorem: neither to seek nor to spurn honors

nec rege, nec populo, sed utrique: neither for king, nor for people, but for both

nec soli cedit: he yields not even to the sun

nec sorte, nec fato: not by chance nor by fate

nec spe, nec metu: without hope, without fear

nec temere nec timide: neither rashly nor timidly

nec timeo nec sperno: neither do I fear nor despise

necessitas non habet legem: necessity has no law; necessity knows no law (Publilius Syrus)

nego argumentum: I refuse the argument

nemo me impune lacessit: no one provokes me with impunity (a motto of Scotland)

nemo sic impar sibi: no one was ever so unlike himself

nemo sine cruce beatus: no one is blessed without the Cross

nemo solus sapit: no one is wise alone (i.e., by himself) (Plautus)

nervis alienis mobile lignum: a puppet moved by sticks in the hands of another

nihil alienum: nothing foreign

nihil ex nihilo: nothing comes from nothing

nihil largiundo gloriam adeptus est: he acquired glory without bribery (Sallust)

nihil obstabit eunti: nothing shall oppose him as he goes

nihil quod tetigit non ornavit: he touched nothing which he did not adorn

nihil reliqui: nothing remains

nihil sine labore: nothing without labor

nihil sub sole novum (or, **nihil sub sole novi,** or, **nil novi sub sole**): there is nothing new under the sun (after Ecclesiastes 1:9)

nihil unquam peccavit, nisi quod mortua est: she never once sinned but when she died (inscription on a wife's tomb in Rome)

nihil verius: nothing truer

nihilo nisi cruce: with nothing but the Cross

nil admirari: to wonder (or marvel) at nothing (Horace)

nil clarius astris: nothing brighter (or clearer) than the stars

nil conscire sibi: to be conscious of no guilt

nil consuetudine majus: nothing is greater than custom (or habit) (Ovid)

nil debet: he owes nothing

nil desperandum: nothing must be despaired of; despair at nothing (Horace)

nil desperandum auspice Deo: nothing to be despaired of under the auspices of God

nil dicit: he says nothing (i.e., he has no defense to make)

nil impossibile: nothing is impossible

nil moror ictus: I do not care for blows

nil mortalibus arduum est: nothing is too difficult for mortals (Horace)

nil nisi bonum: nothing unless good (i.e., say nothing but good about the dead)

nil nisi Cruce: nothing except by the Cross; no hope but in the Cross

nil penna sed usus: not the wing, but its use

nil sine causa: nothing without a cause

nil sine Deo: nothing without God

nil sine magno labore: nothing without great labor (motto of Brooklyn College)

nil sine numine: nothing without Providence (motto of Colorado)

nil solidum: nothing is firm or solid

nil temere: nothing rashly

nisi Dominus, frustra: unless the Lord, it is in vain (after Psalm 127:1; motto of the city of Edinburgh, whimsically translated "you can do nothing here unless you are a lord")

nitor in adversum: I strive against opposition (Ovid)

nobilis ira: noble in anger

nobilitas sola est atque unica virtus: virtue is the one and only nobility (Juvenal)

noctemque diemque fatigant: they wear out night and day (Virgil)

nodo firmo: in a firm knot

nodos virtute resolvo: through virtue I untie knots

nolens volens: whether willing or not willing (i.e., willy-nilly)

noli irritare leones: do not provoke the lions (motto of the Lyons family)

noli me tangere: touch me not (St. John 20:17; sometimes said of a person who complains too much)

nolo episcopari: I do not wish to be made a bishop (sometimes said of someone who feigns rejection of the very thing he or she desires)

nomen atque omen: a name as well as an omen (i.e., an omen in a name) (Plautus)

nomen est; res non est: the name exists, the thing does not

nominis umbra: the shadow of a name

nomiz adelphous tous alethinous philous: count true friends as brothers (a Greek saying)

non aqua, sed ruina: not with water, but with ruin

non arbitrio popularis auræ: not by the caprice of popular applause

non cedit umbra soli: shade does not yield to the sun

non compos mentis: not sound in mind

non conscire sibi: conscious of no fault

non credis mihi?: don't you believe me? (Catullus)

non credo tempori: I trust not to time

non crux, sed lux: not the Cross, but its light

non deficiente crumena: the purse not failing (i.e., while the money holds out) (Horace)

non deficit alter: another is not wanting (Virgil)

non degener: not unworthy

non deludere: not to delude

non dolo, sed vi: not by deceit, but by force

non dormis: I sleep not

non dormit qui custodit: the sentinel sleeps not

non erat his locus: this was out of place here (Horace)

non fecimus ipsi: we have not done these things ourselves

non gladio, sed gratia: not by the sword but by grace

non hæc in fœdera: not into such alliances as these (Virgil)

non hæc sine numine: these things are not without sanction of the gods

non immemor beneficii: not unmindful of kindness

non inferiora secutus: having followed nothing inferior (Virgil)

non locus virum, sed vir locum ornat: not the place the man, but the man adorns the place

non mihi, non tibi, sed nobis: not for you, not for me, but for us

non mihi sed Deo et regi: not for myself but for God and the king

non minima sed magma prosequor: I follow not trivial, but important things

non multa, sed multum: not many things, but much

non nimis: not very much; not particularly

non nobis, Domine: not to us, O Lord (Psalm 115:1)

non nobis sed omnibus: not for us but for all

non nobis solum: not for us alone; not merely for ourselves

non nobis solum nati sumus: not for ourselves alone are we born (Cicero)

non nobis solum, sed toto mundo nati: not born for ourselves alone, but for the whole world

non nova sed nove: not new but a new way

non obscura nec ima: neither obscure nor very low

non olet: it has not a bad smell (i.e., money, no matter its source) (Suetonius)

non omnibus dormio: not for all do I sleep (Cicero)

non omnis moriar: not all of me shall die (Horace, referring to his works)

non passibus æquis: not with equal steps (Virgil)

non prudentia sed victoria: not prudence, but victory

non pugnat sed dormit: instead of fighting, he sleeps

non quam diu, sed quam bene: not how long, but how well

non quis, sed quid: not who, but what

non quo sed quomodo: not by whom but in what manner

non rapui, sed recepi: I have not taken by violence, but received

non revertar inultus: I shall not return unavenged

non sibi: not for himself

non sibi sed omnibus: not for himself but for all

non sibi sed patriæ: not for himself but for his country

non sibi, sed suis: not for one's self but for one's people (motto of Tulane University)

non sibi sed toti: not for himself but for all

non sine anchora: not without an anchor

non sine dis animosus infans: a spirited child, thanks to the gods (Horace)

non sine jure: not without right

non sine lege capillis: let not your hair be out of order (Ovid)

non sine numine: not without divine aid or approval

non subito delenda: not to be hastily destroyed

non sufficit orbis: the world does not suffice

non sum qualis eram: I am not now what I once was (Horace)

non tali auxilio: not for such aid as this (Virgil)

non temere: not rashly

non terra, sed aquis: not by land, but by water

non ut edam vivo, sed ut vivam edo: I do not live to eat, but I eat to live (Quintilian)

non vi sed virtute: not by force but by virtue

non relinquam vos orphanos: I will not leave you orphans (St. John 14:18)

non turbetur cor vestrum: let not your heart be troubled (St. John 14:1)

non vobis solum: not for you alone

non vox, sed votum: not a voice, but a wish

non vultus, non color: there is neither the countenance nor the color (i.e., these two do not compare)

nos duo turba sumus: we two are a multitude (Deucalion to Pyrrha after the deluge, in Ovid)

nos nostraque Deo: both we and ours are God's

nosce te ipsum (or, **nosce teipsum**): know thyself

nosce tempus: know your time (i.e., make hay while the sun shines)

noscitur a sociis (also, **noscitur e[x] sociis**): he is known by his companions (i.e., by the company he keeps)

nota bene (N.B.): note well

novacula in cotem: the razor against the whetstone (i.e., he has met his match)

novus homo: a new man (i.e., a person who has risen from obscurity)

novus ordo seclorum: a new order for the ages (a motto of the United States of America)

nox præsidium nostri: the night is our protection

nox senatum dirimit: night breaks upon the session (i.e., the meeting is called on account of darkness)

nuda veritas: the naked truth (Horace)

nugæ canoræ: melodious trifles; a nonsense song (Horace)

nugis addere pondus: to add weight to trifles (Horace)

nugis armatus: armed with trifles

nulla dies sine linea: no day without a line (i.e., no day without something done)

nulla pallescere culpa: not to grow pale at imputation of guilt

nulli desperandum, quamdiu spirat: (fig.) while there is life there is hope

nulli secundus: second to none (Apuleius)

nullius in verba: at the orders of no one

nullo meo merito: I had not deserved it

nullum sine nomine saxum: no stone without a name (or, without a tale to tell) (Lucan, said of the fate of Troy)

nullum quod tetigit non ornavit: there was nothing he touched that he did not adorn (epitaph by Samuel Johnson for Oliver Goldsmith)

nullus dolus contra Casum: no cunning against Chance

numine et virtute: by God's providence and by virtue

numini et patriæ asto: I stand on the side of God and my country

nunc aut nunquam: now or never

nunc dimittis: now let him depart [in peace] (St. Luke 2:29)

nunc est bibendum: now is the time for drinking (Horace)

nunc ille vivit in sinu Abraham: now he lives in Abraham's bosom (St. Augustine)

nunquam dormio: I never sleep (i.e., I am always on guard)

nunquam non paratus: never unprepared (i.e., always ready)

nunquam obliviscar: I will never forget

nunquam retrorsum: never go back

nutrimentum spiritus: nourishment for the spirit (inscription on the Royal Library of Berlin)

O

O dea certe!: O, thou who are a goddess surely! (Virgil)

O mors ero mors tua: O death, I will be your death (motto of the Black Society)

O noctes cœnæque deum!: O nights and suppers of the gods! (Horace)

O passi graviora!: Oh you, who have suffered greater misfortunes than these! (Virgil)

O pudor! O pietas!: O modesty! O piety! (Martial)

O sancta damnatio!: O holy condemnation!

O sancta simplicitas!: O sacred simplicity! (Jan Hus, the martyred Czech religious reformer, upon seeing a woman hurrying to throw a piece of wood on the fire)

O si sic omnis!: O, if all things were thus!

O tempora! O mores!: Oh, the times! Oh, the morals! (Cicero)

O vita, misero longa!: O life, long to the wretched!

ob patriam vulnera passi: having suffered wounds for their country

obiter cantare: to sing by the way (i.e., to sing as one goes along)

oblivio paupertatis parens: forgetfulness, parent of poverty

obscuris vera involvens: concealing truth in obscurity; shrouding the truth in darkness (Virgil; said of political figures)

obscurum per obscurius: explaining something obscure by something more obscure

obsta principiis (also, **principiis obsta**): resist the beginning

obstantia nubila solvet: it will dissolve confronting clouds

obstrepuit inter olores: it clamored among the swans

occasionem cognosce: know your opportunity

occupet extremum scabies: let the plague seize the last (i.e., the Devil take the hindmost!) (Horace)

occurrent nubes: clouds will intervene

oderint dum metuant: let them hate, provided they fear (Cicero and Accius; disapproved by Seneca)

oderint dum probent: let them hate, provided they approve (attributed to Emperor Tiberius)

odi et amo: I hate and I love (Catullus)

odi profanum: I hate whatever is profane

odium theologicum: theological hatred (i.e., the animosity engendered by differences of theological opinion)

odora canum vis: the strong scent of the hounds (Virgil)

olet lucernam: it smells of the lamp (i.e., late-night work)

oleum addere camino: to add fuel to the flame (i.e., to make things worse) (Horace)

oleum et operam perdidi: I have lost both oil and labor (i.e., to lose both time and trouble) (Plautus)

olla male fervet: the pot boils badly (i.e., it does not look hopeful)

omissis jocis: leaving aside joking (Pliny the Younger)

omne bonum Dei donum: every good thing is a gift of God

omne bonum desuper: all good is from above

omne scibile: everything knowable

omne solum forti patria est: to the brave, every land is his homeland (Ovid)

omne trinum perfectum: every perfect thing is threefold

omne vivum ex ovo: everything living comes from an egg

omnem movere lapidem: to move every stone (i.e., to leave no stone unturned)

omnes composui: I have laid them all to rest (i.e., in the grave) (Horace)

omnes eodem cogimur: we are all drawn to the same place (Horace)

omnes stultos insanire: that all fools are insane (Horace)

omni exceptione major: superior to all exception

omni liber metu: free from every fear

omni violentia major: too strong for any violence

omnia ad Dei gloriam: all things for the glory of God

omnia bona bonis: to the good all things are good

omnia bonos viros decent: all things are becoming in good men

omnia desuper (or, **omnia de super**): all things come from above

omnia ejusdem farinæ: all things are of grain (i.e., of the same stuff)

omnia fortunæ committo: I commit all things to fortune

omnia Græce!: everything is Greek! (Juvenal)

omnia jam fient: all things will now come to pass (Ovid)

omnia novit: he knows everything (Juvenal)

omnia orta occident: all things that rise also set (Sallust)

omnia pro bono: all things for the good

omnia subjecisti sub pedibus, oves et boves: you have placed all things beneath our feet, both sheep and oxen (motto of the Butchers' Company)

omnia suspendens naso: turning up his nose at everything

omnia tuta timens: fearing all things, even those that are safe (Virgil)

omnia vanitas: all is vanity

omnia venalia Romæ: all things can be bought at Rome

omnia vincit amor: love conquers all things

omnia vincit veritas: truth conquers all things

omnibus hoc vitium est: all have this vice (Horace)

omnium horarum homo: a man ready for whatever may come (Quintilian)

onus quam gravissimus: a most heavy burden

ope et consilio: with help and counsel

opera Dei mirifica: the works of God are wonderful

opera illius mea sunt: his works are mine

operose nihil agunt: they are busy about nothing (Seneca)

opes parit industria: industry produces riches

opiferque per orbem dicor: I am known over the world as the helper

opinione asperius est: it is harder than I thought

opprobrium medicorum: the disgrace of physicians (said of diseases that defy their skills)

opum furiata cupido: a frenzied lust for wealth (Ovid)

opus Dei: the work of God

opus est: there is work; there is need

ora et labora: pray and work (St. Benedict)

ora pro nobis: pray for us

ora pro nobis peccatoribus: pray for us sinners

orando laborando: by prayer and by toil (motto of Rugby School, England)

orate fratres: pray, brothers

orate pro anima: pray for the soul of ...

orate pro invicem: pray for one another (St. James 5:16)

orate pro nobis: pray for us

orator fit, poëta nascitur: the orator is made, the poet is born

ornat spina rosas, mella tegunt apes: the rose is guarded by thorns, and honey is protected by bees

ore rotundo: with a round mouth (i.e., with polished speech; a well-turned phrase)

oremus: let us pray

ornatur propriis industria donis: the gifts with which industry is crowned are her own

ostendo non ostento: I show, not boast

otiosa sedulitas: leisurely zeal

otium cum dignitate: leisure with dignity (Cicero)

otium omnia vitia parit: leisure is the mother of all evil

otium sine dignitate: leisure without dignity

otium sine litteris mors est: leisure without literature is death

ou gnosis, alla praxis: not knowledge only, but practice (a Greek saying)

P

pabulum Acherontis (or, pabulum Acheruntis): food for Acheron (i.e., marked for death; bound for hell) (Plautus)

pacatum ipse regam avitis virtutibus orbem: I shall rule the world pacified by the virtues of my ancestors

pace tanti viri: if so great a man will forgive me (sometimes said sarcastically)

pacis et armorum vigiles: vigilant in peace and arms

pæte, non dolet: it does not hurt, Pætus (after stabbing herself in 43 BCE) (Arria the Elder)

Pallida Mors: Pale Death (Horace)

palma non sine pulvere: the palm is not obtained without struggle

palma virtuti: the palm to virtue

palmam qui meruit ferat: let him bear the palm who has merited it (motto of Lord Nelson and of the University of Southern California)

panem et circenses: bread and the circus games (according to Juvenal, the sole interest of the plebes)

par bene comparatum: a well-matched pair

par negotiis, neque supra: equal to his business and not above it (i.e., he is suited to his work) (Tacitus)

par nobile fratrum: a noble pair of brothers (Horace)

par pari referto: I give back tit for tat

par sit fortuna labori: let the success be equal to the labor

par ternis suppar: the two are equal to the three

parasiticam cœnam quærit: he seeks the supper of a parasite

paratus et fidelis: ready and faithful

paratus sum: I am prepared

parce, parce, precor: spare me, spare me, I pray

parcere personis, dicere de vitiis: to spare persons, to condemn crimes (Martial)

parcere subjectis, et debellare superbos: to spare the vanquished and subdue the proud (Virgil)

parcus deorum cultor et infrequens: a sparing and infrequent worshipper of the gods (Horace)

parem non fert: he endures no equal

parendo vinces: you will conquer by obedience

pari passu: with equal steps (i.e., neck and neck)

pari ratione: by parity of reason

pars minima sui: the smallest part of itself

Parthis mendacior: more mendacious than the Parthians (Horace)

parva componere magnis: to compare small things with great

parva sub ingenti: the small under the protection of the great (motto of Prince Edward Island)

parvis componere magna: to compare great things with small (Virgil)

parvum non parvæ amicitiæ pignus: a slight pledge of no small friendship

patent oves, timent canes, intrepidus maneo: the sheep are frightened, the dogs fear, I stand intrepid

Pater Noster: Our Father

pater patriæ: the father of the country

pathemata mathemata: we learn from the things we suffer (Æsop, from the Greek)

patientia victrix: patience is victorious

patientia vinces: by patience you will conquer

patitur qui vincit: the one who conquers, suffers

patria cara, carior libertas: dear is my homeland, but liberty is dearer

patria est communis omnium parens: our country is the common parent of all (Cicero)

patria est, ubicumque est bene: wherever we are content, that is our country (Pacuvius and Cicero)

patriæ fidus: faithful to my country

patriæ infelici fidelis: faithful to my unhappy homeland (i.e., it is my country, wrong or right)

patriæ pietatis imago: the image of his filial affection (Virgil)

patriis virtutibus: by hereditary virtue

pauca sed bona: few things, but good (i.e., quality, not quantity)

pauca suspexi, pauciora despexi: I have admired few things, I have despised fewer

pauca verba: few words

paulo majora canamus: let us sing of somewhat greater things (Virgil)

paupertatis pudor et fuga: the shame and banishment of poverty (Horace)

pauperum solatio: for the solace of the poor

pax: peace

pax aut bellum: peace or war

pax Domini sit semper vobiscum: the peace of the Lord be with you always

pax huic domui: peace be to this house

pax in bello: peace in war

pax quæritur bello: peace is sought by war (motto of the Cromwell family)

pax vobiscum (or, **pax vobis**): peace be with you (St. Luke 24:36)

peccavi: I have sinned

pecunia non olet: money does not smell

pedibus timor addidit alas: fear gave wings to his feet (Virgil)

Pelio imponere Ossam: to pile Ossa on Pelion (i.e., to attempt to scale heaven)

Penelopæ telam retexens: unraveling the web of Penelope (Cicero)

per acuta belli: through the perils of war

per angusta ad augusta: through adversity to greatness

per ardua: through difficulties

per ardua ad astra: through adversity to the stars (motto of the Royal Air Force)

per ardua liberi: free through difficulty

per ardua surgo: I rise through difficulties

per aspera ad astra: through adversities to the stars (a variation of **ad astra per aspera**, the motto of Kansas)

per crucem ad coronam: by the Cross to a crown

per deos immortales!: for heaven's sake!

per Deum et ferrum obtinui: I have obtained it by God and my sword

per fas et nefas: through means both fair and foul

per inæqualem motum, respectu totius: by an unequal movement in respect to the whole (i.e., the differing speeds of planetary movements)

per mare: by sea

per mare per terram (or, **per mare per terras**): by sea and by land

per obitum: through the death of …

per saltum: by a leap; all at once

per tela per hostes: through arrows and enemies

per tot discrimina rerum: through all manner of calamitous events (Virgil)

per undas et ignes fluctuat nec mergitur: through water and fire she goes plunging but is not submerged (a motto of Paris, whose symbol is a boat)

per varios casus: by various (mis)fortunes

per varios usus artem experientia fecit: practice has brought skill through different exercises (Manilius)

per viam dolorosam: by the way of sorrows

per vias rectas: by right ways

per virtutem sentiamque: through virtue and sentiment

pereat iste: let him die himself

percontando a peritis: constantly asking questions of experts (Cicero)

percussus resurgo: struck down I rise again

pereunt et imputantur: they (the hours) pass away and are reckoned against us (Martial; a saying on a sundial)

perfer et obdura: bear and endure to the end (Ovid)

perfervidum ingenium Scotorum: the very ardent temper of the Scots

perge sed caute: advance but cautiously

periculosæ plenum opus aleæ: a work full of dangerous hazard (i.e., a business pregnant with danger)

periculum fortitudine evasi: by courage I have escaped danger

periissem ni periissem: I had perished unless I had persisted

permissu superiorum: by permission of the superiors

permitte divis cætera: commit the rest to the gods (Horace)

pernicibus alis: with swift wings

persevera Deoque confide: persevere and trust in God

perseverando: by persevering

perseverantia: by perseverance

personæ mutæ: silent characters in a play

persta atque obdura: be steadfast and endure

perstare et præstare: to persevere and to surpass (motto of New York University)

petit alta: he seeks high things

petitio principii: begging the question in a debate

philosophia vero omnium mater artium: philosophy, the true mother of all the arts (Cicero)

pia desideria: the desire after things religious (motto of the Pietistic movement)

pia fraus: a pious fraud

pie repone te: repose in pious confidence

pie vivere et Deum et patriam diligere: to live piously and to love God and country

pietas tutissima virtus: piety is the surest virtue

piscem natare docere: to teach a fish how to swim

placet: it pleases

pluries: at several times

plurima mortis imago: death in very many a form (Virgil)

plus uno maneat perenne sæclo: may it live and last for more than a century (Catullus)

pollicitus meliora: one who gave promise of better things (Horace)

pompholoks ho anthropos: man is an air bubble (a Greek saying)

pons asinorum: the asses' bridge; a severely difficult test or venture (a reference to the fifth proposition in the First Book of Euclid, so named because of its difficulty)

popularis aura: the popular breeze (i.e., popular favor) (Cicero)

porcus Epicuri: a pig of Epicurus

porro unum est necessarium: still there is one thing needful

post bellum auxilium: aid after the war

post equitem sedet atra cura: behind the horseman sits dark care (Horace, said of a fugitive from the law)

post est occasio calva: occasion is bald behind (Dionysius Cato)

post festum venisti: you have come after the feast

post funus spes una superstes: after death only one hope survives

post nubila, Phœbus: after the clouds, the sun

post prœlia præmia (also, **post prælia præmia**): after battles come rewards

post tenebras lux: after darkness, light

post tot naufragia portum: after so many shipwrecks we reach port

post virtutem curro: I run after virtue

postera crescam laude: I shall grow in future praise (motto of the University of Melbourne)

potentia amoris: the power of love

potentissimus affectus amor: love, the most powerful passion

potestas vitæ necisque: power over life and death

potius ingenio quam vi: rather by skill than by force

potius mori quam fœdari: rather to die than to be dishonored

potius sero quam nunquam: better late than never (Livy)

præcedentibus instat: he follows close on those who precede

præfervidum ingenium Scotorum: the fervently serious disposition of the Scots

præmium, virtus, honor: reward, virtue, honor

præmonitus, præmunitus: forewarned, forearmed

præstat opes sapientia: wisdom surpasses wealth

præstat sero quam nunquam: better late than never

præsto et persto: I stand in front and I stand firm

preces armatæ: armed prayers (i.e., with weapons to back them up)

premi, non opprimi: to be pressed, not oppressed

pretium laborum non vile: no cheap reward for our labors (motto of the Order of Golden Fleece)

pretium scientiæ: the price of knowledge

primum mobile: the first motion; the prime mover (i.e., that which sets everything else into motion)

primus inter pares: the first among equals

Primus Motor: the First Mover (i.e., the Creator)

primus ultimusque in acie: first and last in battle

principia, non homines: principles, not men

principiis obsta: stop it from the first (i.e., nip the evil at the bud) (Ovid)

prior tempore, prior jure: first by time, first by right (i.e., first come, first served)

prisco stirpe Hibernico: of ancient Irish stock

pristinæ virtutis memores: mindful of ancient valor (or, of former days)

prius frangitur quam flectitur: he is sooner broken than bent

prius mori quam fidem fallere: die rather than betray trust

pro aris et focis: for our altars and our hearths (i.e., for civil and religious liberty) (Cicero)

pro bono malum: evil for good

pro bono publico: for the public good

pro Christo et patria: for Christ and country

pro Christo et patria dulce periculum: for Christ and country, danger is sweet

pro Deo et Ecclesia: for God and the Church

pro Deo et patria: for God and country

pro Deo et rege: for God and king

pro Ecclesia et patria: for the Church and the country (motto of Trinity College)

pro Ecclesia et Pontifice: for Church and Pope

pro Ecclesia, pro Texana: for the Church, for Texas (motto of Baylor University)

pro et contra (also, **pro et con**): for and against

pro fide ablectus: chosen for fidelity

pro fide et patria: for faith and country

pro libertate patriæ: for the liberty of my country

pro Magna Charta: for the Great Charter

pro mitra coronam: a crown for a miter

pro mundi beneficio: for the benefit of the world (motto of Panama)

pro patria: for the country; for one's country

pro patria et rege: for country and king

pro patria et religione: for country and religion

pro patria invictus: for our unconquered country

pro patria vivere et mori: to live and die for our country

pro patriæ amore: for the love of country

pro pelle cutem: the hide for the sake of the fur (motto of the Hudson Bay Company)

pro rege et patria: for king and country

pro rege et populo: for the king and the people

pro rege et religione: for king and religion

pro rege, lege, et grege: for king, law, and the people (i.e., for ruler, rule, and ruled)

pro rege sæpe, pro patria semper: for king often, for country always

pro salute animæ: for the welfare of the soul

pro scientia et sapientia: for knowledge and wisdom (motto of the University of Mississippi)

pro veritate: for truth

pro virtute: for virtue

pro virtute bellica: for valor in war

probitas verus honor (or **honos**)**:** honesty (or integrity) is true honor

probitate et labore: by honesty and labor

procul a Jove, procul a fulmine: far from Jove, far from his thunderbolts

procul omen abesto!: far be that fate from us! (Ovid)

prodesse civibus: to be of advantage to my fellow citizens

prodesse non nocere: to do good, not evil

prodesse quam conspici: to be of service rather than to be conspicuous

professoria lingua: an expert's (or pendant's) tongue (Tacitus)

prope ad summum, prope ad exitum: near the summit, near the end

propositi tenax: tenacious of purpose

propria virtute audax: daring by my own valor

proprie communia dicere: to speak commonplace things as if they were original

proprio vigore: of one's own strength

prosequitor quodcunque petit: he pursues whatever he seeks

provehito in altum: launch forth into the deep (motto of the Memorial University of Newfoundland)

providentia: providence

providentia divina: by divine providence

proximus sum egomet mihi: I am my nearest neighbor (or nearest of kin); also, I am my own best friend (Terence)

prudens simplicitas: a prudent simplicity

prudens ut serpens, simplex ut columba: wise as a serpent, harmless as a dove (after St. Matthew 10:16)

prudentia et constantia: by prudence and constancy

prudentia et honor: prudence and honor

psyches iatreion: a physic for the mind (i.e., books) (a Greek phrase)

publica salus mea merces: the public safety is my reward

publica virtuti per mala facta via est: a highway is open to virtue through the midst of misfortunes (Ovid)

publicum meritorum præmium: the public reward for public services

pugna pro patria: fight for your country

pugnis et calcibus: with fists and heels (i.e., with all one's might)

pulchre!, bene!, recte!: beautiful!, good!, right! (Horace)

pulchritudo sine fructu: beauty without fruit

pulchritudo vincit: beauty conquers

pulvis et umbra sumus: we are but dust and shadow (Horace)

punctum quæstionis: the point at issue; the crux of the question

Punica fides: Punic faith (i.e., treachery)

puri sermonis amator: a lover of pure speech (Julius Cæsar, said of Terence)

pyr machaira me skalenein: to stir fire with a sword (Pythagoras, from the Greek)

Q

qua vincit victos protegit ille manu: with the same hand with which he conquers he protects the conquered (Ovid)

quæ ante pedes: things at our feet

quæ infra nos nihil ad nos: the things that are below are nothing to us

quæ sequimur fuimus: we flee what we follow

quæ supra: which things are above

quæ sursum volo videre: I desire to see the things that are above

quæ vernant crescent: things that are green will grow

quæcumque (sunt) vera: whatsoever things are true (motto of Northwestern University and the University of Alberta)

quære verum: seek after truth

quærens quem devoret: seeking someone to devour

quærite prime regnum Dei: seek ye first the kingdom of God (a motto of Newfoundland, after St. Matthew 6:33)

qualis ab incepto: the same as from the beginning

qualis artifex pereo!: what an artist dies in me! (dying words of Emperor Nero)

qualis pater, talis filius: like father, like son

qualis rex, talis grex: as is the king, so are the people

qualis vita, finis ita: as in life, so in death

quam diu se bene gesserit: as long as he shall conduct himself properly

quam male conveniunt: how ill-matched they are

quam non terret hyems: which winter does not frighten (i.e., nip with cold)

quam (or quem) te Deus esse jussit: what God commands you to be

quando ullum inveniemus parem?: when shall we find (or look upon) his like again? (after Horace)

quanti fama?: at what price fame?

quantum mutatus ab illo!: how changed from what he once was (Virgil)

quare impedit?: why does he hinder?

quasi vestigias nostras insistere: as if to tread in our footsteps

quem nunc amabis?: whom will you love now? (Catullus)

quem (or quam) te Deus esse jussit: what God commands you to be

qui conducit: he who leads

qui laborat, manducat: he who works, shall eat

qui laborat orat: the one who labors prays (St. Augustine)

qui leges juraque servat: he maintains the laws and justice (Horace)

qui me alit me extinguit: the one who nourishes me extinguishes me (from Shakespeare's *Pericles*)

qui nucleum vult, nucem frangat: who so wishes the kernel must crack the nut (after Plautus)

qui parcit virgæ odit filium: the one who spares the rod hates the child

qui patitur vincit: the one who endures conquers

qui potest capere capist: let him take who can take

qui pro quo: who for whom (i.e., one instead of another)

qui tacet consentit: he who is silent consents

qui tam: who as well

qui trans: who is beyond

qui transtulit sustinet: He who transplanted sustains (motto of Connecticut)

quicquid agunt homines nostri est farrago libelli: all the acts and employments of humankind shall be the subject of this publication (a motto for publishers of newspapers and periodicals) (Juvenal)

quicunque vult servari: whoever will be saved (the beginning of the Creed of Athanasius, or the Quicunque Vult)

quid est veritas?: what is truth? (Pontius Pilate, St. John 18:38)

quid non ebrietas designat?: what does drunkenness not affect? (Horace)

quid nunc?: what now? (i.e., a newsmonger)

quid pro quo: one thing for another (i.e., tit for tat)

quid si nunc cœlum ruat?: what if the sky should now fall? (Terence)

quid verum atque decens: what is true and becoming

quidni?: why not?

quidni pro sodali?: why not for a companion?

quis contra nos?: who is against us?

quis separabit?: who shall separate [Britain from Ireland]? (motto of the Order of St. Patrick)

quo celerius eo melius: the faster the better

quo fas et gloria ducunt: where duty and glory lead

quo Fata vocant: whither the Fates may call

quo jure quaque injuria: right or wrong (Terence)

quo nihil majus meliusve terris: than whom was never anything greater or better on earth (Horace)

quo pax et gloria ducunt: where peace and glory lead (motto of the Duke of York and of the Duke of Clarence)

quo sursum volo videre: I am resolved to look upward

quo vadis?: whither goest thou? (St. John 16:5)

quo warranto?: by what warrant?

quod Anglicana ecclesia libera sit: that the English church shall be free (from the Magna Carta)

quod avertat Deus!: which may God avert! (i.e., God forbid!)

quod Deus bene vertat!: may God grant success!

quod di omen avertant: may the gods avert this omen (Cicero)

quod dixi dixi: what I have said I have said

quod eorum minimis mihi: as to the least of them, so to me (St. Matthew 25:40)

quod erat demonstrandum (Q.E.D.): which was to be proved (after Euclid)

quod ero spero: I hope that I shall be

quod est absurdum: which is absurd

quod est faciendum: which was to be done

quod fors feret, feremus æquo animo: whatever fortune brings, we will patiently bear (Terence)

quod licet Jovi, non licet bovi: what is allowed to Jove is not allowed to the ox

quod me alit me extinguit: that which nourishes me extinguishes me

quod potui perfeci: I have done what I could do

quod scripsi scripsi: what I have written I have written (Pontius Pilate, St. John 20:22)

quod sit, esse velit, nihilque malit: who is pleased with what he is and desires nothing else (Martial)

quod sursum volo videre: I wish to see that which is above

quod verum tutum: what is true is safe

quondam his vicimus armis: we were once victorious with these arms

quorsum vivere mori? Mori vita: wherefore live to die? To die is life

quot capita, tot sensus: so many heads, so many opinions (Terence)

quot homines tot sententiæ (also, **tot homines quot sententiæ**): so many men, so many opinions (Terence)

quot rami tot arbores: so many branches, so many trees (motto of the University of Allahabad)

quot servi tot hostes: so many servants, so many enemies

R

radii omnia lustrant: his rays illuminate all things

rami felicia poma ferentes: branches bearing fruit of good fortune (Ovid)

rara avis (in terris): a rare bird (on earth) (i.e., a prodigy) (Juvenal)

rara bonitas: goodness is rare

rari nantes: swimming here and there (i.e., one here and another there) (Virgil)

ratio est radius divini luminis: reason is a ray of divine light

re infecta: the matter left undone; an unfinished task (Julius Cæsar)

re secunda fortis, dubia fugax: in prosperity courageous, in danger timid (Phædrus)

recte et suaviter: justly and mildly

recto cursu: in a right course

rectus in curia: upright in the court (i.e., innocent of the charges)

reddite Deo: render unto God

redeat miseris, abeat fortuna superbis: may fortune revisit the wretched, and forsake the proud (Horace)

redintegratio amoris: the renewal of love

redire ad nuces: to return to the nuts (i.e., to resume childish interests)

redolet lucerna (or, **redolet lucernam**): it smells of the lamp (a reference to a literary work whose labor was great)

refricare cicatricem: to reopen a wound

regnat populus (adapted from **regnant populi**): the people rule (motto of Arkansas)

relata refero: I tell it as it was told to me (whether truthful or not)

relicta non bene parmula: having dishonorably left my shield behind (Horace)

rem acu tetigisti (or **tetigit**): you have (or he has) touched it with a needle (i.e., you have hit the nail on the head)

remedium tempestivum sit: let there be a timely remedy

remis velisque: with oars and sails (i.e., with all one's might, or with all available power)

remis ventisque: with oars and wind (i.e., with all one's might, or with all available power)

renascentur: they will rise again

renovate animos: renew your courage

renovato nomine: by a revived name

repetens exempla suorum: repeating the example of his ancestors (Virgil)

requiem æternam dona eis, Domine: grant them eternal rest, O Lord

requiescant in pace: may they rest in peace

requiescat in pace: may he or she rest in peace

rerum cognoscere causas: to understand the cause of all things (motto of the London School of Economics and Political Science)

rerum concordia discors: the harmonious discord of things (Horace)

rerum sapientia custos: wisdom is the guardian of all things

res accedent luminis rebus: one light shines upon others

res angusta domi: in straitened circumstances at home (Juvenal)

res crescunt concordia: things grow with harmony

res in cardine est: the matter is on the hinge (i.e., at a point of crisis)

res ipsa loquitur (or, **res loquitur ipsa**): the matter speaks for itself (Cicero)

res non verba: facts not words

res severa est verum gaudium: true joy is an earnest thing (Seneca)

resistite usque ad sanguiam: resist even to bloodshed

respice, adspice, prospice: examine the past, examine the present, examine the future (motto of the City University of New York)

respice, et prospice: look backward and forward

respice finem: look to the end; consider the outcome

resurgam: I shall rise again

retinens vestigia famæ: retracing the footsteps of fame (i.e., the achievements of an honorable ancestry)

revirescimus: we flourish again

revirescit: it flourishes again

reviresco: I flourish again

revocate animos: rouse your courage (Virgil)

rex bibendi: king of drinkers; king of the revelers

rex nunquam moritur: the king never dies

ride si sapis: laugh, if you are wise (Martial)

ridere in stomacho: to laugh inwardly (i.e., in one's sleeve)

ridiculus mus: a ridiculous mouse (Horace)

rore vixit more cicadæ: he lived upon dew like a grasshopper

rosam ne rode: gnaw not the rose

ruat cœlum (or, **ruat cælum**): though the heavens fall (or, let the heavens fall)

ruat cœlum, fiat voluntas tua: your will be done, though the heavens should fall

rudis indigestaque moles: a rude and disordered mass (Ovid)

rupto robore nati: we are born from the broken oak (an allusion to the acorn from which the new oak grows)

rus in urbe: the country in the city (Martial)

rustica veritas: rustic truth

S

sæva indignatio: fierce wrath (Virgil)

sævis tranquillus in undis: calm amid the raging waters (motto of William I of Orange)

sal Atticum: Attic salt (i.e., a keen wit) (Pliny the Elder)

saltem cursu prætervehor omnes: I leap past all in the race

salus extra ecclesiam non est: there is no salvation outside the Church (St. Augustine)

salus in fide: salvation by faith

salus per Christum: salvation through Christ

Salus per Christum Redemptorem (S.C.R.): Salvation through Christ the Redeemer

salus populi suprema est lex: the welfare of the people is the supreme law (Cicero)

salus populi suprema lex esto: let the welfare of the people be the supreme law (after Cicero, the motto of Missouri)

salus populi: the welfare of the people (motto of the University of Missouri)

salus publica: the public good

salva conscientia: with safety to conscience (i.e., without compromising one's conscience)

salva dignitate: with safety to dignity (i.e., without compromising one's dignity)

salva fide: with safety to faith (i.e., without compromising one's faith or promise)

salva res est: the matter is safe (Terence)

salvam fac reginam, O Domine: (fig.) may God save the queen

salve, magna parens: hail, thou great parent (Virgil)

salvo jure: saving the right

salvo jure regis: saving the king's right

salvo ordine: without dishonor to one's order

salvo pudore: saving decency; without offense to modesty

salvum fac regem, O Domine: (fig.) may God save the king

Samnitico non capitur auro: he is not captured by Samnitic gold

sancte et sapienter: with holiness and wisdom

sanctum sanctorum: holy of holies; also, a study or private room

sane baro: a baron indeed

sanguinis pretium sanguis: blood is the price of blood

sapere aude: dare to be wise (Horace)

sapere et tacere: to be wise and silent

sapiens dominabitur astris: the wise will rule the stars

sapientem pascere barbam: to nurse a wise beard (i.e., to appear outwardly wise, as in the philosopher)

sapienti sat: enough for the wise (Plautus)

sapientia donum Dei: wisdom is the gift of God

sapientia et doctrina: wisdom and doctrine (motto of Fordham University)

sapientia humana, stultitia est apud Deum: human wisdom is folly before God

sapientissimus in septem: the wisest of the seven (Cicero, said of Thales)

sapientum octavus: the eighth of the wise men (Horace)

sardonicus risus: a sardonic laugh (i.e., a forced or scoffing laugh)

Sartor Resartus: The Tailor Patched (title of a book by Thomas Carlyle)

sat cito, si sat bene: soon enough, if but well enough (St. Jerome)

sat pulchra, si sat bona: beautiful enough, if good enough (i.e., beauty is as beauty does)

satis diu vel naturæ gloriæ: long enough for the demands both of nature and glory

satis superque (est): enough and more than enough (i.e., enough and some to spare)

satis verborum: enough of words (i.e., enough said)

satis vixi; invictus enim morior: I have lived enough; I die unvanquished (Epaminondas in Cornelius Nepos)

sauciat et defendit: it wounds and defends

scandalum magnatum: an offense against a person of high standing

scandit sublima virtus: virtue scales great heights

scientia est potentia: knowledge is power

scientia sol mentis: knowledge is the light of the mind (motto of the University of Delaware)

scire facias: cause it to be known

scribere jussit amor: love bade me write (Ovid)

scripta manent: writings remain

scuto amoris Divini: with the shield of Divine love

scuto bonæ voluntatis tuæ coronasti nos: with the shield of your good will you (God) have surrounded us

se defendendo: in his own defense

se inserit astris: he places himself among the stars

secundis dubiisque rectus: upright both in prosperous and doubtful circumstances

secundo amne defluit: he floats with the stream

securus judicat orbis terrarum: the verdict of the world is conclusive (St. Augustine)

sed de me ut sileam: but to say nothing of myself (Ovid)

sed hæc prius fuere: but all this is over (Catullus)

sed post est occasio calva: but opportunity is bald behind (i.e., has passed us by)

sed sine labe decus: honor without a stain

sedulitate: by diligence

semel abbas, semper abbas: once an abbot, always an abbot

semel et semper: once and always

semel et simul: one and the same; once and together

semper: always; forever

semper augustus: always an enlarger of empire (Symmachus)

semper avarus eget: the miser is ever in want (Horace)

semper eadem: always the same (motto of Queen Elizabeth I)

semper et ubique: always and everywhere

semper felix: always happy; ever fortunate

semper fidelis (pl. semper fideles): always faithful (motto of the U.S. Marine Corps)

semper honos, nomenque tuum, laudesque manebunt: your honor, your renown, and your praises will last forever (Virgil)

semper idem (masc. and neuter forms): always the same

semper paratus: always ready (motto of the U.S. Coast Guard)

semper patriæ servire præsto: always ready to serve my country

semper præcinctus: ever ready

semper sic: always thus

semper sitiens: always thirsty

semper vigilans: always watchful

semper viret: it always flourishes

semper vivit in armis: he lives ever in arms

seniores priores: the elder ones first

sepulto viresco: I revive from my burial

sequitur patrem non passibus æquis: he follows his father with unequal steps (after Virgil)

sequor non inferior (or, sequor nec inferior): I follow, but I am not inferior

sermoni consona facta: deeds agreeing with words

sero sapiunt Phryges: the Phrygians (or Trojans) became wise too late

sero sed serio: late, but seriously (or, late, but in earnest)

serus in cælum redeas: late may you return to heaven (i.e., long may you live)

serva jugum: preserve the yoke (i.e., preserve the bond of love)

servabit me semper Jehovah: Jehovah will always preserve me

servabo fidem: I will keep faith

servari et servare meum est: my duty is to guard myself and others

servata fides cineri: faithful to the memory of my ancestors

serviendo guberno: I govern by serving (or, by ruling I serve)

servire Deo sapere: to know how to serve God

servitute clarior: more illustrious by serving

Servus Servorum Dei: Servant of the Servants of God (a papal title)

sesquipedalia verba: words a foot and a half long (Horace)

sexu fœmina, ingenio vir: in sex a woman, in natural ability a man (epitaph of Empress Maria Theresa of Austria)

si Deus nobiscum, quis contra nos?: if God be with us, who shall be against us? (after St. Paul in Romans 8:31)

si dis placet (or, **si diis placet**): if it pleases the gods

si fallor, sum: if I am deceived, then I exist (St. Augustine's refutation of skepticism through one's self-awareness of deception)

si fortuna juvat: if fortune favors

si monumentum requiris, circumspice: if you seek his monument, look around you (epitaph of Sir Christopher Wren, architect of London)

si non errasset, fecerat ille minus: if he had not committed an error, his glory would have been less (Martial)

si peccavi, insciens feci: if I have sinned, I have done so unknowingly (Terence)

si quæris monumentum, circumspice: if you seek a monument, look around you (an alternate version of Christopher Wren's epitaph)

si quæris peninsulam amœnam, circumspice: if you seek a pleasant peninsula, look around you (motto of Michigan)

si quis adhuc precibus locus: if there is still any place for prayers (Virgil)

si sic omnes!: if all did thus!

si sit prudentia: if there be but prudence (Juvenal)

si vitam puriter egi: if I have led a pure life (Catullus)

sic ætas fugit: thus does life flee

sic erat in fatis: so stood it in the decrees of fate (Ovid)

sic eunt fata hominum: so go the destinies of men

sic frustra: thus in vain

sic itur ad astra: thus is the way to the stars (i.e., thus the way to immortal fame) (Virgil)

sic me servavit Apollo: thus Apollo preserved (or protected) me (Horace)

sic nos sic sacra tuemur: thus we guard our sacred rights

sic passim: thus in passing (i.e., occurring throughout the pages of a book)

sic prædæ patet esca sui: thus to catch its prey it offers itself as bait

sic semper tyrannis: thus always to tyrants (motto of Virginia)

sic spectanda fides: thus is faith to be examined (from Shakespeare's *Pericles*)

sic transit gloria mundi: thus passes the glory of the world (traditionally recited during the coronation of a new pope)

sic viresco: thus I flourish

sic vita humana: thus is human life

sic volo, sic jubeo: thus I will, thus I command (after Juvenal)

sic vos non vobis nidificatis aves: thus do you birds build nests for others (Virgil)

sica inimicis: a dagger to his enemies

sicut ante: as before

sicut columba: as a dove

sicut lilium: as a lily

sicut meus est mos: as is my habit (Horace)

sicut patribus, sit Deus nobis: as with our fathers, may God also be with us (motto of Boston)

sicut quercus: as the oak

sidere mens eadem mutato: although the constellations change, the mind is constant (motto of the University of Sydney)

sidus adsit amicum: let my propitious star be present

silentio et spe: in silence and hope

simile gaudet simili: like delights in like

simili frondescit virga metallo: a bough grows in its place leaves of the same metal (Virgil)

similia similibus curantur: like cures like

simplex munditiis: simple in elegance (i.e., elegant but not gaudy) (Horace)

simplex sigillum veri: simplicity is the seal of truth (motto of Herman Boerhaave)

simplex signum veri: simplicity is the sign of truth

simul astu et dentibus utor: I use my cunning and my teeth simultaneously

sine cortica natare: to swim without corks

sine cruce, sine luce: without the Cross, without light

sine cura: without care (i.e., to receive a salary for an office that requires no work)

sine fine: without end

sine invidia: without envy

sine ira et studio: without anger and without partiality (Tacitus)

sine justitia, confusio: without justice, confusion

sine labe: without dishonor

sine labe lucebit: he shall shine unblemished

sine macula: without stain or blemish

sine metu: without fear

sine odio: without hatred

sine qua non: without which not (i.e., an indispensable condition)

sint ut sunt, aut non sint: let them be as they are, or not at all

siste, viator!: stop, traveler!

sit pro ratione voluntas: let (good)will stand for reason

sit sine labe decus: let my honor be without stain

sit tibi terra levis, mollique tegaris arena: light lie the earth upon you, soft be the sand that covers you (Martial; a Roman epitaph)

sit tua terra levis: may the earth rest lightly upon you (Seneca; a Roman epitaph)

sit ut est, aut non sit: let it be as it is, or let it not be

sit venia verbis: pardon my words

sitio: I thirst (St. John 19:28; one of the Seven Last Words of Christ)

situ et tempore: in place and time

sol lucet omnibus: the sun shines on all

sol occubuit; nox nulla secuta est: the sun is set; no night has followed (i.e., your greatness shines brighter than your predecessor)

sola cruce: only the Cross

sola Deo salus: salvation is from God alone; safety is in God alone

sola juvat virtus: virtue alone assists

sola nobilitas virtus: virtue alone is true nobility

sola salus servire Deo: our only salvation is in serving God

sola virtus invicta: virtue alone is invincible

sola virtus nobiltat: virtue alone ennobles

sola virtus præstat gaudium perpetuum: virtue alone guarantees perpetual joy

solem fero: I bear the sun

solem ferre possum: I can bear the sun

soli Deo: to God alone

soli Deo gloria: to God alone be the glory

soli Deo honor et gloria: to God alone be honor and glory

solo Deo salus: salvation from God alone

solvuntur risu tabulæ: the case is dismissed amid laughter

spe: with hope (motto of the State University of New York, Buffalo)

spe posteri temporis: in hope of the latter time

spe vivitur: we live in hope

spectas et tu, spectaberis: you see, and you shall be seen

spectemur agendo: let us be seen (or judged) by our actions

spem bonam certamque domum reporto: I bring home with me a good and certain hope

spem gregis: the hope of the flock (Virgil)

spem pretio non emo: I do not give money for mere hopes (Terence)

spem reduxit: hope restored (motto of New Brunswick)

spera in Deo: hope in God

sperandum est: it is to be hoped

sperat infestis, metuit secundis: he hopes in adversity and fears in prosperity (after Horace)

sperate et vivite fortes: hope and live bold(ly)

speratum et completum: hoped for and fulfilled

speravi: I have hoped

speravimus ista dum fortuna fuit: we hoped for that once, while fortune was favorable (Virgil)

spero: I hope

spero et captivus nitor: I hope and, though a captive, I strive

spero infestis me tuo secundis: in prosperity I fear, in adversity I hope

spero meliora: I hope for better things (Cicero)

spes: hope

spes alit: hope nourishes

spes anchora vitæ: hope, the anchor of life

spes bona: good hope (motto of Cape Colony)

spes bona dat vires: good hope gives strength

spes durat avorum: the hope of my ancestors continues

spes gregis: the hope of the flock or the common herd (Virgil)

spes infracta: my hope is unbroken

spes lucis æternæ: the hope of eternal light (or life)

spes mea Christus: Christ, my hope

spes mea in Deo: my hope is in God

spes proxima: hope is near

spes tutissima cœlis: the safest hope is in heaven

spiritus intus alit: the spirit within nourishes (Virgil)

Spiritus Sanctus in corde: the Holy Spirit in the heart

splendida vitia: splendid vices (Tertullian, said of pagan virtues)

splendide mendax: splendidly false (Horace)

splendor sine occasu: splendor without diminishment (motto of British Columbia)

spolia opima: the richest of the spoils

stabit: it shall stand

stabit quocunque jeceris: it shall stand, whichever way you throw it (from the legend on the three-legged crest of the Isle of Man)

stabo: I shall stand

stans cum rege: standing with the king

stans pede in uno: standing upon one leg (i.e., done without effort) (Horace)

stant cætera tigno: the rest stand on a beam

stant innixa Deo: they stand supported by God

stare decisis, et non movere quieta: to stand by things as decided, and not to disturb those that are tranquil

stare super antiquas vias (or, **stare super vias antiquas**): to stand upon the old ways

stat fortuna domus: the good fortune of the house stands

stat magni nominis umbra: he stands, the shadow of a great name (Lucan)

stat pro ratione voluntas: the will stands in place of reason

stat promissa fides: the promised faith remains

stat veritas: truth stands

statio bene fida carinis: a safe harborage for ships

status quo (also, **statu quo**): the state in which it was

status quo ante bellum: the state of things before the war

stemmata quid faciunt?: of what use are pedigrees? (Juvenal)

stella monstrat viam: the star shows the way

stet: let it stand

stet fortuna domus: may the fortune of the house endure (motto of Harrow)

stet pro ratione voluntas: let (good)will stand for reason

stimulat, sed ornat: it stimulates, but it adorns

sto pro veritate: I stand in the defense of truth

stratum super stratum: one layer upon another

strenua inertia: energetic idleness (Horace)

strenua nos exercet inertia: busy idleness urges us on (Horace)

studendo et contemplando indefessus: unwearied in studying and meditation

studiis et rebus honestis: by honorable pursuits and studies (motto of the University of Vermont)

studiis florentem ignobilis oti: indulging in the studies of inglorious leisure (Virgil)

studio minuente laborem: the enthusiasm lessening the fatigue (Ovid)

studium immane loquendi: an insatiable desire for talking (Ovid)

stulta maritali jam porrigit ora capistro: he is now stretching out his foolish head to the matrimonial harness (Juvenal)

stylo inverso: with stylus inverted (i.e., erasing or revising what has been written)

stylum vertere: to correct or change the style

sua cuique utilitas: to everything its own use (Tacitus)

sua cuique voluptas: to each his own pleasure

su se robore firmat: he strengthens himself by his own might

suave mari magno: how pleasant when on a great sea (Lucretius)

suaviter et fortiter: gently and firmly

suaviter in modo, fortiter in re: gently in manner, firmly in deed

sub cruce candida: under the pure white Cross

sub cruce salus: salvation under the Cross

sub cruce veritas: truth under the Cross

sub hoc signo vinces: under this sign you will conquer (variation of **in hoc signo vinces**)

sub Jove: under Jove (i.e., in the open air)

sub lege libertas: liberty under the law

sub libertate quietem: rest under liberty

sub reservatione Jacobæo: with St. James's reservation (i.e., if the Lord wills; see St. James 4:15)

sub robore virtus: virtue under strength

sub silentio: in silence

sub sole, sub umbra virens: increasing both in sunshine and in shade

sub specie æternitatis: under the aspect of eternity (i.e., as a particular manifestation of a universal law) (Spinoza)

sub tegmine fagi: beneath the canopy of the spreading beech (Virgil)

sublimi feriam sidera vertice: with head lifted, I shall strike the stars (Horace)

sublimiora petamus: let us seek higher things

suggestio falsi: the suggestion of falsehood

sui generis: of its own kind; one of a kind

sui juris: of his own right

sui oblitus commodi: regardless of his own interest

suis stat viribus: he stands by his own strength

sum quod eris, fuit quod es: I am what you will be, I was what you are (sometimes used as a tombstone inscription)

sum quod sum: I am what I am

summa rerum vestigia sequor: I follow the highest tracks of things

summa summarum: all in all (Plautus)

summo studio: with the greatest zeal (Cicero)

summum bonum: the highest good (Cicero)

summum jus, summa injuria: extreme law, extreme injury (i.e., the law, strictly interpreted, may be the greatest of injustices) (Cicero)

sumus: we are

sunt lacrimæ (or lacrymæ) rerum: tears are the nature of things (Virgil)

sunt sua præmia laudi: his rewards are his praise

suo Marte: by his own ability or prowess (Cicero)

suo sibi gladio hunc jugulo: with his own sword do I stab him (Terence)

super abissus ambulans: walking on precipices

superest quod supra est: what is above lives on

supra vires: beyond one's powers (Horace)

supremum vale: a last farewell (Ovid)

surgit amari aliquid: something bitter rises (Lucretius)

surgit post nubila Phœbus: the sun rises after the clouds

sursum: upward

sursum corda: lift up your hearts

sus Minervam: a pig teaching Minerva (the goddess of wisdom and commerce)

suscipere et finire: to undertake and to accomplish

suspendens omnia naso: turning up one's nose at everything; sneering at everything (Horace)

suspiria de profundis: sighs from the depths of the soul

sustine et abstine: bear and forbear

sustinet nec fatiscit: he holds up and does not weary

suum cuique: to each his own; to everyone his due (Cicero)

T

ta neura tou polemou: the sinews of war (a Greek phrase)

tabula ex naufragio (or, tabula in naufragio): a plank from a shipwreck

tabula rasa: a smoothed tablet; a blank slate; any blank surface

tace: be silent

tace aut fac: say nothing or do

tacent satis laudant: their silence is praise enough (Terence)

tædet me: I am bored

tædium vitæ: weariness of life (Aulus Gellius)

taliter qualiter: such as it is

tam facti quam animi: as much in action as in intention

tam interna quam externa: as much internal as external

tam Marte quam Minerva: as much by Mars as by Minerva (i.e., as much by war as by wisdom; or, as much by courage as by genius)

tam Marti quam Mercurio: as much for Mars as for Mercury (i.e., qualified as much for war as for trade)

tamquam alter idem: as if a second self (Cicero)

tandem fit surculus arbor: a shoot at length becomes a tree

tandi!: so much for that!

tangere ulcus: to touch a sore (i.e., to reopen a wound; to renew one's grief)

tanquam in speculo: as in a mirror

tanquam nobilis: noble by courtesy

tanquam ungues digitosque suos: as well as his nails and fingers (i.e., at his fingers' end)

tantæ molis erat: so great a task it was

tantas componere lites: to settle such great disputes

tanto fortior, tanto felicior!: the more pluck, the better luck!

tanto homini fidus, tantæ virtutis amator: a faithful friend to so great a man, and a steady admirer of such great virtue

tanto monta: so much does he excel

tantum in superbos: only against the proud

tantus amor scribendi: so great a passion for writing (Horace)

tarde sed tute: slow but sure

te Deum laudamus: we praise thee, O God

te ipsum nosce (also, te nosce or nosce teipsum): know thyself

te stante, virebo: with you standing, I shall flourish

tecum habita: live with yourself (i.e., live within your means)

teloque animus præstantior omni: a spirit superior to every weapon (Ovid)

telos oran macrou biou: to see the end of a long life (Chilon, one of the Seven Sages of Greece, from the Greek)

telum imbelle sine ictu: a feeble dart (or spear) thrown to no effect (i.e., a weak and ineffectual argument) (Virgil)

templa quam dilecta!: temples how beloved! (punning motto of the Temple family)

tempus abire tibi est: it is time for you to depart (Horace)

tempus anima rei: time is the essence of the matter

tempus edax rerum: time, the devourer of all things (Horace and Ovid)

tempus et patientia: time and patience

tempus omnia revelat: time reveals all things

tempus omnia terminat: time ends all things

tempus rerum imperator: time is ruler over all things

tenax et fidelis: steadfast and faithful

tenax propositi: tenacious of purpose

tendit ad astra fides: faith reaches toward heaven

tene fortiter: hold firmly

teneat luceat floreat: may it hold, may it shine, may it flourish

tenebo: I will hold

tenebras expellit et hostes: he expels the darkness and the enemy

tentanda via est: a way must be tried (Virgil)

ter quaterque beatus: thrice and four times blest (Virgil)

teres atque rotundus: polished smooth and rounded (i.e., a polished and well-rounded person) (Horace)

terminus a quo: the point from which it begins (i.e., the starting point)

terminus ad quem: the point at which it ends (i.e., the ending point)

terra firma: solid earth; dry land

terra, flatus, ignis, aqua: earth, air, fire, water

terra incognita: an unknown land or region

terra marique fide: with faith by land and sea

terra marique potens: mighty by land and sea

terræ filius: a son of the earth (i.e., a person of low or unknown origin) (Persius)

terram cœlo miscent (or, terram cælo miscent): they mingle heaven and earth

terras irradient: they shall illuminate the earth (motto of Amherst College)

terrere nolo, timere nescio: I wish not to intimidate, and know not how to fear

tertium quid: a third something (produced by the union of two opposites)

tertius e cœlo cecidit Cato: a third Cato has come down from heaven (Juvenal; said mockingly)

teterrima belli causa: most shameful cause of war (Horace)

tetigisti acu: you have touched it with a needle (i.e., you have hit the nail on the head) (Plautus)

tibi poëma feci: I made a poem for you (Catullus)

tibi soli: to thee alone

time Deum, cole regem: fear God, honor the king

timeo Danaos dona ferentes: I fear the Greeks bearing gifts (Virgil)

timet pudorem: he fears shame

timor addidit alas: fear gave him wings (Virgil)

timor Domini fons vitæ: the fear of the Lord is a fountain of life

timor Domini initium sapientiæ: the fear of the Lord is the beginning of wisdom (or, humorously, the fear of the master/lecturer is the beginning of wisdom) (motto of the University of Aberdeen)

tolle lege, tolle lege: take up and read, take up and read (St. Augustine)

tot homines, quot sententiæ (also, **quot homines, tot sententiæ**): so many men, so many opinions (Terence)

tot rami, quot arbores (also, **quot rami, tot arbores**): so many branches, so many trees

totidem hostes esse quot servos: some many servants, so many enemies (quoted by Seneca)

toto cœlo: by the whole heavens

totum in eo est: all depends on this

totus mundus agit histrionem: all the world plays the actor (i.e., all the world's a stage; reputedly the words on a sign hung at Shakespeare's Globe Theater)

totus mundus exercet histrionem (or, **mundus universus exercet histrioniam**): all the world plays the comedian (or actor) (Petronius)

totus teres atque rotundus: entire, smooth, and round (i.e., complete in itself)

tou aristeuein eneka: in order to excel (a Greek phrase)

traditus non victus: yielded but not conquered

transeat in exemplum: let it stand as an example (or a precedent)

transfixus sed non mortuus: wounded but not dead

tria juncta in uno: three joined in one (a reference to the Christian Trinity; also, a reference to a coalition of three members; motto of the Order of the Bath)

Trinitas in Trinitate: Trinity in Trinity

triumphali e stipite surgens alta petit: rising from triumphal stock it seeks the heights

triumpho morte tam vita: I triumph in death as in life

Troja fuit: Troy was

truditur dies die: day presses on the heels of day (Horace)

Tu, Domine, gloria mea: Thou, O Lord, are my glory

tu ne cede malis: yield not to misfortunes (or evils)

tu quoque: you too (Ovid)

tu quoque, Brute!: you too, Brutus! (a variation of **et tu, Brute**)

Tu solus sanctus: Thou alone art holy

tu vincula frange: break your chains

tua res agitur: it is a matter that concerns you

tuebor: I will defend; I will protect

tunica propior pallio est: my tunic is nearer (my skin) than my cloak (Plautus)

turris fortis mihi Deus: God is a tower of strength to me

turris fortissima est nomen Jehovah: an exceedingly strong tower is the name of Jehovah

tuta timens: fearing even safety (Virgil)

tutor et ultor: the protector and the avenger

tutum monstrat iter: he showed a safe road

tutum refugium: a safe refuge

tutum te littore sistam: I shall set you safe upon the shore

tuum est: it is yours (or, your own)

U

uberrima fides: super-abundant faith (or confidence)

ubi amor, ibi fides: where there is love, there is faith

ubi bene, ibi patria: where it is well with me, there is my country

ubi dolor, ibi digitus: where the pain is, there the finger will be

ubi homines sunt, modi sunt: where there are persons, there are manners

ubi lapsus?, quid feci?: where have I slipped?, what have I done?

ubi libertas, ibi patria: where there is liberty, there is my country

ubi mel, ibi apes: where there is honey, there are bees (Plautus)

ubi reddunt ova columbæ: where the pigeons lay their eggs (i.e., the roosts of eminence) (Juvenal)

ubi sæva indignatio cor ulterius lacerare nequit: where bitter indignation cannot lacerate my heart anymore (epitaph of Jonathan Swift)

ubi scriptum?: where is it written?

ubi uber, ibi tuber: where the soil is rich, there you will find roots (Apuleius)

ubique: everywhere

ubique patriam reminisci: everywhere to remember our homeland

ulcus tangere: to touch a sore

ultima ratio regum: the last argument of kings (i.e., military force; said to have been engraved on a cannon by order of Louis XIV)

ultima Thule: remotest Thule (Virgil)

ultimum moriens: the last to die

ultimus Romanorum: the last of the Romans

ultorum ulciscitur ultor: avenger avenges avenger

ultra vires: beyond the powers

ultus avos Troiæ: he has avenged his Trojan ancestors

una et eadem persona: one and the same person

una manu latam libertati viam faciet: with one hand he will make for himself a broad path to freedom (Seneca)

una voce: with one voice; unanimously

unguibus et rostro: with talons and beak (i.e., tooth and nail)

unguibus et rostro, atque alis armatus in hostem: armed with talons, beak, and wings against the enemy

unguis in ulcere: a claw in the wound (i.e., a knife in the wound) (Cicero)

uni æquus virtuti, atque ejus amicis: a friend equally to virtue and to virtue's friends (Horace)

unica semper avis: the bird that is ever unique

unica virtus necessaria: virtue is the only thing necessary

unita: united

unitas: unity

unitate fortior: stronger by being united

uno ictu: at one blow; at once

uno impetu: in one motion

unum pro multis dabitur caput: one will be sacrificed for many (Virgil)

unus atque unicus amicus: one and only friend (Catullus)

unus et idem: one and the same

unus vir, nullus vir: one man, no man (i.e., two are better than one)

urbem latericiam (or lateritiam) invenit, marmoream reliquit: he found a city of brick, and left it one of marble (Suetonius, said of Cæsar Augustus)

urbi et orbi: for the city (Rome) and the world

urbs in horto: a city in a garden (motto of Chicago)

usque ad aras: to the very altars (i.e., to the last extremity)

usque ad sidera tellus: the earth rises up to the stars

usque recurrit: it always returns

usus est tyrannus: custom is a tyrant

usus me docuit: practice (or experience) has taught me

ut apes geometriam: as bees practice geometry

ut canis e Nilo: like a dog by the Nile (i.e., drinking and running)

ut incepit fidelis sic permanet: as loyal as she began, so she remains (motto of Ontario)

ut mos est: as the custom is (Juvenal)

ut pictura, poësis (erit): as with a picture, so (it will be) with a poem (Horace)

ut prosim: that I may be of use

ut quocunque paratus: prepared on every side

ut redeat miseris, abeat fortuna superbis: that fortune may leave the proud, and return to the wretched (Horace)

ut reficiar: that I may be refreshed

ut vivas vigila: watch that you may live

utcunque placuerit Deo: as it shall please God

utere loris: use the reins

uterque bonus belli pacisque minister: a good administrator equally in peace as in war (Ovid)

uti non abuti: to use, not to abuse

uti possidetis: as you now possess (Justinian)

utile dulci: the useful with the delightful (or with the agreeable) (Horace)

utilium sagax rerum: sagacious in making useful discoveries (Horace)

utinam noster esset: would that he were ours

Utopia: no place (the title of Thomas More's satirical book about a perfect world)

V

vade ad formicam: go to the ant

vade in pacem (also, **vade in pace**): go in peace

vade mecum: go with me (i.e., a constant companion; a handbook)

vade post me, satana!: get thee behind me, you satan! (St. Matthew 16:23)

vade retro!: avaunt!; begone!

væ soli: woe to the solitary person (Ecclesiastes 4:10)

væ victis!: woe to the vanquished! (Livy, attributed to King Brennus; also Plautus)

valeat quantum valere potest: let it pass for what it is worth

valeat res ludicra: farewell to the drama (also, farewell to the ridiculous) (Horace)

valet ancora (or **anchora**) **virtus:** virtue is a strong anchor

valete ac plaudite: farewell and applaud (Terence; the final line of Roman actors at the end of a performance)

vanitas vanitatum, omnia vanitas: vanity of vanities, all is vanity

varia sors rerum: the changeable lot of circumstances (Tacitus)

vehimur in altum: we are carried out into the depths

vel cæco appareat: it would be obvious to the blind

vel Jovi cedere nescit: he does not yield, even to Jove

vel prece vel pretio: with either prayer or price (i.e., for either love or for money)

velis et remis: with sails and oars (i.e., by all possible means)

velle bene facere: to wish to do well

velocem tardus assesquitur: the slow overtakes the swift

velut ægri somnia: like the dreams of the sick (Horace)

velut arbor ævo: as a tree with the passage of time (motto of the University of Toronto)

velut inter ignis luna minores: as shines the moon among the lesser fires (Horace)

veluti in speculum: even as in a mirror

venale pecus: the venal herd (Juvenal)

vendere fumos: to sell smoke (i.e., to make empty promises)

vendidit hic auro patriam: he sold his country for gold (Virgil)

veni, Creator Spiritus: come, Creator Spirit

veni, vidi, vici: I came, I saw, I conquered (Julius Cæsar's message to the Roman Senate, declaring his victory over the king of Pontus)

venia sit dicto: pardon the expression (or remark)

venite, adoremus Dominum: come, let us adore the Lord

ventis secundis: with favorable winds

vento intermisso: the wind having died down

ventum ad supremum est: a wind has come, we are at our last shift (i.e., we have a crisis on our hands) (Virgil)

ventura desuper urbi: destined to come down on the city from above (after Virgil)

ver non semper viret: Spring does not always flourish (motto of Lord Vernon, rendered "vernon" always flourishes)

verax atque probus: trustworthy and honest

verba rebus aptare: to fit words to things (i.e., to call something what it is)

verba togæ sequeris: you follow words of the toga (i.e., the language of the cultured class) (Persius)

verbatim et literatim: word for word and letter for letter

verbera, sed audi: whip me, but hear me

verbis ad verbera: from words to blows

verbo tenus: as far as the word goes

verbum caro factum est: the Word was made flesh (after St. John 1:14)

verbum sapienti: a word to the wise

veritas: truth (motto of Harvard University)

veritas et virtus vincunt: truth and virtue conquer

veritas liberabit: truth will liberate

veritas magna est et prævalet: truth is great and prevails

veritas nunquam perit: truth never dies

veritas omnia vincit: truth conquers all things

veritas prævalebit: truth will prevail

veritas temporis filia: truth, the daughter of time

veritas victrix: truth the conqueror

veritas vincit: truth conquers

veritas vos liberabit: the truth shall set you free (motto of the Johns Hopkins University, after St. John 8:32)

veritate et justitia: with truth and justice

vero nihil verius: nothing truer than truth

verso pollice: with thumb turned [down] (Juvenal)

vertitur ad solem: it turns toward the sun

vertitur in lucem: it is changed into light

verus ad finem: true to the end

verus et fidelis semper: always true and faithful

vestigia morientis libertatis: the footprints of dying liberty (Tacitus)

vestigia terrent: the footprints frighten me (Horace)

vestis virum facit: the garment makes the man

vestras spes uritis: you burn your hopes (Virgil)

veteris vestigia flammæ: the traces of my former flame (Virgil)

vi et armis: by force and arms

vi et industria: by strength and industry

vi et veritate: by force and by truth

vi et virtute: by strength and valor

vi victa vis: force overcome by force (Cicero)

vi vivo et armis: I live by force and arms

via crucis, via lucis: the way of the Cross [is] the way of light

via media: the middle way

via trita, via tuta: the beaten path, the safe path

vicarius non habet vicarium: a vicar cannot have a vicar

vicisti, Galilæe: You have conquered, O Galilean (the dying words of Julian the Apostate)

vicit, pepercit: he conquered, he spared

victi vicimus: conquered, we conquer (after Plautus)

victis honor: honor to the vanquished

victor mortalis est: the conqueror is mortal

victoria: victory

victoria concordia crescit: victory is increased by concord

victoria, et per victoriam vita: victory, and by victory he assured his life

victoria, et pro victoria vitam: victory, and for victory he sacrificed his life

victoria mihi Christus: Christ is victory to me

victoria Pyrrhica: a Pyrrhic victory, in which the victor is worse off than the vanquished

victoriæ gloria merces: glory is the reward of victory

victoriam coronat Christus: Christ crowns the victory

victoriam malle quam pacem: to prefer victory to peace (Tacitus)

victrix fortunæ sapientia: wisdom, conqueror of fortune (Juvenal)

victus vincimus: conquered, we conquer (Plautus)

vide et crede: see and believe

video, et taceo: I see, and I am silent

vigilans et audax: vigilant and bold

vigilans non cadit: the vigilant man falls not

vigilanter: watchfully; vigilantly

vigilantia: vigilance

vigilantia non cadit: vigilance does not fall

vigilantia, robur, voluptas: vigilance, strength, pleasure

vigilantibus: to be watchful

vigilate: watch; be watchful

vigilate et orate: watch and pray

vigilo: I watch

vigilo et spero: I watch and I hope

vincam aut moriar: I will conquer or die

vincere aut mori: to conquer or die

vincere vel mori: to conquer or die

vincit amor patriæ: the love of country conquers (Virgil)

vincit cum legibus arma: he conquers arms by laws

vincit omnia pertinax virtus: stubborn virtue conquers all

vincit omnia veritas: truth conquers all things

vincit omnia virtus: virtue conquers all things

vincit pericula virtus: virtue conquers dangers

vincit qui patitur: he conquers who endures

vincit veritas: truth conquers

vincit virtute: virtue conquers

vindictæ trahit exitium: revenge brings with it ruin

vino tortus et ira: tormented by wine and anger (Horace)

vinum incendit iram: wine kindles wrath (Seneca)

vir bonus, dicendi peritus: a good man, skilled in speaking (Cato the Elder)

vir super hostem: a man above an enemy

vires acquirit eundo: it gathers strength as it goes along (Virgil, said of fame)

vires artes mores: strength, arts, customs (motto of Florida State University)

vires et honor: strength and honor

virescit vulnere virtus: virtue flourishes from a wound

viret in æternum: it flourishes forever

viribus unitis: with united strength

virtus ariete fortior: virtue is stronger than a battering ram

virtus basis vitæ: virtue is the basis of life

virtus castellum meum: virtue my castle

virtus clara æternaque habetur: virtue is bright and everlasting (Sallust)

virtus est militis decus: valor is the soldier's honor (Livy)

virtus et honestas: virtue and honesty

virtus hominem jungit Deo: virtue unites man with God (Cicero)

virtus in actione consistit: virtue consists in action

virtus in arduis: virtue (or valor) in difficulties

virtus incendit vires: virtue kindles one's strength

virtus invicta: unconquered virtue

virtus invicta gloriosa: unconquered virtue is glorious

virtus mille scuta (or, **virtus millia scuta**): virtue is a thousand shields

virtus nobilitat: virtue ennobles

virtus non stemma: virtue, not pedigree

virtus non vertitur: virtue (or valor) does not turn

virtus paret robur: virtue begets strength

virtus post nummos: virtue after money (Horace)

virtus potentior auro: virtue is more powerful than gold

virtus probata florescit (or **florebit**): virtue tested flourishes (or blooms)

virtus repulsæ nescia sordida: virtue unconscious of base repulse

virtus requiei nescia sordidæ: virtue that knows no mean repose

virtus semper viridis: virtue is always green (i.e., virtue never fades)

virtus sibi aureum: virtue is worth gold to itself

virtus sola nobilitat: virtue alone confers nobility

virtus sub cruce crescit, ad æthera tendens: virtue increases under the Cross, and looks to Heaven

virtus sub pondere crescit: virtue increases under burden

virtus unita, valet: virtue united, prevails

virtus vincit invidiam: virtue conquers envy

virtute: by virtue

virtute cresco: I grow by virtue

virtute et armis: by valor and arms (motto of Mississippi)

virtute et claritate: by virtue and renown

virtute et fide: by virtue and faith

virtute et fidelitate: by virtue and fidelity

virtute et fortuna: by virtue and fortune

virtute et labore: by virtue and labor

virtute et numine: by virtue and the gods

virtute et opera: by virtue and industry

virtute et valare luceo non uro: by virtue and valor I shine, but do not burn

virtute fideque: by virtue and faith

virtute me involvo: I wrap myself in virtue

virtute non astutia: by virtue not by craft

virtute non verbis: by virtue not by words

virtute, non viris: by virtue, not by men

virtute officii: by virtue of office

virtute parta tuemini: defend what is acquired by valor

virtute probitate: by virtue and honesty

virtute quies: in virtue there is rest

virtute res parvæ crescunt: small things increase by virtue

virtute securus: secure through virtue

virtute vici: I have conquered by virtue

virtutem sequitur fama: fame follows virtue

virtutes et honor: virtue and honor

virtutes parvæ crescunt: small things increase by virtue

virtuti: to virtue

virtuti fortuna comes: fortune, companion of virtue

virtuti nihil obstat et armis: nothing can stand against valor and arms

virtuti non armis fido: I trust to virtue not to arms

virtuti paret robur: strength follows virtue

virtutis amor: the love of virtue

virtutis amore: from love of virtue

virtutis avorum præmium: the reward of the virtue (or valor) of my ancestors

virtutis fortuna comes: fortune is the companion of valor (motto of the Duke of Wellington)

virtutis gloria merces: glory, the reward of virtue

virtutis præmium: virtue's reward

virtutis regia merces: royal is the reward of virtue

virtutis trophæa novæ non degener addet: in keeping with family tradition, he will add new trophies of valor

virum volitare per ora: to fly through the mouths of men (i.e., to spread like wildfire)

vis amoris: the force of love

vis est ardentior intus: the power is more ardent within

vis fortibus arma vigor: vigor is arms to brave men

vis nescia vinci: a power that knows not defeat

vis unita fortior: power is strengthened by union; union is strength

vis viva: the living power

vita brevis, ars longa: life is short, art is long (Horace and Seneca, after Hippocrates)

vita est hominum quasi quum ludas tesseris: the life of man is like a game of dice (Terence)

vita et pectore puro: with pure life and heart

vita sine litteris (or **literis**) **mors est:** life without literature is death

vitæ philosophia dux, virtutis indagatrix: O philosophy, guide of life and discoverer of virtue (Cicero)

vitæ postscenia celant: they conceal the behind-the-scenes part of life

vitæ via virtus: virtue is the way of life

vitam impendere vero: to expend one's life for the truth (Juvenal)

vivamus atque amemus: let us live and let us love (Catullus)

vivant rex et regina: long live the king and queen

vivat regina: long live the queen

vivat respublica: long live the republic

vivat rex: long live the king

vive hodie: live for today

vive memor Lethi: live ever mindful of death (Lethe, a reference to the underworld, was the river whose waters brought forgetfulness of the past) (Persius)

vive ut semper vivas: so live that you may live forever

vive ut vivas: live that you may truly live

vive, vale (or, **vive, valeque**): long life to you, farewell (Horace)

vivere est cogitare: to live is to think (Cicero)

vivere militare est: to live is to fight (Seneca)

vivere sat vincere: to conquer is to live enough

vivida vis animi: the strong force of the mind (Lucretius)

vivimus aliena fiducia: we live by trusting one another (Pliny the Elder)

vivimus in posteris: we live in our posterity

vivit ad extremum: it lives to the end

vivit Leo de Tribu Juda: the Lion of the Tribe of Judah lives

vivitur ingenio: he lives by skill

vix ea nostra voco: I can scarcely call these things our own (Ovid, an allusion to one's ancestry)

vixere fortes ante Agamemnona multi: many brave men lived before Agamemnon (Horace)

vocat in certamina divos: he calls the gods to arms (Virgil)

volando, reptilia sperno: flying, I despise reptiles

volat ambiguis mobilis alis hora: the shifting hour flies with doubtful wings (Seneca)

volat hora per orbem: time flies through the world (Lucretius)

volens et potens: willing and able

volens et valens: willing and able

volente Deo: God willing (Virgil)

volo, non valeo: I am willing but unable

volventibus annis: with revolving years (i.e., as the years roll on)

vota vita mea: my life is devoted

vox clamantis in deserto: the voice of one crying in the wilderness (St. John 1:23; motto of Dartmouth College)

vox et præterea nihil: a voice and nothing more (i.e., sound without sense)

vox faucibus hæsit: the voice stuck in the throat (i.e., dumbstruck) (Virgil)

vox manet: the voice remains (Ovid)

vox omnibus una: one cry was common to them all (Virgil)

vox populi, vox Dei: the voice of the people [is] the voice of God

vox, veritas, vita: voice, truth, life (motto of the California State University)

vulneratur non vincitur: wounded, not vanquished

vulneratus non victus: wounded but not conquered

vulnere sano: I cure by a wound

vulneror, non vincor: I am wounded, but not vanquished

Z

zoë kai psyche: life and soul (a Greek phrase)
zonam perdidit: he has lost his money belt (i.e., he is ruined!; all is lost!) (Horace)

FAMILIAR LATIN QUOTATIONS

A

a diis quidem immortalibus quæ potest homini major esse pœna, furore atque dementia?: what greater punishment can the immortal gods inflict upon man than madness or insanity? (Cicero)

A!, virgo infelix, herbis pasceris amaris!: ah, unfortunate maiden, you will have to graze on bitter herbs! (Calvus)

abiit, excessit, evasit, erupit: he has left, gone off, escaped, broken away (Cicero, said of Catiline's flight)

absentem qui rodit amicum, qui non defendit, alio culpante; hic niger est; hunc tu, Romane, caveto: he who attacks an absent friend, or who does not defend him when spoken ill of by another; that man is a dark character; you, Romans, beware of him (Horace)

absentes tinnitu aurium præsentire sermones de se receptum est: it is generally admitted that those absent are warned by a ringing in the ears when they are being talked about (Pliny the Elder)

abstineas igitur damnandis; hujus enim vel una potens ratio est, ne crimina nostra sequantur ex nobis geniti; quoniam dociles imitandis turpibus ac pravis omnes sumus: let us refrain from doing ill; for one powerful reason, lest our children should follow our crimes; we are all too prone to imitate whatever is base and depraved (Juvenal)

ac primam scelerum matrem, quæ semper habendo plus sitiens patulis rimatur faucibus aurum, trudis avaritiam: expel avarice, the mother of all wickedness, who, always thirsty for more, opens wide her jaws for gold (Claudian)

accipe nunc Danaum insidias, et crimine ab uno disce omnes: learn now of the treachery of the Greeks, and from one example the character of the nation may be known (Virgil)

accipe nunc, victus tenuis quid quantaque secum afferat. In primis valeas bene: now learn what and how great benefit a moderate diet brings with it. Before all, you will enjoy good health (Horace)

accipiunt leges, populus quibus legibus exlex: they consent to laws that place the people outside the law (Lucilius)

ad nullum consurgit opus, cum corpore languet: when the body is indisposed, it is in vain that we call on the mind for any strenuous application (Gallus)

ad populum phaleras, ego te intus et in cute novi: to the vulgar herd with your trappings, I know you both inside and outside (i.e., I know that person too well to be deceived by appearances) (Persius)

adde cruorem stultitiæ, atque ignem gladio scrutare: to your folly add bloodshed, and stir the fire with the sword (Horace)

adde quod ingenuas didicisse fideliter artes emollit mores nec sinit esse feros: add the fact that to have studied faithfully the liberal arts softens behavior, not allowing it to be savage (Ovid)

adeone homines immutari ex amore, ut non cognoscas eundem esse?: that a person should be so changed by love, as not to be known again as the same person? (Terence)

adeste, fideles, læti triumphantes; venite, venite in Bethlehem: O come, all ye faithful, joyful and triumphant; O come, ye, O come, ye, to Bethlehem (a Christian hymn)

adhuc neminem cognovi poëtam, qui sibi non optimus videretur: I have never yet known a poet who did not think himself super-excellent (Cicero)

adulandi gens prudentissima laudat sermonem indocti, faciem deformis amici: the skillful class of flatterers praises the discourse of the ignorant and the face of the disfigured friend (Juvenal)

æquam memento rebus in arduis servare mentem, non secus in bonis ab insolenti temperatam lætitia: when things are steep, remember to stay level-headed and to restrain yourself from immoderate joy in prosperity (Horace)

æstuat infelix angusto limite mundi: the unhappy man frets at the narrow limits of the world (Juvenal)

ætas parentum pejor avis tulit nos nequiores, mox daturos progeniem vitiosiorem: the age of our fathers, which was worse than that of our ancestors, produced us, who are shortly to raise a progeny even more vicious than ourselves (Horace)

agere considerate pluris est quam cogitare prudenter: it is of more consequence to act considerately than to think sagely (Cicero)

agnosco veteris vestigia flammæ: I recognize some traces of my former flame (i.e., my passion is not wholly extinguished) (Virgil)

Agnus Dei, qui tollis peccata mundi, miserere nobis, dona nobis pacem: Lamb of God, who takes away the sins of the world, have mercy on us, grant us peace (from the Catholic Mass)

ah!, quam dulce est meminisse: ah!, how sweet it is to remember

ah!, vitam perdidi operose nihil agendo: alas!, I have lost my life in laboring over nothing (Grotius)

alea jacta est: the die is cast (Julius Cæsar, after crossing the Rubicon in 49 BCE)

aliena negotia centum per caput, et circa saliunt latus: a hundred troubles of other people leap through my head and at my side (Horace)

aliena negotia curo, excussus propriis: I attend to the business of other people, having lost my own (Horace)

alieni appetens, sui profusus: greedy for the things of others, lavish with his own (Sallust, in reference to Catiline)

aliquod crastinus dies ad cogitandum dabit: tomorrow will give some food for thought (Cicero)

alter remus aquas, alter mihi radat arenas: let me strike the water with one oar, and with the other scrape the sands (i.e., let me stay close to shore) (Propertius)

alter rixatur de lana sæpe caprina propugnat nugis armatus: another frequently disputes about goat's wool and rises in arms for trifles (Horace)

altera manu fert lapidem, panem ostentat altera (or **altera panem ostentat**): he carries a stone in one hand, and shows bread in the other (Plautus)

alterius sic altera poscit opem res et conjurat amice: thus one thing demands the aid of the other and both unite in friendly assistance (Horace)

alterutra clarescere fama; sive bonum, sive malum, fama est: to become famous in one way or the other; whether it be good or bad, it is fame

amabilis insania; mentis gratissimus error: a delightful insanity; a most pleasing error of the mind (Horace)

ambiguas in vulgum spargere voces: to scatter ambiguous reports among the people (Virgil)

amor et melle et felle est fœcundissimus: gustu dat dulce, amarum ad satietatem usque aggerit: love has both honey and gall in abundance: it gives sweetness to the taste, but it also brings bitterness to satiety (Plautus)

amori finem tempus, non animus facit: it is time, not the mind, that puts an end to love (Publilius Syrus)

amoto quæramus seria ludo: joking aside, let us turn to serious matters (Horace)

amphora cœpit institui; currente rota cur urceus exit?: a vase was begun; why from the revolving wheel does it turn out a worthless pitcher? (i.e., what began with great fanfare turned out to be something of little note) (Horace)

ampliat ætatis spatium sibi vir bonus; hoc est vivere bis vita posse priore frui: the good man extends the terms of his life; it is to live twice to be able to enjoy one's former life (Martial)

an dives sit omnes quærunt, nemo an bonus: everyone inquires if he is rich, no one asks if he is good

an nescis, quantilla prudentia mundus (or **orbis**) **regatur?:** do you not know with how very little wisdom the world is governed?

an præter esse reale actualis essentiæ sit aliud esse necessarium, quo res actualiter existat?: whether, besides the real being of the actual being, there be any other being necessary to cause a thing to be? (Martinus Scriblerus, said as a jibe against philosophers)

an quidquid stultius, quam quos singulos contemnas, eos aliquid putare esse universos?: can there be any greater folly than the respect you pay to men collectively when you despise them individually? (Cicero)

an quisquam est alius liber, nisi ducere vitam cui licet, ut voluit?: is there a man free, other than he, who has the power of passing life in what manner he pleases? (i.e., the essence of freedom is to do as one pleases without injury to another) (Persius)

anima certe, quia spiritus, in sicco habitare non potest; ideo in sanguine fertur habitare: the soul, which is spirit, cannot dwell in dust; it is carried along to dwell in the blood (St. Augustine)

animal bipes implume (or, **animal implume, bipes**): a two-legged animal without feathers (Plato's definition of man, ridiculed by Diogenes as a "plucked chicken")

animoque supersunt jam prope post animam: their spirit seems even to survive their breath (Sidonius Apollinaris)

animum pictura pascit inani: he fills his mind with an idle picture (Virgil)

animus hoc habet argumentum divinitatis suæ, quod illum divina delectant: the soul has this proof of its divinity, that divine things delight it (Seneca)

animus hominis semper appetit agere aliquid: the mind of man is always longing to do something (Cicero)

animus quod perdidit optat atque in præterita se totus imagine versat: the mind yearns after what is gone and loses itself in dreaming of the past (Petronius)

ante, inquit, cicumspiciendum est, cum quibos edas et bibas, quam quid edas et bibas: he (Epicurus) says that you should rather have regard to the company with whom you eat and drink, than to what you eat and drink (Seneca)

ante senectutem curavi ut bene viverem, in senectute (curo) ut bene moriar; bene autem mori est libenter mori: before old age I took care to live well; in old age I take care to die well; but to die well is to die willingly (Seneca)

ante tubam tremor occupat artus: before the trumpet sounds he trembles all over (Virgil)

antequam incipias, consulto; et ubi consulueris, facto opus est: before you begin, consider well; and when you have considered, act (Sallust)

apparent rari nantes in gurgite vasto: they appear thinly scattered and swimming in the vast deep (i.e., brilliant thoughts are sometimes lost in an ocean of words) (Virgil)

aquam hercle plorat, quom lavat, profundere: he will even weep to throw away the water he has washed with (Plautus)

Arcades ambo, et cantare pares, et respondere parati: Arcadians both, and both equally skilled in the song, and ready in the response (Virgil)

arcanum neque tu scrutaberis ullius unquam; commissumque teges et vino tortus et ira: never inquire into another man's secret; but conceal that which is entrusted to you, though tortured both by wine and passion to reveal it (Horace)

ardeat ipsa licet, tormentis gaudet amantis: though she is aflame herself, she takes joy in the torments of her lover (Juvenal)

ardua cervix, argumtumque caput, brevis alvos, obessaque terga, luxuriatque toris animosum pectus: his neck is high and erect, his head replete with intelligence, his belly short, his back full, and his proud chest swells with hard muscles (Virgil)

ardua molimur; sed nulla nisi ardua virtus: I attempt an arduous task; but there is no virtue that is not of difficult achievement (Ovid)

argentum accepi, dote imperium vendidi: I have received money, and sold my authority for her dowry (Plautus)

argilla quidvis imitaberis uda: you may model (or mold) any form you please out of moist clay (Horace)

arma amens capio; nec sat rationis in armis: I madly take arms; but have not wit enough to use them to any purpose (Virgil)

arma, viri, ferte arma!; vocat lux ultima victos, nunquam omnes hodie moriemur inulti: arms, ye men, bring me arms!; their last day summons the vanquished; not all of us shall die unavenged this day (Virgil)

arma virumque cano, Troiæ qui primus ab oris Italiam fato profugus Laviniaque venit litora, multum ille et terris jactatus et alto vi superum, sævæ memorem Iunonis ob iram: I sing of arms and the man who first from the shores of Troy came destined an exile to Italy and the Lavinian beaches, much buffeted he on land and on the deep by force of the gods because of fierce Juno's never-forgetting anger (Virgil, opening lines of the *Aeneid*)

ars est sine arte, cujus principium est mentiri, medium laborare, et finis mendicare: it is an art without art, which has its beginning in falsehood, its middle in toil, and its end in poverty (i.e., alchemy)

arte citæ veloque rates remoque moventur; arte levis currus, arte regendus amor: by arts, sails, and oars, ships are rapidly moved; arts move the light chariot, and establish love (Ovid)

artificis Naturæ ingens opus aspice: look upon the immense work of the artist Nature

asperges me, Domine, hyssopo, et mundabor: sprinkle me with hyssop, Lord, and I shall be clean (from the Catholic Mass)

asperges me hyssopo, et mundabor; lavabis me, et super nivem dealbabor: sprinkle me with hyssop and I shall be clean; wash me and I will be made whiter than snow (Psalm 51:7)

assiduo labuntur tempora motu, non secus ad flumen. Neque enim consistere flumen. Nec levis hora potest: time glides by with constant movement, not unlike a stream. For neither can a stream stay its course, nor can the fleeting hour (Ovid)

at cum longa dies sedavit vulnera mentis, intempestive qui fovet illa novat: when time has assuaged the wounds of the mind, he who unseasonably reminds us of them opens them afresh (Ovid)

at ingenium, ingens inculto latet hoc sub corpore: yet under this rough exterior lies concealed a mighty genius (Horace)

at non effugies meos iambos: but you cannot escape my iambics (Catullus)

at pater ut gnati, sic nos debemus amici si quod sit vitium non fastidire: but at least we might do for a friend what a father does for his child, and not be disgusted by a blemish (Horace)

at pulchrum est digito monstrari et dicier, hic est: it is pleasing to be pointed at with the finger and then have it said, there he is (Persius)

at tuba terribili sonitu taratantara dixit: but the trumpet sounded with its terrible taratantara (Ennius)

at vindicta bonum vita jucundius ipsa; nempe hoc indocti: but revenge is a blessing sweeter than life itself; or so rude men feel (Juvenal)

atque in perpetuum, frater, ave atque vale: and so, brother, hail and farewell forever (Catullus)

atque in rege tamen pater est: and yet in the king there is the father (Ovid)

atque inter silvas Academi quærere verum: and seek for truth in the groves of the Academy (Horace)

atqui vultus erat multa et præclara minantis: and yet you had the look of one who threatened (i.e., promised) many fine things (Horace)

audax omnia perpeti gens humana ruit per vetitum et nefas: in its boldness to dare all things, the human race rushes into that which is wicked and forbidden (Horace)

aude aliquid brevibus Gyaris et carcere dignum, si vis esse aliquis—probitas laudatur et alget: dare to do something worthy of transportation and imprisonment, if you wish to be somebody—virtue is praised but left out to freeze (Juvenal)

auferre, trucidare, rapere, falsis nominibus imperium, atque; ubi solitudinem faciunt, pacem appellant: to rob, to ravage, to murder, in their imposing language, are the arts of civil policy. Where they have made the world a desert, they call it peace (Tacitus)

augescunt aliæ gentes, aliæ minuuntur inque brevi spatio mutantur sæcula animantum et quasi cursores vitai lampada tradunt: some nations increase, others are reduced, and in a short while the generations of living creatures are changed, and like runners relay the torch of life (Lucretius)

aurea nunc vere sunt sæcula; plurimus auro venit honos; auro conciliatur amor: the age we live in is the true age of gold; by gold men attain to the highest honor and win even love (Ovid)

auream quisquis mediocritatem diligit, tutus caret obsoleti sordibus tecti, caret invidenda sobrius aula: whoever loves the golden mean is serene, and exempted equally from the filth of an old mansion and from the cares of a splendid court (Horace)

auro pulsa fides, auro venalia jura, aurum lex sequitur, mox sine lege pudor: by gold all good faith has been banished, by gold our rights are abused, the law itself follows gold, and soon there will be an end to every modest restraint

aurum irrepertum et sic melius situm: gold discovered and all the better for being so (Horace)

aurum vis hominemne? Habeas? Hominem?, quid ad aurum?: the man or his gold? Which will you take? The man?, when you could have the gold? (Lucilius)

aut formosa fores minus, aut minus improba vellem. Non facit ad mores tam bona forma malos: I would that you were either less beautiful, or less corrupt. Such perfect beauty does not suit such imperfect morals (Ovid)

aut insanit homo, aut versus facit: the fellow is either mad or he is composing verses (i.e., writing poetry) (Horace)

aut nihil est sensus animis a morte relictum aut mors ipsa nihil: either the soul feels nothing after death, or death itself is nothing (Lucan)

aut petis aut urgues ruiturum, Sisyphe, saxum: either you pursue or push, O Sisyphus, the stone destined to keep rolling (Ovid)

aut virtus nomen inane est, aut decus et pretium recte petit experiens vir: either virtue is an empty name, or the man of enterprise justly aims at honor and reward (Horace)

ave Cæsar, morituri te salutant (or **salutamus**)**:** hail Cæsar, those (or we) who are about to die salute you (Suetonius, a salutation of the gladiators to the Roman emperor)

ave Maria, gratia plena, Dominus tecum; benedicta tu in mulieribus, et benedictus fructus ventris tui, Jesus: hail Mary, full of grace, the Lord is with you; blessed are you among women, and blessed is the fruit of your womb, Jesus (11th Century salutation to the Virgin Mary)

ave verum corpus, natum ex Maria Virgine: hail the true body, born of the Virgin Mary (a 14th Century Eucharistic hymn)

B

barbarus hic ego sum, quia non intelligor ulli: I am a barbarian here, for no one understands what I say (Ovid)

beatus ille qui procul negotiis, ut prisca gens mortalium, paterna rura bobus exercet suis, solutus omni fœnore: happy the man who, remote from busy life, is content, like the earlier race of mortals, to plough his paternal lands with his own oxen, freed from all borrowing and lending (Horace)

beatus vir qui timet Dominum, in mandatis ejus volet nimis: happy is the man who fears the Lord, who is all the more willing to follow his commands (Psalm 112:1)

bella, horrida bella, et Thybrim multo spumantem sanguine cerno: wars, horrible wars, and the Tiber foaming with much blood (Virgil)

bellaque matribus detestata: and the wars that mothers detest (Horace)

bellum autem ita suscipiatur, ut nihil aliud, nisi pax, quæsita videatur: let war be carried out in such a way that nothing but peace may seem to be its aim (Cicero)

bellum magis desierat, quam pax cœperat: it was rather a cessation of war than a beginning of peace (Tacitus)

bene merenti bene profuerit, male merenti par erit: to a well-deserving man, God will show favor, to an ill-deserving man, God will be simply just (Plautus)

bene nummatum decorat Suedela Venusque: the goddesses of persuasion and love adorn the train of the well-moneyed man (Horace)

bene si amico feceris, ne pigeat fecisse, ut potius pudeat si non feceris: if you have acted kindly to your friend, do not regret that you have done so, as you should rather be ashamed of having acted otherwise (Plautus)

benedicite, omnia opera Domini, Domino; laudate et superexaltate eum in secula: bless the Lord, all the works of the Lord; praise him and exalt him above all things forever (Daniel 3:57)

benefacta male locata, malefacta arbitror: favors injudiciously conferred I reckon evils (Cicero)

benefacta sua verbis adornant: they enhance their favors by their words (Pliny)

beneficia usque eo læta sunt dum videntur exsolvi posse; ubi multum antevenere, pro gratia odium redditur: benefits are acceptable, while the receiver thinks he may return them; but once exceeding that, hatred is given instead of thanks (i.e., no one wants to be indebted for a favor that is greater than can be repaid) (Tacitus)

beneficus est qui non sua, sed alterius causa benigne facit: the one who is beneficent acts kindly not for his own benefit, but for another's (Cicero)

bis vincit qui se vincit in victoria: he conquers twice who, at the moment of victory, conquers (or restrains) himself (Publilius Syrus)

blanda truces animos fertur mollisse voluptas: alluring pleasure is said to have softened the savage dispositions [of early mankind] (Ovid)

Bœotum in crasso jurares aëre natum: you would swear that he was born in the thick air of the Bœotians (i.e., he's not very smart) (Horace)

bona malis paria non sunt, etiam pari numero; nec lætitia ulla minimo mœrore pensanda: the blessings of life do not equal its ills, even when of equal number; nor can any pleasure, however intense, compensate for even the slightest pain (Pliny the Elder)

bono vinci satius est quam malo more injuriam vincere: the good would rather suffer defeat than defeat injustice by evil means (Sallust)

bonosque soles effugere atque abire sentit, qui nobis pereunt et imputantur: each of us feels the good days speed and depart, and they are lost and counted against us (Martial)

bonum certamen certavi, cursum consummavi, fidem servavi: I have fought the good fight, I have finished the race, I have kept the faith (St. Paul, 2 Timothy 4:7)

bonum summum quo tendimus omnes: that supreme good to which we all aspire (Lucretius)

bos alienus subinde prospectat foras: another person's ox every now and then turns its eyes wistfully to the door

breve tempus ætatis satis est longum ad bene honesteque vivendum: a short term on earth is long enough for a good and honorable life (Cicero)

brevis a natura nobis vita data est; at memoria bene redditæ vitæ est sempiterna: the life given to us by nature is short; but the memory of a well-spent life is eternal (Cicero)

brevis esse laboro, obscurus fio: in trying to be concise, I become obscure (Horace)

bruta fulmina et vana: thunderbolts that strike blindly and in vain (Pliny the Elder)

C

cadit statim simultas, ab altera parte deserta; nisi pariter, non pugnant: a quarrel is quickly settled when deserted by one party: there is no battle unless there be two (Seneca)

cæca invidia est, nec quidquam aliud scit quam detrectare virtutes: envy is blind, and can only disparage the virtues of others (Livy)

cælum prospexit stellis fulgentibus aptum: she looked up at the sky studded with glittering stars (Ennius)

Cæsarem vehis, Cæsarisque fortunam: fear not, you carry Cæsar and his fortunes (Julius Cæsar, remarking to the ship's captain during a storm)

cætera fortunæ, non mea, turba fuit: the rest of the crowd were friends of my fortune, not of me (Ovid)

campos ubi Troja fuit: the fields where Troy once stood (Lucan)

canam mihi et Musis: I will sing to myself and the Muses (i.e., if no one else will listen)

candida de nigris, et de candentibus atra: he makes black white and white he turns to black (Ovid)

candidus in nauta turpis color; æquoris unda debet et a radiis sideris esse niger: a fair complexion is a disgrace in a sailor; he ought to be tanned from the spray of the sea and the rays of the sun (Ovid)

canis a non canedo: a dog cannot sing (and, thus, it is called "canis") (Varro)

canis ingens, catena vinctus, in pariete erat pictus superque quadrata littera scriptum, Cave Canem: a large dog, tied to a chain, was painted on the wall and over the picture was written in block letters, Beware the Dog (Petronius)

cantate Domino canticum novum, quia mirabilia fecit: sing to the Lord a new song, because he has done marvelous things (Psalm 97:1)

cantilenam eandem canis: you are always singing the same tune (Terence)

captum te nidore suæ putat ille culinæ: he thinks that you are taken with the smell of his kitchen (i.e., you have become a parasite) (Juvenal)

caput artis est, decere quod facias: the chief thing in any art you may practice is that you do only the one for which you are fit

cari sunt parentes, cari liberi, propinqui, familiares; sed omnes omnium caritates, patria una complexa est: dear are our parents, dear our children, our relatives, and our associates; but all our affections for all these are embraced in our affection for our native land (Cicero)

carmen perpetuum primaque origine mundi ad tempora nostra: a song for all ages, and from the first origin of the world to our own times (adapted from Ovid)

carmina nil prosunt; nocuerunt carmina quondam: my songs are of no use; they once wrought me harm (Ovid)

carmina spreta exolescent; si irascare, agnita videntur: if you show contempt for abuse, it will gradually die away; if you show irritation, it will be seen as deserved (Tacitus)

carmine di superi placantur, carmine manes: the gods above and the gods below are alike propitiated by song (Horace)

carmine fit vivax virtus; expersque sepulcri, notitiam seræ posteritatis habet: by song virtue is made immortal; and, exempt from burial, it obtains the homage of remote posterity (Ovid)

Castor gaudet equis, ovo prognatus eodem pugnis: Castor delights in horses, he has sprung from the same egg in boxing (Horace)

castrant alios, ut libros suos, per se graciles, alieno adipe suffarciant: they castrate the books of other men, in order that with the fat of their works they may lard their own lean volumes (a reference to plagiarism) (Jovius)

casus ubique valet; semper tibi pendeat hamus. Quo minime credas gurgite, piscis erit: there is scope for chance everywhere; let your hook be always ready. In the eddies where you least expect it, there will be a fish (Ovid)

Cato esse, quam videri, bonus malebat: Cato would rather be good, than seem good (Sallust)

causa et origo est materia negotii: the cause and beginning is the matter of the business (i.e., if trouble or harm results, it is assumed that the perpetrator entered with that intent)

causa latet, vis est notissima: the cause is hidden but its strength (or effect) is well noted (Ovid)

cautus enim metuit foveam lupus, accipiterque suspectos laqueos, et opertum miluus hamum: for the wolf once cautioned dreads the pitfall, the hawk the suspected snare, and the fish the concealed hook (Horace)

caveant consules ne quid res publica detrimenti caperet: let the consuls see to it that no harm come to the Republic (after Cæsar Augustus)

cavendum est ne major pœna, quam culpa, sit; et ne iisdem de causis alii plectantur, alii ne appellentur quidem: care should be taken in all cases, that the punishment not exceed the guilt; and also that some men may not suffer for offenses which, when committed by others, are allowed to pass with impunity (Cicero)

cedant arma togæ, concedat laurea linguæ: let arms yield to the toga, let the victor's laurel yield to the orator's tongue (Cicero)

cedant carminibus reges, regumque triumphi: kings, and the triumphs of kings, must yield to the power of song (Ovid)

cedat amor rebus; res age, tutus eris: let love give way to business; give attention to business, and you will be safe (Ovid)

cede repugnanti: cedendo victor abibis: yield to the one who opposes; by yielding you will obtain the victory (Ovid)

cedite, Romani scriptores; cedite, Graii: give place, Roman writers; give place, Greeks (Propertius)

cedunt grammatici; vincuntur rhetores turba tacet: the grammarians give way; the rhetoricians are beaten off and all the assemblage is silent (Juvenal)

centum doctum hominum consilia sola hæc devincit dea Fortuna: this goddess, Fortune, single-handedly frustrates the plans of a hundred learned men (Plautus)

cereus in vitium flecti, monitoribus asper: pliable as wax to vice, obstinate under reproof (Horace, in reference to youth)

cernis ut ignavum corrumpant otia corpus ut capiant vitium ni moveantur aquæ: you see how sloth wastes the sluggish body, as water is corrupted unless it moves (Ovid)

certum est quia impossibile est: it is true because it is impossible (Tertullian, in reference to Christianity)

cessante causa, cessat (et) effectus: when the cause ceases, the effect must (also) cease (Coke)

chairete, nikomen: greetings, we win (Philippides, before dying, having run to Athens from Marathon to bring news of the Greek defeat of the Persian army)

cignoni non sine causa Apoloni dicata sint, quod ab eo divinationem habere videantur, qua providentes quid in morte boni sit, cum cantu et voluptate moriantur: the swan is not dedicated to Apollo without cause, because foreseeing his happiness in death, he dies with singing and pleasure (Cicero)

cineres credis curare sepultos?: do you think that the ashes of the dead can be affected by this? (i.e., do you think the dead can be affected by the thoughts or actions of the living?)

citharœdus ridetur chorda qui semper obberrat eadem: the harpist who is always at fault on the same string is derided (Horace)

cito fit quod dii volunt: what the gods want happens soon (Petronius)

civitas ea autem in libertate est posita, quæ suis stat viribus, non ex alieno arbitrio pendet: the state alone is free that rests upon its own strength, and depends not on the arbitrary will of another (Livy)

claudite jam rivos, pueri; sat prata biberunt: close up the sluices now, boys; the meadows have drunk enough (Virgil)

cœlo tegitur qui non habet urnam: the one who has no urn to hold his bones is covered by the vault of heaven (Lucan)

cœlum ipsum petimus stultitia: in our foolishness, we assail heaven itself (Horace)

cœpisti melius quam desinis. Ultima primis cedunt: you begin better than you end. The last is inferior to the first (Ovid)

cogitatio nostra cœli munimenta perrumpit, nec contenta est, id, quod ostenditur, scire: our thoughts break through the defenses of heaven and are not satisfied with knowing what is offered to sense observation (Seneca)

committunt multi eadem diverso crimina fato, ille crucem sceleris pretium tulerit, hic diadema: how different the fate of men who commit the same crimes, for the same villainy one man goes to the gallows and another is raised to a throne

commodat in lusus numina surda Venus: Venus lends deaf ears to love's deceits (Ovid)

commune vitium in magnis liberisque civitatibus, ut invidia gloriæ comes sit: it is a usual fault in great and free states that envy should be the companion of glory (Cornelius Nepos)

componitur orbis regis ad exemplum; nec sic inflectere sensus humanos edicta valent, quam vita regentis: the world is fashioned according to the example of kings, and edicts have less effect on the people than the life of the ruler (Claudian)

compositum miraculi causa: a narrative made up only for the sake of the wonder that it may occasion (Tacitus)

condicio dulcis sine pulvere palmæ: the happy state of getting the victor's palm without the dust of racing (Horace)

condo et compono quæ mox depromere possim: I compose and lay up what I may soon after be able to bring forward (Horace)

confiteor Deo omnipotenti: I confess to God the Almighty (from the Catholic Mass)

conjunx est mihi, sunt nati: dedimus tot pignora fatis: I have a wife, I have sons; all of them hostages given to fate (Lucan)

conscia mens recti famæ mendacia risit (or ridet): sed nos in vitium credula turba sumus: the mind conscious of integrity scorns the lies of rumor; but we are a crowd always ready to believe a scandal (Ovid)

conscia mens ut cuique sua est, ita concipit intra pectora pro facto spemque metumque suo: according to the state of a man's conscience, so in his mind do hope and fear arise on account of his deeds (Ovid)

constitit hic arcumque manu celerisque sagittas corripuit fidus quæ tela gerebat Achates: hereupon he stopped and took up in his hand a bow and swift arrows, the weapons that trusty Achates carried (Virgil)

conticuere omnes, intentique ora tenebant: all were at once silent and listened with intent (Virgil)

contra verbosos noli contendere verbis; sermo datur cunctis, animi sapientia paucis: do not contend with words against wordy people; speech is given to all, wisdom to few (Dionysius Cato)

conveniens homini est hominem servare voluptas. Et melius nulla quæritur arte favor: it is a pleasure appropriate to man for him to save a fellow man; and gratitude is acquired in no better way (Ovid)

corpore sed mens est ægro magis ægra; malique in circumspectu stat sine fine sui: the mind is sicker than the sick body; in contemplation of its sufferings it becomes hopeless (Ovid)

corporis et fortunæ bonorum, ut initium, finis est. Omnia orta occidunt, et aucta senescunt: the blessings of good health and good fortune, as they have a beginning, must also have an end. Everything rises but to fall, and grows but to decay (Sallust)

corrumpunt bonos mores colloquia prava: evil (or depraved) conversation will corrupt good morals (Erasmus, after St. Paul)

cras amet qui nunquam amavit, quique amavit cras amet: let those love now who never loved before; let those who always loved, now love all the more

cras ingens iterabimus æquor: tomorrow we will be back on the vast ocean (Horace)

credat Judæus Apella: let Apella the Jew believe it (i.e., only the credulous believe it) (Horace, in derogation of monotheistic religious faith)

crede mihi, miseris cœlestia numina parcunt; nec semper læsos, et sine fine, premunt: believe me, the gods spare the afflicted, and do not always oppress those who are unfortunate (Ovid)

credo in unum Deum, Patrem omnipotentem, factorem cœli et terræ, visibilium omnium et invisibilium: I believe in one God, the omnipotent Father, maker of heaven and the earth, and of all things visible and invisible (from the Catholic Mass)

credo pudicitiam Saturno rege moratam in terris: I believe that during the reign of Saturn (the Golden Age), chastity dwelt upon the earth

credula vitam spes fovet, et fore cras semper ait melius: credulous hope cherishes life, and ever whispers to us that tomorrow will be better (Tibullus)

crescentem sequitur cura pecuniam, majorumque fames. Multa petentibus desunt multa. Bene est cui Deus obtulit parca quod satis est manu: the accumulation of wealth is followed by an increase of care and by an appetite for more. The one who seeks for much will ever be in want of much. It is best with him to whom God has given that which is sufficient, though every satisfaction be withheld (Horace)

crescit indulgens sibi dirus hydrops: the fatal dropsy gains on the patient from his gratifying his thirst (Horace)

creta an carbone notandi?: are they to be marked with chalk or charcoal? (i.e., as good or bad) (Horace)

crine ruber, niger ore, brevis pede, lumine læsus, rem magnam prestas Zoile si bonus es: red-haired, black-mouthed, lame, squint-eyed; it is a wonder, Zoilus, if you are a good man

crudelis ubique luctus, ubique pavor, et plurima mortis imago: everywhere is heart-rending wail, everywhere consternation, and death in a thousand shapes (Virgil)

crux criticorum, medicorum, mathematicorum, et cetera: the greatest difficulty that can occur to critics, physicians, mathematicians, etc.

cui dono lepidum novum libellum?: to whom do I give my new charming little book? (Catullus)

cui flavam religas comam, simplex munditiis?: for whom are you fixing your golden hair, simply but elegantly? (Horace)

cui Fortuna ipsa cedit: to whom Fortune herself yields (Cicero)

cui—gratia, fama, valetudo contingat abunde, et mundus victus, non deficiente crumena: to whom—endowed with grace, fame, and health, with decent fare, and a purse not ill-supplied (Horace)

cui lecta potenter erit res nec facundia deseret hunc nec lucidus ordo: the speaker who has chosen a theme suited to his powers will never be at a loss for felicitous language or lucid arrangement (Horace)

cui licet quod majus, non debet quod minus est non licere: he to whom the greater thing is lawful, has certainly a right to do the smaller thing

cui mens divinior atque os magna sonaturum des nominis hujus honorem: to the one whose soul is more than ordinarily divine, and who has the gift of uttering lofty thoughts, you may justly concede the honorable title of poet (Horace)

cui non conveniat sua res, ut calceus olim, si pede major erit, subvertet, si minor, uret: as a shoe, when too large, is apt to trip one, and when too small, to pinch the feet, so it is with the one whose fortune does not suit him (Horace)

cui peccare licet peccat minus. Ipsa potestas semina nequitiæ languidiora facit: he who has it in his power to commit sin is less inclined to do so. The very idea of being able weakens the desire (Ovid)

cui Pudor, et Justitiae Soror, incorrupta Fides, nudaque Veritas; quando ullum invenient parem?: when will Honor and Justice's sister, uncorrupted Faith, and naked Truth, find anyone equal to him?

cuicunque aliquis quid concedit, concedere videtur et id, sine quo res ipsa esse non potest: to whomsoever someone grants a thing, the same one grants that without which the thing cannot be enjoyed (i.e., the use of something is implied in the giving of it)

cujus conatibus obstat res angusta domi: one whose efforts are opposed by straitened circumstances at home (Horace)

cujus rei libet simulator atque dissimulator: an accomplished pretender and dissembler (Sallust)

cujus tu fidem in pecunia perspexeris, verere ei verba credere?: can you fear to trust the word of a man whose honesty you have known in his handling of money? (Terence)

cujus vulturis hoc erit cadaver?: to which vulture shall this carcass fall? (Martial)

cujuslibet rei simulator atque dissimulator: a man who could, with equal skill, pretend to be what he was not, and not to be what he really was (Sallust, said of Catiline)

cum altera lux venit jam cras hesternum consumpsimus; ecce aliud cras egerit hos annos, et semper paulum erit ultra: when another day has arrived, we will find that we have consumed our yesterday's tomorrow; another morrow will urge on our years, and still be a little beyond us (Persius)

cum ames non sapias aut cum sapias non ames: when you are in love you are not wise, or rather, when you are wise you do not fall in love (Publilius Syrus)

cum autem sublatus fuerit ab oculis, etiam cito transit e mente: once he was taken from our sight, his memory quickly passed out of our minds (Thomas à Kempis)

cum dubia et fragilis sit nobis vita tributa, in morte alterius spem tu tibi ponere noli: since we have received a precarious and frail life, beware of placing your hopes in the death of others (Cato)

cum fortuna manet, vultum servatis amici; cum cedit, turpi vertitis ora fuga: while fortune lasts, you have always the service of friends; but, when it ceases, you will turn your backs in shameful flight (Ovid)

cum frueris felix quæ sunt adversa caveto; non eodem cursu respondent ultima primis: when fortune is lavish of her favors, beware of adversity; events do not always succeed each other in one train of fortunes (Cato)

cum insanientibus furere: to rave with the insane (Petronius)

cum jam fulva cinis fuero: when I will be nothing but a heap of yellow ashes (Calvus)

cum multis aliis quæ nunc perscribere longum est: with many other matters that it would be tedious now to write in full (i.e., etc., etc., etc.)

cum odio sui cœpit veritas. Simul atque apparuit, inimica est: the first reaction to truth is hatred. The moment it appears, it is treated as an enemy (Tertullian)

cuncti adsint, meritæque expectent præmia palmæ: let all attend, and expect the rewards due to well-earned laurels (Virgil)

cunctis servatorem liberatoremque acclamantibus: all having him as savior and deliverer

cur valle permutem Sabina divitias operosiores?: why should I exchange my Sabine valley for riches that bring with them more trouble? (Horace)

cura pii dis sunt, et qui coluere, coluntur: the pious-hearted are cared for by the gods, and those who reverence them are reverenced (Ovid)

curatio funeris, conditio sepulturæ, pompæ exequiarum, magis sunt vivorum solatia, quam subsidia mortuorum: the care of the funeral, the place of the burial, and the pomp of obsequies, are consolations to the living, but of no advantage to the dead (Cæsar Augustus)

curtæ nescio quid semper abest rei: a nameless something is always wanting to our imperfect fortune (Horace)

D

da mi basia mille, deinde centum, dein mille altera, dein secunda centum, deinde usque altera mille, deinde centum: give me a thousand kisses, then a hundred, then another thousand, then a second hundred, then yet another thousand, then a hundred (Catullus)

da mihi castitatem et continentiam, sed noli modo: give me chastity and continency, but not yet (St. Augustine)

da quod jubes et jube quod vis. Imperas nobis continentiam: give what you command, and command what you give. You impose continence upon us (St. Augustine)

da spatium vitæ, multos da, Jupiter, annos!: God grant us life, God grant us many years! (Juvenal)

da ubi consistam, et terram movebo: give me a place to stand and I will move the earth (after Archimedes)

dabit Deus his quoque finem: God will put an end to these troubles as well (Virgil)

damnant quod non intelligunt: they condemn what they do not understand (Cicero and Quintilian)

dantur opes nulli nunc nisi divitibus: wealth nowadays goes all to the rich (Martial)

dapibus supremi grata testudo Jovis: the lyre is a welcome accompaniment at the banquets of sovereign Jove (Horace)

dat Galenus opes, dat Justinianus honores, sed Moses sacco cogitur ire pedes: Galen gives wealth, Justinian honors, but Moses must go on foot with a beggar's wallet (Robert Burton)

dat inania verba, dat sine mente sonum: he utters empty words; he utters sound without meaning (Virgil)

dat veniam corvis, vexat censura columbas: he pardons the ravens, but visits the doves with censure (i.e., they clip the wings of doves but let birds of prey fly freely) (Juvenal)

date, et dabitur vobis: give and it shall be given to you (St. Luke 6:38)

date obolum Belisario: give alms to Belisarius (a Roman general who, according to legend, was reduced to poverty)

Davus sum, non Œdipus: I am Davus (a plain man), not Oedipus (who solved the riddle of the Sphinx) (Terence)

de alieno largitor, et sui restrictor: lavish of what is another's, restrained with what is his own (Cicero)

de asini umbra disceptare: to argue about the shadow of an ass (i.e., to argue over trifling matters)

de fide et officio judicis non recipitur quæstio: no question can be entertained respecting the good intention and duty of the judge

de hoc multi multa, omnis aliquid, nemo satis: of this many have said many things, all something, no one enough

de nihilo nihil fit, in nihilum nil posse reverti: out of nothing comes nothing, and nothing can be reduced to nothing (attributed to the Epicureans)

de non apparentibus et (de) non existentibus eadem est ratio: the reasoning must be the same with respect to things that do not appear as to things that do not exist (Coke)

de omni re scibili et quibusdam aliis: of all things knowable and certain others (i.e., to have a great deal of knowledge; a "know it all") (quoted by Mirandola)

de omnibus rebus et quibusdam aliis: about everything, and certain other things (i.e., a book that rambles on and on)

de profundis clamavi ad te, Domine; Domine, exaudi vocem meam: from the depths I have cried unto you, O Lord; O Lord, hear my voice (Psalm 129:1)

debetis velle quæ velimus: you ought to wish as we wish (Plautus)

decet affectus animi neque se nimium erigere nec subjicere serviliter: we ought to allow the affections of the mind to be neither too much elated nor abjectly depressed (Cicero)

decipit frons prima multos; rara mens intelligit quod interiore condidit cura angulo: the first appearance deceives many; our understandings rarely reach to that which has been carefully reposed in the inmost recesses of the mind (i.e., looks can be deceiving, but actions produced under trial reveal the true character of the person)

Dei jussu non unquam credita Teneris: God commanded that she be believed by none of her Trojan countrymen (Virgil, said of Cassandra)

delere licebit quod non edideris; nescit vox missa reverti: it will be permitted to blot out written words that you do not publish; but it is not possible to recall the spoken word (Horace)

deliberat Roma, perit Saguntum: while Rome deliberates, Saguntum perishes (i.e., while we talk, our allies perish)

deliciæ illepidæ atque inelegantes: unmannerly and inelegant pleasures (Catullus)

delirant reges, plectuntur Achivi: the kings err, the Greeks are punished (Horace)

delphinum silvis appingit, fluctibus aprum: he portrays a dolphin in the woods and a boar in the waves (i.e., he introduces objects unsuited to the scene) (Horace)

demens judicio vulgi, sanus fortasse tuo: mad in the judgment of the mob, sane, perhaps, in your own (Horace)

deos agere curam rerum humanarum credi, ex usu vitæ est: pœnasque maleficiis, aliquando seras, nunquam autem irritas esse: it is advantageous that the gods should be believed to attend to the affairs of man; and the punishment of evil deeds, though sometimes late, is never fruitless (Pliny the Elder)

deos enim reliquos accepimus, Cæsares dedimus: the other gods were handed down to us, but we ourselves made the Cæsars gods (Valerius Maximus)

deridet, sed non derideor: he laughs, but I am not laughed at

desiderantem quod satis est, neque tumultuosum sollicitat mare, non verberatæ grandine vineæ fundusque mendax: a storm at sea, a vine-wasting hail tempest, a disappointing farm, cause no anxiety to him who is content with enough (Horace)

desine de quoquam quicquam bene velle mereri, aut aliquem fieri posse putare pium: give up wanting to deserve any thanks from anyone, or thinking that anybody can be grateful (Catullus)

desinit in piscem mulier formosa superne: a woman elegantly formed above, ending in nothing but a fish (i.e., a mermaid, but applied to literary works that begin with much promise but end in great disappointment) (Horace)

desipere in loco: to act foolishly at the proper time (i.e., to unwind occasionally) (Horace)

despicio terrena et solem contemplor: I despise earthly things and contemplate the sun

deteriores omnes sumus licentia: we are all the worse for license (Terence)

detur aliquando otium quiesque fessis: let ease and rest be sometimes granted to the weary (Seneca)

Deus non immolationibus et sanguine multo colendum: quæ enim ex trucidatione immerentium voluptas est?; sed mente pura, bono honestoque proposito. Non templa illi, congestis in altitudinem saxis, struenda sunt; in suo cuique consecrandus est pectore: God is not to be worshipped with sacrifices and blood, for what pleasure can He have in the slaughter of the innocent?; but with a pure mind, a good and honest purpose. Temples are not to be built for Him with stones piled on high; God is to be consecrated in the breast of each man (Seneca)

Deus hæc fortasse benigna reducet in sedem vice: perhaps God, by some gracious change, will restore things to their proper place (Horace)

Deus quædam munera universo humano generi dedit, a quibus excluditur nemo: God has given some gifts to the whole human race from which none is excluded (Seneca)

di bene fecerunt, inopis me quodque pusilli finxerunt animi, raro et perpauca loquentis: the gods be praised for having made me of a poor and humble mind, with a desire to speak but seldom and briefly (Horace)

di faciles, peccasse semel concedite tuto: id satis est. Pœnam culpa secunda ferat: indulgent gods, grant me to sin once with impunity: that is sufficient. Let a second offense bear its punishment (Ovid)

dicam insigne, recens, adhuc indictum ore alio: I will utter something striking, something fresh, something as yet unsung by another's lips (Horace)

dicebamus hesterno die: we were saying yesterday (Luis de Leon, on resuming a lecture interrupted by his arrest and five years' imprisonment)

dicenda tacenda locutus: saying things that should be said, and things that should not be said (Horace)

dicere quæ puduit, scribere jussit amor: what I was ashamed to say, love has commanded me to write (Ovid)

dies iræ, dies illa, sæclum solvet in favilla teste David cum Sibylla: the day of wrath, that day shall dissolve the world in ashes, as David and the Sibyl attest

dies iste, quem tamquam extremum reformidas, æterni natilis est: this day, which you fear as your last, is the birthday of eternity (Seneca)

dies si in obligationibus non ponitur, præsenti die debetur: a bond may be enforced immediately, when the day on which it is to be fulfilled is not specified

difficile est saturam (or **satiram**) **non scribere:** it is difficult not to write satire (Juvenal)

difficilis facilis, jucundus acerbus es idem: nec tecum possum vivere nec sine te: difficult or easy, pleasant or bitter, you are the same you: I cannot live with you nor without you (Martial)

difficilis, querulus, laudator temporis acti: harsh, complaining, and the eulogist of times that are past (said of the aged who complain about the present while extolling the past) (Horace)

diffugere nives, redeunt jam gramina campis arboribusque comæ: the snows have dispersed, and the grass returns to the fields and the leaves to the trees (Horace)

diffugiunt, cadis cum fæce siccatis, amici, ferre jugum pariter dolosi: when the wine casks are drained to the lees, our friends soon disperse, too faithless to bear as well the yoke of sorrow

digito monstrari et dicier, hic est: to be pointed at by the finger and to have it said, there he is (Persius)

dignum laude virum Musa vetat mori: the Muse forbids the virtuous man to die (Horace)

diis proximus ille est quem ratio, non ira movet, qui facta rependens consilio punire potest: he is next to the gods, whom reason, not passion, impels, and who, after weighing the facts, can measure the punishment with discretion (Claudian)

dilexi justiciam et odi iniquitatem, propterea morior in exilio: I have loved justice and hated injustice, therefore I die an exile (Pope Gregory VII, on his deathbed)

dilige et quod vis fac: love and do what you will (St. Augustine)

diruit, ædificat, mutat quadrata rotundis: he pulls down, he builds up, he changes square into round (i.e., he is acting out of caprice) (Horace)

disce, puer, virtutem ex me, verumque laborem, fortunam ex aliis: learn, my son, virtue and true labor from me, good fortune from others (Virgil)

discit enim citius, meminitque libentius illud quod quis deridet quam quod probat et veneratur: each learns more readily, and retains more willingly, what makes him laugh than what he approves of and respects (Horace)

discite justitiam moniti, et non temnere divos: warned by me, learn justice, and not to despise the gods (Virgil)

discrepant facta cum dictis: the facts do not agree with the statements (Cicero)

disertissime Romuli nepotum: most eloquent of the descendants of Romulus (Catullus, to Cicero)

disjice compositam pacem, sere crimina belli: cast aside the patched-up peace, sow the seeds of wicked war (Virgil)

dissimiles hic vir, et ille puer: how different from the present man was the youth of earlier days (Ovid)

dives agris, dives positis in fœnore nummis: rich in lands, rich in money laid out at interest (Horace)

divine Plato escam malorum appeliat voluptatem, quod ea videlicet homines capiantur, ut pisces hamo: Plato divinely calls pleasure the bait of evil, inasmuch as men are caught by it as fish by a hook (Cicero)

divitiæ grandes homini sunt, vivere parce æquo animo: it is great wealth to a man to live frugally with a contented mind (Lucretius)

divitiarum et formæ gloria fluxa atque fragilis; virtus clara æternaque habetur: the glory of wealth and of beauty is fleeting and frail; virtue is bright and everlasting (Sallust)

dixeris egregie notum si callida verbum reddiderit junctura novum: you will have spoken well if, by skillful arrangement of your words, you have made the ordinary seem new (Horace)

doceo insanire omnes: I teach that all men are mad (Horace)

dolore affici, sed resistere tamen: to be affected by grief, but still to resist it (after Pliny the Younger)

doloris medicinam a philosophia peto: I look to philosophy to provide an antidote to sorrow (Cicero)

doloris omnis privatio recte nominata est voluptas: what we rightly call pleasure is the absence of all pain (Cicero)

dolus an virtus quis in hoste requirat?: who shall ask of an enemy whether he succeeded by strategy or by valor? (Virgil)

Domine, non sum dignus ut intres sub tectum meum; sed tantum dic verbo, et sanabitur anima mea: Lord, I am not worthy that you should enter under my roof; but only say the word, and my soul shall be healed (from the Catholic Mass)

Dominus vobiscum; et cum spiritu tuo: the Lord be with you; and with your spirit (from the Catholic Mass)

donec gratus eram tibi: in the days when I was dear to you (Horace)

donec virenti canities abest morosa: so long as youth is green and old age is far off (Horace)

donum exitiale Minervæ: the fatal gift to Minerva (i.e., the Trojan horse) (Virgil)

duas tantum res anxius optat, panem et circenses: only two things does he worry about or long for, bread and circus entertainment (Juvenal)

duce tempus eget: the time calls for a leader (Lucan)

ducimus autem hos quoque felices, qui, ferre incommoda vitæ, nec jactare jugum, vita didicere magistra: we also deem those happy who, from the experience of life, have learned to bear its ills, and without remarking on their weight (Juvenal)

dulces moriens reminiscitur Argos: as he died he remembered Argos, the home of his youth (Virgil)

dulcique animos novitate tenebo: and I will hold your mind captive with sweet novelty (Ovid)

dulcis amor patriæ, dulce videre suos: sweet is the love of one's country, sweet it is to see one's kindred people (Ovid)

dulcis et alta quies, placidæque simillima morti: sweet and deep repose, very much resembling quiet death (Virgil)

dum deliberamus quando incipiendum incipere jam serum est: while we are deliberating to begin, the time to begin is past (Quintilian)

dum loquimur, fugerit invida ætas; carpe diem, quam minimum credula postero: while we are talking, time flies without favor; seize the day, not trusting the slightest in what is to come (Horace)

dum ne ob malefacta peream, parvi æstimo: so long as I do not die for doing evil, I care little for dying (Plautus)

dum vires annique sinunt, tolerate laborem; jam veniet tacito curva senecta pede: whilst your strength and years permit, you should endure and encounter labor; remember that crooked age, with silent steps, will soon arrive (Ovid)

dummodo sit dives, barbarus ipse placet: provided he be only rich, the very barbarian pleases us (Ovid)

durum!; sed levius fit patientia quicquid corrigere est nefas: it is hard!; but that which we are not permitted to correct is rendered lighter by patience (Horace)

E

e cœlo descendit, gnothi seauton: from heaven came down the precept, know thyself (Juvenal)

ea sola voluptas solamenque mali: that was his sole delight and solace in his woe (Virgil)

ea sub oculis posita negligimus; proximorum incuriosi, longinqua sectamur: we disregard the things that lie under our eyes; indifferent to what is close at hand, we inquire after things that are far away (Pliny the Younger)

ecce spectaculum dignum, ad quod respiciat intentus operi suo Deus. Ecce par Deo dignum, vir fortis cum mala fortuna compositus: behold a worthy sight, to which the God, turning his attention to his own work, may direct his gaze. Behold an equal thing, worthy of a God, a brave man matched in conflict with evil fortune (Seneca)

ego consuetudinem sermonis vocabo consensum eruditorum; sicut vivendi, consensum bonorum: I consider as the rule of language the style of the learned; as the rule of life the manners of the good (Quintilian)

ego de caseo loquor, tu de creta respondes: while I talk to you of cheese, you talk to me of chalk (Erasmus)

ego nec studium sine divite vena, nec rude quid prosit video ingenium: I see not what good can come from study without a rich vein of genius untrained by art (Horace)

ego, si bonam famam mihi servasso, sat ero dives: if I keep my good character, I shall be rich enough (Plautus)

ego si risi quod ineptus pastillos Rufillus olet, lividus et mordax videar?: if I smile at the perfumes with which Rufillus is scented, must I therefore be regarded as envious or ill-natured? (Horace)

ego sum qui sum: I am who I am (Exodus 3:14)

ego sum rex Romanus et supra grammaticam: I am king of the Romans and above grammar (Emperor Sigismund at the Council of Constance)

ego sum via et veritas et vita: I am the way and the truth and the life (St. John 14:6)

ego sum vitis vera, et Pater meus agricola est: I am the true vine, and my Father is the vinedresser (St. John 15:1)

ego verum amo, verum volo mihi dici; mendacem odi: I love truth and wish to have it always spoken to me; I hate a liar (Plautus)

egregii mortalem, altique silenti: a being of extraordinary and profound silence (Horace)

eheu!, fugaces, Posthume, Posthume, labuntur anni; nec pietas moram rugis et instanti senectæ afferet, indomitæque morti: alas!, Posthumus, the years glide swiftly away; nor can even piety delay the wrinkles of approaching age, or the progress of indomitable death (Horace)

eheu!, quam brevibus pereunt ingentia fatis (or **causis**)**:** alas!, By what slight means are great affairs brought to destruction (Claudian)

eloquentia, alumna licentiæ, quam stulti libertatem vocabant: eloquence, the foster-child of license, which fools call liberty (Tacitus)

emori nolo, sed me esse mortuum nihil curo: I would not die, but I care not to be dead (variant of Epicharmos, as quoted by Cicero)

emori nolo: sed me esse mortuum nihil æstimo: I do not wish to die; but I care not if I were dead (Epicharmos, as quoted by Cicero)

entia non sunt multiplicanda præter necessitatem: no more things should be presumed to exist than are absolutely necessary (attributed to William of Occam, known as Occam's razor)

equitis et quoque jam migravit ab aure voluptas omnis ad incertos oculos, et gaudia vana: our gentry no longer receives any pleasure through the ear, and relish only delusive shows and empty pomp (Horace)

equo ne credite, Teucri. Quidquid id est, timeo Danaos et dona ferentes: do not trust the horse, Trojans. Whatever it is, I fear the Greeks even when they are bearing gifts (Virgil)

erant in officio, sed tamen qui mallent imperantium mandata interpretari, quam exsequi: they attended to their duties, but still as if they would rather debate the commands of their superiors than obey them (Tacitus)

eripe turpi colla jugo. Liber, liber sum, dic age: tear away your neck from the yoke. Come, say free, I am free (Horace)

errare malo cum Platone, quam cum istis vera sentire: I'd rather be wrong with Plato than think right with those men (Cicero)

erubuit; salva res est: he blushed; the affair is safe (Terence)

esse est percipi: to be is to be perceived (Berkeley)

esse quam videri bonus malebat; ita quo minus petebat gloriam, eo magis illum sequebatur: he chose to be good rather than to seem good; and so, the less he strove for fame, the closer it followed after him (Sallust)

est animus tibi rerumque prudens, et secundis temporibus dubiisque rectus: you possess a mind both sagacious in the management of affairs and steady at once in prosperous times (Horace)

est animus tibi, sunt mores et lingua, fidesque: you have a man's soul, good manners and powers of speech, and fidelity (Horace, said of a gentleman)

est bonus, ut melior vir non alius quisquam: he is so good that no man can be better (Horace)

est brevitate opus, ut currat sententia: there is need of conciseness, as the thought may run on (Horace)

est deus in nobis, et sunt commercia cœli. Sedibus ætheriis spiritus ille venit: there is a god within us, and we hold commerce with heaven. That spirit comes from abodes on high (Ovid)

est enim lex nihil aliud nisi recta et a numine deorum tracta ratio, imperans honesta, prohibens contraria: for law is nothing else but right reason supported by the authority of the gods, commanding what is honorable and prohibiting the contrary (Cicero)

est hic, est ubi vis, animus si te non deficit æquus: it is here, it is everywhere, if only a well-regulated mind does not fail you (Horace, said of happiness)

est modus in rebus; sunt certi denique fines quos ultra citraque nequit consistere rectum: there is a mean (or middle) in everything. There are fixed limits beyond which and short of which right is not able to find a place (Horace)

est multi fabula plena joci: it is a story full of fun (Ovid)

est profecto Deus, qui quæ nos gerimus auditque et videt; neque id verum existimo, quod vulgo dicitur, Fortuna humana fingit aptatque, ut lubet: there is certainly a God who sees and hears the things that we do; I cannot believe that which is ordinarily said, that Fortune makes and unmakes all human affairs at pleasure (Plautus)

est quadam (or quoddam) prodire tenus, si non datur ultra: it is something to proceed thus far, if it be not permitted to go farther (Horace)

est tempus quando nihil, est tempus quando aliquid, nullum tamen est tempus in quo dicenda sunt omnia: there is a time when nothing may be said, a time when something may be said, but no time when all things may be said

estne Dei sedes nisi terra, et pontus, et aër, et cœlum, et virtus? Superos quid quærimus ultra? Jupiter est, quodcunque vides, quodcunque moveris: has God a dwelling other than earth and sea and air and heaven and virtue? Why do we seek the gods beyond? Whatever you see, wherever you go, there is Jupiter (Lucan)

esto peccator et pecca fortiter, sed fortius fide et gaude in Christo: be a sinner and sin strongly, but more strongly have faith and rejoice in Christ (Martin Luther)

esto quod es; quod sunt alii, sine quemlibet esse; quod non es, nolis; quod potes esse, velis: be what you are; let whoever will be what others are; do not be what you are not; but resolutely be what you can be

esurientes implevit bonis, et divites dimisit inanes: he has filled the hungry with good things, and the rich he has sent away empty (St. Luke 1:53)

et campos ubi Troja fuit: and the fields where Troy once was (Virgil)

et cum spiritu tuo: and with thy spirit (liturgical response to **Dominus vobiscum,** the Lord be with you)

et ego in Arcadia: I too have been to Arcadia (i.e., I know all about it)

et errat longe mea quidem sententia qui imperium credit gravius esse aut stabilius, vi quod fit, quam illud quod amicitia adjungitur: it is a great error, according to my opinion, in those who believe that a government is more firm, or more assured, when it is supported by force, than when it exists by kindness and voluntary obedience (Terence)

et facere et pati fortiter Romanum est: bravery and endurance make a man a Roman (Livy)

et illa erant fercula, in quibus mihi esurienti te inferebatur sol et luna: and these were the dishes wherein to me, hunger-starved for you, they served up the sun and moon (St. Augustine)

et ipse quidem, quamquam medio in spatio integræ ætatis ereptus, quantum ad gloriam, longissimum ævum peregit: and he, though carried off in the prime of life, had lived long enough for glory (Tacitus)

et jam summa procul villarum culmina fumant, majoresque cadunt altis de montibus umbræ: and now the cottage roofs yonder smoke, and the shadows fall longer from the mountain tops (Virgil)

et mea cymba semel vasta percussa procella illum, quo læsa est, horret adire locum: my raft, once shaken by the overpowering storm, shrinks from approaching the spot where it has been shattered (Ovid)

et meæ, si quid loquar audiendum, vocis accedet bona pars: if any opinion of mine is worthy of attention, it shall be given freely in his favor (Horace)

et mihi res, non me rebus, subjungere (or **submittere**) **conor:** I try to subject (or submit) circumstances to myself, not myself to circumstances (Horace)

et nati natorum, et qui nascentur ab illis: and the children of our children, and those who shall be born to them (i.e., for our many generations to come) (Virgil)

et nomen pacis dulce est et ipsa res salutaris, sed inter pacem et servitutem plurimum interest. Pax est tranquilla libertas, servitus postremum malorum omnium non modo bello, sed morte etiam repellendum: the name of peace is sweet and the thing itself is salutary, but there is a great difference between peace and slavery. Peace is freedom in tranquility, slavery is the worst of all evils, to be resisted not only by war, but even by death (Cicero)

et nos quoque tela sparsimus: we too have hurled javelins (i.e., we too are proud warriors, or veterans of war)

et nova fictaque nuper habebunt verba fidem, si Græco fonte cadunt parce detorta: and new and lately invented terms will be well received, if they descend, with slight deviation, from a Grecian source (Horace)

et nulli cessura fides, sine crimine mores, nudaque simplicitas, purpureusque pudor: and I have good faith that will yield to none, and ways without reproach, and unadorned simplicity, and blushing modesty (Ovid)

et nunc magna mei sub terras currit imago: and now my shade shall descend illustrious to the grave (Virgil)

et penitus toto divisos orbe Britannos: even to Britannia, that land completely separated from the world (Virgil)

et Phœbo digna locuti, quique sui memores alios fecere merendo: omnibus his nivea cinguntur tempora vitta: those who spoke things worthy of Phœbus, and those who made men recollect them for their merits: all have their temples bound with a snow-white ribbon (a reference to Elysium) (Virgil)

et pudet, et metuo, semperque eademque precari, ne subeant animo tædia justa tuo: I am ashamed to be always begging and begging the same things, and fear lest you should conceive for me the disgust I merit (Ovid)

et quæ sibi quisque timebat unius in miseri exitium conversa tulere: and what each man feared for himself was easily borne, when it was turned to the destruction of a single wretch! (Virgil, in reference to casting lots to sacrifice one of a number of people)

et quorum pars magna fui: and in which I played a prominent part (Virgil)

et res non semper, spes mihi semper adest: my hopes are not always realized, but I always hope (Ovid)

et tu, Brute (fili mi): you too, Brutus (my son) (Julius Cæsar; Suetonius reports that this was said in Greek: **kai su, teknon,** you too, my son)

etenim omnes artes, quæ ad humanitatem pertinent, habent quoddam commune vinculum, et quasi cognatione quadam inter se continentur: all the arts, which belong to polished life, are held together by some common tie, and connected, as it were, by some intimate relation (Cicero)

etiam quæ sibi quisque timebat unius in miseri exitium conversa tulere: what each man feared would happen to himself did not trouble him when he saw that it would ruin another (Virgil)

etiam sanato vulnere cicatrix manet: though the wound is healed, a scar remains

evolare rus ex urbe tanquam ex vinculis: to fly from the town into the country, as though from bonds (Cicero)

ex diuturnitate temporis omnia præsumuntur esse solemniter acta: everything established for a length of time is presumed to have been done in due form

ex humili magna ad fastigia rerum extollit, quoties voluit fortuna jocari: whenever Fortune is in a joking mood, she raises men from a humble station to the imposing summit of affairs (Juvenal)

ex quovis ligno non fit Mercurius: the god Mercury is not to be fashioned from just any piece of wood (Horace)

ex vita discedo, tanquam ex hospitio, non tanquam ex domo: I depart from life as from an inn, not as from a home (Cicero)

ex vultibus hominum mores colligere: to construe men's characters by their looks

exacto contentus tempore vita cedat uti conviva satur: content with his past life, let him take leave of life like a satiated guest (Horace)

excepto quod non simul esses, cætera lætus: except that you were not with me, in other respects I was happy

exeat aula qui vult esse pius: let him who will be good retire from the court (a reference to the corruption that surrounds the court system) (Lucretius)

exemplo quodcunque malo committitur, ipsi displicet auctori: whatever is committed from a bad example is displeasing even to its author (i.e., we hate the faults in others that we see in ourselves) (Juvenal)

exigite ut mores teneros ceu pollice ducat, ut si quis cera vultum facit: require him as with his thumb to mold their youthful morals, just as one fashions a face with plastic wax (Juvenal)

exigo a me non ut optimis par sim, sed ut malis melior: I require myself not to be equal to the best, but to be better than the bad (Seneca)

exigua est virtus præstare silentia rebus; at contra, gravis est culpa tacenda loqui: slight is the merit of keeping silence on a matter; on the other hand, serious is the guilt of talking on things whereon we should be silent (Ovid)

exigui numero, sed bello vivida virtus: small in number, but their valor is quick for war (Virgil)

exilioque domos et dulcia limina mutant atque alio patriam quærunt sub sole jacentem: they exchange their home and sweet thresholds for exile, and seek another country under another sun (Virgil)

exitio est avidium mare nautis: the greedy sea is destruction to sailors (Horace)

expende Hannibalem: quot libras in duce summo invenies?: weigh Hannibal: how many pounds will you find in that great leader? (Juvenal)

explorant adversa viros; perque aspera duro nititur ad laudem virtus interrita clivo: adversity tries men; and virtue struggles after fame regardless of the adverse heights (Silius Italicus)

exuerint sylvestrem animum, cultuque frequenti, in quascunque voces artes, haud tarda sequentur: they lay aside their rustic ideas, and by repeated instruction will advance apace into whatever arts you may initiate them (Virgil)

F

Fabius Verrucosus beneficium ab homine duro aspere datum, panem lapidosum vocabat: Fabius Verrucosus called a favor roughly bestowed by a hard man bread made of stone (Seneca)

fabula, nec sentis, tota jactaris in urbe: though you do not know it, you are the talk of the town (Ovid)

facetiarum apud præpotentes in longum memoria est: men in power long remember the jests of which they have been the subject (Tacitus)

facies non omnibus una, nec diversa tamen; qualem decet esse sororum: the features were not the same in them all, nor yet are they quite different; but such as we would expect in sisters (i.e., a reference to family resemblance) (Ovid)

facile esse momento, quo quis velit, cedere possessione magnæ fortunæ; facere et parare eam difficile atque arduum esse: it is easy at any moment to surrender a large fortune; to build one up is a difficult and arduous task (Livy)

facile omnes cum valemus recta consilia ægrotis damus. Tu si hic sis aliter senties: it is easy for us to give the right advice to the sick when we all are well. Were you in my place, you would feel otherwise (Terence)

facilis descensus Averno (est), noctes atque dies patet atri janua Ditis; sed revocare gradum superasque evadere ad auras, hoc opus, hic labor est: the descent to Avernus (hell) is easy; night and day the gate of gloomy Dis (Hades) stands open; but to retrace your steps and escape to the upper air, this is work, this is toil (Virgil)

facilius per partes in cognitionem totius adducimur: we are more easily led part by part to an understanding of the whole (Seneca)

facis de necessitate virtutem: you make a virtue of necessity (St. Jerome)

faciunt næ intelligendo, ut nihil intelligant: they are so knowing, that they know nothing (Terence)

facta canam; sed erunt qui me finxisse loquantur: I am about to sing of facts; but some will say I have invented them (Ovid)

facta ejus cum dictis discrepant: his actions do not square with his words (Cicero)

facte nova virtute, puer; sic itur ad astra: go on and increase in valor, young man; thus the path to immortality (Virgil)

fænum habet in cornu, longe fuge: he has hay on his horns; flee far away (Horace)

fallacia alia aliam trudit: one falsehood thrusts aside another (i.e., leads to more) (Terence)

fallentis semita vitæ: the narrow path of an unnoticed (or deceptive) life (Horace)

fallit enim vitium, specie virtutis et umbra, cum sit triste habitu, vultuque et veste severum: vice can deceive under the shape and shadow of virtue, when sad and severe in its dress and countenance (Juvenal)

fallitur, egregio quisquis sub principe credit servitium. Nunquam libertas gratior extat quam sub rege pio: whoever thinks it slavery to serve under an eminent prince is mistaken. Liberty is never more gracious than under a pious king (Claudian)

falso damnati crimine mortis: condemned to die on a false charge (Virgil)

falsus honor juvat et mendax infamia terret quem nisi mendosum et mendacem?: whom does false honor aid and calumny deter but the vicious and the liar? (Horace)

fama est obscurior annis: the fame (or rumor) has become obscure through the years (Virgil)

fama, malum quo non aliud velocius ullum, mobilitate viget, viresque acquirit eundo: rumor, than which no evil thing of any kind is more swift, increases with travel and gains strength by its progress (Virgil)

fama volat parvam subito vulgata per urbem: the rumor forthwith flies abroad, dispersed throughout the small town (Virgil)

famem fuisse suspicor matrem mihi: I suspect that hunger was my mother (Plautus)

fecisti nos ad te et inquietum est cor nostrum, donec requiescat in te (or, fecisti enim nos ad te, et cor inquietum donec requiescat in te): you (God) have created us for yourself, and our heart cannot be quieted until it finds rest in you (St. Augustine)

felices ter et amplius quos irrupta tenet copula, nec, malis divulsus querimoniis, suprema citius solvet amor die: happy three times over are those who enjoy uninterrupted union, and whose love, unbroken by evil complaints, shall not dissolve until the last day (Horace)

fere libenter homines id quod volunt credunt: men willingly believe what they wish to believe (Julius Cæsar)

fertilior seges est alienis semper in agris, vicinumque pecus grandius uber habet: the crop is always greater in the lands of another, and the cattle of our neighbor are deemed more productive than our own (Ovid)

fervens difficili bile tumet jecur: my hot passion swells with savage wrath (Horace)

festinare nocet, nocet et cunctatio sæpe; tempore quæque suo qui facit, ille sapit: it is bad to hurry, and delay is often as bad; the wise person is the one who does everything in its proper time (Ovid)

festinat decurrere velox flosculus angustæ, miseræque brevissima vitæ portio; dum bibimus, dum serta, unguenta, puellas poscimus, obrepit non intellecta senectus: the flower of our brief and narrow existence fades rapidly into decline, its course is quickly ended; whilst we drink, and call for garlands, for perfumes, and for girls, old age steals upon us by surprise (Juvenal)

festinatione nil tutius in discordiis civilibus: nothing is safer than dispatch in civil quarrels (Tacitus)

fictis meminerit nos jocari fabulis: be it remembered that we are amusing you with tales of fiction (Phædrus)

fidem fati virtute sequemur: with my own virtue I shall strive to achieve the promise given to me by destiny

fidem qui perdit, quo se servet relicuo?: the one who has lost his honor, what has he left to live upon? (Publilius Syrus)

fides quærens intellectum (or, **fidens quærens intellectum**): faith seeking understanding (i.e., belief before understanding) (St. Augustine)

fiere non potest, ut filius istarum lacrimarum pereat: it is not possible that the son of these tears should be lost (St. Augustine)

finge datos currus, quid agas?: suppose the chariot (of the sun) be committed to you, what would you do? (Ovid, Apollo to Phæthon)

fingit equum tenera docilem cervice magister ire viam qua monstret eques: the trainer trains the docile horse to turn, with his sensitive neck, whichever way the rider indicates (Horace)

fingunt se medicos quivis idiota, sacerdos, Judæus, monachus, histrio, rasor, anus: any untrained person, priest, Jew, monk, play actor, barber, or old wife is ready to prescribe for you in sickness

flebit, et insignis tota cantabitur urbe: he shall regret it and be a marked man, the butt of some merry song (Horace)

flere licet certe: flendo diffundimus iram; perque sinum lacrimæ, fluminis instar enim: truly it is allowed us to weep: by weeping we disperse our wrath; and tears go through the heart, even like a stream (Ovid)

floriferis ut apes in saltibus omnia libant, omnia nos itidem despascimur aurea dicta: as bees taste of everything in the flowery meadows, so we feed on every golden word that falls from his lips (i.e., one who selects the best of everything that is encountered) (Lucretius)

fœcunda culpæ sæcula nuptias primum inquinavere et genus et domos: this age, fertile of guilt, has first polluted the marriage bed, and with it our people and our houses (Horace)

fœnum habet in cornu, longe fuge, dummodo risum excutiat sibi, non hic cuiquam parcit amico: he has a wisp of hay on his horn, flee far from him; if only he raise a laugh for himself, there is no friend he would spare (Horace)

foliis tantum ne carmina manda; ne turbata volent rapidis ludibria ventis: neither commit your oracles to leaves of paper, lest they fly about dispersed, the sport of rushing winds (Virgil)

formidinem mortis vicit aurum: gold has conquered the fear of death (Apuleius)

formosa virgo est; dotis dimidium vocant isti, qui dotes neglegunt uxorias: the girl is pretty; this is half the dowry, say those men who are not interested in a dowry (Lucius Afranius)

formosos sæpe inveni pessimos, et turpi facie multos cognovi optimos: I have often found good-looking people to be very base, and I have known many ugly people most estimable (Phædrus)

forsan et hæc olim meminisse juvabit; durante, et vosmet rebus servate secundis: perhaps it will be a delight to us some day to recall these misfortunes; bear them, therefore, and reserve yourselves for better times (Virgil)

forsan miseros meliora sequentur: perhaps a better fate awaits the afflicted (Virgil)

forsitan et nostrum nomen miscebitur istis: perhaps my name will be linked with theirs (Ovid)

fortem posce animum mortis terrore carentem, qui spatium vitæ extremum inter munera ponat Naturæ: pray for a strong soul free from the fear of death, which regards the final period of life among the gifts of Nature (Juvenal)

fortes creantur fortibus et bonis; est in juvencis, est in equis patrum virtus, nec imbellem feroces progenerant aquilæ columbam: brave men are begotten by the brave and good; there is in steers and in horses the virtue of their sires, nor does the fierce eagle beget the dove (Horace)

fortes et strenuos etiam contra fortunam insistere, timidos et ignoros ad desperationem formidine properare: the brave and bold persist even against fortune; the timid and cowardly rush to despair through fear alone (Tacitus)

fortes in fine assequendo et suaves in modo assequendi simus: let us be resolute in prosecuting our purpose and mild in the manner of attaining it (Aquaviva)

fortuito quodam concursu atomorum: certain fortuitous concourse of atoms (Cicero)

fortuna amorem pejor infammat magis: when fortune frowns, love's flame burns fiercer (Seneca)

fortuna belli semper ancipiti in loco est: the fortune of war stands ever on the verge (Seneca)

fortuna miserrima tuta est: nam timor eventus deterioris abest: the most wretched fortune is safe; for there is no fear of anything worse (Ovid)

fortunæ majoris honos, erectus et acer: an honor to his distinguished position, upright and brave (Claudian)

fragili quærens illidere dentem offendet solido: he (my adversary), in trying to fix a tooth in some tender part, shall strike it against the solid (i.e., shall find firm resistance) (Horace)

fragrantia durant Herculea collecta manu: when gathered by Hercules's hand, they keep their fragrance

frater, ave atque vale: brother, hello and goodbye (Catullus)

frustra retinacula tendens ferter equis auriga, neque audit currus habenas: in vain, as he tugs at the reins, is the charioteer borne along by the steeds, and the chariot heeds not the curb (Virgil)

frustra vitium vitaveris illud, si te alio pravus detorseris: in vain do you avoid one fault if you perversely turn aside into another (Horace)

fuge magna; licet sub paupere tecto reges et regum vita præcurrere amicos: avoid greatness; under a poor roof there may be found more happiness than kings and their courtiers in palaces enjoy (Horace)

fugit improbus, ac me sub cultro linquit: the rogue runs away and leaves me with the knife at my throat (i.e., to be sacrificed) (Horace)

fuimus Troës, fuit Ilium, et ingens gloria Teucrorum: we Trojans are no more; Ilium is no more, and the great glory of the Teucrians (Virgil)

fuit hæc sapientia quondam, publica privatis secernere, sacra profanis, concubitu prohibere vago, dare jura maritis, oppida moliri leges incidere ligno: this of old was accounted wisdom: to separate public from private property, things sacred from profane, to restrain from vagrant concubinage, to ordain laws for married people, to build cities, to engrave laws on tablets (Horace)

fumum et opes strepitumque Romæ: the smoke, the wealth, the din of Rome (Juvenal and Horace)

fungar inani munere: I shall discharge a fruitless and unavailing duty (Virgil)

fungar vice cotis, acutum reddere quæ ferrum valet, exsors ipsa secandi: I shall perform the office of a whetstone, which can make other things sharp, though it is itself incapable of cutting (Horace)

G

Gallia est omnis divisa in partes tres: all of Gaul is divided into three parts (Julius Cæsar)

garrit aniles ex re fabellas: he tells a fable according to the circumstance (i.e., his argument is more fable than fact) (Horace)

gaudeamus igitur, juvenes dum sumus; post jucundam juventutem, post molestam senectutem, nos habebit humus: let us rejoice, therefore, while we are young; after the pleasures of youth and after the weariness of old age, the earth will hold us (a students' song dating from the 13th century)

gaudent prænomine molles auriculæ: his delicate ears are delighted with the title (Horace)

gaudet equis, canibusque, et aprici gramine campi: he delights in horses, dogs, and the grass of the sunny plain (Horace)

gaudete vosque, O Lydiæ lacus undæ; ridete quidquid est domi cachinnorum: rejoice you too, waters of the Lydian lake, and laugh out loud all the laughter you have at your command (Catullus)

gaudetque viam fecisse ruina: he rejoices at having made his way by ruin (Lucan, said of Julius Cæsar)

genus et proavos et quæ non fecimus ipsi, vix ea nostra voco: birth, ancestry, and what we have ourselves not done, I would hardly call our own (Ovid)

genus humanum superavit: he surpassed the human race in natural ability (Lucretius)

genus immortale manet, multosque per annos stat fortuna domus, et avi numerantur avorum: the race continues immortal, and through many years the fortune of the house stands steadfast, and it numbers grandchildren of grandchildren (Virgil)

gigni de nihilo nihil; in nihilum nil posse reverti: nothing can be produced from nothing; nothing can be returned into nothing (Persius)

gigni pariter cum corpore, et una crescere sentimus pariterque senescere mentem: we see that the mind is born with the body, that it grows with it, and also ages with it (Lucretius)

gloria in excelsis Deo, et in terra pax hominibus bonæ voluntatis. Laudamus te, benedicimus te, adoramus te, glorificamus te: glory to God in the highest, and peace on earth to men of good will. We praise you, we bless you, we adore you, we glorify you (from the Catholic Mass)

gloria Patri, et Filio, et Spiritui Sancto. Sicut erat in principio, et nunc, et semper, et in sæcula sæculorum: glory be to the Father, and to the Son, and to the Holy Spirit. As it was in the beginning, is now, and ever shall be, world without end (from the Catholic Mass)

Græcia capta ferum victorem cepit, et artes intulit agresti Latio: Greece, once conquered, in turn conquered its uncivilized conqueror, and brought the arts to rustic Latium (Horace)

Græculus esuriens in cœlum jusseris ibit: command the hungry Greek to go to heaven, and he will go (i.e., he will attempt the impossible) (Juvenal)

Grais ingenium, Grais dedit ore rotundo Musa loqui: to the Greeks the Muse gave ingenuity, to the Greeks it gave eloquent speech (Horace)

Gram. loquitur, Dia. vera docet, Rhe. verba colorat, Mu. canit, Ar. numerat, Geo. ponderat, As. docet astra: Grammar speaks, Dialectics teaches the truth, Rhetoric gives color to speech, Music sings, Arithmetic numbers, Geometry weighs and measures, and Astronomy teaches the stars (i.e., the seven liberal arts)

grammatici certant, et adhuc sub judice lis est: the grammarians quibble and still the case (or question) is unresolved (Horace)

grammaticus, rhetor, geometres, pictor, aliptes, augur, schœnobates, medicus, magus, omnia novit Græculus esuriens: in cælum jusseris ibit: grammarian, rhetorician, geometrician, painter, athletic trainer, diviner, tightrope walker, doctor, magician, the hungry Greek can do everything: send him to heaven, and he'll go there too (Juvenal)

gratia, Musa, tibi. Nam tu solatia præbes; tu curæ requis, tu medicina mali: thanks to you, my Muse. For you afford me comfort; you are a rest from my cares, a cure for my woes (Ovid)

gratia, quæ tarda est, ingrata est: gratia namque cum fieri properat, gratia grata magis: a favor tardily bestowed is no favor: for a favor quickly granted is a more agreeable favor (Ausonius)

gratis anhelans, multa agendo nihil agens: panting without a cause, and, in pretending to do much, really doing nothing (Phædrus)

gratulor quod eum quem necesse erat diligere, qualiscunque esset, talem habemus, ut libenter quoque diligamus: I am glad that the one whom I must have loved from duty, whatever he might have been, is the same one whom I can love from inclination (Trebonius, according to Tullium)

gratum hominem semper beneficium delectat; ingratum semel: a kindness is always delightful to a grateful person; to the ungrateful, only at the time of its receipt (Seneca)

grave pondus illum magna nobilitas premit: his exalted rank weighs heavy on him as a grievous burden (Seneca)

gutta cavat lapidem, consumitur annulus usu, et teritur pressa vomer aduncus humo: the drop hollows the stone, the ring is worn by use, and the crooked ploughshare is frayed away by the pressure of the earth (Ovid)

H

habemus luxuriam atque avaritiam, publice egestatem, privatim opulentiam: we have luxury and avarice, public debt and private opulence (Sallust, attributed to Cato, said of Rome)

habet aliquid ex iniquo omne magnum exemplum, quod contra singulos, utilitate publica rependitur: every great example of punishment has in it some tincture of injustice, but the wrong to individuals is compensated by the promotion of the public good (Tacitus)

habet cerebrum sensus arcem; hic mentis est regimen: the brain is the citadel of the senses: this guides the principle of thought (Pliny the Elder)

habet iracundia hoc mali, non vult regi: there is in anger this evil, that it will not be controlled (Seneca)

hac quoque de causa, si te proverbia tangunt, mense malos Maio nubere vulgus ait: for this reason, if you believe proverbs, let me tell you the common one: "It is unlucky to marry in May" (Ovid)

hæ tibi erunt artes, pacisque imponere morem, parcere subjectis et debellare superbos: these shall be your arts, to set forth the law of peace, to spare the conquered, and to subdue the proud (Virgil)

hæc amat obscurum; volet hæc sub luce videri, judicis argutum quæ non formidat acumen; hæc placuit semel; hæc decies repetita placebit: one (poem) courts the shade; another, not afraid of the critic's keen eye, chooses to be seen in a strong light; the one pleases but once, the other will still please if ten times repeated (Horace)

hæc ego mecum compressis agito labris; ubi quid datur oti, illudo chartis: these things I revolve around myself with compressed lips; when I have any leisure, I amuse myself with my writings (Horace)

hæc est condicio vivendi, aiebat, eoque responsura tuo nunquam est par fama labori: such is the lot of life, he said, and so your merits will never receive their due reward of praise (Horace)

hæc perinde sunt, ut illius animus, qui ea possidet. Qui uti scit, ei bona, illi qui non utitur recte, mala: these things are exactly according to the disposition of the one who possesses them. To the one who knows how to use them, they are blessings; to the one who does not use them rightly, they are evils (Terence)

hæc prima lex in amicitia sanciatur, ut neque rogemus res turpes, nec faciamus rogati: be this the first law established in friendship, that we neither ask of others what is dishonorable, nor ourselves do it when asked (Cicero)

hæc scripsi non otii abundantia, sed amoris erga te: I have written this, not as having abundance of leisure, but out of love for you (Cicero)

hæc studia adolescentiam alunt, senectutem oblectant, secundas res ornant, adversis solatium ac perfugium præbent, delectant domi, non impediunt foris, pernoctant nobiscum, peregrinantur, rusticantur: these (literary) studies are the food of youth and the consolation of old age; they adorn prosperity and are the comfort and refuge of adversity; they are pleasant at home and are no encumbrance abroad; they accompany us at night, in our travels, and in our rural retreats (Cicero)

hæc sunt jucundi causa cibusque mali: these things are at once the cause and food of this delicious malady (Ovid)

hæc vivendi ratio mihi non convenit: this mode of living does not suit me (Cicero)

hæret lateri lethalis arundo: the deadly arrow sticks in his (or her) side (Virgil)

hanc personam induisti, agenda est: you have assumed this part, and you must act it out (Seneca)

hanc veniam petimusque damusque vicissim: we give this privilege and receive it in turn (Horace, a reference to the author as critic)

has pœnas garrula lingua dedit: this punishment a prating tongue brought on him (Ovid)

has vaticinationes eventus comprobavit: the event has verified these predictions (Cicero)

haud facile emergunt quorum vitutibus obstat res angusta domi: it is not easy for people to rise out of obscurity when they have to face straitened circumstances at home (Juvenal)

haud scio an pietate adversus deos sublata fides etiam et societas generi humani et una excellentissima virtus justitia tollatur: in all probability the disappearance of piety toward the gods will entail the disappearance of faith and sodality among men as well as justice, the greatest of all the virtues (Cicero)

Hectora quis nosset, si felix Troja fuisset? Publica virtuti per mala facta via est: who would have known of Hector if Troy had been fortunate? A highway is open to virtue through the midst of misfortunes (Ovid)

hei mihi!, difficile est imitari gaudia falsa, difficile est tristi fingere mente jocum: oh my!, it is hard to feign the joys one does not feel, hard to feign merriment when one's heart is sad (Tibullus)

hei mihi!, qualis erat!, quantum mutatus ab illo Hectore, qui redit, exuvias indutus Achilli: oh my!, how sad he looked!, how changed from that Hector who returned in triumph arrayed in the spoils of Achilles (Virgil)

hei mihi!, quam facile est (quamvis hic contigit omnes), alterius lucta fortia verba loqui!: oh my!, how easy it is (how much all have experienced it), to indulge in brave words in another person's trouble! (Ovid)

heu, cadit in quemquam tantum scelus!: alas, that so great a crime falls upon anyone! (Paradin)

heu, melior quanto sors tua sorte mea!: alas, how much better is your fate than mine! (Ovid)

heu!, quantum fati parva tabella vehit!: alas!, with what a weight of destiny is this one small plank carried! (Ovid)

heu!, totum triduum!: alas!, three whole days! (Terence, a reference to the separation of lovers)

hi motus animorum atque hæc certamina tanta pulveris exigui jactu compressa quiescent: these passions of their souls, these conflicts so fierce, will cease, and be repressed by the casting of a little dust (Virgil)

hi narrata ferunt alio; mensuraque ficti crescit et auditus aliquid novus adjicit auctor: some report elsewhere whatever is told them; the measure of fiction always increases, and each fresh narrator adds something to what he has heard (Ovid)

hic dies, vere mihi festus, atras eximet curas: this day, for me a true holiday, shall banish gloomy cares (Cicero)

hic est enim sanguis meus novi testamenti: this is the new covenant in my blood (St. Matthew 26:28)

hic gelidi fontes, hic mollia prata, Lycori, hic nemus, hic toto tecum consumerer ævo: here are cool springs, Lycoris, here soft meadows, here a grove; here with you could I pass my whole life (Virgil)

hic locus est partes ubi se via findit in ambas: this is the spot where the way divides into two branches (Virgil)

hic murus aheneus esto, nil conscire sibi, nulla pallescere culpa: let this be your brazen wall of defense, to have nothing on your conscience, no guilt to make you turn pale (Horace)

hic niger est; hunc tu, Romane, caveto: this fellow is a dark heart; be careful of him, Roman (Horace)

hic nigræ succus loliginis, hæc est ægrugo mera: this is the very venom of dark detraction; this is pure malignity (Horace)

hic patet ingeniis campus, certusque merenti stat favor; ornatur propriis industria donis: here is a field open for talent, and here merit will have certain favor, and industry graced with its due reward (Claudian)

hic rogo, non furor est ne moriare mori?: I ask, is it not madness to die that you may not die? (Martial)

hic situs est Phaëthon currus auriga paterni; quem si non tenuit, magnis tamen excidit ausis: here lies buried Phaëthon, the driver of his father's carriage, which he did not manage, still he perished in a great attempt (Ovid)

hic transitus efficit magnum vitæ compedium: this change effects a great savings of life (i.e., of time)

hic ubi nunc urbs est, tum locus urbis erat: here, where the city now stands, was at that time nothing but its site (Ovid)

hic ver assiduum, atque alienis mensibus æstas: here is ceaseless spring, and summer in months in which summer is alien (Virgil, referring to Italy)

hic victor cæstus artemque repono: here victorious I lay aside my gauntlet and my net (Virgil)

hic vivimus ambitiosa paupertate omnes: here we all live in a state of ostentatious poverty (Juvenal)

hinc illæ lacrimæ (or lacrymæ)!, hæc illa 'st misericordia: hence these tears!, and hence all that compassion (Terence)

hinc omne principium, huc refer exitum: to them ascribe every undertaking, to them the issue (Horace, referring to the gods)

hinc subitæ mortes atque intestata senectus: hence sudden deaths and intestate old age (Juvenal)

hinc totam infelix vulgatur fama per urbem: hence the unhappy news is spread abroad through the whole city (Virgil)

hinc usura vorax, avidumque in tempore fænus, et concussa fides, et multis utile bellum: hence arise devouring usury, grasping interest, shaken credit, and war of advantage to many (Lucan, said of the ambition of Cæsar)

hinc venti dociles resono se carcere solvunt, et cantum accepta pro libertate rependunt: hence the obedient winds are loosed from their sounding prison, and repay the liberty they have received with a tune (said of an organ)

his lachrymis vitam damus, et miserescimus ultro: to these tears we grant him life, and pity him besides (Virgil)

his legibus solutis respublica stare non potest: with these laws repealed, the republic cannot last (Cicero)

his saltem accumulem donis, et fungar inani munere: let me at least bestow upon him those last offerings, and discharge a vain and unavailing duty (Virgil)

hoc erat in votis; modus agri non ita magnus; hortus ubi, et tecto vicinus jugis aquæ fons, et paulum silvæ super his foret: this was in my prayers: a piece of ground not too large, with a garden, and a spring of never-failing water near my house, and a little woodland besides (Horace)

hoc est quod palles?; cur quis non prandeat, hoc est?: is it for this you look so pale?; is this a reason why one should not dine? (Persius)

hoc fonte derivata clades in patriam populumque fluxit: from this source has the destruction flowed, which overwhelmed the country and its people (Horace)

hoc Herculi, Iovis satu edito, potuit fortasse contingere, nobis non item: this might perchance happen to Hercules, of the royal seed of Jove, but not to us (Cicero)

hoc patrium est, potius consuefacere filium sua sponte recte facere, quam alieno metu: it is a father's duty to accustom his son to act rightly of his own free will rather than from fear of the consequences (Terence)

hoc per se nihil est, sed si minimum addideris maximum fieret: this by itself is nothing, but if you should add even the least to it, it would become the greatest

hoc præstat amicitia propinquitati, quod ex propinquitate benevolentia tolli potest, ex amicitia non potest: friendship has this advantage over kinship, that kinship can exist without goodwill but friendship cannot (Cicero)

hoc scito, nimio celerius venire quod molestum est, quam id quod cupide petas: be sure of this, that that which is disagreeable comes more speedily than that which you eagerly desire (Plautus)

hoc volo, sic jubeo, sit pro ratione voluntas: this I wish, thus I command, let my will stand in place of reason (Juvenal)

hodie mecum eris in paradiso: today, you shall be with me in Paradise (St. Luke 23:43; one of the Seven Last Words of Christ)

hoi pleiones kakai: the majority of humanity is bad (Bias, one of the Seven Greek Sages, from the Greek)

homine imperito nunquam quidquam injustius qui, nisi quod ipse fecit, nihil rectum putat: nothing so unjust as an ignorant man, who thinks nothing right but what he himself has done (Terence)

homines amplius oculis quam auribus credunt: longum iter est per præcepta, breve et efficax per exempla: men trust their eyes rather than their ears: the way by precept is long and tedious, by example short and effectual (Seneca)

homini amico et familiari non est mentiri meum: it is not my habit to lie to friends or family (Lucilius)

homo ad res perspicacior Lynceo vel Argo, et oculeus totus: a man more clear-sighted for business than Lynceus or Argus, and eyes all over (Appuleius)

homo antiqua virtute ac fide: a man of the ancient virtue and loyalty (Terence)

homo constat ex duabus partibus, corpore et anima, quorum una est corporea, altera ab omni materiæ concretione sejuncta: man is composed of two parts, body and soul, of which the one is corporeal, the other separated from all combination with matter (Cicero)

homo est animal bipes rationale: man is a two-footed reasoning animal (Boëthius)

homo qui erranti comiter monstrat viam, quasi lumen de suo lumine accendit, facit; nihilominus ipsi luceat, cum illi accenderit: the one who kindly shows the way to one who has gone astray, acts as though he had lighted another's lamp from his own, which both gives light to the other and continues to shine for himself (Cicero)

honestum quod vere dicimus, etiamsi a nullo laudatur, laudabile est sua natura: that which we truly call honorable is praiseworthy in its own nature, even though it should be praised by no one (Cicero)

horæ cedunt, et dies, et menses, et anni, nec præteritum tempus unquam revertitur: hours and days, months and years, pass away, and time once past never returns (Cicero)

horror ubique animos, simul ipsa silentia terrent: everywhere horror seizes the soul, and the very silence is dreadful (Virgil)

hos ego versiculos feci, tulit alter honores; sic vos non vobis fertis aratra boves; sic vos non vobis mellificatis apes; sic vos non vobis vellora fertis aves; sic vos non vobis nidificatis aves: I wrote these lines, another received the credit; thus do you oxen bear the yoke for others; thus do you bees make honey for others; thus do you sheep wear fleeces for others; thus do you birds build nests for others (Virgil)

hos successus alit: possunt, quia posse videntur: success encourages them: they can because they think they can (Virgil)

hospes nullus tam in amici hospitium devorti potest, quin ubi triduum continuum fuerit jam odiosus siet: no one can be so welcome a guest that he will not become an annoyance when he has stayed three continuous days in a friend's house (Plautus)

huc propius me, dum doceo insanire omnes, vos ordine adite: come near me all in order, and I will convince you that you are mad, every one (Horace)

huic maxime putamus malo fuisse nimiam opinionem ingenii atque virtutis: we think that what harmed him the most was that he entertained too high an opinion of his own talents and virtue (Cornelius Nepos, said of Alcibiades)

huic versatile ingenium sic pariter ad omnia fuit, ut natum ad id unum diceres, quodcunque ageret: this man's genius was so versatile, so equal to every pursuit, that you would pronounce him to have been born for whatever thing in which he was engaged (Livy, said of Cato the Elder)

hunc tu, Romane, caveto: of him, Romans, do thou beware (Horace)

I

i demens!, et sævas curre per Alpes, ut pueris placeas, et declamatio fias: go madman!, and run over the savage Alps to please schoolboys, and become the subject of declamation (Juvenal, in reference to Hannibal)

iam seges est ubi Troia fuit: now are cornfields where Troy once was (Ovid)

iam ver egelidos refert tepores: now Spring restores balmy warmth (Catullus)

ibi omnis effusus labor: by that one (negligence) all his labor was lost (Virgil)

ibis, redibis, non morieris in bello: you shall go, you shall return, you shall not die in the wars (an ambiguous quote that can also be rendered: **ibis, redibis non, morieris in bello**: you shall go, you shall not return, you shall die in the wars)

id mutavit, quoniam me immutatum videt: he has changed his mind because he sees me unchanged (Terence)

id quod est præstantissimum maximeque optabile omnibus sanis et bonis et beatis, cum dignitate otium: the thing that is the most outstanding, and chiefly to be desired by all healthy and good and well-off persons, is leisure with honor (Cicero)

idoneus quidem mea sententia, præsertim quum et ipse eum audiverit, et scribat de mortuo; ex quo nulla suspicio est amicitiæ causa eum esse mentitum: a competent person in my opinion, as he was accustomed often to hear him, and published his sentiments after the subject of them ceased to exist; there is no reason therefore to suppose that his partiality has misled him from the truth (Cicero)

ignavissimus quisque, et, ut res docuit, in periculo non ausurus, nimio verbis et lingua ferox: every coward, who, as experience has proved, will fly in the hour of danger, is the most boastful in his words and language afterward (Tacitus)

ignavum fucos pecus a præsepibus arcent: they (bees) drive from their hives the drones, a lazy bunch (Virgil)

ignoranti quem portum petat, nullus suus ventus est: if a person does not know to which port he is steering, no wind is favorable to him (Seneca)

ignorent populi, si non in morte probaris, an scieris adversa pati: the world would not know, if you did not prove by your death, that you knew how to bear up against adverse circumstances (Lucan, in reference to Pompey)

ignotis errare locis, ignota videre flumina gaudebat, studio minuente laborem: he delighted to wander over unknown regions, to visit unknown rivers, the interest lessening the fatigue (Ovid)

iliacos intra muros peccatur et extra: sin is committed as well within the walls of Troy as without (i.e., both sides are to be blamed) (Virgil and Horace)

ilicet infandum cuncti contra omina bellum contra fata deum, perverso numine poscunt: forthwith, against the omens and against the oracles of the gods, all to a man, under an adverse influence, clamor for unholy war (Virgil)

illa est agricolæ messis iniqua suo: that is a harvest that ill repays its husbandman (Ovid)

illa injusta bella sunt, quæ sunt sine causa suscepta; nam extra ulciscendi aut propulsandorum hostium causam bellum geri justum nullum potest: those wars are unjust that are undertaken without provocation; for only a war waged for revenge or defense can be just (Cicero)

illa laus est, magno in genere et in divitiis maximis, liberos hominem educare, generi monumentum et sibi: it is a merit in a man of high birth and large fortune to train up his children so as to be a credit to his family and himself (Plautus)

illa placet tellus in qua res parva beatum me facit, et tenues luxuriantur opes: that spot of earth has special charms for me, in which a limited income produces happiness, and moderate wealth abundance (Martial)

illam, quicquid agit, quoquo vestigia flectit, componit furtim, subsequiturque decor: in whatever she does, wherever she turns, grace steals into her movements and attends her steps (Tibullus)

ille fuit vitæ Mario modus, omnia passo quæ pejor Fortuna potest, omnibus uso quæ melior: such was the complexion of the life of Marius, that he had suffered the worst inflictions of Fortune, and enjoyed her choicest blessings (Lucan)

ille igitur nunquam direxit brachia contra torrentem; nec civis erat qui libera posset verba animi proferre et vitam impendere vero: he never was that citizen who would attempt to swim against the torrent, who would freely make his opinions known, and stake his life for the truth (Juvenal)

ille per extentum funem mihi posse videtur ire poëta, meum qui pectus inaniter angit irritat mulcet falsis terroribus implet ut magus: et modo me Thebis, modo ponit Athenis: that man seems to me able to walk on the tightrope who, as a poet, tortures my breast with fictions, can rouse me, then soothe me, fill me with unreal terrors like a magician, set me down either at Thebes or Athens (Horace)

ille potens sui lætusque degit, cui licet in diem dixisse, vixi: cras vel atra nube polum pater occupato vel sole puro: the man lives master of himself and cheerful, who can say day after day, I have lived; tomorrow let the Father above overspread the sky either with cloud or with clear sunshine (Horace)

ille quidem dignum virtutibus suis vitæ terminum posuit: he ended his days in a manner befitting his virtues (Apuleius)

ille vir haud magna cum re, sed plenus fidei: he is a man, not of large fortune, but full of good faith

illi inter sese multa vi brachia tollunt in numerum, versantque tenaci forcipe massam: they (the Cyclops), keeping time, one by one raise their arms with mighty force, and turn the iron lump with the biting tongs (Virgil)

illi robur et æs triplex circe pectus erat, qui fragilem truci commisit pelago ratem primus: that man had oak and triple brass around his breast who first entrusted his frail raft to the savage sea (Horace)

illud amicitiæ sanctum ac venerabile nomen nunc tibi pro vili sub pedibusque jacet: the sacred and venerable name of friendship is now despised by you and trodden under foot (Ovid)

imago animi vultus est, indices oculi: the countenance is the portrait of the soul, and the eyes mark its intentions (Cicero)

immo id, quod aiunt, auribus teneo lupum nam neque quomodo a me amittam, invenio: neque, uti retineam scio: it is true, they say, I have caught a wolf by the ears: for I know neither how to get rid of him nor how to keep him in restraint (Terence)

immoritur studiis, et amore senescit habendi: he is killing himself with his efforts, and in his greed of gain is becoming an old man (Horace)

immortale odium et nunquam sanabile vulnus: a deadly hatred, and a wound that can never be healed (i.e., religious disagreement) (Juvenal)

improbæ crescunt divitiæ, tamen curtæ nescio quid semper abest rei: riches increase to an enormous extent, yet something is ever wanting to our still imperfect fortune (Horace)

improbe amor, quid non mortalia pectora cogis?: cruel love, what is there to which you do not drive mortal hearts? (Virgil)

in æquali jure melior est conditio possidentis: where the right is equal, the claim of the party in possession is the best (or, possession is nine-tenths of the law)

in amore hæc omnia insunt vitia; injuriæ, suspiciones, inimicitiæ, induciæ, bellum, pax rursus: in love there are all these evils, wrongs, suspicions, enmities, treaties, and alternate war and peace (Terence)

in furias ignemque ruunt; amor omnibus idem: they rush into the flames of passion; love is the same in all (Virgil)

in illo viro, tantum robur corporis et animi fuit, ut quocunque loco natus esset, fortunam sibi facturus videretur: in that man there was such oak-like strength of body and mind that whatever his rank by birth might have been, he gave promise of attaining the highest place in the lists of fortune (Livy, said of Cato the Elder)

in manus tuas commendo spiritum meum: into Thy hands I commend my spirit (Luke 23:46; one of the Seven Last Words of Christ)

in melle sunt sitæ linguæ vestræ atque orationes, corda felle sunt lita atque aceto: your tongues and your words are steeped in honey, but your hearts are in gall and vinegar (Plautus)

in mercatura facienda multæ fallaciæ et quasi præstigiæ exercentur: in commerce many deceptions, not to say legerdemain, are practiced

in nova fert animus mutatas dicere formas corpora: I am inclined to speak of bodies changed into new forms (Ovid)

in nullum reipublicæ usum ambitiosa loquela inclaruit: he became celebrated for an affected and ambitious verbosity attended with no advantage whatsoever to the republic (Tacitus)

in omnibus negotiis prius quam aggrediare, adhibenda est præparatio diligens: in all matters, before beginning, a diligent preparation should be made (Cicero)

in pretio pretium est, dat census honores, census amicitias; pauper ubique jacet: worth lies in wealth; wealth purchases honors and friendships; the poor man everywhere is neglected (Ovid)

in principatu commutando, civium nil præter domini nomen mutant pauperes: in a change of masters, the poor change nothing except their master's name (Phædrus)

in principio erat Verbum, et Verbum erat apud Deum, et Deus erat Verbum: in the beginning was the Word, and the Word was with God, and the Word was God (St. John 1:1)

in scirpo nodum quæris: you are looking for a knot in a bullrush (Plautus)

in solo vivendi causa palato est: to gratify the palate is the sole object of their existence (Juvenal)

in te, Domine, speravi; non confundar in æternum: Lord, I have set my hope in thee; I shall not be destroyed forever

in turbas et discordias pessimo cuique plurima vis: pax et quies bonis artibus indigent: in seasons of tumult and discord, the worst men have most power; mental and moral excellence require peace and quietness (Tacitus)

incedis per ignes suppositos cineri doloso: you are treading on fires hidden under a treacherous crust of ashes (after Horace)

inceptis gravibus plerumque et magna professis, purpureus, late qui splendeat, unus et alter adsuitur pannus: oftentimes to lofty beginnings and to such as promise great things, one or two purple patches are stitched on in order to make a brilliant display (Horace)

incerta hæc si tu postules ratione certa facere, nihilo plus agas, quam si des operam ut cum ratione insanias: if you require reason to make that certain which is uncertain, you are simply attempting to go mad by the rules of reason (Terence)

incidit in Scyllam qui vult vitare Charybdim: he falls into Scylla in struggling to escape Charybdis (i.e., to fall into one danger while trying to avoid another) (Horace)

incipe; dimidium facti est cœpisse. Supersit dimidium: rursum hoc incipe, et efficies: begin; to begin is half the work. Let half still remain; begin this again, and you will have finished (Ausonius)

incipe, parve puer, risu cognoscere matrem: begin, little boy, to recognize your mother with a smile (Virgil)

indica tigris agit rabida cum tigride pacem perpetuam; sævis inter se convenit ursis; ast homini ferrum letale incude nefanda produxisse parum est: the Indian tigers live in perpetual peace with each rabid tigress; savage bears agree among themselves; but man without remorse beats out the deadly sword on the accursed anvil (Juvenal)

indignor quandoque bonus dormitat Homerus: I am indignant when sometimes even Homer nods off (Horace)

indignor quidquam reprehendi, non quia crasse compositum, illepideve putetur, sed quia nuper: I feel indignant when a work is censured not as uncouth or rough, but as new

indocti discant, et ament meminisse periti: let the unlearned learn, and the learned take pleasure in refreshing their memories (Hénault, after Pope)

inerat Vitellio simplicitas ac liberalitas, quæ, nisi adsit modus, in exitium vertuntur: Vitellius possessed both simplicity and liberality, qualities which, unless taken in moderation, are generally ruinous to the possessor (Tacitus)

inertis est nescire, quid liceat sibi. Id facere, laus est, quod decet; non, quod licet: it is the act of the indolent not to know what he may lawfully do. It is praiseworthy to do what is becoming, and not merely what is lawful (Seneca)

inest virtus et mens interrita lethi: he has a valiant heart and a soul undaunted by death (Ovid)

infandum, regina, jubes renovare dolorem: a grief too great to be told, O queen, you bid me renew (Virgil, Aeneas's reply to Dido)

infantem nudum cum te natura creavit, paupertatis onus patienter ferre memento: nature having created you and made you come into the world naked, remember to bear poverty with patience (Cato)

infelix Dido nulli bene jucta marito: hoc pereunte fugis, hoc fugiente peris: unhappy Dido ill-provided with husband and lover: the former by dying causes your flight, the latter by fleeing causes your death (Ovid)

infinita est velocitas temporis, quæ magis apparet respicientibus: the swiftness of time is infinite, as is most evident to those who look back (Seneca)

inflatum plenumque Nerone propinquo: puffed up and full of his relationship to Nero (Juvenal)

infortunia nostra, alienis collata, leviora: our misfortunes, compared with those of others, become lighter (from the *Emblemata* of Alciato)

ingeniis patuit campus, certusque merenti stat favor: ornatur propriis industria donis: the field is open to talent and merit is sure of its reward: the gifts with which industry is crowned are her own

ingenio arbusta ubi nata sunt non obsitu: where trees have grown by nature's art, not planted by human hands (Nævius)

ingenium cui sit, cui mens divinior, atque os magna sonaturum, des nominis hujus honorem: the one who possesses genius, a superior mind, and eloquence to display great things, is entitled to the honored name of poet (Horace)

ingenium ingens inculto latet hoc sub corpore: a great genius lies hid under this coarse body (or rough exterior) (Horace)

ingenium magni detractat livor Homeri: envy depreciates the genius of the great Homer (Ovid)

ingentes animos angusto in corpore versant: they have mighty souls at work within a stinted body (Virgil)

ingrata patria, ne ossa quidem mea habebis: ungrateful country, you shall not have even my bones (Scipio Africanus)

ingratus est, qui beneficium accepisse se negat, quod accepit: ingratus est, qui dissimulat; ingratus, qui non reddit; ingratissimus omnium, qui oblitus est: he is ungrateful who denies that he has received a kindness which has been bestowed upon him: he is ungrateful who conceals it; he is ungrateful who makes no return for it; most ungrateful of all is he who forgets it (Seneca)

ingrediturque solo, et caput inter nubila condit: she (fame) walks on the earth, and her head is concealed in the clouds (Virgil)

insani sapiens nomen ferat, æquus iniqui, ultra quod satis est virtutem si petat ipsam: let the wise man bear the name of fool, and the just of injust, if he pursue virtue itself beyond the proper bounds (Horace)

insanire parat certa ratione modoque: he is preparing to act the madman with a certain degree of reason and method (i.e., there is a method in his madness) (Horace)

integer vitæ scelerisque purus non eget Mauris jaculis neque arcu: the man of upright life and free from crime has no need of Moorish javelin or bow (Horace)

inter cetera mala, hoc quoque habet stultitia proprium, semper incipit vivere: among other evils, folly has also this special characteristic, it is always beginning to live (Seneca)

inter Græcos græcissimus, inter Latinos latinissimus: in Greek he is the most accomplished Grecian, and in Latin the most thorough Latinist (said of Erasmus)

inter spem curamque, timores inter et iras, omnem crede diem tibi diluxisse supremum; grata superveniet quæ non sperabitur hora: in the midst of hope and care, in the midst of fears and passions, believe each day that dawns on you is your last; more gratefully will you greet the hour that is not expected (Horace)

interea gustus elementa per omnia quærunt, nunquam animo pretiis obstantibus; interius si attendas, magis illa juvant, quæ pluris emuntur: in the meantime, they search for relishes through all the elements, with minds regardless of expense; look at it closely, those things please more that cost the higher price (Juvenal)

intus et in jecore ægro nascuntur domini: masters spring up in our own breasts, and from a sickly liver (Persius)

inveni portum, Spes et Fortuna valete, sat me lusistis, ludite nunc alios: I have reached the port; Hope and Fortune, farewell; you have made sport enough of me, make sport of others now (the final lines of Le Sage's novel *Gil Blas*)

invidus alterius macrescit rebus opimis; invidia Siculi non invenere tyranni majus tormentus: the envious man grows lean at the prosperity of another; no greater punishment than envy was devised by Sicilian tyrants (Horace)

invidus, iracundus, iners, vinosus, amator, nemo adeo ferus est, ut non mitescere possit, si modo culturæ patientem commodet aurem: the envious, the passionate, the indolent, the drunken, the lewd, none is so savage that he cannot be tamed, if only he lend a patient ear to culture (Horace)

invisa potentia, atque miseranda vita eorum, qui se metui quam amari malunt: the power is detested, and the life wretched, of those who would rather be feared than loved (Cornelius Nepos)

ipsæ rursum concedite sylvæ: once again, ye woods, I say good-bye (Virgil)

ipse dixit. Ipse autem erat Pythagoras: he himself said it. This himself was Pythagoras (Cicero)

ipse docet quid agam; fas est et ab hoste doceri: he himself teaches me what to do; it is right to be taught by the enemy (Ovid)

ipse pavet; nec qua commissas flectat habenas, nec scit qua sit iter; nec, si sciat, imperet illis: scared himself, he knows neither how to turn the reins entrusted to him, nor which way to go; nor, if he did, could he control the horses (Ovid, said of Phaëthon)

ipse quis sit, utrum sit an non sit, id quoque nescit: he knows not who he is, nor if he is, nor if he is not (Catullus)

ira furor brevis est; animum rege, qui, nisi paret, imperat; hunc frenis, hunc tu compesce catena: anger is a brief madness; control your temper, for unless it obeys, it commands you; restrain it with bit and chain (Horace)

irarum tantos volvis sub pectore fluctus?: do you roll such billows of wrath within your breast? (Virgil)

iras et verba locant: they let out for hire their passions and their words (Martial)

ire tamen restat, Numa quo devenit et Ancus: it still remains for you to go where Numa has gone, and Ancus before you (Horace)

is habitus animorum fuit, ut pessimum facinus auderent pauci, plures vellent, omnes paterentur: such was the public temper, that some few dared to perpetrate the vilest crimes, more were desirous to do so, and all looked passively on (Tacitus)

is mihi demum vivere et frui anima videtur, qui aliquo negotio intentus, præclari facinoris aut artis bonæ famam quærit: he alone appears to me to live and to enjoy life, who, being engaged in some business, seeks reputation by some famous action, or some useful art (Sallust)

is mihi videtur amplissimus qui sua virtute in altiorem locum pervenit: he is in my regard the most illustrious man who has risen by his own virtues (Cicero)

is ordo vitio careto, cæteris specimen esto: let that order be free from vice, and afford an example to all others (from the *Twelve Tables*, in reference to the Patricians)

ista decens facies longis vitiabitur annis; rugaque in antiqua fronte senilis erit: your comely face will be marred by length of years; and the wrinkle of age will one day scar your aged brow (Ovid)

ita feri ut se mori sentiat: strike him so that he can feel that he is dying (Suetonius, attributed to Caligula)

ita me Dii ament!, ubi sim nescio: may God love me!, for I know not where I am (Terence)

ita oportuit intrare in gloriam suam: so in that way he was obliged to enter in his glory

J

jacet ecce Tibullus, vix manet e toto parva quod urna capit: see, here Tibullus lies, of all that he was there hardly remains enough to fill a little urn (Ovid)

jam nunc minaci murmure cornuum perstringis aures; jam litui strepunt: even now you stun our ears with the threatening murmur of horns; already I hear the clarions sound (Horace)

jam pauca aratro jugera regiæ moles relinquent: soon will regal piles leave but few acres to the plough (Horace)

jam portum inveni, Spes et Fortuna valete!; nil mihi vobiscum est, ludite nunc alios: now I have gained the port, Hope and Fortune, farewell!; I have nothing more to do with you, now go make sport of others (an epitaph)

jam redit et Virgo, redeunt Saturnia regna: now the Virgin goddess of justice returns, now the reign of Saturn (the return of Astræa, goddess of Justice, was thought by Romans to be a signal for the return of the Golden Age) (Virgil)

jam seges est ubi Troja fuit, resecandaque falce luxuriat Phrygio sanguine pinguis humus: new fields of corn wave where Troy once stood, and the ground enriched with Trojan blood is luxuriant with grain ready for the sickle (Ovid)

jam summa procul villarum culmina fumant: now the high tops of the far-off villas send forth their smoke (Virgil)

jam ver egelidos refert tepores: now Spring restores balmy warmth (Catullus)

jamque dies, ni fallor adest quem semper acerbum semper honoratum (sic dii voluistis) habebo: that day I shall always recollect with grief; with reverence also (for the gods so willed it) (Virgil)

jamque opus exegi quod nec Jovis ira, nec ignis, nec poterit ferrum, nec edax abolere vetustas: I have now completed a work that neither the wrath of Jove, nor fire, nor sword, nor the consuming tooth of time, shall be able to destroy (Ovid, meant as irony)

Jasper fert myrrham, thus Melchior, Balthazar aurum. Hæc quicum secum portet tria nomina regum, solvitur a morbo, Domini pietate, caduco: Jasper brings myrrh, Melchior frankincense, and Balthazar gold. Whoever carries with him the names of these three kings will, by the grace of the Lord, be exempt from the falling sickness (a medieval European charm)

jubilate Deo, omnis terra; servite Domino in lætitia: sing joyfully to God, all the earth; serve the Lord with gladness (Psalm 99:2)

jucunda atque idonea dicere vitæ (or, **jucunda et idonea dicere vitæ**): to describe whatever is pleasant and proper in life (Horace)

judice te mercede caret, per seque petenda est externis virtus incomitata bonis: in your judgment virtue needs no reward, and is to be sought for its own sake, unaccompanied by external benefits (Ovid)

junctæque Nymphis Gratiæ decentes: the beauteous Graces linked hand in hand with the Nymphs (Horace)

jungere equos Titan velocibus imperat Horis: Titan commands the swift-flying Hours to yoke the horses of the sun (Ovid)

Jupiter in multos temeraria fulmina torquet, qui pœnem culpa non meruere pati: Jupiter hurls his reckless thunderbolts against many who have not by guilt deserved such punishment (Ovid)

jura negat sibi nata, nihil non arrogat armis: he denies that laws were made for him, and claims everything by force of arms (Horace)

juravi lingua, mentem injuratam gero: I have sworn with my tongue, but my mind is unsworn (Cicero)

jus omnium in omnia, et consequenter bellum omnium in omnes: the right of all to everything, and therefore of all to make war on all (Hobbes)

jus sanguinis, quod in legitimis succesionibus spectatur, ipso nativitatis tempore quæsitum est: the right of blood, which is regarded in all lawful inheritances, is found in the very time of nativity

justitia nihil exprimit præmii, nihil pretii: per se igitur expetitur: justice extorts no reward, no kind of price; it is sought, therefore, for its own sake (Cicero)

justitia non novit patrem nec matrem, solum veritatem spectat: justice knows neither father nor mother, it regards the truth alone

justitia tanta vis est, ut ne illi quidem, qui maleficio et scelere pascuntur, possint sine ulla particula justitiæ vivere: there is such force in justice, that even those who live by crime and wickedness cannot live without some small portion of it among them (Cicero)

justum bellum quibus necessarium, et pia arma quibus nulla nisi in armis relinquitur spes: war is just to those for whom it is necessary, and to take up arms is a sacred duty with those who have no other hope left (Livy)

justum et tenacem propositi virum, non civium ardor prava jubentium, non vultus instantis tyranni mente quatit solida: not the rage of the citizens commanding wrongful measures, not the aspect of the threatening tyrant, can shake from his firm purpose the person who is just and resolute (Horace)

L

labitur et labetur in omne volubilis ævum: the stream flows, and will go on flowing forever (Horace)

labitur occulte, fallitque volubilis ætas, ut celer admissis labitur amnis aquis: time rolls on steadily, and eludes us as it steals past, like the swift river that glides on with rapid stream (Ovid)

labor omnia vincit improbus, et duris urgens in rebus egestas: persevering labor overcomes all difficulties, and want that urges us on in the pressure of things (Virgil)

lacrimus oculos suffusa nitentis: her glittering eyes filled with tears (Virgil)

lacrymæque decoræ, gratior et pulchro veniens in corpore virtus: his tears become him, and even virtue becomes more pleasing when it shows itself in a fairer form (Virgil)

lætus in præsens animus, quod ultra est oderit curare, et amara lento temperet risu. Nihil est ab omni parte beatum: the mind that is cheerfully contented with the present will shrink from caring about anything beyond, and will temper the bitter things of life with an easy smile. There is nothing that is blessed in every respect (Horace)

lætus sum laudari me abs te, pater, a laudato viro: I am pleased it is you, father, a man highly praised, who praises me (Nævius and Cicero, quoting the words of Hector)

lapsus ubi?, quid feci?, aut officii quid omissum est?: where did I err?, what did I accomplish?, or what duty was left undone? (from the *Emblemata* of Alciato)

latius regnes, avidum domando spiritum, quam si Libyam remotis Gadibus jungas, et uterque Pœnus serviat uni: by subduing an avaricious spirit you will rule a wider empire than if you united Libya to the far-off Gades, and the Carthaginian on both shores should be subject to you alone (Horace)

latrantem curatne alta Diana canem?: does the high-stepping Diana care for the dog that bays her?

laudant illa sed ista legunt: they praise those works, but they are not the ones they read (Martial)

laudate Dominum, omnes gentes; laudate eum, omnes populi: praise the Lord, all nations; praise him, all peoples (Psalm 117:1)

laudatus abunde, non fastiditus si tibi, lector, ero: abundantly, reader, shall I be praised if I do not cause you disgust (Ovid)

laudem virtutis necessitati damus: we give to necessity the praise of virtue (Quintilian)

laudibus arguitur vini vinosus: he is convicted of being a wine-bibber by his praise of wine (Horace)

laudo Deum verum, plebem voco, congrego clerum, defunctos ploro, pestem fugo, festa decoro: I praise the true God, I summon the people, I call together the clergy, I bewail the dead, I put to flight plague, I celebrate festivals (inscription on a church bell)

laudo manentem; si celeres quatit pennas, resigno quæ dedit, et mea virtute me involvo probamque pauperiem sine dote quæro: I praise her (Fortune) while she stays with me; if she flaps her swift feathers, I resign all she has given me, and wrap myself up in my own virtue and pay addresses to honest undowered poverty (Horace)

legum ministri magistratus, legum interpretes judices; legum denique idcirco omnes servi sumus, ut liberi esse possimus: the magistrates are the ministers of the laws, the judges their interpreters; we are all, in short, servants of the laws, so that we may be a free people (Cicero)

legum servi sumus ut liberi esse possimus: we are slaves of the law so that we may be able to be free (Cicero)

leniter ex merito quidquid patiare ferendum est, quæ venit indigne pœna dolenda venit: whatever you suffer deservedly should be borne with resignation; the penalty that comes upon us undeservedly comes as a matter for just complaint (Ovid)

lepus tute es; et pulpamentum quæris!: you are a rabbit; yet you seek game! (Livius Andronicus)

lex est ratio summa insita in natura, quæ jubet ea, quæ facienda sunt, prohibetque contraria: law is the highest reason implanted in nature, which commands what ought to be done and forbids what is contrary (Cicero)

libera Fortunæ mors est; capit omnia tellus quæ genuit: death is not subject to Fortune; the earth holds everything that she ever brought forth (Lucan)

libera me ab homine malo, a meipso: deliver me from the evil man, from myself (St. Augustine)

libertas, quæ sera, tamen respexit inertem: liberty, which, though late, regarded me in my helpless state (Virgil)

libertas ultima mundi quo steterit ferienda loco: in the spot where liberty has made her last stand she was fated to be smitten (Lucan, attributed to Julius Cæsar)

licet quot vis vivendo condere sæcla; mors æterna tamen nilo minus illa manebit: you may live to complete as many generations as you will, nevertheless, that everlasting death will still be waiting (Lucretius)

lingua melior, sed frigida bello dextera: excels in speech, but of a right hand slow to war (Virgil)

linguæ centum sunt, oraque centum, ferrea vox: it (rumor) has a hundred tongues, a hundred mouths, a voice of iron (Virgil)

linquenda tellus, et domus, et placens uxor, neque harum, quas colis, arborum, te, præter invisas cupressos, ulla brevem dominum sequetur: your estate, your home, and your pleasing wife must be left, and of these trees that you are rearing, not one shall follow you, their short-lived owner, except the hateful cypresses (the cypress being used to mark graveyards) (Horace)

litoria litoribus contraria, fluctibus undas imprecor, arma armis; pugnent ipsique nepotes!: I pray that shore shall clash with shore, and wave with billow; let them fight themselves and their descendants! (Virgil)

longa est injuria, longæ ambages: the account of this injury is long, and longer for the telling of it (Virgil)

longa mora est, quantum noxæ sit ubique repertum enumerare; minor fuit ipsa infamia vero: it would take long to enumerate how great an amount of crime was everywhere perpetrated; even the report itself came short of the truth (Ovid)

longe mea discrepat istis et vox et ratio: both my language and my sentiments differ widely from theirs (Horace)

longumque illud tempus cum non ero magis me movet quam hoc exiguum, quod mihi tamen longum videtur: that long time to come when I shall not exist has more affect on me than this short present time, which seems endless (Cicero)

luctantem Icariis fluctibus Africum mercator metuens, otium et oppidi laudat rura sui; mox reficit rates quassas, indocilis pauperiem pati: the merchant, dreading the southwest wind wrestling with the Icarian waves, praises retirement and the rural life of his native town; but soon he repairs his shattered boat, incapable of being taught to endure poverty (Horace)

lucus a non lucendo: the grove does not shine (a play on the words *lucus*, grove, and *lucendo*, shine)

ludit in humanis divina potentia rebus, et certam præsens vix habet hora fidem: the powers above seem to play with human affairs, so that we can scarcely be assured of the present hour [which itself is passing] (Ovid)

lupo agnum eripere postulant: they insist on snatching the lamb from the wolf (Plautus)

lupus est homo homini, non homo, quom qualis sit non novit (or simply, **homo homini lupus**)**:** man is a wolf to man, not a man, when he has not yet found out what he is like (Plautus)

lusisti satis, edisti satis, atque bibisti; tempus abire tibi est: you have amused yourself, you have eaten and have drunk enough; it is time for you to depart (Horace)

luxuriant animi rebus plerumque secundis; nec facile est æqua commoda mente pati: the feelings generally run riot in prosperity; and to bear good fortune with evenness of mind is no easy task (Ovid)

M

macies et nova febrium terris incubuit cohors: a wasting disease and an unheard-of battalion of fevers have swooped down on the earth (Horace)

macte nova virtute, puer, sic itur ad astra: persevere in virtue (or valor), my son, thus is the way to the stars (Virgil)

maculæ quas incuria fudit: the blemishes (or errors) that carelessness has produced

magister artis ingeniique largitor venter: the belly is the teacher of arts, and the bestower of genius (i.e., hunger [necessity] is the mother of invention) (Persius)

magna eloquentia, sicut flamma, materia alitur, et motibus excitatur et urendo clarescit: it is the eloquence as of a flame; it requires material to feed it, motion to excite it, and it brightens as it burns (Tacitus)

magna est admiratio copiose sapienterque dicentis: great is our admiration of the orator who speaks with fluency and discretion (Cicero)

magna fuit quondam capitis reverentia cani, inque suo pretio ruga senilis erat: great was the respect formerly paid to the hoary head, and great the honor to the wrinkles of age (Ovid)

magna vis est, magnum nomen, unum et idem sentientis senatus: great is the power, great the authority, of a senate which is unanimous in its opinions (Cicero)

Magne Pater Divum, sævos punire tyrannos, haud alia ratione velis: virtutem videant, intabescantque videndo: Great Father of the Gods, devise for tyrants no punishment but this: let them contemplate virtue and wither in despair at having forsaken it (Persius)

magnificat anima mea Dominum; et exsultavit spiritus meus in Deo salutari meo: my soul magnifies the Lord; and my spirit rejoices in God my savior (the Hymn of the Virgin Mary at the Annunciation, St. Luke 1:46-47)

magno de flumine mallem quam ex hoc fonticulo tantundem sumere: I had rather take my glass of water from a great river like this than from this little fountain (Horace, criticizing those who store large quantities of things and never use them)

magnum hoc ego duco quod placui tibi qui turpi secernis honestum: I account it a great honor that I have pleased a man like you, who knows so well to discriminate between the base and the honorable (Horace)

magnus ab integro sæculorum (or **sæclorum**) **nascitur ordo:** the mighty cycle of the ages begins its turn anew (Virgil)

major privato visus dum privatus fuit, et omnium consensu capax imperii nisi imperasset: he seemed much greater than a private citizen while he was a private citizen, and had he never become emperor everyone would have agreed that he had the capacity to be emperor (Tacitus, said of Emperor Galba)

major rerum mihi nascitur ordo: a greater succession of events presents itself to my muse (Virgil)

major sum quam cui possit Fortuna nocere multaque ut eripiat, multo mihi plura relinquet. Excessere metum mea jam bona: I am above being injured by Fortune; though she snatch away much, more will remain to me. The blessings I now enjoy transcend fear (Ovid)

majore tumultu planguntur nummi quam funera, nemo dolorem fingit in hoc casu. ... Ploratur lacrimis amissa pecunia veris: money is bewailed with a greater tumult than death; no one feigns grief in this case. ... The loss of money is wept over with true tears (Juvenal)

mala mali malo mala contulit omnia mundo; causa mali tanti fœmina sola fuit: man's jaw and an apple brought all evils in the world; and the cause of all this mischief was the woman

mala merx hæc, et callida est: she is a bad bargain and a crafty one (Plautus)

male si mandata loquaris, aut dormitabo aut ridebo: if you deliver badly what is committed to you, I shall either laugh or fall asleep (Horace)

malim indisertam prudentiam, quam stultitiam loquacem: I prefer sense that is faulty in expression to loquacious folly (Cicero)

malo cum Platone errare, quam cum aliis recte sentire: I had rather be wrong with Plato than think right with others (Cicero)

malus est enim custos diuturnitatis metus, contraque benevolentia fidelis vel ad perpetuitatem: fear is a bad custodian of that which is intended to last; whereas mildness and goodwill ensure fidelity forever (Cicero)

manet alta mente repostum, judicium Paridis spretæque injuria formæ: deep-seated in her mind remains the judgment of Paris and the wrong done to her slighted beauty (Virgil, referring to Juno's vengeance)

Mantua me genuit, Calabri rapuere, tenet nunc Parthenope, cecini pascua, rura, duces: Mantua gave me birth, Calabri snatched me away, now Parthenope holds me; I sang of shepherds, pastures, and heroes (Virgil's epitaph)

Mantua, væ!, miseræ nimium vicina Cremonæ: Mantua, alas!, too near the unhappy Cremona (quoted by Jonathan Swift upon seeing a woman accidentally sweep a violin off a table with her dress)

manum non verterim, digitum non porrexerim: I would not turn my hand or stretch out my finger (Cicero)

mare quidem, commune certo est omnibus: the sea surely is common to all (Plautus)

maria montesque polliceri cœpit: he began to promise seas and mountains (Sallust)

marmoreo Licinus tumulo jacet, at Cato parvo, Pompeius nullo. Quis putet esse deos? Saxa premunt Licinum, levat altum Fama Catonem, Pompeium tituli. Credimus esse deos: Licinus lies in a marble tomb, Cato in a humble one, Pompey in none. Who can believe that the gods exist? Heavy lies the stone on Licinus; Fame raises Cato on high; his glories raise Pompey. We believe that the gods do exist

martyres non facit pœna sed causa: not the punishmnent but the cause makes the martyr (St. Augustine)

materiem, qua sis ingeniosus, habes: you have a subject on which to show your ingenuity (i.e., a task upon which to display your talents) (Ovid)

maxima debetur puero reverentia, si quid turpe paras, nec tu pueri contempseris annos: we owe the greatest reverence to a child; if you ever have something base in mind, do not ignore your son's tender years (Juvenal)

me justum esse gratis oportet: it is my duty to show justice without recompense (Seneca)

me miseram, quod amor non est medicabilis herbis!: oh, unhappy me, that there should be no herbs to cure love!

me nemo ministro fur erit: no one shall become a thief with my help (Juvenal)

me non solum piget stultitiæ meæ, sed etiam pudet: I am not only annoyed at my folly, I am ashamed of it

mea mihi conscientia pluris est quam omnium sermo: my own conscience is more to me than what the world says (Cicero)

mea virtute me involvo: I wrap myself in my virtue (Horace)

mecum facile redeo in gratiam: I easily recover my goodwill myself (Phædrus)

medio de fonte leporum, surgit amari aliquid, quod in ipsis floribus angat: from the midst of the very fountain of delight, something bitter arises to vex us even amid the flowers themselves (Lucretius)

mediocribus esse poëtis non di (or **dii**), **non homines, non concessere columnæ:** mediocrity in poets is condemned by gods and men, and booksellers too (Horace)

mel in ore, verba lactis, fel in corde, fraus in factis (also, **mel in ore et verba lactis, sed fel in corde et fraus in factis**): honey in his mouth, words of milk; gall in his heart, deceit in his deeds

melius non tangere, clamo: I cry out, better it is not to touch (Horace)

melius, pejus, prosit, obsit, nil vident nisi quod libuerit: better or worse, for good or for harm, they see nothing but what they please (Terence)

membra reformidant mollem quoque saucia tactum; vanaque sollicitis incutit umbra metum: the wounded limb shrinks from even a gentle touch, and the unsubstantial shadow strikes the timid with alarm (Ovid)

memini etiam quæ nolo, oblivisci non possum quæ volo: I remember what I would not, and I cannot forget what I would (Themistocles, as quoted by Cicero)

men servasse ut essent qui me perderent?: did I save them that they might destroy me? (Pacuvius)

mene salis placidi vultum fluctusque quietos ignorare jubes? Mene huic confidere monstro?: do you desire that I should not distrust the appearance of the placid sea, and of the waves which are now quiet? Do you wish that I should confide in such a monster? (Virgil)

mens immota manet; lachrymæ volvuntur inanes: the mind remains unmoved; tears are shed in vain (Virgil)

mens peccat, non corpus, et unde consilium abfuit culpa abest: it is the mind that sins, not the body, and where there was no intention there is no criminality (Livy)

mensuraque juris vis erat: and might was the measure of right (Lucan)

meo sum pauper in ære: I am poor, but I am not in debt (Horace)

meos tam suspicione quam crimine judico carere oportere: I judge that members of my family should never be suspected of breaking the law (Julius Cæsar)

merses profundo; pulchrior evenit: plunge it into the depths; it comes forth all the fairer (Horace)

meum est propositum in taberna mori, ut sint vina proxima morientis ori. Tunc cantabunt lætius angelorum chori, sit Deus propitius huic potatori: I desire to end my days in a tavern drinking, may my neighbor hold for me the glass when I am sinking; that the chorus of angels may cry, God be merciful to this the one who has been drinking (a 12th-century poem)

meus hic est; hamum vorat: he's mine; he has swallowed my hook (Plautus)

meus mihi, suus cuique (est) carus: mine is dear to me, and dear is his to everyone (Plautus)

migravit ab aure voluptas omnis: all pleasure has fled from the ear (Horace)

mihi forsan, tibi quod negarit, porriget hora: the hour will perhaps extend to me what it has denied to you (Horace)

mihi istic nec seritur nec metitur: there is neither sowing nor reaping in that affair for me (i.e., there is no profit in it for me) (Plautus)

mihi res, non me rebus, subjungere conor: my aim is to subject circumstances to me, not myself to them (Horace)

mihi tarda fluunt ingrataque tempora: for me the time passes away slowly and joyously (Horace)

militat omnis amans et habet sua castra Cupido: every lover is a soldier and has his camp in Cupid (Ovid)

mille hominum species et rerum discolor usus; velle suum cuique est, nec voto vivitur uno: there are a thousand kinds of men, and different hues they give to things; each one follows his own inclination, neither wishing to live the same way (Persius)

millia frumenti tua triverit area centum, non tuus hinc capiet venter plus ac meus: though your threshing-floor should yield a hundred thousand bushels of grain, will your belly therefore hold more than mine? (Horace)

minor in parvis fortuna furit, leviusque ferit leviora Deus: fortune is gentle to the lowly, and God strikes what is weak with less power (Seneca)

minus habeo quam speravi; sed fortasse plus speravi quam debui: I have less than I had hoped for; but maybe I had hoped for more than I ought (Seneca)

mirantur taciti, et dubio pro fulmine pendent: they stand in silent astonishment, and wait for the fall of the yet doubtful thunderbolt (Statius)

miremur te non tua: let me have something to admire in yourself, not in what belongs to you (Juvenal)

mirum videtur quod sit factum jam diu?: does it seem wonderful because it was done long ago? (Livius Andronicus)

miscebis sacra profanis: you will mix sacred things with profane (Horace)

miscuit utile dulci: he mixes what is useful and sweet (Horace)

miser Catulle, desinas ineptire, et quod vides perisse perditum ducas: poor Catullus, drop your silly fancies, and what you see is lost, let it be lost (Catullus)

misericordia Domini inter pontem et fontem: between bridge and stream the Lord's mercy may be found (St. Augustine)

miseris succurrere disco: I am learning to help the distressed (Virgil)

miserum est aliorum incumbere famæ ne collapsa ruant subductis tecta columnis: it is a wretched thing to lean upon the fame of others, lest the roof should fall in ruins when the pillars are withdrawn (Juvenal)

mobilitate viget, viresque acquirit eundo: it grows by moving, and gathers strength as it speeds on (Virgil, said both of rumor and fame)

modeste tamen et circumspecto judicio de tantis viris pronunciandum est, ne, quod plerisque accidit, damnent quæ non intelligunt: we should, however, pronounce our opinions of such men with modesty and circumspect judgment, lest, as is the case with many, we should be found condemning what we do not understand (Quintilian)

modo me Thebis, modo ponit Athenis: he now places me in Thebes, and now at Athens (Horace, said of a playwright able to change scenes without interrupting the continuity of the story)

molle meum levibus cor est violabile telis: my tender heart is vulnerable by his (Cupid's) light arrows (Ovid)

mollissima corda humano generi dare se natura fatetur, quæ lachrymas dedit: hæc nostri pars optima sensus: nature confesses that she gave the most tender hearts to the human race when she gave them tears: this is the best part of our senses (Juvenal)

molliter austerum studio fallente laborem: the interest in the pursuit gently beguiling the severity of the toil (Horace)

momento mare vertitur; eodem die ubi luserunt, navigia sorbentur: in a moment the sea is agitated, and on the same day ships are swallowed up where lately they sported (Seneca)

monstro quod ipse tibi possis dare; semita certe tranquillæ per virtutem patet unica vitæ: I show you what you can do for yourself; the only path to a tranquil life lies through virtue (Juvenal)

monstrum horrendum, informe, ingens, cui lumen ademptum: a monster horrendous, hideous, and vast, deprived of sight (Virgil, of the blinded Cyclops, Polyphemus)

monstrum nulla virtute redemptum a vitiis: a monster whose vices are not redeemed by a single virtue (Juvenal)

moriamur et in media arma ruamus. Una salus victis nullam sperare salutem: let us die even as we rush into the thick of the fight. The only safe course for the defeated is to expect no safety (Virgil)

moribus antiquis res stat Romana virisque: the Roman republic stands by its ancient manners and men (Ennius)

mors hominum felix quæ se nec dulcibus annis inserit et mæstis—sæpe vocata venit: death is kind to men when it comes not during the sweet but during the sad years—then, indeed, it is often prayed for (Boëthius)

mors infanti felix, juvenis acerba, nimis sera est seni: death is favorable for the child, bitter to the youth, too late for the old (Publilius Syrus)

mors terribilis iis, quorum cum vita omnia exstinguuntur, non iis quorum laus emori non potest: death is full of terrors for those to whom loss of life means complete extinction, not for those who leave behind them an undying name (Cicero)

mortalia facta peribunt; nedum sermonum stet honos et gratia vivax: all a mortal's works must perish; how much less shall the power and grace of language long survive! (Horace)

mortalium rerum misera beatitudo: the miserable bliss of all mortal things (Boëthius)

morte carent animæ, semperque priore relicta sede novis domibus vivunt habitantque receptæ: souls are immortal and are admitted, after quitting their first abode, into new homes, and they live and dwell in them forever (Ovid)

movet cornicula risum furtivis nudata coloribus: the crow, stripped of its stolen colors, provokes our ridicule (i.e., there is nothing more amusing than a proud pig stripped of its feathers) (Horace)

mulier cupido quod dicit amanti, in vento et rapida scribere oportet aqua: what a woman says to an ardent lover ought to be written on the winds and in the swiftly flowing water (Catullus)

mulier profecto nata est ex ipsa mora: woman is surely born of tardiness itself (Plautus)

multa dies, variusque labor mutabilis ævi, retulit in melius; multos alterna revisens lusit, et in solido rursus Fortuna locavit: time and the changed labor of ages have restored many things; and Fortune, after many capricious alterations, has placed them upon solid ground (Virgil)

multa fero ut placeam genus irritabile vatum: much I endure to soothe (or appease) the irritable race of poets (Horace)

multa ferunt anni venientes commoda secum; multa recedentes adimunt: the coming years bring with them many advantages; as they recede they take many away (Horace)

multa me docuit usus, magister egregius: necessity, that excellent master, has taught me many things (Pliny the Younger)

multa petentibus desunt multa. Bene est, cui Deus obtulit parca, quod satis est manu: those who long for much are in want of much. Happy is he to whom God has given, with sparing hand, as much as is enough (Horace)

multa quidem scripsi; sed quæ vitiosa putavi, emendaturis ignibus ipse dedi: much have I written; but what I considered faulty I myself committed to the correcting flames (Ovid)

multa renascentur quæ jam cecidere, cadentque quæ nunc sunt in honore vocabula, si volet usus, quem penes arbitrium est, et jus, et norma loquendi: many words now in disuse will revive, and many now in vogue will be forgotten, if usage wills it, in whose hands is the choice and the right to lay down the law of language (Horace)

multa rogant utenda dari; data reddere nolunt: they ask many a sum on loan; but they are loath to repay (Ovid)

multa tulit fecitque puer, sudavit et alsit, ut posset contingere metam: he suffered and did much in youth, he bore heat and cold, in order to reach the goal

multi committunt eadem diverso crimina fato, ille crucem sceleris pretium tulit, hic diadema: many commit the same crimes with a different destiny; one bears a cross as the price of his villainy, another wears a crown (Juvenal)

multi mortales, dediti ventri atque somno, indocti incultique vitam sicuti peregrinantes transiere; quibus profecto contra naturam corpus voluptati, anima oneri: many men have passed through life like travelers in a strange land, without spiritual or moral culture, and given up to the lusts of appetite and indolence, whose bodies, contrary to their nature, were enslaved to indulgence, and their souls a burden (Sallust)

multis ille bonis flebilis occidit nulli flebilior quam tibi (or mihi): he fell lamented by many good men, by none more lamented than by you (or by me) (Horace, said of Quintilian)

multis parasse divitias non finis miseriarum fuit, sed mutatio; non est in rebus vitium sed in animo: the acquisition of riches has been to many, not the end of their miseries, but a change in them; the fault is not in the riches, but in the disposition (Seneca)

multorum te etiam oculi et aures non sentientem, sicuti adhuc fecerunt, speculabuntur atque custodient: without your knowledge, the eyes and ears of many will see and watch you, as they have done already (Cicero)

multos castra juvant, et lituo tubæ permistus sonitus, bellaque matribus detestata: the camp and the clang of the trumpet mingled with the clarion, and wars detested by mothers, have delights for many (Horace)

multos qui conflictari adversis videantur, beatos; ac plerosque, quanquam magnas per opes, miserrimos: si illi gravem fortunam constanter tolerent, hi prospera inconsulte utantur: there are many who appear to encounter adversity who are happy; while there are some in the midst of riches who are miserable; all depends on the fortitude with which the former bear pressure, and on the unadvised manner in which the latter employ their wealth (Tacitus)

mundæque parvo sub lare pauperum cœnæ, sine aulæis et ostro, sollicitam explicuere frontem: a neat, simple meal under the humble roof of the poor, without hangings and purple, has smoothed the wrinkles of an anxious brow (Horace)

munditiæ, et ornatus, et cultus hæc feminarum insignia sunt, his gaudent et gloriantur: neatness, ornament, and dress, are peculiar badges of women; in these they delight and glory (Livy)

munditiis capimur: non sine lege capillis: we are captivated by neatness: let not your hair be out of order (Ovid)

munera accipit frequens, remittit nunquam: he frequently accepts presents, but never gives any in return (Plautus)

munera, crede mihi, capiunt hominesque deosque; placatur donis Jupiter ipse datis: gifts, believe me, captivate both men and gods; Jupiter himself is won over and appeased by gifts (Ovid)

N

nam de mille fabæ modiis dum surripis unum, damnum est, non facinus mihi pacto lenius isto: if from a thousand bushels of beans you steal one, my loss, it is true, is in this case less, but not your villainy (Horace)

nam ego illum periisse duco, cui quidem periit pudor: I regard that man as lost who has lost his sense of shame (Plautus)

nam et majorum instituta tueri sacris cerimoniisque retinendis, sapientis est: for it is the part of a wise man to protect the institutions of his forefathers by retaining the sacred rites and ceremonies

nam neque divitibus contingunt gaudia solis, nec vixit male qui natus moriensque fefellit: joys do not fall to the rich alone, nor has he lived ill of whose birth and death no one took note (Horace)

nam neque quies gentium sine armis, neque arma sine stipendiis, neque stipendia sine tributis haberi queunt: for the quiet of nations cannot be maintained without arms, nor can arms be maintained without pay, nor pay without taxation (Tacitus)

nam pro jucundis aptissima quæque dabunt di (or dii); carior (or charior) est illis homo quam sibi: the gods will give what is most suitable rather than what is most pleasing; man is dearer to them than he is to himself (Juvenal)

namque sub Aurora jam dormitante lucerna somnia quo cerni tempore vera solent: those dreams are true that we have in the morning, as the lamp begins to flicker (Ovid)

namque tu solebas meas esse aliquid putare nugas: for you used to think my trifles were worth something (Catullus)

narratur et prisci Catonis sæpe mero caluisse virtus: it is said that the virtue even of the elder Cato was often warmed by wine (Horace)

natales grate numeras?, ignoscis amicis?, lenior et melior fis accendente senecta?: do you count your birthdays thankfully?, forgive your friends?, grow gentler and better with advancing age? (Horace)

natura beatis omnibus esse dedit, si quis cognoverit uti: nature has granted to all to be happy, if we only knew how to use its benefits (Claudian)

natura dedit usuram vitæ tanquam pecuniæ nulla præstitua die: nature has lent us life at interest, like money, and has fixed no day for its payment (Cicero)

natura ipsa valere, et mentis viribus excitari, et quasi quodam divino spiritu afflari: to be strong by nature, to be urged on by the powers of the mind, and to be inspired, as it were, by a divine spirit (Cicero; said of genius)

Natura, quam te colimus inviti quoque!: O Nature, how we bow to you even against our will! (Seneca)

naturæ debitum reddiderunt: they paid the debt of nature (i.e., death) (Cornelius Nepos)

natus sum, esuriebam, quærebam; nunc repletus requiesco: I was born, I felt hungry, and sought for food; now that I am satiated, I lay me down to rest

ne Æsopum quidem trivit: neither has he come across Aesop (i.e., as a student, he knows nothing)

ne pereant lege mane rosas: cito virgo senescit: pick roses in the morning, lest they wither: a maiden soon grows old (Florus)

ne pueros coram populo Medea trucidet: you will not let Medea slay her sons before the people (Horace)

ne quid falsi dicere audeat, ne quid veri non audeat: let him not dare to say anything that is false, nor let him dare say what is not true (Cicero)

ne te longis ambagibus ultra quam satis est morer: not to detain you by long digressions more than enough (i.e., to make a long story short) (Horace)

nec audiendi qui solent dicere, vox populi, vox Dei, quum tumultuositas vulgi semper insaniæ proxima sit: and those people should not be listened to who keep saying, the voice of the people is the voice of God, since the riotousness of the crowd is very close to madness (Alcuin, in a letter to Charlemagne)

nec historia debet egredi veritatem, et honeste factis veritas sufficit: history should not overstep the limits of truth, and indeed, in recording noble deeds, the truth is sufficient (Pliny the Younger)

nec me pudet, ut istos, fateri nescire quod nesciam: I am not ashamed, as some are, to confess my ignorance of that which I do not know (Cicero)

nec meus audet rem tentare pudor, quam vires ferre recusent: my modesty does not permit me to attempt a thing which my powers are not equal to accomplish (Virgil)

nec mihi mors gravis est posituro morte dolores: death is not grievous to me, for by death shall I lay aside my pains (Ovid)

nec minor est virtus, quam quærere, parta tueri: casus inest illic; hic erit artis opus: it is no less merit to keep what you have got than to gain it: in the one there is chance; the other will be a work of art (Ovid)

nec, quæ præteriit, iterum revocabitur unda; nec, quæ præteriit, hora redire potest: neither can the wave which has passed by be again recalled, nor can the hour which has passed ever return (Ovid)

nec quies gentium sine armis, nec arma sine stipendiis, nec stipendia sine tributis haberi queunt: neither can the quiet of nations be maintained without arms, nor can arms be maintained without pay, nor pay without taxation (after Tacitus)

nec satis est pulchra esse poëmata; dulcia sunto: it is not enough that poetry should be so polished as to satisfy the judgment; it should appeal to our feelings and imagination (Horace)

nec sit terris ultima Thule: nor shall Thule be the extremity of the world (Seneca)

nec tamen est quisquam, sacros qui lædat amantes: no one would hurt a lover, for lovers are sacred (Propertius)

nec tibi quid liceat, sed quid fecisse decebit occurrat; mentemque domet respectus honesti: do not consider what you may do, but what it will become you to have done; and let the sense of honor subdue your mind (Claudian)

nec Veneris pharetris macer est, aut lampade fervet: inde faces ardent, veniunt a dote sagittæ: he is not made lean by Venus's quiver, nor does he burn with her torch; it is from this that his fires are fed, from her dowry the arrows come (Juvenal)

nec verbum verbo curabis reddere fidus interpres: as a true translator you will take care not to render (or translate) word for word (Horace)

nec vero me fugit, quam sit acerbum, parentum scelera filiorum pœnis lui: it does not escape me that it is a cruel thing for the children to suffer for their parents' misdeeds (Cicero)

nec vidisse semel satis est, juvat usque morari, et conferre gradum, et veniendi discere causas: nor is it enough to have once seen him; they are delighted to linger near him, and to keep step with him, and to learn the reason for his coming (Virgil)

negatas artifex sequi voces: he attempts to express himself in a language that nature has denied him (Persius)

negotium populo Romano melius quam otium committi: the Roman people understand work better than leisure (Appius Claudius)

nemini credo, qui large blandus est dives pauperi: I trust no rich man who is officiously kind to a poor man (Plautus)

nemo malus felix, minime corruptor: no evil person is happy, least of all a corrupter of morals (Juvenal)

nemo mathematicus genium indemnatus habebit: no mathematician will be held a genius until he is condemned (Juvenal)

nemo parum diu vixit, qui virtutis perfectæ perfecto functus est munere: no one has lived too short a life who has discharged the perfect work of perfect virtue (Cicero)

nemo potest personam diu ferre fictam: no one can play a feigned part for long (Seneca)

nemo quam bene vivat, sed quamdiu, curat: quum omnibus possit contingere ut bene vivat, ut diu nulli: no one cares how well they live, but only how long; it is within the reach of every one to live well, it is within no one's power to live long (Seneca)

nemo tam divos habuit faventes, crastinum ut possit sibi polliceri: nobody has ever found the gods so much his friends that he can promise himself another day (Seneca)

nequaquam nobis divinitus esse creatam naturam mundi, quanta stat prædita culpa: the nature of the universe has by no means been made through divine power, seeing how great are the faults that mar it (Lucretius)

nequaquam satis in re una consumere curam: it is by no means enough to spend all our care on a single object (Horace)

neque extra necessitates belli præcipuum odium gero: I bear no particular hatred beyond the necessity of war

neque (enim) quies gentium sine armis, neque arma sine stipendiis, neque stipendia sine tributis haberi queunt: the quiet of nations cannot be maintained without arms, nor can arms be maintained without pay, nor pay without taxation (Tacitus)

neque salsum neque suave esse potest quicquam, ubi amor non admiscetur: not a thing can be either salt or sweet without a dash of love (Plautus)

neque semper arcum tendit Apollo: nor does Apollo always keep his bow drawn (Horace)

nequeo monstrare, et sentio tantum: what I can experience but cannot express (Juvenal)

nequiquam, quoniam medio de fonte leporum surgit amari aliquid quod in ipsis floribus angat: all is vanity, since from the very fountain of enchantment rises a drop of bitterness to bring torment among all the flowers (Lucretius)

nescio qua natale solum dulcedine captos (or **cunctos**) **ducit, et immemores non sinit esse sui:** our native land charms us with inexpressible sweetness and never allows us to forget that we belong to it (Ovid)

nescio qua præter solitum dulcedine læti: elated beyond the usual by some unaccountable delight (Virgil)

nescio quid majus nascitur Iliade: something greater than the Iliad now springs to life (Propertius)

nescire autem quid ante quam natus sis acciderit, id est semper esse puerum. Quid enim est ætas hominis, nisi (ea) memoria rerum veterum cum superiorum ætate contexitur?: not to know what occurred before you were born is to remain always a child. For what is the worth of human life, unless it is woven into the life of our ancestors by the records of history? (Cicero)

nihil agit qui diffidentem verbis solatur suis; is est amicus qui in re dubia re juvat, ubi re est opus: he does nothing who seeks to console a desponding person with words; a friend is one who aids with deeds at a critical time where deeds are called for (Plautus)

nihil cupientium nudus castra peto: naked I repair to the camp of those who desire nothing (Horace)

nihil enim legit, quod non excerperet. Dicere etiam solebat, nullum esse librum tam malum, ut non aliqua parte prodesset: he reads no book from which he did not make extracts. He also used to say, no book was so bad but good of some kind might be got out of it (Pliny the Elder)

nihil est aptius ad delectationem lectoris, quam temporum varietates, fortunæque vicissitudines: nothing contributes more to the delight of a reader than the changes of times and the vicissitudes of fortune (Cicero)

nihil est (autem) tam volucre quam maledictum, nihil facilius emittitur, nihil citius excipitur, nihil latius dissipatur: nothing is so swift as calumny, nothing more easily uttered, nothing more readily received, nothing more widely disseminated (Cicero)

nihil est incertius vulgo, nihil obscurius voluntate hominum, nihil fallacius ratione tota comitiorum: nothing is more uncertain than the masses, nothing more obscure than human will, nothing more deceptive than the whole electoral process (Cicero)

nihil est quod credere de se non possit, quum laudatur dis æqua potestas: there is nothing of which it (power) cannot believe itself capable, when it is praised as equal to that of the gods (Juvenal)

nihil infelicius eo, cui nihil unquam evenit adversi, non licuit enim illi se experiri: there is no one more unfortunate than the man who has never been unfortunate, for it has never been in his power to try himself (Seneca)

nihil peccat nisi quod nihil peccat: his only sin is that he does not sin (Pliny the Younger)

nihil scriptum miraculi causa: nothing is written here to excite wonder (i.e., for effect) (Tacitus)

nihil tam absurdum, quod non dictum sit ab aliquo philosophorum: there is nothing so absurd that has not at sometime been said by some philosopher (after Cicero)

nihil turpius est quam gravis ætate senex, qui nullum aliud habet argumentum, quo se probet diu vixisse, præter ætatem: there is nothing more disgraceful than an old man who has no other proof to offer, of his having lived long in the world, than his age (Seneca)

nil actum credens, dum quid superesset agendum: he believed nothing done so long as anything remained to be done (Lucan, said of Julius Cæsar)

nil actum reputans, si quid superesset agendum: thinking that nothing was done, if anything remained to be done (Lucan)

nil admirari prope est res una, Numici, solaque, quæ possit facere et servare beatum: to marvel at nothing, Numicius, is almost the one and only thing that can make and keep men happy (Horace)

nil æquale homini fuit illi: there was no consistency in that man (Horace)

nil conscire sibi, nulla pallescere culpa: to be conscious of no guilt, and to turn pale at no charge (Horace)

nil (or nihil) cupientium nudus castra peto: naked myself, I make for the camp of those who desire nothing (Horace)

nil desperandum Teucro duce et auspice Teucro: there is no ground for despair while Teucer is leader and Teucer is under his auspices (Horace)

nil dictu fœdum visuque hæc limina tangat, intra quæ puer est: let nothing filthy, either heard by the ear or seen by the eye, enter this threshold, within which there is a child (Juvenal)

nil ego contulerim jucundo sanus amico: as long as I have my senses, there is nothing I would prefer to an agreeable friend (Horace)

nil erit ulterius quod nostris moribus addat posteritas; eadem cupient facientque minores; omne in præcipiti vitium stetit: there will be nothing left for posterity to add to our manners; our descendants will wish for and do the same things as we do; every vice has reached its culminating point (Juvenal)

nil fuit unquam sic impar sibi: never before was there such an inconsistent person (Horace)

nil fuit unquam tam dispar sibi: nothing was ever so unlike itself (Horace)

nil igitur fieri de nilo posse fatendum'st: therefore we must conclude that nothing comes from nothing (Lucretius)

nil igitur mors est ad nos neque pertinet hilum, quandoquidem natura animi mortalis habetur: death therefore is nothing to us nor does it concern us a bit, seeing that the nature of the spirit we possess is something mortal (Lucretius)

nil intra est oleam, nil extra est in nuce duri: [if this be not true, then] there is no pit in the olive, nor has the nut any shell (Horace)

nil me officit unquam, ditior hic, aut est quia doctior; est locus uni cuique suus: it never in the least annoys me that another is richer or more learned than I; everyone has his own place assigned to him (Horace)

nil mihi rescribas, tu tamen ipse veni!: write nothing back to me, and you yourself come! (Ovid)

nil obstet tibi, dum ne sit te ditior alter: nothing stops you, so long as there is not another wealthier than yourself (Horace)

nil oriturum alias, nil ortum tale fatentes: confessing that none like you had arisen before, or will likely arise in the future (Horace, said of Cæsar Augustus)

nil rectum nisi quod placuit sibi ducunt: they deem nothing right except what seems good to themselves (Horace)

nil sine te mei prosunt honores: the honors I obtain are nothing without you (Horace, to the Muse)

nil sole et sale utilius: nothing so useful as the sun and salt

nil temere uxori de servis crede querenti; sæpe etenim mulier quem conjux diligit, odit: do not rashly believe a wife who complains of servants; for often the wife hates those whom the husband prefers (Dionysius Cato)

nimia illæc licentia profecto evadet in aliquod magnum malum: this excessive license will most certainly eventuate in some great evil (Terence)

nimia subtilitas in jure reprobatur, et talis certitudo certitudinem confundit: too much subtlety in law is condemned, and so much certainty confounds certainty

nimirum insanus paucis videatur, eo quod maxima pars hominum morbo jactatur eodem: he appears insane to only a few, because the majority is infected with the same disease (Horace)

nimius in veritate, et similitudinis quam pulchritudinis amantior: too meticulous as regards truth, and with a greater liking for exactness than beauty (Quintilian)

nisi Dominus ædificaverit domum, in vanum laboraverunt qui ædificant eam. Nisi Dominus custodierit civitatem, frustra vigilat qui custodit eam: Unless the Lord builds the house, its builders have labored in vain. Unless the Lord guards the city, those who guard need not be vigilant (Psalm 126:1)

nitor in adversum, nec me, qui cætera vincit impetus, et rapido contrarius evehor orbi: I struggle against an opposing current; the torrent that sweeps away others does not overpower me, and I make headway against the on-rushing stream (Ovid)

nobis non licet esse tam disertis, qui Musas colimus severiores: we who cultivate the Muses of a graver spirit cannot indulge ourselves in such license (Martial)

noctemque diemque fatigat: he wears out both night and day at his work (Virgil)

nocturna versate manu, versate diurna: let these be your studies by night and by day

nolo barbam vellere mortuo leoni: I do not wish to pluck the beard of a dead lion (Martial)

non adeo cecidi, quamvis abjectus, ut infra te quoque sim; inferius quo nihil esse potest: though cast off, I have not fallen so low as to be beneath you; than which nothing can be lower (Ovid)

non agitur de vectigalibus, non de sociorum injuriis; libertas et anima nostra in dubio est: it is not a question of our revenues, nor of the wrongs of our allies; our liberty and very lives are in peril (Sallust)

non alias cælo ceciderunt plura sereno: never till then so many thunderbolts from cloudless skies (i.e., a bolt from the blue) (Virgil)

non amo nimium diligentes: I do not like those who are too diligent (Scipio Africanus)

non amo te, Sabidi, nec possum dicere quare; hoc tantum possum dicere, non amo te: I do not love you, Sabidius, nor can I say why; this only can I say, I do not love you (Martial)

non ampliter sed munditer convivium; plus salis quam sumptus: the entertainment was more neat than ample; there was more of relish than of meat (Cornelius Nepos)

non Angli, sed angeli: not Angles, but angels (Pope Gregory the Great, upon seeing English youths for sale in the Roman slave market)

non bene junctarum discordia semina rerum: the discordant seeds of things ill joined (Ovid)

non canimus surdis, respondent omnia silvæ: I sing not to deaf ears, for all the forest gives an answer (Virgil)

non convivere, nec videre saltem, non audire licet; nec urbe tota quisquam est tam prope, tam proculque nobis: I may not live with him, nor even see him or hear him; in all the city there is no one so near me and so far away (Martial)

non deerat voluntas, sed facultas: not the will, but the ability, was wanting

non eadem est ætas, non mens: my age is no longer the same, nor my inclination (Horace)

non eadem ratio est, sentire et demere morbos; sensus inest cunctis; tollitur arte malum: to be aware of disease and to remove it is not the same thing: the sense of it exists in all; by skill alone is disease removed (Ovid)

non ebur neque aureum mea renidet in domo lacunar: in my dwelling no ivory gleams, nor paneled roof covered with gold (Horace)

non ego avarum cum te veto fieri, vappam jubeo ac nebulonem: when I say, be not a miser, I do not bid you to become a worthless prodigal (Horace)

non ego illam mihi dotem esse puto, quæ dos dicitur, sed pudicitiam, et pudorem, et sedatam cupidinem: in my opinion, a woman's true dowry is not that which is called a dowry, but virtue, modesty, and restrained desires (Plautus)

non ego mordaci distrinxi carmine quenquam; nec meus ullius crimina versus habet: I have not attacked anyone with biting satire, nor does my poetry contain a charge against anyone (Ovid)

non ego mordaci distrinxi carmine quenquam; … nulla venenato litera mista joco est: I have not attacked anyone with biting satire; … nor does any venomous jest lurk concealed in what I have written (Ovid, an alternate version)

non ego omnino lucrum omne esse utile homini existimo: I do not at all consider that every kind of gain is useful to a man (Plautus)

non ego paucis, offendar maculis, quas aut incuria fudit, aut humana parum cavit natura: I shall not be offended with a few faults, ones that arise either from inadvertence or from the frailty of our nature (Horace)

non ego ventosæ venor suffragia plebis: I do not hunt after the votes of the fickle multitude (Horace)

non enim gazæ neque consularis summovet lictor miseros tumultus mentis et curas laqueata circum tecta volantes: for neither regal treasure, nor the consul's lictor, nor the cares that hover about fretted ceilings, can remove the unhappy tumults of the mind (Horace)

non equidem invideo, miror magis: in truth I feel no envy, I am greatly surprised (Virgil)

non equidem studeo, bullatis ut mihi nugis pagina turgescat, dare pondus idonea fumo: I do not study to swell my page with pompous trifles, suited only to give weight to smoke (Persius)

non esse consuetudinem populi Romani, ullam accipere ab hoste armato conditionem: it is not the custom of the Roman people to accept terms from an armed enemy (Julius Cæsar)

non esse cupidum pecunia est; non esse emacem vectigal est; contentum vero suis rebus esse, maximæ sunt, certissimæque divitiae: not to be avaricious is money; not to be extravagant is a revenue; to be truly content with our own is the greatest and most certain wealth of all (Cicero)

non est ad astra mollis e terris via: there is no easy way from the earth to the stars (Seneca and Cicero)

non est, crede mihi, sapientis dicere "vivam"; sera nimis vita est crastina; vive hodie: believe me, the wise do not say "I shall live"; life tomorrow will be too late; live today (Martial)

non est de pastu omnium quæstio, sed de lana: it is not a question of feeding the sheep, but of wool (i.e., of fleecing them) (attributed to Pius II)

non est de sacco tanta farina tuo: all this flour is not from your sack (said of a plagiarist)

non est nostri ingenii: it is not within my range of ability (Cicero)

non est paupertas, Nestor, habere nihil: it is not poverty, Nestor, to have nothing (Martial)

non fumum ex fulgore, sed ex fumo dare lucem: not to bring smoke from light, but from smoke to bring light (said of an accomplished novelist) (Horace)

non hoc ista sibi tempus spectacula poscit: the present moment is not one to indulge in spectacles of this kind (Virgil)

non hominis culpa, sed ista loci: it is not the fault of the man, but of the place (Ovid)

non id videndum, conjugum ut bonis bona, at ut ingenium congruat et mores moribus; probitas, pudorque virgini dos optima est: in marriage the relative proportion of property is not so much to be considered, as the union of mind, and the identity of manner and disposition; chastity and modesty form the best portion that a virgin can bring to her husband (Terence)

non ignara mali, miseris succerrere disco: no stranger myself to misfortune, I am learning to aid those in misery (Virgil)

non illa colo calathisve Minervæ femineas assueta manus: her feminine hands were not trained to the basket (or distaff) of Minerva (Virgil)

non ille pro charis amicis, aut patria timidus perire: he dares for his country or his friends to die (Horace)

non ingenerantur hominibus mores tam a stirpe generis ac seminis quam ex iis rebus, quæ ab ipsa natura nobis ad vitæ consuetudinem suppeditantur, quibus alimar et vivimus: our character is not so much the product of race and heredity as of those circumstances by which nature forms our habits, by which we are nourished and live (Cicero)

non magni pendis, quia contigit: you do not value it highly, because it came by luck (Horace)

non me pudet fateri nescire quod nesciam: I am not ashamed to confess myself ignorant of what I do not know (Cicero)

non mihi si linguæ centum sint oraque centum, ferrea vox, omnes scelerum comprendere formas omnia pœnarum percurrere nomina possim: not if I had a hundred tongues, a hundred mouths, and a voice of iron, could I repeat all the types of wickedness, and run over all the names of penal woes (Virgil)

non modo proditori, sed ne perfugæ quidem locus in meis castris cuiquam fuit: not only no traitor, but no deserter, has found a place in my camp (Cicero)

non nobis, Domine, non nobis; sed nomini tuo da gloriam: not to us, Lord, not to us; but to your Name give glory (Psalm 113:9)

non nostrum (inter vos) tantas componere lites: it is not for us to settle such disputes (among you) (Virgil)

non numero hæc judicantur sed pondere: these things are not to be judged by their number, but by their weight (Cicero)

non nunc agitur de vectigalibus, non de sociorum injuriis; libertas et anima nostra in dubio est: the question is not now respecting our revenues, or injuries to our allies; our liberties and lives are all at stake (Cicero)

non omnis moriar; multaque pars mei vitabit libitinam: not all of me shall die; and a great part of me will escape the grave (Horace)

non opus est magnis placido lectore poëtis; quamlibet invitum difficilemque tenent: great poets have no need of an indulgent reader; they hold captive everyone however unwilling and hard to please he may be (Ovid)

non placet quem scurræ laudant, manipulares mussitant: I do not like the man whom the gentry praise, but of whom the people of his own class say nothing (Plautus)

non possidentem multa vocaveris recte beatum. Rectius occupat nomen beati, qui deorum muneribus sapienter uti, duramque callet pauperiem pati, pejusque leto flagitium timet: you would not justly call him blessed who has many possessions; more justly does he claim the name blessed who knows how to use wisely the gifts of the gods and to bear the hardships of poverty, and who fears disgrace worse than death (Horace)

non possum ferre, Quirites, Græcam urbem: I cannot, Romans, endure a Greek city (Juvenal)

non pronuba Juno, non Hymenæus adest, non illi Gratia lecto; Eumenides stravere torum: no Juno guardian of the marriages rites, no Hymenæus, no one of the Graces, stood by that nuptial couch (Ovid)

non qui soletur, non qui labentia tarde tempora narrando fallat, amicus adest: there is no friend near to console me, none to beguile the weary hours with his talk (Ovid)

non quisquam fruitur veris odoribus, Hybleos latebris nec spoliat favos, si frontem caveat, si timeat rubos: ornat spina rosas, mella tegunt apes: he will never obtain the flowery sweets of spring, nor the honeyed treasures of Mount Hyblo, who cannot face the difficulties that surround them: the rose is guarded by thorns, and honey is protected by bees

non satis est pulchra esse poëmata; dulcia sunto, et quocumque volent animum auditoris agunto: it is not enough that poems be beautiful; they must also be affecting, and move at will the hearer's soul (Horace)

non tali auxilio, nec defensoribus istis tempus eget: the times require other aid and other defenders than those you bring (Virgil)

non tam commutandarum, quam evertendarum rerum cupidi: desiring not so much to change things as to overturn them (Cicero)

non tam portas intrare patentes, quam fregisse juvat: nec tam patiente colono arva premi, quam si ferro populetur et igni. Concessa pudet ira via: the conqueror is not so much pleased by entering into open gates as by forcing his way: he desires not the fields to be cultivated by the patient husbandman, he would have them depopulated by fire and sword. It would be his shame to go by a way already granted to his passage (Lucan)

non tamen adeo virtutum sterile seculum, ut non et bona exempla prodiderit: yet the age was not so utterly destitute of virtues but that it produced some good examples (Tacitus)

non tu corpus eras sine pectore. Di tibi formam, di tibi divitias dederant, artemque fruendi: you were at no time ever a body without a soul. The gods have given you beauty, the gods have given you wealth, and the skill to enjoy it (Horace, to Tibullus)

non usitata, nec tenui ferar penna: I will be borne on no common, no feeble, wing (Horace)

non ut diu vivamus curandum est, sed ut satis: our care should not be so much to live long, but to have lived enough (Seneca)

nondum amabam, et amare amabam. ... quærebam quid amarem, amans amare: not yet I loved, yet I loved to love. ... I sought what I might love, in love with loving (St. Augustine)

nonumque prematur in annum, membranis intus positis: delere licebit quod non edideris; nescit vox missa reverti: let it be kept until the ninth year, the manuscript put away at home; you may destroy whatever you have not published; once let out, what you have said cannot be called back (Horace)

noris quam elegans formarum spectator siem: you will see how nice a judge of beauty I am (Terence)

nos fragili vastum ligno sulcavimus æquor: we have plowed the vast ocean in a fragile boat (Ovid)

nos hæc novimus esse nihil: we know that these things are nothing (i.e., mere trifles) (Martial)

nos patriæ fines et dulcia linquimus arva: we leave the confines of our native country and our delightful plains (Virgil)

nos te, nos facimus, Fortuna, deam: it is we, O Fortune, we who make you a goddess (Juvenal)

noscenda est mensura sui spectandaque rebus in summis minimisque: a man should know his own measure, and have regard to it in the smallest matters as well as the greatest (Juvenal)

nosque ubi primus equis Oriens adflavit anhelis illic sera rubens accendit lumina Vesper: and when the Rising Sun has first breathed on us with its panting horses, over there the red Evening Star is lighting his late lamps (Virgil)

nostra sine auxilio fugiunt bona. Carpite florem: our advantages fly away without aid. Pluck the flower (Ovid)

notandi sunt tibi mores: the manners of men are to be carefully observed (Horace)

novem Iovis concordes filiæ sorores: you nine daughters of Jupiter, sisters of one heart (Nævius)

novi ego hoc sæculum, moribus quibus siet: I know this age, what its character is (Plautus)

novi ingenium mulierum, nolunt ubi velis, ubi nolis cupiunt ultro: I know the nature of women; when you will they won't, when you won't they long for it (Terence)

novum et ad hunc diem non auditum: new and unheard of till this day (Cicero)

nox atra cava circumvolat: black night envelopes them with its hollow shade (Virgil)

nudo detrahere vestimenta me jubes: you order me to strip the clothes from a naked man (Plautus)

nulli negabimus, nulli differemus justitiam: we shall not negate, nor delay, the justice that is due (from the Magna Carta)

nulli vendemus, nulli negabimus aut differemus, rectum aut justitiam: to no one will we sell, nor deny, nor delay, right or justice (from the Magna Carta)

nullius addictus jurare in verba magistri, quo me cunque rapit tempestas, deferor hospes: bound to swear by the opinions of no master, I present myself a guest wherever the storm drives me (Horace)

nullum ab labore me reclinat otium: no period of rest releases me from labor (Horace)

nullum numen habes, si sit prudentia; nos te nos facimus, Fortuna, deam cœloque locamus: you have no divine power where there is prudence; it is we, O Fortune, we who make you a goddess and place you in heaven (Juvenal)

nullus difficilis cupienti labor: no labor is difficult if you wish to do it (St. Jerome)

num barbarorum Romulus rex fuit?: Romulus was not a king of barbarians, was he? (Cicero)

num flatus telluris honor?: surely honor is not simply a blast [of air] from the earth?

numerisque fertur lege solutis: he is borne along in numbers free from law (Horace)

numerus certus pro incerto ponitur: a certain number is put for an uncertain number (i.e., without trying to be exact)

numquam se minus otiosum esse quam cum otiosus, nec minus solum quam cum solus esset: never less idle than when wholly idle, nor less alone than when wholly alone (Cicero)

numquam sis ex toto otiosus, sed aut legens, aut scribens, aut orans, aut meditans, aut aliquid utilitatis pro communi laborans: never to be completely idle, but either reading, or writing, or praying, or meditating, or working at something useful for all in common (Thomas à Kempis)

nunc animis opus, Ænea, nunc pectore firmo: now, Aeneas, you have need of courage, now a resolute heart (Virgil)

Nunc Dimittis servum tuum, Domine, secundum verbum tuum in pace: now let your servant depart in peace, Lord, according to your word (St. Luke 2:29)

nunc est bibendum, nunc pede libero pulsanda tellus: now for drinking, now for dancing to a lively beat (Horace)

nunc omnis ager, nunc omnis parturit arbor; nunc frondent sylvæ, nunc formosissimus annus: now every field is green, and every tree in bloom; the woods are in full leaf, and the year is in its highest beauty (Virgil)

nunc patimur longæ pacis mala; sævior armis luxuria incubuit, victumque ulciscitur orbem: now we suffer the evils of a long peace; luxury more cruel than war broods over us and avenges a conquered world (Juvenal)

nunc positis novus exuviis nitidusque juventa: now, all new, his slough cast off, and shining in youth (Virgil)

nunc scio quid sit amor: now I know too well what love is (Virgil)

nunquam se plus agere, quam nihil quum ageret; nunquam minus solum esse, quam quum solus esset: he said he never had more to do than when he had nothing to do, and never was less alone than when alone (Cicero, quoting Scipio Africanus)

nunquam sero te venisse putabo, si salvus veneris: I shall never think that you are late arriving, provided you arrive safely (Cicero)

nunquam sunt grati qui nocuere sales: never agreeable are those witty remarks that are meant to injure

nutritur vento, vento restinguitur igni: lenis alit flammas, grandior aura necat: fire is fed by the wind and extinguished by the wind: a gentle breeze feeds it, too strong a blast puts it out (Ovid)

O

O cæca nocentum consilia! O semper timidum scelus!: O the blind counsels of the guilty! O how ever cowardly the wicked! (Statius)

O cives, cives, quærenda pecunia primum est; virtus post nummos: O citizens, citizens, you must first seek for wealth, for virtue after money (Horace)

O Corydon, Corydon, secretum divitis ullum esse putas? Servi ut taceant, jumenta loquentur, et canis, et postes, et marmora: O Corydon, Corydon, do you think anything a rich man does can be kept secret? Even if his servants say nothing, his beasts of burden, and dogs, and door posts, and marble slabs will speak (Juvenal)

O curas hominum! O quantum est in rebus inane!: O human cares! O how much emptiness is in their affairs! (Persius and Lucilius)

O curvæ in terris animæ et cœlestium inanes!: O you souls bent down to earth and void of everything heavenly! (Persius)

O di, reddite mi hoc pro pietate mea: O gods, grant me this in return for my piety (Catullus)

O diem lætum, notandumque mihi candidissimo calculo: O happy day, and one to be marked for me with the whitest of chalk (Pliny the Younger)

O faciles dare summa deos, eademque tueri difficiles: O, how easily the gods give high circumstances, and how reluctant they are to ensure them when given (Lucan)

O fallacem hominum spem: O, how deceitful is the hope of men (Cicero)

O fama ingens, ingentior armis!: O great in fame, greater still in deeds!

O formose puer, nimium ne crede colori: O handsome child, trust not too much in your youthful color (Virgil)

O Fortuna, velut luna, statu variabilis, semper crescis aut decrescis: O Fortune, like the moon, you are changeable, ever waxing and waning (from the *Carmina Burana*)

O fortunatam natam me consule Romam!: O fortunate Rome, born when I was consul! (Cicero)

O fortunate adolescens, qui tuæ virtutis Homerum præconem inveneris: O happy youth, to have Homer as the publisher of your valor (Alexander the Great, at the tomb of Achilles)

O fortunatos nimium, sua si bona norint, agricolas!; quibus ipsa, procul discordibus armis, fundit humo facilem victum justissima tellus: O, how happy are the tillers of the ground, if only they knew their blessings!; for whom, far from the clash of arms, the most just earth pours forth from its soil an easy sustenance (Virgil)

O homines ad servitutem paratos!: O men, how you prepare yourselves for slavery! (Tacitus)

O imitatores, servum pecus!: O imitators, you servile herd! (i.e., you miserable apes!) (Horace)

O laborum dulce lenimen: O sweet solace of labors (Horace, in reference to Apollo's lyre)

O lente, lente, currite moctis equi: O slowly, slowly, run ye horses of the night (Ovid)

O magna vis veritatis, quæ ... facile se per se ipsa defendit: O mighty force of truth, that by itself so easily defends itself (Cicero)

O major tandem, parcas, insane, minori: O you, who are a greater madman, spare me, I pray, who am not so far gone (Horace)

O matre pulchra filia pulchrior: O what a beautiful mother, and a still more beautiful daughter (Horace)

O Meliboee, deus nobis hæc otia fecit: O Meliboee, it is a god who has made this leisurely life for us (Virgil)

O mihi præteritos referat si Iuppiter annos: O, if only Jupiter would restore to me those bygone years (Virgil)

O miseras hominum mentes! O pectora cæca!: O, how wretched are the minds of men! O, how blind their hearts! (Lucretius)

O miseri quorum gaudia crimen habent!: O you wretched, whose joys are tainted with guilt! (Pseudo-Gallus)

O morte ipsa mortis tempus indignius!: O, more cruel than death itself was the moment of death! (Pliny the Younger)

O munera nondum intellecta deum: O that the gifts of the gods should not yet be understood (Lucan)

O nimium nimiumque oblite tuorum: O too, too forgetful of your kin (Ovid)

O passi graviora, dabit deus his quoque finem: O you who have suffered greater misfortunes than these, God will grant an end to them as well (Virgil)

O præclarum custodem ovium lupum!: O what an excellent protector of sheep, the wolf! (Cicero)

O qualis facies et quali digna tabella!: O what a face and what a picture it would have been a subject for! (Juvenal)

O quam cito transit gloria mundi!: O how quickly the world's glory passes away! (Thomas à Kempis)

O quam contempta res est homo, nisi supra humana surrexerit!: O what a contemptible thing is man, unless he rises above human concerns! (or, the human condition) (Seneca)

O quanta qualia sunt illa Sabbata, quæ semper celebrat superna curia: O what their joy and their glory must be, those endless Sabbaths the blessed ones see (Peter Abelard)

O quanta species cerebrum non habet!: O that such beauty should be devoid of brains! (Phædrus)

O quantum caliginis mentibus nostris objicit magna felicitas!: O how our minds are darkened by excess of happiness! (Seneca)

O quantum in rebus inane!: O what a void there is in things! (Persius)

O rus quando te aspiciam?, quandoque licebit nunc veterum libris, nunc somno et inertibus horis ducere sollicitæ jucunda oblivia vitæ?: O country, when will I see you?, and when will I be permitted to quaff a sweet oblivion of anxious life, now from the books of the ancients, now from sleep and idle hours? (Horace)

O sæclum insapiens et infacetum!: O this crude and ignorant age! (Catullus)

O Salutaris Hostia: O saving Victim (first words of the hymn used at the beginning of the Benediction of the Blessed Sacrament)

O si tacuisses, philosophus mansisses: O if you had only remained silent, you would have remained a philosopher (Boëthius)

O terque quaterque beati!: O thrice, four times happy they! (Virgil)

O Tite tute Tati tibi tanta tyranne tulisti!: O Titus Tatius, you tyrant, so much you have brought upon yourself! (Ennius)

O ubi campi!: O where are those fields!; O for life in the country! (Virgil)

O vita!, misero longa felici brevis: O life!, long to the wretched, short to the happy (Publilius Syrus)

O vitæ philosophia dux!: O philosophy, life's guide! (Cicero)

obruat illud male partum, male retentum, male gestum imperium: let that power fall that has been wrongfully acquired, wrongfully retained, and wrongfully administered (Cicero)

obsecro, tuum est?; vetus credideram: pray, is it yours?; I thought it something old

observantior æqui fit populus, nec ferre negat, cum viderit ipsum auctorem parere sibi: the people become more observant of justice, and do not refuse to submit to the laws when they see them obeyed by their enactor (Claudian)

obstupui, steteruntque comæ, et vox faucibus hæsit: I was astounded, my hair stood on end, and my voice stuck fast in my throat (Virgil)

obtrectatio ac livor pronis auribus accipiuntur; quippe adulationi fædum crimen servitutis, malignitati falsa species libertatis inest: disparagement and calumny are devoured with a greedy ear; flattery wears the badge of servitude, whilst malignity speaks the tone of independence, and is therefore well received (Tacitus)

occasiones namque hominem fragilem non faciunt, sed qualis sit ostendunt: circumstances do not make a man weak, but they show what manner of man he is (Thomas à Kempis)

occidit miseros crambe repetita magistros: cabbage repeated is the death of the wretched masters (Juvenal)

odero si potero. Si non, invitus amabo: I will hate [you] if I can. If not, then unwillingly will I love [you] (Ovid)

oderunt hilarem tristes, tristemque jocosi, sedatum celeres, agilem gnavumque remissi: the sad detest the cheerful, and the cheerful the sad; the swift dislike the sedate, and the careless dislike the busy and industrious (Horace)

odi et amo: quare id faciam, fortasse requiris. Nescio, sed fieri sentio et excrucior: I hate and I love: why I do so you may well inquire. I do not know, but I feel it happen and am in agony (Catullus)

odi profanum vulgus et arceo. Favete linguis: I hate the profane masses and keep them at a distance. Favor by your tongues (i.e., keep silent) (Horace)

odi puerulos præcoci ingenio: I hate boys of precocious talent (Cicero)

odi summussos; proinde aperte dice quid sit quod times: I hate the whisperers; say out loud what it is you fear (Nævius)

odia in longum jaciens, quæ reconderet, auctaque promeret: he lays his resentment aside, but stores it up to bring it forward with greater bitterness (Tacitus)

odimus accipitrem quia semper vivit in armis: we hate the hawk because it always lives in arms (Ovid)

odit populus Romanus privatam luxuriam, publicam magnificentiam diligit: the Romans hate private luxury, but they love public magnificence (Cicero)

ohe!, jam satis est!: hey!, that's enough already! (Horace)

omne capax movet urna nomen: in the spacious urn of death is shaken every name (Horace)

omne corpus mutabile est; ita efficitur ut omne corpus mortale sit: everybody is subject to change; hence it comes to pass that everybody is subject to death (Cicero)

omne epigramma sit instar apis, aculeus illi, sint sua mella, sit et corporis exigui: every epigram should be like a bee: have a sting like it, honey, and a small body (Martial)

omne tulit punctum qui miscuit utile dulci, lectorem delectando pariterque monendo: he gains universal applause who mingles the useful with the agreeable, at once delighting and instructing the reader (Horace)

omnes amicos habere operosum est; satis est inimicos non habere: it is an arduous task to make all men your friends; it is enough to have no enemies (Seneca)

omnes autem et habentur et dicuntur tyranni, qui potestate sunt perpetua, in ea civitate quæ libertate usa est: all men are considered as tyrants who possess themselves of perpetual power in a state that once enjoyed the blessings of liberty (Cornelius Nepos)

omnes eodem cogimur; omnium versatur urna serius, ocius, sors exitura, et nos in æternum exsilium impositura cymbæ: we are all driven to the same ferry; the lot of each is shaken in the urn, destined sooner or later to come forth, and place us in Charon's boat for the exile (Horace)

omnes homines, qui de rebus dubiis consultant, ab odio, amicitia, ira, atque misericordia vacuos esse decet: all men who consult on doubtful matters should be void of hatred, friendship, anger, and pity (Sallust)

omnes omnium caritates patria una complectitur: our country alone embraces all our affections for all (Cicero)

omnes, quibus res sunt minus secundæ, magis sunt, nescio quomodo suspiciosi: ad contumeliam omnia accipiunt magis; propter suam impotentiam se credunt negligi: all those whose affairs are not prosperous are, somehow or other, extremely suspicious: they take every hint as an affront, and think the neglect with which they are treated is due to their humble position (Terence)

omni autem in re consensio omnium gentium lex naturæ putanda est: but in every matter the consensus among all nations is to be regarded as the law of nature (Cicero)

omnia fanda nefanda, malo permista furore, justificam nobis mentem avertere deorum: the confusion of the right and wrong, in this accursed war, has deprived us of the protecting care of the gods (Catullus)

omnia Græce!, cum sit turpe magis nostris nescire Latine: all things must be in Greek!, when it is more shameful for our Romans to be ignorant of Latin (Juvenal)

omnia jam fient, fieri quæ posse negabam; et nihil est de quo non sit habenda fides: all things will now come to pass that I used to think impossible; and there is nothing that we may not hope to see take place (Ovid)

omnia mea mecum porto (or, **omnia mea porto mecum**): all that is mine I carry with me (Bias, one of the Seven Greek Sages, and Cicero)

omnia mea mecum sunt: all I have (my worldly goods) I carry with me (Seneca)

omnia mutari, et nil vere interire, ac summam materiæ prorsus eandem manere, satis constat: that all things are changed, and that nothing really perishes, and that the sum of matter remains exactly the same, is sufficiently certain (Francis Bacon)

omnia perdidimus, tantummodo vita relicta est: we have lost everything, only life is left (Ovid)

omnia profecto, cum se a cœlestibus rebus referet ad humanas, excelsius magnificentiusque et dicet et sentiet: when a man descends from heavenly things to human, he will certainly both speak and feel more loftily and nobly on every theme (Cicero)

omnia quæ nunc vetustissima creduntur, nova fuere; ... et quod hodie exemplis tuemur, inter exempla erit: everything that is now regarded as very ancient was once new; ... and what we are defending today by precedent, will sometime later be a precedent itself (Tacitus)

omnia scelera etiam, ante effectum operis, quantum culpæ satis est, perfecta sunt: all crimes are committed, so far as the blame attaching to them is concerned, before they are actually carried into effect (Seneca)

omnia serviliter pro dominatione: servile in all his actions for the sake of power (Tacitus, of Emperor Otho)

omnibus a suprema die eadem, quæ ante primum; nec magis a morte sensus ullus aut corpori aut animæ quam ante natalem: his last day places man in the same state as he was before he was born; not after death has the body or soul any more feeling than they had before birth (Pliny the Elder)

omnibus hoc vitium est cantoribus, inter amicos ut nunquam inducant animum cantare rogati, injussi nunquam desistant: this is a general fault of all singers, that among their friends they never make up their minds to sing, however, pressed; but when no one asks them, they will never stop (Horace)

omnibus hostes reddite nos populis, civile avertite bellum: commit us to hostility with every other nation, but avert from us civil war (Lucan)

omnibus in terris, quæ sunt a Gadibus usque Auroram et Gangem, pauci dignoscere possunt vera bona, atque illis multum diversa, remota erroris nebula: in all the lands which stretch from Gades even to the region of the Dawn and the Ganges, there are few who are able, by removing the mist of error, to distinguish between what is really good and what is widely diverse (Juvenal)

omnibus invideas, Zoile; nemo tibi: you may envy all men, Zoilus; but no man envies you (Martial)

omnibus modis, qui pauperes sunt homines miseri vivunt; præsertim quibus nec quæstus est, nec didicere artem ullam: the poor live wretchedly in every way; especially those who have no means of livelihood and have learned no craft (Plautus)

omnis dolor aut est vehemens, aut levis; si levis, facile fertur, si vehemens, certe brevis futurus est: all pain is either severe or slight; if slight, it is easily borne; if severe, it will no doubt be brief (Cicero)

omnis enim res virtus, fama, decus, divina humanaque pulchris divitiis parent; quas qui construxerit, ille clarus erit, fortis, justus: all things divine and human, as virtue, fame, and honor, defer to fair wealth; and the one who has amassed it will be illustrious, brave, and just (Horace)

omnium artium domina eloquentia: eloquence, the mistress of all the arts (after Tacitus)

omnium rerum, ex quibus aliquid acquiritur, nihil est agricultura melius, nihil uberius, nihil dulcius, nihil homine libero dignius: of all pursuits from which profit accrues, nothing is superior to agriculture, nothing more productive, nothing more enjoyable, nothing more worthy of a free man (Cicero)

operosa parvus carmina fingo: I, a little one, compose laborious songs (Horace)

optima quæque dies miseris mortalibus ævi prima fugit: subeunt morbi tristisque senectus, et labor; et duræ rapit inclementia mortis: all the best days of life slip away from us poor mortals first: diseases soon come, and sad old age, and decay; and the cruelty of unmerciful death snatches us away (Virgil)

orator est vir bonus dicendi peritus: an orator is a good man skilled in speaking (Cato the Elder)

os homini sublime dedit cœlumque tueri jussit; et erectos ad sidera tollere vultus: to man, the gods gave an upright countenance to survey the heavens, and to look upward to the stars (Ovid)

os, orare, vale, communio, mensa negatur: speech, prayer, greeting, association, and food are forbidden (i.e., the sentence of excommunication)

osculo Filium hominis tradis?: you betray the Son of Humanity with a kiss? (St. Luke 22:48)

P

pallida mors æquo pulsat pede pauperum tabernas, regumque turres: pale death approaches with equal step, and kicks its way equally into the tents of the poor and the turrets of kings (Horace)

pange, lingua, gloriosi prœlium certaminis: sing, my tongue, of the battle in the glorious struggle (St. Venantius Fortunatus)

parce, puer, stimulis et fortius utere loris: boy, spare the whip and grasp the reins more firmly (Ovid)

parcus deorum cultor, et infrequens, insanientis dum sapientiæ consultus erro; nunc retrorsum vela dare, atque iterare cursus cogor relictos: a sparing and infrequent worshipper of the gods, as long as I strayed from the way by senseless philosophy; I am now forced to turn my sail back and retrace the course I had deserted (Horace)

pars hominum vitiis gaudet constanter, et urget propositum; pars multa natat, modo recta capessens, interdum pravis obnoxia: a part of humanity rejoices consistently in its vices and pursues its purpose; many more waver between doing what is right and complying with what is wrong (Horace)

parta meæ Veneri sunt munera; namque notavi ipse locum aëriæ quo congessere palumbes: I have found out a gift for my fair Venus; I have found where the wood-pigeons breed (Virgil)

pars magna bonitatis est velle fieri bonum: a great step toward goodness is the desire to be good (Seneca)

parturiunt montes, nascetur ridiculus mus: the mountains are in labor, a ridiculous mouse will be born (Horace, said of works that promise much at the outset but yield little in the end)

parva sunt hæc; sed parva ista non contemnendo majores nostri maximam hanc rem fecerunt: these are small things; but it was by not despising these small things that our forefathers made the republic so great (Livy)

parvula (nam exemplo est) magni formica laboris ore trahit quodcunque potest atque addit acervo, quem struit, haud ignara ac non incauta futuri: the ant (for example) is a creature of great industry, drags with its mouth all it can, and adds to the heap it piles up, not ignorant or improvident of the future (Horace)

pascitur in vivis livor, post fata quiescit; tunc suus, ex merito, quemque tuetur honos: envy feeds upon the living, after death it rests; then the honor a man deserves protects him (Ovid)

Pater, in manus tuas commendo spiritum meum: Father, into Your hands I commend my spirit (St. Luke 23:46; one of the Seven Last Words of Christ)

pater ipse colendi haud facilem esse viam voluit, primusque per artem movit agros, curis acuens mortalia corda: the father of tillage himself, did not wish the way to be easy; he was the first to raise the soil by art, inciting the human heart by anxiety (Virgil)

pauca Catonis verba, sed a pleno venientia pectore veri: the words of Cato were few, but they came from a heart full of truth (Lucan)

paulo hoc melius quam mediocre, hoc minus malum quam ut pessumum: it is a little better than mediocre, a little less bad than worst (Lucilius)

pauper enim non est cui rerum suppetit usus. Si ventri bene, si lateri pedibusque tuis, nil divitiæ poterunt regales addere majus: that man is not poor who has a sufficiency for all his wants. If it is well with your stomach, your lungs, and your feet, the wealth of kings cannot add more (Horace)

pauper sum, fateor, patior; quod di dant fero: I am poor, I admit; I put up with it; what the gods give I bear with (Plautus)

pax Cererem nutrit, pacis alumna Ceres: peace is the nurse of Ceres; Ceres is the nursling of peace (Ovid)

peccare docentes fallax historias movet: he falsely relates stories that are merely lessons in vice (Horace)

peccavi nimis cogitatione, verbo, et opere, mea culpa, mea culpa, mea maxima culpa: I have sinned greatly in thought, word, and deed, through my fault, through my fault, through my most grievous fault (from the Catholic Mass)

pecunia non olet; atqui e lotio est: money has no smell; yet that is money made from urine (Vespasian's answer to Titus's objection to levying a tax on public latrines; and Titus's reply to Vespasian)

Pelion imposuisse Olympo: I have piled Pelion on Olympus (i.e., I have scaled heaven) (Horace)

pelle moras; brevis est magni fortuna favoris: away with delay; brief is the time of fortune's great favor (Silius Italicus)

penitus toto divisos orbe Britannos: the Britons, completely separated from all the world (Virgil)

per varios casus, per tot discrimina rerum: through various misfortunes, and so many perils (i.e., after such a strange variety of adventures) (Virgil)

peragit tranquilla potestas quod violenta nequit; mandataque fortius urget imperiosa quies: power can accomplish more by calmness than by violence, and calmness best enforces the imperial mandate (Claudian)

peras imposuit Jupiter nobis duas; propriis repletam vitiis post tergum dedit. Alienis ante pectus suspendit gravem: Jupiter has laid two knapsacks on us; he has placed one behind our backs filled with our own faults, and he has hung another before us, heavy with the faults of other people (Phædrus)

percunctatorem fugito, nam garrulus idem est; nec retinent patulæ commissa fideliter aures: avoid an inquisitive person, for he is sure to be a talker; ears always open to hear will not keep faithfully what is entrusted to them (Horace)

perdis, et in damno gratia nulla tuo: you lose, and for your loss you get no thanks (Ovid)

perfida, sed quamvis perfida, cara tamen: faithless, but, though faithless, still dear (Tibullus)

perge; decet, forsan miseros meliora sequentur: persevere; it is fitting, for a better fate awaits the afflicted (Virgil)

pergis pugnantia secum frontibus adversis componere: you are attempting to reconcile things that are opposite in their natures (Horace)

periculosæ plenum opus aleæ tractas, et incedis per ignes suppositos cineri doloso: the work you are treating is one full of dangerous hazard, and you are treading over fires lurking beneath treacherous ashes (Horace)

periculosum est credere et non credere; ergo exploranda est veritas, multum prius quam stulta prave judicet sententia: it is equally dangerous to believe and to disbelieve; therefore search diligently into the truth rather than form foolish ideas that would pervert your judgment (Phædrus)

perierat totus orbis, nisi iram finiret misericordia: the whole world would perish if pity did not put an end to anger (Seneca the Elder)

periere mores, jus, decus, pietas, fides, et qui redire nescit cum perit, pudor: we have lost all morals, justice, honor, piety, and faith, and with them that sense of shame which, once lost, can never be restored (Seneca)

perierunt tempora longi servitii: my long period of service has led to no advancement (Juvenal)

perpetuus nulli datur usus, et hæres hæredem alterius, velut unda supervenit undam: perpetual possession is allowed to none, and one heir succeeds another as wave follows wave (Horace)

personam tragicam forte vulpes viderat. O quanta species, inquit, cerebrum non habet!: a fox happened to see a tragic actor's mask. How beautiful, he said, but it has no brains! (Phædrus)

pharmaca das ægroto, aurum tibi porrigit æger, tu morbum curas illius, ille tuum: you give medicine to a sick man, he hands you gold; you cure his sickness and he cures yours

philosophia stemma non inspicit. Platonem non accepit nobilem philosophia, sed fecit: philosophy does not look into pedigrees. It did not receive Plato as noble, but it made him such (Seneca)

Phœnices primi, famæ si creditur, ausi mansuram rudibus vocem signare figuris: the Phœnicians, if rumor may be trusted, were the first who dared to write down the fleeting word in rude letters (Lucan)

pictoribus atque poëtis quidlibet audendi semper fuit æqua potestas: the power of daring anything their fancy suggests has always been conceded to the painter and the poet (Horace)

piger scribendi ferre laborem; scribendi recte; nam, ut multum, nil moro: too indolent to bear the toil of writing, I mean of writing well; for I say nothing about the quantity of his composition (Horace, said of someone who is a prolific writer, but not a prolific rewriter)

Pindarum quisquis studet æmulari, ceratis, ope Dædalea, nititur pennis, vitreo daturus nomina ponto: the one who imitates the poet Pindar relies on wings affixed with wax, as by the art of Dædalus, and is sure to give his name to a glassy sea (Horace)

placato possum non miser esse Deo: if God be appeased, I cannot be wretched (Ovid)

plausibus ex ipsis populi, lætoque furore, ingenium quodvis incaluisse potest: at the applause of the public, and at its transports of joy, every genius may grow warm (Ovid)

plausus tunc arte carebat: in those days applause was unaffected (Ovid)

plenus annis abiit, plenus honoribus: he is gone from us, full of years and full of honors (Pliny the Younger)

plerique enim lacrimas fundunt ut ostendant; et toties siccos oculos habent, quoties spectator definit: many shed tears merely for show; and have their eyes quite dry whenever there is no one to observe them (Seneca)

ploravere suis non respondere favorem speratum meritis: they lamented that their merits did not meet with the gratitude for which they hoped (Horace)

plura sunt quæ nos terrent, quam quæ premunt; et sæpius opinione quam re laboramus: there are more things to alarm us than to harm us; and we suffer much more often in apprehension than in reality (Seneca)

plures efficimus quoties metimur a vobis, semen est sanguis Christianorum: as often as we are mown down by you, the more we grow in numbers; the blood of Christians is seed (Tertullian)

plurimum facere, et minimum ipse de se loqui: to do the most and say the least of himself as possible (Sallust)

pluris est oculatus testis unus quam auriti decem. Qui audiunt, audita dicunt; qui vident, plane sciunt: one eyewitness is better than ten who have heard. Hearers can only tell what they have heard; those who see, know what they have seen (Plautus)

plus ægri ex abitu viri, quam ex adventu voluptatis cepi: I have felt more displeasure at his going than pleasure at his coming (Plautus)

plus est quam vita salusque, quod perit; in totum mundi prosternimur ævum: more than life and safety is lost in the present conflict; we are laid prostrate even to the last generation of the world (Lucan)

plus etenim fati valet hora benigni quam si nos Veneris commendet epistola Marti: a moment of smiling fortune is of more avail [to a soldier] than if he were recommended to Mars by a letter from Venus (Juvenal)

pœna potest demi, culpa perennis erit: the punishment can be remitted; the crime is everlasting (Ovid)

poëtica surgit tempestas: a storm is gathering in the poetic world (Juvenal)

pol!, me occidistis, amici: by heaven!, my friends, you have destroyed me (i.e., with friends like you, who needs enemies) (Horace)

ponamus nimios gemitus; flagrantior æquo non debet dolor esse viri, nec vulnere major: let us dismiss excessive laments; a man's grief should not be immoderate, nor greater than the wound received (Juvenal)

pone seram, cohibe; sed quis custodiet ipsos custodes? Cauta est, et ab illis incipit uxor: apply locks and restraint; but who shall guard your own guards? Your wife is cunning, and will begin by seducing them (Juvenal)

ponto nox incubat atra, intonuere poli et crebris micat ignibus æther: black night sits brooding on the deep; the heavens thunder and the ether gleams with incessant flashes (Virgil)

populumque falsis dedocet uti vocibus: he instructs the people to forget false rumors and false impressions (Horace)

populus me sibilat; at mihi plaudo ipse domi, simul ac nummos contemplor in arca: the people boo me; but at home I applaud myself when I contemplate the money in my chest (Horace, said of the miser)

poscentes vario multum diversa palato: requiring, with various taste, things widely different from each other (Horace)

possunt quia posse videntur: they can because they think they can (or, appear as though they were able) (Virgil)

post mediam noctem visus quum somnia vera: he appeared to me in a vision after midnight, when dreams are true (Horace)

præbet mihi littera linguam; et, si non liceat scribere, mutus ero: this letter gives me a tongue; and were I not allowed to write, I should be dumb (Ovid)

præcipuum munus annalium reor, ne virtutes sileantur, utque pravis dictis factisque ex posteritate et infamia metus sit: the principal office of history I take to be this, to prevent virtuous actions from being passed over in silence, and that evil words and deeds should fear an infamous reputation with posterity (Tacitus)

præsertim ut nunc sunt mores, adeo res redit, si quisquis reddit, magna habenda est gratia: in the present state of manners, the matter is brought to this point, that, if any man pays a debt, the creditor must accept it as a favor (Terence)

pravo vivere naso, spectandum nigris oculis, nigroque capillo: with an ugly nose, to be remarkable for fine black eyes and hair (i.e., the beauty of one thing is overlooked by a noticeable flaw elsewhere) (Horace)

prima urbes inter, divum domus, aurea Roma: first among cities, home of the gods, is golden Rome (Ausonius)

primo avulso non deficit alter aureus: the first being wrenched away, another of gold succeeds (Virgil)

primus vere rosam atque autumno carpere poma: to pick the first rose of spring and the first apples of autumn (Virgil)

principibus placuisse viris non ultima laus est. Non cuivis homini contingit adire Corinthum: it is not the least praise to have pleased leading men. Not everyone is lucky enough to go to Corinth (Horace)

principiis obsta; sero medicina paratur, cum mala per longas convaluere moras: stop it at the beginning; a cure is attempted too late when, through long delay, the illness has gained strength (Ovid)

privatus illis census erat brevis, commune magnum: their private fortunes were small, the wealth of the public was great (Horace)

pro patria, pro liberis, pro aris atque focis suis certare: to fight for our country, for our children, for our altars, and for our hearths (Sallust)

pro superi!, quantum mortalia pectora cæcæ noctis habent!: heavens!, how dark the night that shrouds the hearts of men! (Ovid)

pro virtute felix temeritas: instead of valor, successful rashness (Seneca, said of Alexander the Great)

probam pauperiem sine dote quæro: I court virtuous poverty without a dowry (Horace)

procul hinc, procul este, severæ!: away from here, keep far away, cruel women! (Ovid)

procul hinc, procul esto profani!; conclamat vates, totoque absistite luco: away from here, be far away, you profane ones!; and quit entirely the sacred grove (Virgil)

procul, O procul este, profani!: keep away, oh keep far away, you profane ones! (Virgil)

prodigus et stultus donat quæ spernit et odit. Hæc seges ingratos tulit, et feret omnibus annis: the spendthrift and fool gives away what he despises and hates. This seed has ever borne, and will bear, an ungrateful brood (Horace)

proditionem amo, sed proditorem non laudo: I love the treason but I do not praise the traitor (Plutarch)

projicit ampullas et sesquipedalia verba: he throws away his inkwell and his foot-and-a-half-long words (Horace)

propemodum sæculi res in unum illum diem fortuna cumulavit: it may almost be said that into that day fate crowded the events of a century (Curtius, of the Battle of Arbela)

propriæ telluris herum natura, neque illum, nec me, nec quemquam statuit. Nos expulit ille; illum aut nequities, aut vafri inscitia juris, postremo expellet certe vivacior hæres: nature has appointed neither him nor me, nor anyone, lord of this land in perpetuity. That one has ejected us; either some villainy or quirk at law, at any rate, an heir surviving him, will at last eject him (Horace)

proque sua causa quisque disertus erat: everyone was eloquent in his own cause (Ovid)

protectio trahit subjectionem, et subjectio protectionem: protection involves allegiance, and allegiance protection

provocarem ad Philippum, inquit, sed sobrium: I would appeal to Philip, she said, but to Philip sober (Valerius Maximus)

proximus ardet Ucalegon: the house of your neighbor, Ucalegon, is on fire (i.e., beware that it might spread to your own) (Virgil)

prudens futuri temporis exitum caliginosa nocte premit Deus; ridetque, si mortalis ultra fas trepidat: God in his wisdom veils in the darkness of night the events of the future; and smiles if a mortal is unduly solicitous about what he is not permitted to know (Horace)

pudet hæc opprobria nobis et dici potuisse, et non potuisse refelli: it is shameful that such reproaches should be cast upon us and that we are unable to meet them with a refutation (Horace)

pudore et liberalitate liberos retinere, satius esse credo, quam metu: it is better to keep children to their duty by a sense of honor, and by kindness, than by the fear of punishment (Terence)

pugna magna victi sumus: in a great battle we were defeated (Livy)

pulchrum est benefacere reipublicæ: etiam bene dicere haud absurdum est: it is commendable to act well for the republic: even to speak well should not be without its praise (Sallust)

Q

quadrupedante putrem sonitu quatit ungula campum: hooves, with their four-footed galloping sound, are shaking the powdery plain (Virgil)

quæ caret ora cruore nostro?: what coast is without our blood? (Horace)

quæ culpare soles, ea tu ne feceris ipse; turpe est doctoris cum culpa redarguit ipsum: do not do yourself what you generally blame in others; it is improper for a doctor to indulge in what he forbids others (Cato)

quæ lædunt oculum festinas demere; si quid est animum, differs curandi tempus in annum: if anything affects your eye, you hasten to have it removed; but if anything affects your mind, you postpone the term of cure for a year (Horace)

quæ lucis miseris tam dira cupido?: how is it that the wretched have such an infatuated longing for light? (i.e., for life) (Virgil)

quæ potest esse vitæ jucunditas sublatis amicitiis?: what sweetness is left in life if you take away friendship? (Cicero)

quæ regio in terris nostri non plena laboris?: what region of the earth is not full of the story of our calamities? (Virgil)

quæ sint, quæ fuerint, quæ mox ventura trahantur: what is, what has been, and what shall in time be (Virgil)

quæ supra nos nihil ad nos: the things that are above us are nothing to us

quæ te dementia cepit?: what madness has seized you? (Virgil)

quælibet concessio fortissime contra donatorem interpretanda est: every man's grant shall be taken most strongly against himself (i.e., the author of the document shall suffer the loss)

quæque ipse miserrima vidi et quorum pars magna fui: and the most miserable things that I myself saw and of which I was a major part (Virgil)

quærenda pecunia primum, virtus post nummos: money must be sought for in the first instance, virtue after riches (Horace)

qualis sit animus, ipse animus nescit: what the soul is, the soul itself knows not (Cicero)

quam inique comparatum est, hi qui minus habent ut semper aliquid addant divitioribus!: how unjust is the fate that ordains that those who have less should be always adding to the store of the more wealthy! (Terence)

quam seipsum amans sine rivale: how much in love with himself, and that without a rival (i.e., loved by self, hated by all) (Cicero)

quamdiu se bene gesserit: so long as he conducts himself well

quamquam longissimus, dies cito conditur (or simply, **longissimus dies cito conditur**): and yet, the longest day soon comes to an end (Pliny the Younger)

quamvis digressu veteris confusus amici laudo tamen: though distressed at the departure of my old friend, yet I commend him for going (Juvenal)

quando ullum invenient parem?: when shall they find (or look upon) his like again? (Horace)

quandoque bonus dormitat Homerus: sometimes even the good Homer gets sleepy (Horace)

quanta est gula, quæ sibi totos ponit apros, animal propter conviva natum: how great a glutton is the one who has whole boars served up for him, an animal created only for banquets (Juvenal)

quanto plura recentium seu veterum revolvo, tanto ludibria rerum mortalium cunctis in negotiis observantur: the more I go over in my mind the transactions of the ancients, the more frivolity and absurdity I observe in human affairs (Tacitus)

quanto quisque sibe plura negaverit, a diis plura feret. Nil cupientium nudus castra peto; multa petentibus desunt multa: the more a man denies himself, the more will he receive from the gods. Naked, I seek the camp of those who desire nothing; those who require much are ever more in want (Horace)

quantum mutatus ab illo Hectore qui redit exuvias indutus Achilli!: how greatly changed from that Hector who comes home wearing the armor stripped from Achilles! (Virgil)

quantum nobis notrisque hace fabula de Christo profuerit notum est: everyone knows what a godsend this story about Christ has been to us and to our order (attributed to Pope Leo X)

quare facit opium dormire? Quia in eo est virtus dormitiva: why does opium induce sleep? Because it has in it a sleeping quality (attributed to Molière, in mockery of circular argumentation)

quare, si fieri potest, et verba omnia et vox hujus alumnum urbis oleant; ut oratio Romana plane rideatur, non civitate donata: wherefore, if it can be done, all your words and your voice will give the fragrance of a student of this city, that your speech may appear to be truly that of Rome, and not that of a foreigner on whom it has bestowed its freedom (Quintilian)

quare videmus araneam aut muscam aut formicam, in electro, monumento plus quam regio, sepultas, æternizari: whence we see spiders, flies, or ants entombed in amber, a more than royal tomb (Francis Bacon)

quare vitia sua nemo confitetur? Quia etiam nunc in illis est. Somnum narrare vigilantis est: why does no one confess his vices? It is because he is yet in them. It is for a waking man to tell his dreams (Seneca)

quas aut incuria fudit, aut humana parum cavit natura: faults originating from carelessness, or of which human nature was not sufficiently aware (Horace)

quatuor sunt genera Idolorum quæ mentes humanas obsident. Iis (docendi gratia) nomina imposuimus; ut primum genus, Idola Tribus; secundum, Idola Specus; tertium, Idola Fori; quartum, Idola Theatri vocentur: there are four classes of Idols that beset human minds. To these (for the sake of distinction), I have assigned names; the first class, Idols of the Tribe; the second, Idols of the Cave; the third, Idols of the Marketplace; the fourth, Idols of the Theater (Francis Bacon)

quem semper acerbum, semper honoratum—sic dii voluistis—habebo: that day that I will always recall with grief, but—as the gods have willed it—with reverence (Virgil)

quem Venus arbitrum dicet bibendi?: who will Venus seat as judge of drinking? (Horace)

qui amans egens ingressus est princeps in amoris vias, superavit ærumnis suis ærumnas Herculi: the lover who first set out on the highway of love with an empty purse went in for labors harder than the labors of Hercules (Plautus)

qui amicus est amat; qui amat non utique semper amicus est. Itaque amicitia semper prodest; amor etiam aliquando nocet: he who is a friend must love; but he who loves is not always a friend. Thus friendship is always advantageous, while love is sometimes injurious (Seneca)

qui Bavium non odit, amet tua carmina, Mævi: the one who does not despise Bavius, may love your songs, O Mævius (reputedly two of the worst poets of antiquity) (Virgil)

qui blandiendo dulce nutrivit malum, sero recusat ferre, quod subiit, jugum: the one who has fostered the sweet poison of love by fondling it, finds it too late to refuse the yoke that he has of his own accord assumed (Seneca)

qui cupit optatam cursu contingere metam, multa tulit fecitque puer, sudavit et alsit: the one who desires to reach with speed the desired goal must in his youth have suffered and labored much through the extremes of heat and cold (Horace)

qui Curios simulant et Bacchanalia vivunt: those who pretend to be Curii and live like Bacchanals (i.e., who feign prudence but live profligate lives) (Juvenal)

qui fingit sacros auro vel marmore vultus, non facit ille deos: qui rogat, ille facit: the one who fashions sacred things of gold or marble is not the one who makes them gods: he makes them such who prays to them (Martial)

qui fit, Mæcenas, ut nemo, quam sibi sortem seu ratio dederit, seu fors objecerit, illa contentus vivat; laudet diversa sequentes?: how does it happen, Mæcenas, that no one lives content with the lot that either reason has chosen for him or chance has thrown in his way; but that he praises the fortune of those who follow other pursuits? (Horace)

qui legitis flores et humi nascentia fragra, frigidus, O pueri fugite hinc, latet anguis in herba: you children who pluck flowers and strawberries on the ground, run away, a snake lurks in the grass (Virgil)

qui mores hominum multorum vidit et urbes: he who saw the manners of many men and cities (Horace, said of Ulysses)

qui mori didicit, servire dedidicit. Supra omnem potentiam est, certe extra omnem: the one who has learned to die has learned how to avoid being a slave. Such a person is most certainly beyond the reach of all human power (Seneca)

qui nil molitur inepte: one who works at nothing ineptly (i.e., whose efforts are always successful) (Horace)

qui non vult fieri desidiosus, amet: let the one who does not wish to be idle fall in love (after Ovid)

qui nunc it per iter tenebricosum illuc unde negant redire quemquam: now he goes along the darksome way from whence they say no one returns (Catullus)

qui recte vivendi prorogat horam rusticus expectat dum defluat amnis, at ille labitur et labetur in omne volubilis ævum: the one who postpones the hour for living aright is like the yokel who waits till the river flows by; but it glides and will glide on to all eternity (Horace)

qui se ultro morti offerant, facilius reperiuntur, quam qui dolorem patienter ferant: it is easier to find men who will volunteer to die than men who will endure pain with patience (Julius Cæsar)

qui semel a veritate deflexit, hic non majore religione ad perjurium quam ad mendacium perduci consuevit: he who has once deviated from the truth usually commits perjury with as little scruple as he would tell a lie (Cicero)

qui semel aspexit quantum dimissa petitis præstant, mature redeat, repetatque relicta: let him who has once perceived how much what he has given up is better than what he has chosen, immediately return and resume what he has relinquished (Horace)

qui semel est læsus fallaci piscis ab hamo, omnibus unca cibis æra subesse putat: the fish, once wounded by the treacherous hook, thinks the barb concealed in every food (Ovid)

qui simulat verbis, nec corde est fidus amicus, tu quoque fac simile; et sic ars deluditur arte: if anyone feigns with you in speaking and is not a sincere friend, do the same with him, and thus let art be foiled by art (Dionysius Cato)

qui statuit aliquid, parte inaudita altera, æquum licet statuerit, haud æquus est: the one who decides in any case, without hearing the other side of the question, though he might determine justly, is not therefore just (Seneca)

qui studet optatam cursu contingere metam multa tulit fecitque puer, sudavit et alsit: he who would reach the desired goal must, while a boy, suffer and labor much and bear both heat and cold (Horace)

qui utuntur vino vetere sapientis puto et qui libenter veteres spectant fabulas: I regard those men as wise who take old wine and love to see old plays (Plautus)

quia me vestigia terrent, omnia te adversum spectantia, nulla retrorsum: [said the fox to the sick lion] those footprints frighten me, because all are going toward you but none are coming back (Horace)

quia te non capio, tu capies me: because I do not grasp you, you will grasp me (i.e., to be captivated by a complex subject) (attributed to Aristotle)

quicquid agunt homines, votum, timor, ira, voluptas, gaudia, discursus, nostri est farrago libelli: everything humanity does, its wishes, fear, anger, pleasures, joys, runnings to and fro, form the medley of my book (Juvenal)

quicquid Amor jussit non est contemnere tutum. Regnat, et in dominos jus habet ille deos: it is not safe to despise what Love commands. Love reigns supreme, and rules the mighty gods (Ovid)

quicquid servatur, cupimus magis: ipsaque furem cura vocat. Pauci, quod sinit alter, amant: we covet what is guarded; the very care invokes the thief. Few love what they may have (Ovid)

quid brevi fortes jaculamur ævo multa? Quid terras alio calentes sole mutamus?: why do we, whose life is so brief, aim at so many things? Why do we change to lands warmed by another sun? (Horace)

quid deceat, quid non obliti: neglectful of what is seemly and what is not (Horace)

quid dem?, quid non dem?; renuis tu quod jubet alter: what shall I give?, what shall I withhold?; what you decline, another demands (Horace)

quid dignum tanto feret hic promissor hiatu?: what will this promiser produce worthy of such boastful language? (Horace)

quid fit, Mæcenas, ut nemos, quam sibi sortem seu ratio dederit, seu sors objecerit, illa contentus vivat, laudet divera sequentes?: how comes it, Mæcenas, that no person is contented with his course in life, whether selected by choice, or thrown in his way by chance, but that all praise those who follow a different pursuit? (Horace)

quid me alta silentia cogis rumpere?: why force me to break the deep silence? (Virgil)

quid non ebrietas designat? Operta recludit; spes jubet esse ratas; in prælia trudit inertem (or inermem); sollicitis animis onus eximit; addocet artes: what does drunkenness not affect? It unlocks secrets; bids our hopes to be realized; urges the listless (or unarmed) to the fight; lifts the load from troubled minds; teaches accomplishments (Horace)

quid nos dura refugimus ætas? Quid intactum nefasti liquimus?: what have we, a hardened generation, shrunk from? What have we, in our impiety, left inviolate? (Horace)

quid prodest, Pontice, longo sanguine censeri, pictosque ostendere vultus majorum?: what good is it, Ponticus, to be accounted of a long line and to display the painted busts of our ancestors? (Juvenal)

quid rides? Mutato nomine de te fabula narratur: why do you laugh? Change the name and the story is told of you (Horace)

quid Romæ faciam?; mentiri nescio: what should I do at Rome?; I know not how to lie (i.e., how can I be at home in a place whose morals are far worse than my own?) (Juvenal)

quid sit pulchrum, quid turpe, quid utile, quid non: what is becoming, what is base, what is useful, and what is not (i.e., the aim of all moral inquiry) (Horace)

quid velit et possit rerum concordia discors: what the discordant concord of things means and can educe (Horace)

quid verum atque decens curo et rogo, et omnis in hoc sum: my care and study are in what is true and becoming, and in this I am wholly absorbed (Horace)

quid voveat dulci nutricula majus alumno, quam sapere, et fari posse quid sentiat?: what can a nurse wish better for her child than to be wise, and to have the ability of communicating such ideas (Horace)

quidquid agunt homines, votum timor ira voluptas gaudia discursus nostri farrago libelli est: everything humanity does, its hope, fear, rage, pleasure, joys, business, are the medley of my little book (Juvenal)

quidquid delirant reges plectuntur Achivi: for any madness of their kings, it is the Greeks who take the beating (Horace)

quidquid præcipies, esto brevis, ut cito dicta percipiant animi dociles, teneantque fideles omne supervacuum pleno de pectore manat: whatever you teach be brief; what is quickly said the mind readily receives and faithfully retains, everything superfluous runs over as from a full vessel (Horace)

quieta movere magna merces videbatur: just to stir things up seemed a great reward in itself (Sallust)

quin corpus onustum hesternis vitiis animum quoque prægravat una, atque affigit humo divinæ particulam auræ: and the body, overloaded with yesterday's excess, weighs down the soul also along with it, and fastens to the ground a particle of the divine aura (Horace)

Quintili Vare, legiones redde: Quintilius Varus, give me back my legions (Cæsar Augustus, quoted in Suetonius)

quique sui memores alios fecere merendo: those who have ensured their remembrance by their merits (Virgil)

quis expedivit psittaco suum chaira?: who taught that parrot his "hello"? (Persius)

quis furor, O cives, quæ tanta licentia ferri?: what fury, O citizens, what dreadful outrages of the sword? (Virgil)

quis iniquæ tam patiens urbis, ut teneat se?: who can be so patient in this city, and who so steeled as to contain himself? (Juvenal)

quis nescit, primam esse historiæ legem, ne quid falsi dicere audeat?; deinde ne quid veri non audeat?: who does not know that it is the first law of history not to dare to say anything that is false?; and the second not to dare to say anything that is not true? (Cicero)

quis novus hic nostris successit sedibus hospes? Quam sese ore ferens!: what new guest is this who has approached our dwelling? How proudly he bears himself! (Virgil)

quis talia fando temperet a lacrymis?: who, in speaking such things, can abstain from tears? (Virgil)

quis tulerit Gracchos de seditione querentes?: who can endure the Gracchi complaining of sedition? (the Gracchi were seditious men) (Juvenal)

quisnam igitur liber? Sapiens qui sibi imperiosus; quem neque pauperies neque mors neque vincula terrent: responsare cupidinibus, contemnere honores fortis, et in seipso totus teres atque rotundus: who then is free? The one who is wisely in command of himself; whom neither poverty, nor death, nor chains terrify; who is strong to resist his appetites and despise honors, and is complete in himself, smooth and round like a globe (Horace)

quo me cunque rapit tempestas, deferor hospes: wherever the storm may blow me, it carries a willing guest (Horace)

quo mihi fortunam, si non conceditur uti?: of what use is fortune to me, if I am not permitted to use it? (Horace)

quo more pyris vesci Calaber jubet hospes: in the same manner that a Calabrian would insist on your eating pears (i.e., to force on someone what is neither liked nor valued) (Horace)

quo res cunque cadent, unum et commune periclum, una salus ambobus erit: whatever may be the issue, we have both one common peril and one safety (Virgil)

quo teneam vultus mutantem Protea nodo?: by what knot shall I hold this Proteus who is ever changing his shape? (Horace)

quo usque tandem abutere, Catilina, patientia nostra?: how long will you abuse our patience, Catiline? (Cicero)

quocunque aspicio, nihil est nisi mortis imago: wherever I look, I see nothing but some image of death (Ovid)

quod crebro videt non miratur, etiamsi cur fiat nescit. Quod ante non vidit, id si evenerit, ostentum esse censet: a man does not marvel at what he sees frequently, even though he be ignorant of the reason. If anything happens that he has not seen before, he calls it a prodigy (Cicero)

quod enim ipsi experti non sunt, id docent ceteros: they are teaching others an art in which they themselves have no experience (Cicero)

quod medicorum est promittunt medici, tractant fabrilia fabri scribimus indocti doctique poëmata passim: physicians practice what belongs to physicians and workers handle the tools they have been trained to use, but all of us everywhere, trained and untrained alike, write poems (Horace)

quod petiit spernit, repetit quod nuper omisit: he despises what he sought, and he seeks that which he lately threw away (i.e., said of a capricious person) (Horace)

quod petis hic est—est Ulubris: what you seek is here—it is at Ulubræ (i.e., happiness was here all along) (Horace)

quod prestare potes, ne bis promiseris ulli, ne sis verbosus, dum vis urbanus haberi: promise nobody twice the service you can render him, and be not talkative, so that you do not appear a prattler when you wish to show someone your kindness

quod semper, quod ubique, (et) quod ab omnibus creditum est: what is always, what is everywhere, (and) what is believed by all (St. Vincent of Lerins)

quod sequitur, fugio; quod fugit, usque sequor: what follows I flee; what flees I ever pursue (Ovid)

quod si deficiant vires, audacia certe laus erit; in magnis et voluisse sat est: even though strength should fail, surely boldness will have its praise; in great attempts it is enough to dare (Propertius)

quod spiro et placeo, si placeo, tuum est: that I am inspired and give pleasure, if I give pleasure, it is because of you (Horace)

quod tantis Romana manus contexuit annis, proditor unus iners, angusto tempore vertit: what Roman hands had raised in so many years, one single traitor destroyed in one pull (Claudian)

quod tuum'st meum'st; omne meum est autem tuum: what is thine is mine, and all mine is thine (Plautus)

quod verum est, meum est: what is true belongs to me (Seneca)

quod vile est carum, quod carum est vile; putato, sic tibi nec parcus, nec avarus habeberis ulli: consider what is vile as dear, and what is dear as vile; by such acting you will not feel the want of it, neither be considered as avaricious (Dionysius Cato)

quodcunque ostendis mihi sic, incredulus odi: whatever you show me in an overwrought way, I detest and disbelieve (Horace)

quodsi me lyricis vatibus inseres, sublimi feriam sidera vertice: but if you give me a place among the lyric poets, I shall rise up till my head strikes the stars (Horace)

quorum pars magna fui: of which things I was an important part (Virgil)

quot capita tot sententiæ, suus cuique mos est: so many heads, so many minds, each has his own way (attributed to Terence)

quot cœlum stellas, tot habet tua Roma puellas: there are as many girls in your Rome as there are stars in the sky (Ovid)

quousque tandem abutere, Catilina, patientia nostra?: how long will you abuse our patience, Catiline? (Cicero)

quum talis sis, utinam noster esses!: how I wish you were one of us, since I find you so worthy!

R

rara avis in terris, nigroque simillima cygno (or **cycno**)**:** a bird rarely seen on earth, and very much resembling a black swan (i.e., something unique) (Juvenal)

rara temporum felicitate, ubi sentire quæ velis, et quæ sentias dicere licet: such was the happiness of the times, that you might think as you chose and speak as you thought (Tacitus, said of the reigns of Nerva and Trajan)

rari nantes in gurgite vasto: swimming one here and another there in a vast abyss (i.e., good ideas drowning in an ocean of poorly chosen words) (Virgil)

rari quippe boni; numero vix sunt totidem quot Thebarum portæ, vel divitis ostia Nili: rare indeed are the good; in number they are scarcely as many as the gates of Thebes or the mouths of the Nile (Juvenal)

rarus sermo illis, et magna libido tacendi: their conversation was rare, and their seeming desire was to be silent (Juvenal)

re ipsa repperi, facilitate nihil esse homini melius, neque clementia: I have learned by experience that nothing is more advantageous to a person than courtesy and compassion (Terence)

rebus angustis animosus atque fortis appare; sapienter idem contrahes vento nimium secundo turgida vela: wisely show yourself spirited and resolute when perils press you; likewise reef your sails when they swell too much by a favoring breeze (Horace)

recedant vetera, nova sint omnia: let ancient things depart and all things around be new (from the *Sacris Solemniis*)

recta actio non erit, nisi recta fuit voluntas, ab hac enim est actio. Rursus, voluntas non erit recta, nisi habitus animi rectus fuerit, ab hoc enim est voluntas: an action will not be right unless the intention is right, for from it comes the action. Again, the intention will not be right unless the state of the mind has been right, for from it proceeds the intention (Seneca)

rectius vives, Licini, neque altum semper urgendo, neque, dum procellas cautus horrescis, nimium premendo littus iniquum: you will live more prudently, Licinius, by neither always keeping out to sea, nor, while with caution you shrink from storms, hugging too closely the treacherous shore (Horace)

reddere personæ scit convenientia cuique: he knows how to assign to each character what it is proper and becoming to each person (Horace, said of a playwright)

reddere qui voces jam scit puer, et pede certo signat humum, gestit paribus colludere, et iram colligit ac ponit temere, et mutatur in horas: the boy who just knows how to talk and treads the ground with firm foot, (and) delights to play with his friends, is easily provoked and easily appeased, and changes every hour (Horace)

redit agricola labor actus in orbem, atque in se sua per vestigia volvitur annus: the husbandman's toil returns in a circle, and the year rolls in its former footsteps (Virgil)

reges dicuntur multis urgere culullis, et torquere mero, quam perspexisse laborent, an sit amicitia dignus: kings are said to press with many a cup, and test with wine the man whom they desire to test whether he be worthy of their friendship (Horace)

regibus boni quam mali suspectiores sunt, semperque his aliena virtus formidolosa est: the good are more suspected by kings than the bad, and virtue in other men is to them always a source of dread (Sallust)

regis ad exemplum totus componitur orbis: the world is fashioned according to the example of kings (i.e., "the sentiments of the court have a great influence on the sentiments of all people" — Matthew Henry) (Claudian)

regnare nolo, liber ut non sim mihi: I would not be a king and forfeit my liberty (Phædrus)

regnavit a ligno Deus: God reigned from the wood (St. Venantius Fortunatus)

regum æquabat opes animis; seraque revertens nocte domum, dapibus mensas onerabat inemptis: he equaled the wealth of kings in contentment of mind, and at night, returning home, would load his table with unbought dainties (Virgil, said of the husbandman)

reipublicæ forma laudari facilius quam evenire, et si evenit, haud diuturna esse potest: it is easier to praise a republican form of government than to establish one; and when it is established, it cannot be of long duration (Tacitus)

rem facias, rem, si possis, recte; si non, quocunque modo rem: make a fortune honestly if you can; if not, make it by any means (Horace)

requiem æternam dona eis, Domine; et lux perpetua luceat eis: grant them eternal rest, O Lord; and let perpetual light shine on them (from the Catholic Mass for the Dead)

res ad triarios rediit: the situation has come down to the triarii, the third line of defense (i.e., the situation is critical) (Livy)

res est blanda canor; discant cantare puellæ: singing is a charming accomplishment; let girls learn to sing (Ovid)

res humanæ ita sese habent: in victoria vel ignavis gloriari licet, adversæ res etiam bonos detrectant: this is how it is with human affairs: in victory even cowards boast, whereas in defeat even the brave are discredited (Sallust)

res rustica sic est: si unam rem sero feceris, omnia opera sero facies: this is how it is with farming: if you put off doing one thing, you will be late with everything (Cato the Elder)

res sacros non modo manibus attingi, sed ne cogitatione quidem violari fas fuit: not only should sacred things not be touched with the hands, but they should not be violated in thought (Cicero)

respicere exemplar vitæ morumque jubebo doctum imitatorem, et veras hinc ducere voces: I would advise the one who wishes to imitate well to look closely into life and manners and thereby learn to express them with truth (Horace)

restat iter cœlo; cœlo tentabimus ire; da veniam cœpto, Juptier alte, meo: there remains a way through the heavens; through the heavens we will attempt to go; high Jupiter, pardon my bold design (Ovid, of Dædalus, who escaped the labyrinth on wings)

revocate animos, mœstumque timorem mittite: rouse your courage, and cast off desponding fear (Virgil)

rex datur propter regnum, non regnum propter regem. Potentia non est nisi ad bonum: a king is given for the sake of the kingdom, not the kingdom for the sake of the king. His power is only from the public good

ridet argento domus: the house is smiling with silver (Horace)

risum teneatis, amici?: could you keep from laughing, friends? (Horace)

rixatur de lana sæpe caprina: he often quarrels about goat's wool (i.e., he often disputes the obvious, or about nothing worth disputing) (Horace)

Roma locuta est; causa finita est: Rome has spoken; the case is settled (St. Augustine)

Romæ rus optas, absentem rusticus urbem tollis ad astra levis: at Rome, you long for the country, in the country you laud the distant city to the stars (Horace)

Romæ Tibur amem, ventosus, Tibure Romam: fickle as the wind, I love Tibur when at Rome, and Rome when at Tibur (Horace)

Romam cuncta undique atrocia aut pudenda confluunt celebranturque: all things atrocious and shameless flow from all parts to Rome (Tacitus)

rorate, cœli, desuper, et nubes pluant justum; aperiatur terra, et germinet salvatorem: drop down dew, heavens, from above, and let the clouds rain down righteousness; let the earth be opened, and a savior spring to life (Isaiah 45:8)

rusticus expectat dum defluat amnis; at ille labitur et labetur in omne volubilis ævum: the yokel waits until the river flows by; but it still glides on, and will glide on forever (i.e., someone who waits for change in vain) (Horace)

S

sæpe audivi, non de nihilo, dici, mendacem memorem esse oportere: I have often heard it said, and with good reason, that a liar should have a good memory (Apuleius)

sæpe Faunorum voces exauditæ, sæpe visæ formæ deorum: the voices of the Fauns are often heard and the shapes of gods often seen

sæpe grandis natu senex nullum aliud habet argumentum, quo se probet diu vixisse, præter ætatem: often a man who is very old in years has no evidence to prove that he has lived a long life other than his age (Seneca)

sæpe stylum vertas, iterum quæ digna legi sint scripturus; neque, te ut miretur turba, labores contentus paucis lectoribus: you must often make erasures if you mean to write what is worthy of being read a second time; labor not for the admiration of the crowd, but be content with a few choice readers (Horace)

sæpius locutum, nunquam me tacuisse pœnitet: I have often regretted having spoken, never having kept silent (Publilius Syrus)

sæpius ventis agitatur ingens pinus, et celsæ graviore casu decidunt turres, feriuntque summos fulmina (or **fulgura**) **montes:** the huge pine is more frequently shaken by the winds, high towers fall with a heavier crash, and it is the mountain tops that the thunderbolts strike (Horace)

sæva paupertas, et avitus apto cum lare fundus: cruel poverty, and an ancestral piece of land with a dwelling to match (Horace)

sævit amor ferri, et scelerata insania belli: the passions are in arms, and nothing is heard of but the insane wickedness of war (Virgil)

sævitque animis ignobile vulgus, jamque faces et saxa volant; furor arma ministrat: the rude rabble are enraged, now the firebrands and stones are seen to fly about; their fury supplies them with arms (Virgil)

saltabat elegantius (or **melius**), **quam necesse est probæ mulieri:** she danced more elegantly (or much better) than what becomes a virtuous woman (Sallust, said of Sempronia)

saltat Milonius, ut semel icto accessit fervor capiti, numerusque lucernis: Milonius dances as soon as the wine gets into his heated head, and the lights are doubled to his view (Horace)

salve, Regina, mater misericordiæ, vita, dulcedo et spes nostra, salve!: hail, Queen, mother of mercy, hail our life, our sweetness, and our hope! (an 11th-century hymn to the Virgin Mary)

sanctus haberi justitiæque tenax factis dictisque mereris?; agnosco procerem: dare to be held a man without blame, and tenacious of justice both in word and deed; then I recognize in you the nobleman (Juvenal)

sanitas sanitatum, omnia sanitas: sanity of sanity, all is sanity (Ménage, 1693)

sapientia quoque perseveranit mecum: wisdom also continued with me (Francis Bacon)

satis diu vel naturæ vixi, vel gloriæ: I have lived long enough both in years and in glory (Julius Cæsar)

satis est orare Jovem, quæ donat et aufert; det vitam, det opes, æquum mi animum ipse parabo: it is enough to pray to Jove for those things that he gives and takes away; let him grant life, let him grant wealth; I will provide myself with a well-poised mind (Horace)

satis superque me benignitas tua ditavit: your generosity has enriched me enough, and more than enough (Horace)

satura tota nostra est: satire is wholly ours (Quintilian, a reference to Roman character)

saucius ejurat pugnam gladiator, et idem immemor antiqui vulneris arma capit: the wounded gladiator forswears fighting, and yet, forgetful of his former wound, he takes up arms again

scimus, et hanc veniam petimusque damusque vicissim: this we know, and this allowance we give and admit in turn (Horace)

scio enim cui credidi: I know in whom I have believed (2 Timothy 1:12)

scio quid valeant humeri, et quid ferre recusent: I know what shoulders can bear, and what they cannot support

scio: tu coactus tua voluntate es: I know it: you are constrained by your will (Terence)

scire, deos quoniam propius contingis, oportet: you ought to know, since you live near the gods (Horace)

scire potestates herbarum usumque medendi: to know the potential of herbs and their use in healing (Virgil)

scire volunt secreta domus, atque inde timeri: they wish to know of the family secrets, and so to be feared (Juvenal)

scit genius, natale comes qui temperet astrum: the genius, our companion who rules our natal star, knows (Horace)

scribimus indocti, doctique poëmata passim: we, both the learned and unlearned, are in the habit of writing poetry (Horace)

scripta ferunt annos; scriptis Agamemnona nosti, et quisquis contra vel simul arma tulit: writings survive the years; it is by writings that you know Agamemnon, and those who fought for or against him (Ovid)

secreta hæc murmura vulgi: those secret whisperings of the crowd (Juvenal)

secretum iter et fallentis semita vitæ: a quiet journey in the untrodden paths of life (Horace)

secundas res splendidiores facit amicitia, et adversas partiens communicansque leviores: friendship makes prosperity brighter while it lightens adversity by sharing its griefs and anxieties (Cicero)

secundæ res acrioribus stimulis animum explorant; quia miseriæ tolerantur, felicitate corrumpimur: prosperity tries the soul with sharper temptations; while hardships may be endured, one is corrupted by good fortune (Tacitus)

sed nisi peccassem, quid tu concedere posses? Materiam veniæ sors tibi nostra dedit: had I not sinned, what had there been for you to pardon? My fate has given you the material for mercy (Ovid)

sed notat hunc omnis domus et vicinia tota, introrsum turpem, speciosum pelle decora: but all his family and the entire neighborhood regard him as inwardly base, and only showy outside (Horace)

sed nunc amoto quæramus seria ludo: but now, laying banter aside, let us look to more serious matters (Horace)

sed nunc non erat his locus: but there was at this time no place for these matters (Horace)

sed quum res hominum tanta caligine volvi adspicerem, lætosque diu florere nocentes, vexarique pios: rursus labefacta cadebat religio: when I beheld human affairs involved in such dense darkness, the guilty exulting in their prosperity, and pious men suffering wrong, what religion I had began to reel backward and fall (Claudian)

sed summa sequar fastigia rerum: but I will trace the footsteps of the chief events (Virgil)

sed taciti fecere tamen convicia vultus: but still her silent looks loudly reproached me (Ovid)

sed te nos facimus, Fortuna, deam, cœloque locamus: we, O Fortune, make you a goddess, and place you in the heavens

sed tu ingenio verbis concipe plura meis?: but do you of your own ingenuity take up more than my words? (Ovid)

sed vatem egregium cui non sit publica vena, qui nihil expositum soleat deducere, nec qui communi feriat carmen triviale moneta, hunc qualem nequeo monstrare, et sentio tantum, anxietate carens animus facit: a poet of superior merit, whose vein is of no vulgar kind, who never tosses off anything trite, nor coins a trivial poem at the public mint, I cannot describe, but only recognize as a person whose soul is free from all anxiety (Juvenal)

segnem ac desidem, et circo et theatris corruptum militem: a slothful and listless military, debauched by the circus and the theaters (Tacitus)

semel profecto premere felices Deus cum cœpit, urget; hos habent magna exitus: once God has begun to throw down the prosperous, he overthrows them altogether; such is the end of the mighty (Seneca)

semen est sanguis Christianorum: the blood of the Christians is seed (Tertullian, in reference to Roman persecution of the Church)

semper ad eventum festinat et in medias res non secus ac notas auditorem rapit: he always hurries to the main event and whisks his audience into the middle of things as though they already knew (Horace)

semper eris pauper, si pauper es, Æmiliane: if you are poor, Emilian, you will always be poor (Martial)

semper habet lites alternaque jurgia lectus, in quo nupta jacet; minimum dormitur in illo: the bed in which a wife lies is always the scene of quarrels and mutual recriminations; there is very little chance of sleep there (Juvenal)

senex cum extemplo est, jam nec sentit, nec sapit; ajunt solere eum rursum repuerascere: when the elderly man reaches the last stage of life, without senses or mentality, they say that he has grown a child again (Plautus)

senilis stultitia, quæ deliratio appellari solet, senum levium est, non omnium: the foolishness of old age, which is termed dotage, does not characterize all who are old, but only those who are frivolous (Cicero)

seria cum possim, quod delectantia malim scribere, tu causa es, lector: that I dwell on lighter topics when I could handle those that are more serious, you, reader, are the cause (Martial)

series implexa causarum: the complicated series of causes (Seneca)

sero respicitur tellus, ubi fune soluto currit in immensum panda carina salum: it is late to look back upon the land, when, the cable being loosed, the vessel is making its way into the immense deep (Ovid)

sero te amavi, pulchritudo tam antiqua et tam nova, sero te amavi; et ecce intus eras et ego foris, et ibi te quærebam: too late came I to love you, O beauty both so ancient and so new, too late came I to love you; and behold, you were within me, and I out of myself, where I made search for you (St. Augustine)

serpentes avibus geminentur, tigribus agni: let serpents couple with birds, and lambs with tigers (Horace)

serpentum major concordia; parcit cognatis maculis similis fera. Quando leoni fortior eripuit vitam leo?: there is greater agreement among serpents than among men; a wild beast of a like kind spares kindred spots. When did a stronger lion deprive another of life? (Juvenal)

serus in cœlum redeas, diuque lætus intersis populo: late may you return to heaven, and long may you continue to delight your people with your presence (Horace, addressed to Cæsar Augustus)

seseque i perire mavolunt ibidem quam cum stupro redire ad suos popularis: they would rather die on the spot than go back to their people in disgrace (Nævius)

sex horas somno, totidem des legibus æquis: quatuor orabis, des epulisque duas. Quod superest ultra, sacris largire Camenis: give six hours to sleep, as many as to the study of law: four hours you shall pray, and two give to meals. Devote what is beyond that to the sacred Muses (Coke)

si antiquitatem spectes, est vetustissima; si dignitatem, est honoratissima; si jurisdictionem, est capacissima: if you consider its antiquity, it is most ancient; if its dignity, it is most honorable; if its jurisdiction, it is most extensive (Coke, said of the English House of Commons)

si bene commemini, causæ sunt quinque bibendi; hospitis adventus, præsens sitis, atque futura, aut vini bonitas, aut quælibet altera caus: if I remember correctly, there are five excuses for drinking: the visit of a guest, present thirst, thirst to come, the goodness of the wine, or any other excuse you choose (Père Sermond)

si componere magnis parva mihi fas est: if I may be allowed to compare small things with great (Ovid)

si computes annos, exiguum tempus; si vices rerum, ævum putes: a brief time if you count the years; an age if you count the changes it brought forth (Pliny the Younger)

si foret in terris, rideret Democritus: if Democritus were on earth, he would laugh (Horace)

si foret in terris, rideret Heraclitus: if Heraclitus were on earth, he would laugh

si fractus illabatur orbis, impavidum ferient ruinæ: if the world should break in pieces around him, the ruins would leave him undaunted (i.e., nothing can shatter the steadfastness or resolve of an upright man) (Horace)

si fueris Romæ, Romano vivito more; si fueris alibi, vivito sicut ibi: if you are at Rome, live in the Roman style; if you are elsewhere, live as they live there (i.e., when in Rome, do as the Romans) (St. Ambrose)

si genus humanum, et mortalia temnitis arma; at sperate deos memores fandi atque nefandi: if you despise the human race and mortal arms, yet be hopeful that the gods will not be forgetful of right and wrong (Virgil)

si leonina pellis non satis est, assuenda vulpina: if the lion's skin is not enough, we must sew on the fox's

si mihi pergit quæ vult dicere, ea quæ non vult audiet: if he proceeds to state what he pleases against me, he shall have something in return that it will not please him to hear (Terence)

si nihil attuleris, ibis Homere fora: if you do not bring anything, Homer, you will go outside

si numeres anno soles et nubila toto, invenies nitidum sæpius isse diem: if you count the sunny and the cloudy days of the whole year, you will find that the sunshine predominates (Ovid)

si pace frui volumus, bellum gerendum est; si bellum omittimus, pace nunquam fruemur: if we desire to enjoy peace, we must first wage war; if we shrink from war, we shall never enjoy peace (Cicero)

si parva licet componere magnis: if it be allowable to compare small things with great (Virgil)

si pecasse negamus, fallimur, et nulla est in nobis veritas: if we say that we have no sin we deceive ourselves, and there is no truth in us (from Marlowe's play *Faust*, after 1 John 1:8)

si possem sanior essem; sed trahit invitam nova vis; aliudque Cupido, mens aliud suadet: if it were in my power, I would be wiser; but a newly felt power carries me off in spite of myself; love leads me one way, my understanding another (Ovid)

si quoties homines peccant sua fulmina mittat Jupiter, exiguo tempore inermis erit: if Jupiter hurled his thunderbolt as often as men sinned, he would soon be out of thunderbolts (Ovid)

si sursum non efferor alis, saltem cursu prætervehor omnes: though I do not soar high on my wings, I fly by all who are in the race

si una eademque res legatur duobus, alter rem, alter valorem rei: if one and the same thing is bequeathed to two people, one should have the thing, the other the value of the thing (Justinian)

si veris magna paratur fama bonis, et si successu nuda remoto inspicitur virtus, quicquid laudamus in ullo majorum, fortuna fuit: if honest fame attends the truly good, if, setting aside the ultimate success, virtue and valor are alone to be considered, then was his fortune as proud as any to be found in the records of our ancestry (a tribute to Pompey by Lucan)

si vis me flere, dolendum est primum ipsi tibi: if you wish me to weep, you must first show grief yourself (Horace)

si volet usus, quem penes arbitrium est et jus norma loquendi: if usage wills, within whose power are the laws and rules of speech (Horace)

sic ait, et dicto citius tumida æquora placat: so speaks the god, and quicker than he speaks he calms the swelling seas (Virgil)

sic aliud ex alio numquam desistet oriri vitaque mancipio nulli datur, omnibus usu: so one thing will never cease to arise from another, and no one possesses life as an owner, but all are tenants (Lucretius)

sic canibus catulos similes, sic matribus hædos noram; sic parvis componere magna solebam: thus I knew that pups are like dogs and kids like goats; so I used to compare great things with small (Virgil)

sic delatores, genus hominum publico exitio repertum, et ne pœnis quidem unquam satis coërcitum, per præmia eliciebantur: thus were informers, a race of men discovered for public destruction, and never sufficiently restrained by pains or penalties, allured and brought forward by rewards (Tacitus)

sic ego nec sine te nec tecum vivere possum; et videor voti nescius esse mei: thus neither with you nor without you can I live; and I seem not to know my own wishes (Ovid)

sic enim dilexit Deus mundum, ut Filium suum unigenitum daret: for God so loved the world that he gave his only-begotten Son (St. John 3:16)

sic leve, sic parvum est, animum quod laudis avarum subruit ac reficit: so light, so insignificant a thing is that which casts down or revives a soul that is greedy of praise (Horace)

sic quisque pavendo dat vires famæ, nulloque auctore malorum, quæ finxere timent: thus each person by his fears gives wings to rumor, and, without any real source of apprehension, men fear what they themselves have fashioned (Lucan)

sic, sic juvat ire sub umbras: thus, thus, it is my choice to go beneath the shadows (i.e., to Hades) (Virgil)

sic visum Veneri, cui placet impares formas, atque animos sub juga ahenea sævo mittere cum joco: such is the will of Venus, whose pleasure it is in cruel sport to subject to her brazen yoke persons and tempers ill-matched (Horace)

sic vos non vobis mellificatis apes; sic vos non vobis nidificatis aves; sic vos non vobis vellera fertis oves: thus you bees make honey not for yourselves; thus you birds build nests not for yourselves; thus you sheep bear fleeces not for yourselves (Virgil, as a challenge to Bathyllus who claimed authorship of a set of verses that Virgil himself had composed)

Sicelides Musæ, paulo majora canamus: Sicilian Muses, let us sing of slightly grander things (Virgil)

sicut modo geniti infantes, rationabile, sine dolo lac concupiscite: after the fashion of newborn babes, desire the sincere milk of the word (1 Peter 2:2)

simul et jucunda et idonea dicere vitæ: to tell at once what is pleasant and proper in life (Horace)

simul flare sorbereque haud facile est: ego hic esse et illic simul, haud potui: to blow and to swallow at the same time is not easy; I cannot at the same time be here and also there (Plautus)

sine Cerere et Baccho, friget Venus: without Ceres and Bacchus, Venus is cold (i.e., without food and drink, love is cold) (adapted from Terence)

sine Cerere et Libero friget Venus: without the aid of Ceres (bread) and Liberty, Venus (love) freezes (adapted from Terence)

sine pennis volare haud facile est; meæ alæ pennas non habent: it is not easy flying without feathers; my wings are not yet fledged (Plautus)

sine virtute esse amicitia nullo pacto potest; quæ autem inter bonos amicitia dicitur, hæc inter malos factio est: there can be no friendship without virtue; for among good men it is called friendship, among bad men it is called faction (Sallust)

singula quæque locum teneant sortita decenter: let each thing keep the place that it occupies with propriety (Horace)

singula quid referam?; nil non mortale tenemus, pectoris exceptis ingeniique bonis: why do I go into details?; we have nothing that is not mortal except what our hearts and our intellects endow us with (Ovid)

singuli enim decipere et decipi possunt: nemo omnes, neminem omnes fefellunt: individuals indeed may deceive and be deceived; but no one has ever deceived all men, nor have all men ever deceived anyone (Pliny the Younger)

siqua recordanti benefacta priora voluptas est homini: if a man can take any pleasure in recalling the kindnesses he has done (Catullus)

sit mihi fas audita loqui: let me have permission to state what I have heard (Virgil)

sit mihi quod nunc est, etiam minus; ut mihi vivam quod superest ævi, si quid superesse volunt di: may I continue to possess what I have now, or even less; so I may live the remainder of my days after my own manner, if the gods will that any should remain (Horace)

sit tua cura sequi; me duce tutus eris: be it your care to follow; with me for your guide, you will be safe (Ovid)

sive pium vis hoc, sive hoc muliebre vocari; confiteor misero molle cor esse mihi: whether you call my heart affectionate, or you call it womanish, I confess that to my misfortune it is soft (Ovid)

Socratem audio dicentem, cibi condimentum essa famem, potionis sitim: I hear Socrates saying that the best seasoning for food is hunger, for drink, thirst (Cicero)

Socrates quidem quum rogaretur cujatem se esse diceret, Mundanum, inquit, totius enim mundi se incolam et civem arbitrabatur: when Socrates was asked of what country he professed to be a citizen, he answered, "of the world," for he considered himself an inhabitant and citizen of the whole world (Cicero)

solem præ jaculorum multitudine et sagittarum non videbis; in umbra igitur pugnabimus: you will not see the sun for the clouds of javelins and arrows; then we will fight in the shade (Cicero; the Persian's challenge to Leonides at Thermopylæ, and Leonides's reply)

solitudinem faciunt, pacem appellant: they make a desert and call it peace (i.e., they exterminate a people and say that peace has been restored) (Tacitus)

sollicitant alii remis freta cæca, ruuntque in ferrum; penetrant aulas, et limina regum: some disturb unknown seas with oars, some rush upon the sword; some push their way into the courts and portals of kings (Virgil)

solventur risu tabulæ, tu missus abibis: the case is dismissed with a laugh, the court is dismissed, and you are sent away (Horace)

somnium narrare vigilantis est, et vita sua confiteri sanitatis indicium est: the one who is awake can recount his dream, and, similarly, the confession of sin indicates a sound mind (Seneca)

somnus agrestium lenis virorum non humiles domos fastidit, umbrosamque ripam: the gentle sleep of the country folk disdains not humble dwellings and the shady bank (Horace)

sors tua mortalis; non est mortale quod optas: your lot is mortal; and you wish what no mortal may (Ovid)

spargere voces in vulgam ambiguas: spreading ambiguous rumors among the common crowd (Virgil)

spatio brevi spem longam reseces; dum loquimur, fugerit invida ætas; carpe diem, quam minimum credula postero: from the short space of life you should exclude distant hopes; for while we speak, the envious hours are passing away; seize the day, trusting little as possible to what comes after (Horace)

spectatum admissi, risum teneatis, amici?: can even the friends who are admitted to see the work refrain from laughter? (Horace)

spectatum veniunt, veniunt spectentur ut ipsæ: the women come to see, they come also to be seen (Ovid)

sperat infestis, metuit secundis alteram (ad) sortem bene præparatum pectus: a well-prepared heart hopes in adversity and fears in prosperity for a change of fortune (Horace)

spes bona dat vires, animum quoque spes bona firmat; vivere spe vidi qui moriturus erat: good hope gives strength, good hope also confirms resolution; the one who was on the point of death, I have seen hope revive

spes donare novas largus, amaraque curarum eluere efficax: mighty to inspire new hopes, and able to drown the bitterness of cares (Horace, said of wine)

spiritalis enim virtus sacramenti ita est ut lux: etsi per immundos transeat: non inquinatur: the spiritual virtue of a sacrament is like light; although it passes among the impure, it is not polluted (St. Augustine)

spiritus intus alit, totamque infusa per artus mens agitat molem et magno se corpore miscet: the spirit within nourishes, and the mind that is diffused throughout the living parts of nature activates the whole mass and mingles with the vast body of the universe (Virgil)

spretæ injuria formæ: the insult offered to her slighted beauty (Virgil)

sta, viator, heroëm calcas: stop, traveler, you trample upon a hero (an epitaph)

stabant orantes primi transmittere cursum tendebantque manus ripæ ulterioris amore: they stood begging to be the first to make the voyage over and they reached out their hands in longing for the further shore (Virgil)

stabat mater dolorosa juxta crucem lacrymosa qua pendebat filius: the sorrowing mother stood, weeping by the cross where her son hung dying (opening words of the Stabat Mater)

stat sua cuique dies; breve et irreparabile tempus omnibus est vitæ; sed famam extendere factis, hoc virtutis opus: each one has his appointed day; short and irreparable is the brief life of all; but to extend our fame by our deeds, this is the work of manhood (or virtue) (Virgil)

statim daret, ne differendo videretur negare: he would give at once, lest by delaying he should seem to deny the favor (Cornelius Nepos)

status enim reipublicæ maxime judicatis rebus continetur: the standing of a republic is very largely bound up in its judicial decisions (Cicero)

stemmata quid faciunt? Quid prodest, Pontice, longo sanguine censeri pictosque ostendere vultus?: of what use are pedigrees? Of what advantage, Ponticus, is it to be counted by the length of your bloodline, or the display of family portraits? (Juvenal)

stimulos dedit æmula virtus: he was spurred on by rival valor (Lucan)

strangulat inclusus dolor, atque exæstuat intus, cogitur et vires multiplicare suas: suppressed grief suffocates, it rages within the breast, and is forced to multiply its strength (Ovid)

strenua nos exercet inertia; navibus atque quadrigis petimus bene vivere; quod petis hic est: busy idleness urges us on; we seek to live aright by sailing and chariot-driving; what you seek for is here (Horace)

stulte, quid est somnus, gelidæ nisi mortis imago? Longa quiescendi tempora fata dabunt: fool, what is sleep but the image of icy death? The fates shall give us a long period of rest (Ovid)

suave mari magno, turbantibus æquora ventis, e terra magnum alterius spectare laborem: how delightful it is when on the great sea the winds have raised its waters into billows, to witness the perils of another from the land (Lucretius)

subdola cum ridet placidi pellacia ponti: when the calm sea shows its false, alluring smile (Lucretius)

substantia prior et dignior est accidente: the substance should be considered as prior to, and of more weight than, the accident

subtilis veterum judex et callidus audis: you are known as a fine and skillful judge of things old (Horace)

successore novo vincitur omnis amor: all love is vanquished by a new love (Ovid)

sufficit huic tumulus, cui non suffecerit orbis: a tomb now suffices for him for whom the world did not suffice (said of Alexander the Great)

sumite materiam vestris, qui scribitis, æquam viribus, et versate diu, quid ferre recusent, quid valeant humeri: you who write, choose a subject suited to your abilities, and long ponder what your powers are equal to, and what they are unable to perform (Horace)

summa petit livor: perflant altissima venti: envy assails the highest: the winds howl around the highest peaks (Ovid)

summa sequor fastigia rerum: I will trace the principal heads of events (Virgil)

summam (or summum) nec metuas diem, nec optes: you should neither fear nor wish for your last day (Martial)

sunt bona, sunt quædam mediocria, sunt mala plura quæ legis: of those that you read, some are good, some are middling, but more are bad (Martial, referring to books)

sunt delicta tamen, quibus ignovisse velimus: there are some faults, however, that we are willing to pardon (Horace)

sunt Jovis omnia plena: all things are full of the god Jove (Virgil)

superstitio, in qua inest inanis timor Dei; religio, quæ Dei pio cultu continetur: there is in superstition a senseless fear of God; religion consists in the pious worship of him (Cicero)

supremus ille dies non nostri extinctionem sed commutationem affert loci: the last day does not bring extinction to us, but change of place (Cicero)

suum cuique incommodum ferendum est, potius quam de alterius commodis detrahendum: every one should bear his own grievances and inconveniences, rather than detract from or abridge the comforts of another (Cicero)

T

tabesne cadavera solvat, an rogus, haud refert: it makes no difference whether corruption, or the funeral pyre, dissolve the carcass (Lucan)

tacitæ per amica silentia lunæ: through the friendly silence of the soundless moonlight (Virgil)

tacitum vivit sub pectore vulnus: the secret wound still lives within the heart (Virgil)

tale tuum carmen nobis, divine poëta, quale sopor fessis in gramine: your song is to us, O heavenly poet, as sleep to the weary on the soft grass (Virgil)

talibus ex adyto dictis Cumæa Sibylla horrendas canit ambages, antroque remugit, obscuris vera involvens: in words like these the Sybil utters her fearful oracles of dubious import, and sounds them forth from her cavern, blending truth with obscurity (Virgil)

tam bonus gladiator rudem tam cito accepisti?: has so great a gladiator so quickly accepted a wooden foil? (i.e., retired) (Cicero)

tam felix utinam, quam pectore candidus essem: oh, that I were as happy as I am clear in conscience (Ovid)

tamen illic vivere vellem, oblitusque meorum obliviscendus et illis: yet I could find it in my heart to live there, forgetting my friends and being forgotten by them (Horace)

tamen me cum magnis vixesse invita fatebitur usque invidia: nevertheless, even envy, however unwilling, will have to admit that I have lived among great men (Horace)

tandem poculum mœroris exhausit: he has exhausted at last the cup of grief (Cicero)

tandem tandem justitia obtinet: at last, at last, justice prevails

tantæ molis erat Romanam condere gentem: so great a task it was to found the Roman people (Virgil)

tantum religio potuit suadere malorum: so potent was religion in persuading to evil deeds (Lucretius, in reference to the sacrifice of Iphigenia)

tantum se fortunæ permittunt, etiam ut naturam dediscant: they give themselves up so much to fortune, as even to forget their nature (Curtius)

tantum series juncturaque pollet tantum de medio sumptis accedit honoris: of such force are order and arrangement that so much honor may be imparted to subjects from common life (Horace)

tantum vertice in auras ætherius quantum radice in Tartara tendit: its summit stretches as far into the upper ether as its roots into Tartarus (i.e., the nether world)

tarda sit illa dies, et nostro serior ævo: slow may that day approach, and long after our time (Ovid)

te, Fortuna, sequor; procul hinc jam fœdera sunto; credidimus fatis, utendum est judice bello: you, Fortuna, I follow; hence far all treaties past; to fate I commit myself, and the arbitration of war (Lucan, on Cæsar crossing the Rubicon)

te matutinus flentem conspexit Eous et flentem paulo vidit post Hesperus idem: Eos saw you weeping at dawn, and at sunset Hesperus found you weeping still (Cinna, referring to Zmyrna, mother of Adonis)

te propter nullos tellus tua postulat imbres, arida nec pluvio supplicat herba Jovi: because of you, your land never pleads for showers, nor does its parched grass pray to Jove for rain (Tibullus, in reference to the Nile River)

te sine nil altum mens inchoat: without you my mind originates nothing lofty (Virgil, to Mæcenas)

te spectem, suprema mihi cum venerit hora, et teneam moriens deficiente manu: may I be looking at you when my last hour has come, and dying may I hold you with my weakening hand (Tibullus)

tecum vivere amem, tecum obeam libens: with you I should love to live, with you be ready to die (Horace)

tempora labuntur, tacitisque senescimus annis; et fugiunt fræno non remorante dies: time glides away and we grow older through the silent years; the days flee away and are restrained by no rein (Ovid)

tempus abire tibi est, ne ... rideat et pulset lasciva decentius ætas: it is time for you to be gone, lest ... the age more decent in its wantonness should laugh at you and drive you off the stage (Horace)

tempus erat quo prima quies mortalibus ægris incipit et dono divum gratissima serpit: it was the time when first sleep begins for weary mortals and, by the gift of the gods, creeps over them most welcomely (Virgil)

tempus est quædam pars æternitatis: time is a certain fraction of eternity (Cicero)

tempus ferax, tempus edax rerum: time the producer, time the devourer of things (after Ovid)

tempus in agrorum cultu consumere dulce est: it is delightful to spend one's time in the tillage of the fields (Ovid)

tendimus huc omnes; metam properamus ad unam. Omnia sub leges mors vocat atra suas: we are all bound thither; we are hastening to the same common goal. Black death calls all things under the sway of its laws (Ovid)

tene magis salvum populus velit an populum tu? Servet in ambiguo, qui consulit et tibi et Urbi, Iuppiter: is your life dearer to the people than the people's life to you? May Jupiter, who keeps watch over you and Rome, leave the answer in doubt (Varius)

teneris, heu, lubrica moribus ætas!: alas!, the slippery nature of tender youth (Claudian)

tentanda via est qua me quoque possim tollere humo, victorque virum volitare per ora: I, too, must attempt a way by which I may raise myself above the ground and soar victorious through the mouths of men (Virgil)

ter conatus ibi collo dare brachia circum, ter frustra comprensa manus effugit imago: three times I attempted to throw my arms there around her neck, and three times clutched in vain, her image eluded my grasp (Virgil)

terminat hora diem, terminat auctor opus: the hour ends the day, the author ends the work (from Marlowe's play *The Jew of Malta*)

terra antiqua, potens armis atque ubere glebæ: an ancient land, powerful in arms and in the fertility of its soil (Virgil, of Italy)

terretur minimo pennæ stridore columba unguibus, accipiter, saucia facta tuis: the dove, O hawk, that has once been wounded by your talons is frightened by the least movement of a wing (Ovid)

tibi nullum periculum esse perspicio, quod quidem sejunctum sit ab omnium interitu: I can see no danger to which you are exposed, other than that which threatens the destruction of us all (Cicero)

timeo Danaos et dona ferentes: I fear the Greeks, even when they bear gifts (i.e., beware of Greeks bearing gifts) (Virgil)

timeo hominem unius libri: I fear the man of one book (St. Thomas Aquinas)

Titus, amor et deliciæ humani generis: Titus, the darling and delight of the human race (Suetonius)

tollimus in cælum curvato gurgite, et idem subducta ad manes imos descendimus unda: we are carried up to the heaven by the circling wave, and immediately the wave subsiding, we descend to the lowest depths (Virgil)

torva leæna lupum sequitur, lupus ipse capellam, florentem cytisum sequitur lasciva capella, te Corydon, O Alexi: trahit sua quemque voluptas: fierce lioness goes after wolf, that same wolf after a goat, the wanton goat goes after the flowering clover, and I go after you, O Alexis: each follows its own delight (Virgil)

totus hic locus est contemnendus in nobis, non negligendus in nostris: this place [where we are buried] is wholly to be disregarded by us, but not to be neglected by our surviving friends (Cicero)

totus in toto, et totus in qualibet parte: wholly complete and complete in every part (ancient definition of the human mind; also said of the human heart)

trahit ipse furoris impetus, et visum est lenti quæsisse nocentem: the very violence of their rage drags them on, and to inquire who is guilty were [for them] a waste of time (Lucan)

tribus Anticyris caput insanabile: a head incurable by three Anticyræ (i.e., a person incurably insane) (Horace)

tristia mæstum vultum verba decent; iratum, plena minarum; ludentem, lasciva; severum, seria dictu: sorrowful words become the sorrowful; angry words suit the passionate; light words befit a playful expression; serious words suit the grave (Horace)

Tros Tyriusve mihi nullo discrimine agetur: Trojan or Tyrian, it shall make no difference to me (i.e., I treat all the same) (Virgil)

truditur dies die, novæque pergunt interire lunæ: day presses on the heels of day, and new moons hasten to their wane (Horace)

tu est Christus, filius Dei vivi: you are the Christ, the son of the living God (St. Matthew 16:16)

tu ne quæsieris, scire nefas, quem mihi, quem tibi finem di dederint, Leuconoë: do not inquire, for it is not permitted to know such things, Leuconoë, what end the gods have in store for me and for you (Horace)

tu nihil invita dices faciesve Minerva: you must say and do nothing against Minerva (i.e., against the one who inspires you) (Horace)

tu quamcunque Deus tibi fortunaverit horam, grata sume manu; nec dulcia differ in annum, ut quocunque loco fueris, vixisse libenter te dicas: receive with a thankful hand every hour that God may have granted you, and defer not the comforts of life to another year; that in whatever place you are, you may say you have lived freely (Horace)

tu regere imperio populos, Romane, memento: You, Roman, remember to rule peoples with your power (Virgil)

tu vero felix, Agricola, non vitæ tantum claritate, sed etiam opportunitate mortis: you were truly lucky, Agricola, not only in the distinction of your life, but also in the opportune timing of your death (Tacitus)

tui me miseret, mei piget: I pity you and vex myself (Ennius)

tum, ut adsolet in amore et ira, jurgia, preces, exprobratio, satisfactio: then there is the usual scene when lovers are excited with each other, quarrels, entreaties, reproaches, and then fondling reconciliation (Tacitus)

tuo tibi judicio est utendum. Virtutis et vitiorum grave ipsius conscientia pondus est; qua sublata jacent omnia: you must use your own judgment on yourself. Great is the weight of conscience in deciding on your own virtues and vices; if that be taken away, all is lost (Cicero)

turba Remi sequitur fortunam, ut semper, et odit damnatos: the Roman mob follows the lead of fortune, as it always does, and hates those who are condemned (Juvenal)

turpis et ridicula res est elementarius senex: juveni parandum, seni utendum est: nothing can be as shameful or ridiculous as to see an old man in his rudiments: it is for youth to acquire, and for age to use those acquirements (Seneca)

tuta petant alii. Fortuna miserrima tuta est; nam timor eventus deterioris abest: let others seek security. My most wretched fortune is secure; for there is no fear of worse to follow (Ovid)

U

uberibus semper lacrymis, semperque paratis in statione sua, atque expectantibus illam quo jubeat manare (modo): with tears always in abundance, and always ready at their station, and awaiting her signal to flow as she bids them (Juvenal)

ubi plura nitent in carmine, non ego paucis offendar maculis, quas aut incuria fudit, aut humana parum cavit natura: when many beauties appear in a work, I will not cavil at a few faults that proceed either from negligence or from the imperfection of our nature (Horace)

ubi summus imperator non adest ad exercitum, citius quod non facto 'st usus fit, quam quod facto 'st opus: when the emperor is not with the army, that is sooner done which need not to be done than that which requires to be done (Plautus)

ubi sunt qui ante nos fuerunt? (or, ubi sunt?): where are those who lived before us?

udum et molle lutum es; nunc nunc properandus, et acri fingendus sine fine rota: you are now but soft and moist clay, and therefore instantly and incessantly to be formed by the glowing wheel (Persius)

ultima semper expectanda dies homini (est), dicique beatus ante obitum nemo supremaque funera debet: a person should ever look to his last day, and no one should be accounted happy before he is dead, or until his funeral rites have been performed (Ovid)

unde ingenium par materiæ?: where can we find talent equal to the subject? (Juvenal)

uni odiisque viro telisque frequentibus instant. Ille velut rupes vastum quæ prodit in æquor, obvia ventorum furiis, expostaque ponto, vim cunctam atque minas perfert cœlique marisque, ipsa immota manens: they attack this one man with their hate and their shower of weapons. But he is like some rock that stretches into the vast sea and that, exposed to the fury of the winds and beaten against by the waves, endures all the violence and threats of heaven and sea, himself standing unmoved (Virgil)

uni quippe vacat, studiis odiisque carenti, humanum lugere genus: there is only one person, who, being equally free from attachments and resentments, is at leisure to weep for the miseries of the human race (Lucan, said of Cato)

uno avulso, non deficit alter: when one is plucked away, another shall not be wanting (i.e., when you save one, another person in need will appear) (Virgil)

unus homo nobis cunctando restituit rem; non ponebat enim rumores ante salutem: one man, by delaying, restored the state; for he preferred the public safety to idle report (i.e., sometimes victory comes through partial engagements with the enemy over time, rather than by one direct assault) (Ennius, said of Fabius's battles against Hannibal)

unus Pellæo juveni non sufficit orbis; æstuat infelix angusto limite mundi: one world is not enough for the youth of Pella; the unhappy man frets at the narrow limits of the world (Juvenal, said of Alexander the Great)

urbem quam dicunt Romam, Meliboee, putavi, stultus ego, huic nostræ similem: the city, Meliboeus, that they call Rome, I foolishly imagined to be like this town of ours (Virgil)

urbem venalem et mature perituram, si emptorem invenerit: a city for sale and ripe for ruin, once it finds a purchaser (Sallust, referring to Rome)

urbes constituit ætas: hora dissolvit. Momento fit cinis diu sylva: it takes an age to build a city, an hour to ruin it. A forest is long in growing, but in a moment it may be reduced to ashes (Seneca)

urit enim fulgore suo, qui prægravat artes infra se positas; exstinctus amabitur idem: the one who weighs down the merits of those beneath him blinds them by his very splendor; but when his light is extinguished, he will be admired (Horace)

Usus me genuit, mater peperit Memoria. Sophiam vocant me Graii, vos Sapientiam: Practice was my father, Memory my mother. The Greeks call me Sophia, you call me Wisdom (Lucius Afranius)

ut ignis aquam conjectus, continuo restinguitur et refrigeratur, sic refervens falsum crimen in purissimam et castissimam vitam collatum, statim concidit et extinguitur: as fire when thrown into water is cooled down and put out, so also a false accusation, when brought against a man of the purest and holiest character, boils over and is at once dissipated and vanishes (Cicero)

ut nec pes, nec caput uni reddatur formæ: so that neither the foot nor the head shall belong to the same form (i.e., an incongruous picture or situation) (Horace)

ut nemo in sese tentat descendere nemo; sed præcedenti spectatur mantica tergo, quæsieris: you ask why no man attempts to descend into himself, but looks to the knapsack on the shoulders of him who proceeds (i.e., they see the faults of the ones who go ahead, but not the faults they themselves carry) (Persius)

ut solet accipiter trepidas agitare columbas: as the hawk is wont to pursue the trembling doves (Ovid)

ut turpiter atrum desinat in piscem mulier formosa superne: so that which is a beautiful woman on top ends in a dark ugly fish (Horace, referring to a mermaid tale)

ut vellum, his potius nugis tota illa dedisset tempora sævitiæ!: would to heaven he had given up to trifles like these all the time, which he devoted to savage and cruel purposes! (Juvenal)

utendum est ætate; cito pede præterit ætas; quam cuperes votis hunc revocare diem?: use the occasion, for it passes swiftly by; with how many wishes would you not then endeavor to recall the present day? (Ovid)

utinam populus Romanus unam cervicem haberet!: if only the Roman people had one neck! (Suetonius, attributed to Emperor Caligula)

utinam tam facile vera invenire possem, quam falsa convincere: I wish that I could as easily discover the truth as I can detect falsehood (Cicero)

utque alios industria, ita hunc ignavia ad famam protulerat: while other men have attained to fame by their industry, this man has done so by his indolence (Tacitus)

uvaque conspecta livorem ducit ab uva: the grape gains its purple tinge by looking at another grape (Juvenal)

uxorem accepi, dote imperium vendidi: I have taken a wife, I have sold my sovereignty for a dowry (Plautus)

uxorem, Posthume, ducis? Dic qua Tisiphone, quibus exagitare colubris?: are you marrying a wife, Posthumous? By what Fury, say, by what snakes are you driven mad? (Juvenal)

uxori nubere nolo meæ: I will not marry a wife to be my master (Martial)

V

væ!, puto deus fio: woe is me!, I think I am becoming a god (Vespasian, said when fatally ill)

valeant mendacia vatum: away with the lies of poets! (also, of prophets) (Ovid)

valeat res ludicra, si me palma negata macrum, donata reducit opimum: farewell to the drama, if the palm as it is granted or denied makes me happy or miserable (Horace)

valet ima summis mutare, et insignem attenuat Deus, obscura promens: God can change the lowest into the highest, can extinguish the proud, and bring the obscure into prominence (Horace)

vana quoque ad veros accessit fama timores: idle rumors were also added to well-founded fears (Lucan)

vanescit absens et novus intrat amor: the absent love vanishes and the new love enters (i.e., absence makes the heart grow fonder—for someone else) (Ovid)

vanitas vanitatum, dixit Ecclesiastes; vanitas vanitatum, et omnia vanitas: vanity of vanities, says the Preacher; vanity of vanities, and everything is vanity (Ecclesiastes 1:2)

Vare, Vare, redde mihi legiones meas!: Varus, Varus, give me back my legions! (Suetonius; the exclaim of Cæsar Augustus upon hearing news of the rout of his troops commanded by Varus)

vehemens in utramque partem, aut largitate nimia aut parsimonia: ready to rush to either extreme of liberality or thrift (Terence)

Veiosque habitante Camillo, illic Roma fuit: when Camillus lived at Veii, Rome was there (Lucan)

velim mehercule cum istis errare, quam cum aliis recte sentire: by Hercules, I would rather err with those men than think rightly with these others

vellem nescire literas: I wish I never knew how to write (Emperor Nero, as quoted by Suetonius, upon signing his own death warrant)

velocius ac citius nos corrumpunt vitiorum exempla domestica, magnis cum subeant animos auctoribus: the examples of vice at home more easily and more quickly corrupt us than others, since they steal into our minds under the highest authority (Juvenal)

venator sequitur fugientia; capta relinquit; semper et inventis ulteriora petit: the hunter follows things that flee from him; he leaves them when they are taken; and ever seeks for that which is beyond what he has found (Ovid)

vendentem thus et odores: selling frankincense and perfumes (Horace, in reference to books or writings destined for use as wrapping paper)

venerationi mihi semper fuit non verbosa rusticitas, sed sancta simplicitas: I have always revered not crude verbosity, but holy simplicity (St. Jerome)

venient annis sæcula seris, quibus Oceanus vincula rerum laxet, et ingens pateat tellus, Tiphysque novos detegat orbes; nec sit terris ultima Thule: in later years a time will come when Oceanus shall relax his bars and a vast territory shall appear, and Tiphys shall discover new worlds, and Thule shall be no longer the remotest spot on earth (Seneca, predicting the discovery of the New World)

venit summa dies et ineluctabile tempus Dardaniæ: the last day and inevitable hour of Troy is come (Virgil)

veniunt a dote sagittæ: the arrows were shot from the dowry (Juvenal)

vera redit facies, dissimulata perit: our natural countenance comes back, the assumed mask falls off (Petronius)

verba animi proferre, et vitam impendere vero: to speak the words of the mind, and to stake one's life for the truth (Juvenal)

verborum paupertas, imo egestas: a poverty of words, or rather an utter want of them (Seneca)

verbosa ac grandis epistola venit a Capreis: a lengthy and momentous letter came from Capri (Juvenal, in reference to Emperor Tiberias' missive from his residence at Capri condemning Sejanus in 31 CE; also rendered derisively as "a grand and wordy letter from Capri")

verbum Domini manet in æternum: the word of the Lord remains forever (1 Peter 1:25)

verbum non amplius addam: I will not add another word (Horace)

versus inopes rerum, nugæque canoræ: verses devoid of substance, melodious trifles (Horace)

vertere seria ludo: to turn from serious to playful (Horace)

verum ubi plura nitent in carmine, non ego paucis offendar maculis: but where many beauties shine in a poem, I will not be offended at a few blemishes (Horace)

vetat dominans ille in nobis deus, injussu hinc nos suo demigrare: the divinity who rules within us, forbids us to leave this world without his command (Cicero)

vexilla regis prodeunt, fulget crucis mysterium; qua vita mortem pertulit, et morte vitam protulit: the banners of the king advance, the mystery of the Cross shines bright; on which his life endured death, and by death brought forth life (St. Venantius Fortunatus)

viamque insiste domandi, dum faciles animi juvenum, dum mobilis ætas: enter upon the way of training while the spirits in youth are still pliant, while they are at that period when the mind is docile (Virgil)

victrix causa diis placuit, sed victa Catoni: the victorious cause pleased the gods, that of the vanquished by Cato (Lucan)

video barbam et pallium; philosophum nondum video: I see the beard and cloak, but I don't yet see a philosopher (Aulus Gellius)

video meliora proboque deteriora sequor: I see and approve the better things but I follow the worse (Ovid)

videtis quantum scelus contra rem publicam vobis nuntiatum sit?: how great an evil do you see that may have been announced by you against the Republic? (Cicero)

vidit et erubit lympha pudica Deum: the modest water saw God and blushed (a reference to Christ's first miracle, the turning of water into wine in St. John 2:1–11)

vincere scis, Hannibal, victoria uti nescis: you know how to conquer Hannibal, but you know not how to profit by your victory (Livy)

vir bonus est quis? Qui consulta patrum, qui leges juraque servat: what man is to be called good? The one who keeps the decrees of the fathers, and who maintains the laws and justice (Horace)

Virgilium vidi tantum: so far I have only seen Virgil (Ovid)

virtus est vitium fugere, et sapientia prima stultitia caruisse: to flee vice is the beginning of virtue, and the beginning of wisdom is to have gotten rid of folly (Horace)

virtus præmium est optimum. Virtus omnibus rebus anteit profecto. Libertas, salus, vita, res, parentes, patria et prognati tutantur, servantur; virtus omnia in se habet; omnia assunt bona, quem penes est virtus: virtue is the highest reward. Virtue truly goes before all things. Liberty, safety, life, property, parents, country, and children are protected and preserved. Virtue has all things in herself; he who has virtue has all things that are good attending him (Plautus)

virtus, recludens immeritis mori cœlum, negata tentat iter via; cœtusque vulgares, et udam spernit humum fugiente penna: virtue, opening heaven to those who deserve not to die, explores its way by a path denied to others, and spurns with soaring wing the vulgar crowds and the foggy earth (Horace)

virtus repulsæ nescia sordidæ intaminatis fulget honoribus; nec sumit aut ponit secures arbitrio popularis auræ: virtue, which knows no base repulse (or disgrace of defeat), shines with unsullied honors, neither receives nor resigns the badges of office at the will of popular whim (Horace)

virtute ambire oportet, non favitoribus. Sat habet favitorum semper, qui recte facit: we should try to succeed by merit, not by favor. He who does well will always have favor enough (Plautus)

virtutis expers verbis jactans gloriam ignotos fallit, notis est derisui: a fellow who brags of his fame but is devoid of valor imposes on strangers what is the jest of those who know him (Phædrus)

virtutum primam esse puta compescere linguam: proximus ille deo est qui scit ratione tacere: I think that the first virtue is that of holding the tongue: he approaches the gods, who, though in the right, can be silent (Cato)

virum mihi, Camena, insece versutum: tell me, O Muse, of the skillful man (Livius Andronicus)

vis consilii (or consili) expers mole ruit sua; vim temperatam dii (or di) quoque provehunt in majus; iidem (or idem) odere vires omne nefas animo moventis (or moventes): strength or force, lacking judgment, collapses by its own weight; when power is governed by moderation, it is aided by the gods; but they hate it when directed to all manner of wickedness (Horace)

vita data utenda; data est sine fœnore nobis mutua, nec certa persolvenda die: life is given to us to be used; it is a loan without interest, and we have no date fixed for repayment (Pedo Albinovanus)

vita dum superest, bene est: if only life remain, I am content (Mæcenas)

vitæ post-scenia celant: they conceal what goes on behind the scenes (i.e., the secret actions of their lives) (Lucretius)

vivamus, mea Lesbia, atque amemus: let us live, my Lesbia, and let us love (Catullus)

vive sine invidia, mollesque inglorius annos exige, et amicitias sic tibi junge pares: live free from envy and spend your peaceful years without fame, and thus live in friendship with your peers (Ovid)

vive, vale: si quid novisti rectius istis, candidus imperti; si non, his utere mecum: farewell and live well: if you know of any precepts better than these, be so candid as to communicate them; if not, partake of these with me (Horace)

vivendi recte qui prorogat horam, rusticus expectat dum defluat amnis; at ille labitur et labetur in omne volubilis ævum: he who postpones the hour of living rightly is like the yokel who waits till the river shall have passed by; but that river still flows and will continue to flow for all eternity (Horace)

vivendum est recte, cum propter plurima, tum his præcipue causis, ut linguas mancipiorum contemnas; nam lingua mali pars pessima servi: you should live virtuously for many reasons, but particularly on this account, that you may be able to despise the tongues of your domestics; the tongue is the worst part of a bad servant (Juvenal)

vivere si nequis recte, discede peritus: if you know not how to live rightly, leave the society of those who do (Horace)

vivitur exiguo melius: natura beatis omnibus esse dedit, si quis cognoverit uti: men live best upon a little; nature has ordained all to be happy, if they would but learn to use their talents (Claudian)

vivitur parvo bene, cui paternum splendet in mensa tenui salinum; nec leves somnos timor aut cupido sordidus aufert: he lives well on little on whose frugal table the paternal salt-cellar shines, and whose soft slumbers are not disturbed by fear or the sordid passion for gain (Horace)

vivo et regno, simul ista reliqui, quæ vos ad cœlum fertis rumore secundo: I live and am king, as soon as I have left those interests of the city that you exalt to the skies with such praise (Horace)

vivunt in Venerem frondes, etiam nemus omne per altum felix arbor amat; nutant ad mutua palmæ fœdera, populeo suspirat populus ictu, et platani platanis, alnoque assibilat alnus: the leaves live to love, and over the whole lofty grove each happy tree loves; palm nods to palm in mutual pledge of love; the poplar sighs for the poplar's embrace; plane tree whispers to plane tree, and alder to alder (Claudian)

vivunt in Venerum frondes omnisque vicissim felix arbor amat; nutant ad mutua palmæ fœdera: the leaves live but to love, and in all the lofty grove the happy trees love each his neighbor (Claudian)

vix a te videor posse tenere manus: I feel hardly able to keep my hands off you (Ovid)

vixere fortes ante Agamemnona multi; sed omnes illacrymabiles urgentur, ignotique longa nocte, carent quia vate sacro: many brave men lived before Agamemnon; but all of them, unwept and unknown, are overwhelmed in endless night, because they are without a sacred bard to sing their praises (Horace)

vixerunt: they have lived (i.e., they are dead) (Cicero, said of the Catilinarian conspirators)

vixi dubius, anxius morior, nescio quo vado: I have lived in doubt, I die in anxiety, and I know not whither I go

vixi, et quem dederat cursum fortuna, peregi: et nunc magna mei sub terras currit imago: I have lived, and I have run the course that fortune allotted me; and now my shade shall descend illustrious to the grave (Virgil)

volat ambiguis mobilis alis hora; nec ulli præstat velox Fortuna fidem: the shifting hour flies with doubtful wings; nor does swift Fortune keep faith with anyone (Seneca)

vox tantum atque ossa supersunt; vox manet: the voice and bones are all that is left; the voice remains (Ovid)

vulgus ignavum et nihil ultra verba ausurum: a cowardly populace that will dare nothing beyond talk (Tacitus)

vulnus alit venis, et cæco carpitur igni: he (or she) nourishes the poison in the veins, and is consumed by the hidden fire (Virgil, said of love that is hidden)

vulturus in silvis miserum mandebat homonem. Heu!, quam crudeli condebat membra sepulchro!: in the woods a vulture was eating a wretched man. Alas!, what a cruel grave into which his limbs were being buried! (Ennius)

ABBREVIATIONS

A.D. (anno Domini): in the year of our Lord
ad inf. or **ad infin.** (ad infinitum): to infinity (i.e., forever)
ad us. (ad usum): according to usage
æt. or **ætat.** (ætatis; anno ætatis suæ): of the age; in his/her lifetime
a.h.l. (ad hunc locum): at this place
a.h.v. (ad hanc vocem): at this word
A.U.C. (anno urbis conditæ): in the year (or from the time) of the founded
    city (Rome, founded about 753 BCE)
BCE: before the Common Era (i.e., **B.C.**)
b.v. (bene vale): farewell
c. or **ca.** (circa): about
c. or **circ.** (circiter): about
c. or **circ.** (circum): about
CE: in the Common Era (i.e., **A.D.**)
cf. (confer): compare
e.g. or **ex. gr.** (exempli gratia): for example
et al. (et alibi): and elsewhere
et al. (et alii or et aliæ): and others
etc. (et cetera): and so forth
et seq. (et sequens): and the following
et seq. (et sequentes): and what follows
ex. gr. or **e.g.** (exempli gratia): for example
f. or **fem.** (femininum): feminine
fig.: figurative
fl. or **flor.** (floruit): flourished
ib. or **ibid.** (ibidem): in the same place (in a book)
id. (idem): the same as above
i.e. (id est): that is
ign. (ignotus): unknown
inf. (infra): below
i.q. (idem quod): the same as
l.c. (loco citato): in the place cited
loc. cit. (loco citato): in the place cited

m. or **masc.** (masculinum): masculine
m.m. (mutatis mutandis): with the necessary changing being made
MS (manuscriptus): manuscript
MSS (manuscripta): manuscripts
n. (natus): born
N.B. or **n.b.** (nota bene): note well
non obs. (non obstante): notwithstanding
non seq. (non sequitur): it does not follow
o.c. (opere citato): in the work cited
op. cit. (opere citato): in the work cited
pass. (passim): throughout
pct. (per centum): by the hundred
per cent. or **p.c.** (per centum): by the hundred
pl. (pluralis): plural
PPS (post postscriptum): an additional postscript
PS (postscriptum): a postscript
ptc. (participium): a participle
q.e. (quod est): which is
qq.v. (quæ vide): (pl.) which see
q.v. (quod vide): (sing.) which see
sc. (scilicet): that is to say, namely
sec. (secundum): according to
seq. (sequens): (sing.) the following
seq. (sequitur): it follows
seqq. (sequentia): (pl.) the following (things)
sg. or **sing.** (singularis): singular
sup. (supra): above
t. or **temp.** (tempore): in the time of
u.s. (ubi supra): where (mentioned) above
ut inf. or **ut i.** (ut infra): as stated or shown below
ut sup. or **u.s.** (ut supra): as stated or shown above
v. or **vs.** (versus): against
v. (vide): see
v.i. (vide infra): see below
viz. (videlicet): namely
v.s. (vide supra): see above
V.V. or **v.v.** (vice versa): conversely

MAIN AUTHORS CITED

Author	Dates	Type/Genre of Work
Accius (or Attius)	170–c. 86 BCE	Tragedy, Poetry
Afranius	c. 160–120 BCE	Poetry, Comedy
Apuleius	c. 125–? CE	Novel
St. Augustine	354–430 CE	Ecclesiastical writings
Augustus	63 BCE–14 CE	Emperor
Ausonius	c. 310–395 CE	Poetry
Bacon, Sir Francis	1561–1626	Philosophy
Boëthius	c. 480–524 CE	Ecclesiastical writings
Cæcilius Statius	c. 219–166 BCE	Poetry
Caligula (Gaius)	12–41 CE	Emperor
Calvus	82–47 BCE	Oratory, Poetry
Cato "the Censor"	234–149 BCE	Oratory, History
Catullus	c. 84–54 BCE	Poetry
Celsus	fl. c. 14–37 CE	Encyclopædia
Cicero	106–43 BCE	Oratory
Claudian	c. 370–404 CE	Poetry
Coke, Sir Edward	1552–1634	Jurisprudence
Cornelius Nepos	c. 100–25 BCE	History
Curtius	1st Century CE	History
St. Cyprian	c. 200–258 CE	Ecclesiastical writings
Dionysius Cato	c. 200 CE	Ethical Prose
Domitian	51–96 CE	Emperor
Ennius	239–169 BCE	Poetry, Tragedy
Erasmus	1466–1536	Classical scholar
Florus	2nd Century CE	History
Gellius (Aulus Gellius)	c. 130–180 CE	Criticism, Anecdotes
Grotius, Hugo	1583–1645	Jurisprudence
Horace	65–8 BCE	Poetry
St. Jerome (Hieronymus)	c. 347–420 CE	Ecclesiastical writings
Jesus of Nazareth	c. 4 BCE–30 CE	Sermons and Parables

Author	Dates	Type/Genre of Work
Julius Cæsar	102–44 BCE	History
Justinian	482–565 CE	Emperor
Juvenal	c. 60–140 CE	Satire
Laberius	c. 105–43 BCE	Poetry, Mimes
Lactantius	c. 245–325 CE	Ecclesiastical writings
Livy	59 BCE–17 CE	History
Lucan	39–65 CE	Poetry
Lucretius	c. 98–55 BCE	Poetry, Philosophy
Macrobius	fl. c. 400 CE	Scholar
Manilius	1st Century CE	Poetry
Martial	c. 40–104 CE	Poetry
Nævius	c. 270–190 BCE	Poetry, Drama
Nero	37–68 CE	Emperor
Ovid	43 BCE–18 CE	Poetry
Pacuvius	c. 220–130 BCE	Poetry
St. Paul	c. 10–64 CE	Ecclesiastical writings
Persius	34–62 CE	Poetry
Petronius	c. 26-66 CE	Poetry, Satire
Phædrus	c. 15 BCE–50 CE	Poetry, Fables
Plautus	c. 254–184 BCE	Comedy
Pliny the Elder	23–79 CE	History, Biography
Pliny the Younger	61–113 CE	Oratory
Propertius	c. 50–16 BCE	Poetry
Prudentius	c. 348–405 CE	Poetry
Publilius Syrus	fl. 40 BCE	Poetry, Epigrams, Mimes
Quintilian	c. 35–95 CE	Oratory
Sallust	86–35 BCE	History
Scipio Africanus	236–183 BCE	Military
Seneca	c. 4 BCE–65 CE	Rhetoric, Philosophy
Seneca the Elder	c. 55 BCE–40 CE	Oratory, Rhetoric
Sidonius Apollinaris	430–480 CE	Poetry
Silius Italicus	c. 25–101 CE	Poetry
Statius	c. 45–96 CE	Poetry
Suetonius	c. 70–140 CE	History
Symmachus	c. 340–402 CE	Oratory
Tacitus	c. 55–118 CE	History
Terence	185–159 BCE	Comedy
Tertullian	c. 160–230 CE	Ecclesiastical writings
Tiberius	42 BCE–37 CE	Emperor

Author	Dates	Type/Genre of Work
Tibullus	c. 55–19 BCE	Poetry
Titus	39–81 CE	Emperor
Valerius Maximus	fl. c. 15–35 CE	History
Varro	116–27 BCE	Scholar
Vegetius	fl. c. 380 CE	Military
Verrius Flaccus	fl. c. 10 BCE–14 CE	Scholar / Critic
Vespasian	9–79 CE	Emperor
Virgil	70–19 BCE	Poetry

SELECTED ENGLISH–LATIN INDEX

A

a bird in the hand is worth two in the bush (fig.): **ad præsens ova cras pullis sunt meliora**

a blank slate: **tabula rasa**

a body without a soul: **corpus sine pectore**

a book worm: **helluo librorum**

a child of fortune: **fortunæ filius**

a city for sale and ripe for ruin: **urbem venalem et mature perituram**

a claw in the wound: **unguis in ulcere**

a common danger begets unity: **commune periculum concordiam parit**

a constant drip hollows a stone: **stillicidi casus lapidem cavat**

a daughter more beautiful than her beautiful mother: **matre pulchra filia pulchrior**

a dear mother: **alma mater**

a deceiver deals in generalities: **dolosus versatur in generalibus**

a delegate cannot delegate: **delegatus non potest delegare**

a delightful insanity: **amabilis insania**

a disorderly patient makes the physician cruel: **crudelem medicum intemperans æger facit**

a document does not blush: **charta non erubescit**

a dog cannot sing: **canis a non canedo**

a dog in the manger: **canis in præsepi**

a favor ought to be returned: **gratiam referendam**

a favorite son: **fortunæ filius**

a field becomes exhausted by constant tillage: **continua messe senescit ager**

a friend is half of one's soul: **amicus animæ dimidium**

a friend is one soul in two bodies: **amicus est unus animus in duobus corporibus**

a friend is proven in time of necessity: **amicus in necessitate probatur**

a friend is the solace of life: **amicus vitæ solatium**

a friend of the human race: **amicus humani generis**

a friend to the court: **amicus curiæ**

a gift worthy of Apollo: **munus Apolline dignum**

a gilded bit does not make for a better horse: **non faciunt meliorem equum aurei freni**

a god from a machine: **deus ex machina**

a golden key opens any door: **auro quæque janua panditur**

a good judge is one who prevents litigation: **boni judicis est lites dirimere**

a good man is always learning: **bonus vir semper tiro**

a good mind possesses a kingdom: **mens bona regnum possidet**

a government within a government: **imperium in imperio**

a great fortune is a great slavery: **magna servitus est magna fortuna**

a great genius lies hid under this rough exterior: **ingenium ingens inculto latet hoc sub corpore**

a great man can come from a hut: **potest ex casa magnus vir exire**

a great mind becomes a great fortune: **magnam fortunam magnus animus decet**

a great revenue is thrift: **magnum vectigal est parsimonia**

a great step toward goodness is the desire to be good: **pars magna bonitatis est velle fieri bonum**

a guardian of morals: **custos morum**

a guide to those in doubt: **ductor dubitantium**

a hand from the clouds: **manus e nubibus**

a handsome face is a silent recommendation: **formosa facies muta commendatio est**

a harmless thunderbolt: **fulmen brutum** or **brutum fulmen**

a judge is the law speaking: **judex est lex loquens**

a just balance preserves justice: **libra justa justitiam servat**

a knife in the wound (fig.): **unguis in ulcere**

a last farewell: **supremum vale**

a learned person always has riches within: **homo doctus in se semper divitias habet**

a letter does not blush: **epistola non erubescit**

a liar should have a good memory: **mendacem memorem esse oportet**

a life without purpose is an aimless one: **vita sine proposito vaga est**

a madman is punished by his madness: **furiosus furore suo punitur**

a man dies as often as his friends die: **homo totiens moritur quotiens amittit suos** a man is lent, not given, to life: **homo vitæ commodatus non donatus**

a man of great learning: **homo multarum literarum**

a man of no party: **homo nullius coloris**

a man of one book: **homo unius libri**

a man should be religious, not superstitious: **religentem esse oportet, religiosum nefas**

a man, when angry, is beside himself: **homo extra est corpus suum cum irascitur**

a man's oldest friend is his best: **quam veterrimus homini optimus est amicus**

a match for the whole world: **nec pluribus impar**

a mind conscious of integrity: **conscia mens recti**

a mouse does not rely on just one hole: **mus non uni fidit antro**

a new order for the ages: **novus ordo seclorum**

a noble pair of brothers: **par nobile fratrum**

a partner in evil will also be a partner in punishment: **qui socius est in malo, consors erit in supplicio**

a passion for praise: **laudumque immensa cupido**

a picture is a silent poem: **mutum est pictura poëma**

a pig of Epicurus: **porcus Epicuri**

a pious fraud: **pia fraus**

a pleasing countenance is no small advantage: **auxilium non leve vultus habet**

a poet is born, not made: **poëta nascitur, non fit**

a poverty of words: **verborum paupertas**

a precipice before me, wolves behind me: **a fronte præcipitium a tergo lupi**

a quiet journey in the untrodden paths of life: **secretum iter et fallentis semita vitæ**

a rare bird on earth: **rara avis in terris**

a rolling stone gathers no moss: **lapis qui volvitur algam non generat**

a shipwreck of fortune: **fortunæ naufragium**

a single light suffices in the darkness: **sufficit unum lumen in tenebris**

a slip of the tongue: **lapsus linguæ**

a small kitchen does not suffice for two gluttons: **parvam culinam duobus ganeonibus non sufficere**

a snake in the grass: **anguis in herba**

a son of the earth: **terræ filius**

a sound conscience is a bronze wall: **murus æneus conscientia sana**

a sound mind in a healthy body: **mens sana in corpore sano**

a storm is gathering in the poetic world: **poëtica surgit tempestas**

a strong shield is the safety of leaders: **forte scutum, salus ducum** a thing desired: **desideratum**

a tree is known by its fruit: **fructo cognoscitur arbor**

a tree makes progress when transplanted: **translata proficit arbos**

a true friend is a rare bird: **amicus verus rara avis**

a venal flock: **grex venalium**

a very small spark has often kindled a great conflagration: **parvula scintilla sæpe magnum suscitavit incendium**

a vicar cannot have a vicar: **vicarius non habet vicarium**

a whetstone to their wit: **cos ingeniorum**

a will-o'-the-wisp (fig.): **ignis fatuus**

a word once spoken cannot be recalled: **verbum emissum non est revocabile**

a word to the wise: **verbum sapienti**

a word to the wise is sufficient: **verbum sat sapienti**

a worthless vessel is seldom broken: **malum vas non frangitur**

a year filled with wonders: **annus mirabilis**

abnormally wise: **abnormis sapiens**

abstain from license: **licentiam retrœna**

abundance has made him poor: **inopem copia fecit**

abundant caution does no harm: **abundans cautela non nocet**

abuse does not take away use: **abusus non tollit usum**

act according to your strength: **agite pro viribus**

act your office: **age officium tuum**

adversity reminds men of religion: **adversæ res admonent religionum**

adversity tries men: **explorant adversa viros**

advise with salt (discretion): **mone sale**

after death no pleasure remains: **post mortem nulla voluptas**

after sexual intercourse, every animal is sad: **post coitum omne animal triste**

after the fact: **ex post facto**

against good morals: **contra bonos mores**

age carries everything away, even the mind: **omnia fert ætas, animum quoque**

aim at a sure thing: **certum pete finem**

alas!, the years glide swiftly away: **eheu!, fugaces labuntur anni**

alert at the beginning, careless at the end: **acribus initiis, incurioso fine**

all a mortal's works must perish: **mortalia facta peribunt**

all art is an imitation of nature: **omnis ars imitatio est naturæ**

all at once: **per saltum**

all beginnings are small: **omnia rerum principia parva sunt** all in all: **summa summarum**

all is vanity: **omnia vanitas**

all love is vanquished by a new love: **successore novo vincitur omnis amor**

all of Gaul is divided into three parts: **Gallia est omnis divisa in partes tres**

all that is mine I carry with me: **omnia mea mecum porto**

all that is most ancient is a lie: **antiquissima quæque commenticia**

all the world plays the actor: **totus mundus agit histrionem**

all things are common among friends: **communia esse amicorum inter se omnia**

all things are full of God: **Dei plena sunt omnia**

all things are full of the god Jove: **sunt Jovis omnia plena**

all things are good to the good: **bonis omnia bona**

all things are obedient to money: **pecunia obediunt omnia**

all things at Rome may be bought for a price: **omnia Romæ cum pretio**

all things change, and we ourselves change with them: **omnia mutantur, nos et mutamur in illis**

all things come from above: **omnia desuper** or **omnia de super**

all this flour is not from your sack: **non est de sacco tanta farina tuo**

all together and all as one: **semel et simul**

always and everywhere: **semper et ubique**

always faithful: **semper fidelis**

always happy: **semper felix**

always ready: **semper paratus**

always ready to serve my country: **semper patriæ servire præsto**

always the same: **semper eadem** or **semper idem**

always watchful: **semper vigilans**

among friends all things are common: **inter amicos omnium rerum communitas**

among the living: **inter vivos**

an angry lover tells himself many lies: **amans iratus multa mentitur**

an ass at the lyre: **asinus ad lyram**

an eagle does not catch flies: **aquila non capit muscas**

an empire within an empire: **imperium in imperio**

an empty cask is easily rolled: **dolium volvitur**

an empty threat (fig.): **fulmen brutum** or **brutum fulmen**

an enemy of the human race: **hostis humani generis**

an error that is not resisted is approved: **error qui non resistitur approbatur**

an evil gain equals a loss: **lucrum malum æquale dispendio**

an evil tongue is the proof of an evil mind: **lingua mali loquax malæ mentis est indicium** an honorable death is better than a dishonorable life: **honesta mors turpi vita potior**

an Iliad in a nutshell: **in nuce Iliad**

an Iliad of woes: **Ilias malorum**

an incurable passion to write: **insanabile cacoëthes scribendi**

an indispensable condition: **sine qua non**

an itch for disputation is the mange of the Church: **disputandi pruritas ecclesiarum scabies**

an itch for finding fault: **cacoëthes carpendi**

an itch for speaking: **cacoëthes loquendi**

an itch for writing: **cacoëthes scribendi**

an offense against a person of high standing: **scandalum magnatum**

an old man is twice a boy: **senex bis puer**

an opportunity is often lost through deliberation: **deliberando sæpe perit occasio**

an ox on the tongue: **bos in lingua**

an undazzled eye to the sun: **illæso lumine solum**

an unknown land or region: **terra incognita**

and seek for truth in the groves of the Academy: **atque inter silvas Academi quærere verum**

and the fields where Troy once was: **et campos ubi Troja fuit**

and yet in the king there is the father: **atque in rege tamen pater est**

and yet, the longest day soon comes to an end: **quamquam longissimus, dies cito conditur**

anger assists hands however weak: **quamlibet infirmas adjuvat ira manus**

anger is a brief madness: **ira furor brevis est**

anger manages everything badly: **male cuncta ministrat impetus**

another and the same: **aliud et idem**

applause is the reward of virtue: **merces virtutis laus est**

Arcadians both: **Arcades ambo**

arms are the buttresses of peace: **arma pacis fulcra**

arms cause laws to be respected: **leges arma tenent sanctas**

arms maintain peace: **arma tuentur pacem**

art for art's sake: **ars gratia artis**

art is long, life is short: **ars longa, vita brevis**

as bees taste of everything in the flowery meadows: **floriferis ut apes in saltibus omnia libant**

as in life, so in death: **qualis vita, finis ita**

as is the face so is the mind: **facies qualis mens talis**

as long as the pot boils, friendship lasts: **fervet olla, vivit amicitia**

as to yourself so to another: **ut tibi sic alteri**

as you have sown, so also shall you reap: **ut sementem feceris ita et metes**

at last, at last, justice prevails: **tandem tandem justitia obtinet**

at the point of death: **in articulo mortis**

at war and at peace: **domi militiæque**

at what price fame?: **quanti fama?**

Athanasius against the world: **Athanasius contra mundum**

Attic wit: **sal Atticum**

avarice is rich, while modesty is poor: **est aviditas dives, et pauper pudor**

avoid excess: **ne quid nimis**

away with the lies of poets!: **valeant mendacia vatum!**

B

bad advice is often fatal to the adviser: **malum consilium consultori pessimum**

bad faith: **mala fides**

bad grammar does not vitiate a contract: **mala grammatica non vitiat chartam**

bad hen, bad egg: **mala gallina, malum ovum**

bad mind, bad designs: **mala mens, malus animus**

be as wise as the serpent and gentle as the dove: **esto prudens ut serpens et simplex scut columba**

be busy and you will be safe: **res age, tute eris**

be first, that you may be of service: **præsis ut prosis**

be it unsaid: **indictum sit**

be silent: **tace**

be silent and you will pass for a philosopher: **sile et philosophus esto**

be what you seem to be: **etiam quod esse videris**

bear patiently with a rival: **rivalem patienter habe**

beauty is a flower, fame is a breath: **forma flos, fama flatus**

beauty is a fragile good: **forma bonum fragile est**

before the court of conscience: **in foro conscientiæ**

behind the horseman sits dark care: **post equitem sedet atra cura**

behold the Lamb of God: **ecce Agnus Dei**

behold the man: **ecce homo**

behold the sign: **ecce signum**

believe that you have it, and you have it: **crede quod habes, et habes**

beneath one's dignity: **infra dignitatem**

better death than dishonor: **malo mori quam fœdari**

better late than never: **potius sero quam nunquam** or **præstat sero quam nunquam**

better things to come: **in dies meliora**

between hope and fear: **inter spem et metum**

between the hammer and the anvil: **inter malleum et incudem**

beware of the dog: **cave canem**

beware of the double-tongued: **bilingues cavendi**

beware of the man of one book: **cave ab homine unius libri**

beware what you say, when, and to whom: **cave quid dicis, quando et cui**

beyond one's powers: **supra vires**

beyond the walls: **extra muros**

blessed are the peace makers: **beati pacifici**

blessed are the poor in spirit: **beati pauperes spiritu**

blessed is the one who comes in the name of the Lord: **benedictus qui venit in nomine Domini**

blessed is the one-eyed person in the country of the blind: **beati monoculi in regione cærcorum**

bodies are slow in growth, rapid in decay: **corpora lente augescunt, cito extinguuntur**

bones for those who come late: **sero venientibus ossa**

born to consume the fruits of the earth: **fruges consumere nati**

bound for hell (fig.): **pabulum Acherontis**

boys read books one way, men another, old men another: **aliud legunt pueri, aliud viri, aliud senes**

brave men are begotten by the brave and good: **fortes creantur fortibus et bonis**

brave men have no need of walls: **viris fortibus non opus est mœnibus**

bread and the circus games: **panem et circenses**

but hope is not broken: **at spes non fracta**

but hope is unbroken: **at spes infracta**

but who will guard the guardians themselves?: **sed quis custodiet ipsos custodes?**

but you cannot escape my iambics: **at non effugies meos iambos**

by a leap: **per saltum**

by all possible means (fig.): **velis et remis**

by common consent: **communi consensu**

by divine favor: **benigno numine**

by divine providence: **providentia divina**

by God's favor: **favente Deo**

by pruning it grows green: **abscissa virescit**

by sea and by land: **per mare per terram**

by the favor of heaven: **benigno numine**

by the grace of God: **Dei gratia**

by this sign you will conquer: **in hoc signo vinces**

by virtue of office: **ex officio**

C

cabbage repeated is the death of the wretched masters: **occidit miseros crambe
repetita magistros**

Cæsar has no authority over the grammarians: **Cæsar non supra grammaticos**

calm amid the raging waters: **sævis tranquillus in undis**

care brings grey hairs: **cura facit canos**

Carthage must be destroyed: **Carthago delenda est**

catch as catch can: **capiat qui capere possit**

Cato against the world: **Cato contra mundum**

caught between a wolf and a cliff: **a fronte præcipitium a tergo lupi**

caught in the act: **flagrante delicto**

cause it to be done: **fieri facias**

cause it to be known: **scire facias**

change but the name, and the tale is told of you: **mutato nomine, de te fabula narratur**

charity begins at home: **prima caritas incipit a seipso**

cheerful for others, wise for himself: **aliis lætus, sapiens sibi**

close your mouth, open your eyes: **claude os, aperi oculos**

cobbler, stick to your last: **sutor, ne supra crepidam**

come, let us adore the Lord: **venite adoremus Dominum**

comity among nations: **comitas inter gentes**

conscience is as a thousand witnesses: **conscientia mille testes**

consent makes law: **consensus facit legem**

consider the outcome: **respice finem**

control your temper: **compesce mentem**

could you keep from laughing, friends?: **risum teneatis, amici?**

counsel is of no effect after the fact: **post factum nullum consilium** craftier than a cuckoo: **astutior coccyge**

create in me a clean heart, O God: **cor mundum crea in me, Deus**

crocodile tears: **crocodili lacrimæ** or **lacrimæ simulatæ**

cruel necessity: **dira necessitas**

cruel poverty: **sæva paupertas**

D

dare to be wise, begin at once: **sapere aude, incipe**

day presses on the heels of day: **truditur dies die**

dead men tell no tales (fig.): **mortui non mordant**

death dissolves all things: **mors omnia solvit**

death is a swift rider: **cita mors ruit**

death is common to all things: **mors omnibus communis**

death is common to every age: **omni ætati mors est communis**

death is everywhere: **undique mors est**

death is the gate of life: **mors janua vitæ**

death is the last boundary of things: **mors ultima linea rerum est**

death levels all things: **omnia mors æquat**

death pursues the man even as he flees from it: **mors et fugacem persequitur virum**

death rather than disgrace: **mors potius macula**

deceit deserves deceit: **fraus meretur fraudem**

deeds not words: **facta non verba**

deep calls unto deep: **abyssus abyssum invocat**

defend what you have won: **parta tueri**

defender of the faith: **fidei defensor** or **defensor fidei**

delays in the law are odious: **dilationes in lege sunt odiosæ**

deliver us from evil: **libera nos a malo**

deliver yourself from the fear of death: **libera te metu mortis**

deny it, if you did it: **nega, si fecisti**

different strokes for different folks: **suus cuique mos est**

difficult things become easier with practice: **dura usu molliora**

direct us, O Lord: **dirige nos, Domine**

disaster awaits the wicked on every side: **malo undique clades**

disgrace is immortal: **hominum immortalis est infamia**

divide and rule: **divide et impera**

do not aim at too much popularity: **cupias non placuisse nimis**

do not celebrate your triumph before you have conquered: **ante victoriam ne canas triumphum**

do not disturb things at rest: **quieta non movere**

do not do what is done: **actum ne agas**

do not entrust a sword to a boy: **ne puero gladium**

do not go forward in your hatred: **ulterius ne tende odiis**

do not pluck the beard of a dead lion: **noli barbam vellere mortuo leoni**

do not provoke the lions: **noli irritare leones**

do not stir the fire with a sword: **ignem ne gladio fodito**

do not trumpet your almsgiving: **noli tuba canere Eleemosynam**

do not trust the horse, Trojans: **equo ne credite, Teucri**

do this and you shall live: **hoc fac et vives**

do to another as to yourself: **alteri sic tibi**

do you count your birthdays thankfully?: **natales grate numeras?**

drunkenness kills more than the sword: **plures crapula quam gladius**

dry land: **terra firma**

during life: **durante vita**

E

each one is drawn by his own delight: **trahit sua quemque voluptas**

each person is the architect of his own fortune: **faber est quisque fortunæ suæ**

each person's homeland is dear to him: **patria cuique chara**

eagles do not beget doves: **non generant aquilæ columbas**

earth, air, fire, water: **terra, flatus, ignis, aqua**

easy come, easy go: **male parta male dilabuntur**

easy is the descent to hell: **facilis est descensus Averni**

eggs today are better than chickens tomorrow: **ad præsens ova cras pullis sunt meliora**

either death or victory: **aut mors aut victoria**

either I will find a way or make one: **aut inveniam viam aut faciam**

either victory or death: **aut vincere aut mori**

elder ones first: **seniores priores**

eloquence is difficult: **facundia difficilis**

eloquence, the mistress of all the arts: **omnium artium domina eloquentia**

enough said: **satis verborum**

entrust trifles to fools: **fatuis levia committito**

envy aims very high: **summa petit livor**

envy feeds upon the living: **pascitur in vivis livor**

envy is blind: **cæca invidia est**

equity follows the law: **æquitas sequitur legem**

even a fly gets angry: **habet et musca splenem**

even a hair has its shadow: **vel capillus habet umbram suam**

even ants get angry: **inest et formicæ sua bilis**

even brave men are alarmed by sudden terrors: **etiam fortes viros subitis terreri**

even one hair has a shadow: **etiam capillus unus habet umbram**

even savage bears agree among themselves: **sævis inter se convenit ursis**

even tears at times have the weight of speech: **interdum lacrimæ pondera vocis habent**

even the fountains complain of thirst: **fontes ipsi sitiunt**

even the gods love jokes: **jocos et dii amant**

even the ruins have perished: **etiam periere ruinæ**

even war has its laws: **habet et bellum suas leges**

even while they teach, men learn: **homines dum docent discunt**

ever faithful: **semper fidelis**

ever fortunate: **semper felix**

ever higher: **excelsior**

ever watchful: **semper vigilans**

every animal loves itself: **omne animal seipsum diligit**

every lover is a soldier and has his camp in Cupid: **militat omnis amans et habet sua castra Cupido**

every lover is demented: **omnis amans amens**

every madman thinks all others insane: **insanus omnis furere credit cæteros**

every man is the maker of his own fortune: **est unusquisque faber ipsæ suæ fortunæ**

every monarch is subject to a mightier one: **omnes sub regno graviore regnum est**

every vice ever stands on a precipice: **omne in præcipiti vitium stetit**

everyone is nearest to himself: **quisque sibi proximus**

everyone's life is dark to himself: **sua cuique vita obscura est**

everything becomes mellower with time: **tempore cuncta mitiora**

everything living comes from an egg: **omne vivum ex ovo**

everything rises but to fall, and grows but to decay: **omnia orta occidunt, et aucta senescunt**

everything unknown is thought to be magnificent: **omne ignotum pro magnifico est**

everything which is born passes away: **deficit omne quod nascitur** everywhere horror seizes the soul: **horror ubique animos**

everywhere the poor man is despised: **pauper ubique jacet**

everywhere to remember our homeland: **ubique patriam reminisci**

expect from Heaven what you have done to another: **ab alto speres alteri quod feceris**

experience bought with pain teaches: **empta dolore docet experientia**

experience is the teacher of fools: **stultorum eventus magister est**

experience teaches: **experientia docet**

external actions indicate internal secrets: **acta exteriora indicant interiora secreta**

extreme law, extreme injury: **summum jus, summa injuria**

extreme law is often extreme wrong: **jus summum sæpe summa malitia est**

F

faith, hope, love: **fides, spes, charitas**

faith is stronger than a lion: **leone fortior fides**

faith seeking understanding: **fides quærens intellectum**

faithful Achates: **fidus Achates**

faithful always: **semper fidelis**

faithful even to death: **fidelis usque ad mortem**

faithful till death: **ad mortem fidelis**

faithful to the end: **ad finem fidelis**

faithful to the memory of my ancestors: **servata fides cineri**

false in one thing, false in everything: **falsus in uno, falsus in omnibus**

falsehood is nothing but an imitation of truth: **nihil est aliud falsitas nisi veritatis imitatio**

fame does not always err; sometimes it chooses well: **haud semper errat fama; aliquando et elegit**

fame never reports things in their true light: **nunquam ad liquidum fama perducitur**

fame nourishes the arts: **honos alit artes**

familiarity breeds contempt: **nimia familiaritas parit contemptum**

farewell and applaud: **valete ac plaudite**

farewell to the drama: **valeat res ludicra**

faster, higher, stronger: **citius, altius, fortius**

fate leads the willing and drags the unwilling: **ducunt volentem fata, nolentem trahunt**

favor with your tongues: **favete linguis**

fear betrays ignoble souls: **degeneres animos timor arguit** fear causes anger to subside: **cadit ira metu**

fear gave wings to his feet: **pedibus timor addidit alas**

few are unwilling to sin, all know how: **peccare pauci nolunt, nulli nesciunt**

fidelity bought with money is overcome by money: **pretio parata vincitur pretio fides**

fields left fallow recover their fertility: **derelicta fertilius revivescunt**

fire from fire: **ab igne ignem**

fire is fed by the wind and extinguished by the wind: **nutritur vento, vento restinguitur ignis**

first by time, first by right: **prior tempore, prior jure**

first come, first served (fig.): **prior tempore, prior jure**

flame is close to smoke: **flamma fumo est proxima**

florets of thought: **flosculi sententiarum**

flying to the heavens: **ad cœlos volans**

food for Acheron: **pabulum Acherontis**

fools are without number: **stulti sunt innumerabiles**

fools laugh at the Latin language: **rident stolidi verba Latina**

footprints do not go backwards: **vestigia nulla retrorsum**

for ages and ages: **in sæcula sæculorum**

for and against: **pro et contra**

for Christ and country: **pro Christo et patria**

for God and country: **pro Deo et patria**

for God so loved the world that he gave his only-begotten Son: **sic enim dilexit Deus mundum, ut Filium suum unigenitum daret**

for heaven's sake!: **per deos immortales!**

for king and country: **pro rege et patria**

for king, law, and the people: **pro rege, lege, et grege**

for the letter kills, but the spirit breathes life: **littera occidit, spiritus vivicat**

for the love of country: **pro patriæ amore**

for the perpetual remembrance of a thing: **ad perpetuam rei memoriam**

for the public good: **pro bono publico**

for the wages of sin is death: **stipendia enim peccati mors est**

for the welfare of the soul: **pro salute animæ**

for there is nothing sillier than a silly laugh: **nam risu inepto res ineptior nulla est**

for whose benefit?: **cui bono?**

for whose detriment?: **cui malo?**

force, lacking judgment, collapses by its own weight: **vis consilii expers mole ruit sua**

forever and ever: **in sæcula sæculorum**

forever faithful: **semper fidelis**

forewarned, forearmed: **præmonitus, præmunitus**

forgive and you will be forgiven: **ferto, fereris**

forgive others often, yourself never: **ignoscito sæpe alteri nunquam tibi**

fortune does not change nature: **fortuna non mutat genus**

fortune favors fools: **fortuna favet fatuis**

fortune favors the brave: **fortuna juvat audaces**

fortune finds us friends: **res amicos invenit**

fortune is blind: **fortuna cæca est**

fortune is gentle to the lowly: **minor in parvis fortuna furit**

Fortune shields more than it makes safe: **plures tegit Fortuna quam tutos facit**

Fortune smiles upon our first effort: **aspirat primo Fortuna labori**

Fortune spurns the prayers of cowards: **ignavis precibus Fortuna repugnat**

foul in the beginning, foul in the end: **fœdum inceptu, fœdum exitu**

friends are proved by adversity: **amici probantur rebus adversis**

friends are thieves of time: **amicos esse fures temporis**

from a high mountain: **de monte alto**

from a pure spring pure water flows: **a fonte puro pura defluit aqua**

from bad morals good laws are produced: **leges bonæ ex malis moribus procreantur**

from bad morals good laws have sprung: **ex malis moribus bonæ leges natæ sunt**

from day to day: **de die in diem**

from head to heel: **a capite ad calcem**

from nothing, nothing is made: **ex nihilo nihil fit**

from one learn all: **ab uno disce omnes** or **ex uno disce omnes**

from one to all: **ab uno ad omnes**

from possibility to actuality: **a posse ad esse**

from sea to sea: **a mari usque ad mare**

from the beginning: **ab initio**

from the bottom of the heart: **imo pectore**

from the depths I have cried unto you, O Lord: **de profundis clamavi ad te, Domine**

from the founding of the city: **ab urbe condita**

from the words of the law there is no departure: **a verbis legis non est recedendum**

from top to bottom (fig.): **a capite ad calcem**

from words to blows: **a verbis ad verbera**

full of men, vacant of friends: **hominibus plenum, amicis vacuum**

G

get thee behind me, you satan!: **vade post me, satana!**

gifts of enemies are unlucky: **inimicorum dona, infausta**

give alms to Belisarius: **date obolum Belisario**

give and it shall be given to you: **date, et dabitur vobis**

give glory to God: **da gloriam Deo**

give me a place to stand and I will move the earth: **da ubi consistam, et terram movebo**

give me a thousand kisses: **da mi basia mille**

give me chastity and continency, but not yet: **da mihi castitatem et continentiam, sed noli modo**

give place to your betters: **da locum melioribus**

give to faith what belongs to faith: **da fidei quæ fidei sunt**

give unto God: **Deo date**

given as a gift: **dono dedit**

giving has no bottom: **largitio fundum non habet**

giving requires good sense: **res est ingeniosa dare**

Glory be to the Father: **Gloria Patri**

glory comes too late after one has died: **post cineres gloria sera venit**

glory to God in the highest, and peace on earth to men of good will: **gloria in excelsis Deo, et in terra pax hominibus bonæ voluntatis**

go in peace: **vade in pacem**

go, the mass is over: **ite, missa est**

go with me: **vade mecum**

God be with you: **Deus vobiscum**

God enriches: **ditat Deus**

God finds out the guilty: **reperit Deus nocentem**

God forbid!: **Deus avertat!**

God gives short horns to the cruel ox: **dat Deus immiti cornua curta bovi**

God grant!: **Deus det!**

God has his dwelling within every good man: **in unoquoque virorum bonorum habitat Deus**

God helping: **juvante Deo**

God is best known in not knowing him: **Deus scitur melius nesciendo**

God is my shepherd: **Deus pastor meus**

God is my shield: **Deus clypeus meus**

God is my strength: **Deus fortitudo mea**

God is the greatest good: **Deus est summum bonum**

God pilots the ship: **Deus gubernat navem**

God will provide: **Deus providebit**

God will put an end to these troubles as well: **dabit Deus his quoque finem**

God willing: **Deo volente**

God wills it: **Deus id vult**

God's beloved are in want of nothing: **cara Deo nihilo carent**

God's will be done: **fiat Dei voluntas**

gold has conquered the fear of death: **formidinem mortis vicit aurum**

good friends appear in difficulties: **in angustis amici boni apparent**

good hope gives strength: **spes bona dat vires**

good laws grow out of evil acts: **bonæ leges malis ex moribus proceantur**

good men ought to fear nothing from the rich: **bonis a divitibus nihil timendum**

good wine makes men's hearts rejoice: **bonum vinum lætificat cor hominis**

grace to you and peace: **gratia vobis et pax**

grant them eternal rest, O Lord: **requiem æternam dona eis, Domine**

grant us peace: **dona nobis pacem**

great city, great solitude: **magna civitas, magna solitudo**

great fear is concealed under daring: **audendo magnus tegitur timor**

great is the force of habit: **magna est vis consuetudinis**

greater is the terror of something unknown: **major ignotarum rerum est terror**

H

hail Mary, full of grace, the Lord is with you: **ave Maria, gratia plena, Dominus tecum**

hale (or hail) and farewell: **ave atque vale**

happiness has many friends: **felicitas multos habet amicos**

happy is the one who owes nothing: **felix qui nihil debet**

haste is late: **festinatio tarda est**

hated governments never last long: **invisa numquam imperia retinentur diu**

he calls a hoe a hoe: **ligonem ligonem vocat**

he conquers twice who conquers himself: **bis vincit qui se vincit**

he conquers who conquers himself: **vincit qui se vincit**

he directs his course towards heaven: **ad cœlum tendit**

he falls into Scylla in struggling to escape Charybdis: **incidit in Scyllam qui vult vitare Charybdim** he fills his mind with an idle picture: **animum pictura pascit inani**

he follows his father with unequal steps: **sequitur patrem non passibus æquis**

he gives twice who gives on time: **bis dat qui temptestive donat**

he gives twice who gives quickly: **bis dat qui cito dat**

he grows worse with the treatment: **ægrescit medendo**

He has favored our undertaking: **annuit cœptis**

he hurts the good who spares the bad: **bonis nocet quisquis pepercerit malis**

he is led, not drawn: **ducitur, non trahitur**

he is wide of the mark: **longe aberrat scopo**

he is wise who watches: **sapiens qui vigilat**

he lives twice who lives well: **bis vivit qui bene vivit**

he lives well who lives industriously: **bene qui sedulo**

he lives well who lives peacefully: **bene qui pacifice**

he mixes what is useful and sweet: **miscuit utile dulci**

he portrays a dolphin in the woods and a boar in the waves: **delphinum silvis appingit,**
    fluctibus aprum

he rejoices at having made his way by ruin: **gaudetque viam fecisse ruina**

he sends his gift with a hook attached: **sua munera mittit cum hamo**

he threatens the innocent who spares the guilty: **minatur innocentibus**
    qui parcit nocentibus

he touched nothing which he did not adorn: **nihil quod tetigit non ornavit**

he trembles before the trumpet sounds: **ante tubam trepidat**

he was spurred on by rival valor: **stimulos dedit æmula virtus**

he was stirring up billows in a ladle: **excitabat fluctus in simpulo**

he who hurts in life, heals in death: **qui vivens lædit morte medetur**

he who is silent consents: **qui tacet consentit**

he who proves too much proves nothing: **qui nimium probat, nihil probat**

he will have most who desires least: **is plurimum habebit qui minimum desiderabit**

hear the other party: **audi alteram partem**

heart and hand: **cor et manus**

heaven at last!: **denique cælum** or **denique cœlum**

help from on high: **auxilium ab alto**

here and everywhere: **hic et ubique**

here and now: **hic et nunc**

here is Rhodes, here leap: **hic Rhodos, hic salta**

here lies: **hic jacet**

his only sin is that he does not sin: **nihil peccat nisi quod nihil peccat** hold your tongue: **favete linguis**

honesty is often goaded to ruin: **ad perniciem solet agi sinceritas**

honesty is praised and is left out to freeze: **probitas laudatur et alget**

honesty is the best policy: **candide secure**

honor has its burdens: **honos habet onus**

honor is the reward of virtue: **honor est præmium virtutis**

honor nourishes the arts: **honos alit artes**

honors are enhanced by merit: **meritus augentur honores**

horrible to see!: **horribile visu!**

horrible to tell!: **horribile dictu!**

horses and poets should be fed, not pampered: **equi et poëtæ alendi, non saginandi**

human affairs are a jest to be wept over: **res sunt humanæ flebile ludibrium**

human nature is greedy of novelty: **natura hominum novitatis avida**

hunger is the best of seasonings: **fames optimum condimentum**

hunger sweetens beans: **fabas indulcet fames**

hunger teaches many things: **multa docet fames**

hunger that impels the crime: **malesuada fames**

hush money (fig.): **bos in lingua**

hypocrites are the offspring of vipers: **hypocritæ progenies viperarum**

I

I am a man: **homo sum**

I am bored: **tædet me**

I am Davus, not Oedipus: **Davus sum, non Œdipus**

I am king of the Romans and above grammar: **ego sum rex Romanus et supra grammaticam**

I am my own friend: **ipse amicus**

I am the good shepherd: **ego sum pastor bonus**

I am the light of the world: **lux sum mundi**

I am the resurrection and the life: **ego sum resurrectio et vita**

I am the true vine: **ego sum vitis vera**

I am the way and the truth and the life: **ego sum via et veritas et vita**

I am what I am: **sum quod sum**

I am who I am: **ego sum qui sum**

I believe in one God: **credo in unum Deum**

I came, I saw, I conquered: **veni, vidi, vici**

I commit the rest to fortune: **fortunæ cætera mando**

I confess to God the Almighty: **confiteor Deo omnipotenti**

I do not like those who are too diligent: **non amo nimium diligentes**

I do not purchase hope for a price: **ego spem pretio non emo**

I do not wish to pluck the beard of a dead lion: **nolo barbam vellere mortuo leoni**

I eat, therefore I am: **edo, ergo ego sum** or **edo, ergo sum**

I fear the Greeks bearing gifts: **timeo Danaos dona ferentes**

I fear the man of one book: **timeo hominem unius libri**

I follow, but I am not inferior: **sequor non inferior** or **sequor nec inferior**

I give back tit for tat: **par pari referto**

I give that you may give: **do ut des**

I had rather buy than beg: **emere malo quam rogare**

I hate and I love: **odi et amo**

I hate the profane masses and keep them at a distance: **odi profanum vulgus et arceo**

I have fought the good fight: **bonum certamen certavi**

I have found it: **eureka**

I have not, I want not, I care not: **nec habeo, nec careo, nec curo**

I have piled Pelion on Olympus: **Pelion imposuisse Olympo**

I have scaled heaven (fig.): **Pelion imposuisse Olympo**

I have sinned: **peccavi**

I have sworn with my tongue, but my mind is unsworn: **juravi lingua, mentem injuratam gero**

I hold a wolf by the ears: **auribus teneo lupum**

I hope for a heavenly crown: **cœlestem spero coronam**

I hope for better things: **spero meliora**

I hope in the Cross: **in cruce spero**

I keep faith: **fidem servo**

I know in whom I have believed: **scio enim cui credidi**

I love: **amo**

I love as I find: **amo ut invenio**

I love the treason but I do not praise the traitor: **proditionem amo, sed proditorem non laudo**

I pity you and vex myself: **tui me miseret, mei piget**

I see and approve the better things but I follow the worse: **video meliora proboque deteriora sequor**

I seek higher things: **altiora peto**

I shall rise again: **resurgam**

I should wish to be rather than to seem: **esse quam videri malim**

I sleep not: **non dormis**

I speak from experience: **expertus dico**

I suspect that hunger was my mother: **famem fuisse suspicor matrem mihi**

I think that the first virtue is that of holding the tongue: **virtutum primam esse puta compescere linguam**

I think, therefore I am: **cogito ergo sum**

I too have been to Arcadia: **et ego in Arcadia**

I will be borne on no common, no feeble, wing: **non usitata, nec tenui ferar penna**

I will sing to myself and the Muses: **canam mihi et Musis**

I wish this unsaid: **hoc indictum volo**

I would rather be ill than idle: **malo mihi male quam molliter esse**

I would rather die than be dishonored: **malo mori quam fœdari**

I wrap myself in my virtue: **mea virtute me involvo**

I wrap myself in virtue: **virtute me involvo**

idleness is the blight of genius: **ærugo animi, rubigo ingenii**

idleness waits for its destiny: **otium sortem exspectat**

if fortune favors: **si fortuna juvat**

if God is for us, who is against us?: **si Deus pro nobis, quis contra nos?**

if I cannot bend heaven then I shall stir up hell: **flectere si nequeo superos, Acheronta movebo**

if I may be allowed to compare small things with great: **si componere magnis parva mihi fas est**

if only life remain, I am content: **vita dum superest, bene est**

if the head aches all the members languish: **si caput dolet omnia membra languent**

if you are at Rome, live in the Roman style: **si fueris Romæ, Romano vivito more**

if you did it, deny it: **si fecisti, nega**

if you seek his monument, look around you: **si monumentum requiris, circumspice**

if you want peace, then prepare for war: **sis pacem, para bellum**

if you want to be loved, then love: **si vis amari, ama**

ignorance is bliss: **ignoti nulla cupido**

ignorance of the fact excuses: **ignorantia facti excusat**

ignorance of the law excuses no one: **ignorantia legis neminem excusat**

ignoring the point at issue: **ignoratio elenchi**

ill-gotten, ill-spent: **male parta male dilabuntur**

in all things love: **in omnibus caritas**

in all things prepared: **in omnia paratus**

in Christ's name: **in Christi nomine**

in desire swiftness itself is delay: **etiam celeritas in desiderio mora est**

in eternal remembrance: **memoria in æterna**

in everlasting remembrance of an event or thing: **in perpetuam rei memoriam**

in everything truth surpasses its imitation: **in omni re vincit imitationem veritas**

in generalities lurks deception: **in generalibus latet dolus**

in generalities lurks error: **in generalibus latet error**

in God we trust: **in Deo speramus**

in good faith: **bona fide**

in heaven is rest: **in cælo quies**

in heaven is salvation: **in cælo salus**

in memory of: **in memoriam**

in peace they are lions, in battle they are deer: **in pace leones, in prælio cervi**

in silence: **sub silentio**

in so many words: **in totidem verbis**

in the likeness of all: **ad instar omnium**

in the Lord we trust: **in Domino confido**

in the name of the Father, the Son, and the Holy Spirit: **in nomine Patris et Filii et Spiritus Sancti**

in the name of the Lord every evil begins: **in nomine Domini incipit omne malum**

in the nature of things: **in rerum natura**

in the night is counsel: **in nocte consilium**

in the open air (fig.): **sub Jove**

in the presence of the people: **coram populo**

in the tail is poison: **in cauda venenum**

in the whole the part is also contained: **in toto et pars continetur**

in the year of our Lord: **anno Domini**

in the year of the founding of the city: **anno urbis conditæ**

in this place: **hoc loco**

in this sign you will conquer: **in hoc signo vinces**

in time of war, the laws are silent: **inter arma leges silent**

in trying to be concise, I become obscure: **brevis esse laboro, obscurus fio**

in war, it is not permitted to err twice: **non licet in bello bis peccare**

in wine is truth: **in vino veritas**

industry enriches: **diligentia ditat**

into Thy hands I commend my spirit: **in manus tuas commendo spiritum meum** iron is sharpened by iron: **ferrum ferro acuitur**

it always flourishes: **semper viret**

it becomes a young man to be modest: **adolescentem verecundum esse decet**

it breaks against a solid: **infringit solido**

it grows as it goes: **crescit eundo**

it hangs by a hair: **de pilo pendet**

it hangs by a thread: **de filo pendet**

it happens in a moment, and happens all year long: **accidit in puncto, et toto contingit in anno**

it is a story full of fun: **est multi fabula plena joci**

it is best to be silent in a bad cause: **mala causa silenda est**

it is best to profit by the madness of others: **aliena optimum frui insania**

it is better to receive than to do an injury: **accipere quam facere præstat injuriam**

it is crushed under its own weight: **mole ruit sua**

it is dangerous to believe and to disbelieve: **periculosum est credere et non credere**

it is delightful to spend one's time in the tillage of the fields: **tempus in agrorum cultu consumere dulce est**

it is difficult not to write satire: **difficile est saturam non scribere**

it is done: **factum est**

it is easier to find fortune than to keep hold of it: **fortunam citius reperias quam retineas**

it is easier to praise a republican form of government than to establish one: **reipublicæ forma laudari facilius quam evenire**

it is easy to add to what has already been invented: **facile est inventis addere**

it is easy to be generous with what is another's: **facile largiri de alieno**

it is easy to rule over the good: **facile est imperium in bonis**

it is finished: **consummatum est**

it is fraud to conceal fraud: **fraus est celare fraudem**

it is human nature to hunt for novelty: **est natura hominim novitatis avida**

it is less to suffer punishment than to deserve it: **estque pati pœnas quam meruisse minus**

it is not easy flying without feathers: **sine pennis volare haud facile est**

it is not easy to repair a damaged reputation: **famæ laboranti non facile succurritur**

it is not good to trifle with the gods: **non est bonum ludere cum diis**

it is not permitted to err twice in war: **bis peccare in bello non licet**

it is one thing to conceal, another to be silent: **aliud est celare, aliud tacere**

it is pleasant at times to play the madman: **aliquando et insanire jucundum est**

it is possible to infer the future from the past: **ab actu ad posse valet illatio**

it is right and fitting: **dignum et justum est**

it is sometimes expedient to forget what you know: **etiam oblivisci quod scis interdum expedit**

it is sometimes prudent to feign stupidity: **stultitiam simulare loco prudentia summa est**

it is sweet to be silly in places: **dulce est desipere in loco**

it is the heart that makes one eloquent: **pectus est quod disertos facit**

it is the will of God: **est voluntas Dei**

it is time for you to depart: **tempus abire tibi est**

it is true because it is impossible: **certum est quia impossibile est**

it is wretched to be found out: **deprendi miserum est**

it seemed otherwise to the gods: **dis aliter visum**

it shines with a borrowed light: **luce lucet aliena**

it will not always be summer: **non semper erit æstas**

J

jokes directed against the unfortunate are inhumane: **adversus miseros inhumanus est jocus**

joys do not fall to the rich alone: **nam neque divitibus contingunt gaudia solis**

judge a tree by its fruit, not by its leaves: **fructu non foliis arborem æstima**

judge not that you be not judged: **nolite judicare ut non judicemini**

Jupiter laughs at lovers' deceits: **perjuria ridet amantum Juppiter**

justice is the queen of virtues: **justitia virtutum regina**

justice renders to every one his due: **justitia suum cuique distribuit**

justice seeks no reward: **justitia nihil expetit præmii**

K

keep between both extremes: **inter utrumque tene**

keep silence: **favete linguis**

kings have many ears and eyes: **multæ regum aures et oculi**

know thyself: **nosce te ipsum** or **nosce teipsum**

know your opportunity: **occasionem cognosce**

knowledge is power: **scientia est potentia**

knowledge itself is power: **ipsa scientia potestas est**

L

labor conquers all things: **labor omnia vincit**

labor is its own reward (fig.): **labor ipse voluptas**

late may you return to heaven: **serus in cœlum redeas**

later, opportunity is bald: **posthac occasio calva**

laughter abounds in the mouth of fools: **risus abundat in ore stultorum**

law is the art of the good and the just: **jus est ars boni et æqui**

laws are subservient to custom: **leges mori serviunt**

lay the burden on the lazy ass: **onus segni impone asello**

lead back the wanderer into the right way: **errantem in viam reductio**

learn to endure: **disce pati**

learned ignorance: **docta ignorantia**

leave poets free to perish as they will: **sit jus liceatque perire poëtis**

leave war to others: **bella gerant alii**

leave well enough alone: **actum ne agas**

leaving aside joking: **omissis jocis**

leisure begets vices: **otia dant vitia**

leisure without literature is death: **otium sine litteris mors est**

let ancient things depart, and all things around be new: **recedant vetera, nova sint omnia**

let arms yield to the toga: **cedant arma togæ**

let deeds suffice for words: **dictis facta suppetant**

let fortune favor: **faveat fortuna**

let him take who can: **capiat qui capere possit**

let his bones softly rest: **molliter ossa cubent**

let it be done: **fiat**

let it be everlasting: **esto perpetuum**

let it pass for what it is worth: **valeat quantum valere potest**

let it stand: **stet**

let justice be done, though the heavens fall: **fiat justitia, ruat cælum**

let my will stand in place of reason: **sit pro ratione voluntas**

let not the sun set on your anger: **sol non occidat super iracundiam vestram**

let not your heart be troubled: **non turbetur cor vestrum**

let perpetual light shine on them: **lux perpetua luceat eis**

let sleeping dogs lie (fig.): **quieta non movere**

let the buyer beware: **caveat emptor**

let the die be cast: **jacta alea esto**

let the one who sins when drunk be punished when sober: **qui peccat ebrius luat sobrius**

let the one who stands be careful lest he fall: **qui stat, caveat ne cadat**

let the punishment equal the crime: **noxiæ pœna par esto**

let the seller beware: **caveat venditor**

let the success be equal to the labor: **par sit fortuna labori**

let the superior answer: **respondeat superior**

let the traveler beware: **caveat viator**

let them hate, provided they fear: **oderint dum metuant**

let there be fire: **fiat ignem**

let there be light: **fiat lux**

let us drink, death is certain: **bibamus, moriendum est**

let us go where our appetite prompts us: **eamus quo ducit gula**

let us live and let us love: **vivamus atque amemus**

let us live, my Lesbia, and let us love: **vivamus, mea Lesbia, atque amemus**

let us live today, forgetting the cares that are past: **hodie vivendum, amissa**
    præteritorum cura

let us pray: **oremus**

let us seek higher things: **sublimiora petamus**

let us then be joyful, therefore, while we are young: **gaudeamus igitur, juvenes dum sumus**

let us turn to better things: **ad meliora vertamur**

let us yield to love: **cedamus amori**

let your desire aim at a fixed limit: **certum voto pete finem**

let your desires be governed by reason: **appetitus rationi pareat**

liberty in the laws: **libertas in legibus**

liberty is a thing of inestimable value: **libertas inæstimabile res est**

liberty under the law: **sub lege libertas**

licking a cub into shape (fig): **lambendo paulatim figurant**

life is changeable: **varia vita est**

life is short, art is long: **vita brevis, ars longa**

life itself is short but evils make it longer: **brevis ipsa vita est sed malis fit longior**

life without literature is death: **vita sine literis mors est**

lift up your hearts: **sursum corda**

light comes from above: **lux venit ab alto**

light griefs find utterance, great ones hold silence: **curæ leves loquuntur, ingentes stupent**

light is the grief that can take counsel: **levis est dolor qui capere consilium potest**

light is the load that is cheerfully borne: **leve fit quod bene fertur onus**

light of the world: **lux mundi**

light-minded men are improvident of the future: **leves homines futuri sunt improvidi**

lightning strikes the mountain tops: **feriunt summis fulmina montes**

like a brook, life flows away: **ut amnis vita labitur**

like cures like: **similia similibus curantur**

like father, like son: **qualis pater, talis filius**

listen, be silent, flee: **aude, tace, fuge**

listen to both sides: **audi alteram partem**

little minds are caught by little things: **parva leves capiunt animas**

live ever mindful of death: **vive memor Lethi**

live for today: **vive hodie**

live, while you can: **dum potes vive**

live within your means: **messe tenus propria vive**

lofty towers fall with a heavier crash: **celsæ graviore casu decidunt turres**

long live the king: **vivat rex**

long live the king and queen: **vivant rex et regina**

long live the queen: **vivat regina**

long live the republic: **vivat respublica**

look to the end: **respice finem**

look upon the immense work of the artist Nature: **artificis Naturæ ingens opus aspice**

look within: **interiora vide**

Lord, have mercy on us: **Kyrie eleison**

love, and a cough, are not concealed: **amor tussisque non celantur**

love bade me write: **scribere jussit amor**

love begets love: **amor gignit amorem**

love conquers all things: **omnia vincit amor**

love has both honey and gall in abundance: **amor et melle et felle est fecundissimus**

love is a kind of warfare: **militiæ species amor est**

love is a thing full of anxious fears: **res est solliciti plena timoris amor**

love is one thing, lust another: **alius est amor, alius cupido**

love is the same in all: **amor omnibus idem**

love is the token of peace: **signum pacis amor**

love of country: **amor patriæ**

love of country leads me: **ducit amor patriæ**

love of neighbor: **amor proximi**

lovers are lunatics: **amantes sunt amentes**

lovers remember everything: **meminerunt omnia amantes**

lucky and unlucky days: **fasti et nefasti dies**

M

make haste slowly: **festina lente**

man alone is either a God or a Demon: **homo solus aut Deus aut Dæmon**

man is a two-footed reasoning animal: **homo est animal bipes rationale**

man is a wolf to man: **homo homini lupus**

man is his own worst enemy: **nihil inimicius quam sibi ipse**

man is the measure: **homo mensura**

man is to man either a God or a wolf: **homo homini aut Deus aut lupus**

man proposes, but God disposes: **homo proponit, sed Deus disponit**

many are called but few are chosen: **multi sunt vocati, pauci vero electi**

many grains make a heap: **ex granis fit acervus**

many hands make work light: **multæ manus onus levius faciunt**

many promises weaken faith: **multa fidem promissa levant**

many things fall between the cup and the lip: **multa cadunt inter calicem supremaque labra**

may he/she rest in peace: **requiescat in pace**

may the earth lie light upon you: **levis sit tibi terra**

may the Lord curse him: **maledicat Dominus**

may they rest in peace: **requiescant in pace**

meanwhile, something is going on: **interim fit aliquid**

memory is the treasury and guardian of all things: **memoria est thesaurus omnium rerum e custos**

men are transformed by pleasures: **homines voluptatibus transformantur**

men are wise as far as their beards: **barbæ tenus sapientes**

men trust their eyes rather than their ears: **homines amplius oculis quam auribus credunt**

men willingly believe that which they wish for: **libenter homines id quod volunt credunt**

mind moves matter: **mens agitat molem**

mind your own business: **sutor, ne supra crepidam**

mine and thine: **meum et tuum**

mine today, yours tomorrow: **hodie mihi, cras tibi**

misfortune is a second master: **magister alius casus**

misfortunes benefit the good man: **juvant aspera probum**

misfortunes come unsought: **mala ultro adsunt**

misfortunes often stir up genius: **ingenium mala sæpe movent**

moderation is the mark of a great heart: **magni pectoris est inter secunda moderatio**

modesty is inborn, it cannot be learned: **pudor doceri non potest, nasci potest**

money does not smell: **pecunia non olet**

money is bewailed with a greater tumult than death: **majore tumultu planguntur nummi quam funera**

money is both blood and life to mortal men: **et sanguis et spiritus pecunia mortalibus**

money is either our master or our slave: **imperat aut servit collecta pecunia cuique**

more lasting than bronze: **ære perennius**

more of good taste than expense: **plus salis quam sumptus**

more relish than meat (fig.): **plus salis quam sumptus**

mortals must bear many ills: **pati necesse est multa mortales mala**

most of man's misfortunes are due to man: **homini plurima ex homine sunt mala**

motion drawing to its end is swifter: **motus in fine velocior**

much in little: **multum in parvo**

my help is from above: **auxilium meum ab alto**

my soul magnifies the Lord: **magnificat anima mea Dominum**

my strength is from heaven: **cælitus mihi vires**

N

naked I repair to the camp of those who desire nothing: **nihil cupientium nudus castra peto**

nature abhors a vacuum: **natura abhorret a vacuo**

nature desires perfection: **natura appetit perfectum**

nature has granted to all to be happy: **natura beatis omnibus esse dedit**

nature never says one thing and wisdom another: **nunquam aliud natura, aliud sapientia dicit**

nature teaches one duty: **officium natura docet**

necessity has no law: **necessitas non habet legem**

necessity is a powerful weapon: **ingens telum necessitas**

necessity is the mother of invention: **mater artium necessitas**

necessity knows no holiday: **feriis caret necessitas**

necessity knows no law (fig.): **necessitas non habet legem**

neck and neck: **pari passu**

neglect of appearance becomes men: **forma viros neglecta decet**

neglected things flourish: **neglecta virescunt**

neither blame nor applaud yourself: **neque culpa neque lauda teipsum**

neither can I live with you nor without you: **nec tecum possum vivere, nec sine te** neither fear nor wish for your last day: **summam nec metuas diem, nec optes**

neither is it permitted to know all things: **nec scire fas est omnia**

neither love nor a cough can be hidden: **nec amor nec tussis celatur**

never acquiesce: **nunquam acquiescere**

never less alone than when alone: **nunquam minus solus quam cum solus**

never trust an alliance with the powerful: **nunquam est fidelis cum potente societas**

never weary of doing good: **bene agendo nunquam defessus**

new fields of corn wave where Troy once stood: **jam seges est ubi Troja fuit**

night is the time for counsel, day for arms: **consiliis nox apta ducum, lux aptior armis**

no evil person is happy: **nemo malus felix**

no god assists the idle: **otiosis nullus adsistit deus**

no good person ever became suddenly rich: **repente dives nemo factus est bonus**

no just man ever became rich quickly: **nunquam vir æquus dives evasit cito**

no man has perpetual good fortune: **nulli est homini perpetuum bonum**

no more beyond: **ne plus ultra**

no occasion to be alert is to be overlooked: **cavendi nulla est dimittenda occasio**

no one becomes extremely wicked all at once: **repente nemo fit turpissimus**

no one becomes guilty by fate: **nemo fit fato nocens**

no one can be happy without virtue: **beatus autem esse sine virtute nemo potest**

no one can escape death: **mortem effugere nemo potest**

no one can give what he does not have: **nemo dat quod non habet**

no one can serve two masters: **nemo potest duobus dominis servire**

no one can wear a mask for very long: **nemo potest personam diu ferre fictam**

no one deserves punishment for a thought: **cogitationis pœnam nemo meretur**

no one has license to sin: **peccare licet nemini**

no one in love sees: **nemo in amore videt**

no one is bound to accuse himself: **nemo tenetur se ipsum accusare**

no one is deceived who is knowingly deceived: **non decipitur qui scit se decipi**

no one is heir of the living: **nemo est hæres viventis**

no one is satisfied with his lot: **nemo sua sorte contentus**

no one is wise alone: **nemo solus sapit**

no one is wise at all times: **nemo mortalium omnibus horis sapit**

no one ought to gain by another person's loss: **nemo debet ex aliena jactura lucrari**

no one provokes me with impunity: **nemo me impune lacessit**

no one should be a judge in his own cause: **aliquis non debet esse judex in propria causa**

no poison is drunk out of earthenware: **nulla aconita bibuntur fictilibus**

no possession is greater than virtue: **virtute nulla possessio major** no sooner said than done: **dictum factum** or **dictum ac factum**

nor is heaven always at peace: **nec sidera pacem semper habent**

not all of me shall die: **non omnis moriar**

not Angles, but angels: **non Angli, sed angeli**

not equal to many: **nec pluribus impar**

not for you alone: **non vobis solum**

not for you, not for me, but for us: **non mihi, non tibi, sed nobis**

not sound in mind: **non compos mentis**

not too much: **de nimium**

not with equal steps: **non passibus æquis**

not yet victory, and there was already dissension: **nondum victoria, jam discordia erat**

note well: **nota bene**

nothing beyond it: **ne plus ultra**

nothing can be created of nothing: **nil posse creari de nilo**

nothing comes from nothing: **nihil ex nihilo**

nothing dries sooner than a tear: **nihil enim lacryma citius arescit**

nothing in life is permanent: **firmum in vita nihil**

nothing is great unless it is good: **nil magnum nisi bonum**

nothing is impossible: **nil impossibile**

nothing is loftier than the love of truth: **nil est amore veritatis celsus**

nothing is swifter than rumor: **fama nihil est celerius**

nothing is swifter than the years!: **nihil est annis velocius!**

nothing is too difficult for mortals: **nil mortalibus arduum est**

nothing is wanting here except a song: **nihil hic nisi carmina desunt**

nothing so useful as the sun and salt: **nil sole et sale utilius**

nothing that relates to man is alien to me: **humani nihil alienum**

nothing too much: **ne quid nimis**

nothing without God: **nil sine Deo**

nothing without great labor: **nil sine magno labore**

nothing without labor: **nihil sine labore**

now or never: **nunc aut nunquam**

now Spring restores balmy warmth: **jam ver egelidos refert tepores**

O

O, how deceitful is the hope of men: **O fallacem hominum spem**

O imitators, you servile herd!: **O imitatores, servum pecus!**

O sacred simplicity!: **O sancta simplicitas!**

O sweet solace of labors: **O laborum dulce lenimen**

O the times! O the morals!: **O tempora! O mores!**

O what a void there is in things!: **O quantum in rebus inane!**

occasion is bald behind: **post est occasio calva**

odd numbers bring luck: **numero omnia impare gaudet**

of blessed memory: **beatæ memoriæ**

of evils to choose the least: **ex malis eligere minima**

of its own kind: **sui generis**

of so much force are system and connection: **tantum series juncturaque pollet**

of sound mind: **compos mentis**

of the dead say nothing but good: **de mortuis nihil nisi bonum**

of the dead say nothing but what is true: **de mortuis nil nisi verum**

of two evils, always choose the lesser: **de duobus malis, minus est semper eligendum**

of what use are pedigrees?: **stemmata quid faciunt?**

often a man is his own worst enemy: **sæpe nihil inimicus homini quam sibi ipse**

Oh, the times! Oh, the morals!: **O tempora! O mores!**

old age is a heavy burden to man: **grave senectus est hominibus pondus**

old age is an incurable disease: **senectus insanabilis morbus est**

old men are twice children: **bis pueri senes**

on one side a wolf besets you, on the other a dog: **hac urget lupus, hac canis**

on the spur of the moment: **ex tempore**

once an abbot, always an abbot: **semel abbas, semper abbas**

once and always: **semel et semper**

one and the same: **semel et simul**

one grieves sincerely who grieves unseen: **illa dolet vere quæ sine teste dolet**

one hand rubs the other: **manus manum fricat**

one hand washes the other: **manus manum lavat**

one heart, one way: **cor unum, via una**

one man can do nothing, two can do much: **unum nihil, duos plurimum posse**

one man sins, the other is punished: **alius peccat, alius plectitur**

one man's loss is another man's gain: **ex damno alterius, alterius utilitas**

one must move with the times: **tempori parendum**

one of a kind: **sui generis**

one ought not to wrestle with ghosts: **cum larvis non luctandum**

one ought to beware of prostitutes: **cavendum a meretricibus** one ought to fear even the tiniest of creatures: **a minimis quoque timendum**

one single bright day will equal the black ones: **æquabit nigras candida una dies**

one wrong does not justify another: **injuria non excusat injuriam**

opportunity makes the thief: **occasio furem facit**

opposite cures opposite: **contraria contrariis curantur**

others' dangers are our warnings: **aliena pericula, cautiones nostræ**

our day is over (fig.): **fuimus Troës**

Our Father: **Pater Noster**

our light comes from God: **a Deo lux nostra**

our temples do not conceal our age: **ætatem non tegunt tempora**

our thoughts are free: **liberæ sunt enim nostræ cogitationes**

out of Africa there is always something new: **ex Africa semper aliquid novi**

out of many one: **e pluribus unum**

out of many things a great heap will be formed: **de multis grandis acervus erit**

out of the same mouth comes blessing and cursing: **ex ipso ore procedit benedictio et maledictio**

out of the smoke into the flame: **de fumo in flammam**

over their cups: **inter pocula**

P

pain makes even the innocent man a liar: **etiam innocentes cogit mentiri dolor**

pale death approaches with equal step: **pallida mors æquo pulsat pede**

pardon my words: **sit venia verbis**

pardon the expression: **venia sit dicto**

past labors are pleasant: **jucundi acti labores**

patience abused becomes fury: **patientia læsa fit furor**

peace be to this house: **pax huic domui**

peace be with you: **pax vobiscum** or **pax vobis**

peace is preferable to war: **pax potior bello**

peace is produced by war: **pax paritur bello**

pearls before swine: **margaritas ante porcos**

perhaps a better fate awaits the afflicted: **forsan miseros meliora sequentur**

philosophy is the true medicine of the mind: **est profecto animi medicina, philosophia**

physician, heal thyself: **medice, cura te ipsum**

pleasure arises out of labor: **e labore dulcedo**

poetic license: **licentia poëtica**

poetry is the wine of demons: **poësis est vinum dæmonum**

poison is drunk from a gold cup: **venenum in auro bibitur**

poison is more often drunk from a gold cup: **sæpius in auro bibitur venenum**

poverty hinders the greatest talents from advancing: **paupertatem summis ingeniis obesse,** **ne provehantur**

poverty inspires genius: **ingenii largitor venter**

practice is the best teacher: **exercitatio optimus est magister**

praise be to God: **laus Deo**

pray and work: **ora et labora**

pray, brothers: **orate fratres**

pray for a strong will: **fortem posce animum**

pray for us sinners: **ora pro nobis peccatoribus**

prayer goes heavenward: **it prex cæli**

precepts guide, but examples drag along: **præcepta ducunt, at exempla trahunt**

precocious things do not last long: **præcocia non diuturna**

prepared for any change of fortune: **in utraque fortuna paratus**

prepared for everything: **in omnia paratus**

prepared in war and peace: **bello ac pace paratus**

presence diminishes fame: **minuit præsentia famam**

princes are mortal, the republic is eternal: **principes mortales, rempublicam æternam**

prudent men abstain from wine: **prudentes vino abstinent**

Punic faith (treachery): **Punica fides**

puppies and pigs have a very different smell: **aliter catuli longe olent, aliter sues**

pursuits become habits: **abeunt studia in mores**

Q

quieter than a fish: **magis mutus quam piscis**

R

rarely are beauty and wisdom found together: **raram facit misturam cum sapientia forma**

read the whole if you wish to know the whole: **lege totum si vis scire totum** ready tears are a sign of treachery, not of grief: **paratæ lacrimæ insidias non fletum indicant**

reason can generally effect more than blind force: **plus ratio quam vis cæca valere solet**

reason is a ray of divine light: **ratio est radius divini luminis**

reason is the spirit and soul of the law: **ratio est legis anima**

refrain from laying the guilt of the few upon the many: **parcite paucarum diffundere crimen in omnes**

religion is not abolished by abolishing superstition: **superstitione tollenda religio non tollitur**

remember death: **memento mori**

remember that you are a man: **te hominem esse memento**

remotest Thule: **ultima Thule**

remove the foundation and the structure falls: **sublato fundamento cadit opus**

render unto God: **reddite Deo**

renew your courage: **renovate animos**

repetition is the mother of study: **repetitio est mater studiorum**

resist the beginning: **obsta principiis**

resolving one controversy by creating another: **litem quod lite resolvit**

respect is greater at a distance: **major e longinquo reverentia**

retracing the footsteps of fame: **retinens vestigia famæ**

revenge brings with it ruin: **vindictæ trahit exitium**

revenge is an inhuman word: **inhumanum verbum est ultio**

riches allow one to be foolish: **stultitiam patiuntur opes**

rivalry is the whetstone of talent: **ingeniorum cos æmulatio**

Rome has spoken; the case is settled: **Roma locuta est; causa finita est**

room for doubt: **ambigendi locus**

ruling men is one thing, entertaining them is another: **alia res sceptrum, alia plectrum**

rumor flies: **fama volat**

rumor grows as it goes: **fama crescit eundo**

rumor never reports things in their true light: **nunquam ad liquidum fama perducitur**

rumor runs away: **fama fert**

rusty mind, blighted genius: **ærugo animi, rubigo ingenii**

S

safety must sometimes be bought with money: **ære quandoque salutem redimendam** said and done: **dictum factum** or **dictum ac factum**

salt seasons everything: **sal sapit omnia**

salvation by faith: **salus in fide**

salvation in God alone: **in solo Deo salus**

salvation under the Cross: **sub cruce salus**

sanity of sanity, all is sanity: **sanitas sanitatum, omnia sanitas**

satire is wholly ours: **satura tota nostra est**

second thoughts are generally wiser thoughts: **posteriores cogitationes sapientiores solent esse**

second to none: **nulli secundus**

see and believe: **vide et crede**

see that it be done: **fieri facias**

seek after truth: **quære verum**

seek not yourself from outside yourself: **ne te quæsiveris extra**

seek ye first the kingdom of God: **quærite prime regnum Dei**

seize the day: **carpe diem**

seize the opportunity that is offered: **oblatam occasionem tene**

self-praise is base: **laus propria sordet**

selling incense and perfumes: **vendentem thus et odores**

serve the Lord with gladness: **servite Domino in lætitia**

seven is a banquet, nine a brawl: **septem convivium, novem convitium**

short cuts are roundabouts: **compendia dispendia**

short-lived pleasure is the parent of pain: **brevis voluptas mox doloris est parens**

simple in elegance: **simplex munditiis**

simplicity is nowadays very rare: **ævo rarissima nostro simplicitas**

simplicity is the seal of truth: **simplex sigillum veri**

simplicity is the sign of truth: **simplex signum veri**

simulated tears (crocodile tears): **lacrimæ simulatæ**

sincerity gives wings to strength: **candor dat viribus alas**

sing joyfully to God, all the earth: **jubilate Deo, omnis terra**

sing to the Lord a new song: **cantate Domino canticum novum**

sleep is the image of death: **somnus est imago mortis**

sleep on it: **in nocte consilium**

slow but sure: **tarde sed tute**

small in number, but their valor is quick for war: **exigui numero, sed bello vivida virtus**

small things become the small: **parvum parva decent**

small things will make a large pile: **de parvis grandis acervus erit** so help me God!: **medius fidius!**

so many men, so many opinions: **quot homines tot sententiæ**

solid earth: **terra firma**

some do the planting, others the reaping: **alii sementem faciunt, alii metentem**

some remedies are worse than the disease: **graviora quædam sunt remedia periculis**

sometimes a fool speaks well: **interdum stultus bene loquitur**

sometimes common error makes law: **communis error facit jus**

sometimes even the good Homer nods off: **aliquando bonus dormitat Homerus**

sometimes sweet things become bitter: **dulcia quandoque amara fieri**

soon ripe, soon rotten: **cito maturum, cito putridum**

sooner or later we hasten to one home: **serius aut citius sedem properamus ad unam**

speak and act: **fare fac**

speak of the devil (fig.): **lupus in fabula**

speech is an indicator of thought: **index animi sermo est**

speech is given to all, wisdom to few: **sermo datur cunctis, animi sapientia paucis**

speech is the mirror of the mind: **imago animi sermo est**

spoken words fly, written words remain: **verba volant, scripta manent**

state secrets: **arcana imperii**

still water runs deep: **aqua profunda est quieta**

strength, lacking judgment, collapses by its own weight: **vis consilii expers mole ruit sua**

strife is the dowry of a wife: **dos est uxoria lites**

success makes some crimes honorable: **honesta quædam scelera successus facit**

such as it is: **taliter qualiter**

suffering follows those who flee: **fugientes afflictio sequitur**

suppression of the truth is the suggestion of falsehood: **suppressio veri suggestio falsi**

sweet association of friends: **dulce sodalicium** or **dulce sodalitium**

sweet danger: **dulce periculum**

sweet home: **dulce domum**

sweet is the love of one's country: **dulcis amor patriæ**

sweet is the memory of past labor: **suavis laborum est præteritorum memoria**

sweet society: **dulce sodalicium** or **dulce sodalitium**

sweet things come after bitter things: **post amara dulcia**

sweeter than honey: **dulcior melle**

swimming here and there: **rari nantes**

T

take heed you do not fall: **cave ne cadas**

take up and read: **tolle lege**

taxes are the sinews of the republic: **vectigalia nervos esse rei publicæ**

teach that you may learn: **doce ut discas**

tears are the nature of things: **sunt lacrimæ rerum**

ten constitute a crowd: **multitudinem decem faciunt**

testimonies are to be weighed, not counted: **ponderanda sunt testimonia, non numeranda**

thanks be to God: **Dei gratias** or **Deo gratias**

that is a harvest which ill repays its husbandman: **illa est agricolæ messis iniqua suo**

that is rightly done which is honestly done: **recte quod honeste**

that which hurts teaches: **quæ nocent docent**

that which pleases is twice repeated: **bis repetita placent**

that would be adding insult to injury: **ad damnum adderetur injuria**

the absent one will not be the heir: **absens hæres non erit**

the abuse of a thing is no argument against its use (fig.): **ab abusu ad usum non valet consequentia**

the abuse of a thing is no argument for its disuse: **ex abusu non argumentum ad desuetudinem**

the act of God does injury to no one: **actus Dei nemini facit injuriam**

the act of the law does injury to no one: **actus legis nulli facit injuriam**

the age we live in is the true age of gold: **aurea nunc vere sunt sæcula**

the anger of the lion is noble: **ira leonis nobilis**

the appearances of things are deceptive: **fallaces sunt rerum species**

the bad end of a bad beginning: **mali principii malus finis**

the beaten path is the safest one: **via trita est tutissima**

the beaten path, the safe path: **via trita, via tuta**

the beginning of wisdom is the fear of the Lord: **initium sapientiæ est timor Domini**

the beginnings of all things are small: **omnium rerum principia parva sunt**

the belly is the giver of genius: **ingenii largitor venter**

the best counselors are the dead: **optimi consiliarii mortui**

the best remedy for anger is delay: **maximum remedium iræ mora est**

the best things await us in heaven: **manent optima cœle**

the blood of the Christians is seed: **semen est sanguis Christianorum**

the brain is the citadel of the senses: **habet cerebrum sensus arcem** the brave always show mercy: **fortes semper monstrant misericordiam**

the brave may fall, but they cannot yield: **fortis cadere, cedere non potest**

the cart draws the ox: **currus bovem trahit**

the case is settled: **causa finita est**

the cautious wolf fears the snare: **cautus metuit foveam lupus**

the Church does not die: **Ecclesia non moritur**

the clamor of the forum: **forensis strepitus**

the cock is proudest on his own dungheap: **gallus in sterquilinio suo plurimum potest**

the comfort derived from the misery of others is slight: **levis est consolatio ex miseria aliorum**

the corruption of the best is the worst: **corruptio optimi pessima**

the country in the city: **rus in urbe**

the coward calls himself cautious, the miser thrifty: **timidus se vocat cautum, parcum sordidus**

the cowl does not make the monk: **cucullus non facit monachum**

the craftsman is known by his work: **opus artificem probat**

the crop is always greater in the lands of another: **fertilior seges est alienis semper in agris**

the Cross is our crown: **a crux nostra corona**

the Cross is the touchstone of faith: **fidei coticula crux**

the crown of old age is authority: **apex est autem senectutis auctoritas**

the dead do not bite: **mortui non mordant**

the deeds of men never escape the gods: **acta deos nunquam mortalia fallunt**

the defense of a just cause is easy: **justæ causæ facilis est defensio**

the delight of mankind: **deliciæ humani generis**

the descent to hell is easy: **facilis est descensus Averni**

the Devil take the hindmost! (fig.): **occupet extremum scabies**

the die is cast: **jacta alea est**

the dread of war is worse than war itself: **pejor est bello timor ipse belli**

the dregs of the people: **fæx populi**

the drop hollows the stone: **gutta cavat lapidem**

the eagle bears me on high: **alte fert aquila**

the ear of the bridled horse is in the mouth: **equo frænato est auris in ore**

the empty-handed traveler sings before the robber: **cantabit vacuus coram latrone viator**

the end crowns the work: **finis coronat opus**

the end of one day is the beginning of another: **finis unius diei est principium alterius**

the ending proves the deeds: **exitus acta probat**

the end justifies the means: **cui licitus est finis, etiam licent media** the exception proves the rule: **exceptio probat regulam**

the face is the index of the soul: **vultus est index animi**

the fatal gift to Minerva: **donum exitiale Minervæ**

the Fates lead the willing and drag the unwilling: **Fata volentem ducunt, nolentem trahunt**

the Fates oppose: **Fata obstant**

the father of the country: **pater patriæ**

the fear of death is worse than death: **timor mortis morte pejor**

the fear of the Lord is the beginning of wisdom: **timor Domini initium sapientiæ**

the fear of war is worse than war itself: **pejor est bello timor ipse belli**

the feelings generally run riot in prosperity: **luxuriant animi rebus plerumque secundis**

the fellow is either mad or he is composing verses: **aut insanit homo, aut versus facit**

the fields where Troy once stood: **campos ubi Troja fuit**

the fig tree splits huge blocks of marble: **ingentia marmora findet caprificus**

the fires of youth have cooled: **adulescentia deferbuit**

the first among equals: **primus inter pares**

the first appearance deceives many: **decipit frons prima multos**

the first reaction to truth is hatred: **cum odio sui cœpit veritas**

the fleeting years glide by: **fugaces labuntur anni**

the flower of youth: **flos juventutis**

the fool is always beginning to live: **stultus semper incipit vivere**

the footprints of dying liberty: **vestigia morientis libertatis**

the footsteps of fortune are slippery: **lubrici sunt fortunæ gressus**

the fortune of the house stands: **stat fortuna domus**

the fortune of war stands ever on the verge: **fortuna belli semper ancipiti in loco est**

the fountain of all living things: **fons omnium viventium**

the fountain of evil: **fons malorum**

the fountain of justice is good faith: **fundamentum justitiæ est fides**

the fruit of sin is bitter: **amarus vitiorum fructus**

the future is inscrutable: **futurum invisibile**

the gain of the one is the loss of the other: **unius compendium, alterius dispendium**

the garment makes the man: **vestis virum facit**

the giver makes the gift precious: **auctor pretiosa facit**

the gods sell all things to hard labor: **dii laboribus omnia vendunt**

the golden mean: **aurea mediocritas**

the good are more suspected by kings than the bad: **regibus boni quam mali suspectiores sunt** the good leader makes good soldiers: **bonus dux bonum reddit militem**

the greatest force is that of nature: **naturæ vis maxima**

the greatest respect is due to a child: **maxima reverentia pueris debetur**

the greatest scholars are not the wisest men: **magis magni clerici non sunt magis sapientes**

the happier the moments, the shorter the time: **tanto brevius omne, quanto felicius tempus**

the heavens tell of the glory of God: **cæli enarrant gloriam Dei**

the highest good: **summum bonum**

the highest justice is often the greatest injustice: **summum jus sæpe summa injuria est**

the highest seat does not hold two: **summa sedes non capit duos**

the hired hand flees from the flock: **mercenarius fugit a grege**

the honest man does not repent: **probum non pœnitet**

the hope of the flock: **spem gregis**

the hour flies: **hora fugit**

the house is smiling with silver: **ridet argento domus**

the house of a friend is the best house: **domus amica domus optima**

the idle are always needy: **otiosi semper egentes**

the indulgence of parents is the bane of children: **indulgentia parentum, filiorum pernicies**

the injured man writes in marble: **scribit in marmore læsus**

the irritable race of poets: **genus irritabile vatum**

the judge is condemned when the guilty is acquitted: **judex damnatur cum nocens absolvitur**

the judge of beauty: **arbiter formæ**

the judge of the drinking: **arbiter bibendi**

the judgment of God: **judicium Dei**

the just shall live by faith: **justus autem ex fide vivit**

the king can do no wrong: **rex non potest peccare**

the king never dies: **rex nunquam moritur**

the king reigns but does not govern: **rex regnat sed non gubernat**

the labor and delay of the file: **limæ labor et mora**

the language of truth is simple: **veritatis simplex oratio est**

the last of the Romans: **ultimus Romanorum**

the law compels no one to do what is impossible: **lex neminem cogit ad impossibilia**

the law does not concern itself with trifles: **de minimis non curat lex**

the law is hard, but it is the law: **dura lex, sed lex**

the law is prospective, not retrospective: **lex prospicit non respicit**

the law of nations: **jus gentium**

the law of the sword: **jus gladii**

the laws are silent in time of war: **silent leges inter arma**

the laws sometimes sleep, but never die: **dormiunt aliquando leges, nunquam moriuntur**

the lesser of two evils: **minima de malis**

the light shines in the darkness: **lux in tenebris lucet**

the living power: **vis viva**

the longest day soon comes to an end: **longissimus dies cito conditur**

the Lord be with you: **Dominus vobiscum**

the Lord has spoken it: **dixit Dominus**

the Lord himself has spoken it: **ipse dixit Dominus**

the Lord is my light: **Dominus illuminatio mea**

the Lord is my rock: **Dominus petra mea**

the Lord will provide: **Dominus providebit**

the loss falls upon its owner: **res perit suo domino**

the loss of money is bewailed with true tears: **ploratur lacrimis amissa pecunia veris**

the love of money increases: **crescit amor nummi**

the love of money is a root to all kinds of evil: **radix omnium malorum est cupiditas**

the madness of one makes many mad: **unius dementia dementes efficit multos**

the madness of scholars: **deliramenta doctrinæ**

the malevolent have hidden teeth: **malevolus animus abditos dentes habet**

the man who is everywhere is never anywhere: **nusquam est qui ubique est**

the manners of men are to be carefully observed: **notandi sunt tibi mores**

the master of taste: **elegantiæ arbiter**

the master of the feast: **arbiter bibendi**

the master suffers the loss: **damnum sentit dominus**

the master's eye makes the horse fat: **oculus domini saginat equum**

the middle way: **via media**

the mighty cycle of the ages begins its turn anew: **magnus ab integro
    sæculorum nascitur ordo**

the mind is sicker than the sick body: **corpore sed mens est ægro magis ægra**

the miser is ever in want: **semper avarus eget**

the miserable bliss of all mortal things: **mortalium rerum misera beatitudo**

the modest water saw God and blushed: **vidit et erubit lympha pudica Deum**

the more men have, the more they want: **homines, quo plura habent,
    eo cupiunt ampliora**

the more pluck, the better luck!: **tanto fortior, tanto felicior!**

the mother of the coward has no occasion to weep: **timidi mater non flet**

the mouse perishes by betraying itself: **sorex suo perit indicio**

the Muse forbids the virtuous man to die: **dignum laude virum Musa vetat mori**

the naked truth: **nuda veritas**

the new drives out the old: **cura cura repulsa nova**

the office shows the man: **magistratus indicat virum**

the one who spares the rod hates the child: **qui parcit virgæ odit filium**

the one who asks timidly courts denial: **qui timide rogat, docet negare**

the one who denies his sins does not atone for them: **non purgat peccata qui negat**

the one who does a thing by another does it himself: **qui facit per alium facit per se**

the one who envies is inferior: **qui invidet minor est**

the one who flees will fight again: **qui fugiebat, rursus prœliabitur**

the one who hates vice, hates humanity: **quis vitia odit, homines odit**

the one who judges in haste repents in haste: **ad pœnitendum properat, cito qui judicat**

the one who labors prays: **qui laborat orat**

the one who teaches learns: **qui docet discit**

the one who wishes for peace must prepare for war: **qui desiderat pacem,**
    præparet bellum

the opinions of men are fallible: **hominum sententia fallax**

the origin of evil: **fons malorum**

the penniless man has nothing to lose (fig.): **cantabit vacuus coram latrone viator**

the people boo me, but I applaud myself: **populus me sibilat, at mihi plaudo**

the people wish to be deceived: **populus vult decipi**

the play is over: **acta est fabula**

the plaything of Fortune: **ludibrium Fortunæ**

the poet's frenzy: **furor poëticus**

the popular breeze: **aura popularis**

the pot boils badly: **olla male fervet**

the power of custom is most weighty: **gravissimum est imperium consuetudinis**

the power of love: **potentia amoris**

the price of knowledge: **pretium scientiæ**

the public good: **salus publica**

the public good is to be preferred to private advantage: **publicum bonum**
    privato est præferendum

the remedy is worse than the disease: **ægrescit medendo**

the remembrance of past labors is pleasant: **acti labores jucundi** the results of war are uncertain: **incerti sunt exitus belli**

the Roman republic stands by its ancient manners and men: **moribus antiquis res stat
Romana virisque**

the roughest seas are far from land: **medio maxima turba mari est**

the ruins strike him undaunted: **impavidum ferient ruinæ**

the same laws hold for peace as for war: **sunt et belli sicut pacis jura**

the same old thing (fig.): **crambe repetita**

the same way by different steps: **gradu diverso, via una**

the scar remains: **cicatrix manet**

the sea surely is common to all: **mare quidem, commune certo est omnibus**

the shadow of a great name: **magni nominis umbra**

the slave rides in the same chariot: **servus curru portatur eodem**

the son of a white hen: **albæ gallinæ filius**

the son of the earth: **filius terræ**

the soul is the nobility: **animus est nobilitas**

the soul of the world: **anima mundi**

the source and origin of the evil: **fons et origo mali**

the spirit is ready, but the flesh is weak: **spiritus promtus est, caro autem infirma**

the stag provoked becomes a lion: **cervus lacessitus leo**

the star shows the way: **stella monstrat viam**

the stars my camp, the gods my light: **astra castra, numen lumen**

the state in which it was: **status quo**

the story relates to you: **de te fabula narratur**

the stronger always succeeds: **plus potest qui plus valet**

the suggestion of falsehood: **suggestio falsi**

the sun of all days has not yet set: **nondum omnium dierum sol occidit**

the sun shines even on the wicked: **et sceleratis sol oritur**

the sun shines on all: **sol lucet omnibus**

the tears of things: **lacrimæ rerum**

the things that are above us are nothing to us: **quæ supra nos nihil ad nos**

the tired ox plants its foot more firmly: **bos lassus fortius figit pedem**

the toastmaster: **arbiter bibendi**

the traveler who has nothing sings before the robber: **vacuus cantat coram latrone viator**

the trumpet sounds attack: **classicum canit**

the truth hates delays: **veritas odit moras**

the truth shall set you free: **veritas vos liberabit**

the uncertainty of law: **alea judiciorum**

the uncertainty of war: **alea belli**

the unknown explained by the unknown: **ignotum per ignotius**

the vigor of youth passes away like a spring flower: **vigor ætatis fluit ut flos veris**

the virtue of parents is a great dowry: **dos est magna parentum virtus**

the voice of one crying in the wilderness: **vox clamantis in deserto**

the voice of the people is the voice of God: **vox populi, vox Dei**

the voice remains: **vox manet**

the weeping of an heir is laughter in disguise: **hæredis fletus sub persona risus est**

the welfare of the people: **salus populi**

the wicked are not swayed by obsequiousness: **improbus a nullo flectitur obsequio**

the wolf changes its coat, not its disposition: **lupus pilum mutat, non mentem**

the wolf in the fable: **lupus in fabula**

the wonderful year: **annus mirabilis**

the word of God endures through eternity: **verbum Dei manet in æternum**

the Word was made flesh: **verbum caro factum est**

the work boils: **fervet opus**

the workmanship surpassed the material: **materiam superabat opus**

the world does not suffice: **non sufficit orbis**

the world is the living image of God: **mundus est Dei viva statua**

the world wishes to be deceived: **mundus vult decipi**

the wrath of God: **Dei irati**

the wrath of kings is always severe: **gravis ira regum est semper**

the written word remains, what is spoken perishes: **litera scripta manet, verbum ut inane perit**

the years are doubled for the just: **justo geminantur anni**

the years glide swiftly by: **fugaces labuntur anni**

their silence is praise enough: **tacent satis laudant**

there are a thousand kinds of men: **mille hominum species**

there are no unmixed blessings: **nihil est ab omni parte beatum**

there is a god within our heart: **deus est in pectore nostro**

there is a god within us, and we hold commerce with heaven: **est deus in nobis, et sunt commercia cœli**

there is a limit to grief, but not to fear: **dolendi modus, timendi non autem**

there is a method in all things: **est modus in rebus**

there is always something new out of Africa: **semper aliquid novi Africam affere**

there is danger in delay: **periculum in mora**

there is honor in sincerity: **in candore decus**

there is no day without sorrow: **nulla dies mærore caret**

there is no desire for what is unknown: **ignoti nulla cupido**

there is no disputing about tastes: **de gustibus non est disputandum**

there is no easy way from the earth to the stars: **non est ad astra mollis e terris via**

there is no life without friendship: **sine amicitia vitam esse nullam**

there is no salvation outside the Church: **extra ecclesiam nulla salus**

there is nothing assured to men: **nil homini certum est**

there is nothing left (fig.): **etiam periere ruinæ**

there is nothing more foolish than a foolish laugh: **risu inepto res ineptior nulla est**

there is nothing new under the sun: **nihil sub sole novum**

there is nothing that God cannot do: **nihil est quod Deus efficere non possit**

there is nothing that is blessed in every respect: **nihil est ab omni parte beatum**

there is room for even more guests at the feast: **locus est et pluribus umbris**

there is safety in many advisors: **salus ubi multi consiliarii**

there is safety in this: **in hoc salus**

there is something in omens: **omina sunt aliquid**

they can because they think they can: **possunt quia posse videntur**

they condemn what they do not understand: **damnant quod non intelligunt**

they make a desert, and call it peace: **solitudinem faciunt, pacem appellant**

they mingle heaven and earth: **terram cœlo miscent**

they rush into the flames of passion: **in furias ignemque ruunt**

they wander from the point: **a re decedunt**

they were sowing the wind, and they shall reap the whirlwind: **ventum seminabant et turbinem metent**

they will pay at the Greek calends: **ad Græcas kalendas soluturos**

things are more pleasant from a distance: **quæ e longinquo magis placent**

things forbidden have a secret charm: **prævalent illicita**

things locked up are safe: **quæ serata secura**

think on eternity: **eternitatem cogita**

this I wish, thus I command: **hoc volo, sic jubeo**

this is my body: **hoc est corpus meum**

this is the new covenant in my blood: **hic est enim sanguis meus novi testamenti**

those secret whisperings of the crowd: **secreta hæc murmura vulgi**

those who are happy at home should stay there: **domi manere convenit felicibus**

those who contemplate the heights, fall: **qui alta contemplantur, cadere**

though ten times repeated, it still is pleasing: **decies repetita placebit**

though the wound is healed, a scar remains: **etiam sanato vulnere cicatrix manet** thrift is a great revenue: **parsimonia est magnum vectigal**

through adversity to greatness: **per angusta ad augusta**

thunderbolts that strike blindly and in vain: **bruta fulmina et vana**

thus always to tyrants: **sic semper tyrannis**

thus passes the glory of the world: **sic transit gloria mundi**

thus you bees make honey not for yourselves: **sic vos non vobis mellificatis apes**

Thy will be done: **fiat voluntas tua**

time cures our griefs: **dies adimit ægritudinem**

time flies: **tempus fugit**

time flies through the world: **volat hora per orbem**

time glides away, and we grow older through the silent years: **tempora labuntur, tacitisque senescimus annis**

time is a certain fraction of eternity: **tempus est quædam pars æternitatis**

time is the best of the healing arts: **temporis ars medicina fere est**

time is the essence of the matter: **tempus anima rei**

time is the greatest innovator: **maximus novator tempus**

time reveals all things: **tempus omnia revelat**

time reveals the truth: **veritatem dies aperit**

time the producer, time the devourer of things: **tempus ferax, tempus edax rerum**

times change, and we change with them: **tempora mutantur, et nos mutamur in illis**

to a T (fig.): **ad unguem**

to accept a favor is to sell one's liberty: **beneficium accipere libertatem vendere est**

to add fuel to the flame: **oleum addere camino**

to add insult to injury: **ad damnum adderetur injuria**

to argue about the shadow of an ass: **de asini umbra disceptare**

to attempt to scale heaven (fig.): **imponere Pelion Olympo** or **Pelio imponere Ossam**

to be is to be perceived: **esse est percipi**

to be loved, be lovable: **ut ameris, amabilis esto**

to call a spade a spade: **ligonem ligonem vocat**

to carry wood to the forest: **in silvam ligna ferre**

to compare great things with small: **parvis componere magna**

to compare small things with great: **parva componere magnis**

to draw water with a sieve: **cribro aquam haurire**

to drink poison from a golden cup: **bibere venenum in auro**

to each his own: **suum cuique**

to each his own beauty: **suum cuique pulchrum**

to each his own custom: **suus cuique mos est**

to each his own pleasure: **sua cuique voluptas**

to err is human: **errare humanum est**

to everyone his due: **suum cuique**

to feed the flame: **alere flammam**

to fetch food from the flames: **e flamma cibum petere**

to fish with a golden hook: **aureo hamo piscari**

to God alone be the glory: **soli Deo gloria**

to God, the Best, the Greatest: **Deo, Optimo, Maximo**

to hold a wolf by its ears: **lupum auribus tenere**

to honors through difficulties: **ad augusta per angusta**

to how many evils does not religion persuade!: **quantum religio potuit suadere malorum!**

to laugh in one's sleeve (fig.): **ridere in stomacho**

to lean against a falling wall: **in caducum parietem inclinare**

to leave no stone unturned: **omnem movere lapidem**

to live an evil life is a type of death: **genus est mortis male vivere**

to live from hand to mouth (fig.): **in diem vivere**

to lose a friend is the greatest of all losses: **amicum perdere est damnorum maximum**

to miss the mark: **aberrare a scopo**

to passion, even haste is slow: **est ipsa cupiditati tarda celeritas**

to pile Ossa on Pelion: **Pelio imponere Ossam**

to pile Pelion on Olympus: **imponere Pelion Olympo**

to pray is to work, to work is to pray: **orare est laborare, laborare est orare**

to put the cart before the ox: **currus bovem trahit**

to raise a tempest in a teapot (fig.): **fluctus in simpulo exitare**

to rave with the insane: **cum insanientibus furere**

to sell smoke: **fumos vendere**

to swear is to call God to witness: **jurare est Deum in testem vocare**

to teach a fish how to swim: **piscem natare docere**

to the devil with you! (fig.): **abi in malam crucem**

to the good all things are good: **omnia bona bonis**

to the greater glory of God: **ad majorem Dei gloriam**

to the highest point: **ad summum**

to the indolent every day is a holiday: **ignavis semper feriæ sunt**

to the Lord, the best, the greatest: **Domino, Optimo, Maximo**

to the memory of: **in memoriam**

to the pure all things are pure: **omnia munda mundis**

to the stars through adversities: **ad astra per aspera**

to the weary, the bare ground is a bed: **fatigatis humus cubile est**

to those who come late the bones: **tarde venientibus ossa**

to throw cold water on a business: **frigidam aquam effundere**

to throw the handle after the hatchet: **ad perditam securim manubrium adjicere**

to touch a sore: **tangere ulcus**

to understand the cause of all things: **rerum cognoscere causas**

to which vulture shall this carcass fall?: **cujus vulturis hoc erit cadaver?**

to whom Fortune herself yields: **cui Fortuna ipsa cedit**

to wish for death is a coward's part: **timidi est optare necem**

to work is to pray: **laborare est orare**

today, you shall be with me in Paradise: **hodie mecum eris in paradiso**

tomorrow will give some food for thought: **aliquod crastinus dies ad cogitandum dabit**

tooth and nail: **unguibus et rostro**

touch me not: **noli me tangere**

treat a thousand dispositions in a thousand ways: **mille animos excipe mille modis**

trial by ordeal: **judicium Dei**

Troy was: **Troja fuit** or **fuit Ilium**

truly the gods use us men as footballs: **enim vero di nos quasi pilas homines habent**

trust but see in whom: **fide sed cui vide**

trust not to appearances: **ne fronti crede**

trust the expert: **experto crede**

truth begets hatred: **veritas odium parit**

truth conquers all things: **veritas omnia vincit**

truth fears nothing but concealment: **veritas nihil veretur nisi abscondi**

truth will prevail: **veritas prævalebit**

two are better than one (fig.): **unus vir, nullus vir**

U

unanimously: **una voce**

unbridled gratification produces unbridled desire: **libido effrenata effrenatam appententiam efficit**

under this sign you will conquer: **sub hoc signo vinces**

union gives strength to the humblest of aids: **auxilia humilia firma consensus facit**

union is strength (fig.): **juncta juvant**

unpleasing is the face that does not smile: **nec grata est facies cui gelasinus abest**

unraveling the web of Penelope: **Penelopæ telam retexens**

unrehearsed: **ex tempore**

until it fills the whole world: **donec totum impleat orbem**

use is the best teacher: **usus est optimum magister**

V

vanity of vanities, all is vanity: **vanitas vanitatum, omnia vanitas**

variety is delighting: **varietas delectat**

various are the opinions of men: **varii hominum sensus**

virtue alone can purchase power: **emitur sola virtute potestas**

virtue alone is true nobility: **sola nobilitas virtus**

virtue is a thousand shields: **virtus mille scuta**

virtue is indeed its own reward: **ipsa quidem virtus pretium sibi**

virtue is praised and left out to freeze: **virtus laudatur et alget**

virtue is the highest reward: **virtus præmium est optimum**

virtue is the safest helmet: **cassis tutissima virtus**

virtue is the strongest shield: **ægis fortissima virtus**

virtue lives on after the grave: **vivit post funera virtus**

virtue shines forth: **fulget virtus**

W

war is always easy to start, but very hard to end: **omne bellum sumi facile, ceterum ægerrume desinere**

war is delightful to the inexperienced: **dulce bellum inexpertis**

warmed-over cabbage: **crambe repetita**

wars, horrible wars: **bella, horrida bella**

wars, the horror of mothers: **bella, detesta matribus**

watch and pray: **vigilate et orate**

we all have power to do harm: **ad nocendum potentes sumus**

we are all consumed by cares: **curis tabescimus omnes**

we are all the worse for license: **deteriores omnes sumus licentia**

we are born but to die: **nascentes morimur**

we are born poets, we become orators: **nascimur poëtæ, fimus oratores**

we are but dust and shadows, born to consume the fruits of the earth: **pulvis et umbra
sumus, fruges consumere nati**

we are corrupted by good fortune: **felicitate corrumpimur**

we become workmen by working: **fabricando fabri fimus**

we cannot command nature except by obeying her: **naturæ enim non imperatur,
nisi parendo**

we covet what is guarded: **quicquid servatur, cupimus magis**

we do not destroy religion by destroying superstition: **nec vero superstitione tollenda
religio tollitur**

we forget our pleasures, we remember our pains: **cui placet obliviscitur, cui
dolet meminit**

we have all been mad once: **semel insanivimus omnes**

we learn by teaching: **docendo discimus**

we lose things certain in pursuing things uncertain: **certa amittimus dum incerta petimus**

we pay when old for the excesses of our youth: **quæ peccamus juvenes ea luimus senes**

we praise thee, O God: **te Deum laudamus**

we two are a multitude: **nos duo turba sumus**

weariness of life: **tædium vitæ**

weigh Hannibal: **expende Hannibalem**

what a difference between a wise man and a fool!: **stulto intellegens quid interest!**

what a fine shepherd a wolf must be!: **optimum custodem ovium quem dicunt
esse lupum!**

what a wonderful revenue lies in thrift!: **quam magnum vectigal sit parsimonia!**

what an artist dies in me!: **qualis artifex pereo!**

what coast is without our blood?: **quæ caret ora cruore nostro?**

what emptiness there is in human affairs!: **quantum est in rebus inane!**

what good are laws when there are no morals?: **quid leges sine moribus vanæ proficiunt?**

what I have said I have said: **quod dixi dixi**

what I have written I have written: **quod scripsi scripsi**

what if the sky should now fall?: **quid si nunc cœlum ruat?**

what is braver than a lion?: **quid leone fortius?**

what is done quickly, perishes quickly: **quod cito fit, cito perit**

what is lawful is not always respectable: **honestum non est semper quod licet**

what is true belongs to me: **quod verum est, meum est**

what is truth?: **quid est veritas?**

what is unseemly is unsafe: **intuta quæ indecora**

what is useful is sweet: **dulce quod utile**

what is useful is valuable: **pretiosum quod utile**

what is violent is not durable: **quod est violentum, non est durabile**

what is well begun is already half done: **dimidium facti qui bene cœpit habet**

what madness has seized you?: **quæ te dementia cepit?**

what now?: **quid nunc?**

what suffices is enough: **satis quod sufficit**

what was hard to suffer is sweet to remember: **quæ fuit durum pati meminisse dulce est**

what were once vices are now customs: **quæ fuerant vitia mores sunt**

whatever begins, also ends: **quicquid cœpit, et desinit**

whatever you teach, be brief: **quidquid præcipies, esto brevis**

when fortune frowns, love's flame burns fiercer: **fortuna amorem pejor infammat magis**

when gold speaks, not even the least reason avails: **auro loquente nihil pollet quævis ratio**

when the cause is removed, the effect ceases: **sublata causa, tollitur effectus**

when you are at Rome, live after the Roman fashion: **quum Romæ fueris, Romano vivite more**

where the law is uncertain, there is no law: **ubi jus incertum, ibi jus nullum**

where there is law there is remedy: **ubi jus, ibi remedium**

where there is smoke, there is fire: **flamma fumo est proxima**

where they create desolation they call it peace: **ubi solitudinem faciunt pacem appellant**

which was to be proved: **quod erat demonstrandum**

while fortune lasted: **dum fortuna fuit**

while Rome deliberates, Saguntum perishes: **deliberat Roma, perit Saguntum**

while the crime blazes: **flagrante delicto**

while there is life, there is hope: **dum vita est, spes est**

while we live, let us live: **dum vivimus, vivamus**

whip me, but hear me: **verbera, sed audi**

whither goest thou?: **quo vadis?**

whither the Fates may call: **quo Fata vocant**

who then is free?: **quisnam igitur liber?**

who will guard the guardians?: **quis custodiet ipsos custodes?**

who would dare to call the sun a liar?: **solem quis dicere falsum audeat?**

wholly complete and complete in every part: **totus in toto, et totus in qualibet parte**

whom does it benefit?: **cui bono?**

whom does it harm?: **cui malo?**

whom have flowing cups not made eloquent?: **fecundi calices quem non fecere disertum?**

whose region, his religion: **cujus regio, ejus religio**

why force me to break the deep silence?: **quid me alta silentia cogis rumpere?**

wickedness takes the shorter road, and virtue the longer: **compendiaria res improbitas, virtusque tarda**

wine kindles wrath: **vinum incendit iram**

wine opens the seals of the heart: **aperit præcordia liber**

wings greater than the nest: **majores pennas nido**

wisdom grows by study: **studio sapientia crescit**

wisdom is the gift of God: **sapientia donum Dei**

wisdom surpasses wealth: **præstat opes sapientia**

wise as a serpent, harmless as a dove: **prudens ut serpens, simplex ut columba**

wise is the person who talks little: **vir sapit qui pauca loquitur**

wise without learning: **abnormis sapiens**

with a grain of salt: **cum grano salis**

with equal steps: **pari passu**

with God's favor: **Deo favente**

with God's help, work prospers: **adjuvante Deo labor proficit**

with heart and hand: **mente manuque**

with how little wisdom the world is governed!: **quam parva sapientia regitur mundus!**

with one voice: **una voce**

with stronger force: **a fortiori**

with talons and beak: **unguibus et rostro**

with the blessed, all things are blessed: **in beato omnia beata**

with the greatest zeal: **summo studio**

with unequal steps: **haud passibus æquis**

without care: **sine cura**

without end: **sine fine**

without envy: **sine invidia**

without fear: **sine metu**

without hatred: **sine odio**

without money all is vain: **absque argento omnia vana**

without the Cross, without light: **sine cruce, sine luce**

woe is me!, I think I am becoming a god: **væ!, puto deus fio**

woe to the vanquished!: **væ victis!**

woman is ever fickle and changeable: **varium et mutabile semper fœmina**

wonderful to behold!: **mirabile visu!**

wonderful to tell!: **mirabile dictu!**

work is itself a pleasure: **labor ipse voluptas**

work is the best of relishes: **optimum obsonium labor**

worship God, serve the king: **Deum cole, regem serva**

Y

yield not to misfortunes: **tu ne cede malis**

yield to no one: **cede nullis**

you are always singing the same tune: **cantilenam eandem canis**

you are building on sand: **in arena ædificas**

you are looking for a knot is a bullrush: **in scirpo nodum quæris**

you are making an elephant out of a fly: **elephantem ex musca facis**

you are teaching a dolphin to swim: **delphinum natare doces**

you are the Christ, the son of the living God: **tu est Christus, filius Dei vivi**

you are trying to get water from a stone: **aquam a pumice nunc postulas**

you are writing in water: **in aqua scribis**

you betray the Son of Humanity with a kiss?: **osculo Filium hominis tradis?**

you cannot escape necessity, but you can overcome it: **effugere non potes necessitates, potes vincere**

you frighten a lion with a mask: **leonem larva terres**

you have eaten and have drunk enough: **edisti satis, atque bibisti**

you have come after the feast: **post festum venisti**

you have entrusted the wolf with the sheep: **lupo ovem commisisti**

you have hit the nail on the head (fig.): **tetigisti acu**

you hold an eel by the tail: **anguillam cauda tenes**

you make a virtue of necessity: **facis de necessitate virtutem**

you must avoid that wicked siren Sloth: **vitanda est improba siren Desidia**

you need only a show of war to have peace: **ostendite modo bellum, pacem habebitis**

you too, Brutus: **et tu, Brute** or **tu quoque, Brute**

you will mix sacred things with profane: **miscebis sacra profanis**

you will stir up the hornets: **irritabis crabones**

your descendants will pick your fruit: **carpent tua poma nepotes**

your years are counted on your face: **facies tua computat annos**

youth seek, the old use: **quære adolescens, utere senex**